Encyclopedia of Modern Worldwide Extremists and Extremist Groups

Encyclopedia of **MODERN WORLDWIDE EXTREMISTS** and **EXTREMIST GROUPS**

Stephen E. Atkins

GREENWOOD PRESS
Westport, Connecticut • London

Library of Congress Cataloging-in-Publication Data

Atkins, Stephen E.
    Encyclopedia of modern worldwide extremists and extremist groups / Stephen E. Atkins.
        p. cm.
    Includes bibliographical references and index.
    ISBN 0–313–32485–9 (alk. paper)
        1. Radicalism—Encyclopedias.   2. Radicals—Encyclopedias.   3. Religious fundamentalism—
Encyclopedias.   4. Religious fanaticism—Encyclopedias.   I. Title.
HN49.R33A85   2004
320.53′03—dc22   2003064256

British Library Cataloguing in Publication Data is available.

Library of Congress Catalog Card Number: 2003064256
ISBN: 0–313–32485–9

First published in 2004

Greenwood Press, 88 Post Road West, Westport, CT 06881
An imprint of Greenwood Publishing Group, Inc.
www.greenwood.com

Printed in the United States of America

∞™

The paper used in this book complies with the
Permanent Paper Standard issued by the National
Information Standards Organization (Z39.48–1984).

10 9 8 7 6 5 4 3 2 1

Contents

List of Entries

Chronology of Events

1858 February 15	Irish republicans found the Irish Republican Army (IRA)
1905	Irish republicans form the Irish political party Sinn Fein (Ourselves Alone)
1912 September	Ulster Loyalists found the Ulster Volunteer Force (UVF) to fight for an independent Northern Ireland
1925	Hindu nationalists form the Hindu supremacy party Rashtriya Swayamsevak Sangh (National Volunteer Organization) (RSS)
1928 March	Hassan al-Banna founds the Muslim Brotherhood in Egypt
1931	Irish Free State government declares the Irish Republican Army (IRA) as an illegal organization
1938	Vladimir Ze'ev Jabotinsky, Abraham Stern, and David Raziel form the Irgun Zvai Leumi (National Military Organization) (IZL)
1940	Abraham Stern breaks with the Irgun Zvai Leumi and founds the Stern Gang
1941 August 26	Mawlana Mawdudi founds the Islamist party Jam'at-i Islami (Islamic Party)
1942 February 12	British kill the leader of the Stern Gang—Abraham Stern
1944 February 1	Menachem Begin leads Irgun in an anti-British terrorist campaign
September 13	Sikh students form the All-India Sikh Students Federation
November 6	Stern Gang assassinates Lord Moyne, former British colonial secretary, in Cairo, Egypt
1945 May	Sayyid Mujtaba Mirlawhi founds the Devotees of Islam (Fida'iyan-i Islam) in Iran
1946 July 22	Members of the Jewish terrorist organization, Irgun Zvai Leumi (IZL), bomb the King David Hotel in Jerusalem, killing over 80 people
December 26	Italian neo-Fascists start the Italian Social Movement (MSI) in Rome

1947	
April	Formation of the Arab Baath Socialist Party in Damascus, Syria
November 29	United Nations votes in favor of partitioning Palestine into two states—Jewish and Arab
1948	
January 30	Hindu nationalist assassinates Mohandas K. Gandhi
April 9	Jewish members of Irgun destroy Arab village of Dir Yassin, killing more than 100 Arabs
April 9	Right-wing terrorists kill the Colombian presidential candidate Jorge Eliécer Gaitán
May 14	Great Britain leaves Palestine and David Ben-Gurion proclaims the state of Israel
May 15	Arab armies invade new state of Israel
September 17	Members of the Stern Gang kill Count Folke Bernadotte of Sweden and French Colonel Andre Serot because of their United Nations activities
December 8	Egyptian government bans the Muslim Brotherhood
December 28	Muslim Brotherhood activists assassinate Egyptian Prime Minister Mahmoud Fahmy el-Nokrashy Pasha because of the defeat of the Arab cause in the war against Israel
1949	
January 7	End of Arab-Israeli War allows Jewish leaders to consolidate the State of Israel
February 12	Egyptian security agents assassinate Hassan al-Banna, founder of the Muslim Brotherhood
1950	Jordan annexes West Bank of the Jordan River
1952 July	Gamal Abdel Nasser comes to power in Egypt

1953	Sheikh Taqiuddin an-Nabhani Filastyni founds the Hizb u Tahrir al-Islami (Islamic Liberation Party) (HT) in Jordan
1956 July 26	Nasser nationalizes the Suez Canal
September 21	Terrorists shoot Anastasio Somoza, president and dictator of Nicaragua, and he dies on September 29, 1956
October	Yasser Arafat and other Palestinian leaders form al-Fatah
October 29	Beginning of the Suez War—Britain, France, and Israel versus Egypt
1959 July 31	Elements of the Basque Nationalist Party and the student group Ekin (Action) form the Basque separatist ETA (Euskadi Ta Askatasune) (Basque Fatherland and Liberty)
1961	Carlos Fonseca Amador, Tomas Borge Martinez, and Silvio Mayorga start the Sandinista National Liberation Front
1964 January	Meeting of Arab countries under the leadership of Gamal Abdel Nasser form the Palestine Liberation Organization (PLO)
May 22	Palestine Liberation Organization approves Palestinian National Charter Organization (PLO)
November 28	German neo-Nazis form the German National Democratic Party (Nationaldemokratische Partei Deutschlands) (NPD)
1965 January	Al-Fatah launches raids into Israel
September 6	Three Iranian engineers form the Mujahedin-e Khalq (MEK) Organization to wage war against the regime of the Shah of Iran

1966
March 13 Jonas Malheiro Savimbi founds the National Union for the Total Independence of Angola (UNITA)

Bal Thackeray forms the Hindu nationalist group Shiv Sena (Sword of Shiva) in Bombay, India

Ulster government declares the Ulster Volunteer Force (UVF) as an illegal organization after the murders of several Catholics

1967
May 25 Naxalite movement forms in West Bengal

June 5–10 Israel conducts preemptive war against Egypt, Syria, and Jordan

1968
March 21 Battle of Karameh between Israelis and Palestinians in Jordan

April 3 Four members of the future Red Army Faction (RAF) firebomb two Frankfurt department stores

April 12 Moshe Levinger and Israeli settlers move into Hebron claiming it as a Jewish city

April 15 Palestine Liberation Organization (PLO) selects Yasser Arafat to become the chair of the Executive Committee

July 28 First aircraft highjacking by the Popular Front for the Liberation of Palestine (PFLP)

December 26 Official date of the forming of the New Peoples Army in the Philippines

1969
April 22 Naxalites organize the Communist Party of India–Marxist-Leninist (CPI-ML)

May 27 Adriano Sofri and dissident communists form the Italian Lotta Continua (Continuous Struggle)

August 29 Leila Khaled and others of the Popular Front for the Liberation of Palestine skyjack a TWA B-707 flight from Rome to Tel Aviv

November 4 Brazilian police kill Carlos Marighela, an urban guerrilla leader, in a gunfight in São Paulo, Brazil

December 28 Split of Irish Republican Army into Official and Provisional groups after IRA Army Convention in Dublin

1970
February Abimael Guzman founds the Peruvian Maoist Communist Shining Path group

May 14-15 Red Army Faction forms in West Germany in the aftermath of Andreas Baader's escape from jail

May 29 Argentine Montoneros kidnap former provisional president of Argentina, General Pedro Eugenio Aramburo

July 1 Montoneros announce execution of General Pedro Eugenio Aramburo

July 31 Uruguayan Tupamaros guerrillas seize Daniel A. Mitrione, a U.S. diplomat, and Aloisio Gomide, a Brazilian diplomat in separate kidnapping incidents

September Renato Curcio, Margherita Cagol, and Alberto Franceschini form the Red Brigades in Italy

September 7 Argentinean police kill two principal leaders of the Montoneros, José Sabino Navarro and Carlos Gustave Ramus

September 10 Jordanian army moves against PLO guerrillas in Jordan, driving them out of the country to Lebanon

1971
January Gerhard Frey founds the extremist German People's Union (DVU)

Chronology of Events

January 8	Uruguayan Tupamoros guerrillas kidnap Sir Geoffrey Jackson, the British Ambassador to Uruguay
May 15	Ulster Loyalists form the Ulster Defence Association (UDA)
August 21	Members of the New Peoples Army explode three grenades, killing members of President Marcos's liberal opposition at the Miranda Plaza in Manila, Philippines
November 28	Members of Black September assassinate Wasfi Tell, Jordan's prime minister, in Cairo, Egypt
December 4	Ulster Volunteer Force (UVF) bombs McGurk's Bar in Belfast, killing 15 Catholics
1972	
January 30	Bloody Sunday, when British army 1st Parachute Regiment kills 13 Catholic civilians in Derry, Northern Ireland
March 2	Black September operatives assassinate three diplomats, including the U.S. Ambassador to Sudan Cleo A. Noel, in Khartoum
May 8	Four members of Black September hijack a Sabena airliner over Zagreb, Yugoslavia, and redirect the aircraft to Tel Aviv's Lod Airport
May 17	Member of the Lotta Continua kills Luigi Calabresi, Milan police commissioner
May 30	Japanese Red Army attacks Israelis at Lod Airport in Israel, killing 24 people and wounding 80 others
June 1	West German police arrest Red Army Faction leaders Andreas Baader and Jan-Carl Raspe in Frankfurt
June 8	West German police arrest Gudrun Ensslin in Hamburg
June 15	West German police arrest Ulrike Meinhof in Hannover
July 21	Provisional Irish Republican Army launch 22 bombings in the Belfast area that kill 11 and wound more than 100
July 28	Leader of the Naxalites Charu Mazumdar dies in captivity
September 5	Black September Organization attacks Israeli Olympic team in Munich Olympics, killing 11 Israelis and 5 Palestinians
October 5	Jean-Marie Le Pen and five veteran French right-wingers form the Front National (FN)
December 28	Black September Organization seizes the Israeli Embassy in Bangkok, Thailand
1973	
March 6	Black September members seize Saudi Embassy in Khartoum, Sudan, and kill two American and one Belgian diplomat
October 6	Egypt and Syria launch Yom Kippur War against Israel
December	Claude Vorilhon establishes the Raelian Movement
December 20	ETA assassinates Spanish Prime Minister Admiral Carrero Blanco in Madrid, Spain, with a bomb
1974	
May 17	Ulster Volunteer Force (UVF) bomb squad explodes bombs in Dublin and Monahan, Republic of Ireland, killing 32 and wounding more than 200
June	Members of the Israeli settlers group form the Gush Emunim
September 8	Italian police arrest the head of the Red Brigades, Renato Curcio
November 13	Yasser Arafat, head of the Palestine Liberation Organization (PLO), speaks before the United Nations General Assembly
November 22	Abu Nidal forms the terrorist group Abu Nidal Organization

1975

February 18   Margherita Cagol leads Red Brigade activists in a prison break that frees Renato Curcio

April   Civil war breaks out in Lebanon between Maronite Christians and PLO guerrillas

April 10   Israeli hit team assassinates three prominent al-Fatah leaders in Beirut, Lebanon

April 26   Six Red Army Faction members seize the West Germany embassy in Stockholm, Sweden, taking 12 hostages

June 4   Italian police kill Margherita Cagol, a leader of the Red Brigades

June 27   Illich Ramirez Sanchez (Carlos the Jackal) shoots two French policemen in Paris killing them as they try to arrest him

July 21   Israeli agents kill Moroccan waiter suspected of being Ali Hasan Salameh in Lillehammer, Norway

December 21   Popular Front for the Liberation of Palestine activists led by Ilyich Ramirez Sanchez (Carlos the Jackal) hold 81 representatives from the Organization of Petroleum Exporting Countries (OPEC) hostage

December 23   Hit team from the Revolutionary Organization 17 November assassinate Richard Welch, a CIA chief in Greece, in Athens, Greece

1976

May 8   Ulrike Meinhof commits suicide by hanging herself in her prison cell

June 24   Joint operation between members of the Popular Front for the Liberation of Palestine and the German Revolutionary Cells skyjacks an Air France Airbus on route from Tel Aviv to Paris and flies it to Entebbe, Uganda, where Israeli commandos free the Jewish passengers

July 2   Members of the Montoneros explode a bomb in the dining room of the federal police security building in Buenos Aires, Argentina, that kills 18 and wounds 66

December 15   Montoneros terrorists explode a bomb at a Defense Ministry building in Buenos Aires, Argentina, that kills 15 and injures 30 military officers and civilians

1977

April 7   Members of the Red Army Faction assassinate Siegfried Buback, the chief federal prosecutor in the prosecution of the imprisoned RAF leaders, and his driver and bodyguard

September 5   Red Army Faction activists kidnap Dr. Hans-Martin Schleyer, prominent West German industrialist and kill his driver and three bodyguards

October 17   German anti-terrorist team assaults skyjackers from the Popular Front for the Liberation of Palestine (PFLP) in Mogadishu, Somalia

October 18   Leaders of the Red Army Faction (RAF) commit suicide in their prison cells

October 18   Learning of the suicide of the Red Army Faction leaders, RAF members kill Dr. Hans-Martin Schleyer

November 8   Philippine agents capture the leader of the New Peoples Army, José María Sison

1978

March   Israel invades south Lebanon and attacks PLO guerrillas

March 16   Members of the Italian Red Brigades kidnap Aldo Moro, a prominent Italian politician

May 9	Police find body of Aldo Moro in a car in Rome
July 2	Bhai Amrik Singh reorganizes the All-India Sikh Students Federation and makes it a radical Sikh group
August 22	Edén Pastora Gomez leads a Sandinista unit in the seizure of the Nicaraguan National Palace and takes 1,500 legislators and staff hostage
September	Camp David Accords signed by Israel, Egypt, and the United States
1979	
January 22	Israeli hit team kills Ali Hasan Salameh, the leader of Black September and the architect of the 1972 Munich Olympic terrorist attack, with a car bomb in Beirut
February 1	Ayatollah Khomeini assumes power in Iran
March 26	Egypt and Israel sign Egyptian-Israeli Peace Treaty
March 30	Irish National Liberation Army (INLA) assassinate Airey Neave, Tory member of Parliament, by exploding a car bomb in London
April 7	Italian police arrest Antonio Negri, the leading Marxist theorist in Italy
August 27	Provisional IRA kill Earl Mountbatten of Burma and members of his family in a bombing attack
October 9	Israeli politicians Yuval Neeman and Geula Cohen form the right-wing extremist Tehiya Party
November 4	Iranian students seize 83 American hostages in the U.S. Embassy in Tehran
1980	
January 16	Members of the Revolutionary Organization 17 November assassinate Major General Pantelis Petrou, deputy commander of the Athens Riot Police, in Athens, Greece
February 27	Members of Colombia's M-19 seize the Dominican Embassy in Bogotá, Colombia and hold 57 hostages
March 24	Salvadorian rightists assassinate Archbishop Oscar Arnulfo Romero in the cathedral in San Salvador
May 17	Shining Path launches first terrorist operation
September 22	Saddam Hussein launches attack against Iran that starts the Iran-Iraq War
December 2	Salvadorean death squad kills 3 Maryknoll order nuns and a Catholic lay social worker near San Salvador, El Salvador
1981	
May 5	Bobby Sands, a member of the Provisional IRA, dies on the 65th day of his prison hunger strike
May 13	Mehmet Ali Agca, a member of the Turkish right-wing extremist group Grey Wolves, wounds Pope John Paul II and 2 others in an assassination attempt in St. Peter's Square in Rome, Italy
August 30	Operative of the Mujahedin-e Khalq (MEK) plants bomb in Tehran that kills the Iranian president and prime minister
October 6	Assassination of President Anwar Sadat of Egypt during a military parade
December 17	Members of the Red Brigades kidnap General James Dozier in Verona and hold him for ransom
1982	
January 28	Italian security forces rescue General James Dozier from an apartment in Padua
June 6	Israel invades Lebanon to destroy the PLO in Lebanon

July	Formation of the Shi'ite Hezbollah in Lebanon
July 20	Provisional Irish Republican Army hit team explodes two bombs in London during military changing of the guard ceremonies, killing 9 soldiers and wounding 49 soldiers and civilians
August 21–31	PLO withdraws from Beirut, Lebanon, and establishes headquarters in Tunis, Tunisia
September 3	Red Brigades hit team assassinates General Carlos Alberto Della Chiesa, the former chief of Italy's war on terrorism
1983	
April 18	Mugniyah's Islamic Jihad launches a truck bomb attack against the U.S. Embassy in Beirut, Lebanon, that kills 63 people and injures 120
June–November	Mutiny against the leadership of Arafat breaks out
September 23	Abu Nidal Group claims responsibility for the downing of a Gulf Air aircraft near Abu Dhabi, United Arab Emirates, that kills 111 passengers and crew
October 23	Mugniyah, leader of Hezbollah's Islamic Jihad, directs the suicide bombing of the U.S. Marine complex in Beirut, Lebanon, killing 241 Marines and Navy personnel
October 23	Hezbollah suicide bomber drives truck filled with explosives into French military complex in Beirut, Lebanon, that kills 58 French paratroopers
November 17	Franz Schönhuber, Franz Handlos, and Ekkehard Voigt, start the German Republican Party (REP) in Bavaria
November 17	Three Indians and 3 Mestizos form the Zapatista Army of National Liberation (EZLN) in Chiapas, Mexico
1984	Sheikh Abdullah Yussuf Azzam and Osama bin Laden establish Mujahideen Services Bureau (MAK) to recruit and train Afghan fighters
January 18	Imad Fayez Mugniyah's Islamic Jihad kills Malcolm Kerr, president of the American University of Beirut, in Lebanon
February 15	Hit team from the Red Brigades kills Leamon R. Hunt, an American diplomat, in Rome
March 16	Mugniyah's Islamic Jihad kidnaps William Buckley, the CIA station chief in Beirut, Lebanon
March 19	Indian government bans the radical Sikh group All-India Sikh Students Federation
June	Victor Polay Campos forms the Tupac Amaru Revolutionary Movement
July 5–6	Indian troops assault the Sikh's Golden Temple in Amritsar, India, killing more than 800 Sikhs, including Jarnail Singh Bhindranwale
October 31	Sikh bodyguards assassinate Indian Prime Minister Indira Gandhi in revenge for the Indian government's attack on the Golden Temple
December 3	Mugniyah's Islamic Jihad kidnaps Peter Kilburn, a librarian at the American University of Beirut, Lebanon
1985	
February 1	Members of the Red Army Faction assassinate Ernst Zimmerman, a prominent West German industrialist
February 21	Revolutionary Organization 17 November members kill Nikos Momferatos, publisher of

	Greece's largest conservative newspaper *Afternooner*, in Athens, Greece
March 16	Terrorists under the command of Imad Fayez Mugniyah kidnap Terry Anderson in Beirut, Lebanon
June 21	Sikh separatists explode bomb on Air India Boeing 747 Flight 182 killing 329 passengers and crew
August 8	Red Army Faction activists explode a car bomb on the U.S. Air Force base at Rhein-Main killing 2 Americans and wounding 20 others
October 7	Members of the Popular Front for the Palestine Liberation seize the Italian cruise ship Achille Lauro
November 6	Members of the Colombian M-19 terrorist group seize the Palace of Justice in Bogotá, Colombia, seizing 100 hostages
1986	
January 26	Sikh leadership forms the Panthic Committee to coordinate Sikh separatist movement
February 10	Members of the New Red Brigades/Communist Combatant Party kill Lando Conti, ex-mayor of Florence and a pro-American supporter
May 3	Liberation Tigers of Tamil Eelam activists explode a bomb in an Air Lanka Tristar aircraft in Colombo, Sri Lanka, that kills 17 people
July 9	Red Army Faction activists assassinate Dr. Karl-Heinz Beckurts, an executive at Siemens electronics company, with a bomb in Munich, West Germany
November 17	Members of the French terrorist group Action Directe assassinate Georges Besse, the president of Renault, in Paris

1987	
January 20	Mugniyah's Islamic Jihad kidnaps Anglican layman Terry Waite during the negotiations for the release of other hostages
March 20	Two members of the New Red Brigades/Communist Combatant Party assassinate General Licio Giorgieri, a pro-NATO military leader, in Rome
April 21	Tamil guerrillas of the Liberation Tigers of Tamil Eelam explode a bomb in a bus station in Colombo, Sri Lanka, that kills 105 people and wounds 200 others
November 8	Provisional IRA explodes bomb in Enniskillen, killing 11 and wounding another 63
December 9	Palestinian Intifada breaks out in Gaza Strip and spreads to the West Bank
December 14	Sheikh Ahmed Yassin organizes Hamas
1988	Sheikh Abdullah Azzam and Osama bin Laden form al-Qaeda
April 16	Mossad hit team assassinates Khalil al-Wazir in Tunis, Tunisia
June 28	Members of the Revolutionary Organization 17 November kill Navy Captain William Nordeen, a U.S. defense attaché in Greece, with a car bomb in Athens, Greece
August 20	Parties negotiate cease-fire in Iran-Iraq War
December	Arafat recognizes Israel and says he renounces terrorism in an address to the UN General Assembly in Geneva
December 21	Libyan agents plant bomb on Pan Am Flight 103 that explodes over Lockerbie, Scotland, killing 270 passengers

1989

February 3 — Peruvian police capture Victor Polay Campos

February 14 — Khomeini issues Iranian fatwa against Salman Rushdie

February 18 — Islamic party Islamic Salvation Front (FIS) forms in Algeria

June 3 — Ayatollah Ruholla Khomeini dies

November 24 — Unknown group assassinates Islamist leader Sheikh Abdullah Azzam in Peshawar, Pakistan, with a car bomb

November 30 — Red Army Faction members assassinate Alfred Herrhausen, chairman of the Deutsche Bank, by a bomb in Frankfurt, West Germany

July 30 — Provisional Irish Republican Army members explode a car bomb that kills Ian Gow, Conservative member of the British Parliament, in the London suburb of Hankham

December — Vladimir Zhirinovsky founds the neo-Fascist Liberal Democratic Party of Russia (LDPR)

1990

March — First Congress of the Liberal Democratic Party of Russia (LDPR) selects Vladimir Zhirinovsky as its head

August — Iraq invades Kuwait and occupies it

November 5 — Islamist assassinates Rabbi Meir Kahane in New York City

1991

January– February — Gulf War between Iraq and U.S.-led coalition ends in the defeat of Iraq

April 1 — Red Army Faction sniper assassinates Detlev Rohwedder, president of the Trusteeship Office for East German State Property, in Dusseldorf, West Germany

May 21 — Female member of the Liberation Tigers of Tamil Eelam explodes a bomb that kills former Indian Prime Minister Rajiv Gandhi in the southern Indian town of Sriperambudur near Madras, India, along with 17 others

October 16 — Aleksandr Barkashov founds the neo-Fascist Russian National Unity Party in Moscow

1992

March 17 — Hezbollah operatives explode bomb at the Israeli Embassy in Buenos Aires, Argentina, that kills 25 and injures 252

June 10 — Peruvian police arrest Victor Polay Campos, the head of the Tupac Amaru Revolutionary Movement, in Lima, Peru

August 10 — Northern Ireland government bans the Ulster Defence Association (UDA)

September 13 — Peruvian police capture Abimael Guzman, the head of the Shining Path, in Lima, Peru

October 15 — Indian police kill Talwinder Singh Parmar, the leader of the Babbar Khalsa Sikh terrorist group

December — Shiv Sena instigate riots that kill 800 Muslims in Bombay, India

1993

February 26 — Explosion at the World Trade Center in New York City kills 6 and wounds 1,042

May — Eduard Limonov and Alexander Dugin form the National Bolshevik Party in Moscow, Russia

July 2 — FBI agents arrest Sheikh Omar Abdel-Rahman for his role in the February bombing at the World Trade Center in New York City

September 13 — Israel and the PLO sign the Oslo Accords

Chronology of Events

October 4 — Hamas suicide bombing begins in Israel

1994
January 1 — Zapatista National Liberation Army (EZLN) launches offensive against the Mexican government in Chiapas

February 25 — Baruch Goldstein murders 29 Muslims with an automatic weapon in Hebron before survivors beat him to death

July 18 — Hezbollah agents under the command of Mugniyah explode a car bomb in front of two buildings housing Argentine-Israel organizations in Buenos Aires, Argentina, that kill 85 and injure 300

August 31 — Provisional IRA announces a cease-fire

October 8 — Landlords in India form the terrorism group Ranvir Sena

October 13 — Loyalist paramilitaries announce a cease-fire

December — Ivanov-Sukharevsky starts the neo-Nazi skinhead People's National Party

December 19 — Zapatistas in Chiapas declare 38 autonomous municipalities in a direct challenge to the Mexican government

1995
February 7 — Pakistani authorities arrest Ramzi Ahmed Yousef, the leader of the 1993 World Trade Center bombing, in Islamabad, Pakistan

March 20 — Members of the Japanese extremist group, Aum Shinri Kyo, plant sarin nerve gas inside the Tokyo subway system that kills 12 persons and injures another 3,796

April 19 — ETA unsuccessfully tries to assassinate prominent Spanish politician José Maria Aznar

June 26 — Assassination attempt on Egyptian President Hosni Mubarak in Addis Ababa, Ethiopia, by Islamic militants

August 21 — Hamas explodes a bomb on a Jerusalem bus that kills 6 and injures 100

October 12 — Zainon Ismail founds the Malaysian terrorist group Kumplan Militan Malaysia (KMM)

November 13 — Armed Islamic Movement (AIM) kills 5 Americans and 1 Saudi in a bombing in Riyadh, Saudi Arabia

1996
January 31 — Liberation Tigers of Tamil Eelam hit team bombs the Sri Lanka Central Bank in Colombo, Sri Lanka, killing 100 and wounding 1,400

February 9 — Provisional IRA ends cease-fire with a bombing at Canary Wharf in London

February 13 — Communist Party of Nepal starts rebellion against the Nepal government

June 25 — Truck bomb at al-Khobar in Dhahran kill 19 American servicemen and wounds hundreds of others

August 23 — Osama bin Laden announces a jihad against the United States for its occupation of Saudi Arabia

December 17 — Tupac Amaru Revolutionary Movement (MRTA) seize Japanese ambassador's residence taking more than 450 hostages

1997
April — Carlos Castaño combines the Colombian right-wing paramilitary groups into the United Self-Defense Forces of Colombia (AUC)

April 22 — Peruvian security forces raid Japanese ambassador's residence, freeing 72 hostages and killing the 14 guerrillas holding them

September 4 — Three Hamas sucide bombers explode bombs in the Ben Yehuda shopping mall in

Jerusalem, killing 8 persons and wounding nearly 200 others

October 15   Members of the Liberation Tigers of Tamil Eelam explode a bomb at the Colombo World Trade Center, killing 18 people

October 19   Dissidents from the Provisional Irish Republican Army establish the Real Irish Republican Army to continue the armed struggle to unite Northern Ireland with Ireland

December 22   Mexican paramilitary forces kill 45 refugees in Acteal, municipality of Chenalho, in an effort to fight against the Zapatista rebellion

1998
February   Osama bin Laden forms the International Islamic Front for Jihad against Jews and Crusaders

February 23   Osama bin Laden issues declaration of a global jihad against all enemies of Muslims

April 10   Leaders of PIRA and Ulster Loyalists sign Good Friday Accord

August 7   Bombings of U.S. embassies in Nairobi, Kenya, and Dar es Salaam, Tanzania, by representatives of al-Qaeda takes place

August 15   Members of the Real IRA explode a bomb in Omagh, Northern Ireland that kills 28 and wounds 220

August 20   U.S. cruise missiles strike al-Qaeda base camps in Afghanistan

December 18   Death of Ustadz Abdurajak Abubakar Janjalani, the head of the Abu Sayyaf terrorist group, in a gunfight with Philippine troops

1999
May 20   Members of the New Red

Brigades/Communist Combatant Party kills Massimo D'Antona, a Labor Minister advisor to the Italian government, in Rome

July 14   Peruvian military forces capture Shining Path leader Oscar Ramirez Durand

August   Greg Avery, wife Heather James, and other animal rights activists form the Stop Huntingdon Animal Cruelty (SHAC)

August 12   Jose Bove leads members of his Peasant Confederation to the French town of Millau to attack the local McDonald's fast-food restaurant as part of his anti-globalization campaign

November 14   Jaffar Umar Thalib founds the Muslim extremist group Laskar Jihad in Indonesia

2000
January 11   Opening of the David Irving trial

September 28   Outbreak of the al-Aqsa Intifada on the occasion of the Likud leader Ariel Sharon's visit to the Temple Mount

October 12   Al-Qaeda operatives bomb the American destroyer USS *Cole*, killing 17 sailors and injuring 39 others

2001
May 27   Abu Sayyaf rebels kidnap 20 at the Dos Palmas beach resort in the Philippines, including the Burnham missionaries

September 11   Islamic militants crash two American airliners into the Twin Towers of the World Trade Center in New York City, a third into the Pentagon in Washington, D.C., and a fourth in Pennsylvania

October 1   Pakistani Army of Muhammad attacks the Srinagar legislature in Kashmir and kills 38 people

December 13   Pakistani Army of Muhammad assaults India's parliament and kills 15 people

2002
February 22   Angolan forces kill Jonas Savimbi, the head of UNITA

March 19   Members of the New Red Brigades/Communist Combatant Party assassinate Professor Mario Biagi, labor advisor to the Italian government, in Bologna

March 27   Hamas suicide bomber detonates a bomb in a Netanya hotel restaurant, killing 22 persons and wounding 140 others

May 6   Animal rights activist Volkert van der Graaf assassinates Dutch populist leader Pim Fortuyn

June 19   An Aqsa Martyrs Brigades suicide bomb detonates a bomb at a bus stop in Jerusalem, killing 6 persons and wounding 43 others

October 12   Jemaah Islamiyah operatives explode bomb on Bali that kills 188 and wounds hundreds

October 23   Chechen rebels take more than 800 hostages at the Palace of Culture Theater in Moscow

October 26   Russian Special Forces administer gas and storm the theater, killing all the Chechen rebels, but in the rescue attempt 124 hostages die

October 28   Abu Musab al-Zarqawi's group Al Tawhid assassinates Laurence Foley, an administrator of U.S. aid programs in Jordan, in Amman, Jordan

2003
September 9   Two Hamas suicide bombers kill 15 Israelis in Israel

August 5   Suicide bomber Jemaah Islamiyah explodes a car bomb in front of the Marriott Hotel in Jakarta's business district killing 13 and wounding 149

August 11   Thai authorities and the CIA arrest Hambali, one of the leaders of the Jemaah Islamiyah, in Thailand

August 19   Truck bomber affiliated with al-Zarqawi strikes the United Nations headquarters in Baghdad, Iraq, killing Sergio Vieira de Mello, the U.N. representative in Iraq, and 22 others

August 29   Car bomber with ties to al-Zarqawi explodes a bomb outside the Imam Ali Mosque in the Shi'ite Muslim holy city of Najaf, Iraq, killing the Ayatollah Mohammed Baqir al-Hakim and more than 85 others

November 12   Suicide truck bomber affiliated with al-Zarqawi triggers bomb at the Italian military headquarters in Nasiriyah, Iraq, killing 30, including 19 Italians

December 5   Suicide bomber from Shamil Basayev's Chechen forces blow up commuter train near Yessentuki, Russia killing 50 and wounding more than 110

December 9   Suicide bomber from Shamil Basayev's Chechen forces explodes bomb in front of the National Hotel in Moscow that killing 6 and wounding 14

2004
February 6   Chechen terrorist explodes bomb in the Moscow subway that kills 39 and wounds 130

Introduction

Few subjects are as ill defined as political extremism. Terrorism is much easier to define because it begins with a conspiracy and ends with on overt act. Political extremism, however, lurks behind the scenes and may lead to terrorism but not necessarily so. Extremists may lead peaceful and undistinguished lives, but the ideology and ideas that they espouse may cause followers to take actions that produce loss of life and destruction of property. This work is an attempt to penetrate the veil of extremism by looking at a variety of political extremists and extremist groups that have proliferated in the last half century. The year 1945 is especially noteworthy because political extremism assumed a new orientation after the collapse of the two prewar brands of extremism—German Nazism and Italian Fascism.

The history of extremism has been characterized by the development of new forms of extremism. Before World War II, extremism had been represented by the two ideologies of Communism and Fascism. An earlier type of extremism, anarchism, had lost most of its appeal by the end of the 1930s. In the postwar world, different varieties of extremism have surfaced. Both left-wing and right-wing versions appeared shortly after the war, but the left wing had the advantage of the positive legacy of World War II. Left-wing groups benefited at first from the discrediting of Nazism and Italian Fascism.

Wars of national liberation and revolutionary activism combined to stimulate left-wing political activism. Three events served as catalysts: the Chinese Revolution of Mao Tse-tung, the Cuban Revolution of Fidel Castro, and the Vietnam War. These events provided examples of successful revolutionary action. Supporters and sympathizers of these revolutions also had the opportunity to repudiate the actions and policies of the two superpowers of the time—the Soviet and the Western blocs. Student activism stimulated by revolutionary change led to the student revolts in France and the United States in the late 1960s, which spread worldwide. Even after the radical phase of student activism crashed in the early 1970s, left-wing groups proliferated mostly in Europe and the United States but also in Latin America. Intense debate took place among left-wing revolutionaries on the strategy and tactics to produce a successful revolution. Most of the European radicals decided to overthrow the existing regimes by the use of terror tactics in urban settings. Latin American revolutionaries examined both urban and rural insurrectionary strategies. Che Guevara, the Argentinean revolutionary and Cuban Revolution hero, and his theories on rural guerrilla tactics had an impact on all such discussions. In Asia, the revolutionary strategies of Mao Tse-tung echoed Guevara's in Latin America.

Right-wing extremists had a more difficult road to travel to regain political influence. World War II had discredited both Nazism and Italian Fascism. Despite this disfavor, adherents of these ideologies remained in place and determined to reestablish them. De-Nazification in Germany only caught a few top Nazis and soon was a casualty of the Cold War. Nazi supporters realized that Adolf Hitler's brand of Nazism would be impossible to replicate, but a similar type of regime would be possible if Hitler and Nazism could be rehabilitated. The biggest obstacle to any rehabilitation of Nazism was the Holocaust. As long as the Holocaust remained unchallenged as genocide, the subsequent neo-Nazi movement had little chance of success. Holocaust denial became both an article of faith of all neo-Nazis and later an organized international campaign.

Although Italian Fascism was not linked with the legacy of the Holocaust, it did have to fight Benito Mussolini's image as buffoon. Mussolini had organized a corporate dictatorship that revolved around his image as a powerful leader. In the interwar era, Mussolini and his brand of Fascism had a fascinating appeal to European and even American intellectuals. His regime seemed more reputable than Nazi Germany, and Mussolini basked in his reputation as a strong leader. Until World War II, this image held up to public scrutiny, but allied propaganda, the ineptness of Italian military forces, and Mussolini's ignoble death tarnished his image. Italian neo-Fascists had to overcome this image problem before any chance of success in Italian politics. The most prominent Italian neo-Fascist party, the Italian Social Movement, and its successor, the National Alliance, did have the advantage of anti-parliamentarianism in a state that had a tradition of parliamentary instability.

Extremism in the Middle East has followed a different path. The Muslim world has been in political disarray in modern times subject to what Muslim intellectuals and religious leaders perceive as Western cultural and political imperialism. Religious differences between the Sunni majority and the Shi'ite minority proved a barrier to a unified Muslim front. Followers of the various Muslim religious reformers that have appeared over the last two centuries have promoted intolerance of opposing views. Most prominent of the early fundamentalist reform movements were Wahhabism from Saudi Arabia and later the Deobandi Movement from India. The legacy of Western imperialism also produced Muslim political reformers eager to overthrow the influence of Western culture. These religious schisms and political differences made the Muslim world volatile, and the emergence of the Israeli state in 1948 only increased the volatility.

Hostility toward the state of Israel has become an article of faith among Muslim extremists. Myriad groups have formed to fight against Israel with varying degrees of effectiveness. Hostility toward Israel has come from both secular organizations, such as the Palestine Liberation Organization (PLO), and Muslim organizations, such as Hamas. All of these groups consider Israel an interloper in Palestine and a creature of Western imperialism. These beliefs have made it difficult for there to be peace in the Middle East.

The term "Islamist" figures prominently in a number of the citations in this book. This term describes those fundamentalist Muslims who call for the Muslim world to return to a purified Islam from the era of the prophet Muhammad. These Islamists want an adherence to Islamic law (*sharia*) of the Koran. Despite religious differences between Sunni and Shi'ite Muslims, Islamists share the common belief that Western culture and mores have corrupted modern Islam. They hold that only by returning to the precepts of original Islam can the evils of the Western world be driven out. These Islamists have also adopted in common the idea of waging a holy war, or jihad, to reach their goals. Because the Muslim world lacks the military might to fight a conventional war, the Islamist groups have resorted to terrorist tactics. However, even traditional terrorist tactics of assassinations, bombing, and kidnappings have a limited chance of success against a major military organization such as the Israel Defense Forces (IDF). Consequently, several of the Islamist organizations, such as Hamas, Hezbollah, Palestine Islamic Jihad, and al-Qaeda, have resorted to suicide bombings in their war against Israel and the Western powers. Suicide bombings, or martyr operations, depend on the recruitment of idealistic and nationalist youth willing to sacrifice their lives for a cause. There appears to be no shortage of Palestinians or al-Qaeda members volunteering for missions of this type.

The purpose of this book is to give an overview of the most significant extremists and extremist groups in operation in the last half century. A total of 285 citations appear in this book. I easily could have selected another hundred or so, but time and space constraints have made it impossible to do so. A decade of more research would produce a multivolume work but it would be dated within six months of its publication. Information about new groups and new leaders appear almost daily. Just keeping up to date is a daunting task.

Those individuals, groups, and events that I have included in this book have been selected for their importance in the world of extremism. Because over 85 percent of the material covers the period since 1980, I have included some individuals and groups for background. An example is Oswald Mosley and the British Union of Fascists, a group that served as the precursor of the neo-Fascism and neo-Nazism of Colin Jordan, the British National Front, the British National Party, Nick Griffin, and Combat 18.

Years ago, I wrote in another book on terrorism that there were only a limited number of scholars writing in the field. This is no longer the case, as both scholars and journalists are active in extremist and terrorist studies. Because of a wealth of new research and the complexities of research in this field, the problem of shifting though conflicting information has compounded.

In my earlier books on extremism and terrorism, I remarked on the difference in attitude toward publicity by extremists and terrorists. Terrorists in the 1970s and 1980s presented to the researcher a mass of information about themselves, their organizations, and their cause, sometimes with fabrications. In contrast, extremists have always eschewed publicity because they prefer to remain behind the scenes where they are most influential and safe. They developed the tactic of leaderless resistance that would allow small groups of dedicated followers to carry out operations without the active participation of the extremist leaders. The effectiveness of counterterrorism in the 1990s, exemplified by the ability of Israeli intelligence to successfully target Palestinian resistance leaders and eliminate them, caused the terrorists also to reject publicity. So throughout the 1990s, terrorist leaders have increasingly attempted to remain anonymous, and extremist leaders have removed themselves even farther underground. This avoidance of publicity has also complicated research.

Common spelling among Muslim names is another complication. Western names have standardized spellings, but this is not true in the various Middle East languages. Arabic is the biggest problem, as both personal and geographical names vary in spelling. A good example is Fathi Shikaki, the former head of the Palestine Islamic Jihad. His name is spelled both Shikaki and Shiqaqi and it appears each way in the literature. Another significant example is Shi'ite, a member of a branch of Islam. It appears also as Shias, and there are several other versions. I have selected Shi'ite and used it throughout the book. Finally, Hezbollah (Party of God) can be spelled Hizbollah, Hiz'bollah, or Hezballah.

Each of the 285 citations varies in length, ranging from two hundred to two thousand words. Length depended on two factors: the importance of the group, individual, or event and the information available. Each citation has been selected for its political significance. Several groups and individuals are not only politically significant but also could be classified as parts of cults. Two such entities are Japan's Aum Shinri Kyo and France's Raelian Movement. They have been included because the first initiated a poison gas attack in

Tokyo, Japan, and the latter is involved in the politics of cloning.

Writing a book is always a humbling experience. It depends on support from a variety of sources. Each of my books I have dedicated to an individual, but this time I want to mention the following five people: The first is Dr. David Pinkney, my mentor and friend from my days in graduate school at the University of Missouri–Columbia. Next is Dr. Alan Spitzer, the most demanding advisor that a graduate student could ever have and also a friend during my days at the University of Iowa. The next two were friends and supporters during my tenure at the University of Illinois–Urbana–Champaign: Hugh Atkinson, University Librarian, and Patricia Stenstrom, Library Science Librarian. Finally, there is Dr. Fred Heath, the Dean and Director at Texas A&M University Libraries and a good friend. These individuals played a significant role in the writing of this book whether they knew it or not.

I also want to thank my wife, Susan Jordan Atkins, for her support and her tolerance for my book buying. She also boosted my morale during my recent siege with colon cancer. My animal friends are still important—Miss Molly (a dog), Dudley Doright (a cat), and the most recent addition, Terrible Tommy "the Shredder" (a cat). Rocky (a cat) and Tupence (a cat) both succumbed to cancer within the last year and they are both missed.

A

Abdel-Rahman, Sheikh Omar (1938–) (Egypt)

Sheikh Omar Abdel-Rahman is the spiritual leader of the militant Islamic fundamentalist group **Islamic Group** (al-Gama'a al-Islamiyya). He was born on May 3, 1938, in the small village of al-Gamalia in the Nile Delta's Daquahliya Province. His family was poor and Abdel-Rahman lost his eyesight when he was 10 months old, probably because of diabetes. He devoted his life to Islamic studies and by age 11 had memorized a Braille copy of the Koran. In 1965, Abdel-Rahman received a master's degree at Cairo University's School of Theology. He then attended **al-Azhar University**, studying for a degree in Islamic jurisprudence.

The defeat of the Arab forces in the 1967 Arab-Israeli War was a turning point in Abdel-Rahman's political orientation. He turned much of his attention to Islamic politics, and his principal target was the regime of Egyptian President Gamal Abdel Nasser. Taking a sabbatical from his doctorate work, Abdel-Rahman assumed the post of religious scholar and prayer leader at the small village of Fedemin in the Faiyum Oasis, 60 miles south of Cairo. Over the next couple of years, he converted this area to his brand of political Islam. Abdel-Rahman's attacks on Nasser soon attracted the attention of Egyptian authorities. His accusation that Nasser

was acting as a pharaoh led to his dismissal from his religious teaching post in 1969. Then, in 1970, Egyptian authorities placed him under arrest and held him for eight months in prison. After his release, Abdel-Rahman finished his doctorate. His thesis topic was on the verse in the Koran entitled "Repentance," and his interpretation was that it endorsed holy war (jihad) against the enemies of Islam.

The Anwar Sadat regime was at first more tolerant of political dissent, and Abdel-Rahman benefited from this relaxation. By 1973, he had become a professor of theology at the University of Asyut. His militant brand of political Islam led to the formation of the Islamic Group in 1976. Most of the followers were students at the various Egyptian universities. Sadat's government began to crack down on the political opposition, and Abdel-Rahman left Egypt for Saudi Arabia. He held a post on the faculty of the Girls' College of the Imam Muhammad Ibn Saud Islamic University of Riyadh. It was during his stay in Saudia Arabia that Abdel-Rahman met and became close friends with **Hassan al-Turabi**, the leader of Sudan's National Front.

The conclusion of the Egyptian-Israeli Camp David Accords in 1979 brought Abdel-Rahman back to Egypt in 1980. His goals were to overthrow the Sadat government and establish a theocratic Islamic state,

1

and some of his followers assassinated Sadat on October 6, 1981. Abdel-Rahman had been arrested a month before the assassination, but he had escaped. The Egyptian government arrested him again and placed him on trial for the Sadat assassination with 24 others, but he was acquitted. Abdel-Rahman also escaped conviction in a conspiracy trial in which he faced charges of conspiring to overthrow the Egyptian government. Despite these acquittals, Abdel-Rahman spent nearly six years either under house arrest for his anti-Nasser preaching or in prison during the 1980s. In 1985, he traveled to Peshawar, Pakistan, and then to Afghanistan to encourage Afghan fighters against Soviet forces. As long as Abdel-Rahman directed his energies against the Soviets, he received support from the U.S. Central Intelligence Agency (CIA). He continued his anti-government agitation by preaching holy war, martyrdom for the slain, and strict adherence to the laws of the Koran. During his travels in the Middle East, Abdel-Rahman also became friends with **Osama bin Laden**. Bin Laden gave Abdel-Rahman and his supporters financial aid. In July 1990, Abdel-Rahman moved to the United States traveling on a tourist visa. His reason for coming to the United States was to build a militant Islamic group infrastructure. His initial contact was with Mustafa Shalabi at the Alkifah Refugee Center in Brooklyn. Not long afterward, Abdel-Rahman and Shalabi had a serious disagreement, and Shalabi was found murdered in March 1991. By this time, Abdel-Rahman had succeeded **Abdullah Azzam**, who had been killed in a car bombing, as the leading Islamist scholar in the international Islamist movement. On February 26, 1993, Islamic terrorists detonated a bomb in the basement garage of the World Trade Center in New York City. Several of Abdel-Rahman's supporters participated in the plot and were arrested. American authorities arrested Abdel-Rahman on July 2, 1993, and charged him in August 1993 with seditious conspiracy to wage a terrorist war against the United States. In January 1996, he was sentenced in the New York court to life imprisonment in a federal prison. He also faced charges for ordering the murder of **Meir Kahane,** the former head of the Jewish Defense League (JDL), and the plotting of the assassination of Egyptian President Hosni Mubarak. Abdel-Rahman has spent most of the time since his sentence in the basement cell of the U.S. federal prison hospital in Springfield, Missouri. In 2001, he was transferred to a maximum-security medical prison in Minnesota. He has been charged with directing the activities of his Islamic Group from prison through his lawyer and translators. **See also** Islamic Group (al-Gama'a al-Islamiyya); Al-Turabi, Abdallah Hassan; World Trade Center Bombing.

Suggested readings: Joseph P. Fried, "Sheik Sentenced to Life in Prison in Bombing Plot," *New York Times* (January 18, 1996), p. A1; Josh Meyer and John J. Goldman, "U.S. Lawyer Accused of Aiding Imprisoned Cleric in Terror Plot," *Los Angles Times* (April 10, 2002), p. A1; Caryle Murphy and Steve Coll, "The Making of an Islamic Symbol," *Washington Post* (July 9, 1993), p. A1; Simon Reeve, "Blind Sheikh behind New Terror Wave," *Scotland on Sunday* (Edinburgh) (November 23, 1997), p. 17; Mary Anne Weaver, *A Portrait of Egypt: A Journey through the World of Militant Islam* (New York: Farrar, Straus & Giroux, 1999); Mark Tran, "Sheikh Who Stirred 'Witches' Brew,'" *Guardian* (London) (October 2, 1995), p. 8.

Abu Bakr (See Bakr, Yasin Abu)

Abu Nidal (See Nidal, Abu)

Abu Nidal Organization (ANO) (Middle East)

The Abu Nidal Organization was the most notorious terrorist group in the Middle East in the period from 1974 until the early 1990s. Sabri al-Banna founded the group on November 22, 1974, and he assumed the name Abu Nidal (Father of the Revolution). His purpose was to protest the involvement of Syrian forces in the Lebanese civil war. For a time, the group had the name Black June to commemorate the uprising of the Palestinians against the Jordanians in June 1974. He modeled the ANO on the strategy and tactics of the Jewish terrorist group the **Stern Gang**. His opposition to Syrian intervention in Lebanon moderated, and he turned his attention to Israeli targets.

Abu Nidal had success in recruiting activists, and soon the Abu Nidal group had several hundred hard-core members ready to carry out operations. His hit team consisted of three or four members who were to study and then attack a designated target. From 1974 to 1990 the ANO carried out operations in 20 countries, and it killed or injured nearly 900 persons. One such example was the bombing of a Gulf Air aircraft on September 23, 1983, near Abu Dhabi, United Arab Emirates, that killed 111 passengers and crew. During its heyday, the ANO's headquarters was in Baghdad, Iraq, but most of its operations came out of Lebanon. With an operation base in Lebanon, Abu Nidal was able to recruit from the Palestinian refugee camps. Many of the ANO's operations targeted the **Palestine Liberation Organization** and its head, **Yasser Arafat**. A blood feud developed between Abu Nidal and Arafat that continued to Abu Nidal's death.

Since 1990, the Abu Nidal Organization has deteriorated and has become almost inactive. In the 1980s, terrorist experts classified the ANO as one of the most active and dangerous terrorist groups operating. Political pressure from Western and Middle Eastern governments, internal dissention, and the health of Abu Nidal have all played roles in weakening the ANO. Political pressure on Iraq (1983), Syria (1987), Libya (1999), and Egypt (1999) caused the ANO to move its operations to Baghdad, Iraq.

Another major factor in the eclipse of the group was a purge of members of the ANO by Abu Nidal in 1989. Abu Nidal became fearful of dissidents in the ANO at his training camps in Libya. He purged 150 of his 800 followers and had them executed. This action caused two leaders of the ANO, Atef Abu Baker and Abdel Rahman Issa, to break with Abu Nidal in November 1989. In addition, news of the executions hurt the ability of ANO to recruit, and membership has lagged since the purge. Much of ANO's financial support has also dried up because of its lack of support from patron states. Barry Rubin reported in *The Jerusalem Post* in 2002 that Abu Nidal and his supporters "are reported to have killed 300 people and wounded more than 650 others in a wide variety of attacks, most of them in Western Europe."

Abu Nidal had periodic health problems, including a heart condition, and he was in virtual retirement in Baghdad, Iraq. He retained control over the Abu Nidal Organization, but its last major operation was the assassination of a Jordanian diplomat in 1994. Nidal had some form of skin cancer, and he was receiving medical attention in Baghdad until August 2002. On August 14, 2002, Iraqi intelligence agents of the Mukhabarat surrounded the villa where Abu Nidal was living and attacked it. Abu Nidal was either shot or he shot himself to evade arrest. He died in a local hospital later the same day. The Abu Nidal Organization died with him. **See also** Arafat, Mohammed Yasser; Nidal, Abu; Palestine Liberation Organization (PLO).

Suggested readings: Marie Colvin and Sonya Murad, "Executed," *Sunday Times* (London) (August 25, 2002), p. 13; Con Coughlin, "He Who Lives by Terrorism," *Sunday Telegraph* (London) (August 25, 2002), p. 19; Kenneth Labich, James O. Goldsborough, and Tony Clifton, "War among the Terrorists," *Newsweek* (August 14, 1978), p. 25; Yossi Melman, *The Master Terrorist: The True Story behind Abu Nidal* (New York: Adama Books, 1986); Barry Rubin, "A Man Who Showed That Terrorism Pays," *Jerusalem Post* (August 28, 2002), p. 7; Patrick Seale, *Abu Nidal: A Gun for Hire* (New York: Random House, 1992).

Abu Sayyaf Group (Bearer of the Sword) (ASG) (Philippines)

The Abu Sayyaf Group (ASG), founded by **Ustadz Abdurajak Abubakar Janjalani** (Abu Sayyaf), Amilhussin Jumaani, and Wahab Akbar, is one of the leading Muslim separatist groups in the Philippines. This group originated as the Mujahideen Commando Freedom Fighters (MCFF) in the mid-1980s. Leaders renamed it the Abu Sayyaf Group in 1992.

Janjalani was a scholar of Islamic law in Libya before joining the anti-Soviet Afghanistan forces in the early 1980s. Jumaani, who had connections with Iran, and Akbar, who had connections with Syria, were both veterans of the International Islamic Brigade and fought in Afghanistan. It was also in Afghanistan that the leaders of the Abu Sayyaf Group made contact with two significant Islamist leaders: Abdul Rasul Sayyaf and **Osama bin Laden**. Most of the members were previously followers of the **Moro National Liberation Front** (MNLF), but they broke away after the leaders of the MNLF started negotiating with the Philippine government. By June 2001, estimates indicated that the ASG had over 1,000 active fighters and was twice as large as it was in 1994.

The ASG is organized into four line units—hit squads, demolitions, young Moro mujahideen, and recruitment. Operational control is divided between the island provinces of Basilan and Sulu, and sometimes the two factions compete with each other. Janjalani's death on December 18, 1998, led to the division of operational control between various field leaders. Janjalani's brother, Khadafy Janjalani, assumed leadership of one faction of the Abu Sayyaf, and Galib Andang, also called Commander Robot, controlled the other faction. Later, after 1999, Abu Sabaya assumed command of yet a third group. The ASG has conducted operations in different areas with financial support from a variety of sources, including funds gathered from field operations, Libya, and most recently from the **al-Qaeda** network of Osama bin Laden.

The goal of the Abu Sayyaf Group is to establish an Islamic republic in Mindanao, Philippines. Leaders of the ASG belong to the radical wing of the Islamist movement and want to establish an Islamic republic that will have no contact with other religions. They have declared open warfare against other religions and believe any form of criminal acts against Christians is justified in the pursuit of their religion. Moreover, they subscribe to the theory of martyrdom that advocates that death in a "suicide attack against the enemy is the highest form of self-sacrifice." In the pursuit of these ideas, the ASG engaged in a series of kidnaps-for-ransom, arsons, robberies, and murders in the 1990s and early 2000s. The first major operation was on January 12, 1995, when members of the Abu Sayyaf raided the Christian town of Ipil. They killed 53 persons and burned down the town center. Galib Andang's group raided the Malaysian resort on the island of Sipandan on April 23, 2000, and held for ransom 21 international guests before releasing them on the payment of $1 million ransom. Another famous operation was the kidnapping by ASG fighters of 17 tourists and three resort workers at the Dos Palmas beach resort on Palawan Island in southwest Philippines on May 27, 2001. Then on June 2, 2001, ASG members kidnapped 200 more hostages in Lamitan, Philippines. Most of the hostages were released after a ransom payment of several million U.S. dollars, and Philippine military personnel freed others. Among those kidnapped in May 2001, three hostages remained in the hands of Sabaya's faction: American missionaries Martin and Gracia Burnham and Deborah Yap. Among those executed by the Abu Sayyaf was Guillermo Sobero, an American citizen who was beheaded shortly after capture.

In the aftermath of the **September 11, 2001**, terrorist attacks in the United States, the U.S. government decided to assist the Philippine government in its battle against the Abu Sayyaf. U.S. troops have been sent since February 17, 2002, to the southern Philippines to train and assist Philippine soldiers in their fight against the guerrilla forces of the Abu Sayyaf. On April 21, 2002, elements of the Abu Sayyaf exploded bombs in the southern Philippines that killed 14 people. American troops paid special attention to the prospect of freeing the Burnhams. This effort received a setback when Philippine government troops engaged the Abu Sayyaf in Sirawai town on June 7, 2002, resulting in the deaths of Martin Burnham and Deborah Yap and the wounding of Gracia Burnham.

The increased American aid has allowed Philippine forces to harass the Abu Sayyaf. American troops are not allowed to conduct military operations, but advisors can give oral assistance and train Philippine forces. Military pressure has caused the Abu Sayyaf to split into three independent groups. Khadafy Janjalani continues to lead one group and its goal remains to establish an Islamic fundamentalist state. Another group, more interested in banditry, is under the leadership of Hamsiraji Sali. Leadership of the third group is unknown, but it was still active in the winter of 2003. Continuous military pressure is making it difficult for the Abu Sayyaf to continue operations, but it is still able to stage a terrorist attack or a kidnapping. Progress has been made in defeating the Abu Sayyaf, but it has been slow and many of the local Muslims have resented the presence of American advisors. **See also** Janjalani, Ustadz Abdurajak Abubakar; Al-Qaeda (The Base); Sabaya, Abu.

Suggested readings: Phar Kim Beng, "Abu Sayyaf's Tactical Game for Moro Loyalty," *Straits Times* (Singapore) (June 5, 2000), p. 50; Penny Crisp, "A Religious War Comes to Paradise," *Asiaweek* (May 5, 2000), p. 20; Miriam Donohoe, "Filipino Officials Allege Gang, Army in Collusion," *Irish Times* (February 16, 2002), p. 10; Rohan Gunaratna, "The Evolution and Tactics of the Abu Sayyaf Group, *Jane's Intelligence Review* 13, no. 7 (July 1, 2001); Richard Lloyd Parry, "Treasure Island," *Independent* (London) (March 4, 2001), p. 18; Ilene R. Prusher and Simon Montlake, "Across Southeast Asia, Ripple Effect of Attacks on US," *Christian Science Monitor* (September 18, 2001), p. 7; Maria A. Ressa, *Seeds of Terror: An Eyewitness Account of Al-Qaeda's Newest Center of Operations in Southeast Asia* (New York: Free Press, 2003); Marites D. Vitug and Tony Clifton, "A Rebellion with a Cause," *Newsweek* (May 15, 2000), p. 47.

Action Directe (Direct Action) (AD) (France)

Action Directe (AD) is a small group of French left-wing terrorists with anarchist tendencies that carried out a terrorist campaign from 1979, when it was founded by Jean-Marc Rouillan and Nathalie Menignon, to the 1980s. AD was constituted out of two earlier organizations: the International Revolutionary Action Group (Groupes d'action revolutionanaires internationalists) (GARI), an anti-Franco anarchist group, and the New Arms for Popular Autonomy (Noyaux armis pour l'autonomie populaire) (NAPAP), a Maoist group of Parisian urban guerrillas. Both groups had engaged in terrorist acts separately before merging. Action Directe never had a centralized leadership, but certain leaders emerged over the years: Rouillan, Menignon, Andre Olivier, Georges Cipriani, Maxime Frerot, Frederic Oriach, and Regis Schleicher. They share the idea that by attacking the French political structure they could provoke a revolution in France. Each leader or combination of leaders formed a strike force under a symbolic name and carried out operations from assassinations to bombings. The first such operation was an unsuccessful machine-gun attack on a French minister on March 18, 1979.

Action Directe carried out numerous assassinations, bank robberies, and bombings from 1979 to 1982. These operations attracted the attention of French authorities and several of the leaders, Menignon, Rouillan, and Schleicher, were arrested and imprisoned. Other leaders assumed command of strike units and continued operations. Both Menignon and Rouillan were released from jail after short stays and resumed their leadership roles. In 1982, the French government declared the Action Directe an illegal organization.

In 1982, Action Directe divided into two autonomous groups. The Paris wing formed the Action Directe Internationale (ADI) and the Lyons wing the Action Directe Nationale (ADN). The leaders of the ADI, Menignon and Rouillan, wanted to extend the activities of their group to fight against international imperialism. Olivier and Frerot were the leaders of the ADN, and they insisted on retaining the original mission of the AD to destabilize the French regime. ADI members initiated an assassination campaign against international targets. Leaders also cultivated a working relationship with the Belgian revolutionary group **Communist Fighting Cells** (Cellules Communistes Combattantes) (CCC) of Pierre Carette. ADN specialized in bank robberies during which several bank guards were killed or assaulted. These groups made life difficult for French authorities from 1982 to 1987. On November 17, 1986, a hit team of two women assassinated Georges Besse, the president of the automobile firm Renault, in the Montparnasse district of Paris.

This terrorist campaign took a toll on the leadership of both the ADI and ADN. By 1987, most of the leaders of both groups had been arrested and faced a series of state trials. The leaders of the ADI placed the French government on trial by a series of hunger strikes and charges of prison brutality. Their lawyers tried to argue mitigation, but the leaders received sentences from life imprisonment to lengthy prison terms. Leaders of the ADN also confronted the courts by challenging the judges. This tactic also failed and they also received long prison sentences.

The terrorist campaigns of ADI and ADN ended with the leaders of both groups out of circulation. French authorities estimated that there had never been more than 250 members of either group. The number of activists was probably much smaller. With 22 of the 25 known members of Action Directe in prison by 1989, French authorities classified it as inactive in 1990. **See also** Communist Fighting Cells (CCC).

Suggested readings: Yonah Alexander and Dennis Pluchinsky, *Europe's Red Terrorists: The Fighting Communist Organizations* (London: Frank Cass, 1992); Richard Bernstein, "A French Leftist Groups Says It Killed Renault's President," *New York Times* (November 19, 1986), sec. A, p. 1; Edward Cody, "France Sees Trial as Death Knell of Terror Group," *Washington Post* (January 12,

1988), p. A16; Michael Y. Dartnell, *Action Directe: Ultra-Left Terrorism in France, 1979–1987* (London: Frank Cass, 1995); William Echikson, "How the French Police Got Their Men—and Women," *Christian Science Monitor* (February 25, 1987), p. 7; Stanley Meisler, "France Captures Four Leaders of Terrorist Group," *Los Angeles Times* (February 23, 1987), p. 1.

Adair, Johnny "Mad Dog" (1964–) (Northern Ireland)

Johnny "Mad Dog" Adair is the leader of the Protestant loyalist extremist group the **Ulster Freedom Fighters** (UFF). He was born in 1964 and raised in the lower working-class district of Shankill in West Belfast, Northern Ireland. As a teenager, Adair and his buddies from Shankill were neo-Nazi skinheads following the lead of their British counterparts. Adair belonged to the NF Skinz and was a bass guitar player in a neo-Nazi punk band, the Offensive Weapon. Battles between Protestant and Catholic skinheads progressed into all-out wars in the 1980s. Adair and his friends then joined the Protestant loyalist **Ulster Defence Association** (UDA). When the Ulster Freedom Fighters formed, Adair organized his buddies and supporters into the C Company of the UFF to fight against the **Irish Republican Army** (IRA). His campaign of terror against the IRA produced at least 40 Catholic deaths in the early 1990s. His hero was the UFF leader **Billy "King Rat" Wright,** and he tried to emulate him even after Wright's death in December 1997.

Adair's activities against Catholics made him a target of both the IRA and the Northern Ireland government. Several times the IRA initiated assassination attempts against him, but each time he escaped major injury. The most serious attempt was in 1993 when the IRA exploded a bomb in Shankill that killed nine Protestants and one of the bombers in an effort to kill Adair. He was less successful against evading the Royal Union Constabulary (RUC). The RUC arrested him in 1995 and charged him with directing terrorism in Northern Ireland. His conviction earned him a 16-year prison sentence in Sep-

Ulster Freedom Fighters (UFF) leader Johnny "Mad Dog" Adair leaves the Maze Prison, Belfast, Northern Ireland, September 14, 1999, after being released under the terms of the Good Friday Agreement. Police rearrested notorious militant Adair on August 22, 2000, as Britain moved to surpress rising violence among the province's Protestant gangs. UDA flag in the background stands for Ulster Defense Association. (AP Photo/ Peter Morrison)

tember 1995. Authorities released him as a part of the Good Friday Agreement's early release program on September 14, 1999, after serving only five years, and Adair resumed his leadership of the UFF. Soon after his release, he survived a head wound from unknown assailants during a rock concert in Belfast. Despite charges of drug dealing, Adair remains a cult hero among young, working-class Protestants in Belfast.

Adair also has been a leader in the feud between the various Protestant loyalist groups. His UFF group has engaged the **Ulster Volunteer Force** (UVF) in a deadly game of murder. Adair has never accepted peace with the IRA, and his partisans have attacked any Protestant figure that has accepted the peace agreement. In early August 2000, members of the UFF attacked UVA members and their families in Shankill in an effort to drive them out of the neighborhood. On August 22, 2000, the Northern Ireland Secretary Peter Mandelson had Adair arrested for his role in the loyalist feud and imprisoned him in Maghaberry prison. Adair continued to direct of the UFF until his release on May 15, 2002. Much of his efforts in prison focused on trying to woo Wright's **Loyalist Volunteer Force** (LVF) into rejoining the UFF. Since his release from prison, Adair spent most of his attention tightening his control over the UDA and reinventing his political image. His revamped image and desire to run for public office had repercussions within the UDA. In September 2002, the UDA's council expelled Adair from UDA along with his ally John White for becoming too friendly with the LVF. Adair is now caught in the middle of the feud between the UDA and the LVF. His feud with other elements in the UDA led to the Ulster government returning him to prison on January 10, 2003, where he remains. Adair continues to run the UFF from Maghaberry prison, and he is suspected of ordering the assassination of John "Grug" Gregg, a member of UDA's ruling council and one of the failed assassins of Gerry Adams in 1984, on Febuary 3, 2003. This murder and pressure from his former colleagues has caused his wife, family, and close friends to leave the Shankill area of Belfast and move to Scotland. See also Irish Republican Army (IRA); Ulster Defence Association (UDA)/Ulster Freedom Fighters (UFF); Ulster Volunteer Force (UVF).

Suggested readings: Mike Browne, "He'll be Dead by Xmas," *People* (London) (October 6, 2002), p. 4; Ian Bruce, "So Who Will Be the Next Target?" *Herald* (Glasgow) (May 11, 2002), p. 13; Liam Clarke, "Could Mad Dog Be Trying to Replace the King Rat?" *Sunday Times* (London) (July 2000), p. 1; Rosie Cowan, "Loyalists on the Brink of War as UDA Chief Is Shot Dead," *Guardian* (February 3, 2003), p. 5; Roisin Ingle, "Master of Mad Dogs and Orangemen," *Irish Times* (July 15, 2000), p. 9; Tim Luckhurst, "Johnny Rotten," *Daily Mail* (London) (February 7, 2003), p. 12; David McKittrick, "Ulster: 'Mad Dog' at Heart of Convulsions in Loyalists Belfast," *Independent* (London) (August 21, 2000), p. 4; Henry McDonald, "Loyalists at War," *Observer* (London) (August 27, 2000), p. 14; Michael Tierney, "The Jigsaw Man," *Herald* (Glasgow) (August 26, 2000), p. 8.

Adams, Gerry (1948–) (Northern Ireland)
Gerry Adams is the leader of the political wing of the **Provisional Irish Republican Army** (Provos), the **Sinn Fein**. He was born on October 6, 1948, in the Falls Road area of Belfast, Northern Ireland, into an Irish Catholic republican family. His father and several member of his mother's Hannaway family had been active in the **Irish Republican Army** (IRA). Adams was the oldest of 10 brothers and sisters. His father was an unskilled building laborer and his mother worked in linen mills. He attended several Catholic schools before entering St. Mary's Grammar School, and he was a good but not outstanding student. After leaving school in early 1965, he became a barman first at a Belfast Protestant pub, the Ark, and later at the Duke of York. Earlier in 1964, he had joined D Company (D Coy) of the Belfast Brigade of the IRA. His membership was in part because of increasing tensions in Belfast over Protestant loyalist leader **Ian Paisley**'s protests about the displaying of the Irish tricolor in Belfast. Adams participated in the Catholic civil rights movement in the mid-1960s, but he became discouraged about its prospects. Most of his political education came from his membership in the Wolfe Tone Society, an Irish republican literary and debating society. Adams and other young republicans started a political newssheet, the *Spearhead, Voice of Republican North*, as their contribution in the propaganda war in Northern Ireland.

The Ulster loyalist revolt against the Catholic civil rights movement caused Adams to become more militant. Adams commanded the Belfast Brigade of the Provisional IRA before his arrest and imprisonment in Long Kesh prison in 1973. Adams was released briefly to negotiate a truce with the British and the IRA, but he was rearrested shortly after the truce expired. Adams endured beatings in prison that resulted in kidney problems, which he suffers from to this day. Between December 2, 1977, and February 18, 1978, Adams was the IRA's chief of staff. His diplomatic skills led him to become one of the political leaders of the reorganized Provisional Irish Republican Army. Younger leaders were emerging from the ranks of the IRA, and Adams served as their spokesperson. In 1983, Adams became president of the Sinn Fein.

Sinn Fein's Martin McGuinness, left, and President Gerry Adams, right, address a crowd of republicans outside the Belfast City Hall, Northern Ireland, August 10, 1997. An estimated 3,000 Irish Republican Army supporters marched into downtown Belfast that Sunday to demand a negotiated end to British rule. The commemoration officially marked the 26th anniversary since the British government implemented internment. The T-shirt worn by Gerry Adams is in celebration of the West Belfast Festival, with many events throughout that August. (AP Photo/ Paul McErlane)

Several times, Ulster loyalist groups targeted Adams for assassination. The closest call was on April 14, 1984, when three **Ulster Freedom Fighters** (UFF) gunmen shot him four times in downtown Belfast. Only quick medical attention saved his life. Another attempt on Adams's life was made by Michal Stone, a member of the UFF, at an IRA funeral on March 11, 1998. This time Adams escaped injury.

Sometime in the late 1970s Adams became leader of the moderate wing of the Provi-

sional IRA. By the early 1980s, he had converted to acceptance of the political process in Northern Ireland, but he needed followers. Adams formed a political alliance with another former militant, **Martin McGuinness**. Together they began to take steps to moderate the terror tactics of the Provisional IRA without causing widespread defections of militants. These steps led to the Provisional IRA's declaration of a cease-fire in 1994. This strategy of moderation was only partially successful as key dissidents left the Provisional IRA to join other groups willing to continue the war against the Protestants in Northern Ireland. In 1998, Adams was a key participant in the Good Friday Accords that ended the Provisional IRA's open warfare in Northern Ireland.

Adams is now a power in Northern Ireland politics as the head of Sinn Fein, but the animosity built up among Protestants over his role in the terror campaign of the Provisional IRA has not diminished. His sponsorship of McGuinness's role in government, however, helped him win office. Adams has also been in the middle of controversy over the demand by the British government to decommission the arms of the Provisional IRA. He has walked a delicate path between accommodation and stubbornness. His commitment to the peace process has remained steady, but he remains a controversial figure in Northern Ireland politics. **See also** Irish Republican Army (IRA); McGuinness, Martin; Provisional Irish Republican Army (Provos) (PIRA).

Suggested readings: Tim Pat Coogan, *The IRA: A History* (Niwot, CO: Roberts Rinehart, 1993); Simon Hattenstone, "The Survivor," *Guardian* (London) (April 30, 2001), p. 2; Ed Moloney, *A Secret History of the IRA* (New York: Norton, 2002); Gerry Moriarty, "Leaders Strolled Their Way towards History," *Irish Times* (October 27, 2001), p. 8; Kathleen Ochshorn, "An Exclusive Interview with Sinn Fein Leader Gerry Adams," *St. Petersburg Times* (Florida) (July 6, 2003), p. 1D; Fintan O'Toole, "Adams—From IRA Pariah to A-List Celebrity," *Sunday Times* (London) (February 23, 2003), p. 8; David Sharrock and Mark Davenport, *Man of War, Man of Peace: The Unauthorised Biography of Gerry Adams* (London: Pan Books, 1997); Kevin Toolis, "A Not So Simple Sorry Marks the Beginning of the End for the IRA," *Herald* (Glasgow) (July 20, 2002), p. 11.

Advani, Lal Krishna (1928–) (India)

Lal Krishna Advani is one of India's leading Hindu nationalist extremists. He was born in Karachi, India (now in Pakistan), in 1928. Advani attended St. Patrick's Missionary High School in Karachi. On June 20, 1942, Advani heard a lecture by a member of the radical Hindu nationalist group **Rashtriya Swayamsevak Sangh** (RSS). After the lecture, he became a convert to Hindu nationalism and the RSS. His devotion to the RSS intensified after meeting its leader, M. S. Golwalker. After high school, Advani briefly considered a career in engineering before going to law school at Bombay University. He continued his membership in the RSS throughout his schooling. After graduation from law school, he devoted most of his attention to RSS politics.

Advani was a leader of the RSS in Karachi when the partition of India took place in 1947. He had opposed the partition, and his hostility toward Pakistan has never diminished. After the RSS was banned by the Indian government in 1948 because of the assassination of Mohandas K. Gandhi, Advani continued his Hindu nationalist activities. He advanced the radical Hindu Nationalist program called "Hindutva." The goal of Hindutva is to turn India into a Hindu state and exclude all other religions in India. In 1980, he cofounded the Hindu nationalist party Bharatiya Janata Party (BJP). He was the BJP general secretary and then president of BJP in the 1980s and 1990s. In 1992, he led a months-long Hindu campaign to destroy the Muslim Babri Mosque in Ayodyha, which sparked riots throughout India that caused the death of more than 3,000. Hindu leaders had claimed that the Muslim Mosque had been built on the site of the birthplace of the Hindu god Ram. Advani later decried the loss of life, but his daughter-in-law, in a March 2002 written submission to an inquiry commission investigating the destruction of the mosque, alleged that he had ordered its demolition.

Advani's political ascendancy in Indian politics has been the result of the electoral success of the BJP. The victory of the BJP in the 1998 election and the elevation of Atal Bihari Vajpayee as prime minister have made Advani the number-two politician in the Indian government. Advani has long been an opponent of Pakistan and a hawk over Kashmir. His advocacy of the use of India's nuclear arsenal in any conflict with Pakistan is public knowledge. He favored military action against Pakistan during the border standoff between India and Pakistan over Kashmir in 2001–2002. Advani still is active promoting India as a Hindu state with no tolerance for other religions or beliefs. On June 29, 2002, Advani was appointed Deputy Prime Minister, and many consider him as the heir apparent to Prime Minister Vajpayee. **See also** Rashtriya Swayamsevak Sangh (National Volunteer Organization) (RSS).

Suggested readings: Rahul Bedi, "Hindus in India Target Other Religions," *Irish Times* (November 14, 2000), p. 16; Prabhu Chawla, Swapan Dasgupta, and Rajeev Deshpande, "L. K. Advani: 'I am Vajpayee's Voice for He Heads the Government'," *India Today* (July 22, 2002), p. 1; H.D.S. Greenway, "Rising Threat of Hindu Extremism," *Boston Globe* (July 12, 2002), p. A15; Manjeet Kripalani, "A Hard-Liner at the Helm?" *Business Week* (August 26, 2002), p. 22; Robert Marquand, "India's Leader-in-Waiting Fans Hindu Nationalism," *Christian Science Monitor* (July 26, 2002), p. 1; Shaikh Azizur Rahman, "In-Law Blames Hindu Official of '92 Riots," *Washington Times* (March 8, 2002), p. A17.

Afghan Arabs (Middle East)

The unintended consequence of the Afghanistan-Soviet War in the 1980s was the formation of a cadre of Afghan Arabs willing to carry on a war with the West. Among fundamentalist Muslims, the war against the atheistic Soviets was a jihad, or holy war. Volunteers had come from all over the Muslim world to fight in this holy cause. These volunteers started arriving in 1986, partly stimulated by Saudi Arabian Airlines giving a 75 percent discount on flights to Peshawar, Pakistan, for those joining the mujahideen. Religious support came from Pakistan and other Arab states, but weaponry and supplies came from the United States. Pakistani security authorities kept the Americans away from the Afghanistan fighters. At least 25 countries had natives fighting in the Afghanistan War. Estimates of the number of Afghan Arabs that

fought in Afghanistan range from the CIA estimate of 17,000 to the British intelligence source of *Jane's Intelligence Review's* 14,000. *Jane's* also broke down the totals by nationality—5,000 Saudis, 3,000 Yemenis, 2,800 Algerians, 2,000 Egyptians, 400 Tunisians, 370 Iraqis, 200 Libyans, and a score of other nationalities. One observer noted that, for the Afghan Arabs, "Afghanistan was like a university which introduced a new ideology and school of thought." After the war, most of these Afghan Arabs returned to their native lands full of devotion to the Islamist cause. Other Afghan Arabs moved to western cities, especially London and Frankfurt, because they were unwelcome in their native lands.

In the past decade, whenever an opportunity arose to advance the Islamist cause, Afghan Arabs appeared on the scene. Algerian Afghan Arabs provided the military leaders and fighters for the **Armed Islamic Group** and the **Islamic Salvation Front** in the Algerian civil war in the 1990s. Next, Afghan Arabs appeared in Albania to train the Kosovo Liberation Army (KLA) and then to fight in Kosovo. Another group appeared in the Philippines to form the **Abu Sayyaf** terrorist group. Afghan Arabs have also been active in Chechnya fighting Russian military forces. Many Afghan Arabs also returned to Afghanistan and fought for the Taliban.

A number of leaders emerged among the Afghan Arabs. Most notable among these **Osama bin Laden** and **Ayman al-Zawahiri**. It is from the cadre of Afghan Arabs that bin Laden has been able to recruit members for his **al-Qaeda** network of terrorist organizations. **See also** Bin Laden, Osama; Al-Qaeda (The Base); Taliban (Students of Religious Schools).

Suggested readings: Mark Huband, *Warriors of the Prophet: The Struggle for Islam* (Boulder, CO: Westview Press, 1999); Roland Jacquard, *In the Name of Osama Bin Laden: Global Terrorism and the Bin Laden Brotherhood* (Durham, NC: Duke University Press, 2002); Elizabeth Shogren and Douglas Frantz, "U.S. Aid to Afghan Rebels Proves a Deadly Boomerang," *Los Angeles Times* (August 2, 1993), p. A1.

Afrikaner Resistance Movement (Afrikaner Weerstandsbeweging) (AWB) (South Africa)

The Afrikaner Resistance Movement (AWB) is the leading neo-Nazi group in South Africa. Its current leader is **Eugene Terre Blanche**. Terre Blanche founded the AWB in 1976 and it gained notoriety because members of the AWB trained the Inkatha hit squads that fought a war with the African National Congress (ANC). Terre Blanche operated the AWB from his headquarters at Venterdorp until he had to sell it in 1994 to pay legal fees. He formed the AWB as an openly militaristic organization to lead the fight to preserve white dominance in South Africa. A commando unit, the AWB Victory Commando (Wendocommando), forms the strike force for the AWB. In 1990, the AWB had about 3,600 hard-core members, but in the agitation of the 1992 national elections, membership increased to around 18,000. An estimate of the size of the Victory Commando shock troops at that time was in the 8,000 to 9,000 ranges. The leader of the AWB's military wing is Kirk Ackerman and he has retained close personal ties to Terre Blanche. Additional aid for the AWB in case of an insurrection comes from supporters in the South African military. Without this support, the AWB is too lightly armed to fight South African security forces. In 1992, the Afrikaner Resistance Movement joined the Afrikaner People's Front (Afrikaner Volkfront) (AVF) in a common right-wing unity movement to pressure the de Klerk government for a white homeland in South Africa. Efforts were made on the political front to disrupt negotiations between the African National Congress (ANC) and the de Klerk government to gather arms for a possible insurrection. A member of the AWB, Janusz Walus, murdered the popular black politician and head of the South African Communist Party, Chris Hani, on April 10, 1993. Walus's support from two officials of the Conservative Party and the rank-and-file of the AWB showed the strength of popular support among Afrikaners. Divisions among the extreme right caused the Afrikaner vote in the general elections on April 27, 1994, to split between General Constand Viljoen's Freedom Front and Terre Blanche's AWB. Terre Blanche had called for a general boycott of the election. This strategy backfired on the AWB and the movement became almost marginalized. No longer has the AWB been able to terrorize its opponents as it did before the election. Terre Blanche has also lost considerable prestige because of his failure to mount an insurrection to prevent a Mandela government. He has continued to campaign for an Afrikaner homeland, but the more radical wing of the AWB has left to form the **Boer Resistance Movement** (Boere Weerstandsbeweging, or BWB).

An offshoot of the Afrikaner Resistance Movement was the White Wolves (Die Wit Wolwe). Under the leadership of Barend Strydom, it declared open war against the South African government of President Frederik W. de Klerk and the ANC in the early 1990s. Besides outright terrorism, members also conducted psychological warfare by issuing bomb threats to all of its perceived enemies. It claimed responsibility for the firebombing of a church orphanage in Pretoria, South Africa, in March 1992 in which seven black children were killed. Much of the White Wolves' activities were directed toward destabilizing South Africa before the April 1994 national election. Instead, the White Wolves and its sponsor, the Afrikaner Resistance Movement, ensured that Nelson Mandela and the African National Congress were victorious. After the election, members of the White Wolves returned to the Afrikaner Resistance Movement and other white separatist groups. **See also** Boer Resistance Movement (Boere Weerstandsbeweging) (BWB); Terre Blanche, Eugene Ney.

Suggested readings: Richard Ellis, "Afrikaners Threaten Guerrilla Campaign," *Sunday Times* (London) (June 27, 1993), p. 1; Joseph Lelyveld, "Extremist South African Group Arouses Concern," *New York Times* (August 23, 1981), sec. 1, p. 3; Edward O'Loughlin, "Terre Blanche's AWB Awaits Dawn of Bloodshed," *Irish Times* (August 8, 1995), p. 7; David B. Ottaway, "White Militants Challenge S. African Reforms," *Washington Post* (February 3, 1992), p. A13;

David B. Ottaway, "White Terrorism Increases in South Africa," *Washington Post* (July 21, 1990), p. A16.

Ahmeti, Ali, (1959–) (Macedonia)

Ali Ahmeti is the leader of the Albanian-Macedonian National Liberation Army (NLA). He was born on January 4, 1959, into an Albanian Muslim family in Kicevo, Macedonia. His early life was spent in the village of Zajas near Kicevo. He studied philosophy at the University of Pristina in Kosovo (then in Yugoslavia). Yugoslavian authorities imprisoned him for two months for his activities in the 1981 uprising of Albanian students at the University of Pristina. After his release from prison, Ahmeti fled to Switzerland. In Switzerland, Ahmeti joined the Movement for an Albanian Socialist Republic in Yugoslavia. His political views at this time were those of an Albanian nationalist with a strong Marxist-Leninist orientation.

Ahmeti decided in the early 1990s to return to the Balkans and organize forces against Yugoslavia and Macedonia. By 1993, he was back in Macedonia organizing guerrilla groups. During the Kosovo War, he became affiliated with the Kosovo Liberation Army (KLA) and fought beside the KLA in that war. After the success of the KLA in Kosovo, Ahmeti decided to adopt the same guerrilla strategy in Macedonia. This strategy was to initiate open guerrilla warfare followed by a willingness to negotiate to attract the Western powers to intervene on his side against the Macedonian government. He also had an experienced army because many of the military leaders and fighters in the National Liberation Army had fought in Kosovo and they brought their weapons with them. The National Liberation Army launched its offensive in February 2001. This strategy of inviting outside powers was successful, with the Western powers intervening in the civil war on the side of the Albanian minority and ensuring a political settlement. Ahmeti continued to claim that constitutional and political guarantees were his only goals, and in early June 2002, he established a new political party. This party, the Democratic Union for Integration, is the personal creation of Ahmeti, and he used his reputation as an Albanian military leader to challenge the Macedonian government in the September 2002 elections. This gamble was successful, as his party is now one of the two coalition parties heading the government. Ahmeti has made the transition from guerrilla leader to politician, but his inclusion on the Bush administration's list of outlawed Albanian terrorists still leaves his status questionable.

Suggested readings: Timothy Garton Ash, "Is There a Good Terrorist?" *New York Review of Books* XLVIII, no. 19 (November 29, 2001); Ian Fisher, "Shadowy Rebel Assures Macedonia That He Seeks Peace," *New York Times* (August 17, 2001), p. A3; Ashley Fantz, "Yesterday's Terrorist, Today's Peacemaker," http://salon.com/ (accessed September 17, 2002); Richard Mertens, "Once a Rebel, Now a Reformer," *Christian Science Monitor* (July 18, 2002), p. 6; Alissa J. Rubin, "Rebel Leader No Longer Persona Non Grata," *Los Angeles Times* (August 20, 2001), p. A5; Daniel Simpson, "An Uphill Fight in Macedonia to Fend Off Chaos," *New York Times* (June 14, 2002), p. A6; R. Jeffrey Smith, "Birth of New Rebel Army," *Washington Post* (March 30, 2001), p. A1; Nicholas Wood, "Macedonian Rebel Chief Calls Off War," *Guardian* (London) (September 28, 2001), p. 18.

Alex Boncayao Brigade (ABB) (Philippines)

The Alex Boncayao Brigade (ABB) is a Philippine Communist urban terrorist group that operates in Manila. This group is named after Alex Boncayao, a Philippine labor leader in the **New Peoples Army** (NPA) who was killed by the Philippine Army in 1983 in an engagement in Nueva Ecija province. Urban guerrillas affiliated with the New Peoples Army formed the ABB in Manila in 1984 to carry the guerrilla war to the Philippine capital city. This group specialized in assassinations. Its first victim, in May 1984, was Brigadier General Tomás Karingal, the commander of Manila's northern sector.

Members of this group splintered off from the Maoist Communist New Peoples Army

(NPA) in May 1993. Felimon Lagman, a rival to José María Sison as leader of the Communist Party of the Philippines (CPP), is the head of the ABB. Lagman was unhappy with the dictatorial leadership of Sison, and he wanted to change revolutionary strategy in the Philippines. Sison's strategy was to control the countryside following the peasant-oriented strategy developed by the Chinese Communist leader Mao Tse-tung. Lagman believed that the revolutionary struggle should shift to the cities. He started out with 50 operatives from the NPA, but by March 1995, Lagman claimed in an interview with the *Christian Science Monitor* that his group had 13,000 supporters. A more recent estimate in 2000 by the staff of the *Journal of Counterterrorism and Security International* placed the strength of the ABB at around 500. Special targets for the ABB have been Manila businessmen and government officials. At last count, the members of the ABB had killed around 100 of them. Unlike the New Peoples Army, the leadership of the ABB has had no contact with the Muslim insurgents in the southern Philippines. **See also** New Peoples Army (NPA).

Suggested readings: Cameron W. Barr, "Philippines' Communists Losing Enemies, Keep the Faith," *Christian Science Monitor* (March 21, 1995), p. 7; Nirmal Ghosh, "Divided Philippine Communists Appear to Be Shifting Strategy," *Straits Times* (Singapore) (December 28, 1995), p. 15; Gregg R. Jones, *Red Revolution: Inside the Philippine Guerrilla Movement* (Boulder, CO: Westview Press, 1989); IACSP Staff, "Terrorists at War in the Philippines," *Journal of Counterterrorism and Security International* 6, no. 4 (Summer 2000).

Amal (Lebanon)

Amal is a Lebanese Shi'ite group that has resorted to terrorism. **Musa al-Sadr** founded the political party Harakat al-Mahrumin (Movement of the Deprived) in 1974 to represent the interests of the Shi'ite population in Lebanon. In July 1975, he formed the militia wing Amal (Harakat Amal) (Movement of Hope). Amal comes from the acronym AMAL, from Afwaj al-Muqawama al-Lubnaniya (Lebanese Resistance Detachment). Al-Sadr used Amal as a fighting force to protect the Shi'ites in southern Lebanon. At first, al-Sadr had Amal cooperate with Kamal al-Jumblatt's Lebanese National Movement, but he found Jumblatt's role in the Lebanese civil war in 1975 unsatisfactory. The Amal found itself caught in the middle of the civil war and sometimes had to fight on one side or the other. The presence of the **Palestine Liberation Organization** (PLO) complicated the situation. Caught in the middle of the struggle between the PLO and Israel, Amal forces found that they had difficulties with both sides. The Israeli invasion of Lebanon in 1978 caused even more chaos. Al-Sadr's disappearance and probable murder during a visit in **Muammar Qaddafi**'s Libya in August 1978 produced a change of leadership in Amal.

The loss of al-Sadr changed the orientation of Amal. His prestige as a religious leader could not be matched. Husain al-Husaini, a Shi'ite parliamentary leader, replaced al-Sadr, but he proved to be ineffective as a leader. Nabih Berri, a lawyer who had studied at the Sorbonne University in Paris, replaced al-Husaini in 1980. In the interval, the Iranian Revolution of 1979 had changed the political landscape for Shi'ites. Ayatollah Khomeini's fundamentalist Islamic regime in Iran revitalized Lebanon's Shi'ites. Membership in Amal had always been small, but the number of sympathizers had been large. Much of its financial support came from urban Shi'ites, but they did little of the fighting. Relations between Amal and the leaders of Syria have always been good, and in the 1980s, Syrian president Hafiz al-Asad counted on its support during the Syrian intervention in eastern Lebanon.

Amal's Syrian ties and opposition to PLO activities in southern Lebanon led to fighting between Amal and the PLO in 1982. Amal leaders were uncertain about the Israeli invasion in 1982 until it became apparent that the Israelis wanted to occupy southern Lebanon. Amal has had an anti-Israel orientation, but its bad relationship with the PLO had deteriorated to the point that its defeat was watched with some satisfaction. Israeli efforts to incorporate the Amal into a militia group to support Israeli occupation failed, and hostilities opened between the Amal and Israeli military forces.

Berri's leadership of Amal has had to withstand several serious challenges. Husain Musawi, a member of Amal's Command Council, broke with Amal in the summer of 1982. He wanted to recast Amal as a pro-Khomeini group and found a Shi'ite Islamic state. After leaving Amal, Musawi founded the Islamic Amal Movement. Another challenger was the Shi'ite religious leader Mufti Muhammad Mahdi Shams al-Din. He led the religious wing of Amal in a revolt against Berri, but in early 1983, he left Amal to engage in Shi'ite politics on the national level. Berri has been able to withstand these challenges, but he remains first among equals, and much of his energy is devoted to persuasion rather than the giving of orders.

The most serious threat to Amal has come from the Iran-sponsored **Hezbollah**. Whereas most of the leadership of Amal is secular, the leadership of Hezbollah is clerical. These fundamentalist Shi'ite clerics called for a Shi'ite Islamic state modeled after Ayatollah Khomeini's regime in Iran and attracted significant support from militant Shi'ites, taking members away from Amal. These differences led to a civil war between Amal and Hezbollah that broke out in May 1988. Syrian President Hafiz al-Asad distrusted Hezbollah because of its close ties to Iran. This civil war only lasted until January 1989, when the Damascus Agreement was signed under the auspices of Syria. Both groups then turned their attention to the fight against Israel.

Gradually the leadership of Amal has turned away from military operations against Israel to a greater involvement in Lebanese politics. Hezbollah's leaders have attacked Berri for being too moderate and as an enemy of an Islamic revolution in Lebanon. These attacks led Berri to adopt more militant tactics in the late 1980s, but his entry into mainstream Lebanese politics in the 1990s reduced his interest in the war against Israel. Berri's election as president of the Lebanese parliament on November 20, 1992, is an indication of his more moderate image. **See also** Hezbollah (Party of God); al-Sadr, Musa.

Suggested readings: Fouad Ajami, *The Vanished Imam: Musa al Sadr and the Shia of Lebanon* (Ithaca, NY: Cornell University Press, 1986); Hala Jaber, *Hezbollah: Born with a Vengeance* (New York: Columbia University Press, 1997); Augustus Richard Norton, *Amal and the Shi'a: Struggle for the Soul of Lebanon* (Austin, TX: University of Texas Press, 1987); Robin Wright, *Sacred Rage: The Wrath of Militant Islam* (New York: Simon & Schuster, 1985).

Amir, Yigal (1970–) (Israel)

Yigal Amir is the Israeli religious extremist who assassinated Israeli Prime Minister Yitzhak Rabin. He was born in 1970 in Herzliya, a suburb of Tel Aviv. His parents were both Yemenite immigrants to Israel. They were members of the extreme Orthodox Haredi Sephardi community. Amir was one of eight children, four boys and four girls. At age six, Amir began schooling at the Haredi Wolfsohn School in Herzliya. Then at twelve, he entered the elite Yishev Hadash (New Community) Yeshiva in Tel Aviv. Amir was a dedicated but difficult student noted for his dogmatic religious views. Although Amir could have escaped military service, he allowed himself to be drafted into the Israel Defense Forces (IDF). Amir joined the 13th Battalion of the Golani Brigade. During the 1987 Palestinian Intifada, his battalion was sent into the occupied territories to quell the riots. His strong religious views caused him to have arguments with the more secular soldiers, and he also earned a reputation for his harsh conduct towards Palestinians. After leaving the Israel Defense Forces, he began study at the Kerem D'Yavneh Yeshiva. In the summer of 1992, his yeshiva sent him to Riga, Latvia, to serve as a counselor in summer camps for Jewish youth. He also voted in the 1992 elections for the radical right-wing Moledet (Homeland) Party. In 1993, he entered Bar-Ilan University to study law and computer science.

Yigal Amir, Israeli Prime Minister Yitzhak Rabin's assassin, gives the thumbs up in the Tel Aviv District Court, September 11, 1996, moments before Amir, together with his brother Haggai and friend Dror Adani, were all found guilty of conspiracy to kill the prime minister. Yigal Amir, who was already convicted of murder and received a life term, was sentenced October 3, 1996, with Haggai Amir and Adani on the most recent charges. (AP Photo/ Nati Harnik)

Amir became a convert to the Greater Israel movement. This movement grew after the 1967 Arab-Palestinian War when Israel seized land outside Israel proper. Under the leadership of Rabbi Zvi Yehuda Kook, an Orthodox rabbi who headed the Mercaz Harav (Rabbi's Center) Yeshiva in Jerusalem, the Greater Israel movement gained adherents. His preaching to reestablish the Israel of biblical times meant Israeli expansion into the West Bank, Gaza, and Jordan. The **Gush Emunim** (Bloc of the Faithful) formed in January 1974 with the goal of establishing Israeli settlements in the West Bank and Gaza. These nearly 300,000 settlers and their political allies in Israel have opposed any settlement that would restore Palestinian lands or the formation of a Palestinian state. Any Israeli politician that proposed or backed a peaceful agreement with the Palestinians was classified as a traitor. The series of agreements culminating in the Oslo Agreement negotiated by Rabin were constantly attacked. A number of Jewish rabbis, both in Israel and the United States, declared Rabin to be in *din rodef* (duty to kill a Jew who imperils the life or property of another) for agreeing to a Palestinian state.

Once Amir learned of the rabbis' ruling, he began making preparations to assassinate Rabin. He recruited his brother Haggai Amir, and Dror Adani, a friend of Yemenite background, into the conspiracy. Later, he brought his girlfriend, Margalit Har-Shefi, and others into the planning. After studying several assassination scenarios, Amir decided to act alone. Amir picked a political rally on November 4, 1995, where Rabin would be making a speech. As Rabin left the rally, Amir came up behind him and fired three shots from his nine-millimeter Beretta. Two of the hollow-point bullets hit Rabin, and the third bullet wounded his bodyguard. Shabak, Israel security officers, and policemen seized Amir and disarmed him. Rabin was rushed to a hospital, where he died an hour and a half later at 11:00 P.M. Police arrested the other conspirators in a matter of days. On March 27, 1996, Amir was convicted of the assassination of Rabin and sentenced to life imprisonment plus six years for the wounding of Rabin's bodyguard. In a second trial, Amir received another five-year sentence for conspiracy to harm Arabs. On December 20, 2001, the Israeli parliament (the Knesset) passed a bill that barred a pardon or commutation of a sentence for any convicted killer of a prime minister if he or she is found to have acted with a political motive. This bill earned the title of "Yigal Amir Bill" because it was so obviously directed against him.

The assassination of Rabin exposed the bitter political divisions within Israel. Some Orthodox right-wing Israelis and adherents of the Greater Israel movement have adopted Amir as a hero. More secular Israelis condemned the assassination, and they have been surprised at the outpouring of support for Amir. A poll in the summer of 1996 found almost a sixth of Israelis condoned the assassination. Many right-wing politicians, however, including Benjamin Netanyahu and Ariel Sharon, backtracked on their attacks against Rabin but not without some embarrassing moments. **See also** Gush Emunim (Bloc of the Faithful).

Suggested readings: Joel Greenberg, "New Law Bars Rabin's Killer from Pardon or Commutation," *New York Times* (December 20, 2001), sec. A, p. 16; Michael Karpin and Ina Friedman, *Murder in the Name of God: The Plot to Kill Yitzhak Rabin* (New York: Metropolitan Books, 1998); Yoram Peri (ed.), *The Assassination of Yitzhak Rabin* (Stanford, CA: Stanford University Press, 2000); Israel Shahak and Norton Mezvinsky, *Jewish Fundamentalism in Israel* (London: Pluto Press, 1999); Ehud Sprinzak, *Brother against Brother: Violence and Extremism in Israeli Politics from Altalena to the Rabin Assassination* (New York: Free Press, 1999).

Angry Brigade (Great Britain)

The Angry Brigade was a British, left-wing, anarchist terrorist group that conducted a bombing campaign in the 1970s. This group of only 12 members came out of the political turmoil on British university campuses in the late 1960s. These students at Cambridge University and Essex University had become alienated from British society, but no common ideology united them. Politics of action attracted them into violence against the establishment. Key members were John Barker, Christopher Bott, Hilary Creek, Stuart Christie, James Greenfield, Kate McLean, Anna Mendleson, Jake Prescott, Ian Purdie, and Angela Weir. They decided to form a libertarian socialist group in late February 1970 and name it the Angry Brigade.

The members of the Angry Brigade initiated a bombing campaign against the British state. On May 22, 1970, members of the Angry Brigade planted a bomb at the Paddington Green Police Station in London, but it failed to explode. Over the next year and a half they exploded dozens of bombs in a campaign that lasted until August 15, 1971. Targets varied from conservative politicians to the Miss World competition. Bombers were careful to avoid casualties and there were no fatalities, only considerable property damage. At first, the British police were mystified by the bombings, but this ended when the leaders of the Angry Brigade began issuing communiqués justifying the bombings. On January 13, 1971, a communiqué announced the Angry Brigade's responsibility for the bombs at the home of Robert Carr, the Tory secretary of state for employment and productivity. Police began a nationwide hunt for the bombers, especially after another communiqué announced that Prime Minister Edward Heath was a target.

Each successive bombing gave the police more evidence until they had enough evidence to conclude that the Angry Brigade was former students. Police also found evidence that the members of the Angry Brigade were financing operations by writing fraudulent checks on banks. A tip from an unknown person alerted the police to a house occupied by four university dropouts.

The raid on a house on Amhurst Road in London on August 20, 1971, produced enough evidence to arrest the ringleaders of the Angry Brigade. Police found explosives, weapons, and a hand-operated duplicating machine used for the production of the communiqués. Among those arrested at the time were Barker, Creek, Greenfield, and Mendleson. Later the police arrested Bott, Christie, McLean, and Weir. These eight received a trial that lasted from May to December 1972. Barker, Creek, Greenfield, and Mendleson were sentenced to 10 years in prison. The other four defendants were acquitted. Both Creek and Mendleson were let out of prison after only five years, but the men served sentences of more than seven years. All members of the Angry Brigade have slipped into obscurity and no longer are active in politics.

Suggested readings: Martin Bright, "Look Back in Anger," *Observer* (February 3, 2002), p. 17; Gordon Carr, *The Angry Brigade: The Cause and the Case* (London: Gollanz, 1975); Christopher Dobson and Ronald Payne, *The Terrorists: Their Weapons, Leaders and Tactics*, rev. ed. (New York: Facts on File, 1982); Jonathon Green, "The Urban Guerrillas Britain Forgot," *New Statesman* (August 27, 2001), p. 1; Tom Vague, *Anarchy in the UK: The Angry Brigade* (London: AK Press, 1997).

Animal Liberation Front (ALF) (Great Britain)

The Animal Liberation Front is Great Britain's leading animal liberation group that employs direct action tactics. Ronnie Lee, a trainee solicitor's clerk and a vegan, founded the ALF in 1976 with the goal to end animal suffering by attacking those businesses or individuals responsible for their ill treatment. Lee had earlier been an active member of the Hunt Saboteurs Association and the founder of the Band of Mercy in 1973. In 1975, Lee was jailed for arson, but after his release from prison, he decided to form an underground group of animal rights activists to conduct a secret war to protect animals.

Anyone can join the ALF because there is no formal administrative structure and no national leader. Leadership comes from collective decision making. An individual joins the ALF by undertaking an operation against businesses or persons that he or she perceives as perpetrating animal mistreatment. Once this person has proven that he or she is dedicated to the goals of the ALF, acceptance follows. Persons affiliated with the ALF have raided laboratories to free animals, bombed buildings, committed arson against department stores, sent mail bombs to prominent scientists and animal workers, and beaten up employees of businesses associated with what the ALF believes is exploitation of animals. Despite the ALF's lack of formal organization, its activists are protected by an underground that shelters them before and after operations. The ALF even has a public relations officer, Robin Webb, a former British civil servant, who publicizes and justifies ALF activities. Kevin Toolis, in a 1998 article in *The Guardian* (London), estimated the top leadership of the ALF at no more than 20, with a support group of activists at between 300 and 400. Another 3,000 or so back the ALF with money or attendance at animal rights demonstrations.

The British Animal Liberation Front has become the global center of animal rights activism. Soon after its founding in 1976, the idea and the structure of the ALF was exported to the United States, Germany, and the Scandinavian countries. Activity in the United States was particularly heavy. Other groups, including the Earth Liberation Front (ELF) and **Stop Huntingdon Animal Cruelty** (SHAC), have adopted the strategy and tactics of the ALF.

ALF's activities against the use of animals for scientific research have been its most controversial campaign. One such target was a lengthy war with Hillgrove Farm, near

Witney, in Oxfordshire. This farm bred and supplied cats for scientific research. The campaign against Hillgrove Farm started in August 1997 shortly after a similar campaign against Consort Kennels, a business that provided dogs for scientific research, had bankrupted the company. A subsidiary target was launched against Professor Colin Blakemore at Oxford University, who used cats for his brain research.

Recent British legislation has made it more difficult for the Animal Liberation Front to operation. Court decisions have made demonstrations to intimidate executives and workers at Huntington Life Science less effective by establishing 50-yard exclusion zones. Demonstrators have turned to other industries, including chicken factory farms and research guinea pig breeding farms. ALF operations have had an impact by reducing the number of experiments using animals by half in the past 30 years. **See also** Horne, Barry; Lee, Ronnie; Stop Huntingdon Animal Cruelty (SHAC).

Suggested readings: Michael Durham, "Animal Passions," *Observer* (London) (November 12, 1995), p. 19; Oliver Parkinson, "Britain Is Top Exporter of Animal Terrorism, Says FBI," *Independent* (London) (February 25, 2001), p. 5; Stewart Tendler, "Tiny Secret Army Where Prison Is Badge of Commitment," *Times* (London) (April 5, 2001), p. 1; Kevin Toolis, "In for the Kill," *Guardian* (London) (December 4, 1998), p. 8; Polly Toynbee, "Something Has to Stop the Torture and the Horror," *Guardian* (London) (June 10, 1995), p. 1.

Ansar-i Hezbollah (See Defenders of the Party of God)

Anti-Terrorist Liberation Group (Groupo Antiterroristas de Liberacion) (GAL) (Spain)

The Anti-Terrorist Liberation Group (GAL) was a Spanish death squad that carried out assassinations of Spanish Basques living in France in the 1980s. An earlier death squad, the Spanish Basque Battalion (Battalion Vasco Espanol) had conducted a series of assassinations of the leaders of the Basque terrorist group **Basque Fatherland and Liberty** (Euskadi ta Askatasuna) (ETA) both in Spain and in France from 1975 to 1980. During this campaign, 10 ETA leaders were killed in revenge for the assassination of Admiral Luis Carrero Blanco on December 20, 1973. Felipe Gonzalez, the head of the Spanish Socialist Party, became prime minister of the Spanish government in 1982. Among his most serious problems was the terrorist campaign of ETA. This group had undertaken an offensive to provoke a coup against the Socialist government by assassinations of public servants, soldiers, and police officials. In September 1982, the minister of interior, Jorge Barrionuevo, authorized the creation of a death squad to retaliate against the ETA and provided funds for it. The intent was to cripple ETA leadership by removing its leaders and convince the French to end its safe haven for ETA members. Top police officials had the responsibility to recruit hit team members from the police and from mercenary groups. Mercenaries were paid $15,000 per murder.

GAL's terror campaign lasted from 1983 to 1987. Within this time frame, GAL carried out 27 assassinations and wounded 30. Most of the operations were in southern France. GAL operatives used a variety of methods from bombs to submachine guns. They were also sloppy; nine of their victims, including two young girls ages three and five, had no connections with the ETA. Although Spanish public opinion supported this dirty war against terrorists, enough negative publicity brought the GAL to suspend operations in 1987. Also a factor was that France had agreed by this time to deport ETA activists from southern France. This campaign had brought fear into the ranks of ETA activists, but it never hindered the ability of the ETA to undertake its operations.

Although there was always speculation that the GAL had operated with Spanish government approval, news that high government authorities had sanctioned and supported its activities caused a national scandal. The discovery of the bodies of missing ETA operatives and supporters in graves gave further impetus to the scandal. Soon charges reached as high as Felipe Gonzalez, the Socialist prime minister. In 1998, Jose Barrionuevo, the former interior minster in the Gonzalez government, and Rafael Vera, former secretary of state for security, were found guilty of the kidnappings and murders of alleged ETA activists. Other convictions followed, but the Spanish Supreme Court refused in November 1996 to allow the questioning or charging of Gonzalez. **See also** ETA (Euskadi Ta Askatasuna) (Basque Fatherland and Liberty).

Suggested readings: John Darnton, "Basque Exiles in France Live in Fear," *New York Times* (April 15, 1984), sec. 1, p. 3; Adela Gooch, "Ex-Minister Faces Jail Over 'Dirty War,'" *Guardian* (London) (July 24, 1998), p. 13; Wilbur G. Landrey, "Spain Anti-Terror Campaign Tars Leaders," *Los Angeles Times* (February 28, 1996), p. 2A; Daniel Williams, "ETA Scandal Refuses to Go Away," *The Washington Post* (May 18, 1996), p. A15; Paddy Woodworth, *Dirty War, Clean Hands: ETA, the GAL and Spanish Democracy* (Cork, Ireland: Cork University Press, 2001).

Al-Aqsa Intifada (Palestine)

Al-Aqsa Intifada is the latest Palestinian uprising in the occupied territories of Gaza and the West Bank. This uprising started on September 28, 2000, in response to the visit to the Temple Mount, or as the Arabs called it "Haram al-Sharif," in Jerusalem of the Likud political leader Ariel Sharon. Tensions had been building among Palestinians over the failure of the implementation of the Oslo Peace Accords of 1993. Palestinians had received a measure of self-government in the accords with the Palestinian Authority (PA), but the failure of negotiations for the evacuation of Israeli military and settlers from what the Palestinians perceived as their territory was the catalyst for the uprising. The collapse of the Camp David talks in 1998 also frustrated of the Palestinians.

The Aqsa Intifada differed from the 1987 **Intifada** in both motivation and intensity. In 1987, an accident in the Gaza Strip resulted in a spontaneous uprising against the Israelis. In contrast, a symbolic event in Jerusa-

lem led to an organized uprising. Two factors are important to an understanding of this Intifada: the frustration of younger elements in the Palestinian nationalist movement with the old guard around Yasser Arafat and the Palestinian Authority (PA) and the inability of the Arafat's forces to control the Islamists of **Hamas** and **Islamic Jihad**. Soon after the outbreak of violence, younger elements within the Palestinian Authority (PA) organized groups to carry out urban guerrilla tactics against the Israelis. Then, in October 2000, **al-Aqsa Martyrs' Brigades** appeared to fight against the Israel Defense Forces (IDF). Seven members of Arafat's al-Fatah came together and formed the new group. While this group claimed allegiance to Arafat, the leaders maintained no ties with him. Anti-Israeli activity by the Al-Aqsa Martyrs' Brigades joined with Hamas and the Islamic Jihad to carry the battle to the Israelis. A major tactic has been suicide bombings within Israel, but these operations have not been as frequent as those of Hamas. The most serious was on June 19, 2002, when an Aqsa Martyrs Brigades suicide bomber detonated a bomb at a bus stop in Jerusalem that killed 6 persons and wounded 43 others.

The Israelis responded with an emphasis on coercive measures, such as military occupations of refugee camps and major Palestinian urban sites. Economic sanctions against Palestinians have been harsh, including sealing off Israel from the territories. Mass arrests of suspected terrorist leaders have become routine. Finally, Israel has resorted to extrajudicial killings of Palestinian leaders. None of these measures has been effective in ending the Intifada. Palestinians have been fighting the battle for international public opinion almost as much as the war against Israel.

The impact of the Aqsa Intifada has been the almost total breakdown of the Palestinian economy and social life in the occupied territories and the weakening of the Israeli economy. Economic life has ceased to exist for most Palestinians. Frequent military interventions into the occupied territories of Gaza and the West Bank have stopped any attempts to reestablish a functioning economy. Schools and universities have been closed. Suicide strikes and loss of Palestinian labor has also impacted the Israeli economy. Failure of leadership on both the Israeli and Palestinian sides have allowed the Aqsa Intifada to continue long after its political message had been received. The inability of Israel to deal with the settlement problem and the inability of Palestinians to control terrorism have made any attempt to end the Aqsa Intifada futile. See also Al-Aqsa Martyrs' Brigades; Hamas (Haarakat al-Muqawama al-Islami) (Islamic Resistance Movement); Intifada; Islamic Jihad.

Suggested readings: Ghassan Andoni, "A Comparative Study of Intifada 1987 and Intifada 2000," in Roane Carey (ed.), *The New Intifada: Resisting Israel's Apartheid* (London: Verso, 2001); Kirsten E. Schulze, "Camp David and the Al-Aqsa Intifada: An Assessment of the State of the Israeli-Palestinian Peace Process, July–December 2000)," *Studies in Conflict and Terrorism* 24, no. 3 (May–June 2001); Joshua Sinai, "Why Israel Can't Resolve the New Palestinian Intifada," *Journal of Counterterrorism & Security International* 7, no. 3 (Spring, 2001); Khalil Shikaki, "Palestinians Divided," *Foreign Affairs* (January 2002/February 2002), p. 89; Khaled Abu Toameh, "Anatomy of Rage," *Jerusalem Report* (March 26, 2001), p. 22.

Al-Aqsa Martyrs' Brigades (Kataib Shuhada Al-Aqsa) (Palestine)

Al-Aqsa Martyrs' Brigades has been one of the leading terrorist groups operating during the Palestinian **Aqsa Intifad**a. Shortly after the outbreak of the al-Aqsa Intifada on September 28, 2000, seven veterans of Yasser Arafat's al-Fatah met at the Balata Refugee Camp near Nablus on the West Bank and decided to form al-Aqsa Martyrs' Brigades to carry the war to Israel. This meeting was held in October 2000 at Nablus's Balata refugee camp. Among the founders were Nasser Awais, Yasser Badawi, Maged Masri, and Raed Karmi. They named the group after al-Aqsa Mosque in Jerusalem. The leaders have maintained their loyalty to Arafat, but they have had reservations about the leadership in the Palestinian Authority (PA). They claim that the group is independent from Arafat and the Palestinian Authority (PA). They also have strong ties to **Marwan Barghouthi,** the head of al-Fatah's militia, Tanzim.

Members of al-Aqsa Martyrs' Brigades are not as intransigent as those in Islamic **Jihad** or **Hamas,** but they are willing to conduct a guerrilla war against Israel until Israeli troops withdraw from the occupied territories and a Palestinian state exists. At first, most of the operations were against Israeli soldiers and Jewish settlers on the West Bank, but this changed after the violence escalated, and they became willing to use any tactics, including suicide bombers to achieve this goal. Initially, most of the suicide bombers were men, but since 2002 most have been women. These attacks threatened Israeli security so Israeli authorities targeted the leadership of al-Aqsa Martyrs' Brigades for assassination. Raed Karmi and Mahmoud Titi have been killed, and Awais and Masri were captured by the Israelis. Despite these losses, the al-Aqsa Martyrs' Brigades have still initiated operations in Israel.

Efforts by the Palestinian Authority to bring al-Aqsa Martyrs' Brigades under control have been unsuccessful. Militants in leadership positions have refused to heed the calls from al-Fatah to cease terrorist attacks. They believe that the moderate policies of Arafat and the Palestinian Authority will not force the Israelis to come to the bargaining table. The arrest of Barghouthi by the Israelis has been a blow because he had considerable prestige among the rank-and-file of al-Aqsa Martyrs' Brigades. In the middle of 2003, a stalemate began between the leadership of al-Aqsa Martyrs' Brigades on one side and Arafat and the Palestinian Authority on the other side that will not be broken until one or the other concedes. See also Al-Aqsa Intifada; Arafat, Mohammed Yasser; Barghouthi, Marwan bin Khatib.

Suggested readings: Ferry Biedermann, "Secular and Deadly: The Rise of the Martyrs' Brigades," http://Salon.com/ (accessed March 19, 2002); Peter Hermann, "Palestinian Dissension Confounds a 'Martyr,'" *Baltimore Sun* (January

9, 2003), p. 1A; Michael Tierney, "Young, Gifted and Ready to Kill," *Herald* (Glasgow) (August 3, 2002), p. 8; Tracy Wilkinson, "End of the Line for a 'Martyr,'" *Los Angeles Times* (December 31, 2002), p. 1.

Arafat, Mohammed Yasser (1929–) (Palestine)

Yasser Arafat is the leader of the **Palestine Liberation Organization** (PLO). He was born on August 24, 1929, in Cairo, Egypt. His father was related to the Husseini clan, whose head was Haj Amin al-Husseini, the mufti of Jerusalem, and his mother's family was the Abu Saud family of Jerusalem. His parents left Palestine and moved to Cairo, Egypt, in 1927, where his father ran a successful wholesale trading business. His mother died when Arafat was four years of age, and he was sent to live with his uncle, Salim Abu Saud, in Jerusalem. After four years there, Arafat returned to Cairo. His childhood was unhappy and he was always an indifferent student. When he was seventeen, he began running weapons from Egypt to Palestine. In 1948, Arafat entered the University of Fuad the First in Cairo, studying engineering. News of the war between the Jews and the Palestinians caused him to leave school in April 1948 and join in the war. Arafat was disillusioned by the Arab League's conduct of the war and he became an enemy of the Arab states.

After the war, Arafat returned to the university and plunged into politics. He had made contacts with the **Muslim Brotherhood** during the war and he continued these contacts in Egypt. In 1952, Arafat won election to the presidency of the Union of Palestinian Students. Arafat used the presidency to begin campaigning for an independent Palestine liberation movement. He was able to persuade Egyptian authorities to allow him to publish a student publication, *The Voice of Palestine.* In his duties as president of the Palestinian students, Arafat met fellow Palestinian Khalil al-Wazir, and they began plotting military operations against Israel.

Arafat began to attract the attention of Egyptian security officials. In the aftermath of an assassination attempt on Gamal Abdel Nasser by a Muslim Brotherhood member in October 1954, Arafat was arrested and tortured by Egyptian security forces for several weeks. Arafat gained his release from jail and soon afterward was able to persuade Nasser to start training and arming Palestinian fighters. In July 1956, Arafat graduated from the University of Fuad the First with a degree in civil engineering. His graduation caused him to lose his position as president of the Union of Palestinian Students so he started the Union of Palestinian Graduates. He also found a job as an engineer with an Egyptian construction company. During the Suez Canal war in October 1956, Arafat joined the Egyptian army as a second lieutenant in a bomb-disposal unit. After the war, Arafat returned to his engineering job. Arafat and al-Wazir continued to explore ways to build a secret Palestinian army, but Egyptian authorities began to pressure him about his political activities. In 1957, Arafat decided to leave Egypt and took a job in Kuwait. Al-Wazir joined him in Kuwait and together, in October 1957, they formed the secret Fatah underground.

Arafat had a successful business life in Kuwait and his income allowed him to further his political goals. In early 1959, Arafat financed the publication *Our Palestine.* Arafat filled this publication with articles that were anti-Israel, anti-Arab regimes, and anti-Nasser. It was banned in most Arab states. In February 1963, **al-Fatah**'s first Central Committee was formed with 10 members. Arafat was 1 of the 10, but he held no central leadership position. He soon became unhappy about the lack of direction of al-Fatah. Both Arafat and al-Wazir wanted to launch a military movement, but the Central Committee was more circumspect. Khalad Hassan was Arafat's chief opponent on the committee. After an agreement with the Algerian government, al-Wazir was sent to Algeria to begin preparations for a military campaign by opening a secure training and diplomatic base.

In 1964, Arafat finally persuaded the Central Committee of al-Fatah to start military action against Israel. Arafat was denied the leadership of al-Fatah's military operations because Abu Youseff was appointed to this post. Arafat had been wooing the Syrians to give al-Fatah a base of operations, but the Syrian government wanted to control both Arafat and al-Fatah. Despite this danger, Arafat planned and executed a number of raids into Israel during the first three months of 1965. In the spring of 1965, Arafat replaced Youseff as military commander. Arafat assumed command of military operations in Lebanon and ignored instructions from the Central Committee in Kuwait. Soon, a conflict between Arafat and the Central Committee stopped military operations as the committee halted his funding. It took a fund drive among Palestine workers in Germany and among Palestinian students to reestablish the funding. Arafat tried to convince Syrian leaders to support al-Fatah and allow operations to be conducted out of Syria. For a time Arafat believed that he had convinced the Syrians, but a change of regime lost him much of his Syrian support. Nevertheless, Arafat was arrested in May 1966 and kept in jail for two months without charges to intimidate him.

The defeat of Arab forces in the 1967 Arab-Israeli War made it possible to revive al-Fatah's military campaign and improve Arafat's standing. After Arafat was reaffirmed as its military commander, he moved operations to the West Bank and initiated raids in September 1967. This campaign ended in failure, however, for two reasons—Israeli security forces suppressed it and the Palestinian populace was unready for a national uprising. Arafat had several narrow escapes before he had to leave the West Bank. By the end of December 1967, al-Fatah's military operations were in shambles. To save what was left of al-Fatah, Arafat relocated its headquarters to Jordan. When Israeli forces tried to raid the Karamech base camp in Jordan on March 21, 1968, they were repulsed with elements of the Jordanian army fighting on the side of al-Fatah. After news of this victory be-

came public, volunteers flocked to al-Fatah's recruiting offices.

Arafat became head of the PLO in February 1968 and he and Nasser became allies. In this position, Arafat's biggest challenge was restraining the radical elements of the PLO. Several groups espoused ideologies that made them difficult to coalesce. George Habash's **Popular Front for the Liberation of Palestine** (PFLP), a Marxist-Leninist group was one such group. Even more dangerous and unpredictable was **Abu Nidal** and his **Abu Nidal Organization** (ANO). Nidal undertook an assassination campaign against PLO leaders because they pursued a more moderate political agenda than Nidal. More significant than these political rivalries was the loss of Jordan as a staging area for military operations against Israel in September 1970. Arafat had to move the PLO from Jordan to Lebanon, where he authorized the creation of al-Fatah's **Black September** terrorist group. Only when this group had outlived its usefulness was it disbanded in 1974.

By 1974, Arafat was busy transforming the Palestine Liberation Organization into an international cause. This strategy worked when Arafat received an invitation to speak before the United Nations General Assembly. His appearance and speech on November 13, 1974, earned him the reception of a head of state. Arafat used this acclaim to move the PLO toward a more moderate stance on the Israeli-Palestinian issue. This new orientation was not without its costs, as several of the more radical organizations left the PLO to establish the Rejectionist Front. Even the eviction of the PLO from Beirut, Lebanon, by Israel in 1982 only temporarily hurt Arafat and the PLO. Arafat continued to confront Israel on the field of international opinion.

In 1982, the Israeli invasion of Lebanon almost destroyed Arafat and the Palestine Liberation Organization. After expulsion from Jordan, PLO operations had been established in southern Lebanon. Despite tensions and sometimes armed conflict with the Shi'ites in southern Lebanon, Arafat and PLO leaders initiated military operations against Israel. These operations ceased with the intervention of the Israel Defense Forces (IDF) in the summer of 1982. Only foreign intervention saved the PLO from destruction. A truce allowed Arafat to transfer operations to Tunisia. This transfer was a blow to both the prestige and operations of the PLO under Arafat's leadership.

Arafat's removal from the Palestinian scene weakened him on the international scene until the outbreak of the Intifada in December 1987. This uprising caught Arafat and the leadership of the PLO by surprise. It also allowed the development of **Hamas**, a serious rival to Arafat and the PLO. Roots of Hamas had been present in the Palestinian branch of the Muslim Brotherhood, but now it was a political force. Arafat tried to gain control of the Intifada with only limited success. A benefit was that the uprising led to the negotiations and signing of the Oslo Peace Accords in 1993. For the first time, this agreement gave Arafat and the PLO a chance for an independent Palestine. It also allowed the Palestinian Authority (PA) to be established as the political entity to represent the Palestinian people.

Arafat had a resurgence of prestige after the Oslo Peace Accords, but his image had become tarnished by the end of the 1990s. His desire for a secular Palestinian state has been challenged by Hamas. Leaders of Hamas want an Islamist Palestinian state and they have rejected Arafat as the sole spokesperson for the Palestinians. Even elements within al-Fatah have rebelled and created **al-Aqsa Martyrs' Brigades**. Besides these internal difficulties, Arafat has made decisions on the international scene that have weakened his position. In late 2000, the then president William Clinton tried to negotiate a final settlement between Israel and the Palestinians, but Arafat rejected the final product. This rejection; his inability to control terrorism by Hamas, **Islamic Jihad**, and al-Aqsa Martyrs' Brigades; and the refusal of Israeli Prime Minister Ariel Sharon to negotiate with him have come together to challenge Arafat's leadership. International pressure and internal charges of corruption within the Palestinian Authority led to Arafat agreeing

to appoint a Palestinian prime minister in the spring of 2003. His choice was his longtime deputy in the PLO, Mahmud Abbas, but they were unable to compromise on the issue of control of the PA's security forces. Abbas resigned and he was replaced by Ahmed Qureia. Whether or not Arafat will concede more political authority to Qureia than to Abbas remains to be seen. **See also** Al-Fatah; Muslim Brotherhood (al-Ikhwan al-Muslimun); Palestine Liberation Organization (PLO).

Suggested readings: Said K. Aburish, *Arafat: From Defender to Dictator* (New York: Bloomsbury, 1998); Andrew Gowers and Tony Walker, *Behind the Myth: Yasser Arafat and the Palestinian Revolution* (New York: Olive Branch Press, 1992); Alan Hart, *Arafat: Terrorist or Peacemaker?* (London: Sidgwick & Jackson, 1984); Thomas Kiernan, *Arafat, the Man and the Myth* (New York: Norton, 1976); Laura King, "Ignored and Isolated, Arafat Survives," *Los Angeles Times* (February 8, 2002), p. 3; Shaul Mishal, *The PLO under Arafat: Between Gun and Olive Branch* (New Haven, CT: Yale University Press, 1986); Diana L. Reische, *Arafat and the Palestine Liberation Organization* (New York: Watts, 1991); Janet Wallach, *Arafat: In the Eyes of the Beholder* (Secaucus, NJ: Carol, 1997).

ARENA (Alianza Republicana Nacionalista, or National Republican Alliance) (El Salvador)

ARENA (Alianza Republicana Nacionalista or National Republican Alliance) is an extreme right-wing party in El Salvador. **Roberto D'Aubuisson**, a right-wing former officer in the El Salvadorean Army, founded ARENA in 1981. He used the civil war in El Salvador between the Salvadorean state and the **Farabundo Martí National Liberation Front** (FMLN) to form an organization to terrorize Salvadorian leftists. His use of anti-Communism earned him support from the Reagan administration in 1982. Earlier, D'Aubuisson had used another of his organizations, Broad National Front (Frente Amplio Nacional), to organize **death squads**. One of these death squads had assassinated Archbishop Oscar Romero on March 23,

1980. These death squads continued under D'Aubuisson's control after the formation of ARENA.

D'Aubuisson also used ARENA as a political party. In the 1982 elections, ARENA won 19 out of the 60 seats available. D'Aubuisson was able to negotiate electoral alliances with other right-wing parties to gain the presidency of the National Assembly. This position gave respectability to both D'Aubuisson and ARENA. He continued to direct death squad operations from a security office on the second floor of the National Assembly. His failure to win the Salvadorean presidency in 1984 hurt him with both ARENA's rank-and-file and the Reagan administration. Growing dissatisfaction with his leadership led to his replacement by Alfredo Cristiani in 1988.

Cristiani's leadership of ARENA restored it as a political force in El Salvador. He had also been active in directing death squads as a leader of ARENA. Despite this liability, Cristiani won the Salvadorean presidency in 1989. D'Aubuisson's subsequent death from throat cancer in February 1992 removed him as an embarrassment to Cristiani and ARENA. Since then, the ARENA candidate has won every presidential election. Despite opposition of the FMLN as an opposition party, ARENA candidates have won by a combination of propaganda, money, and American help. Each time that a FMLN candidate comes close to winning an election, American scare tactics ensure that the ARENA candidate wins. **See also** D'Aubuisson Arrieta, Roberto; Death Squads.

Suggested readings: Robert Armstrong and Janet Shenk, *El Salvador, the Face of Revolution* (Boston: South End Press, 1982); Hugh Byrne, *El Salvador's Civil War: A Study of Revolution* Boulder, CO: Lynne Rienner, 1996); James LeMoyne, "El Salvador's Forgotten War," *Foreign Affairs* (Summer 1989), p. 105; Carlos Mario Marquez, "Rightwing ARENA Party Wins El Salvador Election Vote," Agence France Presse (March 17, 2003), p. 1; Tommie Sue Montgomery, *Revolution in El Salvador: From Civil Strife to Civil Peace,* 2nd ed. (Boulder, CO: Westview Press, 1995).

Argentine Anti-Communist Alliance (Alianza Argentina Anti-Comunista) (Triple A) (Argentina)

The Argentine Anti-Communist Alliance, or Triple A, was the umbrella organization under which Argentinean death squads operated in the 1970s. Perónist and conservative elements in the Argentinean government were fearful of radical left-wing groups and decided in 1974 to eradicate them. Jose Lopez Rega, an advisor to Juan Domingo Perón and the minister of social welfare in Isabel Perón's government, founded the Triple A. Activities of the Triple A were at first coordinated by the Federal Police, and policemen and military men were recruited. Later in 1975, the government issued Decree No. 261, which mandated that all subversive elements in Argentinean society were to be eradicated. The groups targeted were the Perónist left-wing **Montoneros**; the Maoist People's Revolutionary Army (ERP); and the two radical leftists, Revolutionary Armed Force (FAR) and the People's Armed Forces. Total membership of these groups numbered only around 2,000, but in the previous decade members of these groups had carried out 697 assassinations.

Roving bands of members of the Argentine Anti-Communist Alliance carried out a campaign of terror in cities and on college campuses. Any potential opposition to the Argentinean government was targeted. Those targeted often saw their names in the newspapers or at locations with the warning that the Triple A was coming to get them. People would simply disappear, sometimes at night and at other times in the daytime. Hit teams traveled in unmarked and unlicensed green Ford Falcons and often left their victims in ditches or along roads. Anyone associated with unions or involved in any political activities on the left was especially in danger. Members of the Triple A assassinated the Jesuit priest Father Carlos Mugica, a close associate of the Montoneros, in May 1974. In the period from 1974 to 1975, approximately 100 students and faculty of the national University of La Plata were assassinated or disappeared and were never to be seen again. Other universities suffered the same fate. Any student or faculty member who had a reputation for liberalism or left-wing views was in danger. Moreover, most members of the Triple A were anti-Semitic and pro-Nazi and they concentrated on Jewish intellectuals. Labor leaders and journalists were also potential victims. These conditions continued until the Generals Coup of March 24, 1976, that overthrew the Isabel Perón regime. The Triple A disappeared into the Argentinean government and was replaced by the Argentinean military. This war against dissidents became part of the general's Process for National Reorganization and the beginning of the "Dirty War." Many members of the Triple A joined the government by running concentration camps, such as the **Naval Mechanics School** in Buenos Aires. **See also** Naval Mechanics School (EMSA).

Suggested readings: Marguerite Feitlowitz, *A Lexicon of Terror: Argentina and the Legacies of Torture* (New York: Oxford University press, 1998); Patricia Marchak and William Marchak, *God's Assassins: State Terrorism in Argentina in the 1970s* (Montreal, Canada: McGill-Queen's University Press, 1999).

Armata Corsa (Corsican Army) (Corsica)

The Armata Corsa (Corsican Army) is a small terrorist group in Corsica that seeks independence for Corsica from France. Jean-Michel Rossi and Francois "the Iguana" Santoni founded Armata Corsa in 1999. Both of them had been members of the **Front de la Liberation Nationale de la Corse** (Front for the National Liberation of Corsica) (FLNC), but they became disillusioned with its leadership and policies. Besides wanting independence for Corsica, this group has the goal of eradicating organized crime in Corsica. Members of the Armata Corsa have participated in attacks on banks and military and police buildings and assassinations of key political figures. Most of these attacks have been restricted to Corsica, but some have been in France. Between 1999 and 2001, members of the Armata Corsa exploded 20 bombs and killed three people.

Most of its efforts have been directed toward sabotaging the Matignon Accords, which grants Corsica limited autonomy.

The future of Armata Corsa is in question because of the loss of its top leaders. In August 2000, unknown assassins killed Rossi and his bodyguard in the Corsican village of L'Ile-Rousse. Then in 2001, French authorities arrested Santoni and sentenced him to a four-year jail term for extortion. Santoni was let out of jail in time for an assassin to murder him on August 16, 2001. The Armata Corsa has never had a large membership, probably no more than 30 activists. A successor to Rossi and Santoni as head of the group is probably Jean-Dominique Allegrini-Simonetti, but French police arrested him shortly after the assassination of Santoni. The Armata Corsa has an imposing number of enemies, including the French police, Corsican-organized crime organizations, and its rival, the FLNC. **See also** Front de la Liberation Nationale de la Corse.

Suggested readings: Agence France Press, "Corsican Peace Process under Threat from Separatist Feud," *Agence France Press* (August 27, 2001), p. 1; Catherine Field, "Bloody Vendettas Big Threat to Self-Rule Plan for Corsica," *New Zealand Herald* (August 29, 2001), p. 1; Lara Marlowe, "Cold-Blooded Iguana Will Not Be Missed," *Irish Times* (August 18, 2001), p. 13.

Armed Islamic Group (Groupes Islamiques Armés) (GIA) (Algeria)

The Armed Islamic Group (GIA) is the most active terrorist group in Algeria. This group was formed shortly after the Algerian military seized control of the Algerian government in 1992. Members of the GIA advocate an Islamist state and are willing to use unrestricted terror to achieve this end. Djaffar Alghani, an early leader, conducted a campaign against the Algerian intelligentsia, killing administrators, teachers, and journalists. Over 40 journalists have been assassinated in almost a decade. The GIA has also targeted foreigners, including Christian priests and tourists. This campaign by the GIA has contributed to the bulk of the more than 70,00 people killed in this religious civil war against the Algerian state.

The Armed Islamic Group had good relations with the **Islamic Salvation Front** (FIS) until its violence alienated the FIS leadership. By the mid-1990s, however, hostilities had broken out between the two groups. Even the moderates in the GIA, Mohammed Said and Abderazak Redjam, were executed by the more exteme GIA leader, Djamel Zitouni, in 1994. Algerian authorities killed a number of the GIA's leaders as well, including its military leaders Mourad Sid Ahmed and Antar Zouabri. New leaders emerged and carried out terrorist operations against both the Algerian government and civilian targets. By the beginning of the 2000s so much bloodshed had taken place that even the most radical GIA leaders began to have reservations about continuing the campaign of terror. Isolated incidents of terrorism have continued, but the prospect of the Algerian government becoming more accommodating to the demands of the Islamic fundamentalists has led to a decrease in agitation by them. **See also** Islamic Salvation Front (FIS).

Suggested readings: Ed Blanche, "Death Toll Mounts in Algerian Bloodbath," *Jane's Intelligence Review* 9, no.1 (March 1, 1997), p. 119; Elie Chalala, "Killing Fields," *In These Times* (January 10, 1999), p. 12; James Ciment, "The Battle of Algiers," *In These Times* 22 (December 28, 1997) p. 19; William B. Quandt, *Between Ballots and Bullets: Algeria's Transition from Authoritarianism* (Washington, DC: Brookings Institution Press, 1998); Milton Viorst, "Algeria's Long Night," *Foreign Affairs* (November–December 1997), p. 86; Michael Willis, *The Islamist Challenge in Algeria: A Political History* (Washington Square: New York University Press, 1996).

Armed Revolutionary Forces of Colombia (See Revolutionary Armed Forces of Colombia) (FARC) (Colombia)

Asahara, Shoko (Chizuo Matsumoto) (1955–) (Japan)

Shoko Asahara is the leader of the extremist religious sect the **Aum Shinri Kyo** (Supreme Truth Sect, or AUM). He was born Chizuo Matsumoto in March 1955 in Yatsushiro, Kyushu, Japan. His father was a maker of tatami mats. Born with poor eyesight, Asahara was educated at a prefectural school for the sight-impaired. While at school, he earned a certificate in acupuncture. At the age of 21, Asahara moved to Tokyo and in 1978 married his wife Tomoko. He started business life by setting up a store in Chiba that specialized in Chinese-style herbal medicine, but he went bankrupt after being arrested in 1982 for selling products without a permit. In 1984, he started another company, "AUM," which published books and built yoga-training centers. Sometime during this period, Asahara claims to have achieved enlightenment as the result of an ascetic experience in the Himalayas. He founded the Aum Shinri Kyo sect in 1987. In August 1989, he received the approval of the Tokyo metropolitan government for the Aum Shinri Kyo to become a religious foundation. Asahara also learned in the same year that he had hepatic cirrhosis.

The growth of AUM has been the result of its appeal to Japanese youth. Asahara's religious views attract Japanese youth disillusioned by the competitive nature of Japanese society and their personal shortcomings. Another factor is the type of mind manipulation practiced by Asahara. He teaches his followers that the only way to attain salvation is to be completely devoted to the faith. Proof of this is divestment of personal wealth to the sect and working for its expansion. Asahara has also incorporated a doomsday vision into his religion. He preaches that there will be an Armageddon, or third world war, and AUM would survive and become the ultimate world religion. While Asahara is rather indistinct about the date of Armageddon, he claimed that it would happen in 1997 or 1999. Despite the passage of these dates, Asahara has not adjusted his vision. As AUM grew and prospered, Asahara began to expand his organization into other businesses and into politics. In 1992, the AUM opened a branch in Moscow, Russia. In the next year, other branches were launched in New York,

Bonn, and Sri Lanka. Also in 1993, AUM expanded into the computer business by opening shops in Tokyo and Osaka. His financial empire continued to expand until he ran into legal problems over AUM's use of sarin gas at the Tokyo subway on March 20, 1995. The Japanese government closed Asahara's businesses, causing him to go bankrupt in 1996. However, the government was reluctant to outlaw the sect, and so the AUM has been able to recover financially.

Asahara's legal troubles have kept him in legal proceedings since April 1996. He has been charged with 17 offenses ranging from sanctioning murders to being responsible for the 1995 sarin gas attack at the Tokyo subway. His team of 12 lawyers and the incoherence of Asahara have complicated the government's prosecution. Most of the leaders of AUM have been sentenced to lengthy prison terms for their participation in various crimes. In the meantime, Asahara's followers camp outside the court, following the proceeding and proclaiming his innocence of all charges. Asahara's trial ended in October 2003, and he received the death sentence in February 2004. **See also** Aum Shinri Kyo (Supreme Truth Sect) (AUM).

Suggested readings: D.W. Brackett, *Holy Terror: Armageddon in Tokyo* (New York: Weatherhill, 1996); Mark Juergensmeyer, *Terror in the Mind of God: The Global Rise of Religious Violence* (Berkeley: University of California Press, 2000); Ian Reader, *Religious Violence in Contemporary Japan: The Case of Aum Shinrikyo* (Honolulu: University of Hawaii Press, 2000).

Atef, Mohammad (1944–) (Egypt)

Mohammad Atef was the head of military operations for **al-Qaeda** until his death in November 2001. He was born in 1944 and raised in Egypt. Little is known about his early career except that he had training as a policeman. Sometime in the late 1970s Atef joined Islamist extremists and the group Islamic Jihad led by **Ayman al-Zawahiri**. This group had been active in the assassination of President Anwar Sadat in October 1981. Atef escaped the crackdown on the Islamic Jihad launched by the Egyptian police and intelligence forces. In 1983, he left Egypt to join the Mujahideen fighters in Afghanistan. There he became an associate of **Abdullah Azzam** and later of **Osama bin Laden**. After the end of the Afghan-Soviet War, Atef remained in Afghanistan.

Atef became the head of military operations for al-Qaeda. He shared duties with Ubaidah al-Banshiri until al-Banshiri's death in a boat disaster in 1996. Atef planned the bombing operations in both Nairobi, Kenya, and Dar es Salaam, Tanzania. These operations alerted Western intelligence to Atef's role, and the Federal Bureau of Investigation (FBI) placed a $5 million reward on Atef's head. American intelligence concluded soon after the **September 11**, 2001, attack on the World Trade Center and the Pentagon that Atef had a role in the planning of this operation. The reason for this supposition was that Atef had been the supervisor of training of new al-Qaeda members in Afghanistan. Then in January 2001, bin Laden's eldest son married Atef's daughter, cementing an already close personal relationship between Atef and bin Laden. Atef continued to be a key advisor to bin Laden until his death in a bombing raid by U.S. aircraft on al-Qaeda barracks in Kabul on November 18, 2001. **See also** Bin Laden, Osama; Al-Qaeda (The Base); Al-Zawahiri, Ayman Muhammad Rabi.

Suggested readings: Dan Eggen and Serge F. Kovaleski, "Bin Laden Aide Implicated; Egyptian Is Identified as a Key Planner of Attacks," *Washington Post* (October 7, 2001), p. A1; Roland Jacquard, *In the Name of Osama Bin Laden: Global Terrorism and the Bin Laden Brotherhood* (Durham, NC: Duke University Press, 2002); Michael James and Gail Gibson, "Top Lieutenants of Terrorism," *Baltimore Sun* (October 9, 2001), p. 9A; Daniel McGrory, "Military Chief Shows His Face, but Where Are the Other Henchmen? *Times* (London) (October 9, 2001), p. 1.

Atta, Mohamed al-Amir Awad al-Sayed (1968–2001) (Egypt)

Mohamed Atta was the leader of **al-Qaeda**'s teams that hijacked four American airlines and used them as weapons on **September 11, 2001.** He was born on September 1, 1968, in the village of Kafr el-Sheikh in the Egyptian Delta. His father was a middle-class lawyer with ties to the **Muslim Brotherhood.** In 1978, the family of one son and two daughters moved to a Giza suburb of Cairo. Atta attended high school in Cairo. After graduation, he enrolled in 1986 at Cairo University, where he studied architecture. Atta graduated in 1990 from college, and he began to study German. In July 1992, he traveled to Hamburg, Germany, to begin a study of town planning at the Hamburg-Harburg Technical University. His area of specialty was the preservation of the Islamic quarters of old cities. Although he received free tuition, Atta found a job as a draftsman with a local design company, Plankontor. His contemporaries at school and at work in Hamburg noted his strong religious views. In 1994, he traveled to Turkey and Syria to study Muslim town planning. Atta then traveled in 1995 on a pilgrimage to Mecca. It was in Mecca that Atta first made contact with al-Qaeda recruiters. He grew a beard to proclaim his religious convictions. After a short trip to Egypt to study Cairo city planning, he returned to Germany to finish his degree.

Atta's trips to Mecca and then Cairo changed his life. He became disturbed by what he perceived as the Americanization of Egyptian society. After his return to Hamburg in 1996, he started attending the local mosque, where his recruitment to radical Islam was completed. Atta had two successful sisters, one a medical doctor and the other a zoologist, but he was always puritanical and authoritarian in his views about women. His attitude was that women and sex were polluting, and he would not allow them to distract him from the path of righteousness.

Atta decided to devote his life to al-Qaeda. In 1997, Atta abruptly left his job and left Germany. He traveled first to Pakistan and then to Kandahar, Afghanistan. Atta received military and terrorist training at the Qaeda camp at Khaldan. This camp was al-Qaeda's most demanding training camp. Atta proved to be one of the better trainees so he was recruited for a future suicide mission. Al-Qaeda's leadership sent him back to Hamburg, Germany, to prepare for a future mission. Atta spent much of his time finishing his thesis on city planning, but behind the scenes he was the head of a Qaeda cell in Hamburg. After completing his thesis in 1999 and receiving his degree, Atta left Germany for his mission in the United States.

Atta arrived in the United States on June 3, 2000, with the intent to carry out a suicide mission. He and Marwan al-Shehhi traveled from New Jersey to Venice, Florida. They enrolled in a flying school to take pilot lessons. Other members of his cell enrolled in flying schools around the country. By December 2000, Atta and two of his compatriots, al-Shehhi and Ziad Jarrah, qualified as light-aircraft commercial pilots. Several times Atta flew back and forth on commercial flights between Germany and the United States in 2001 to coordinate parts of the mission. Each time he had an expired visa, but the Immigration and Naturalization Service (INS) allowed him to reenter the United States.

Atta was the leader of the terrorist cell and he was the only one in it to know the nature of the mission. He was also active in scouting out potential targets from the Watts Bar Dam in Tennessee near a nuclear plant and investigating cities most vulnerable to chemicals dropped from crop dusting planes. His traveling caused a minor problem when he was arrested for driving without a valid driver's license on April 26, 2001, by a Broward County, Florida, sheriff's deputy. He was released and scheduled for a court date five weeks later. Atta ignored the May 2001 court date and a warrant was issued for his arrest, but nothing came out of the arrest warrant because the police were too busy to handle it.

Atta gathered most of the members of his cell together in Florida in early June 2001. Only a few members were absent because they were still in training trying to qualify as pilots. Most of the newcomers were Saudis with clean records of terrorist activities.

Atta was the acknowledged leader with the pilots, his closest confidants. The newcomers had no idea of the nature of the operation except that it was a suicide mission. Atta formed four teams with at least one pilot attached to each team. Teams took test flights throughout the summer of 2001 to examine airline procedures and security. These test flights determined that airline security was weak and that the best time to hijack a plan was on a Tuesday morning. They also calculated how long it took an aircraft to reach cruising speed and that the seats in first-class gave them the best access to the cockpit. In July 2001, Atta returned to Europe and spent time in Spain conferring with al-Qaeda representatives.

Atta issued final instructions about the mission on the night of September 10. Three of the teams had five members and the fourth team only four members. **Zacharias Moussaoui**'s arrest in Minneapolis, Minnesota, had deprived the fourth team of its fifth participant. One-way tickets for flights on September 11, 2001, were brought with credit cards in late August. Atta made arrangements to have excess funds transferred back to al-Qaeda on September 4. The night of September 10 was spent in prayer and various preparations.

Atta commanded the first team, which hijacked American Airlines Flight 11 flying out of Logan Airport in Boston, Massachusetts. Logan Airport had the reputation of being one of the more lax airports in security. His team had seats in the first-class section in the Boeing 767. Fifteen minutes after take-off, Atta's team seized control of the jet with their weapons of box cutters. Atta directed the aircraft into the North Tower of the New York Trade Center at 8:45 A.M. The other teams also accomplished their missions, except for the fourth team, whose aircraft crashed in a field in west Pennsylvania. **See also** Moussaoui, Zacharias; Al-Qaeda (The Base); September 11th.

Suggested readings: Jane Corbin, *Al-Qaeda: The Terror Network That Threatens the World* (New York: Columbia University Press, 2002); Peter Finn, "A Quiet Path to Horror at World Trade Center," *Washington Post* (September 23, 2001), p. A14; Yosri Fouda and Nick Fielding, *Masterminds of Terror: The Truth behind the Most Devastating Terrorist Attack the World Has Ever Seen* (New York: Arcade Publishing, 2003); Elena Lappin, "Portrait: Atta in Hamburg," *Prospect* (August 29, 2002), p.1; John Miller and Michael Stone, *The Cell: Inside the 9/11 Plot and Why the FBI and CIA Failed to Stop It* (New York: Hyperion, 2003).

AUC (See United Self-Defense Forces of Colombia) (Autodefensas Unidas de Colombia) (AUC) (Colombia)

Aum Shinri Kyo (Supreme Truth Sect) (AUM) (Japan)

The Aum Shinri Kyo (Supreme Truth Sect, or AUM) is Japan's most extreme religious sect. Its leader is **Shoko Asahara**, who began a company "Aum" in 1984 that specialized in book publishing and yoga training centers. Asahara converted his yoga school into the Aum Shinri Kyo sect in 1987. In 1989, the AUM was recognized by the Tokyo metropolitan government as a religious foundation. The sect promises spiritual experiences through a version of Tibetan-style mysticism, but most of the rewards would go to the most fervent that devoted themselves entirely to a communal life. To join this community of true believers, the adherents contribute all of their savings to the AUM and live an austere life.

The expansion of AUM has been rapid and not without controversy. While Asahara remained the leader of AUM, others began to play important roles. Among those was Yoskihiro Inoue, who was AUM's intelligence minister. AUM's main headquarters is in Fujinomiya, with a Tokyo branch in Minato Ward. AUM started building a complex at Kamikuishiki, near Mt. Fuji west of Tokyo in 1992. Neighbors of the complex initiated several lawsuits during construction. A lawyer representing former adherents of AUM disappeared in November 1989 along with his wife and child, and they were found buried in mountain locations in September 1995. Besides dealing with defections and critics, the leadership of the AUM decided to enter politics. Twenty-four members of AUM, including Asahara, ran for seats in the general elections for the Lower House of Parliament, but none of them won a seat. In 1992, AUM expanded abroad, opening a branch in Moscow, Russia. Soon afterward, branches were established in New York, Bonn, and Sri Lanka. In 1993, the business side of AUM opened a number of computer shops in Tokyo and Osaka. By the mid-1990s, AUM had more than 15,000 followers, and about 1,400 had joined the sect's monastic lifestyle. In June 1994, the first case of possible use by AUM members of sarin gas became public. Eight people in Matsumoto, central Japan, were killed by sarin gas, including three judges presiding over a case concerning an AUM land purchase. Several incidents of members trying to extort money from families of adherents were reported to the police. On March 20, 1995, a sarin gas attack on five Tokyo subway trains during rush hour killed 12 people and injured 3,796. Despite denials, police found evidence of sarin gas manufacturing at AUM installations. After massive police raids on AUM facilities, Japan's top-tanked police chief was seriously wounded by a police member of the AUM on March 30, 1995. On May 16, 1995, Asahara was arrested for his part in the Tokyo subway gas attack. In December 1995, the Japanese government disbanded AUM, citing it as a public safety threat due to its anti-state ideology and its stockpiling of weapons and poisonous gases. Then in August 1996, the government tore down the complex at Kamikuishiki because of the sarin production capacity at this site. Despite its threat to public safety, the Japanese government rescinded its disbanding of the AUM in January 1997 because of its fears that the Anti-subversive Activities Law was unconstitutional.

The trial of Asahara and the leaders of the AUM opened in April 1996 and it concluded in October 2003. Besides the Tokyo subway attack, other charges have been introduced,

from the 1994 sarin gas attack in Matsumoto to the murder of the anti-AUM lawyer and his family in 1989. Asahara has been charged with 17 counts, and the verdict in his trial will come in early 2004. Many of the other leaders have received lengthy prison sentences, from seven years to life, and Kazuaki Okazaki was sentenced to death for murdering four people in two separate attacks.

Despite the publicity of the trials, the AUM made a comeback. It regrouped and is recruiting new members both in Japan and abroad and is raising vast sums of money. Japanese authorities report that the group in October 1998 had about 5,000 followers, including 500 following the monastic life. By operating 28 installations at 18 branches, AUM is reaching a multitude of potential recruits. Its current leadership is using the Internet and chat rooms to raise large sums of money. In 1998, government authorities report that the AUM bought at least $1.65 million in Japanese real estate. Japanese authorities are concerned about the future direction of AUM, but the refusal of the Japanese government to allow security officials to outlaw the sect means that it will continue to grow. See also Asahara, Shoko (Chizuo Matsumoto).

Suggested readings: D.W. Brackett, *Holy Terror: Armageddon in Tokyo* (New York: Weatherhill, 1996); Mark Juergensmeyer, *Terror in the Mind of God: The Global Rise of Religious Violence* (Berkeley: University of California Press, 2000); Ian Reader, *Religious Violence in Contemporary Japan: The Case of Aum Shinrikyo* (Honolulu: University of Hawaii Press, 2000).

Australian Civil Liberties Union (ACLU) (Australia)

The Australian Civil Liberties Union (ACLU) is Australia's leading neo-Nazi group. John Bennett, a Melbourne lawyer, founded the ACLU in 1980 to promote a neo-Nazi agenda. After graduation from the University of Melbourne, he served as secretary of the Victorian Council for Civil Liberties from 1966 to 1980. Bennett claims that his 1979 reading of Arthur Butz's *The Hoax of the Twentieth Century* converted him to **Holocaust denial**. Shortly afterward, he founded the Australian Civil Liberties Union to serve as a forum for his views. Bennett has been president and main spokesperson for the ACLU since its inception.

In an effort to rehabilitate Nazi Germany, Bennett has become Australia's leading Holocaust denier. He maintains that no evidence exists of the Holocaust. He has established close ties with the American anti-Semitic Institute for Historical Review (IHR) and he has served on its board of directors. Bennett has periodically invited speakers from the IHR to Australia. He has also established working relationships with Fredrick Töben's Adelaide Institute and **Pauline Hanson's One Nation Party**. Bennett owns a bookstore in Melbourne that sells and distributes neo-Nazi and anti-Semitic literature. Most of his recruiting successes have been among the Australian working classes suffering from bad economic times. In 1998, Bennett protested the banning of the British historian and Holocaust denier **David Irving** from visiting Australia.

Bennett has made anti-Americanism part of ACLU's campaign. He had long been a self-styled champion of civil rights. After the terrorist attack on **September 11**, 2001, in the United States, the Australian government proposed a series of anti-terrorist laws that the ACLU attacked as infringement on the basic civil rights of Australians. He blamed the American government for the introduction of these laws. His opposition helped water down these laws. Bennett also opposed the American-British war in Iraq in 2003 as unnecessary and to the benefit of Israel. **See also** Hanson, Pauline; Holocaust Denial; Irving, David John Cawdell; One Nation Party (ONP).

Suggested readings: AAP Information Services, "Liberties Union Says Anti-Terrorist Laws Over-Reaction," AAP Newsfeed (May 17, 2002), p. 1; Deborah Lipstadt, *Denying the Holocaust: The Growing Assault on Truth and Memory* (New York: Plume, 1993).

Austrian Freedom Party (Freiheitliche Partei Osterreichs) (FPO) (See Haider, Jörg)

Autonomous Movement (Europe)

The Autonomous Movement is a complex alliance of European groups and communes that reject traditional economic, political, and social organizations. Because members of the Autonomous Movement reject hierarchical organizations, class distinctions, and personality cults, they seek to control their lives by avoidance of political institutions. The autonomous movement has no unified ideology. Closest to a philosophy is the desire to abolish the existing social system because they see it as exploitative and inhumane. George Katsiaficas describes it as the "politics of the first person." Many of the Autonomous Movement's beliefs and conclusions resemble early 20th-century anarchism more than any other ideology. Autonomists, however, deny that they are anarchists, but some acknowledge the similarities. They remain hostile toward both communism and socialism, finding both ideologies outmoded. Activists in this movement are willing to fight for causes that are important to them, and they rarely avoid confrontations with the authorities and the police. This movement also developed a counterculture of the youth that reinforced the estrangement from the establishment.

The Autonomous Movement originated in northern Italy in the autumn of 1969. Initial agitation came from blue- and white-collar workers who revolted against both industry and trade unions. They conducted strikes for better working conditions but also to change the nature of work. These strikers wanted more control over their lives. Students in universities and high schools soon joined the movement for autonomy, and this alliance of workers and students caused considerable social unrest. Several groups formed out of this unrest: Lotta Continua (Continuous Struggle); Potere Operaio (Workers' Power); Autonomia Operaia (Workers' Autonomy); Metropolitan Indians; and, finally, the Red

Brigades. Radical feminism also became a part of the movement when Rivolta Femminile (Female Revolt) and Lotta Feminista (Female Struggle) formed in the early 1970s to fight for abortion rights and to elevate the status of women in Italy.

The Italian Autonomous Movement went to war against the Italian state in 1977, and it was brutally repressed by the Italian government. After neo-Fascist groups attacked students at the universities, students revolted against the university's hierarchy by occupying buildings. In the meantime, the Italian Communist Party had joined the Italian government, and it allied with the police to put down the revolt. Students fought pitched battles often led by members of the radical student autonomous group Metropolitan Indians. Throughout April and March 1977, fighting continued in a mini–civil war between students and the Italian state. By the end of 1977, the student Autonomous Movement had been crushed through a combination of police action and repressive legislation passed by the Italian Parliament. Some of the student leaders resorted to guerrilla warfare and others joined Italian leftist terrorist groups, including the Red Brigades, Front Line (Prima Linea), and the Armed Proletarian Nuclei.

At the time that the Autonomous Movement was going into decline in Italy, the movement spread to West Germany. It emerged out of the anti–nuclear power movement, the peace movement, the environmental movement, and the feminist movement. Added to these movements was the increasing lack of housing, which produced a squatter's movement whose members began occupying abandoned buildings. An organization, Autonomen, appeared in the late 1970s and combined elements from these movements. Autonomen had no centralized structure, but it had an activist orientation. With no recognized national leadership, local Autonomen activists mobilized against West German government policies by organizing mass demonstrations. These mass demonstrations included a willingness to confront the police. Throughout the 1980s

mass demonstrations protesting nuclear power and environmental exploitation took place in West Germany. By the late 1980s, the German movement had developed new enemies that included the world banking system and multinational corporations.

The center of the Autonomen movement is in Hamburg's Hafenstrasse, where activists first occupied houses in 1981. After police failed to oust the squatters by force, the Hamburg municipal government recognized its existence by allowing it to form an independent corporation in 1987. The battles over the Hafenstrasse staged the first appearance of the **Black Bloc**, an outgrowth of the Autonomous Movement, as fighters against the police.

By 1988, the Autonomous Movement had become a European phenomenon. Anti-government agitation spread from Germany into Austria, Denmark, England, Holland, Italy, and the United States. Activists gathered at conferences and meetings in various countries to establish a common front. Alliances and friendships developed and the violent tactics of the Autonomen in Germany soon became widespread in other countries. The lack of affordable housing was an issue that united all of the European autonomous groups. Another issue that united the international Autonomous Movement was opposition to South Africa's apartheid policies. A Dutch group, Anti-Racist Action Group (RARA), began attacking in 1985 the Shell Oil Company for its investment in South Africa. **See also** Black Bloc.

Suggested readings: George Katsiaficas, *The Subversion of Politics: European Autonomous Social Movements and the Decolonization of Everyday Life* (Atlantic Heights, NJ: Humanities Press International, 1997); Sylvere Lotringer and Christian Marazzi (eds.), *Autonomia: Post-Political Politics* (New York: Semiotext[e], 1980).

Avery, Greg (1967–) (Great Britain)

Greg Avery is the leader of the British radical animal rights group **Stop Huntingdon Animal Cruelty** (SHAC). Born in 1967, his family had a tailoring business, which he joined after finishing his education. At an early age, Avery became a convert to the animal rights movement. He and his wife Heather James met at a demonstration against live animal exports in 1995 and soon married. They became active in the Save the Hill Grove Cats campaign against cat breeding for laboratory testing in Witney, Oxfordshire, and the dog breeding for research of the Consort Kennels near Ross-on-Wye, in Herefordshire. Their activities led to both these operations going out of business. Several times Avery has been arrested; the most serious charge, conspiracy to commit arson, occurred in 1996. He was found innocent, but his co-defendant, David Callender, was found guilty. Most of the other arrests were for disturbing the peace, and he has served brief jail terms.

In August 1999, Avery, his wife, and veterans of the Hill Grove formed the Stop Huntingdon Animal Cruelty. This campaign was to target the animal research on beagles at Huntingdon Life Sciences (HLS). In 1997, after two staff members had been found guilty of abusing animals, leaders of SHAC decided to target Huntingdon Life Sciences for animal cruelty. Avery formulated the strategy of attacking HLS at its financial base. Because SHAC has only around a dozen active members, the chief weapons were the Internet and media events. Besides demonstrations and Internet traffic directed against the executives, scientists, and staff of HLS, Avery directed a harassment campaign against the financial supporters of HLS. A combination of bad publicity and harassment caused British banking to sell its interests in HLS to banks and individuals in the United States. This shift across the Atlantic Ocean, however, has not stopped Avery and SHAC from attacking those institutions and individuals. His tactics attracted the attention of British authorities, and Avery was arrested in the summer of 2001. In November 2001, he was given a yearlong sentence for inciting a public nuisance, but the British government released him in April 2002. Even the absence of Avery did not stop SHAC's campaign against HLS. Because of the harassment of HLS, the British government insured the

laboratory for future damages in January 2003. **See also** Stop Huntingdon Animal Cruelty (SHAC).

Suggested readings: Ross Hawkins, "Experienced Activists Lead British Animal Rights Group," *Sunday Business* (London) (January 21, 2001), p. 1; Patrick Jenkins, "A Ruthless Hunter," *Financial Times* (London) (January 12, 2002), p. 9; Kevin Toolis, "In for the Kill," *Guardian* (London) (December 4, 1998), p. 8; Giles Trendle, "Anti-Corporate Activism," *Enterprise* (October 1, 2002), p. 18; Bruce Wallace, "Battle Reaches Home Front: Guerrilla Tactics," *Edmonton Journal* (April 15, 2001), p. E4.

Al-Azhar University (Egypt)

Al-Azhar University in Cairo, Egypt, is the leading Islamist institution of higher education in the Middle East. It was founded in A.D. 977, making the university the oldest institution of higher education in the world. Al-Azhar has served as the model for the European universities founded in medieval times. The major part of the university's curriculum traditionally is the study of Sunni Islam, but philosophy, the social sciences, and medical specialties have been added to the curriculum in the last century. In 1962, women were allowed to enroll, but they are instructed separately from the men. Al-Azhar University attracts students from all over the Muslim world, and by the end of the 1990s, its enrollment exceeded 125,000 students. The chief religious leader at al-Azhar University is also considered the supreme religious authority in Egypt.

Al-Azhar University has become a hotbed of Islamist theology. Religious leaders at al-Azhar have traditionally provided the Egyptian ruler religious legitimacy in return for their services as advisors and consultants. In 1961, Gamal Abdel Nasser, the head of the Egyptian state, nationalized al-Azhar University and made its clerics (*ulema*) paid civil servants. All of the recent leaders of Egypt, from Anwar Sadat to Hosni Mubarak, have been careful to cultivate the religious leaders of al-Azhar University. Sadat increased al-Azhar's budget and allowed it to raise funds from other Muslim countries. Kuwait and

Saudi Arabia have been generous benefactors. Financial support has allowed the leading religious leaders at al-Azhar University more independence.

Religious leaders have in the past been reluctant to challenge the Egyptian government, but over the years partisans of the **Muslim Brotherhood** have infiltrated the university and influenced both faculty and students. This militancy has come despite the leadership of the Grand Imam Sheikh Muhammad Sayed al-Tantawi. Al-Tantawi has been reluctant to challenge the Egyptian government, but he has attempted to have al-Azhar be given a censorship role on books published in Egypt to prevent the appearance of un-Islamic books. Since 1989, religious leaders of al-Azhar University have become increasingly critical of the Egyptian government's peace with Israel and more aggressive in advancing its Islamist theology. The assassination of Dr. Farag Fouda, an Egyptian human rights activist, on June 7, 1992, by an assassin with contacts to al-Azhar University is another sign of the growth of extremism at the university. Such extremism was revealed again when Islamic scholars at al-Azhar threatened to proclaim a holy war, or jihad, against the United States for its invasion of Iraq in the spring of 2003. Graduates of al-Azhar disseminate the Islamist ideas being taught at the university throughout the Islamic world. **See also** Muslim Brotherhood (al-Ikhwan al-Muslimun).

Suggested readings: Karim Alrawi, "University of the Extreme," *Guardian* (London) (June 23, 1992), p. 19; Douglas Jehl, "Moderate Muslims Fear Their Message Is Being Ignored," *New York Times* (October 21, 2001), sec. 1B, p. 1; Judith Miller, *God Has Ninety-Nine Names: Reporting from a Militant Middle East* (New York: Touchstone Books, 1996); Anthony Shadid, "Islamic Scholars Urge Jihad in Event of Iraq War," *Washington Post* (March 11, 2003), p. A12.

Azzam, Sheikh Abdullah Yussuf (1941–1989) (Pakistan)

Sheikh Abdullah Azzam was one of the spiritual leaders of the radical Islamist movement in Pakistan and Afghanistan. He was born in 1941 in the small village of Selat al-Harithis near Jenin, Palestine. Most of his schooling was in religious schools in Jordan. In the early 1960s, he attended the Sharia College of Damascus University where he obtained in 1966 a bachelor's degree in Sharia (Islamic law). He also joined the **Muslim Brotherhood**. After leaving the West Bank because of the Israeli occupation in 1967, he traveled to Egypt and worked on a master's degree in Sharia at Cairo's **al-Azhar University**. He taught for a couple of years in Egyptian religious schools before returning in 1971 to al-Azhar University, where he received a Ph.D. in Islamic jurisprudence in 1973. Al-Azhar has been a hotbed of militant Islamists and Azzam came to share their views. The secular orientation of the **Palestine Liberation Organization** (PLO) disturbed him, so he took a teaching job in Saudi Arabia at King Abdul Aziz University in Jeddah. **Osama bin Laden** was a student at the university at the same time that Azzam was teaching there.

Azzam was a proponent of the doctrine that jihad (holy war) is central to the liberation of the Muslim world from the tyranny of the secular West. He taught this doctrine in his lectures at King Abdul Aziz University. Azzam decided to place his Islamist doctrine and himself at the service of the Afghan fighters against the Soviets. He believed that his role was to teach the doctrine of resistance, but this decision caused Saudi authorities to expel him from his teaching post. Next, he moved to Peshawar, Pakistan, where he founded an organization, Bait-ul-Ansar, to train fighters for the Afghanistan War. He worked closely with bin Laden in forming the Mujahideen Services Bureau (Maktab al-Khidamat) in 1984. Throughout the 1980s, Azzam made frequent trips into Afghanistan preaching global jihad. These sermons reached most of the 16,000 to 20,000 Afghanistan War volunteers, and they carried his ideas back to their countries after the war. He paid special attention to those Muslims with connections to and in the United States.

Azzam's ideas became more radical as the Afghanistan War progressed. Heavy losses of

Afghan fighters at Jalalabad convinced him that there was a conspiracy on the part of the Pakistani and American governments to weaken the Islamic cause. He preached this message both in Afghanistan and Pakistan. In 1987, Azzam conceptualized the idea of an Islamist vanguard, or al-Qaeda al-Sulbah (The Solid Base), to carry out his ideas on the creation of a purified Islamist society. His chief disciple, Osama bin Laden, seized on this idea, and he created **al-Qaeda**. Later, Azzam and bin Laden's relationship deteriorated because Azzam disagreed with bin Laden over the export of terrorism. Azzam wanted to concentrate on building an Islamist society in Afghanistan, and he opposed launching a terrorist campaign against Arab regimes. On November 24, 1989, a bomb exploded under Azzam's automobile in Peshawar, Pakistan,

killing him, two of his sons, and a companion. Although no group or individual has claimed responsibility for his assassination, suspicion had centered first on Pakistani security forces. Rohan Gunaratna, an authority on al-Qaeda, believes that bin Laden sponsored a hit-team to conduct the assassination. His death has not silenced Azzam's call for a global jihad, however, because his supporters continue to advance his cause. **See also** Bin Laden, Osama; al-Qaeda (The Base).

Suggested readings: Yossef Bodansky, *Bin Laden: The Man Who Declared War on America* (New York: Forum, 2001); Rohan Gunaratna, *Inside Al Qaeda: Global Network of Terror* (New York: Columbia University Press, 2002); Chris Suellentrop, "Abdullah Azzam," *Slate Magazine* (April 16, 2002), p. 1; Penny Wark, "What Fuels His Hatred," *Times* (London) (October 19, 2001), p. 1.

B

Baader-Meinhof Gang (See Red Army Faction) (RAF)

Baader, Andreas (1943–1977) (West Germany)

Andreas Baader was one of the leaders of the most notorious West German terrorist organizations, the **Red Army Faction** (RAF). He was born in Munich, Germany, on May 6, 1943. His father was a historian and archivist, but he was drafted into the German Army and, after being taken prisoner by the Russians in 1945, was reported missing. His mother never remarried. Baader was always a stubborn and impulsive child. He was intelligent, but he kept changing schools. At 16, he attended a private school in Munich where he was in constant trouble for fighting. Baader left school early and he entered a private art college where he wrote advertising copy. He started frequenting the Munich night scene with artists and underworld types. In 1963, Baader moved to West Berlin. He worked briefly as a journalism trainee on the *Bild-Zeitung* until he was fired for bad conduct. In the meantime, Baader had become a fixture in West Berlin nightlife. He also came to specialize in stealing cars and motorbikes and in small-time theft. Baader considers these antisocial activities as a form of terrorism against the West German

system. In 1967, he met **Gudrun Ensslin** and they became lovers.

Baader, Ensslin, and a compatriot decided to become full-time terrorists by firebombing a couple of department stores in Frankfurt. On April 2, 1968, they ignited firebombs in the Kaufhaus Schneider Department Store and the Kaufhol Department Store. A couple of days later the police arrested the three of them for these offences. In the court trial in October 1968, Baader received a three-year prison sentence. Baader served 14 months of his sentence before being released on appeal on June 13, 1969. After his appeal failed, he and Ensslin went underground. They moved to Paris where Regis Debray, the French revolutionary theorist, harbored them in his apartment for several weeks. Next they traveled to Rome, Italy. Baader and Ensslin then decided to return to West Germany, and they stayed in Berlin with **Ulrike Meinhof**. On April 4, 1970, police arrested Baader after receiving a tip from a German undercover agent. On May 14, 1970, Ensslin, Meinhof, and several accomplices rescued Baader by overpowering security guards on an outing from prison.

Baader assumed the leadership role in the group that was now named the Red Army Faction (RAF). After Baader's escape, the RAF flew in two groups to Lebanon and then to Syria. After a short stay in Syria, the RAF ended up in a Palestinian training camp in Jordan. Baader's obnoxious behavior and demands for special privileges soon alienated his Palestinian instructors. They terminated training and sent the group back to West Germany.

Over the next two years, Baader masterminded the terrorist activities of the Red Army Faction. He planned and led three bank robberies on September 28, 1970. His goal was to raise funds for continuing operations. Baader traveled throughout West Germany orchestrating new bank robberies and narrowly escaped from the police several times. He decided in early 1972 to expand operations to include a bombing campaign. This time he included U.S. military as well as West German targets. On June 1, 1972, German police trapped him in a garage in Frankfurt where the RAF was manufacturing bombs. Baader was shot in the thigh and seriously wounded by a police sniper. After his arrest and that of Holger Meins, Baader was hospitalized.

Baader received special harsh treatment by the German police and by prison guards because of his position as the head of the Red Army Faction. For the first year after his arrest, he was kept in restricted confinement in a prison in Schwalmstadt away from the other members of the RAF. Despite isolation, he was able to start a communication system with other RAF prisoners. In late 1972, he called the first of three hunger strikes. Each of the hunger strikes became more serious, and Meins consequently starved himself to death on November 10, 1974, during the third hunger strike.

Baader used his trial beginning in May 1975 to attack the West German political and judicial system. He, Ensslin, Meinhof, and **Jan-Carl Raspe** engaged in political theater by challenging the judges. The government charged him with nine separate offenses including murder, attempted murder, bombings, and bank robberies. His trial opened on May 21, 1975, and it lasted nearly two years. On April 18, 1977, Baader received a sentence of life imprisonment. He and the RAF prisoners served their sentence in a special section of Stammheim prison.

Baader never adjusted to prison life. He retained his control over the RAF, but he had several periods of depression. Because the prisoners were able to establish communications with those outside the prison, Baader was aware of the failed kidnapping of Jurgen Ponto, a West German banker, on July 30, 1977, and the successful kidnapping of Hans Martin Schlyer, a West German industrialist, on September 5, 1977. Baader placed much of his hopes of freedom on the skyjacking of a Lufthansa aircraft by members of the **Popular Front for the Liberation of Palestine (PFLP)** on October 13, 1977. News of the failure of the skyjacking on the evening of October 17, 1977, led the members of the RAF to decide on a suicide pact. Sometime in the early morning of October 18, Baader used a smuggled pistol to commit suicide. His death in what had been described as the most secure prison in Europe led to speculation on whether or not he had been murdered. Several investigations by West German authorities concluded that Baader and his colleagues in the RAF had committed suicide, but the West German left questioned this verdict. **See also** Ensslin, Gudrun; Mahler, Horst; Meinhof, Ulrike; Raspe, Jan-Carl; Red Army Faction.

Suggested readings: Stefan Aust, *The Baader-Meinhof Group: The Inside Story of a Phenomenon* (London: Bodley Head, 1985); Jillian Becker, *Hitler's Children: The Baader-Meinhof Terrorist Gang* (Philadelphia: Lippincott, 1978); Tom Vague, *Televisionaries: The Red Army Faction* (London: AK Press, 1994).

Bajrang Dal (India)

The Bajrang Dal is a Hindu extremist organization that is trying to rid India of Christianity by conducting a terrorist campaign against Christians. Extremist Hindus founded the Bajrang Dal in 1984 along with its female affiliate, the Durga Vahini, as a way to mobilize Hindu youth. It has a loose affiliation with the Hindu nationalist organization **Rashtriya Swayamsevak Sangh** (RSS). Surendra Kumar Jain is the president of Bajrang Dal and its chief spokesperson. The group's headquarters is in south Delhi in a Hindu temple complex, but it has adherents spread throughout India. By 1999, a reporter for *Newsweek* placed the membership of Bajrang Dal at 1.5 million and growing. It trains its youthful supporters at 30 training camps scattered throughout India. At first, the main activity of the Bajrang Dal was attacking Muslims in an effort to keep a purified Hindu state. Outrages against Muslims caused Bajrang Dal to be briefly outlawed in 1992, but a tribunal overturned the ruling. In the mid-1990s, the leadership began targeting Indian Christians and Christian missionaries. Leaders of the Bajrang Dal started claiming that Christian missionary work was a threat to the survival of Hindu society in India.

Soon after the Hindu nationalist party, Bharatiya Janata Party (BJP), assumed national office in April 1998, the leadership of the Bajrang Dal started gathering information on the 5,000 Christian missionaries working in India and announced their goal to rid India of Christianity. In the summer of 1998, Hindu militants of the Bajrang Dal started attacking Christian missionaries. In September 1998, a Hindu gang in the central Indian state of Madhya Pradesh raped four Catholic nuns. On December 25, 1998, Bajrang Dal activists attacked two Roman Catholic schools, a hospital, and three churches. Indian Christians in Gujarat state were forced to renounce Christianity and convert back to the Hindu religion after a purification ceremony.

The worst excess was the murder of an Australian Protestant missionary and his sons on January 23, 1999. Graham Staines was the director of the Evangelical Missionary Society in the state of Orissa and had been working with lepers for over 30 years. A mob led by Ravinder Kumar Pal, a supporter of the Bajrang Dal, burned alive Staines and his two young sons in their jeep while shouting pro-Bajrang Dal slogans. These murders attracted worldwide attention and caused the Indian government to launch an inquiry into the incident. A Home Ministry report appeared in August 1999 absolving the Dajrang Dal from responsibility, but this report was widely believed to be a cover-up to protect the BJP government and preserve the Hindu nationalist coalition. **See also** Rashtriya Swayamsevak Sangh (National Volunteer Organization) (RSS)

Suggested readings: Barry Bearak, "Indian Report Blames Individual in Killing of Missionary and Sons, *New York Times* (August 7, 1999), sec. 1, p. 4; Suzanne Goldenberg, "Promoters of Hate Blame Missionary for His Own Death," *Guardian* (London) (January 28, 1999), p. 15; Samar Halarnkar and Uday Mahurkar, "Religious Tensions: Burning the Cross," *India Today* (January 11, 1999), p. 22; Robert Marquand, "Anti-Christian Violence in India Builds on Fear of Conversions," *Christian Science Monitor* (October 5, 1998), p. 7; Carla Power, "Gods in the Classroom," *Newsweek* (July 23, 2001), p. 20; Ajay Singh, "The Flames of Religious Hate; Murders Most Foul Put the BJP under Pressure," *Asiaweek* (February 5, 1999), p. 26; N. K. Singh and Uday Mahurkar, "Bajrang Dal: Loonies at Large," *India Today* (February 8, 1998), p. 26; Tavleen Singh, "Ban Bajrang Dal," *India Today* (February 8, 1998), p. 30.

Bakr, Yasin Abu (1930–) (Trinidad)

Born in 1930 in Trinidad, Yasin Abu Bakr is the spiritual leader of the Trinidad Islamist group Jamaat al-Muslimeen (Society of Muslims). His first career was as a policeman. After Bakr became attracted to the American Black Muslim movement and its brand of Islam, he founded the Jamaat al-Muslimeen in 1969 with only 12 members. After establishing a religious community, Bakr developed close ties to Libya's President **Muammar Qaddafi** and made frequent trips to Libya to consult with him. Over the years, the Libyan government has subsidized the growth of Bakr's group. By 2001, the Jamaat al-Muslimeen had between 6,000 and 7,000 members.

Bakr was a minor religious leader in Trinidad until the Jamaat al-Muslimeen attempted a coup against the Trinidad government in 1990. He and followers had been angered over delays in resolving a land dispute with the government. Bakr gathered 114 members of the Jamaat al-Muslimeen for a coup attempt against the government in Port of Spain on July 27, 1990. Their first action was to bomb the police headquarters building. Next, Bakr led his supporters armed with AK-47s to seize the parliament building, known as the Red House, and occupy the Trinidad and Tobago Television (TTT) station. After seizing the building, Bakr held government officials, including Prime Minister Arthur Robinson, hostage. Bakr and the Jamaat al-Muslimeen held the hostages for six days while hostage negotiations proceeded. An acting prime minister signed an amnesty for the hostage-takers, and the hostages were freed on August 1, 1990. Soldiers arrested Bakr and his 114 compatriots and threw them into jail, but lawyers for Bakr and his supporters appealed their arrest. After the Port of Spain courts finally accepted the amnesty, all of the hostage-takers were released from prison in 1992. They also won nearly $1 million from the government for wrongful destruction and occupation of Jamaat al-Muslimeen property. This amnesty and the financial settlement outraged many in Trinidad because 24 people had been killed during the coup attempt.

Bakr and his Jamaat al-Muslimeen remain controversial. Government officials remain nervous about Bakr's political ambitions. His contacts with Qaddafi have kept him in the spotlight as a potential terrorist. The arrest of a man in Florida with an affiliation with the Jamaat al-Muslimeen in late 2001 for attempting to buy assault rifles and machine guns has created further uncertainty. Bakr has made efforts to keep a low political profile while at the same time posing as the champion of the lower classes. Despite fears that he had contacts with terrorists, Bakr condemned the terrorist attacks in the United States on **September 11**, 2001, and he has refused to participate in anti-American demonstrations. **See also** Qaddafi, Muammar.

Suggested readings: David Gonzalez, "Failed Rebel's Boast: At Least He Rules the Street," *New York Times* (January 9, 2002), p. A4; Angela Potter, "After Terrorist Attacks, Trinidad Puts Muslim Rebel Group under Renewed Scrutiny," Associated Press Worldstream (October 28, 2001), p. 1; Peter Richards, "Radical Muslim Group Focus of Trinidad and Tobago Poll," Inter Press Service (October 4, 2002), p.1; Scott Wheeler, "Trinidad and Tobago—Terrorists Develop Island Operations," *Insight* (December 24, 2002), p. 1.

Bakri Mohammed, Sheikh Omar (See al-Muhajiroun)

Al-Banna, Hassan (1906–1949) (Egypt)

Hassan al-Banna was the founder of the **Muslim Brotherhood** in Egypt. He was born in 1906 in the Egyptian Nile Delta town of Muhammadia northwest of Cairo. His father had studied at the **al-Azhar University** and had become a part-time Islamic judge. Al-Banna grew up in a religious environment and learned Islamic law. He was active in the 1919 riots against British rule. After graduation from Cairo Teachers College, he found a job in Ismailiya, Egypt, teaching Arabic at the primary level. While in college, he had been exposed to the leading Islamic scholars of the day, including Muhammad Rashid Rida. In 1928, al-Banna and six associates founded the Muslim Brotherhood in Ismailiya. At first it was intended to be a youth club, but it soon turned into a political organization. After obtaining a teaching job in Cairo in 1932, al-Banna transferred the Muslim Brotherhood to Cairo. In the political environment of Cairo the Muslim Brotherhood began to grow. It offered a total Islamic worldview and a rejection of Western society. The Muslim Brotherhood continued to grow during World War II, reaching a membership of nearly 500,000 in 1945. Al-Banna was always vague about his political goals, but he expressed his admiration for Benito Mussolini and Adolf Hitler and their war against the British.

By the end of World War II, the Muslim Brotherhood had become the most serious political rival of the nationalist Wafd Party. Al-Banna's response to the end of the war was to launch a terror campaign in Egypt that included arson, bombings, and beatings. He organized camps to train terrorists, and these camps attracted others from the Middle East. Al-Banna remained the leading figure in the Muslim Brotherhood, but factional infighting over its future direction hurt the organization. Besides advocating an Islamic state and the adherence to the Islamic law of the Sharia, al-Banna became concerned about the Palestinian problem. Under his leadership, Muslim Brotherhood members received military training and were dispatched to Israel in May 1948 to fight in the Arab-Israeli war. Egyptian authorities learned of these activities and attempted to suppress the Muslim Brotherhood. On December 8, 1948, the Egyptian government dissolved the Muslim Brotherhood on the basis of its potential for terrorism and armed insurrection. The leader of the suppression was Prime Minister Mahmud Fahmi al-Nuqrashi. A member of the Muslim Brotherhood assassinated al-Nuqrashi on December 28, 1948. Egyptian security forces retaliated on February 12, 1949, by murdering al-Banna on a Cairo Street. Al-Banna's death was a serious blow to the Muslim Brotherhood. His followers had their revenge by helping to undermine King Farouq's regime, thus allowing for the military coup to be successful in 1952. **See also** Muslim Brotherhood (al-Ikhwan al-Muslimun).

Suggested readings: Wilhelm Dietl, *Holy War* (New York: Macmillan, 1984); Christina Phelps Harris, *Nationalism and Revolution in Egypt: The Role of the Muslim Brotherhood* (The Hague, Netherlands: Mouton, 1964); Fereydoun Hoveyda, *The Broken Crescent: The "Threat" of Militant Islamic Fundamentalism* (Westport, CT: Praeger, 1998); Mark Huband, *Warriors of the Prophet: The Struggle for Islam* (Boulder, CO: Westview Press, 1999).

Barghouthi, Marwan bin Khatib (1959–) (Palestine)

Marwan Barghouthi is the charismatic leader of the military wing of the Palestinian Authority's (PA) **Tanzim** (Organization). He was born in 1959 in the West Bank village of Kober, where his father was a farmer. Always fascinated by politics, he joined al-Fatah at age 15. Barghouthi attended Bir Zeit University, where he studied history and political science. Twice he was elected head of the student body. After earning a master's degree in international affairs with a thesis on French-Palestinian relations, he entered Palestinian politics. His anti-Israel activities landed him in jail. After serving six years in various Israel jails, Israeli authorities deported him in 1987. Barghouthi moved first to Tunis, Tunisia, and then to Amman, Jordan. By this time, Barghouthi had become an emerging figure in the **Palestine Liberation Organization** (PLO). In 1989, he was elected to the Fatah Revolutionary Council.

Barghouthi returned to the West Bank in 1994 in the aftermath of the Oslo Accords. Soon afterward, **Yasser Arafat**, the head of the PLO, appointed him to be the general secretary of al-Fatah movement in the West Bank, and as such he became the head of Tanzim, the military wing of the Palestinian Authority (PA), giving him control over **Al-Aqsa Martyrs' Brigades** as well as other military forces. In 1996, he was elected to the Palestinian legislature as a representative from Ramallah. His election to the Palestine Liberation Organization Central Council also increased his authority. Barghouthi has remained loyal to Arafat, but he has been critical of the Palestinian Authority, accusing some of its members of corruption.

Barghouthi's role as the head of Tanzim has given him a high profile in al-Aqsa Intifada. Tanzim military operations have rivaled both Hamas and Islamic Jihad in lethal attacks on Israeli soldiers and civilians. His nickname is the "little Napoleon" because of his short stature. He is a hard-liner who insists on an independent Palestinian state in Jerusalem and the right of Palestinians to return. Barghouthi is also disillusioned about the United States and its role in peace making because of its alliance with Israel. These views have made him a popular figure in the Palestinian movement. Recent Palestinian polling organizations, the Palestinian Center for Policy and Survey Research, and Jerusalem Media and Communications Center have determined Barghouthi to be both the most popular and the most trusted Palestinian after Arafat and **Sheikh Ahmed Yassin**, the head of Hamas. His ability to speak both

Marwan Barghouthi marches with bodyguards and Palestinian gunmen in a show of strength through the center of the West Bank town of Ramallah on August 4, 2001. Israeli forces, on April 15, 2002, arrested Marwan Barghouthi, a close aide to Palestinian leader Yasser Arafat, for his alleged involvement in the Palestinian suicide bombings. (AP Photo/Nasser Nasser)

English and Hebrew has allowed him to become an articulate spokesman for the Palestinians.

Barghouthi's leadership in military operations against Israel has made him high on Israel's most-wanted list. Several times he has been able to avoid Israeli assassination attempts. Barghouthi has long been considered by many political analysts to be a logical successor to Arafat. His high profile led to his arrest by Israeli forces on April 15, 2002, in Ramallah, West Bank. Israeli authorities blamed him for the Palestinian suicide bombings, and they brought him to trial on September 4, 2002. His lawyer has maintained that he had been captured in a part of the West Bank that under the Oslo agreements is subject to Palestinian jurisdiction, making his arrest illegal. In addition, supporters have charged that the Israelis have tortured Barghouthi. Barghouthi has refused to respond to the Israeli charges and has claimed that he is a politician being tried illegally. Barghouthi's trial has lasted for more than a year, and a verdict is expected in early 2004. **See also** Arafat, Yasser; Palestine Liberation Organization (PLO).

Suggested readings: James Bennet, "Fatah Leader Defies Israeli Court," *International Herald Tribune* (London) (April 7, 2003), p. 8; Nicholas Jubber and Michael Hirst, "Marwan Barghouthi, Fatah Leader," *Arabies Trends* (September 1, 2001), p. 1; Isabel Kershner, "The Amazing Rise of Marwan Barghouthi," *Jerusalem Report* (February 25, 2002), p. 16; Ben Lynfield, "Political Stock Rises for a Palestinian Firebrand," *Christian Science Monitor* (August 8, 2001), p. 1; Jessica Maccallin, "'Israel Has No Right to Try Me,'" *Sunday Herald* (Edinburgh) (September 8, 2002), p. 21; Charles A. Radin, "Palestinian Activist Tests Extremes of Israeli Policy for Top Militant," *Boston Globe* (March 17, 2002), p. A12.

Barkashov, Aleksandr Petrovich (1953–) (Russia)

Aleksandr Barkashov is the leading neo-Nazi activist in Russia. He was born on October 6, 1953, in Moscow, Russia. His father was an electrician and his mother a nurse. He attended a local school where he distinguished himself in sports and fighting. Because of his belligerent attitude, Barkashov was refused permission to join the Communist Youth League (Komsomol). After leaving school in 1971, he joined the Soviet army. He served in the Soviet army in Belarus and never obtained a rank higher than private. After leaving the army, Barkashov found employment at an underground thermal energy station in Moscow, where he worked for 14 years. His main interests during this period were in karate and making bows and daggers.

Then Barkashov decided to enter extremist politics. In 1985, he joined the anti-Semitic Pamyat group. During the closing days of the Soviet Union, the Pamyat group was backed by hard-line anti-Gorbachev elements that opposed the perestroika reforms. Despite successful promotions within the group, Barkashov became disenchanted with the leadership of Pamyat and left the group in August 1990. He then formed his own

group, **Russian National Unity** (Russkoje Nationalnoje Edinstv, or RNE), on October 16, 1990. Members of the RNE swore a personal loyalty oath to Barkashov. Barkashov openly expressed his admiration for Adolf Hitler and Nazi racial policies. He blames most of Russia's economic, political, and social problems on the Jews.

Barkashov has directed the Russian National Unity group to participate in Russian politics. He supported the August 1991 abortive coup against the Yeltsin government. Failure of this revolt did not discourage Barkashov. The breakup of the Soviet Union and the isolation of nearly 25 million ethnic Russians in other countries disturbed him. He was also upset over the large number of ethnic non-Russians left in Russia. Barkashov used the resentment against foreigners and ethnic minorities to increase political support for his RNE. He also worked to establish relations with other European neo-Nazis, including those in Germany. In the mid-1990s, Barkashov formed an alliance with Aleksandre Stergilov, a former KGB general and notorious anti-Semite, to establish the Russian National Assembly (RNA) group. Barkashov and Stergilov have positioned the RNE on the extreme right wing of Russian politics. They have also called for the reunification of all Slavs living in the former Soviet Union. In September 1993, Barkashov and his followers participated with several extremist groups, including **Eduard Limonov**'s **National Bolshevik Party**, in the storming of the Russian parliament building. After several hundred were killed, Barkashov escaped arrest and hid near Moscow. A few weeks later, Barkashov received a gunshot wound in the hip from a colleague at his hiding spot. While he was recuperating in the hospital, Russian police arrested and imprisoned him for his role in the attack on the Russian parliament building. However, amnesty granted by the Russian parliament in February 1994 allowed Barkashov to be freed from prison.

Barkashov has replaced **Vladimir Zhirinovsky** as Russia's most extreme Russian nationalist politician. Since 1994, he has been actively building the Russian National Unity Party into a national force. Images of the RNE activists in demonstrations around Russia appear on Russian television, giving the impression that the party is on the march under the leadership of Barkashov. By February 2002 an opinion poll quoted by Alexei Pankin in *The Moscow Times* ranked Barkashov as "one of Russia's 10 most recognizable politicians." **See also** Limonov, Eduard; Russian National Unity (Russkoje Nationalnoje Edinstv) (RNE); Zhirinovsky, Vladimir Volfovich.

Suggested readings: Victoria Clark, "Russia's Little Hitler Backs President Yeltsin," *Guardian* (London) (May 29, 1996), p. 13; Martin A. Lee, *The Beast Reawakens* (Boston: Little, Brown, 1997); Alexei Pankin, "Under the Surface of the Skinhead Threat," *Moscow Times* (April 23, 2002), no. 2429; Stephen D. Shenfield, *Russian Fascism: Traditions, Tendencies, Movements* (Armonk, NY: M. E. Sharpe, 2001); Helen Womack, "Fascist Chief Spreads Fear over Russia," *Independent* (London) (January 2, 1999), p. 15.

Basayev, Shamil (1965–) (Chechnya)

Samil Basayev was Chechnya's leading guerrilla leader. He was born in January 1965 and raised in the village of Dyshne-Vedeno, near Vedeno, Chechnya, where his father was a laborer. After finishing school, he served his compulsory military service in the Russian army as a fireman. Basayev then moved to Moscow, intending to study law at Moscow State University, but he was unable to gain admittance. Instead, he ended up studying land management and living in a building with African and Cuban students. Basayev supported himself by selling foreign computers. In August 1991, he participated in the defense of Russian President Boris Yeltsin after Russian right-wingers attempted a coup against him. Soon afterward, Basayev joined the Chechnya independence movement.

Basayev's experiences in the Russian army left him unprepared to become a military leader in Chechnya's military forces, but he soon became one of its major commanders. His first operation in 1991 was in the hijacking of a Russian passenger plane on a flight from Mineralnye Vody in southern Russia to Turkey. In the period 1992–1993, he became commander of a Chechen battalion that fought alongside Abkhaz insurgents in Georgia and helped them defeat the Georgians. In 1994, Basayev traveled to Afghanistan to train with the Afghan military leader Akhmed Shah Masood. During the first Chechen war with Russia, Basayev became a leading military commander. His mission was to head the defense of the Chechen capital of Grozny against the Russian army. He was able to outmaneuver and outfight Russian forces. His attitude hardened in May 1995 when a Russian air raid on Vedeno killed his mother, one of his brothers, one of his sisters, two of his children, and six other relatives. In June 1995, he led a raid into Russia that ended in the occupation of a hospital in the Russian town of Budyonnovsk and the taking of 1,200 hostages. His raid was an attempt to force the Russian government to proclaim a cease-fire with Chechnya. This attempt was successful but at the cost of more than 100 dead, including 20 dead Chechens. Basayev returned to Chechnya a national hero. On April 29, 1996, he was appointed the chief of staff of the Chechen rebel army. In August 1996, he took 1,500 Chechen guerrillas into Grozny and surrounded the Russian forces there. His forces killed more than 1,000 Russian soldiers, and soon afterward hostilities between Russia and Chechnya ceased.

After the fighting ended, Basayev entered Chechen politics. The wartime leader of Chechnya, Dzhokhar Dudayev, had been killed in April 1996 during a Russian rocket attack. His absence led to a power struggle between Aslan Maskhadov, a former colonel in the Russian army and a former military chief of staff in the Chechen army, and Basayev. In the January 1997 election for Chechnya's presidency, Basayev lost out to Maskhadov, obtaining only 23.5 percent of the vote. This loss did not prevent him from being named prime minister of Chechnya in December 1997. Basayev resigned as prime minister in July 1998 to renew the military struggle against Russia.

Chechen rebel warlord Shamil Basayev speaks in Grozny on October 28, 1999, after his residence was destroyed in air bombardments by Russian jets. Basayev has claimed responsibility for both the commuter train bombing at Yessentuki (December 5, 2003) and the bombing of the National Hotel in Moscow (December 9, 2003). (AP Photo/Ruslan Musayev)

Basayev instigated the second Chechen war with Russia by leading Chechen forces into the Republic of Dagestan. He brought about renewed fighting with Russian forces in September 1999 by leading an army of 1,500 fighters to free Dagestan from Russian control. This second war has proven to be less successful than the first. Basayev continues to lead Chechen forces, but he was seriously wounded in 2001. His troops blundered into a minefield and Basayev had to have his left foot amputated. Basayev is still a national hero in Chechnya, but Russian forces have made him public enemy number one and are actively seeking him dead or alive.

Russian interest in Basayev reached a new high in late 2003 and early 2004, when a series of Chechen terrorist attacks in Moscow took place. On October 23, 50 armed Chechen rebels seized more than 800 hostages at the Palace of Culture Theater in Moscow to demand an end to the war in Chechnya. Three days later the Russian Special Forces stormed the theater and killed the 50 Chechen rebels, but in the process 124 hostages died from side effects of an anesthetic gas and the gunfire. Then in January 2004 Basayev claimed responsibility for the commuter train bombing at Yessentuki on December 5, 2003, that killed 50 and wounded more than 110 and the bombing of the National Hotel in Moscow on December 9, 2003, that killed 6 and wounded 14. This intensity has been increased since the February 6, 2004, subway bombing in Moscow that killed 39 and wounded 130.

Suggested readings: Robyn Dixon, "Chechen Warrior Returns as Kremlin's Enemy No. 1," *Gazette* (Montreal) (August 23, 1999), p. A13; David Filipov, "Russian Nemesis Rises Again," *Boston Globe* (August 12, 1999), p. A1; Carolotta Gall and Thomas de Waal, *Chechnya: Calamity in the Caucasus* (New York: New York University Press, 1998); Carlotta Gall, "Rebel Lord of Grozny Revels in His Triumph," *Independent* (London) (August 17, 1996), p. 8; Christopher D. Kondaki, "Chechnya's Vicious War Re-Ignites," *Defense and Foreign Affairs Strategic Policy* (September, 2001), p. 20.

Bashir, Abu Bakar (1937 or 1938–) (Indonesia)

Abu Bakar Bashir is the ideological leader of the Indonesian Islamic extremist group **Jemaah Islamiyah** (Islamic Community) (JI). He was born in either 1937 or 1938 in Jombang, East Java. His first political activity was to join the Darul Islam movement in the 1950s. Members of this movement rebelled against Indonesia's secular constitution, but the government crushed it with brutality. In the 1960s, Bashir studied Islamic law at Gontor, Indonesia's leading Islamic school. It was at school that Bashir developed his strict fundamentalist brand of Islam. After leaving school, he broadcast his religious views from a radical Islamic radio station. In 1973, he formed an Islamic self-governing commune that he named Jemaah Islamiyah. In 1978, the Suharto government arrested him and he was convicted of subversion for advocating a jihad, or holy war, against the enemies of Islam. Bashir served nearly four years of a nine-year sentence, leaving prison in 1982.

In 1985, Bashir fled to Malaysia after the Indonesian Supreme Court reimposed his original nine-year sentence. In Malaysia, he continued to agitate for an Islamic state. It was at this time that Bashir recruited **Hambali.** Together, they revitalized the Jemaah Islamiyah by establishing branches in Malaysia and Singapore. He also formed a good working relationship with the Malaysia Mujahideen Group (KMM). Bashir empowered Hambali and Abu Jibril (Mohammad Iqbal Rahman) to set up a network of JI cells in Indonesia, Malaysia, the Philippines, and Singapore. The mission of these cells was to undertake operations against the regimes in those states.

The collapse of the Suharto regime in 1998 allowed Bashir to return to Indonesia without fear of further charges. He began to run the Mukmin Quranic boarding school in the Ngruki village in Solo, in central Java about 250 miles southeast of Jakarta. By October 2002, he was teaching more than 2,000 students. Bashir has always advocated a strict Islamic state for Indonesia and other Muslim states in the region. He is an unabashed admirer of the **Taliban** of Afghanistan and **Osama bin Laden**, claiming that they have upheld Islam. Bashir has disclaimed any association with **al-Qaeda**, but he is a longtime critic of the United States and what he claims is its anti-Islamic politics. Bashir had been left alone by Indonesian authorities so as not to stir up his radical Islamic supporters. This safe position became untenable after the bombing in Bali on October 12, 2002, when 188 dead and hundreds wounded caused foreign governments to pressure the government of Megawati Sukarnoputri to act against Bashir. Bashir's fragile health has made the government react slowly, but he was questioned about the bombing. He denied any complicity in the bombing.

The Indonesian government decided in October 2002 to arrest Bashir and place him on trial. Police arrested Bashir in a hospital in Solo, Indonesia, on October 28, 2002, and delivered him to the capital city of Jakarta. It took 300 riot police and army troops to control a mob that protested Bashir's arrest. His trial opened in Jakarta on April 23, 2003, with his facing the charges of treason and sponsoring terrorism. Government prosecutors wanted to tie him to the Bali bombing, but there was insufficient evidence to do so. The verdict of the trial showed the influence of Bashir, because he was declared innocent of being the spiritual head of Jemaah Islamiyah but guilty of treason. An appeals court then cleared him of treason and reduced his sentence from four years to three years. The only charge that Bashir is serving prison time for is forging identity documents. **See also** Al-Ghozi, Fathur Rohman; Hambali (Riduan Isamuddin); Jemaah Islamiyah (Islamic Community) (JI).

Suggested readings: Christopher Kremmer, "Recruiting a Holy Army of Hate," *Sydney Morning Herald* (October 19, 2002), p. 9; Andrew Laxon, "Abu Bakar Bashir and Hambali, Indonesia's Masters of War," *New Zealand Herald* (October 16, 2002), p. 1; Ian McPhedran, "Radical Cleric Has Both Terror Links and Motive," *Daily Telegraph* (Sydney) (October 15, 2002), p. 21; Tony Parkinson, "'We Will Fight Until We Run Out of Blood,'" *Age* (Melbourne) (October 15, 2002), p. 13; Jane Perlez and Raymond Bonner, "Indonesia Orders Muslim Cleric to Undergo Questioning," *New York Times* (October 18, 2002), sec. A, p. 14; Sian Powell, "Insulted 'Terror' Cleric Pleads Innocent," *Australian* (Sydney) (April 24, 2003), p. 1; Shefali Rekhi, "JI: From a Village School to a Regional Network of Terror," *Straits Times* (September 29, 2002), p. 1.

Basque Fatherland and Liberty (See ETA)

Batasuna (See Herri Batasuna) (Popular Unity)

Battalion 316 (Honduras)

Battalion 316 was a secret army unit in Honduras that operated in the 1980s as a death squad against Honduran leftists and dissidents. General Gustavo Alvarez Martinez, chief of the Honduras armed forces, directed the formation and operations of this unit. General Alvarez made no secret of his belief in the effectiveness of terror and violence against subversives, and he admired Argentinean army methods of dealing with them. Captain Alexander Hernandez ran the battalion, but he took orders directly from General Alvarez. In 1981, the United States started providing funds for a counterinsurgency operation in Honduras. Members of Battalion 316 were sent to Central Intelligence Agency (CIA) facilities in the United States for training on surveillance and interrogation techniques. After members of Battalion 316 returned to Honduras, some of the instructors in Honduras conducting further training were Argentinean veterans of the Argentinean Dirty War. These veterans had extensive experience in torture and eliminating the leftist opposition.

Over the next decade members of Battalion 316 stalked suspected dissidents and terrorists and kidnapped them. Those arrested were then tortured to make them reveal their secrets. Members of the units that refused to use torture were threatened with removal from the unit and a death sentence. At least four former members of Battalion 316 had been murdered by 1988. Some of the victims were subsequently released with warnings about talking about their experiences, but others were killed and buried in secret graves. One of these deaths was Nelson Mackay, a Honduran lawyer of Australian descent, who was suspected of supplying arms to radicals. His body, which showed signs of torture, was found in 1982. In 1993, the Honduran government admitted that 184 people were victims of Battalion 316 and presumed dead, but critics claim that this total is far too small. Unidentified bodies have been found in rural areas for more than two decades.

The activities of General Alvarez and Battalion 316 became so violent that elements in the Honduras army revolted. On March 31, 1984, officers in the Honduras army seized Alvarez and loaded him on a military plane for Costa Rica. Later in 1984, Alvarez and his family arrived in Miami, Florida, where he stayed for the next five years. Deciding to become a missionary, Alvarez returned to Honduras to preach religion. His past caught up with him, though, on January 25, 1989, when a hit team of five gunmen assassinated him. A group called the Popular Liberation Movement claimed responsibility for the assassination.

Efforts to bring members of Battalion 316 to justice have been blocked by various Honduran governments. Even though evidence of atrocities had become public knowledge by 1987, in 1991 the Honduran government declared a general amnesty for all crimes of both the government and rebels. International human rights organizations, however, have continued to locate members of Battalion 316 and survivors who had been tortured. Evidence of CIA involvement surfaced in the 1990s. Information about the disappearance and murder of an American Roman Catholic priest, James Carney, in 1983 caused a controversy because of the indifference of the American government to his fate. Carney, a graduate of St. Louis University and a Jesuit priest, had been serving as a chaplain to a revolutionary group when he disappeared. Several attempts have been made to bring leaders and members of Battalion 316 to court, but the Honduras army has managed to block each effort.

Suggested readings: Gary Cohn and Ginger Thompson, "Battalion 316: Unearthed; Fatal Secrets," *Sun* (Baltimore) (June 11, 1995), p. 1A; Gary Cohn and Caitlin Francke, "Censored Papers Indicate That CIA Knew of Torture," *Sun* (Baltimore), (August 30, 1997), p. 1A; Anne Manuel, "Death Squad Debris," *Washington Post* (November 28, 1993), p. C5; Joseph E. Mulligan, "The Case of the Disappeared Priest," *St. Louis Post-Dispatch* (January 7, 1997), p. 11B; Julia Preston, "Honduras Accused of Death-Squad Operations," *Washington Post* (November 1, 1988), p. A21; Ginger Thompson and Gary Cohn, "Battalion 316: Torturers' Confessions," *Sun* (Baltimore) (June 13, 1995), p. 1a.

Bhindranwale, Jarnail Singh (1947–1984) (India)

Jarnail Singh Bhindranwale was the leader of the Sikh separatist movement in India. He was born in 1947 in the village of Rodey near Moga in the Fridkot district in a region close to Pakistan. His birth name was Jarnail Singh and he later adopted the name Bhindranwale from the village of Bhinder in the central Punjab. He was the seventh and youngest son of a impoverished small farmer of the Jat caste. Because of the need to work in the field, Bhindranwale only received a mediocre primary level education. His parents then sent him to the Damdami Taksal School. He showed an early aptitude for religious study and became a *sant*, or holy man. His charismatic leadership made him an important figure in the school.

At an early age Bhindranwale became involved in Sikh politics. Many members of the Damdami Taksal School had long been dissatisfied with the policies of the Indian government. After the death of the head of the school, Kartar Singh, Bhindranwale was appointed in his stead. He continued the activism of his predecessor. Several times he had trouble with Indian authorities. In April 1978, his group had an armed battle with a breakaway Sikh group called the Nirankaris. After one such clash that resulted in 18 deaths, Bhindranwale became even more militant. Indian authorities arrested him in September 1981 for his complicity in the murder of the Punhabi Hindu newspaper editor Jagat Narain. Public pressure and demonstration led to his release, and Bhindranwale was never charged with this crime.

Bhindranwale's popularity came from his attacks on the Indian government for maltreatment and discrimination against Sikhs. Because of this alleged mistreatment, Bhindranwale campaigned for independence from India without formally calling for a separate Sikh state to be formed out of the Punjab state of India. Many of his followers, however, were not reluctant to call for a Sikh state to be called Khalistan. Bhindranwale rejected the gradualist approach of the moderate Sikh party Akali Dal (Party of the Servitors of the Timeless God). He managed to recruit able followers, including a former general in the Indian army, Shihbeg Singh, and the president of the All-India Sikh Students Federation, Bhai Amrik Singh.

Bhindranwale's militancy caused the Indian government of Indira Gandhi to take action against him and his followers. After his 1981 troubles with the authorities, Bhindranwale and his most militant supporters fortified themselves in the Sikh's most sacred Golden Temple complex at Amritsar, India. Bhindranwale launched a terrorist campaign of intimidation, assassination, robbery, and sabotage against Hindus to drive them out of the Punjab. The Punjab had been 57 percent Sikh in the early 1970s, but by the early 1980s, this percentage had dropped to 52 percent. Young militants organized themselves into the Dishmish Regiment (Followers of the 10th Guru) and carried out operations against those that they perceived as enemies of the Sikhs. Besides Hindus, these operations also targeted the leaders of the Akali Dal for murder.

Gandhi decided in June 1984 that she could no longer tolerate the lawlessness of Bhindranwale and his followers. The final straw was the proclamation by Bhindranwale of the economic boycott of Punjab by the Sikhs. This action would have caused food shortages throughout India. Gandhi ordered a military assault on the Golden Temple of Amritsar by 5,000 troops. On June 5–6, 1984, Indian troops attacked the Sikh followers of Bhindranwale and heavy fighting ensued. Final reports differed on the number of casualties, but 789 bodies were recovered from the temple. The Indian army claimed 400 Sikhs and 80 Indian solders died in the fighting. Among the dead were Bhindranwale and his two closest advisors, Shihbeg Singh and Amrik Singh. Bhindranwale's death made him a martyr to the Sikh cause. Many of his followers had escaped the assault and continued his campaign of terror. Even moderate Sikhs were outraged over the assault on the Golden Temple.

Suggested readings: Harry Anderson, Patricia J. Sethi, and Sudip Mazumdar, "The Golden Temple Shoot-Out," *Newsweek* (June 18, 1984), p. 44; Sanjoy Hazarika, "Sikh Chiefs: Fundamentalist Priest, Firebrand Student and the Ex-General," *New York Times* (June 8, 1984), p. A6; Mark Juergensmeyer, "The Logic of Religious Violence," in David C. Rapoport, *Inside Terrorist Organizations* (London: Frank Cass, 2001); Cynthia Keppley Mahmood, *Fighting for Faith and Nation: Dialogues with Sikh Militants* (Philadelphia: University of Pennsylvania Press, 1996); Mary Anne Weaver, "Indian Army Apparently Fails to Squelch Militant Sikh Movement," *Christian Science Monitor* (October 17, 1984), p. 13; Mary Anne Weaver, "Sikh Violence Jars India's Wealthiest State," *Christian Science Monitor* (May 9, 1984), p. 9.

Bin Laden, Osama (1957–) (Saudi Arabia)

Osama bin Laden is the most notorious terrorist leader of the last 20 years and the head of **al-Qaeda** terrorist network. He was born on July 30, 1957, in the Malazz neighborhood of Riyadh, Saudi Arabia, into a wealthy Saudi family. His father, Muhammad bin Oud bin Laden, an engineer and architect, ran a successful construction company with close ties to the Saudi regime. Osama was the 17th son of his father, by one of his 11 wives. His mother was from Damascus, Syria, but she was never one of his father's favorite wives. Bin Laden's family moved several times in his youth, from Hijaz to Medina to Jeddah. He went to high school in Jeddah. In 1972, his father died in a helicopter crash. Between 1974 and 1978, bin Laden studied economics and management at King Abdul Aziz University in Jeddah. He left school without a degree in 1979. Several times in the early 1970s, bin Laden had traveled to Beirut, Lebanon, and engaged in an active social life there. In 1975, bin Laden married a young Syrian woman in an arranged marriage.

Beginning in 1973, bin Laden started becoming more religious and made contacts with the Muslim Brotherhood. While at the university, he had taken courses taught by Muhammad Qutb, the brother of the famous Islamist writer **Sayyid Qutb**, and later from his patron **Abdullah Azzam**. This growing religious orientation was furthered by Islamic fundamentalism exported from Egypt and the seizure of the Grand Mosque in Mecca on November 20, 1979, by a group of men under the command of Juhayman ibn-Muhammad-ibn-Sayf al-Utaibi. The Soviet Union's invasion of Afghanistan in late 1979 was the final impetus that caused bin Laden to become a militant Islamist.

Osama bin Laden, left, with his top lieutenant, Egyptian Ayman al-Zawahiri, is seen at an undisclosed location in this television image broadcast October 7, 2001. Bin Laden praised God for the September 11th terrorist attacks and swore America "will never dream of security" until "the infidel's armies leave the land of Muhammad," in a videotaped statement aired after the strike launched that Sunday by the United States and Britain in Afghanistan. Graphic at top right reads "Exclusive to Al-Jazeera." At bottom right is the station's logo, which reads "Al-Jazeera." At top left is "recorded." (AP Photo/Al-Jazeera)

Bin Laden's participation in the Afghanistan War was a turning point in his life. Within days of the Soviet invasion, bin Laden volunteered to go to Afghanistan and fight. His first job, however, was to set up an organization to recruit Arab fighters, and most of the early expenses came out of his personal finances. He also came into contact with Sheikh Abdullah Yussuf Azzam, a leader of the militant wing of Islamic fundamentalism in Pakistan. Together they formed the Mujahideen Services Bureau (Maktab al-Khidanet) (MAK) in 1984 to recruit and train Afghan fighters. Bin Laden also used his Saudi contacts to bring heavy construction equipment to protect the fighters from Soviet artillery and air strikes. By the mid-1980s, the Afghanistan War was the training ground for militant Islamists from all over the Muslim world. Peshawar, Pakistan, became the center of militant Islamic theology.

In the mid-1980s, bin Laden decided to extend his activities to the battlefield. He joined an Arab mujahideen unit and participated in the battle of Jalalabad in 1986. Between battles, bin Laden sponsored the activities of Azzam, who traveled into Afghanistan preaching global jihad (holy war).

Azzam's assassination on November 24, 1989, was a personal loss to bin Laden. At least one al-Qaeda expert, Rohan Gunaratna, maintains that the assassination of Azzam came with the blessing of bin Laden. Azzam and bin Laden's relationship had deteriorated over the future direction of al-Qaeda.

After the end of the Afghanistan War, bin Laden returned to Saudi Arabia as a war hero. His war record made him popular with both the Saudi government and the general populace. He settled down in Jeddah, working for his family's construction firm until Iraq invaded Kuwait on August 2, 1990. This invasion threatened Saudi Arabia, and the Saudi government looked for help from the United States. Bin Laden proposed a defense plan for Saudi Arabia by establishing an anti–Saddam Hussein Arab coalition of mujahideen veterans, but also explained his opposition to non-Muslim forces being stationed on the holy land of Saudi Arabia. Despite this warning, the Saudi government requested assistance from Western powers. Bin Laden made public his opposition to Hussein's invasion of Kuwait and at the same time indicated that he considered non-Muslims in Saudi Arabia as a sacrilege. Once it became obvious that foreign troops would remain in Saudi Arabia after the war, bin Laden became an open opponent of the Saudi regime. To escape persecution by Saudi security forces, bin Laden and his family moved to Pakistan in April 1991. He then launched a campaign against the Saudi family by portraying them as false Muslims. Then **Hassan al-Turabi,** the religious leader in Sudan, invited bin Laden to Sudan. Bin Laden moved the bulk of al-Qaeda's membership and assets to Sudan. There he established a series of businesses. Because bin Laden was not a religious scholar, he formed a religious committee that could issue religious rulings, or fatwas. These fatwas have given him authority to act.

Bin Laden's first operation against the United States was in Somalia in the early 1990s. American intervention resulted in unacceptable casualties brought by Somali forces under the control of Arab Afghan

fighters. His role was at the leadership level, and the victory in Somalia convinced him that the United States could be driven out of Saudi Arabia and ultimately out of the Middle East if pressure were placed on it. His experience in helping first the Muslims in Bosnia and then the Albanian Muslims in Kosovo only reinforced this belief.

By the mid-1990s, bin Laden had enough prestige and influence in the Islamist world that he was able to set up the al-Qaeda network of terrorist organizations. In 1994, bin Laden moved to London, England, to coordinate activities there. On April 7, 1994, he lost his Saudi citizenship and had his financial assets there frozen for anti-Saudi activities. Because of the danger of arrest and extradition, bin Laden returned to Khartoum, Sudan, and the protection of the Turabi government. In a series of conferences in 1994 and 1995 in Tehran, Iran; Khartoum; and Larnaca, Cyprus, the leaders of the Islamist movement planned a coordinated terrorist campaign against the United States, Egypt, Israel, Jordan, Saudi Arabia, and other Arab states participating in Mideast peace initiatives. Bin Laden was not a participant in all of these meetings, but by the end of 1995 he had become the most powerful leader of the terrorist campaign.

Bin Laden opened his campaign against the Saudi regime in November 1995. A car bomb exploded in Riyadh on November 13, 1995, killing 5 Americans and 1 Saudi and wounding more than 60. The Armed Islamic Movement (AIM), a front for bin Laden, claimed credit for the attack. It was his first blow to overthrow the Saudi regime. Then on June 25, 1996, a bomb team exploded a truck bomb at al-Khobar in Dhahran, killing 19 American servicemen and wounding hundreds of others.

In May 1996, bin Laden moved his operations from Sudan to Afghanistan. The Saudi government and the United States placed pressure on the Sudanese government of General Omar al-Bashir to expel bin Laden. Negotiations were in progress to deport him to Saudi Arabia when bin Laden decided to move to Afghanistan. Afghanistan was a natural haven, because of the victory of the **Taliban** in September 1996. This country soon became a safe refuge for Afghan Arabs seeking asylum. Taliban leaders welcomed bin Laden as a hero of the Muslim world. Bin Laden responded by arranging financing from the Arab world for the new regime. Then he was allowed to establish a base camp in the Jalalabad area of Afghanistan. With the assistance of the Taliban, bin Laden organized a series of training camps to train a cadre of terrorists to carry out operations worldwide. Al-Qaeda forces joined the Taliban military units fighting the Northern Alliance Army of General Ahmed Shah Masood.

In June 1996, a conference was held in Tehran that formed an alliance of Sunni and Shi'ites into the Hezbollah International. Representatives stabled a Committee of Three to coordinate planning for this new organization. Mahdi Chamran Savehi, an Iranian nuclear physicist and chief of Iranian External Intelligence, was selected as the head of Hezbollah International. The representative appointed bin Laden as one of the three, with Imad Mughniyah and Ahmad Salah as the other two. Members of the Committee of Three reported to Savehi, but each of them had independence of action. Bin Laden had been building his al-Qaeda network, and his participation with the Hezbollah International helped him. On August 23, 1996, bin Laden issued a call for a jihad against the Americans for their occupation of Saudi Arabia. Then, in February 1998, bin Laden formed the International Islamic Front for Jihad Against Jews and Crusaders. He followed this action by announcing on February 23, 1998, a global jihad against all enemies of Muslims and emphasized that geographical boundaries were immaterial. He also made the statement, "We are Muslims and wish to be martyred."

The first major operations of al-Qaeda were the bombings of the U.S. embassies in Kenya and Tanzania. Bin Laden was the political leader and **Ayman al-Zawahiri** was the operational commander, but Muhammad Sadiq Odeh was the on-site commander. Both bombs exploded on August 7, 1998, one in Nairobi, Kenya, and the other in Dar-es-Salaam, Tanzania. Casualties at both embassies were heavy, with about 250 deaths and more than 5,500 injured. Most of the victims were Africans. The United States responded by a cruise attack on his base camps in Afghanistan on August 20, 1998. This failed attack only reinforced bin Laden's stature in the Muslim world. At the time that his political reputation was growing, bin Laden's health began deteriorating. Reports surfaced that he suffered from stomach and kidney troubles, and that he required a renal dialysis machine. His close associate al-Zawahiri also served as his personal doctor.

Bin Laden approved the plans for the September 2001 attacks in the United States as a way to cripple American economic, military, and political power. Targets were selected for symbolic reasons—the Pentagon, the World Trade Center, and probably the White House. Days before the September assault, two al-Qaeda operatives assassinated the military commander of the Northern Alliance, Masood. Bin Laden expected a vigorous American response to these attacks, and he counted on the harshness of the response to mobilize Muslims worldwide against the United States and the West. Instead, the response was worldwide sympathy for the victims in the United States and the overthrow of the Taliban regime in Afghanistan.

The fall of Afghanistan to the Northern Alliance with the assistance of the U.S. military was a major setback for bin Laden. The ease of the Taliban's fall was unexpected. Loss of key leaders, such as **Mohammad Atef**, was also a blow. Bin Laden retreated into the Tora Bora complex, where he stayed until early December. Bin Laden, his family, and around 1,000 fighters escaped into Pakistan. Efforts by U.S. intelligence have been unable to locate his whereabouts. Most observers believe that he is being protected in the remote areas of northwest Pakistan outside of the reach of the Pakistani government. Even with a low profile, bin Laden is still considered a hero to many Muslims because he stood up to the United States. **See also** Al-

Qaeda (The Base); Taliban (Students of Religious Schools); Al-Zawahiri, Ayman.

Suggested readings: Yossef Bodansky, *Bin Laden: The Man Who Declared War on America* (New York: Forum, 2001); Jane Corbin, *Al-Qaeda: In Search of the Terror Network That Threatens the World* (New York: Thunder's Mouth Press, 2002); Rohan Gunaratna, *Inside Al Qaeda: Global Network of Terror* (New York: Columbia University Press, 2002); Roland Jacquard, *In the Name of Osama Bin Laden: Global Terrorism and the Bin Laden Brotherhood* (Durham, NC: Duke University Press, 2002); Jane Mayer, "The Search for Osama," *New Yorker* (August 4, 2003), p. 26.

Black Bloc (Europe and United States)

The Black Bloc is an international anarchist organization with the goal of fighting globalization. This group originated out of the Autonomen movement in Hamburg, Germany, in 1987. Roots of this movement, however, reach back to the Autonomous Movement of northern Italy in the late 1960s. Members of the **Autonomous Movement** rejected hierarchical organizations, class distinctions, and personality cults. These characteristics carried over to the Black Bloc. The name "Black Bloc" was given to them by the police after their adoption of black clothes to be worn at demonstrations. Except for anarchism and anti-globalization, the Black Bloc does not endorse any philosophy. Because there are no official members, no headquarters, and no general meetings, the Black Bloc operates mainly through the Internet. Whenever there is a meeting of the World Trade Organization (WTO) or similar organizations, word is passed out through the Internet and demonstrations are organized. The most extensive coverage of the Black Bloc is by the Independent Media Center (IMC), a global volunteer newsroom on the Internet.

The Black Bloc specializes in violent demonstrations. First exposure of the violent nature of the Black Bloc was at the WTO meeting in Seattle, Washington, on November 30, 1999. This demonstration was followed by another demonstration in Quebec City, Canada, in April 2001. At each of these demonstrations Black Bloc activists roamed the streets destroying symbols of capitalist society such as automobiles and shop windows. These demonstrations culminated in the July 2001 Group of Eight economic summit in Genoa, Italy. Around 150,000 protesters from various anti-globalization groups combined to clash with 20,000 police. Clashes between the Black Bloc and police produced numerous injuries and one death. Police killed Carlo Giuliani, a Genoese student and anarchist, on July 20, 2001. These clashes caused damages to Genoa totaling approximately $45 million and a political crisis in Italy. Since Genoa, the Black Bloc has retired to wait for the next major globalization target. **See also** Autonomous Movement.

Suggested reading: Daniel Howden, "Greek City Vows 'Never Again' after Latest EU Traveling Circus," *New Zealand Herald* (June 23, 2003), p. 1; Dean Kuipers, "Out of Control," *LA Weekly* (July 27, 2001), p. 19; Lara Marlowe, "Region Besieged by Twin Menace Shuts Down," *Irish Times* (June 2, 2003), p. 9; Glen McGregor, "Who Are Those Masked Men?" *Ottawa Citizen* (March 24, 2001), p. B1.

Black September (Palestine)

Black September was the terrorist wing of the **Palestine Liberation Organization** (PLO). Palestinian camps had been set up in Jordan in the aftermath of the Arab defeat in the 1967 Arab-Israeli War. Adherents of **Yasser Arafat's al-Fatah** used these base camps to launch military operations against Israel. On March 21, 1968, Israeli forces invaded Jordan to attack the Karameh Base camp. A battle ensued during which the Palestinians, with the help of Jordanian army units, were able to fight the Israelis to a stalemate. Palestinian commandos from both al-Fatah and the **Popular Front for the Liberation of Palestine** (PFLP) started treating Jordanian territory as part of a Palestinian state. Affairs deteriorated so much that King Hussein of Jordan unleashed his army against the Palestinian commandos on September 10, 1970. Thousands of al-Fatah and PFLP fighters were killed in the fighting. Subsequently, the leadership of al-Fatah moved its operations to Lebanon, but its military operations were curtailed. In September 1971, Arafat and the central leadership of al-Fatah allowed the militant wing to form a separate terrorist group to be called Black September. Salah Khalaf (also known as Abu Iyad), a former schoolteacher and leader in al-Fatah, became the operational head of Black September. His chief assistant was Abu Youssef. The purpose of the group was to plan and implement special operations, and the top leaders were all officers who recruited troops to carry out secret missions.

Black September carried out a number of spectacular terrorist acts. A six-member terrorist squad assassinated Wasfi Tell, the prime minister of Jordan, on the steps of the Sheraton Hotel in Cairo, Egypt, on November 28, 1971, to avenge his role in the suppression of the Palestinians in September 1970. After several minor operations, four Black September operatives, two men and two women, hijacked a Sabena Flight 517 from Brussels, Belgium, to Tel Aviv, Israel. After the plane landed at Lod Airport in Israel, an Israeli assault team freed the hostages, killed the two men, and captured the two women.

The most notorious operation of Black September was the massacre of the Israeli Olympic Team at the 1972 Munich Olympics. A hit team attacked the Israeli Olympic team at the Olympic Village on September 5, 1972, and the final casualties were 11 Israelis and 5 Palestinians. Planners of this operation knew that the coverage of the Olympics would ensure worldwide coverage. This bloody operation horrified the world, but the Arabs considered it a triumph. Next, members of the Black September seized the Israeli Embassy in Bangkok, Thailand, on December 28, 1972, but this operation ended without the violence of the other attacks. Violence associated with Black September in the Munich operation and later in the killing of three diplomats, including the U.S. Ambassador to Sudan Cleo A. Noel, on March 2, 1973, in Khartoum, Sudan, made these type of operations counterproductive for the Palestinian cause. Palestine Liberation Organization leaders decided in 1974 to cease operations of Black September. Later in 1981, leaders of the Palestine Liberation Organization reconstituted Black September briefly to counter the anti-PLO atrocities of **Abu Nidal** and the **Abu Nidal Organization**.

The Israeli government formed a special unit to avenge the Munich Olympics massacre. Mossad, the Israeli intelligence service, created a special group under the name Wrath of God (Mivtzan Elohim) to seek out and kill those responsible for the massacre. During 1972 and 1973, this group assassinated those key Palestinian terrorist leaders that the Israelis believed responsible for Munich. The Wrath of God killed at least six leaders of Black September. Ali Hasan Salameh was a special target because the Israelis blamed him for Munich. Operations of the Wrath of God came to a sudden end in July 1975 when an Israeli hit team in a case of mistaken identity assassinated a Moroccan waiter on July 21, 1975, in Lillehammer, Norway. Israeli agents thought the waiter was Ali Hasan Salameh. In the aftermath of this bungled affair the Israelis closed down the Wrath of God. This closure did not mean that the Israeli intelligence services gave up on hunting down and killing Salameh. An Israeli hit team blew Salameh up with a car bomb in Beirut, Lebanon on January 22, 1979. **See also** Abu Nidal Organization (ANO); Arafat, Mohammed Yasser; Nidal, Abu; Palestine Liberation Organization (PLO).

Suggested readings: Christopher Dobson, *Black September: Its Short, Violent History* (New York: Macmillan, 1974); Christopher Dobson and Ronald Payne, *The Terrorists: Their Weapons, Leaders and Tactics,* rev. ed. (New York: Facts on File, 1982); Serge Groussard, *The Blood of Israel: The Massacre of the Israeli Athletes: The Olympics 1972* (New York: Morrow, 1975).

Blood and Honor (Great Britain and Germany)

Blood and Honor is a skinhead group that serves as an umbrella organization for more than 30 neo-Nazi **skinhead** groups in Europe and the United States. **Ian Stuart Donaldson,** lead singer of the neo-Nazi skinhead rock group Skrewdriver, founded Blood and Honor in Great Britain in 1987. The name refers to a Nazi SS slogan. Donaldson was able to translate his popularity as a white supremacist singer to advance the cause of Blood and Honor. Leadership has claimed chapters from Australia to South Africa, but most chapters are in Europe. Communications among the various chapters involves the creation of around 350 Web sites on the Internet. At one time the leadership of Blood and Honor had close ties to the British terrorist group **Combat 18**. Blood and Honor's association with Ian Stuart Donaldson ended on September 23, 1993, when Donaldson was killed in an automobile accident in Great Britain.

Blood and Honor's numerous chapters have engaged in political agitation in their native countries, but the most serious incidents have taken place in Germany. The German chapter started up in Berlin in 1994. By 2000, Imre Karacs, a journalist for the *Independent* (London), estimated that the German Blood and Honor had around 300 members. These members have been active in organizing neo-Nazi concerts in Germany. This group has been effective in attracting adherents from former East Germany. In September 2000, the German government decided to outlaw Blood and Honor because of its influence in creating an environment that encouraged violence and idealized Germany's Nazi past. **See also** Skinhead Movement.

Suggested readings: Denis Campbell, "Hitler Youth Moves North," *Scotland on Sunday* (Edinburgh) (December 17, 1995), p. 4; Imre Karacs, "Skinhead Group Is Outlawed in Neo-Nazi Crackdown," *Independent* (London) (September 15, 2000), p. 16; Silke Tudor, "House of Tudor," *SF Weekly* (California) (May 7, 2003), p. 1.

Boer Resistance Movement (Boere Weerstandsbeweging) (BWB) (South Africa)

The Boer Resistance Movement (BWB) is the newest of the neo-Nazi organizations in South Africa. It is a secret organization that Andrew Ford founded in 1991 but made its first public appearance in 1993. Dries Kriel is BWB's secretary-general and spokesperson,

but Ford, an electrician and farmer from the small town of Bethlehem about 150 miles south of Johannesburg, is its acknowledged leader. The military wing of the BWB is the Boer Republican Army (Boere Republiekeinse) (BRL). Most of its members come out of the most radical wing of the **Afrikaner Resistance Movement** (AWB) and left the AWB because of dissatisfaction with its policies. A Boer General Council establishes general policy, but the members are organized into cells to promote security. Each cell can undertake operations independently without authorization from higher authority. Spokespersons for the BWB claim that it had set up 33,000 military cells to restore an Afrikaner homeland, but South African security forces doubt that the BWB has anywhere near that many adherents.

Leadership of the Boer Resistance Movement has ordered several terrorist operations. In October 1993, members bombed an Indian business area at Bronkhorstpruit. On June 1, 1997, members of the BWB, the Boere Boys (Boereseuns) attacked an ammunition depot at Bloemfontein and stole weapons and ammunition. Two army corporals were killed in the attack. The leadership of the BWB defended this operation without claiming direct responsibility. In June 1999, the leadership of the BWB branded both the head of the Freedom Front, General Constand Viljoen, and the head of the Afrikaner Resistance Movement, **Eugene Terre Blanche**, as traitors to the Boer cause. A feud between the BWB and the Afrikaner Resistance Movement led to several assassination attempts against Ford. BWB leadership also volunteered to send forces to Serbia to fight on the side of the Serbs in the Kosovo War, but this initiative died without any members going to Kosovo. **See also** Afrikaner Resistance Movement (Afrikaner Weerstandbeweging) (AWB); Terre Blanche, Eugene Ney.

Suggested readings: Amnesty Committee, "Right-Wing Groups," in *The Intersection Between the Work of the Human Rights Violations Committee and the Amnesty Committee*, vol. 6 (Pretoria, South Africa: South African Government, 2000), sec. 3, chapter 6, p. 444; Jon

Sawyer, "'Racialists' Expect Civil War 'We Want to Fight,' Says South African White; Extremist," *St. Louis Post-Dispatch* (September 30, 1990), p. 1A.

Bossi, Umberto (1941–) (Italy)

Umberto Bossi is the head of the Italian separatist party **Northern League**. He was born on September 19, 1941, in Cassano Magnago, Italy, near Varese. His father held a management position in a factory. He was a good enough student to study medicine, but he left school without finishing a medical degree. After two failed marriages, Bossi decided to enter politics. In 1979, he became attached to the separatist ideas of Bruno Salvadori of the Union Valdotaine. Bossi became converted to the idea that Italy needed to become a federation of regions rather than a single nation-state.

Bossi started agitating for autonomy for the northern Italian Lombardy region. In March 1982, he founded the Lombard League. Bossi started out glorifying the language and culture of Lombardy, but this message lacked appeal. Soon after he began attacking the central Italian government, southern Italians, and the influx of foreign

Northern League leader Umberto Bossi during a speech in Pontida, northern Italy, June 2, 1996. That same year Bossi declared the industrialized region stretching from Genoa to Venice an independent and sovereign republic (the Republic of Padania). While the political statement did attract supporters in the Lombard region, it was essentially ignored by the Italian government. (AP Photo/Luca Bruno/File)

immigrants, his Lombard League attracted followers. Thereafter the league garnered enough, though modest, political backing so that Bossi was elected to the Italian Senate in 1987. Bossi had ambitious plans for the Lombard League and he attempted to combine the various separatist groups into a single political party.

Bossi was able to transform the Lombard League into the Northern League (Lega Nord). This process started at a National Congress of separatist movements in December 1989 with the merger of the Lombard League with two other groups, La Liga Veneta and Piedmont Autonomista. Finally, at another general meeting in February 1991, the Northern League was constituted. Bossi intended that the Northern League become a national party so he began downplaying his criticism of southern Italy, but he intensified his attacks on the central Italian government and immigrants. His goal was to divide Italy into three political regions: north, center, and south. The appeal of this agenda remained limited to northern Italians, and Bossi's Northern League did well with the electorate in the north but nowhere else.

Bossi decided that he needed political allies. Silvio Berlusconi, the right-wing media tycoon, had political ambitions, so Bossi concluded an alliance with him in 1992. Bossi and the Northern League joined Berlusconi's Forza Italia (Go Italy) coalition along with Gianfranco Fini's neo-Fascist National Alliance. This strategy worked and Bossi found himself a power broker with members of the Northern League as ministers. Bossi found it difficult to be secondary to Berlusconi and, after only seven months, he engineered the collapse of the first Berlusconi government. His success in overthrowing Berlusconi proved unsatisfactory, as it isolated Bossi from political power. Even several elections during which the Northern Alliance received higher than expected results did not damper Bossi's frustration. In 1996, Bossi made a political statement by proclaiming northern Italy as the federal, independent, and sovereign Republic of Padania. While the Italian government ignored this political statement,

it did attract a significant number of supporters in the Lombard region. Bossi swallowed his pride and realigned himself with Berlusconi. **See also** Northern League (Lega Nord); Fini, Gianfranco.

Suggested readings: I. Diamonti, "The Northern League: From Regional Party to Party of Government," in S. Gundle and S. Parker (eds.), *The New Italian Republic* (London: Routledge, 1996); Robert Graham, "Rough Words, Smooth Player—Umberto Bossi," *Financial Times* (London) (April 9, 1994), p. 6; Damian Tambini, *Nationalism in Italian Politics: The Stories of the Northern League, 1980–2000* (London: Routledge, 2001); Bill Schiller, "'Dangerous' Bossi Strikes Fear in Italy," *Toronto Star* (September 15, 1996), p. A1; Bill Schiller, "Thousands Cheer Birth of Bossi's 'Padani'," *Toronto Star* (September 16, 1996), p. A1; Peter Semler, "A Sword over Europe," *New Statesman* (May 14, 2001), p. 1.

Bove, Jose (1953–) (France)

Jose Bove is the leader of the French radical left-wing farmers' union Peasant Confederation (Confederation Paysanne) and an international spokesperson against globalization. He was born on June 11, 1953, at Talence near Bordeaux, France, into a family of academics. His family took him to the United States for four years in the late 1950s while both his father and mother studied agricultural sciences at the University of California at Berkeley. After returning to France, Bove attended a private Catholic school. His political activities in the May 1968 student uprising in Paris caused his school to close operations. Bove then attended Bordeaux University, where he majored in philosophy. He left the university without a degree and became a leader in resistance to military service. Bove evaded military service and spent three weeks in jail in 1976 for his opposition to the military.

After settling in the hamlet of Montredon on the Causse du Larzac plateau near Roquefort-sur-Soulzon, Bove became a Roquefort cheese farmer. His cheese-making business, however, did not prevent him from engaging in left-wing politics. In the 1980s, he led the fight

French farmer Jose Bove raises his fist as he leaves the Villeneuve les Maguelonne jail in the south of France, September 7, 1999. Bove, leader of a radical farmers' union, was jailed for nearly three weeks for vandalizing McDonald's restaurant property. The small Farmer's Confederation has made McDonald's the main target in a wave of sometimes violent protests, decrying the fast-food chain as a symbol of American trade hegemony and economic globalization. (AP Photo/ Christophe Ena)

against the French expansion of a military base in the Larzac region. Then, in 1995, Bove headed a delegation of farmers to protest French nuclear testing on the Muroroa testing area in Tahiti.

Bove's claim to fame is his leadership of the Peasant Confederation and his campaign against the multinational globalization movement. In 1987, Bove and a group of French farmers formed the Peasant Confederation to protest economic and environmental issues. The French government had banned American hormone-treated beef, and the United States with the World Trade Organization's approval imposed a 100 percent tax on cer-

tain luxury European foods, including Roquefort cheese. This ban caused an uproar among French farmers. Bove had been active in the campaign against genetically altered food and had helped drench five tons of genetically altered corn in Montpellier in 1998. On August 12, 1999, Bove led around 300 followers in a raid on a McDonald's fast-food restaurant being built in Millau, a small town north of Montpellier. This attack caused $110,000 worth of damages to the building. The reason for the raid, as explained to Simon Hattenstone in a June 2001 interview, was that McDonald's "represented everything they despised—cultural imperialism, capitalism gone mad and, possibly worst of all, tasteless muck, which he labeled malbouffe." Bove and nine other men were arrested and jailed. Only after three weeks did Bove allow others to bail him out of jail. In the meantime, he had become a French national hero. After highly publicized meetings with French President Jacques Chirac and French Prime Minister Lionel Jospin, Bove went on trial on July 1, 2000. Although he received a three-month jail sentence for criminal vandalism, he served only three weeks in jail before being granted an early release. His compatriots were given two-month suspended sentences or were fined about $300. In June 1999, he also participated in the destruction of a genetically modified rice field in southern France. On December 21, 2001, Bove was sentenced to six months in jail by a French court for this offense, but he is appealing this sentence.

Bove has used his position as a French national hero to lobby against the evils of globalization. In 2001, Bove and a collaborator, Francois Dufour, published a book titled *The World Is Not for Sale: Farmers Against Junk Food,* in which they charge that large corporations are employing dangerous food-making technologies that are harmful to both the environment and people. Bove has traveled extensively to Brazil, Canada, Great Britain, Mexico, Switzerland, and the United States, speaking against multinational agricultural companies and the World Trade Organization. He claimed in a June 2001 article in *The Guardian* that "we now have a worldwide dictatorship (governed by multinationals)." His views have changed from the radical socialism of his youth and moved more toward the brand of environmental anarchism advocated by the **Black Bloc** and the other opponents of the World Trade Organization. **See also** Black Bloc.

Suggested readings: Jose Bove, "Revolting Choice," *Guardian* (London) (June 13, 2001), p. 8; Simon Hattenstone, "Pipe Dreamer: When Jose Bove Demolished a Branch of McDonald's He Became a Hero," *Guardian* (London) (June 11, 2001), p. 4; Suzanne Daley, "French Turn Vandal into Hero Against the U.S.," *New York Times* (July 1, 2000), p. A1; Stuart Jeffries, "Jose Bove: What's Your Boeuf?" *Financial Times* (London) (November 12, 2000), p. 27; John Lloyd, "The Trial of Jose Bove," *Financial Times* (London) (July 1, 2000), p. 13; Rory Mulholland, "The Roquefort Revolutionary," *Independent* (London) (February 20, 2000), p. 26.

British National Front (BNF) (Great Britain)

The British National Front (BNF) is one of the latest of the British neo-fascist parties. Leaders of the League of Empire Loyalists (LEL) and the **British National Party** (BNP) decided to merge into an umbrella organization in 1967. Two leaders of this merger were A. K. Chesterton, a veteran neo-fascist and head of the League of Empire Loyalists, and Andrew Fountaine, head of the British National Party. Chesterton was the first president, but he soon engaged in a power struggle with Fountaine that led to his resignation as president in 1970. Fountaine became the new head, but his refusal to use his large family fortune to back the party led to his expulsion from the BNF in 1970. By the 1970s, John Tyndall, who was selected and served as the head the British National Front until the leadership removed him from authority in 1980, was the party's most prominent leader. Leadership problems had continued to haunt the BNF enough so that at times the party has been marginalized.

The British National Front had the same neo-fascist, racist, and anti-immigration orientation of the British National Party. Sometimes the two parties united in demonstrations, but other times members fought against each other. They combined to conduct demonstrations against Asian immigrants in the spring and summer of 2001. Racial tensions had been high over incidents between British whites and Asians in the former industrial towns of Bradford and Oldham. Riots broke out beginning April and did not end before August, leaving several dozen injured and damage to property in the thousands of pounds. **See also** British National Party (BNP).

Suggested readings: Nuala Haughey, "Hate on the Streets," *Irish Times* (August 11, 2001), p. 60; Ian Herbert, "In Oldham's 'No Go' Zone," *Independent* (London) (May 28, 2001), p. 3; Angus Roxburgh, *Preachers of Hate: The Rise of the Far Right* (London: Gibson Square Books, 2002); Peter Webb and Malcolm MacPherson, "Britain's New Ultra-Right," *Newsweek* (August 29, 1977), p. 44.

British National Party (BNP) (Great Britain)

The British National Party (BNP) is one of the leading neo-Nazi parties in Great Britain. Leaders of two neo-Nazi groups—the National Labour Party (NLP) and the White Defence League (WDL)—formed the British National Party in 1960. Andrew Fountaine, a wealthy landowner and a veteran of Franco's army during the Spanish Civil War, became BNP's first president. Other prominent leaders of the BNP were John Bean, a chemist and veteran fascist leader; **Colin Jordan**, a former English and mathematics teacher and former head of the WDL; and John Tyndall, salesman and former head of the NLP and the BNF. This galaxy of leaders soon had to weather leadership disagreements. Jordan's refusal to stop building a separate neo-Nazi movement caused him to be expelled from the BNP in 1962. Tyndall left at the same time, and together they started the National Socialism Movement (NSM).

The ideology of the British National Party was racial nationalism. Protection of England's Nordic heritage from Jews and immigrants from Third World countries was the main preoccupation. Part of this program was to force non-English elements to leave the country. Efforts to turn the BNP into a neo-fascist or neo-Nazi party had adherents in the party, but most of them left with Jordan and Tyndall. Bean remained a party leader, and he directed most of his attention to gaining political influence by running candidates for Parliament. His use of the party's newspaper, *Combat,* was an effective tool to spread propaganda. He was able to capitalize on British unrest about immigration to stage some upsets in the mid-1960s.

In the early 1990s, Tyndall rejoined the British National Party and became its head. During this time, in an effort to help the BNP, American neo-Nazi William Pierce advised the party on political tactics. However, the British National Party went into a period of decline until **Nick Griffin** assumed control of the party in 1999. Griffin had been active in the British National Front until 1989. After flirting with other right-wing neo-fascist groups, he joined the British National Party in 1995. After winning a power struggle with Tyndall, he emerged as the head of the party. He had long emphasized **Holocaust denial** and he led the party in this direction. Soon Griffin decided that anti-immigration agitation was the way for the British National Party to carve out a political constituency. In 2001, Griffin's strategy of anti-immigration demonstrations attracted enough supporters for the British National Party to become an electoral force in British politics. His father's role in the Conservative Party caused a scandal, but Griffin used the opportunity for more publicity. Griffin has also been active in the recruitment of skinheads to serve as shock troops for the BNP. **See also** British National Front (BNF); Holocaust Denial; Jordan, Colin; Skinhead Movement.

Suggested readings: Chris Blackhurst, "World's Leading Nazi Advises British Fascists," *Independent* (London) (March 2, 1997), p. 3; Steve Boggan, "March of the Far-Right," *Evening Standard* (London) (February 3, 2003), p. 16; Sarah Lyall, "Shadowy Party Heats Up British Racial Tensions," *New York Times* (July 4, 2001), sec. A, p. 3; T. R. Reid, "Party Stokes Racial Ire in Britain," *Washington Post* (July 10, 2001), p. A12; Angus Roxburgh, *Preachers of Hate: The Rise of the Far Right* (London: Gibson Square Books, 2002); Richard Thurlow, *Fascism in Britain: From Oswald Mosley's Blackshirts to the National Front* (London: Tauris, 1999); Sarah Wilson, "BNP Feeds Off Docklands Dogged by Racial Prejudice," *Scotsman* (Edinbrough) (April 26, 1997), p. 8.

British Union of Fascists (BUF) (Great Britain)

The British Union of Fascists (BUF) was Great Britain's leading fascist organization from the 1930s to the 1970s. **Oswald**

Mosley, a World War I veteran, founded the BUF in October 1932 and organized it in the image of Benito Mussolini's Fascist movement in Italy. Two other fascist groups, Rotha Lintorn Orman's the British Fascisti and Arnold Leese's Imperial Fascist League (IFL), were in existence in the early 1930s, but Mosley's new BUF absorbed most of their members and discredited their leaders. Mosley's goal for the BUF was to use authoritarian methods to solve British economic and social problems. Mosley organized a disciplined paramilitary force, the Blackshirts, both to serve as a defensive force and to fight with opponents. Mosley believed that fascism would attract a large national following, but his efforts to attract mass support proved unsuccessful. The British public remained suspicious of the BUF, especially after the BUF's reputation for violence grew.

By early 1933, the BUF was the leading fascist organization in Great Britain. Excitement over political change and potential violence were two of the biggest recruiting incentives for new members. Many of the new recruits came from public schools and universities. In June 1933, the BUF participated in a march through London with 1,000 Blackshirts present. Mosley established the headquarters for the BUF in Chelsea at the Black House. Two factors began to mitigate further expansion of the BUF—its growing emphasis on violence and its association with fascism in Germany and Italy. Negative publicity about violence caused the loss of financial support of key backers and hurt recruitment. Secret funds from Benito Mussolini, the Italian dictator, helped offset the party's financial difficulties. As the party lost much of its political appeal, Mosley and his key advisor, G. K. Chesterton, turned in October 1934 to political anti-Semitism to revive the fortunes of the BUF. Instead of increasing the appeal of the BUF, anti-Semitism helped marginalize it even further. Battles on the streets between followers of the BUF and both Communists and Jews led to the passage of the Public Order Act by Parliament in 1936.

British entry into World War II ended the prospects of the British Union of Fascists. The British government interned key leaders, including Mosley, as security risks. Their authority was the Emergency Powers Act of August 24, 1939, and Defence Regulation 18b. Mosley was arrested and interned in late May 1940. British authorities declared the British Union of Fascists a proscribed organization on July 10, 1940. This action and the internment of the BUF's leadership ended the career of Mosley's party. The British government released Mosley from internment in November 1943. After the war, Mosley attempted to reestablish a British Fascist movement, but he was never successful. **See also** Mosley, Oswald.

Suggested readings: Robert Benewick, *The Fascist Movement in Britain*, rev. ed. (London: Allen Lane, 1972); Colin Cross, *The Fascists in Britain* (London: Barrie and Rockliff, 1961); D. S. Lewis, *Illusions of Grandeur: Mosley, Fascism, and British Society, 1931–81* (Manchester, UK: Manchester University Press, 1987); Richard Thurlow, *Fascism in Britain: From Oswald Mosley's Blackshirts to the National Front* (London: Tauris, 1998); Dave Renton, *Fascism, Anti-Fascism and Britain in the 1940s* (New York: St. Martin's Press, 2000).

C

Cagol, Margherita (1945–1975) (Italy)

Margherita Cagol was one of the founders and leaders of the Italian **Red Brigades**. She was born on April 8, 1945, in Sardagna, a small town near Trent, Italy. Her parents were religious, conservative, and well-to-do. They doted on her and she showed unusual music talent performing on the piano at several national music contests. After graduation from high school in 1964, Cagol decided to attend the popular Institute of Sociology at Trent. There she met **Renato Curcio**, a radical student leader, and they became romantically and politically involved. Cagol joined him in working on the Maoist journal *Political Work*. She and Curcio joined the Communist Party of Italy (Marxist-Leninist) in 1968 shortly before it split up into rival factions. Cagol married Curcio in the summer of 1969 after she earned her degree with a thesis entitled *Qualification of the Work Force in Phases of Capitalistic Development*. They then moved to Milan where Cagol and her husband believed that the Italian radical movement was ripe to adopt revolutionary tactics. She shared her husband's belief that the capitalist should be destroyed first in Italy and then elsewhere in the world, and any tactics used to accomplish this were acceptable.

Although Cagol was one of the founders of the Red Brigades, she remained behind the scenes in a supporting role to the other leaders: Curcio, Alberto Franceschini, and **Mario Moretti**. Her role changed after the arrest on September 8, 1974, of Curcio and Franceschini, and she assumed greater leadership in the planning and carrying out of terrorist operations. On February 18, 1975, she led a daring prison rescue of Curcio. This reunion was short, however, because on June 4, 1975, Cagol was killed in a shoot-out with Italian police. Her death paralyzed Curcio, and his removal as head of the Red Brigades after his arrest allowed even more radical elements to seize control of the group. **See also** Curcio, Renato; Red Brigades.

Suggested readings: Richard Drake, *The Revolutionary Mystique and Terrorism in Contemporary Italy* (Bloomington, IN: Indiana University Press, 1989); Robert C. Meade, *Red Brigades: The Story of Italian Terrorism* (New York: St. Martin's Press, 1990); Leonard B. Weinberg and William Lee Eubanks, *The Rise and Fall of Italian Terrorism* (Boulder, CO: Westview Press, 1987).

Carette, Pierre (1952–) (Belgium)

Pierre Carette is the founder and leader of the defunct Belgian terrorist group the **Communist Fighting Cells** (Cellules Communistes Combattantes, or CCC). He was born in 1952 in Charleroi, Belgium, to working-class parents. After an average education, he became a printer. His dissatisfaction with the moderate Belgian leftist parties led him toward extremism. He was also attracted by the activities of the German **Red Army Faction** (RAF) and its war against German society. In 1979, Carette started a cooperative printing company to promote his Marxist-Leninist views. These views began appearing in his journal *Subversion*.

Carette decided that left-wing propaganda was not effective enough and subsequently started the formation of an urban guerrilla group. His problem was that his extreme left-wing views had cut him off from potential recruits. Only by joining the Internationalist Communist Front, a small Communist fringe group, did Carette find others willing to join an urban guerrilla group. Then, in 1982, he met Frédéric Oriach, a French Communist theorist. Oriach introduced him to Jean-Marc Rouillan and Nathalie Menignon, leaders of the French terrorist group **Action Directe**. After receiving guidance from Oriach, Rouillan, and Menignon, Carette founded the Communist Fighting Cells in 1982. Lacking funds for operations, Carette and his small cadre of 10 members robbed several banks. These funds allowed the CCC to began a series of bombings of North Atlantic Treaty Organization (NATO) installations. Carette targeted these installations because of the political controversy over the stationing of cruise missiles in Europe. Over the next 14 months, Carette and the CCC committed 20 terrorist acts against property, mostly NATO facilities. Carette and his associates were careful to destroy property and not lives, but some casualties resulted. On December 16, 1985, Belgian police arrested Carette and three members of the CCC, Didir Chevolet, Bertrand Sassoye, and Pascale Vandergeerde, in Namur. These arrests ended the career of the CCC because without Carette and the other leaders, the CCC was no longer operational. Most of the remaining members of the CCC went underground and then drifted to other groups. After a short trial in 1986, Carette received a life sentence. His colleagues were released earlier, but Carette served 17 years of his sentence at the Leuven Prison before Belgian

authorities released him on February 25, 2003. Under terms of his parole, Carette has to resume his job as a print worker and must avoid contact with former members of the CCC. **See also** Action Directe (Direct Action) (AD); Red Army Faction (RAF).

Suggested readings: "Former Leftwing Militant Freed from Belgian Jail," Agence France Presse (February 25, 2003), p. 1; Yonah Alexander and Dennis Pluchinsky, *Europe's Red Terrorists: The Fighting Communist Organizations* (London: Frank Cass, 1992); Michael Y. Darnell, *Action Directe: Ultra-Left Terrorism in France, 1979–1987* (London: Frank Cass, 1995).

Castaño, Carlos (1966–) (Colombia)

Carlos Castaño is the head of the right-wing paramilitary group **United Self-Defense Forces of Colombia** (AUC). One of 12 children, he was born in 1966 on a milk farm near Antioquia in northern Colombia. He attended school for several years, but dropped out before graduation. Elements of the **Revolutionary Armed Forces of Colombia** (FARC), a Marxist guerrilla group, kidnapped his father in September 1981 and held him for ransom. Because the Castaño family was unable to raise but a third of the $500,000 ransom, the guerrillas killed his father. Although only 15 years of age, Castaño left school to fight against the FARC with his older brother, Fidel "Rambo" Castaño. They served as guides for the Colombian army's Bombona Battalion. Fidel Castaño was a self-made millionaire, investing in cattle ranching and dealing in drugs. Later, Fidel became a feared leader of a death squad that he financed, but he disappeared on January 6, 1994, and was killed by guerrillas. Afterward, Castaño assumed control of his brother's death squad. He was able to attract enough support from right-wing landowners and sympathizers in the Colombian government to form the Peasant Self-Defense Force of Cordoba and Uraba (ACCU). In 1997, Castaño persuaded several other groups to join a new paramilitary group, the Self-Defense Forces of Colombia.

Castaño has made the AUC into a fighting force capable of matching the FARC on the

This is a February 2001 photo of Carlos Castaño, the leader of the right-wing paramilitary group United Self-Defense Forces of Colombia, which has its headquarters in the northwest mountains. (AP Photo)

battlefield and in the countryside. By 2001, his paramilitary force numbered more than 8,000. He recruits them from rural vigilantes, drug protection groups, and former members of the Colombian army. His financial support comes from wealthy landowners and a 20 percent tax on the drug trade, which raises around $1 million a year. These funds allow Castaño to pay his soldiers a salary of $350 a month.

The AUC has been successful in liberating territory from the FARC by a campaign of calculated terror. Castaño decided to outdo the FARC by adopting its tactics and being even more violent. This strategy has resulted in the AUC averaging around 1,000 killings a year. Castaño claimed in a 2001 interview with a reporter for the *Gazette* (Montreal) that "his forces do not kill civilians, but guerrilla spies and collaborators disguised as peasants." A disproportionate number of the victims, however, have been human rights activists, journalists, and Colombian government functionaries. In his book *My Confessions* (2001), Castaño has confessed to committing 50 political murders, including planning the assassination in 1990 of the leftist presidential candidate Carlos Pizarro. His activities led the Colombian government of President Ernesto Samper to offer a $1 million reward for his capture in 1997. As a result, Castaño is cautious and never allows photographs to be taken of him.

Despite this campaign of terror, Castaño is popular among segments of the Colombian population and he has supporters in the Colombian government and armed forces. Castaño has not escaped loss from FARC attacks, as he has lost five of his brothers and sisters to the guerrillas. Castaño has managed to build a force that has been more successful against the FARC than the Colombian army. This success has had a price, as the U.S. Department of State classified the AUC as a terrorist organization in 2001 because of its murders and its affiliation with the drug trade. Castaño is a determined opponent of the efforts of the Colombian government to conclude a peace with the FARC. To Castaño, the war between the AUC and FARC has always been a struggle to the death. In May 2001, Castaño stepped down as head of the AUC and was replaced by a nine-man army council of regional leaders. His new assignment is as head of the AUC's political affairs. Castaño has been feeling political heat from the United States because of his involvement in the cocaine drug trade, but he has been able to withstand American extradition efforts. **See also** Revolutionary Armed Forces of Colombia (FARC); United Self-Defense Forces of Colombia (AUC).

Suggested readings: Andres Cala, "Conversation with a Killer," *Gazette* (Montreal) (March 18, 2001), p. A7; Linda Diebel, "Killer Becomes a Media Darling," *Toronto Star* (February 12, 1999), p. 1; Steven Dudley, "Dead Man's Bluff," *Washington Post* (November 24, 2002), p. W10; Joshua Hammer, "Army of an Angry Son," *Newsweek* (June 2, 1997), p. 16; Jeremy McDermott, "Death Squad Leader Owns Up to 50 Murders," *Daily Telegraph* (London) (December 8, 2001), p 1; Jeremy McDermott, "Million Dollar Murderer with a Shopping List of Victims," *Daily Telegraph* (London) (July 19, 2002), p. 18; Bert Ruiz, *The Colombian Civil War* (Jefferson, NC: McFarland, 2001); Diana Jean Schemo, "Rightist Avengers Become the Terror of Colombia," *New York Times* (March 26, 1997), p. A1; James Wilson, "Colombia's Paramilitary Groups Begin to Feel Heat," *Financial Times* (London) (June 15, 2001), p.6.

Cerpa Cartolini, Nestor (1943–1997) (Peru)

Nestor Cerpa Cartolini was one of the major leaders of Peru's **Tupac Amaru Revolutionary Movement** (Movimiento Revolucionario Tupac Amaru) (MRTA). He was born on August 14, 1943, in the Lima barrio of Balconcillo to a working-class family. The early death of his father caused him to leave school at 17 to find work to support his mother and three siblings. Cerpa Cartolini found work at Cromotex, a Chilean-owned textile plant. After a number of years, he was elected secretary-general of the plant's union. In December 1978, the company went bankrupt and tried to close the plant. Cerpa Cartolini was one of the leaders of an occupation of the plant to prevent its closing. Police stormed the building in February 1979, killing six workers. Afterward, Cerpa Cartolini spent nearly a year in prison for complicity in the death of a police officer who died during the fighting. After his early release from prison in a general amnesty, Cerpa Cartolini turned to radical leftist politics. **Victor Polay Campos**, a leftist intellectual jurist, recruited him into the new Tupac Amaru Revolutionary Movement in 1984.

Cerpa Cartolini was soon one of the major guerrilla leaders of the Tupac Amaru Revolutionary Movement. He left the Marxist ideology to Polay Campos and instead devoted his energies to guerrilla fighting. His group robbed banks and firebombed Kentucky Fried Chicken outlets in and around Lima. After his activities began to attract too much police attention, he moved his group to San Martin province. There he met Nancy Gilvonio and made her his common-law wife. She became his chief assistant and served as an intelligence agent for the group. Polay Campos's arrest in 1989 made Miguel Rincon the leader of the MRTA, and Cerpa Cartolini became number two in the command structure. He commanded his group during several operations, ranging from the assassination of Peru's former defense minister General Enrique Lopez Albujar in January 1990 to several kidnappings of foreign nationals. His loyalty to Polay Campos led him to help Polay Campos and other MRTA activists escape from prison in July 1990. Together they resumed their terrorist campaign until Polay Campos was recaptured in Lima on June 10, 1992.

Cerpa Cartolini spent the next several years planning to once again free Polay Campos and other members of the MRTA from prison. In November 1995, Cerpa Cartolini and his wife planned to seize the Peru Congress and hold the deputies hostage until all MRTA prisoners were released. A tip led the police to raid the house where the MRTA plotters resided on November 30, 1995, and they arrested 30 of them after a gun battle. Among those arrested in this raid and the aftermath were Rincon, an American named Lori Berenson, and Cerpa Cartolini's wife. They were all sentenced to life imprisonment for treason. The loss of his wife left Cerpa Cartolini with two small children and an MRTA in disarray.

Cerpa Cartolini was the only MRTA leader free, and now he had another reason to liberate the MRTA prisoners. His next plan was to recruit a commando squad to undertake a mission that was possibly a suicide mission. On December 17, 1996, Cerpa Cartolini led 13 MRTA members in the seizure of the Japanese ambassador's residence during a reception honoring Japan's emperor. They found themselves with nearly 500 hostages, which was too many to manage. Over the next several weeks, Cerpa Cartolini released all but 72 hostages. These hostages were all prominent figures—generals, politicians, and supreme court justices. Over the next four months, Cerpa Cartolini negotiated with the hard-line President Alberto Fujimori for the release of MRTA prisoners. On April 22, 1997, Peruvian special forces stormed the building, rescuing the hostages and killing all of the guerrillas. With the death of Cerpa Cartolini and his guerrillas, the MRTA ceased to function as an effective guerrilla force in Peru. **See also** Tupac Amaru Revolutionary Movement (MRTA); Polay Campos, Victor.

Suggested readings: Javier Farje, "Nestor Cerpa: Hostage to Peru's History," *Guardian* (London) (April 25, 1997), p. 22; Tom Fennell, Lucien Chauvin, and Showwei Chu, "Rescue in Lima," *Maclean's* (May 5, 1997), p. 38; Joshua Hammer, "Liberated," *Newsweek* (May 5, 1997), p. 36; Joshua Hammer, "Portrait of a Terrorist: Leftist's Common-Law Wife among Imprisoned Comrades," *Ottawa Citizen* (January 18, 1997), p. B4; Sebastian Rotella, "Getting in Was Easy Part for Peruvian Guerrillas," *Los Angeles Times* (January 6, 1997), p. A1; Calvin Sims, "Peru's Rebel leader: An Able Talker and Terrorist," *New York Times* (December 23, 1996), p. A1.

Cohen, Geula (1925–) (Israel)

Geula Cohen is one of the leaders of the Greater Israel movement in Israel. One of 10 children, she was born in 1925 in Tel Aviv, Israel. Both her parents were Sephardi Jews; her father was from Yemen and her mother from Morocco. As a youth of 12, she joined the extremist youth organization Betar. Then Cohen joined the **Irgun**, the armed wing of the Betar, but she became disillusioned because it was not radical enough. Cohen's political activities led to her expulsion from the Levinsky Seminary, where she was a student. Soon afterward at age 16, she migrated to the **Stern Gang**, or Lehi, going underground to carry out an ongoing war with the British. Cohen became a popular speaker on the illegal Lehi radio station. The British secret service arrested her and she was sentenced to nine years in prison, but after a year and a half of imprisonment she escaped.

After the establishment of the Israeli state in 1948, Cohen returned to more peaceful pursuits. She founded a radical magazine, *The Ladder*, on which she served as the editor for 15 years. During that time, she also worked on a degree in philosophy at the Hebrew University in Jerusalem. After graduation, she spent the next 15 years as a reporter for the newspaper *Maariv*, where she rediscovered her interest in politics. Cohen published her life story in a 1960 book, *The Story of a Fighter*. In 1972, after joining the Herut Party, she won election to the Knesset. After Menachem Begin, the head of the Herut Party, became prime minister, Cohen was appointed president of the Knesset's Commission for Immigration and Absorption. She remained a loyal supporter of Begin until he helped negotiate the Camp David Accords. Then she gave her support to the **Gush Emunim** in its dispute with Begin. Her opposition to concessions to the Palestinians caused her to leave the Herut and join with Yuval Neeman to start the political party **Tehiya**. The main idea behind the Tehiya was to provide a forum for a campaign for a Greater Israel. Cohen's belief in Greater Israel led her to propose the legislation in the Knesset for the annexation of the Old City of Jerusalem. Altogether, Cohen served in the Knesset for 19 years. She has been active in supporting the Jewish settlements in the West Bank and in Gaza, and in 1993 she moved into a home in Kiryat Arba, near Hebron. Recent attempts to control or remove Israeli settlements have caused her to threaten insurrection if the Israeli government undertakes such a policy. Another of her projects has been to free Jonathan Pollard, the Jewish American in prison in the United States for spying for Israel. Then, in 1998, Cohen founded the Uri Zvi Greenberg Heritage Center to preserve Israeli culture. In March 2003, Cohen received the Israel Prize for Life Achievement. **See also** Tehiya (Renaissance) (Israel).

Suggested readings: Raphael Mergui and Philippe Simonnot, *Israel's Ayatollahs: Meir Kahane and the Far Right in Israel* (London: Saqi Books, 1987); Sally Quinn, "Fighter in the Promised Land, Geula Cohen and the New Zionism," *Washington Post* (October 11, 1978), p. B1; Carl Schrag, "New Gal on the Block," *Jerusalem Post* (December 31, 1993), p. 14; Joseph B. Treaster, "An Unyielding Warrior: Geula Cohen," *New York Times* (July 31, 1980), sec. A, p. 8; Asher Wallfish, "Geula Cohen's Solo Performance," *Jerusalem Post* (February 9, 1990), p. 1.

Combat 18 (Great Britain)

Combat 18 was Great Britain's leading neo-Nazi terrorist group in the early 1990s. Leaders of the **British National Party** (BNP) formed Combat 18 in 1992 to serve as a self-defense group for the party after anti-Nazi demonstrators had disrupted one of its meetings. Paul Charles Sargent, a former drug dealer from northern London nicknamed Ginger Pit, was the group's first leader. Combat 18 acquired its name by taking the initials of Adolf Hitler's name and converting them to numbers (A=1 in the alphabet, H=8). Harold Covington, the American neo-Nazi leader, served as technical advisor to the organization of Combat 18. Combat 18 resorted to violence to carry out its self-defense mission. Among its targets were left-wing bookshops, gay pubs, anti-apartheid activists, and mixed-marriage couples. Sargent began recruiting British skinheads and the violence became so extreme that the leaders of the British National Party started distancing the BNP from Combat 18. Sargent countered by distrusting the attempts of the BNP to become a mainstream British political party. In 1993, Sargent and 200 members of Combat 18 broke away from the BNP. By openly proclaiming itself as a racist group, much of the support for Combat 18 came from football hooligans and neo-Nazi **skinheads**. The group also made inroads in certain units of the British army. Sargent established ties with the **Ulster Defence Association** (UDA) until that group became suspicious that Sargent was a British agent.

The violent tactics and finances caused internal dissention within Combat 18. Financial support for Combat 18 came from drug dealing and the illegal white-power music business. It was a dispute over the profits of the music business that proved Sargent's undoing. In December 1996, Sargent was expelled from Combat 18 over a feud with other leaders about funds. Some of Sargent's supporters left Combat 18 and founded the National Socialist Alliance. In February 1997, Chris Castle, a leader in Combat 18, tried to act as an intermediary between Sargent and the new leaders of the group to settle the feud. At a meeting between Castle, Sargent, and Martin Cross, an ally of Sargent, Cross stabbed Castle to death. In a trial in January 1998, both Sargent and Cross were sentenced to life imprisonment for the murder.

Although weakened by the loss of Castle, Combat 18 remained active under new leadership. In August 1997, Will Browning started the new Combat 18 magazine *Strikeforce*. However, Combat 18 was further weakened when a dozen of its more radical neo-Nazi members broke away to form the White Wolves in 1999. Later that same year, an investigation by Scotland Yard concluded that Combat 18's two dozen members were no longer able to sustain a race terror campaign. Combat 18 is still in existence in the early 2000s, but it remains much reduced in size and influence. **See also** British National Party (BNP).

Suggested readings: Andrew Buncombe, "Soldiers Recruited by Violent Far Right," *Independent* (London) (March 11, 1999), p. 4; Gerry Gable, "Behind Enemy Lines," *Independent* (London) (February 22, 1997), p. 28; Mark Honigsbaum, "War of the Nazis: Ginger Pig Was the Leader of Combat 18," *Observer* [London] (January 25, 1998), p. 3; Tim Kelsy, "Informer Exposes Neo-Nazi Football Gangs," *Independent* (London) (August 7, 1993), p. 1; Stuart Millar, "Combat Fatigued," *Guardian* (London) (January 22, 1997), p. T6; Stuart Millar, "'We're at War and If That Means More Bombs, So Be It,'" *Guardian* (London) (April 27, 1999), p. 2; Helen Rumbelow, "'White Wolves' Emerge from Hiding," *Times* (London) (April 26, 1999), p. 1; Nick Ryan, "Combat 18: Memoirs of a Street-Fighting Man," *Independent* (London) (February. 1, 1998), p. 4; Rajeev Syal, Olga Craig, and David Bamber, "Neo-Nazis Follow IRA's Strategy," *Ottawa Citizen* (May 2, 1999), p. A3.

Communist Fighting Cells (Cellules Communistes Combattantes) (CCC) (See Carette, Pierre)

Communist Party of Nepal (CPN-Maoist) (Nepal)

The Communist Party of Nepal (CPN-Maoist) is leading a guerrilla movement against the government of Nepal. Nepal has been ruled as a constitutional monarchy since April 1990. Man Mohan Adhikari was the leader of the United Marxist-Leninist Communist Party of Nepal (UML), and he served as prime minister in 1994. His ministry attempted a series of reforms, and he was voted out of office in 1995. In February 1996, the UML split and the Communist Party of Nepal (Maoist) initiated a guerrilla war on February 13, 1996, against the government of Nepal. Pushpa Kamal Dahal, using the name of Comrade Prachanda; Baburam Bhattarai, who holds a doctorate in urban planning; and Mohan Vaidya, alias Kiran, started the rebellion in Gam on February 13, 1996. They adopted Mao Tse-tung's ideology of a people's revolution and the guerrilla warfare tactics of Peru's Shining Path.

After a slow start, the Maoist guerrilla army began attracting adherents from the poorer segments of Nepalese society. Political instability, corruption, and the assassination of King Bhirendra and his family on June 1, 2001, have weakened the Nepalese government. Although widely unpopular, King Gyanendra replaced his brother. In the spring of 2001, the military forces of CPN-Maoist launched a full-scale offensive throughout Nepal. In July 2001, the Nepal government concluded a truce with the CPN-Maoist that lasted until November 2001. In heavy fighting, the Maoist forces inflicted heavy casualties on government troops in the spring of 2002. Fighting continued throughout 2002 and early 2003 until King Gyanendra persuaded the CPN-Maoist to enter negotiations. These lengthy negotiations showed little progress as of the summer of 2003.

Suggested readings: Yuvraj Acharya, "Nepal Government Promises Swift Response to Maoist Ultimatum," *Katmandu Post* (July 29, 2003), p. 1; Farzand Ahmed, "Nepal: On Red Alert," *India Today* (December 10, 2001), p. 34; Farzand Ahmed, "Peace Coup by Palace," *India Today* (February 17, 2003), p. 53; Binod Bhattarai, "Maoist Rebellion Hits Nepal Hard," *Financial Times* (London) (April 24, 2002), p. 9; Joseph Marques, "Insurgency a Cause of Concern for Nepal," *Gulf News* (May 25, 2002), p. 1; Peter Popham, "Nepal Year Zero," *Independent on Sunday* (London) (August 12, 2001), p. 16; Martin Regg, "Paradise No More; Ripe for Revolution," *Toronto Star* (June 24, 2001), p. B1.

Continuity Irish Republican Army (CIRA) (Northern Ireland)

The Continuity Irish Republican Army (CIRA) is a small Irish republican group that has conducted terrorist operations in Northern Ireland. Michael Hegarty and others split from the **Provisional Irish Republican Army** (Provos) in 1986 and formed the Continuity IRA. They opposed **Gerry Adams** and the decision to participate in Northern Ireland's Stormont Assembly. Leaders of CIRA accused Adams and the leadership of the Provos of abandoning republican principles and pledged to continue the armed struggle against British control of Northern Ireland. The title "Continuity" was adopted because the leaders of CIRA claimed direct descent from the original **Irish Republican Army** and did not recognize the legitimacy of the government of the Republic of Ireland. CIRA has a small membership and it is selective in its recruiting. Its policy is to reject former Provisional IRA members and avoid anybody with a criminal record. Suzanne Breen, in a September 1997 article in *The Irish Times*, estimated its membership at no more than 100. Leadership of the CIRA had changed frequently because of the arrests of its leaders. Hegarty was arrested in November 1995 at a farm in Inniskeen while in the process of building a bomb. Others leaders, Josephine Hayden and Co Monaghan, were also arrested in 1995. They are serving long prison terms. New leadership has emerged, but names of these leaders have been kept secret to avoid their being arrested. The political wing of the Continuity Irish Republican Army is the Republican **Sinn Fein** (RSF). Base of operations of the CIRA is in the northern counties of the Republic of Ireland near the border of Northern Ireland.

The leadership of the Continuity Irish Republican Army has developed close ties to both the **Irish National Liberation Army (INLA)** and the **Real Irish Republican Army (RIRA)**. Members of both groups have assisted CIRA in conducting terrorist operations in Northern Ireland by providing training, bomb-making instructions, and weapons. They share a common rejectionist position toward the decommissioning of arms advocated by Adams and the Sinn Fein. Beginning in 1995, the CIRA launched a bombing campaign in Northern Ireland. On September 16, 1997, CIRA activists exploded a bomb in Markethill, Northern Ireland, which caused extensive damage but few casualties. It has been careful to avoid attacks on Protestant loyalists and instead has targeted British installations. When the Real Irish Republican Army (RIRA) announced a cease-fire in August 1998 in the aftermath of the bombing in Omagh, CIRA refused to go along with it. To finance its operations, CIRA has engaged in a number of bank robberies in the Republic of Ireland. Members have also carried out attacks on British military outposts as late as March 2001.

Suggested readings: Suzanne Breen, "CIRA Pledged to 'Armed Struggle,'" *Irish Times* (September 17, 1997), p. 3; Suzanne Breen, "Provisionals Worried by Continuity IRA's Bombing of Markethill," *Irish Times* (September 23, 1997), p. 9; Jim Cusack, "Bombing Attributed to Continuity IRA," *Irish Times* (March 5, 2001), p. 20; Jim Cusack, "CIRA Acquired Bombing Skills and Equipment from Ex-Provisionals," *Irish Times* (February 23, 1998), p. 6; Jim Cusack, "Militants May Rally to Continuity IRA," *Irish Times* (September 9, 1998), p. 6; Jim Cusack, "Small Continuity IRA May Pose Future Threat to Peace in the North," *Irish Times* (December 22, 2000), p. 14.

**Corsican National Liberation Front
(See Front de la Liberation de la
Nationale Corse)**

Curcio, Renato (1941–) (Italy)

Renato Curcio was one of the founders and
the ideological leader of the Italian **Red
Brigades**. He was born in 1941 at Mont-
erotondo, near Rome. Curcio was the
product of a brief love affair between his
wealthy father, Renato Zampa, and his
mother, a housemaid. The mother belonged
to the Waldensian religious sect, but Curcio
was brought up a Catholic. He was moved
around among several family friends until
he finally resided with his mother in Milan.
After a slow start, Curcio became a good
student and in 1962 graduated with a diploma. In 1964, he decided to attend the
Institute of Sociology in Trent. At Trent,
Curcio studied the writings of Karl Marx,
Vladimir Lenin, and Mao Tse-tung and was
converted to Communism. He had also become a member of the Jeune Europe
(Young Europe) movement of **Jean-
Francois Thiriart**. Thiriart was a Belgium
extremist with ties to both the political left
and right, but his principal message was to
rid Europe of American and Soviet influence. Later, in 1964, he met and became
romantically involved with **Margherita
Cagol**. In the fall of 1967, he participated
in founding a Maoist journal, *Political
Work*. In 1968, he and Cagol joined the
Communist Party of Italy (Marxist-
Leninist) shortly before ideological divi-
sions caused it to split into rival factions.
In the summer of 1969, Curcio married
Cagol and they moved to Milan.

Curcio and his wife became leaders in
the radical left movement in Milan. In September 1969, Curcio and representatives
from various factory groups formed the
Metropolitan Political Collective (MPC) to
study urban guerrilla warfare. Curcio was
able to use the MPC to attract the attention of Alberto Franceschini and **Mario
Moretti**. In the summer of 1970, Curcio,
Cagol, and Franceschini decided to adopt
the name Red Brigades for their new revolutionary group. They picked this name to
identity it with the Italian Communist Resistance in World War II and to advance
the goal of a Communist revolution. They
also selected as its symbol a five-pointed
red star enclosed in a circle.

Curcio became the ideological head of
the Red Brigades. He was always more
concerned with Marxist ideology than
planning terrorist operations. On September 8, 1974, Italian police arrested Curcio
while he was trying to recruit a police spy
for the Red Brigades. He was imprisoned
in Casale Monferrato near Turin. On February 18, 1975, Cagol broke him out of
prison in a daring one-person raid. On
June 4, 1975, the Red Brigades kidnapped
a wealthy wine manufacturer. Police found
the hiding place, and in a firefight on June
5 Cagol was killed. The loss of his wife
caused Curcio to go into a deep depression,
and he left the leadership of the Red Brigades to others. In January 1976, Italian
police recaptured him.

Curcio's role as a leader of the Red Brigades was over, but even in prison he remained its principal theoretician. He was
sentenced to a jail term of 24 years. Most
of the spectacular assassinations and
kidnappings of the Red Brigades took
place with Curcio in prison, but he remained unrepentant and supportive. On
October 7, 1998, Italian authorities released Curcio from prison after he had
served 18 years of his 24-year sentence.
Shortly afterward, in May 1999, the senior advisor to Italy's Labor Minister
Massimo D'Antona was assassinated in
Rome, and the Red Brigades claimed
credit. Curcio's role in this murder remains unknown, but he has never renounced his political ideas. **See also**
Cagol, Margherita; Moretti, Mario; Red
Brigades.

Suggested readings: Raymond Carroll, et al., "Inside the Red Brigades," *Newsweek* (May 15, 1978), p. 43; Anthony A. Lukin, "History in the Headlines: The Return of the Red Brigades?" *Journal of Counterterrorism and Security International* 6, no. 1 (Fall 1999); Robert C. Meade, *Red Brigades: The Story of Italian Terrorism* (New York: St. Martin's Press, 1990); Leonard B. Weinberg and William Lee Eubank, *The Rise and Fall of Italian Terrorism* (Boulder, CO: Westview Press, 1987).

D

D'Aubuisson Arrieta, Roberto (1943–1992) (El Salvador)

Robert D'Aubuisson was the leader of the **death squads** in El Salvador and one of the founders of the right-wing party **ARENA**. He was born on August 23, 1943, in Santa Tecla, a small city near San Salvador. His father was a salesman and his mother was a career civil servant. D'Aubuisson's paternal family was of French extraction, and an ancestor had worked for the de Lesseps Company in its ill-fated attempt to build a canal across Central America. His education was punctuated by several expulsions from Jesuit schools for bad behavior. After briefly working in a canning factory as a teenager, he entered a military academy to pursue a military career. After graduation near the bottom of his class, D'Aubuisson joined the National Guard, where he specialized in military intelligence. Soon he became the protégé of the right-wing National Guard Commander Jose Alberto Medrano. In 1970, he was sent to the United States to train at the International Police Academy near Washington, D.C. Later, the U.S. Congress closed this school because of its reputation for teaching torture techniques. D'Aubuisson also traveled to Uruguay and Taiwan to study intelligence and police methods. Later, he attended U.S. Special Forces School in the Panama Canal Zone. In 1975, D'Aubuisson was transferred to the Salvadorean Armed Forces General Command and then promoted to major.

By 1975, D'Aubuisson was one of the leaders of the Salvadorean right wing. He formed the White Warrior's Union (Union de Guerreros Blancos) (UGB) to counter left-wing agitation for land reform. His opposition to land reform gained him political support from the elite Salvadorean landowners, or, as they were called, "the 14 families." Because the Jesuit Order in the Catholic Church supported land reform, the UGB attacked Jesuits, killing some and intimidating others. D'Aubuisson's use of torture to gain intelligence earned him the nickname "Major Blowtorch." In October 1979, liberal elements in the Salvadorean army overthrew the government of President Carlos Humberto Romero. The new government had no use for D'Aubuisson and the Salvadorean rebels of the **Farabundo Martí National Liberation Front** (FMLN). With financial support from the 14 families and political support from elements in the National Guard, D'Aubuisson was dismissed from the army. He went into exile in Guatemala and purchased a rice farm. After this venture failed, he decided to reenter Salvadorean politics.

In 1980, D'Aubuisson returned to El Salvador and became a leader of the right wing in its war against the FMLN. First he founded a new political party, the Broad National Front (Frente Amplio Nacional) to recruit anti-leftist activists. He also formed death squad units that carried out his orders. A member of these units assassinated Archbishop Oscar Arnulfo Romero on March 24, 1980, after Romero had publicly supported land reform. Other units eliminated left-wing politicians and anyone else in D'Aubuisson's way. In May 1980, he attempted and was arrested for a coup d'état that failed, but a military judge freed him. The Salvadorean army had threatened to revolt if D'Aubuisson was not freed. After the government of President Napoleon Duarte tried to arrest him again, D'Aubuisson again fled to Guatemala. His flight did not prevent one of his military death squads from killing three Maryknoll order nuns and a Catholic lay social worker outside the International Airport near San Salvador on December 2, 1980. Returning to El Salvador in 1981, D'Aubuisson was more successful in his efforts to influence Salvadorean politics. He and his political allies formed a new right-wing political party, ARENA (Alianza Republicana Nacionalista). This party was more successful because of its exploitation of anti-Communism and political support from the new Reagan administration. In 1982, ARENA won 19 out of the 60 seats, or 24 percent of the votes to the National Assembly. By an electoral alliance with other right-wing parties, D'Aubuisson became president of the National Assembly. He held this post until March 1983, when he resigned after his failure to reverse the land reform legislation of the previous government. However, he continued to direct death squad operations from a security office on the second floor of the National Assembly.

D'Aubuisson's failure to win the presidency in 1984 started his downfall as a political leader. He had become such a controversial political figure that not even the Reagan administration would help him. American support had been withdrawn before the election, and D'Aubuisson blamed the CIA for his defeat. His association with the death squads continued, but his inability to win national elections hurt him in ARENA. Before the 1988 national election, D'Aubuisson was replaced as head of ARENA by Alfredo Cristiani. Cristiani won the presidency, but D'Aubuisson held no important post in the new government. By this time, his erratic personal behavior had become a problem and rumors emerged about his dependence on alcohol and cocaine. He played a negative role in the peace negotiations with the Salvadorean rebels in the early 1990s. In April 1991, doctors diagnosed D'Aubuisson as having throat cancer. He made several trips to the United States for cancer treatments before dying of complications on February 20, 1992, in San Salvador. D'Aubuisson died a hero to the right wing because the Salvadorean upper classes believed that he had saved El Salvador from Communism. Other segments of Salvadorean society celebrated his death as a good omen for peace in El Salvador. **See also** ARENA (Alianza Republicana Nacionalista, or National Republican Alliance); Death Squads; Farabundo Marti National Liberation Front (FMLN).

Suggested readings: Robert Armstrong and Janet Shenk, *El Salvador the Face of Revolution* (Boston: South End Press, 1982); Douglas Farah, "D'Aubuisson: Death Comes to the Executioner," *Washington Post* (February 23, 1992), p. C4; Guy Gugliotta, "D'Aubuisson Kept U.S. on Its Guard," *Washington Post* (January 4, 1994), p. A1; Isabel Hilton, "Roberto D'Aubuisson," *Independent* (London) (February 22, 1992), p. 46; Douglas Farah, "A Ghost in Salvador's Elections," *Washington Post* (March 17, 1994), p. A31; Marjorie Miller, "Roberto D'Aubuisson, 48; Reputed Head of Salvadoran Death Squads," *Los Angeles Times* (February 21, 1992), p. A26; Tommie Sue Montgomery, *Revolution in El Salvador: From Civil Strife to Civil Peace*, 2nd ed. (Boulder, CO: Westview Press, 1995); Jefferson Morely, "When Reaganites Backed D'Aubuisson, They Unleashed a Political Assassin," *Los Angeles Times* (March 1, 1992), p. M2; Richard Severo, "Roberto D'Aubuisson, 48: Far-Rightist in Salvador," *New York Times* (February 21, 1992), p. A19.

Death Squads (Latin America)

Many countries have used right-wing death squads as a way to combat left-wing guerrilla and terrorist movements. This use of death squads has not been the exclusive tool of governments in Latin American, but it reached its height of popularity in those countries. Military men, policemen, and right-wing volunteers formed these death squads on an ad hoc basis. Often the death squads had sponsors or at least close connections with the government that it was defending. Justification for the death squads was that the only way to defeat guerrilla or terrorist movements was to adopt counterterrorist tactics that resembled those used by the guerrillas or terrorists. The goal was to destroy subversion by any means possible, including assassinations of leaders or potential leaders, massacres of dissident groups, and torture of individuals to gather intelligence. Torture was especially important to the death squads because of the information that could be gained from the victims. Because torture is illegal in each of these countries, the normal procedure has been to cover up the crime by killing the victim of torture. To spread terror, the body either disappeared or was left in a prominent place to spread fear.

Leaders of the death squads borrowed tactics from countries outside Latin America. They studied carefully the tactics used by the French military in Indochina and Algeria. Further reinforcement of tactics came from U.S. military instructors at the School of Americas. The most notorious of the leaders of the death squads have been **Roberto D'Aubuisson** in El Salvador and **Carlos Castaño** in Colombia. D'Aubuisson's death squads claimed the murder of Archbishop Oscar Arnulfo Romero and the Maryknoll nuns in 1980. Castano has conducted a no-holds war against the followers of leftist guerrillas. Other practitioners have been governments in Argentina and Honduras.

Death squads have not been exclusive to Latin America. Other regimes have resorted to death squads to fight guerrilla insurgents. For example, in Sri Lanka, the Sinhalese government unleashed death squads in the late 1980s. This tactic was most successful against the People's Liberation Front of **Rohan Wijeweera**. His death did not stop the Sri Lankan government from further use of death squads to wipe out his followers. **See also** ARENA (Alianza Republicana Nacionalista, or National Republican Alliance); Battalion 316; Castaño, Carlos; D'Aubuisson Arrieta, Roberto; Wijeweera, Rohan.

Suggested readings: Andrew Bilski, Joseph Gannon and William Owther, "Wave of Terror," *Maclean's* (November 27, 1989); Bruce B. Campbell and Arthur D. Brenner (eds.), *Death Squads in Global Perspective: Murder with Deniability* (New York: St. Martin's Press, 2000); Steve Coll, "Silence in the Killing Zone," *Washington Post* (January 16, 1994), p. W16; Anne Manuel, "Death Squad Debris," *Washington Post* (November 28, 1993), p. C5; Jefferson Morley, "Death from a Distance," *Washington Post* (March 28, 1993), p. C1; Craig Pyes, "Death Squad Democracy," *Washington Post* (April 17, 1994), C1; Jeffrey A. Sluka (ed.), *Death Squad: The Anthropology of State Terror* (Philadelphia: University of Pennsylvania Press, 2000).

Defenders of the Party of God (Ansar-i Hezbollah) (Iran)

The Defenders of the Party of God (Ansar-i Hezbollah) is an Iranian vigilante extremist group whose goal is to maintain the political and religious regime of the **Ayatollah Khomeini** revolution. This group had numerous predecessors, but in 1989 18 right-wing political figures decided to form it on an ad hoc basis. In 1993, it adopted the name of Defenders of the Party of God. By 1995, the group had become a political force in Iran. Leaders recruited members out of the hardline partisans of the Ayatollah Khomeini, veterans of the Iran-Iraq War, and students at religious schools. Recognized leaders are Masud Dehnamaki, a veteran of the Iran-Iraqi War; Husayn Allah-Karam, a veteran of the Iran-Iraq war and a doctoral student in management at Tehran University; and Ayatollah Ahmad Jannati, a religious leader and a member of the Council of Guardians since

1980. The Defenders of God has only a few hundred members, but its leadership has extensive political contacts in the Iranian political and religious establishment.

All members of the Defenders of the Party of God share two convictions—anti-Americanism and a hatred of domestic reformers. Both leaders and members blame the United States for the suffering and outcome of the Iran-Iraq War. Anti-Americanism extends to opposition to any manifestation of Western culture. As intense as the feeling against the United States remains, it pales beside the hatred directed toward domestic reformers. Close ties within the Iranian police and security forces allow members of the Defenders of the Party of God to use violence against anyone whom they interpret as a reformer. They interpret reform as a betrayal of the Khomeini revolution. One of its leaders, Jannati, has been chair of the Council of Guardians, the supreme religious authority in Iran, and he is a close associate of the Ayatollah Ali Khameinei, the successor to the Ayatollah Khomeini and the head of the Iranian state.

Sponsorships by religious leaders ensure that the Defenders of the Party of God continue to serve as a bulwark against reform in Iran. This group has declared open warfare against the reform government of President Mohammad Khatami. Despite the group's frequent use of violence, no member of the Defenders of the Party of God has ever been convicted of a crime. This is despite violent attacks on reformers and the July 1999 assault on a Tehran University dormitory that resulted in several deaths. In December 2002, leaders of the Defenders of the Party of God launched a holy war against reformers in Iran. One of the leaders, Masud Dehnamaki, a leading ideologist in the movement, directed an attack against the moderate policies of Mohammad Reza Khatami. More recently, leaders of the group have begun using the Internet to launch verbal attacks against the West and moderate Muslims. The intensity of these attacks increased after the State of the Union Address by President George W. Bush in which he included Iran in the "axis of evil." **See also** Khomeini, Ayatollah Ruholla.

Suggested readings: Stewart Bell, "'Taliban of Iran' Uses Canadian Web Host," *National Post* (Canada) (February 28, 2002), p. A1; Ali Akbar Dareini, "Hard-Line Vigilantes Declare War to 'Clean Up' Iran of Reformers Promoting Western Democracy," Associated Press Worldstream (December 4, 2002), p. 1; Angus McDowall, "Tehran Deploys Islamic Vigilantes to Attack Protesters," *Independent* (London) (July 11, 2003), p. 1; Michael Rubin, *Into the Shadows: Radical Vigilantes in Khatami's Iran* (Washington, DC: Washington Institute for Near East Policy, 2001).

Deobandi Madrasas Movement (India)

The Deobandi Madrasas Movement is a Muslim religious, educational, and philosophical movement that originated in nineteenth-century India and has produced generations of militant Islamists in the 20th century. Mohammad Qasim Nanautvi and his followers founded the Darul Uloom (House of Knowledge) in 1867 in the aftermath of the Indian Sepoy Mutiny. They located the school at Deoband, 90 miles northeast of New Delhi, India. The goal of the founders was to start a religious school, or madrasa, to return Muslims to the basic texts of Islam and reject Western culture. They also wanted to purge Indian Islam of its Hindu influences. Darul Uloom as an institution is considered in the Muslim world second only to **al-Azhar University** in Cairo, Egypt, as a center of Islamic learning.

At the Darul Uloom, madrasa religious scholars teach students the basics of Islam. Special emphasis is placed on the basic texts of the Koran and the prophetic sayings (Hadiths). Further stress is directed toward teaching students correct behavior. Efforts to modernize the curriculum have failed because of opposition of conservative teachers. Students arrive at around age 5 and leave at about 25. In 2001, the madrasas at Deobandi had around 3,000 students. Most of the graduates leave and establish their own madrasas. An estimated 65,000 Islamic scholars have been produced at Deoband in the last half of the 20th century.

In the years since Darul Uloom's founding, Deobandi madrasas have spread throughout the Muslim world. By 2001, there were an estimated 15,000 madrasas in operation, with more opening monthly. Those in India tend to be more moderate, but others in Pakistan and in Afghanistan have become more extreme. The orientation of a madrasa depends heavily on the religious motivations of the teachers. Many of the Deobandi teachers have been identified with the puritanical **Wahhabi** movement of Saudi Arabia. This was the case with the **Taliban** (religious students) in Afghanistan, whose original members were products of the Deobandi madrasas movement. **See also** Taliban (Students of Religious Schools); Wahhabism.

Suggested readings: Moni Basu, "The Taliban: Deobandi Movement," *Atlanta Journal and Constitution* (November 15, 2001), p. 10A; Rahul Bedi, "School That Inspired a Century of Extremists," *Daily Telegraph* (London) (December 6, 2001), p. 17; Sayantan Chakravarty, "SIMI: Simmering Fanaticism," *India Today* (October 15, 2001), p. 56; M. J. Gohari, *The Taliban: Ascent to Power* (Oxford: Oxford University Press, 1999); Edward Luce, "Teachers of the Taliban," *Financial Times* (London) (November 17, 2001), p. 1.

DEV-SOL (Revolutionary Left) (Turkey)

DEV-SOL (Revolutionary Left) is a Turkish urban underground leftist group that has specialized in terrorism. This group was formed in 1978 as a part of the anti-Turkish government movement. Most of its members had formerly been active in the Turkish People's Liberation Party/Front. DEV-SOL participated in violent demonstrations against the government that produced nearly 5,000 deaths. Dursun Karatas, the leader of the DEV-SOL, was arrested and sentenced to life in prison. In 1980, the military government banned DEV-SOL and this ban lasted throughout the decade. Karatas escaped from an Istanbul prison in 1989 to resume leadership of the group. Evidence began to surface in the 1990s that this group had been receiving training in Syrian terrorist training bases in Lebanon. Another ally of DEV-SOL has been the **Kurdistan Worker's Party** (PKK). Together with the PKK, DEV-SOL has engaged in assassinations and bank robberies to finance its activities. Leaders of DEV-SOL have also used extortion among Turkish residents abroad, especially in London, to raise funds for the group. Those who refuse to cooperate have been murdered. Back in Istanbul, Turkey, members of the DEV-SOL assassinated a member of the prominent Sabanci family, his victim's personal secretary, and the manager of the family's auto-making venture in February 1996.

Turkish authorities have been active in suppressing the DEV-SOL. In April 1992, a raid in Istanbul resulted in the death of 11 DEV-SOL militants and the capture of 7 others. Captured in the raid were weapons, money from robberies, fax machines, mobile telephones, and materials to disguise operatives. This setback hurt the DEV-SOL, but it remained a threat to the Turkish government. In September 1994, Karatas was arrested crossing the French border from Italy with false papers. The Turkish government tried to have him extradited from France, but Turkey's use of the death penalty led France to refuse to extradite him.

DEV-SOL resumed operations in 1994, but this time under the name Revolutionary People's Liberation Party/Front (DHKP/C). The loss of Karatas's leadership produced a void that the group never adequately replaced. It took nearly two years before a major operation could be launched. In 1996, a prominent Turkish businessman was assassinated along with two companions. Another operation was an unsuccessful attempt in June 1999 to fire antitank weapons at the U.S. consulate in Istanbul. In the late 1990s, Turkish police were able to arrest most of the activists, who were sentenced to lengthy prison terms. **See also** Kurdistan Worker's Party (PKK).

Suggested readings: Yonah Alexander and Dennis Pluchinsky, *Europe's Red Terrorists: The Fighting Communist Organizations* (London: Frank Cass, 1992); Duncan Campbell, "Murder, Extortion, Racketeering, Shootings, Drugs, Firebombs, Terrorism, Far-Left Plots and Neo-Fascist Groups," *Guardian* (London) (April 29, 1994),

p. 2; Edward DeMarco, "Bold Murders Revive Fears in Turkey," *Newsday* (February 9, 1996), p. A17; Hugh Pope, "50 Die as Turkey Battles Leftist Group," *Los Angeles Times* (April 18, 1992), p. A8; Hugh Pope, "American Civilian Worker at Turkish Base Shot to Death," *Los Angeles Times* (February 8, 1991), p. A10; Paul Wilkinson, "Terrorism and Turkey," *Jane's Intelligence Review* 4, no. 6 (June 1, 1992).

Devi, Phoolan (1963–2001) (India)

Phoolan Devi was the controversial ex-Bandit Queen who became the champion of the lower castes in India. She was born on August 10, 1963, in Shekhpur Gudda, in north India. Her family was poor and it belonged to the lowly Mallah fishermen's caste (Delits, formerly called Untouchables). At age 11, she was married to a much older man. After years of abuse, her marriage broke down. Both her husband and family abandoned her. She returned eight years later to defend her father in a court case over a land dispute. After losing the case, Devi was arrested by the police and raped by them. Devi then joined a band of lower-caste outlaws headed by Vikram Mallah. They became lovers until he was killed. These bandits specialized in murder and robbery of upper-caste victims. In 1980, two gang members turned Devi over to a group of Thakurs, upper-caste landowners, in the village of Behmai. She was raped repeatedly before escaping. Devi rejoined her gang and led them back to the village of Behmai where she executed 22 men. These murders resulted in a massive hunt for her and her gang. In the meantime, her legend as the Bandit Queen grew and she became a positive symbol for India's lower castes. After three years, Devi finally surrendered to Indian authorities in February 1983, but only after she negotiated a favorable surrender package. Negotiations settled that she would not be hanged and that she would serve only eight years for her crimes. Only part of the settlement was fulfilled, as she spent 11 years in prison in the Central Jail in Gwalior. It took the personal intervention of Mulyam Singh Yadav, the chief minister of the state of Uttar Pradesh and an ambitious lower-cast politician, to have her released.

Once out of jail, in 1994 Devi turned to politics. The same year that she was released from prison, a movie of her life, *Bandit Queen,* was released. After a good reception at the Cannes Film Festival, this movie gave Devi considerable publicity. While she found fault with the movie, Devi accept the favorable publicity. It allowed her the opportunity to run for the Indian Parliament. She and other lower-caste politicians formed the Samajvadi Party to support the rights of the lower castes. In 1996, Devi was elected to Parliament from Mirzapur. Because she was illiterate, Devi was reluctant to speak or be active in Parliament. Despite this, she served as a symbol for India's lower castes. On July 25, 2001, three masked gunmen ambushed her as Devi returned home for lunch after a session of Parliament. She died after being shot four or five times in the head.

Suggested reading: Peter Popham, "Trusted Friend Confesses to 'Revenge Killing' of Bandit Queen," *Independent* (London) (July 28, 2001), p.15; Michael Sheridan, "Bandit Queen Assassination Divides India," *Gazette* (Montreal) (July 29, 2001), p. A8; Alex Spillius, "'Bullet to Ballot to Bullet': Slain Bandit Queen Was a Hero to India's Poor," *Gazette* (Montreal) (July 26, 2001), p. A1.

Devi, Savitri (1905–1982) (France)

Savitri Devi was the leading exponent of occult National Socialism in postwar Europe. She was born Maximiani Portas on September 30, 1905, in Lyons, France to a Greek father and British mother. Her early education was in both France and Greece. In the 1920s, she received master's degrees in philosophy and science in French schools. In 1931, she earned a Ph.D. in chemistry. Despite her ability in the sciences, Devi was more interested in politics, philosophy, and religion.

Two influences were to have an impact on Devi's life—attraction to Germany and anti-Semitism. She believed that Germany had been wronged in the settlement at Versailles following World War I. This sympathy for Germany extended to German philosophy and later to Adolf Hitler and Nazism. Her anti-Semitism came out of the right-wing anti-Semitic writers in France present in the interwar period between 1918 and 1939. She concluded that Jews were racial and cultural outsiders to be despised.

Devi's interest in Aryanism led to her attraction with India. In the 1930s, she moved to India and undertook a lifelong study of the Aryan origin myths of classical India. In 1940, Devi married A. K. Mukherji, a pro-Nazi Indian nationalist. This marriage allowed her to have a British passport. During World War II, Devi worked for a Nazi victory by conducting research for a book on a new Aryan religion that would be adopted by the Nazis after the war. The defeat of Nazi Germany, however, frustrated these plans. In 1945, Devi settled in England, where she published the book *A Son of God*. This book was followed in 1946 by another titled *The Impeachment of Man*. In this book, Devi outlined a National Socialist nature religion that has attracted many postwar neo-Nazis. Later in 1946, Devi moved to Iceland, where she became interested in Norse paganism, or Odinism. Her research in Odinism foreshadowed its later adoption as a religion by neo-Nazis.

Devi's attraction to Nazism earned her the enmity of German authorities. In 1948, she traveled to West Germany, where her distribution of neo-Nazi material led to a jail sentence. German authorities arrested her in 1949, and Devi served six months in a German prison. After her release, she left Germany.

Devi spent much of the 1950s writing. She published *Defiance* in 1950, *Gold in the Furnace* in 1952, *The Lightning and the Sun* in 1956, and *Pilgrimage* in 1958. These works solidified her position as the leading neo-Nazi writer in Europe, but she was unhappy about the lack of progress of the neo-Nazi movement. Devi began to look around, first in Europe and then in the United States, for a possible emerging leader. She finally identified a leading contender in the American

George Lincoln Rockwell, the head of the new American Nazi Party.

Devi became the champion of the World Union of National Socialists (WUNS). She believed that a pan-Nazi movement would stimulate the neo-Nazi movement. Devi represented France in the 1962 meeting at Cottswald in England. At this meeting Rockwell; **Colin Jordan**, Britain's leading neo-Nazi; and Devi united to conclude the Cottswald Agreement. This agreement was the theoretical blueprint for the beginning of an international neo-Nazi movement. At the time, Devi had great plans for WUNS. Later, after the assassination of Rockwell in 1967 and much to Devi's disappointment, WUNS slowly began to disintegrate.

Devi then returned to India and her husband. She spent most of her time writing and corresponding with other neo-Nazis. After her conversion to **Holocaust denial**, Devi became one of its leading champions. She served as the "godmother" of the neo-Nazi movement until her death on October 22, 1982. **See also** Holocaust Denial; Jordan, Colin.

Suggested readings: Nicholas Goodrick-Clark, *Hitler's Priestess: Savitri Devi, the Hindu-Aryan Myth, and Occult Neo-Nazism* (New York: New York University Press, 1998); Philip Rees, *Biographical Dictionary of the Extreme Right Since 1890* (New York: Simon and Schuster, 1990); Frederick J. Simonelli, *American Fuehrer: George Lincoln Rockwell and the American Nazi Party* (Urbana: University of Illinois Press, 1999).

Devotees of Islam (Fida'iyan-i Islam) (Iran)

The Devotees of Islam (Fida'iyan-i Islam) extremist group is the oldest active pressure group in Iran. Sayyid Mujtaba Mirlawhi, a young Shi'ite theology student, formed the Devotees of Islam in 1945 after he had become unhappy about the secular drift of Iran. Mirlawhi was born in 1924, probably in Tehran, into a deeply religious family. He was distressed by the influence of Ahmad Kasravi, a historian who had criticized the role of Shi'ism in Iranian history. High-ranking Shi'ite clerics issued fatwas (religious orders) condemning Kasravi to death, and **Ruhollah Khomeini** approved them. In May 1945, Mirlawhi attempted to assassinate Kasravi but only wounded him. After a short term in jail, he directed the Devotees of Islam to fight for the Shi'ite cause. Followers of the Devotees of Islam assassinated Kasravi in May 1946, and they were acquitted shortly after their capture. Over the next several years, Mirlawhi developed a close relationship with Ayatollah Abdul Qassim Kashani, a Shi'ite political leader. Mirlawhi also started a newspaper, *Flag of Islam* (*Parcham-i Islam*) and adopted the war name of Navab Safavi.

The Devotees of Islam launched a widescale assassination campaign in early 1949. The first target was the Shah of Iran, but an attempt on his life at the University of Tehran in February 1949 was unsuccessful. Husayn Imani, a member of the Devotees of Islam, was able to assassinate Abdul Husayn Hazhir, a former prime minister, in central Tehran. This crime led to Imani's hanging, but this sentence did not deter his compatriots. On March 7, 1951, Prime Minister 'Ali Razmara was assassinated in Tehran's Shah Mosque by a member of the Devotees of Islam. This time the assassin, Khalil Tahmasbi, won an acquittal. After the Musaddiq's regime in 1952–1953, the Devotees of Islam renewed their terrorist campaign. An unsuccessful assassination attempt against Prime Minister Husayn 'Ala in November 1955, however, ended this phase. In retaliation, the Iranian government executed Mirlawhi and four of the Devotees of Islam's leaders on January 18, 1956.

The loss of Mirlawhi was a serious blow, but the Devotees of Islam continued to function. Most of the followers went underground. They reappeared in the early 1960s when the Ayatollah Khomeini began his public opposition to the Shah of Iran. Operating under the name of the Islamic Coalition Association (ICA), operatives assassinated Prime Minister Hassan 'Ali Mansur in January 1965. Even after Khomeini's exile, the members of the Devotees of Islam kept in close contact with him. They distributed cassettes of Khomeini's sermons, speeches, and writings, thus keeping his ideas alive in Iran.

In 1978, the Devotees of Islam came out in the open as supporters of Khomeini. Ayatollah Sadiq Khalkhali, a close associate of Khomeini and a member of the group since his student days, became head of the Devotees of Islam in May 1979. Under his leadership, the Devotees of Islam launched a terrorist campaign against the enemies of Khomeini. Khalkhali orchestrated the December 1979 assassination of Shahyar Mustafa Chafik, a nephew of the Shah of Iran, in Paris. As soon as Khomeini consolidated power in Iran, Khalkhali became chairman of the Revolutionary Courts. His brutality as head of the Revolutionary Courts earned him such a bloodthirsty reputation that he alienated even his supporters and he was deposed in December 1980. Khomeini had gained complete ascendancy in Iran, and in 1981 the Devotees of Islam formally disbanded.

The Devotees of Islam group has reappeared during the Khatami regime in the late 1990s. President Muhammad Khatami came to power as a moderate with the idea of reform. His initiatives to open dialogue with the West in 1998 caused the defunct Devotees of Islam to revitalize. This time the driving force was a virulent anti-Americanism. Besides threatening and carrying out attacks on Americans, the leaders of the Devotees of Islam turned attention on moderates. Two victims, husband and wife Darius Foruhar and Parvaneh Iskandari, were murdered in Tehran in November 1998. Other murders followed with the Devotees of Islam trademark of the murder of moderate Iranians on them. Evidence exists that Iranian intelligence services had a hand in the resurrection of the Devotees of Islam, but the suspected leader of the group, Sa'id Imami, allegedly committed suicide in an Iranian prison on June 19, 1999. A government investigation has uncovered little information, but enough was found to discredit several of the top intelligence leaders, which led to several key resignations.

Suggested readings: Shahrough Akhavi, *Religion and Politics in Contemporary Iran:*

Clergy-State Relations in the Pahlavi Period (Albany, NY: State University of New York Press, 1980); Fereydoun Hoveyda, *The Broken Crescent: The "Threat" of Militant Islamic Fundamentalism* (Westport, CT: Praeger, 1998); Michael Rubin, *Into the Shadows: Radical Vigilantes in Khatami's Iran* (Washington, DC: Washington Institute for Near East Policy, 2001).

Donaldson, Ian Stuart (1957–1993) (Great Britain)

Ian Stuart Donaldson was the lead singer of the neo-Nazi rock group Skrewdriver and one of the most influential **skinheads** in Great Britain. He was born on August 11, 1957, at Pouton-le-Fylde in Lancashire, England. His father was a businessman and his mother a housewife. He was raised in nearby Blackpool, England. In the early 1970s, the skinheads had become a presence in Great Britain and Donaldson was attracted to their lifestyle. He started a skinhead political action group, White Noise, with a strong affiliation to the National Front. He also formed a rock group, Tumbling Dice, which mainly performed standards of the Rolling Stones and The Who. After this group folded, Donaldson formed the skinhead rock group Skrewdriver in early 1977 and the group moved to London. This group had a contract with Chiswick Records but soon lost it due to the band's reputation for violence. Subsequently, Skrewdriver disbanded and Donaldson moved to Manchester in northern England and found a job in a textile factory.

Donaldson became as involved in politics as in the music scene. By this time Donaldson had shortened his name to Ian Stuart. Under the name of Stuart he emerged as one of the major leaders of the British skinheads. Stuart and his skinheads had developed a neo-Nazi ideology that was anti-immigrant, anti-Communist, anti-Semitic, anti-gay, and anti-**Irish Republican Army** (IRA). He realized the political shortcomings of the skinheads, so his first tactic was to join the neo-Nazi **National Front**. Stuart decided that his contribution to

the National Front was through his music. In the summer of 1982, he reconstituted Skrewdriver. This time Skrewdriver made no pretense about its racist orientation. Its records *White Power* in 1982, *Hail the New Dawn* in 1984, and *Blood and Honour* in 1985 made it plain that Skrewdriver was an advocate of white supremacy. Stuart's political advocacy landed him in jail in December 1985 after he had a fight with Nigerians on December 11, 1985. He received a 12-month prison sentence in Wayland Prison in Norfolk. After his release from prison, Stuart made *White Rider* in 1987. By this time, Stuart had become suspicious of the National Front leadership. Leaders of the National Front had tried to censor some of Skrewdriver's lyrics, and Stuart was uncertain how the funds that his concerts were raising were being spent. Later in 1987, Stuart resigned from the National Front. In its stead, Stuart formed the neo-Nazi skinhead organization **Blood and Honor**. This group served as an umbrella organization for more than 30 skinhead groups.

Stuart and Skrewdriver had an international reputation, and invitations to play came from all over Europe. In 1990, Skrewdriver was invited to Cottbus, Germany. The band appeared a few days before the concert, but when riots broke out, Stuart and the members of Skrewdriver were arrested. Stuart was released but the rest of the band stayed in Moat Prison in Berlin for over a month. In September 1992, violence broke out at a concert that was called "The Battle of Waterloo." Stuart continued to make records and create controversy. On the night of September 23, 1993, Stuart was killed in a car crash in Derbyshire, England. Stuart left a white power legacy in his music, and no leader of his caliber has emerged since in the British skinhead movement. In the meantime Blood and Honor has continued to grow, and some of its leaders developed contacts with the neo-Nazi terrorist group **Combat 18. See also** Combat 18; Front National.

Suggested readings: Anti-Defamation League, *The Skinhead International: A World-*

wide Survey of Neo-Nazi Skinheads (New York: Anti-Defamation League, 1995); Mark S. Hamm, *American Skinheads: The Criminology and Control of Hate Crime* (Westport, CT: Praeger, 1994; Silke Tudor, "House of Tudor," *SF Weekly* (California) (May 7, 2003), p. 1.

Dugin, Alexander Gelevich (1962–) (Russia)

Alexander Dugin was one of the founders of the **National Bolshevik Party** and is now active in the newly created Eurasia Political Party. He was born in 1962 to a family with a history of producing military men. Near the end of the 1970s, he entered the Moscow Aviation Institute to pursue a military career. This career choice came despite his growing alienation from Soviet society. He also became a part of the Golovin Circle. Yevgeny Golovin, a scholar in European mystical literature and poetry, had gathered two others, Yuri Mamleyev, a Christian philosopher, and Geidar Jema, a specialist in Islam studies, to study mysticism. Dugin was a natural member of this circle because he had mastery of nine foreign languages. His first contribution was translation into Russian of Julius Evola's *Pagan Imperialism*. When Soviet authorities learned of his contacts with the Golovin Circle, he was dismissed from the Moscow Aviation Institute. To earn a living, Dugin became a Moscow street sweeper, but continued his study of right-wing and neo-Fascist thought.

The introduction of more freedoms after 1987 allowed Dugin to enter Russian politics. In 1987, he joined the anti-Semitic Pamyat (Memory) group. Leaders of Pamyat appreciated his abilities and, in late 1988, he assumed a seat on Pamyat's Central Council. By the middle of 1989, Dugin decided that he could no longer associate with Pamyat because of its low intellectual level. He decided to travel to Western Europe and contact leading neo-Fascist figures. On his travels, he had talks with Alain de Benoist, the French intellectual, and **Jean-François Thiriart**, the Belgian neo-Fascist. They reinforced his distaste for the Ameri-canized European culture and led him back to Russian traditionalism. Dugin returned to Russia and established his own publishing house, Arktogeya, and a bookstore. He used the publishing house to publish a series of books authored by him. These books outlined his vision of a conservative social revolution for Russia. This conservative social revolution included an emphasis on authority, collectivism, hierarchy, spirituality, and tradition.

Dugin was one of the founders of the **National Bolshevik Party**. He became acquainted with **Eduard Limonov** sometime in late 1992 or early 1993. Limonov had just broken with Vladimir Zhirinovsky and the Liberal-Democratic Party of Russia and he was looking for a way to advance his political views. They decided to create a National Bolshevik Party in May 1993. Limonov was to be the leader of the party and Dugin the chief theoretician. This arrangement worked for five years until Dugin left the party in 1998. His chief complaint was that the party had watered down his ideas to make them almost incoherent.

After leaving the National Bolshevik Party, Dugin began to explore other options. He made contacts with the Communist Party of the Russian Federation (CPRF), the successor party to the Communist Party in the Soviet Union. His role as advisor to Gennady Seleznev, speaker of the Russian Parliament (Duma), gave him access to power. Dugin also formed the New Ideological Movement to spread his political and geopolitical views to Russian students in Moscow.

Dugin's geopolitical ideology led him to become one of the founders of the Eurasia Nationwide Political Movement. A Eurasianist movement had developed in the 1930s with the leadings figures two Russian émigrés—Pyotr Savitsky and Prince Nikolai Trubetskoi. This movement advocated a Pan-Asia/Europe grouping that would rival the Atlanticism of the United States and its allies. Lev Gumilyov, a philosopher, had kept the Eurasian idea alive, but political events left this movement as a relic of a bygone age until Dugin adopted it. Dugin gathered allies, from Mufti Talgat Tadzhuddin on the Muslim side to Rabbi Avrom Shmulevich on the Jewish side, to form the Eurasia Nationwide Political Movement on April 21, 2001. Since then, Dugin has been active building the movement and attracting political allies. He has been wooing Russian President Vladimir Putin to adopt the Eurasian concept as an alternative to the American alliance. Dugin found the American-British invasion of Iraq in the spring of 2003 to be an attempt by the United States to establish worldwide hegemony. In several articles, he advised the Putin government to oppose American policies. **See also** Limonov, Eduard; Thiriart, Jean-François.

Suggested readings: Yelena Dorofeyva, "Eurasia Movement Created in Russia," TASS (April 21, 2001), p. 1; Aleksandr Dugin, "Columnists Eye War's Implications for Russia, World," *Current Digest of the Post-Soviet Press*, vol. 55, no. 15 (May 14, 2003); Aleksandr Dugin, "Russia Watches Europe Split over Iraq," *Current Digest of the Post-Soviet Press*, vol. 55, no. 7 (March 19, 2003); Grigory Nekhoroshev, "'Eurasians' Decide to Rely on Vladimir Putin," *Current Digest of the Post-Soviet Press* (May 23, 2001), p. 14; Stephen D. Shenfield, *Russian Fascism: Traditions, Tendencies, Movements* (Armonk, NY: M. E. Sharpe, 2001).

Durand, Oscar Ramirez (1954–) (Peru)

Oscar Durand was the successor to **Abimael Guzman** as head of the **Shining Path** in Peru. He was born in 1954 in Arequipa, Peru. His father was a senior officer in the Peruvian army and retired as a general. Durand's early education was at the Franciscan Catholic school Colegio San Francisco. In 1971, he entered the National Engineering University in Lima. Durand began to spend more time on politics than on his studies. At first he was a follower of Che Guevara, the Argentine-Cuban revolutionary martyr, and his brand of revolution. His contacts with a Maoist student leader, Margie Clavo, resulted in his conversion to Maoism. By 1973, he was a dedicated

revolutionary and he broke with his family, accusing his father of being part of the forces of repression.

Durand moved to Ayacucho, Peru, where he became a follower of Guzman, a philosophy professor at the local university, and the founder of the Maoist group the Shining Path. Soon afterward, Durand became a member of Guzman's inner circle of advisors. In 1979, he was appointed to the Central Committee. His abilities as a military commander made him one of the Shining Path's military strategists. By the early 1990s, Durand was number three in the hierarchy of the Shining Path, behind Guzman and Elena Iparraguirre. His operational name was Comrade Feliciano. Guzman's capture in September 1992 was a serious blow to the Shining Path. Durand assumed control of the most radical wing, the Red Path (Sendero Rojo) of the Shining Path, and, after a period of reorganization, he renewed guerrilla operations. He was wounded in the leg in an operation in 1992 that left him with a pronounced limp. Durand concentrated his military operations in the jungle and isolated villages in the Ayacucho area. In 1995, his terrorist activities led to a business organization offering a $100,000 reward for his capture. In early 1999, he traveled to Colombia to study military tactics with the **Revolutionary Armed Forces of Colombia** (FARC). On July 14, 1999, Peruvian security forces captured Durand with five associates near Juancayo in the Ayacucho area. A secret military tribunal sentenced Duran to life imprisonment on August 31, 1999. He is serving his sentence in a high-security prison in Lima alongside Guzman. In early January 2003, Durand petitioned Peru's Constitutional High Court for a new trial. His appeal was turned down on January 6, 2003. In the summer of 2003, Durand was one of the imprisoned rebel leaders who apologized for the death toll caused by his actions in the Shining Path. **See also** Guzman, Abimael; Shining Path (Sendero Luminoso).

Suggested readings: Drew Benson, "Peruvian Court Rejects Petition by Jailed Top Rebel

Leader," Associated Press Worldstream (January 7, 2003), p. 1; Anthony Faiola, "Shining Path Rebel Leader Is Captured in Peru," *Washington Post* (July 15, 1999), p. A19; "Imprisoned Rebel Leaders in Peru Ask for Forgiveness," Agence France Presse (June 10, 2003), p. 1; William R. Long, "Grim Hunt for a Rebel Leader," *Los Angeles Times* (March 14, 1995), p. 3.

E

ELN (Ejército de Liberación) (National Army of Liberation) (Colombia)

The ELN (Ejército de Liberación, or National Army of Liberation) is one of the Colombian guerrilla groups at war with the Colombian state. Colombian students had traveled to Cuba in the early 1960s, where they had become converted to the guerrilla warfare theories of the revolutionary leader Che Guevara. These students returned to Colombia in 1964 and formed the ELN. Many of them had been former members of the **Revolutionary Armed Forces of Colombia** (FARC).

Many of the followers of the ELN came out of the Liberation Theology movement and a commitment to the Colombian lower classes. This movement, in turn, came out of the Catholic Church's Second Vatican Council and its call for the church to become more involved in the welfare of the poor. Camilo Torres Restrepo, a Colombian priest, was one of the first priests to join the ELN. Shortly after his adherence to the ELN, he was killed in a battle with the Colombian military. Later, Manuel Pérez Martinez, a former Basque priest, became one of the principal leaders of the ELN until his death from hepatitis in 1996.

The ELN has always been a small, highly disciplined guerrilla group. Only in the mid-1980s did the ELN gain a number of supporters from other guerrilla groups. Dissidents from FARC joined the ELN in 1984 when the FARC negotiated a truce with President Belisario Betancur's government. In contrast to FARC, leaders of the ELN opposed any agreements with the Colombian government up until the late 1990s, when they finally engaged peace talks with the Peruvian government. In 1998, the then Colombian president, Andres Pastrana, made peace overtures with the ELN. This overture collapsed in 2002 when the right-wing paramilitary group, **United Self-Defense Forces of Colombia,** of **Carlos Castaño** launched an offensive into ELN territory. The next Colombian president, Alvaro Uribe, tried again, but he was more reluctant to give concessions to the ELN. Uribe's attempt to conclude peace with Colombian right-wing paramilitary groups caused ELN's leadership to withdraw from negotiations in January 2003. In comparison to FARC, the ELN's 4,500-strong army makes it a junior partner in the civil war against the Colombian state.

A specialty of the ELN is economic sabotage, and its fighters have frequently targeted foreign oil companies operating in Colombia. Tactics, including extortion and kidnapping, have also been adopted to destabilize the Colombian society. Unlike other guerrilla groups in Colombia, the ELN has been careful to avoid the drug trade. This refusal to accept funds from the drug trade has made the ELN the only Colombian terrorist group with financial problems. Antonio Garcia is the present military commander of the ELN. **See also** Castaño, Carlos; Revolutionary Armed Forces of Colombia (FARC); United Self-Defense Forces of Colombia (AUC).

Suggested readings: Ana Carrigan, *The Palace of Justice: A Colombian Tragedy* (New York: Four Walls Eight Windows, 1993); Garry M. Leech, *Killing Peace: Colombia's Conflict and the Failure of U.S. Intervention* (New York: Information Network of the Americas, 2002); Bert Ruiz, *The Colombian Civil War* (Jefferson, NC: McFarland, 2001); James Wilson, "ELN May Attempt Dignified Exit from Years of Revolution," *Financial Times* (London) (June 18, 2002), p. 3.

Ensslin, Gudrun (1940–1977) (West Germany)

Gudrun Ensslin was one of the leaders of the West German terrorist group **Red Army Faction** (RAF). She was born in 1940 in the village of Bartholoma in Swabia, Germany, the fourth of seven children. Her father was a Protestant minister. Ensslin went to grammar school in Tuttlingen, Germany. She spent 1958–1959 in the United States in Pennsylvania as a foreign exchange student. Although her American family became fond of her, she was critical of the conservative society in the United States. After returning to West Germany, Ensslin attended Tubingen University, where she studied German and English language and literature as well as educational theory to prepare for a teaching career. She met Bernward Vesper, son of the poet Will Vesper, and together they started a small publishing house called Studio for New Literature. After winning a university grant, she and Vesper enrolled in 1962 in the Free University in West Berlin, where Ensslin became active in the student movement. Her relationship with Vesper ended several months before she gave birth to a son in May 1967. Shortly before the birth, Ensslin met **Andreas Baader**. After the birth, she and Baader became lovers.

Ensslin started her career as a terrorist almost as a lark. She, Baader, and Thorwald Proll decided to firebomb two department stores in Frankfurt. On April 2, 1968, they left firebombs in both the Kaufhaus Schneider Department Store and the Kaufhof Department Store. Two days later the police arrested the three of them. In the subsequent court trial in October 1968, Ensslin received a three-year prison sentence. Her stay in prison only lasted 14 months before she was released on appeal. After the appeal was rejected, she and Baader went underground, traveling to Paris. Regis Debray, the French revolutionary theorist, sheltered them for several weeks before they moved on to Italy. In early 1970, they moved back to West Germany. After Baader's arrest on April 4, 1970, Ensslin spent the next six weeks planning Baader's escape from prison. On May 14, 1970, Ensslin, **Ulrike Meinhof**, and other accomplices overpowered prison security guards when Baader was temporarily out of prison. They soon named their group the Red Army Faction.

Ensslin's relationship with Baader and her strong personality made her number two in the Red Army Faction, behind only Baader. She traveled with Baader and Meinhof to Jordan to receive terrorist training from the Palestinians. This training caused problems, as both Ensslin and Baader were always challenging accepted practices. After the training was terminated, Ensslin returned with Baader to West Berlin. On September 28, 1970, she participated in one of the three bank robberies to gather funds for the RAF. She acted as second-in-command to Baader throughout the terrorist campaign in 1971–1972. She was devastated when Baader was wounded and arrested on June 1, 1972. Less than a week later on June 7, 1972, police arrested her in a Hamburg dress boutique shop trying on clothes.

German authorities treated Ensslin with special attention as a leader of the Red Army Faction. She was held in a jail in Essen away from other leaders of the RAF. Despite this effort to isolate them, an informal communication system was built. Baader called for a series of hunger strikes. Ensslin participated in two of the hunger strikes, but both of them ended prematurely. Her trial started on May 21, 1975, And she participated with Baader, Meinhof, and **Jan-Carl Raspe** in turning the trial into political theater. She received a life sentence on April 28, 1977, for murder, attempted murder, and for having formed a criminal association. Ensslin was housed in a special section of the Stammheim prison reserved for the RAF. She spent much of her time trying to keep Baader's spirits positive. She learned on the evening of October 17 that the attempt to free them by means of a Lufthansa skyjacking had failed, and afterward Ensslin joined the other RAF prisoners in a suicide pact. Sometime in the morning of October 18, 1977, she used a loudspeaker cable to hang herself. Her death and the others' caused the West German government to conduct an investigation to prove that it was suicide rather than murder. A committee concluded that Ensslin had committed suicide. **See also** Baader, Andreas; Mahler, Horst; Meinhof, Ulrike; Raspe, Jan-Carl; Red Army Faction (RAF).

Suggested readings: Stefan Aust, *The Baader-Meinhof Group: The Inside Story of a Phenomenon* (London: Bodley Head, 1985); Jillian Becker, *Hitler's Children: The Baader-Meinhof Terrorist Gang* (Philadelphia: Lippincott, 1978); Barry Davies, *Terrorism: Inside a World Phenomenon* (London: Virgin Books, 2003).

EOKA (Ethniki Organosis Kyrion Agoniston) (National Organization of Cypriot Fighters) (Cyprus)

EOKA (National Organization of Cypriot Fighters) was the terrorist organization under which Greek Cypriots in Cyprus fought against the British in the late 1950s. Colonel **George Grivas**, a native of Cyprus and formerly an officer in the Greek army, founded EOKA in early January 1955. Grivas had landed in Cyprus on November 10, 1954, to launch a guerrilla war against the British. He spent the time between November and January gathering equipment and organizing personnel. From the beginning, Grivas split the EOKA into two operational units: one to conduct guerrilla activities and sabotage, and the other to engage in political activities involving demonstrations and riots. He also concluded a tenuous political alliance with Archbishop Makarios, the Greek Orthodox religious leader of Cyprus. Their goal was union with Greece (Enosis).

EOKA's military operations opened on April 1, 1955, with a series of bombings in different parts of Cyprus. Grivas wanted to destabilize the British administrative structure and the police. Initial results were discouraging because the EOKA operatives were inexperienced and the number of activists was too low. Grivas reacted by organizing EOKA into small operational cells modeled on those of the Communist Party. Many of the new recruits were teenage schoolboys. The British government responded with a State of Emergency proclaimed on November 16, 1955.

Grivas ordered an all-out attack on British troops and civilians, and on Greek Cypriots whom he considered as collaborators with the British. The British army committed 17,000 troops to putting down the guerrilla warfare. Grivas conducted a guerrilla campaign, but the political side was left to Makarios. British authorities began to seek a political solution in negotiations in London between British Greek and Turkish representatives. Continuation of terrorist attacks and the refusal of Makarios to compromise led to Makarios's exile from Cyprus. After a general strike in April 1958, Grivas and the EOKA declared a truce. British, Greek, Turkish, and Cypriot leaders signed the London Agreement to give Cyprus independence on February 19, 1959. EOKA declared a ceasefire on December 24, 1959. Grivas was a national hero in both Greece and Cyprus, and he was promoted to general in the Greek army. This victory gave Cyprus independence, but it was only the first step in the struggle between Greek and Turkish Cypriots that led to the partition of Cyprus into Greek and Turkish areas. **See also** Grivas, George; Sampson, Nicos Giorgiades.

Suggested readings: Nancy Crawshaw, *The Cyprus Revolt: An Account of the Struggle for Union with Greece* (London: Allen and Unwin,

1978); Charles Foley and W. I. Scobie, *The Struggle for Cyprus* (Stanford, CA: Hoover Institution Press, 1975).

ETA (Euskadi ta Askatasuna) (Basque Fatherland and Liberty) (Spain)

ETA is a Basque separatist movement that has adopted terrorism as a way to establish a Basque state in Spain. The Franco government punished the Basque Country for its support for the Republican side during the Spanish Civil War by banning the use of the Basque language and other punitive measures. On July 31, 1959, elements from the Basque Nationalist Party (Partido Nacionalista Vasco, or PNV) and university students from the spin-off study group Ekin (Action) united to form the ETA. The initial goal of the ETA was full independence for the seven Basque provinces in northern Spain. In July 1961, the ETA conducted a failed effort to derail a train carrying Francoist veterans to a Spanish Civil War ceremony. More than a hundred ETA activists were arrested by the Franco government, and, in the aftermath of these arrests, the leadership of the ETA decided to avoid further direct action. An assembly of delegates in 1962 gave the ETA its form, structure, and philosophy. Members agreed that the ETA was a Basque revolutionary national liberation movement with the goal of establishing a socialist Basque state. Those members who

Two masked men raise their clenched fists in the air by the coffin of Basque separatist ETA member Ignacia Ceberio during a memorial rally in her hometown of Lizartza, northern Spain, June 7, 1998. Ceberio was killed in a shoot-out with police in Guernica during a raid on a suspected ETA safehouse. At right is an ETA flag with the group's snake and axe symbol. (AP Photo/Arenberri)

disagreed with this leftist orientation left the ETA. At first, members of the ETA limited their activities to political action, but beginning in 1965 the leadership initiated a terrorist campaign.

This terrorist campaign has continued into the 21st century. Initial operations were against banks to obtain funds to finance the movement, but in 1968, the ETA started including assassinations in its strategy. After the assassination of the chief of the political police, Meliton Manzanas, in Guipuzcosin August 1968, the Franco government tried the 16 leaders of the ETA in a military tribunal in Burgos in December 1970. This tribunal issued nine death sentences and sentenced the others to 30 years in prison, but the head of the Spanish state, Francisco Franco, commuted the death sentences to 30 years in prison. This loss of leadership hurt the operations of the ETA, but new leaders emerged. Its most spectacular operation was the assassination of Spanish Prime Minister Admiral Carrero Blanco on December 20, 1973, by a command-detonated bomb. Carrero Blanco was the heir apparent to the leadership of Franco Spain after General Franco's death. In 1974, the ETA split into two competing factions—the ETA-M and the ETA-PM. The leaders of the ETA-M wanted to continue the military struggle, and those of the ETA-PM turned to the political struggle. This separation lasted until the ETA-PM disbanded in 1983. In the early and mid-1990s, the ETA reorganized itself. Even in its new form the ETA continued its terrorist campaign, including an attempt to assassinate José Maria Aznar, then a prominent politician and now the two-term Spanish prime minister, on April 19, 1995. In 1998, the ETA declared a cease-fire to negotiate with the Spanish government for a Basque state. These negotiations collapsed and the ETA resumed terrorist operations in November 1999.

Leadership of ETA has changed over the years as Spanish authorities have arrested or killed many of its leaders. An Executive Committee of three to five members directs the operations of ETA. Known members of the Executive Committee in 2001 are Mikel Albisu Iriate, Asier Oyarzabal Chaparteque, and Jose Luis Arrieta Zubimendi. ETA is organized into three parts—military, political, and logistical. Each of these parts is subdivided down to the cell level. Secrecy is ensured by compartmentalization, with members of each cell ignorant of the activities of other cells.

Since its first assassination in 1968, the ETA has targeted its enemies in a bloody campaign of terror. By 2001, the ETA had killed 811 individuals and wounded more than 2,000. The list of its victims includes a total of 360 dead and 1,358 wounded politicians, journalists, and judges. Next largest total of 356 dead and 541 wounded comes from attacks on the Spanish government's security forces. Finally, the Spanish army has suffered 95 dead and 101 wounded.

The leadership of the ETA has also concluded alliances and partnerships with other terrorist organizations. Early in its existence, the ETA made contacts with various Latin American Terrorist groups in Argentina, Chile, Guatemala, Nicaragua, and El Salvador. Later in the 1970s, ETA members received training at camps run by Middle East terrorist groups, including those of the **Popular Front for the Liberation of Palestine (PFLP)**. Close contacts were also formed with other European Marxist groups—the **Red Army Faction** in Germany, the **Red Brigades** in Italy, and the **Action Directe** in France. More recently, ETA leaders have cooperated with the Breton and Corsican separatists.

The Spanish government has taken a series of steps to curtail ETA activities. First among them has been to ban the ETA's political wing, **Herri Batasuna**. This action intended to end the political power of the ETA in Basque country municipalities. Increased police and military pressure on ETA leadership has been the next step. This pressure has caused many ETA activists to flee to France. Diplomatic overtures to France have caused the ETA to lose much of its sanctuary in France. Despite these actions, the ETA still has considerable strength among the Basque population of northern Spain, and it is still able to undertake terrorist acts throughout Spain. **See also** Herri Batasuna (Popular Unity); Popular Front for the Liberation of Palestine (PFLP).

Suggested readings: J. Agirre, *Operation Ogro: The Execution of Admiral Luis Carrero Blanco* (New York: Quadrangle, 1975); Yonah Alexander, Michael S. Swetnam, and Herbert M. Levine, *ETA: Profile of a Terrorist Group* (Ardsley, NY: Transnational, 2001); Robert P. Clark, *The Basque Insurgents* (Madison: University of Wisconsin Press, 1984); Paddy Woodworth, *Dirty War, Clean Hands: ETA, the GAL, and Spanish Democracy* (Cork, Ireland: Cork University Press, 2001).

Evola, Julius Cesare Andrea (1898–1974) (Italy)

Julius Evola was the leading philosopher of the European neo-fascist movement. He was born on May 19, 1898, in Rome, Italy. Evola descended from an aristocratic Sicilian family and was raised a strict Catholic. In his early education, Evola showed an aptitude for art and literature. He started out as a Dada artist and poet before turning to journalism. In 1917, he joined the Italian army as an artillery officer. After the war ended, Evola returned to Rome where he wrote for the Dada journal *Revue Bleu*. His intellectual interests began to shift from literature to philosophy, and he became a student of magic, the occult, alchemy, and Eastern religions.

After witnessing Benito Mussolini's March on Rome in 1922, Evola became fascinated with fascism. Although he never joined Mussolini's Fascist Party, Evola accepted the Fascist state. In the 1920s and 1930s, he wrote several books on political philosophy, some of which were critical of the Mussolini regime. Evola was critical of the Fascist regime because it was not fascist enough. In 1927, his book *Pagan Imperialism* (*Imperialismo pagano*) appeared, and in it he attacked the Catholic Church. Later he opposed the Lateran Accords that made peace between the Mussolini regime and the Catholic Church. He also served as the cultural writer of the influential journal, *The Fascist Regime* (*Il Regime Fascista*). Later, Evola became influential with Mussolini, but only through his writings. Evola's brand of racism, which emphasizes the spiritual side, especially attracted Mussolini's attention.

As much as Evola was supportive of Mussolini, he admired Adolf Hitler and the Nazi regime more. Evola believed that the Nazis had created fascism in its most sublime form, and his books and lectures were popular in Germany. He spent the last two years of World War II in Germany working with the Nazis in the Security Service of the Reichsführer SS, or SD (Sicherheilsdienst des Reichführers-SS). He wanted Germany and Italy to have a spiritual unity that would provide a new order in Europe after a German victory. In 1945, Evola was seriously wounded during the Russian aerial bombardment of Vienna. His spinal cord was damaged and he was in a wheelchair the rest of his life. During the immediate postwar world, Evola remained in a hospital in Bad Ischl in Upper Austria. He returned to Rome, Italy, in 1948.

In the postwar world, Evola continued his writings on political philosophy, but he still refused to join any political party. Leaders of the neo-fascist **Italian Social Movement** (MSI) claimed him as their philosopher-king, but he barely tolerated their attention. In June 1951, Italian authorities arrested Evola and other neo-fascists for plotting to overthrow the Italian state. After a lengthy trial that lasted from June to November 1951, he was acquitted.

Evola's philosophy was a complete rejection of modern society and its mores. Franco Ferraresi, a professor of political sociology at the University of Turin, characterized Evola's philosophy as "antiegalitarian, antiliberal, antidemocratic and antipopular." It was also characterized by a severe pessimism about the direction of modern civilization. Evola had made his views known in his 1934 book *Revolt against the Modern World* (*Rivolta control il mondo moderno*). Evola believed that European society had declined since the French Revolution. In his view, capitalism and Marxism were symptoms of this decline.

His solution was that the state must have primacy over civil society. Rulers of the state were to be an elite that would be imbued with spiritual ideals. His idea of a worthy elite was an organization similar to the Nazi SS or the Rumanian Iron Guard. These organizations attracted him because of the nihilism and emphasis on heroic violence. Evola also espoused racial purity that excluded inferiors, but it was a spiritual racism that differed from the raw racism of the Nazis. His negative attitude toward women caused him to exclude them from any serious consideration.

Evola was frustrated by the inability of the Italian right to unite and establish his form of society. In 1953, he published the book *Men among the Ruins* (*Gli Uomini e le Robine*) in which expressed his political views. His pessimism with modern society attracted Italian youth and young neo-fascists around Europe. He also attracted attention from neo-Nazis such as the American Francis Parker Yockey. Even Evola's death on August 11, 1974, has not limited his influ-ence. Two of his disciples, Girogio Freda and Adriano Romualdi, continued to advance his ideas. After scattering Evola's ashes in the Italian Alps, his admirers established the Foundation Evola to advance his ideas. In the Internet age, a Web site exists that serves as a forum to discuss Evola's ideas. **See also** Italian Social Movement (Movimento Sociale Italiano) (MSI).

Suggested readings: Kevin Coogan, *Dreamer of the Day: Francis Parker Yockey and the Postwar Fascist International* (Brooklyn, NY: Autonomedia, 1999); Richard Drake, *The Revolutionary Mystique and Terrorism in Contemporary Italy* (Bloomington, IN: Indiana University Press, 1989); Franco Ferraresi, *Threats to Democracy: The Radical Right in Italy after the War* (Princeton, NJ: Princeton University Press, 1996); H. T. Hansen, "Julius Evola's Political Endeavors," in Julius Evola, *Men among the Ruins: Post-War Reflections of a Radical Traditionalist* (Rochester, VT: Inner Traditions, 2002); Leonard B. Weinberg, *After Mussolini: Italian Neo-Fascism and the Nature of Fascism* (Washington, DC: University Press of America, 1979); Leonard B. Weinberg and William Lee Eubank, *The Rise and Fall of Italian Terrorism* (Boulder, CO: Westview Press, 1987).

F

Fadlallah, Sayyid Muhammad Husayn (1935–) (Lebanon)

Sayyid Fadlallah is the spiritual mentor of the radical Shi'ite **Hezbollah** group in Lebanon. He was born in 1935 in Najaf, Iraq. His father was a Shi'ite cleric. Although his family had lived for generations in Iraq, the family was originally from Lebanon. He received a classical Islamic education in the Shi'ite schools of Najaf. In 1966, Fadlallah moved to Beirut, Lebanon, where he soon earned a reputation as a Shi'ite theologian. There he established the Circle of Brotherhood and the Islamic Legal Institute. His Friday sermons at a Beirut mosque attracted large crowds. His preachings extolled the virtues of an Islamic state and attracted numerous followers among the impoverished Shi'ites of southern Lebanon. After 1982, he was instrumental in the formation of the Shi'ite Hezbollah group, but only as spiritual advisor.

Fadlallah's relationship with Hezbollah has always been close. He is the leading exponent of religious issues in the Hezbollah, but he has maintained independence from it on politics. Fadlallah was an earlier follower of **Ayatollah Khomeini**'s views on the need for clerical leadership in an Islamic state, but later he became critical of Khomeini and Iran's actions. He has been more reluctant to accept terrorism, and his position on Hezbollah's suicide missions has been lukewarm. In his 1976 two-volume book *Islam and the Logic of Force*, however, he justified the use of violence in the defense of Islam. Fadlallah has long been hostile to the United States and Saudi Arabia. His hostility to the United States is partly because he believes that American agents tried to kill him in a 1985 bombing attempt that killed 85 people. Fadlallah survived five assassination attempts in the early and mid-1980s without injury. He also is convinced in the inevitability of America's fall as a world power and the eventual triumph of Islam. Fadlallah considers Saudi Arabia and its claim of devotion to Islamic law a fraud. His prestige in Lebanon is immense among mainstream Shi'ites in Lebanon. **See also** Hezbollah (Party of God) (Lebanon).

Suggested readings: Hala Jaber, *Hezbollah: Born with a Vengeance* (New York: Columbia University Press, 1997); Judith Miller, "Faces of Fundamentalism: Hassan al-Turabi and Muhammed Fadlallah," *Foreign Affairs* (November–December 1994), p. 123; Amal Saad-Ghorayeb, *Hizbu'llah: Politics and Religion* (London: Pluto Press, 2002); Robin Wright,

Grand Ayatollah Sayyid Muhammad Husayn Fadlallah, speaks at the American University of Beirut on October 30, 2001. Fadlallah accused U.S. forces of trying out their weaponry against Afghans and of killing civilians. In 1995 President Clinton ordered Fadlallah's assets frozen as part of Clinton's anti-terror campaign. (AP Photo/Hussein Malla)

Sacred Rage: The Wrath of Militant Islam (New York: Simon & Schuster, 1985).

Farabundo Martí National Liberation Front (FMLN) (El Salvador)

The Farabundo Martí National Liberation Front (FMLN) was the Marxist guerrilla group that fought a war against El Salvador from 1980 to 1992. It was named after Farabundo Martí, the Communist insurgent leader executed by the Salvadorean military in the 1932 Communist uprising. Revolutionary agitation had increased after the electoral frauds of the 1972, 1974, and 1977 elections. Right-wing death squads operated with impunity, killing those that the military considered leftists. Five guerrilla groups came together in 1980 to form the FMLN: Popular Liberation Front—Farabundo Martí (FPL), Popular Revolutionary Army (ERP), National Resistance (RN), Central American Workers Party (PRTC), and the Armed Forces of Liberation (FAL). Cayetano Carpio, a former baker, had organized the FPL after breaking away from the Salvadorean Communist Party (PCS) in 1970. Another splinter group from the PCS was the ERP, which left the PCS in 1972. Joaquin Villalobos and Guadalupe Martinez were its leaders. Ernesto Jovel separated also in 1972 from the ERP and formed the RN. Not long afterward, Roberto Roca founded the PRTC. FAL, the armed wing of the Salvadorean Communist Party began operations in 1979 under the combined leadership of the brothers Shafik Handal and Farid Handal. The success of the Nicaraguan Revolution in July 1979 provided the impetus for the unification of the groups into the FMLN. By naming the new movement after the revolutionary hero Farabundo Martí, the FMLN attached itself firmly into the Salvadorean revolutionary tradition.

Because the Farabundo Martí National Liberation Front served as an umbrella organization for the five guerrilla groups, the administrative structure assumed added importance. A five-person directorate, the Unified Revolutionary Directorate (DRU), handled executive functions. Each member of the directorate represented one of the of the five guerrilla groups. Headquarters of the DRU always remained in Managua, Nicaragua. In theory, each member of the directorate had equal authority. In practice, however, the representatives of the two largest groups, ERP and FPL, had more influence. Two political organizations reported to the DRU: the Popular Revolutionary Bloc (BPR) and the Democratic Revolutionary Front (FDR). The BPR had responsibility for domestic politics and the FDR for international politics.

The military operational structure of the FMLN was built to support the field operations of five groups. Five military leaders of each group formed the General Command (CG). These 25 military leaders planned military strategy for the FMLN. Once general strategy had been decided within the General Command, orders were sent out to the military commands of the five groups. Operational control resided in the local units. This system allowed for operational flexibility, and, at least in the beginning, it also allowed for confusion because not all the groups cooperated with each other. Later, cooperation between groups improved and military operations were more successful.

Because no political or military ideology predominated within the FMLN, the military leadership adopted a multifaceted approach to warfare. The overall theme always remained prolonged popular war, but various approaches to this theme were adopted. Three operational strategies were adopted: guerrilla warfare, conventional maneuver warfare, and attrition warfare. Each group within the FMLN had its preferred approach, and the leaderships of these groups carried out different types of operations in their respective areas of operation. The goal of the FMLN from the beginning, however, was to build a well-equipped army of 15,000 men and women able to defeat the Salvadorean army in the field.

The leadership of the FMLN launched a military campaign on January 10, 1981. These leaders had high hopes of victory. After several initial successes, the offensive bogged down in February 1981. A key factor was the growing American aid to El Salvador's government. In December 1981 the Salvadorean army killed around 1,000 villagers near the village of El Mozote. A lengthy guerrilla war lasted for the next decade with the FMLN able to control large parts of El Salvador, but it was unable to defeat the Salvadorean military forces in the field. Help for the FMLN in the form of military supplies came from the **Sandinista National Liberation Front** (FSLN) in Nicaragua, but it was not enough for victory. In 1986, talks between the Salvadorean government and the FMLN took place without results. Talks resumed in 1988 in Mexico and Costa Rica. In November 1989, the FMLN launch its last major offensive attacking military centers in major cities.

The combination of military and political stalemate led to the FMLN to negotiate a permanent armistice in January 1992. This time, the United Nations sponsored the negotiations between the FMLN and the Salvadorean government. On January 16, 1992, the two sides signed the Chapultepec Peace Accord, which ended the civil war in El Salvador. Since the peace accord, the FMLN has operated as a political party with indifferent success.

The lack of success has caused a split between factions in the FMLN. Members of the party have been divided into the orthodox faction that remains committed to the original communist/socialist agenda and the reformer faction that is more pragmatic and tends toward social democracy. A center faction, the institutionalists, has formed a third force to merge over the differences between the two more extreme wings of the party. This divergence of views has led to the purging of the reformist leader Facundo Guardado in October 2001. **See also** Sandinista National Liberation Front (Frente Sandinista de Liberación Nacional) (FSLN).

Suggested readings: Robert Armstrong and Janet Shenk, *El Salvador, the Face of Revolution* (Boston: South End Press, 1982); Terry Lynn Karl, "El Salvador's Negotiated Revolution," *Foreign Affairs* (March–April 1992), p. 147; Tommie Sue Montgomery, *Revolution in El Salvador: From Civil Strife to Civil Peace*, 2nd ed. (Boulder, CO: Westview, 1995); Jose Angel Moroni Bracamonte and David E. Spencer, *Strategy and Tactics of the Salvadoran FMLN Guerrillas: Last Battle of the Cold War, Blueprint for Future Conflicts* (Westport, CT: Praeger, 1995); Alan Riding, "Salvador Rebels: Five-Sided Alliance Searching for New, Moderate Image," *New York Times* (March 18, 1982), sec. A, p. 1; Margaret Swedish, *Central America/Mexico Report*, http://www.rtfcam.org/report/volume_21/No_4/article_8.htm/ (accessed October 2001).

FARC (See Revolutionary Armed Forces of Colombia) (Columbia)

Al-Fatah (Palestine)

The Fatah terrorist group is one of the founding members of the **Palestine Liberation Organization** (PLO). **Yasser Arafat**, Khalil Wazir, and three other Palestinian activists started al-Fatah in Kuwait in October 1957 as an underground movement to lead military operations against Israel. The name al-Fatah means "the conquest," but it was created as a reverse acronym for Harakat al-Tarir al-Filistini (Palestinian Liberation Movement). After the three other founding members left al-Fatah, Arafat and Wazir began a recruitment campaign among the Palestinians. They published a monthly magazine, *Our Palestine*, to help recruitment and to attack their enemies. In February 1963, al-Fatah's first Central Committee was formed with 10 members. Arafat was 1 of the 10 members of a collective leadership. He soon became restless and started lobbying for more responsibility. His chief opponent on the Central Committee was Khalad Hassan, who opposed premature military action. At first, al-Fatah was no more than a discussion group, with the members of the Central Committee always discussing strategy. Arafat and Wazir pressured for military operations against Israel, but the other members insisted on support from Arab states before engaging in military force.

The establishment of the Palestine Liberation Organization (PLO) in 1964 almost destroyed al-Fatah. Many of the military cadre in al-Fatah left it to join the military wing of the PLO—the Palestine Liberation Army (PLA). One estimate is that at least 80 percent of al-Fatah's members left to join the PLA. Only after it became apparent that the sponsors of the PLO and the PLA—Gamal Abdel Nasser and the Arab states—had no intention of launching hostilities against Israel did al-Fatah recover.

Arafat and Wazir were finally able to persuade al-Fatah's Central Committee to start military operations against Israel. Abu Youseff was appointed military leader, much to Arafat's displeasure. Although the first few raids in early January 1965 were disappointing, 10 sabotage raids were carried out in the first three months of 1965. To fool their enemies, al-Fatah launched operations under the codename "al-Assifa" (The Storm). Arafat replaced Youseff as military commander in the spring of 1965. He soon found himself in opposition to the Central Committee over reducing military operations, and so Arafat simply ignored their directives. Khalad Hassan and the committee tried to regain control by depriving Arafat and his military command of funding. By this time,

Arafat had left Lebanon and was operating out of Damascus, Syria. Funding from Palestinians working in Germany and from students saved Arafat and his military command, but al-Fatah's military operations ceased until the funds arrived.

The defeat of Arab forces in the 1967 Arab-Israeli War made it possible to revive al-Fatah's military campaign. After Arafat was reaffirmed as its military commander, he moved al-Fatah's military operations to the West Bank. They planned to begin raids on August 28, 1967, but actual operations commenced in early September. This campaign ended in failure because Israeli security forces suppressed it and the Palestinian population only tolerated the Fatah fighters. By the end of December, al-Fatah had been defeated in the field. Arafat decided to relocate operations in Jordan. When Israeli forces raided the Karameh base camp in Jordan on March 21, 1968, al-Fatah fighters and the Jordanian army repulsed the raid. This victory helped recruitment, but the number of volunteers was too many to be easily absorbed in the existing command structure.

Al-Fatah moved its operations with the PLO into Lebanon after the expulsion from Jordan by the Jordanian army. Bitter fighting by the PLO with the Jordanians in September 1970 led to military defeat. A faction of al-Fatah formed the terrorist group Black September to avenge the defeat. Al-Fatah's move into Lebanon allowed it to reestablish military and terrorist operations against Israel. It also led to friction with the Shi'ite majority in southern Lebanon. The Israeli invasion of Lebanon in 1982 was another defeat for al-Fatah. Al-Fatah left Lebanon with the PLO and moved its headquarters to Tunisia.

The **Intifada** in 1987 allowed al-Fatah to revitalize. Much like the rest of the PLO, the leaders of al-Fatah were surprised by the outbreak of the Intifada. Good relations had earlier been established with the **Palestine Islamic Jihad** in the Gaza Strip, but the formation of **Hamas** in December 1987 posed a new threat to al-Fatah. Leaders of Hamas wanted noth-

ing to do with the secularism of either the PLO or al-Fatah. This incompatibility between secularism and Islamist ideology has never been bridged. Even the prospect of more Palestinian autonomy as outlined in the Oslo Accords did not improve relationships.

The formation of the Palestinian Authority (PA) in the aftermath of the Oslo Accords made al-Fatah into a government. Rivalry between al-Fatah and Hamas continued unabated. Efforts by Arafat to make the Palestinian Authority the de facto Palestinian government by making agreements with the Israeli government began to cause friction within al-Fatah. The military wing of al-Fatah, the al-Aqsa Martyrs' Brigades, began to act independently. Al-Fatah leaders, such a **Marwan Barghouthi**, claimed loyalty to Arafat but at the same time attacked the corruption and actions of the Palestinian Authority. Efforts to end terror attacks in the fall of 2002 caused both leaders of al-Fatah and rank-and-file members to migrate to the more extreme Hamas and Palestine Islamic Jihad. Mahmud Abbas, the Palestinian prime minister in 2003 and member of al-Fatah, caused even more defections because of his attempts to work with the Israeli government. The collapse of the Abbas government has left al-Fatah still in the hands of Arafat, but it is no longer a unified group. **See also** Arafat, Yasser; Barghouthi, Marwan bin Khatib; Hamas (Haarakat al-Muqawama al-Islami) (Islamic Resistance Movement); Palestine Islamic Jihad (PIJ); Palestine Liberation Organization (PLO).

Suggested readings: James Bennet, "For Fatah, Only a War Can Bring Peace to Mideast," *New York Times* (March 7, 2002), sec. A, p. 8; Alan Hart, *Arafat: Terrorist or Peacemaker?* (London: Sidgwick & Jackson, 1984); Isabel Kosher, "Order in the House," *Jerusalem Report* (February 10, 2003), p. 32; Khaled Abu Toameh and Gil Hoffman, "Call to End Terror Attacks Sparks Fatah Split," *Jerusalem Post* (September 11, 2002), p. 2.

Faurisson, Robert (1929–) (France)

Robert Faurisson has been the leading Holocaust denier in France for over two decades. He was born in 1929 in Great Britain. After academic training in France, he became a professor of contemporary literature at the University of Lyons. Faurisson first became notorious for his article in the French publication *Le Monde* on December 28, 1978, when he first attacked the existence of Nazi gas chambers. His thesis was that the Holocaust never happened and therefore the Germans never used gas chambers. He claimed that Jewish witnesses to the Holocaust are liars and are part of a Jewish conspiracy. An anarcho-Marxist press, La Vieille Taupe (The Old Mole), decided to publish Faurisson's books. Because of his viewpoint, Faurisson has had a long association with the American Institute for Historical Review (IHR). Besides speaking at conferences of the IHR, he wrote articles for IHR's *Journal of Historical Review*. He also supported the French **Holocaust denial** journal *Annales of Revisionist History* (*Annales d'histoire revisionniste*).

Faurisson's anti-Holocaust activities have resulted in legal troubles for him. In 1990, the French Parliament passed a law against "criminal revisionism." Faurisson was convicted of violating this law in a Paris trial in March 1991. His offense was claiming that the Nazis had no extermination plan and had built no gas chambers. He was fined $20,000. This judgment did not prevent him from helping found another Holocaust denial journal, the *Revue of Revisionist History* (*Revue d'histoire revisionniste*). Faurisson retired from the University of Lyons, but he still travels around France and Europe lecturing on literature and politics. His views have made him unpopular enough that he was mugged near his home in Vichy, France, in September 1989. This assault left him with a badly shattered jaw. He has since recovered from his injury and it has not prevented him from presenting his Holocaust denial arguments. See also Holocaust Denial.

Suggested readings: Suzanne Lowry, "Rewriters of Holocaust Face Wrath of Zionists," *Sunday Telegraph* (London) (September 24, 1989), p. 14; Kenneth S. Stern, *Holocaust Denial* (New York: American Jewish Committee, 1993);

Pierre Vidal-Naquet, *Assassins of Memory: Essay on the Denial of the Holocaust* (New York: Columbia University Press, 1992); John C. Zimmerman, *Holocaust Denial: Demographics, Testimonies and Ideologies* (Lanham, MD: University Press of America, 2000); Michel Zlotowski, "Furor at Holocaust Denier's Trial," *Jerusalem Post* (March 24, 1991), p. 1.

Fida'iyan-i Islam (See Devotees of Islam)

Fini, Gianfranco (1952–) (Italy)

Gianfranco Fini is the leading neo-fascist in Italian politics. He was born in 1952 in Bologna, Italy, to a middle-class family. His father was a civil servant and his mother a teacher. Fini's grandfather had been a Communist, but his father had been a Fascist who fought for Mussolini in the last days of World War II. In 1968, he joined the youth movement of the neo-fascist Italian Social Movement (Movimento Sociale Italiano [MSI]). His family moved to Rome in 1971, and Fini attended the University of Rome, studying psychology. He continued his political activities with the MSI and in 1977 was made secretary of the MSI's Youth Front. In 1983, he was elected to parliament as a representative of the MSI. His growing popularity both inside and outside the party led the MSI to pick him to lead the party in 1987, replacing Giorgio Almirante.

Fini decided to take the MSI into the mainstream of Italian politics. A corrupt Italian political system gave him the opportunity. In 1993, he ran for the post of mayor of Rome and received 47 percent of a runoff vote. His moderate stance on the issues earned him popularity among the Italian voters. A key supporter was Alessandra Mussolini, the granddaughter of former Italian dictator Benito Mussolini and the niece of actress Sophia Loren. Fini made headlines by calling Benito Mussolini the 20th century's "greatest statesman." Besides supporting the Mussolini's regime, Fini was able to mine anti-immigration sentiment to attract voters. He also called for the reunification of Italy with Yugoslavian territory.

Fini has won more respectability by his service in the Berlusconi governments. Fini's drive for respectability led to his disbanding of the MSI in January 1994. He replaced the MSI with a new party with a new name, the National Alliance. After a purge of the rougher elements within the MSI, most of the neo-fascists of the MSI joined him in the new party. Later in 1994, Fini concluded an alliance with Silvio Berlusconi, a media tycoon and right-wing politician. In return for his electoral support, Fini was given a ministerial post and four MSI supporters served in the government. Since then, Fini and his National Alliance had been stalwarts in the last two Berlusconi governments. Despite his ideological baggage, Fini remains one of the most popular politicians in Italian politics. **See also** Italian Social Movement (Movimento Sociale Italiano) (MSI).

Suggested readings: James Blitz, "Fini Looking to Complete His Long March to Power," *Financial Times* (London) (March 27, 2001), p. 8; Martin A. Lee, "Citizen Kane on Steroids," *In These Times* (June 25, 2001), p. 12; Peter Popham, "Il Duce's Disciple," *Independent* (London) (March 25, 1995), p. 20; Angus Roxburgh, *The Rise of the Far Right* (London: Gibson Square Books, 2002).

Fonseca Amador, Carlos (1936–1976) (Nicaragua)

Carlos Fonseca Amador was one of the founders and a key leader of the **Sandinista National Liberation Front** (Frente Sandinista de Liberación Nacional, or FSLN) in its war against the Somoza regime in Nicaragua. He was born on June 23, 1936, as the illegitimate son of the principal administrator of the agricultural properties of the Somoza family and a domestic servant in the employment of the Somozas. His mother raised him in Matagalpa, Nicaragua, and he showed early academic promise. Fonseca attended a high school in Matagalpa beginning in 1950. While in high school, he joined the Nicaraguan Communist Party (Partido Socialista Nicaragilense, or PSN). After graduation from high school, he attended the National Autono-

mous University in Managua in 1956. Fonseca soon became a prominent leftist student leader and the editor of the student newspaper *El Universitario*. He also formed a lasting friendship with Tomas Borge Martinez, a law student and student activist. Fonseca's political activities and friendships led the police to arrest him in the aftermath of the assassination of General Anastasio Somoza Garcia on September 29, 1956.

After his early release from prison, Fonseca devoted the rest of his life to being a full-time revolutionary. In 1957, the PNS sent him to the Soviet Union for further study on politics. After returning to Nicaragua in 1958, the Somoza government deported him to Guatemala as a political undesirable. Fonseca traveled to Mexico and then to Cuba in 1959 just in time to witness the triumph of the guerrilla movement of Fidel Castro. His contacts with Cuban revolutionaries convinced him that a guerrilla movement could overthrow the Somoza regime in Nicaragua. In June 1959, Fonseca joined other guerrillas under the command of Eden Pastora Gomez in an abortive invasion of Nicaragua from Honduras. He suffered a wound at the Battle of El Chaparral, but he was able to escape back to Honduras. His revolutionary activities made his membership in the more moderate PSN difficult, so he resigned from it.

After experimenting with several groups, Fonseca decided to form his own revolutionary guerrilla group. On July 23, 1961, Fonseca and his friends Tomas Borge Martinez and Silvio Mayorga formed the Sandinista National Liberation Front. In the beginning, the FSLN had only about 20 members, and its first operations were bank robberies to raise funds to support the group. Recruiting successes among students and leftists soon had the FSLN number in the lower hundreds. Early clashes with the Nicaraguan National Guard found the FSLN outgunned, and it suffered significant losses, considering its small number of fighters. Leadership mistakes also compounded the problems facing the FSLN. Recruitment became increasingly difficult because the FSLN could only operate in the remote areas of northern Nicaragua.

Often the revolutionaries had to seek refuge in Honduras.

Both in 1963 and 1967, the FSLN launched offensives, but each time it suffered defeats. Of the 85 guerrillas in the 1963 Bocay campaign only 15 survived. In January 1965, Foncesca was arrested in Guatemala in the aftermath of a bank robbery. Several FSLN members hijacked an aircraft of the U.S. United Fruit Company and they were able to bargain for the release of Fonseca and his fellow captives. In 1966, Somoza declared an amnesty and Fonseca returned to Nicaragua. Fonseca and the military leadership planned for the next guerrilla campaign throughout the remainder of 1966. Shortly after the guerrilla forces had reached staging areas, the Nicaraguan National Guard wiped out most of the guerrillas. The biggest lost was the death of Mayorga in 1967. Foncesca escaped, but in 1969 authorities in Costa Rica arrested him and kept him in jail until 1970.

After his release from jail, Foncesca returned to the guerrilla war. By then, the Sandinista National Liberation Front had become a serious threat to the Somoza regime and Fonseca's leadership role began to diminish. Several other leaders had emerged during his absence and he commanded only one of the numerous guerrilla forces. The December 1972 Managua earthquake and the inability of the Somoza regime to avoid taking advantage of relief funds encouraged more recruits into the FSLN. Fonseca died in 1976 leading FLN forces in northern Nicaragua. His death was a blow to the FSLN, but by 1976 a new generation of leaders had emerged to replace him. After the triumph of the FSLN in 1979, Fonseca was buried in a concrete tomb in Managua's Revolution Plaza. He has become a beloved martyr for the FSLN cause. Opponents of the FSLN exploded a bomb at Fonseca's tomb in November 1991, damaging it slightly, which led to major riots in Managua. See also Sandinista National Liberation Front (Frente Sandinista de Liberación Nacional) (FSLN).

Suggested readings: John A. Booth, *The End and the Beginning: The Nicaraguan Revolution* (Boulder, CO: Westview Press, 1985); Timothy C. Brown (ed.), *When the AK-47s Fall Silent: Revolutionaries, Guerrillas, and the Dangers of Peace* (Stanford, CA: Hoover Institution Press, 2000); Stephen Kinzer, *Blood of Brothers: Life and War in Nicaragua* (New York: Putnam's, 1991); Matilde Zimmermann, *Sandinista: Carlos Fonseca and the Nicaraguan Revolution* (Durham, NC: Duke University Press, 2000).

Fortuyn, Pim (1948–2002) (The Netherlands)

Pim Fortuyn was The Netherlands' leading right-wing, populist politician until his assassination in May 2002. He was born on February 19, 1948, in Velzen, The Netherlands, into a respectable Catholic family. His father was a traveling salesman and Fortuyn grew up in the village of Driehuis, just outside Amsterdam. After local schooling, he attended The Netherlands Business School in Breukelen, where he studied economics, history, law, and sociology. At this time, Fortuyn considered himself a Marxist. He was also active in the Dutch student movement. After graduating in 1970, he went to study sociology at the University of Amsterdam, where he received a doctorate in 1971. Next he enrolled at the Rilksuniversiteit Groningen for further study in sociology, and in 1980 he received his doctorate in the social sciences. After service in both government and private industry, Fortuyn obtained a teaching position at the Erasmus University in Rotterdam in 1990. While he was a successful professor, Fortuyn became fascinated with politics.

Fortuyn pursued a political career as a populist and a libertarian. Soon after taking his position at Erasmus University, he began writing in newspapers expressing his views. He began to question his Marxist views and soon developed a right-wing viewpoint. He began attacking the liberal consensus of the Dutch government, and, in particular, its open immigration policies. His target was Muslim immigration, because he believed that Muslims could not be assimilated into Dutch society. In a series of books, including *Against the Islamicisation of Our Culture*;

Pim Fortuyn, the right-wing politician accused of promoting racism, wipes his face after a protester threw a pie at him in The Hague, March 14, 2002. Fortuyn was on his way to present his book outlining his political platform. Fortuyn, who had been critical of environmental and animal rights groups, would be shot to death two months late by animal rights activist Volkert van der Graaf. (AP Photo/Phil Nijuis)

Fifty Years Israel, but for How Long?; and *The Orphaned Community*, he attacked Islamic fundamentalism as incompatible with Western life. His anti-immigrant viewpoint corresponded closely to that of the French and Austrian right-wing leaders, **Jean-Marie Le Pen** and **Jörg Haider**, respectively, but Fortuyn rejected both because of their neo-Nazism and anti-Semitism. Fortuyn openly flouted his gay lifestyle and he advanced its cause in public. His other views included opposition to the European Union, the advocacy of drug legalization, the promotion of laxer rules on euthanasia, and the advocacy of a libertarian view of government.

Fortuyn's political viewpoint was becoming increasingly popular with Dutch voters. He had joined and become the leader of the Liveable Netherlands (Leefbaar Nederland) party in November 2001. He turned this party toward the radical right, but he was removed from leadership of the party in February 2002 because of his charge to abolish the Dutch constitution's Article One, which bans discrimination. He reacted by establishing his own party, List Fortuyn, to contest the Dutch March elections. His success in these elections gave him hope that he could play a leading role in the Dutch government by winning in the May 2002 elections. Fortuyn knew that his confrontational style had risks, so he employed bodyguards. Among his controversial statements had been dismissive remarks about the environmental and animal rights movements. On May 6, 2002, after Fortuyn left a radio station in

Hilversum near Amsterdam, animal rights activist Volkert van der Graaf shot him six times, killing him. Police arrested van der Graaf and found the murder weapon on him. Despite Fortuyn's death, his party won a resounding victory at the polls and it participated in the creation of a new Dutch government. Fortuyn had been popular and his funeral was widely attended. **See also** Haider, Jörg; Le Pen, Jean-Marie.

Suggested readings: David Brooks, "The 'Fascist' and the 'Activist,'" *Weekly Standard* (London)] (Mary 20, 2002), vol. 7, p. 13; Ambrose Evans-Pritchard, "Holland's High-Camp Hero of New Politics," *Daily Telegraph* (London) (May 4, 2002), p. 16; Stryker McGuire, "Sudden Death," *Newsweek* (May 20, 2002), p. 30; Andrew Osborn, "Gay Mr. Right Woos the Dutch," *Observer* (London) (April 14, 2002), p. 21; Stephen Robinson, "Colourful Crusader Who Touched a Raw Nerve until his Death," *Daily Telegraph* (London) (May 8, 2002), p. 17; Angus Roxburgh, *Preachers of Hate: The Rise of the Far Right* (London: Gibson Square Books, 2002).

Frey, Gerhard (1933–) (Germany)

Gerhard Frey is the leader of the German extremist political party the **German People's Union** (Deutsche Volksunion, or DVU). He was born in 1933 in northern Bavaria. His family was wealthy department store owners. Frey received an education at good schools. He also earned a law degree and a Ph.D. in political science. Instead of pursuing an academic career, Frey went into the publishing business. After a stint working as a freelance journalist for the *German Soldiers' Paper* (*Deutsche Soldatenzeitung*), he bought the newspaper in the late 1950s. He renamed it the *German National Paper* (*Deutsche Nationalzeitung*) and then he started the *German Weekly Newspaper* (*Deutsche Wochenzeitung*). These newspapers served as the foundation for a publishing empire that in 1998 was estimated to be worth between $300 and $500 million. Frey also has a profitable mail order business that specializes in right-wing materials. Headquarters for Frey and his businesses are in Munich, Germany.

After establishing his business empire, Frey turned to right-wing politics. His newspapers have always touted nationalism, anti-Semitism, and anti-immigrant views. In January 1971, he founded the German People's Union as a right-wing lobby group. Then in 1987, Frey tuned the DVU into a political party. This party depends exclusively on Frey for its financial support and in return it serves as an outlet for his political ideas. Frey is not a charismatic figure and he is more comfortable operating behind the scenes. He has been careful not to let any rivals for leadership into the DVU. Frey's party has been moderately successful in German state elections. Several times it has been rumored that Frey had concluded an electoral alliance with other German right-wing parties, but each time Frey had backed out. The German government estimated in 2000 that the DVU had around 15,000 active members, but Frey claims that this figure is much too low. His party has been able to capitalize on the general economic and political malaise among young Germans following reunification in the early 1990s.

Frey has developed extensive contacts with neo-Nazis and other extremists both in Germany and in Europe. He has always been careful to skirt on the edge of German law against **Holocaust denial** and Nazism. He has espoused Germany's claim to land that formerly belonged to the German Reich under the Nazis, and he has opposed efforts for European unification. Frey developed a relationship with Franz Schönhuber and the **Republican Party**, but this relationship cost Schönhuber his leadership of that party. His friendship with the British historian and Holocaust denier **David Irving** led him to collaborate with Irving on exposing the Nazi ties of German political figures. Frey has close ties with France's right-wing political leader **Jean-Marie Le Pen** and Russia's neo-fascist leader **Vladimir Zhirinovsky**. His relationship with other German right-wing leaders is less cordial because they distrust him and they fear that his financial resources will overwhelm them. **See also** German People's Union (Deutsche Volksunion) (DVU); Republican Party (REP).

Suggested readings: Markus Krah, "Danger on the Right," *Jerusalem Report* (July 6, 1998), p. 30; Martin A. Lee, *The Beast Reawakens* (Boston: Little, Brown, 1997); David Marsh, "West German Right-Wing Publisher Combs Nazi Files in Berlin," *Financial Times* (London) (March 14, 1988), p. 3; Cas Mudde, *The Ideology of the Extreme Right* (Manchester, UK: Manchester University Press, 2000); Philip Sherwell, "Bavarian Tycoon Fans Flames of Racism," *Ottawa Citizen* (May 3, 1998), p. F8; Philip Sherwell, "Secretive Tycoon's Poll Victory Raises Nazi Fears," *Sunday Telegraph* (London) (May 3, 1998), p. 29; Denis Staunton, "Far-Right Party Little More Than One Wealthy Fanatic's Toy," *Irish Times* (April 28, 1998), p. 11.

Front de la Liberation Nationale de la Corse (Front for the National Liberation of Corsica) (FLNC) (France)

The Front de la Nationale Liberation de la Corse (Front for the National Liberation of Corsica) (FLNC) is the oldest Corsican nationalist group fighting for Corsica's independence from France. Corsican nationalists founded the FLNC in 1976. Since its inception, members of the FLNC have conducted a terrorist offensive of assassinations and bombings in Corsica and in metropolitan France. Most of the bombings have destroyed property with few people being hurt. Funding for the FLNC comes from a revolutionary tax on Corsican businesses and wealthy individuals.

The FLNC has suffered from numerous factional splits. In the early 1980s, the FLNC developed two factions: the Canal historique (Historical Faction) and the Canal habituel Usual Faction). Despite this factionalism, the FLNC continued its bombing campaign. Leaders of the FLNC declared a cease-fire and adhered to it until 1989. In 1990, a third faction, Rezistanza (Resistance), emerged. Other factions have appeared throughout the 1990s. These various factions still claim allegiance to the FLNC, but on occasions each undertakes operations against a rival faction. Throughout the 1990s, members of the FLNC have conducted an average of more than 200 bombings annually. By 2000, activists had assassinated 17 individuals.

By the late 1990s, the FLNC attracted the attention of French authorities. Negotiations of the Matignon Accords focused on the autonomy of Corsica in 2000. The French government believed that the issue of Corsican autonomy would never go away until a political settlement was reached. Helping them understand this was the contact between the FLNC and the **Irish Republican Army** (IRA). Jean-Guy Talamoni, a Corsican lawyer who is a leader in the FLNC, was active in the final negotiations. Leaders of the FLNC still have as their goal the independence of Corsica, but they accepted autonomy as the first step. In 2001, the French government and the leaders of the FLNC participated in the ongoing negotiations for the Matignon Accords. However, when the French government made changes to the settlement, the FLNC rejected the accords. The subsequent defeat of the French proposal by a 51 to 49 percent of Corsican voters ended this initiative. Leaders of the FLNC proclaimed a cease-fire on December 13, 2002, but it ended on July 11, 2003, after eight Corsicans convicted for the murder of French official Claude Erignac in 1998 were sentenced to prison for terms ranging from 15 years to life. Throughout late July and August 2003, members of the FLNC carried out a series of bombing attacks in Corsica against holiday homes, three banks, and a police station. See also Irish Republican Army (IRA).

Suggested readings: "Corsican Nationalists End Truce, Claim Attacks," *Agence France Presse* (July 18, 2003), p. 1; "Corsican Separatist Group Claims Bomb Blasts," *Agence France Presse* (August 3, 2003), p. 1; Lara Marlowe, "Independent Corsica May Be a Place Too Far for the French," *Irish Times* (August 26, 2000), p. 11; Robert Ramsay, *The Corsican Time Bomb* (Manchester, UK: Manchester University Press, 1983).

Front National (FN) (France)

The Front National (FN) is France's leading extreme right-wing political party. **Jean-Marie Le Pen**, a veteran right-wing politician; Francois Brigneuay; anti-Semitic journalists Pierre Bousquet, a veteran of the Nazi Waffen-SS, and Pierre Duran, a close friend and supporter of Le Pen; Roger Holeindre, a right-wing journalist; and Alain Robert, a leader of the neo-fascist Ordre Nouveau (New Order) founded the Front National on October 5, 1972. The initial goal of the FN was to unite all of France's right-wing parties into a coalition party that could make a serious effort to gain control of the French state by parliamentary means. Leaders of the new party elected Le Pen as its president on October 8, 1972. Le Pen's strategy was to appeal to the disaffected in France with the motto "France for the French." An essential part of this strategy included verbal attacks on immigrants, Israel, and the United States.

Supporters of the FN tend to be male and have proven to be the most loyal of any members of French political parties. FN members typically are anxious about the future and fear immigrants, crime, and social breakdown. In addition, they believe that the main mission of French women is to marry and have children, and therefore they advocate the restriction of women's rights. Party newspapers *National Hebdo* and the *Present* promote the Front National's program.

The Front National had limited electoral success during its first few years. It had almost no impact on the 1973 National Assembly elections. Le Pen ran for the French presidency in the 1974 election to replace Georges Pompidou, but he was unsuccessful. In 1981, Le Pen failed to be placed on the presidential ballot because he was unable to obtain the necessary signatures from the 500 notables. The failure of the economic policy of François Mitterrand's Socialist government and bad economic times, however, gave Le Pen and the Front National an opening. A skillful tactic of blaming immigration for French unemployment, street crime, and drugs gave the Front National an opportunity to attract French voters. After winning several municipal elections, and with the change of the French electoral law in 1985 to proportional representation, the Front National was able to win 35 seats in the 1986 elections to the National Assembly. Le Pen and the other FN deputies, however, gar-

nered negative publicity because of their bad manners and disruptions in the assembly, and FN's political success tapered after 1986. Efforts of the leaders of the FN to collaborate with other right-wing parties proved unsuccessful.

From the beginning, the Front National has been identified with its charismatic leader, Le Pen. He organized the party in an authoritarian manner with Jean-Pierre Stirbois as the party's secretary-general. Stirbois ran the FN's daily operations and he appointed hard-liners to key positions. Both Le Pen and Stirbois allowed no discussion or dissent from subordinates. This intolerance toward dissenting views led to a constant turnover of party members. Still, Harvey Simmons reported in his book on the Front National that it had 50,000 members in the 1990s, and he characterized the FN as "the most powerful and influential extreme right political party in Europe."

Stirbois's death in an automobile accident in 1988 allowed another hard-liner, **Bruno Mégret**, to succeed him as number two in the FN's hierarchy. This alliance between Le Pen and Mégret was of short duration because of the ambitions on both sides. In 1998, Mégret bolted from the FN and formed a rival right-wing party, the National Republican Movement (Mouvement National Republicain, or MNR).

Despite the schism within the Front National, Le Pen led the party to a stunning success in the first round of France's 2002 presidential election. He received 16.8 percent of the vote in the April 21, 2002, presidential vote. This result stunned French political pundits. President Jacques Chirac was able to gather allies and resoundingly defeated Le Pen in the second round of the election, but the image of Le Pen as a political force remained on the French agenda. Le Pen has used the 2002 success to begin grooming his youngest daughter, Marine Le Pen, to replace him as head of the Front National. **See also** Le Pen, Jean-Marie; Mégret, Bruno.

Suggested readings: Julian Barnes, "French Farce," *Guardian* [London] (May 3, 2002), p. G2;

James Cohen, "Le Pen's Pitchfork Populism," *In These Times* 20 (October 28–November 10, 1996), p. 25; Christopher Flood, "Organizing Fear and Indignation: The Front National in France," in Richard J. Golsan (ed.), *Fascism's Return: Scandal, Revision, and Ideology since 1980* (Lincoln: University of Nebraska Press, 1998); Harvey G. Simmons, *The French National Front: The Extremist Challenge to Democracy* (Boulder, CO: Westview Press, 1996); Alex Duval Smith, "Racist Party Wins Over the Workers," *Guardian* (London) (November 3, 1996), p. 21.

G

GAL (See Anti-Terrorist Liberation Group)

Al-Gama'a al-Islamiyya (See Islamic Group)

Genoud, François (1915–1996) (Switzerland)

François Genoud was a Swiss banker who assisted extremist groups from neo-Nazis to Middle East terrorists. He was born in 1915 in Lusanne, Switzerland. After a trip to Germany and a meeting with Adolf Hitler, Genoud became a Nazi sympathizer. He then became a member of the Swiss Nazi Party. During World War II, he played an active role in the negotiations between Allen Dulles, the head of the American OSS (Office of Strategic Services), and Nazi SS agents trying to end the war. After the war, Genoud acquired the publication rights to the works of Hitler, Martin Bormann, and Joseph Goebbels. He was also active in the postwar neo-Nazi movement and had contacts with former Nazi leader General **Otto Remer** and others.

Genoud became the banker of choice of both the neo-Nazi movement and Middle East extremist groups, earning the nickname the "Black Banker." After developing con-

tacts with the Egyptian government of President Gamal Abdel Nasser, he started shipping arms to the Algerian independence movement FLN (National Liberation Front). By 1954, Genoud was serving as the FLN's banker. After Algerian independence, he was appointed head of the Arab Popular Bank (Banque Populaire Arabe) in Algiers. After his involvement in a feud among Algerian leaders, Genoud was arrested in October 1964 for an illegal transfer of funds. This ended his involvement with Algeria.

In the late 1960s, Genoud turned his attention to supporting anti-Israel groups. His friendship with Wadi Haddad, the operational head of **Popular Front for the Liberation of Palestine** (PFLP), led him to back PFLP operations with funding and legal support. He also established a working relationship with the leaders of the **Palestine Liberation Organization** (PLO). Genoud openly applauded Black September's attack on Israeli athletes at the Olympic games in Munich, Germany.

While he supported anti-Israel groups, Genoud retained his neo-Nazi contacts. In 1982, Klaus Barbie, the accused Nazi war criminal, was extradited from Bolivia to France. Genoud and his close associate Jacques Vergès provided the funds and the legal defense for Barbie. They used the trial to attack Barbie's accusers and at the same time to highlight France's crimes against Algeria. Despite their defense, Barbie was convicted of war crimes.

Genoud's last contribution to extremism was his support for the terrorist **Ilich Ramirez Sánchez**, or Carlos the Jackal. After the Sudanese government relinquished Sánchez to French authorities on August 15, 1994, he was brought to France to stand trial for the killing of two French policemen. Genoud arranged the defense for Sánchez, but despite Genoud's efforts, Sánchez was convicted. Genoud took the occasion to express his admiration for Sánchez as a hero of the Palestinian struggle. By this time Genoud was considered by extremists as the grand old man of extremist causes. Despondent about his increasing ill health, Genoud committed suicide by drinking a cocktail of drugs in his home in Pully, a district of Geneva, Switzerland, on May 30, 1996. **See also** Palestine Liberation Organization (PLO); Popular Front for the Liberation of Palestine (PFLP); Remer, Otto Ernst; Sánchez, Ilich Ramirez (Carlos the Jackal).

Suggested readings: Kevin Coogan, *Dreamer of the Day: Francis Parker Yockey and the Postwar Fascist International* (Brooklyn, NY: Autonomedia, 1999); John Follain, *Jackal: The Complete Story of the Legendary Terrorist, Carlos the Jackal* (New York: Arcade, 1998); Martin A. Lee, *The Beast Reawakens* (Boston: Little, Brown, 1997).

German Alternative (Deutsche Alternative) (DA) (Germany)

The German Alternative was the leading neo-Nazi party in Germany in the early 1990s. **Michael Kühnen** founded the group in May 1989 to unify the various German neo-Nazi groups. Kühnen had been active in German right-wing politics and believed that a successful neo-Nazi party could achieve political power in Germany. He believed in a peaceful transition of power and avoided unnecessary violence, using Hitler's electoral tactics. Kühnen's plan was to appeal to all discontented elements in German society by providing them with Hitler's type of authoritarian leadership. The party had success in attracting neo-Nazis from the former East

Germany. A program of anti-immigrant agitation and the formation of "foreign-free zones" was popular among younger Germans. This party never had more than 1,000 members, but it had a significant following among neo-Nazis and **skinheads**. Much of the propaganda for the DA came from Gary Lauck and his propaganda mill in Lincoln, Nebraska.

The biggest problem for the German Alternative was with leadership. Kühnen was an effective leader, but his death from complications from AIDS in April 1991 left a leadership vacuum. Gottfried Kussel, a veteran Austrian neo-Nazi, succeeded Kühnen as head of the German Alternative. Kussel believed in more violent tactics and soon the members of the German Alternative began having legal problems. On January 7, 1992, Kussel was arrested in Vienna for Nazi activities and sent to prison. His successor was Frank Hubner, a former official in the East German Communist youth movement. The German government banned the German Alternative on December 10, 1992, and informed Hubner that he was forbidden to hold party meetings or spread neo-Nazi propaganda. **See also** Kühnen, Michael; Republican Party (REP).

Suggested readings: Marc Fisher, "Bonn Bans Neo-Nazis' Main Party" *Washington Post* (December 11, 1992), p. A43; Paul Hockenos, *Free to Hate: The Rise in Post-Communist Eastern Europe* (New York: Routledge, 1993); Francine S. Kiefer, "German Crackdown Signals Commitment to End Violence," *Christian Science Monitor* (December 11, 1992), p. 3; Michael Schmidt, *The New Reich: Violent Extremism in Unified Germany and Beyond* (New York: Pantheon Books, 1993).

German National Democratic Party (Nationaldemokratische Partei Deutschlands) (NPD) (Germany)

The German National Democratic Party (Nationaldemokratische Partei Deutschlands, or NPD) is the oldest of the German neo-Nazi parties. In the mid-1950s, leading neo-Nazis formed the German Reich Party (Deutsche Reichspartei) and it had some successes in the 1959 local elections. Several right-wing groups, including the German Reich Party, merged on November 28, 1964, to form the German National Democratic Party. Fritz Thielen was the first party chairperson, but the major leader was Adolf von Thadden. A majority of the leaders of the NPD were former members of the National Socialist German Worker's Party (NSDAP), or Nazi Party. In 1967, Thadden replaced Thielen after a short power struggle. From the beginning, the NPD wanted to reestablish the 1937 German borders. Territorial demands included the incorporation into Germany of East Germany, Alsace-Lorraine from France, the former Sudetenland from the Czech Republic, East Prussia from Russia, and former German lands in western Poland.

The German National Democratic Party had high hopes of electoral success in the 1969 federal elections. These high hopes were crushed after it gained only 4.3 percent of the votes and no seats in the Bundestag. This defeat caused the leadership to reexamine its political strategy. Since then, electoral successes have become even more difficult as other neo-Nazi groups have formed to challenge the dominance of the NPD.

Internal dissension also weakened the German National Democratic Party. Leadership struggles and the formation of the **German People's Union** in 1971 caused a membership drain. In November 1971, Thadden stepped down as leader, and he was replaced with Martin Mussgnug. Many of the newer neo-Nazi groups have been able to attract younger members because of their encouragement and acceptance of violence. The NPD was the first right-wing party to discover the political advantages of attacking foreign workers. Elements of the NPD contacted **skinhead** groups to establish a working relationship at election time. Despite this alliance, leaders of the NPD have been reluctant to commit further to violence and possible revolution. They prefer to attain political power at the ballot box. Leaders of the NPD welcomed German unification as a positive first step in the revival of Germany's natural frontiers. The NPD has managed to survive, but by the 1990s it was only a shadow of its former size and prestige. **See also** German People's Union (Deutsche Volksunion) (DVU); Skinhead Movement.

Suggested readings: Anti-Defamation League, *The Skinhead International: A Worldwide Survey of Neo-Nazi Skinheads* (New York: Anti-Defamation League, 1995); Paul Hockenos, *Free to Hate: The Rise of the Right in Post-Communist Eastern Europe* (New York: Routledge, 1993); Cas Mudde, *The Ideology of the Extreme Right* (Manchester, UK: Manchester University Press, 2000).

German People's Union (Deutsche Volksunion) (DVU) (Germany)

The German People's Union (DVU) is the second-largest neo-Nazi party in Germany. **Gerhard Frey**, a wealthy publisher, along with 13 others, founded the DVU in January 1971 after a split with the **German National Democratic Party** (NPD). Headquarters for the DVU is in Munich. The DVU is Frey's party, and without him the party would disappear. Frey has made the DVU into the defender of Nazi Germany, including its anti-Semitism. The party's newspaper, *German National Newspaper* (*Die Deutsche National Zeitung*), published from Munich, has a circulation of around 100,000 subscribers and advances a neo-Nazi line that includes **Holocaust denial**.

For a time, it seemed that the newer **Republican Party** would supplant the DVU as the leading neo-Nazi party in the 1980s, but the DVU survived and Frey was able to lead the DVU to several local election successes in the early 1990s. Frey, an admirer of the Russian right-wing politician **Vladimir Zhirinovsky**, concluded a strategic alliance with Russian extremists. He became Zhirinovsky's principal German contact and they agreed to a German-Russian alliance that would divide Eastern Europe between Germany and Russia. During the Cold War, Frey backed the North Atlantic Treaty Organization (NATO), but he later became a critic of NATO and reversed his position. Frey also backed Saddam Hussein during the Gulf War in 1991.

Frey led the German People's Union to a surprisingly strong showing in Saxony-Anhalt in 1998. His party was able to capitalize on economic distress in Saxony-Anhalt and political unrest. Frey pumped an estimated $1.7 million into an election campaign to attract young Germans from former East Germany. By winning 13 percent of the vote in April 1998, the DVU became a player on the national German political scene. **See also** Holocaust Denial; Zhirinovsky, Vladimir Volfovich.

Suggested readings: Tony Czuczka, "German Rightist Extremist Triumphs," Associated Press News Service (April 27, 1998), p.1; Andress Goh, "Germany's Ultra Right-Wing" *Straits Times* (Singapore) (May 5, 1998), p. 42; Martin A. Lee, *The Beast Reawakens* (Boston: Little, Brown, 1997); Cas Mudde, *The Ideology of the Extreme Right* (Manchester, UK: Manchester University Press, 2000); Tony Paterson, "Rise of Germany's Far-Right Could Spell Defeat for Schroder's SPD," *Sunday Telegraph* (London) (September 5, 1999), p. 22.

Al-Ghozi, Fathur Rohman (1971–2003) (Indonesia)

Fathur Rohman al-Ghozi is one of the leading operatives of the Indonesian Islamic extremist group **Jemaah Islamiyah** (JI). He was born on February 17, 1971, in Kebonzar on the island of Java. His father was a member of East Java's provincial parliament. Al-Ghozi was the eldest of four children. Because of al-Ghozi's early interest in religion, his parents sent him at age 12 to a religious school at Sekola Dasar, where he stayed from 1978 to 1984. Then he attended the radical Islamist religious school in the Ngruki village in Solo, central Java. Abu Bakar Bashir ran this school with an emphasis on building a strict Islamic society. Al-Ghozi remained there throughout the late 1980s and early 1990s. After winning a scholarship, he continued his religious studies in Lahore, Pakistan. It was at this school that al-Ghozi was recruited to the Jemaah Islamiyah in 1992. Twice, in 1993 and 1994, he traveled to Afghanistan for weapons and explosives training. After this training, al-Ghozi was considered trained enough to be sent on a mission to the Philippines in 1996.

Al-Ghozi spent the next four years in and out of the Philippines. He established close working relationships with the **Moro National Liberation Front** (MNLF). In 1998, al-Ghozi worked as an instructor at an MNLF camp in Mindanao training various nationalities in terrorist tactics and explosives. Later in December 2000, al-Ghozi planned and then coordinated the December 30, 2000, bombing campaign in Manila, Philippines. Five bombs exploded around Manila, killing 22 and wounding over 100 people.

After the Philippines mission, al-Ghozi's handlers in Jemaah Islamiya sent him to Singapore for operations there. He acquired explosives and weapons for a series of major terrorist attacks in Singapore. However, authorities arrested him on January 15, 2002, in Manila after finding explosive components in his possession. Unlike other captured Islamist terrorists, al-Ghozi began cooperating with Western intelligence. He gave testimony that revealed the association between Jemaah Islamiya and **al-Qaeda** as well as the nature of the training and operations of the MNLF. He remained in a Philippine prison serving a 12-year sentence for possession of explosives until he escaped on July 13, 2003. His escape with two other convicted terrorists has caused a major scandal in the Philippine government. Al-Ghozi was free for over three months until Philippine police caught up with him on October 12, 2003. A rebel informant fingered him for the police, and in a gun battle al-Ghozi was killed. **See also** Bashir, Abu Bakar; Hambali (Riduan Isamuddin); Jemaah Islamiyah (Islamic Community) (JI); Moro National Liberation Front (MNLF); Al-Qaeda (The Base).

Suggested readings: Rohan Gunaratna, *Inside Al Qaeda: Global Network of Terror* (New York: Columbia University Press, 2002); Kimina Lyall, "How al-Ghozi Walked Out of Jail," *Weekend Australian* (Sydney) (July 19, 2003), p. 1; Dan Murphy, "Al Qaeda's Asian 'Quartermaster,'" *Christian Science Monitor* (February 12, 2002), p. 6; Philip P. Pan, "Philippine Arrest Offers Clues to Web of Asian Terrorists," *Washington Post* (Feb. 9, 2002), p. A18; Raissa Robles, "Terrorism's Old

Boys' Network," *South China Morning Post* (June 29, 2003), p. 11.

Giotopoulos, Alexandros (1944–) (Greece)

Alexandros Giotopoulos was the ideological head of the Greek terrorist group **Revolutionary Organization 17 November** (17 November). He was born in 1944 in Paris into a prominent Trotskyist family. His father, a close friend of Leon Trotsky until they had a falling out, had fought in the Spanish Civil War, and he had headed a powerful Greek movement, the Archeio Marists, in Greece's civil war. His father later began compromising with the Greek right wing against the Greek Communists, and this action caused his son much unhappiness. Since Giotopoulos held dual French and Greek citizenship, he traveled with his family back and forth between France and Greece. Most of his education was in France and he studied at the Paris University Faculty of Law and Social Sciences. In 1968, he participated in the student uprisings in France as the head of the Greek Student Union of France. His opposition to the Greek military dictatorship led to his joining the Greek Communist Party. In 1969, he founded the May 29 Movement as a group to lead an armed rebellion against the Greek government. Giotopoulos also traveled to Cuba to study revolutionary strategy and tactics. After the May 29 Movement dissolved, he formed another group, the Revolutionary Popular Struggle. After an argument over tactics, this group also disappeared.

Giotopoulos returned to Greece in 1974 after the collapse of the Greek military dictatorship. In 1974, he was one of the founders of 17 November, a small urban terrorist group that never numbered more than a dozen at any one time. The group adopted the name 17 November after the date of the suppression of student demonstrations in Athens on November 17, 1973. Giotopoulos operated behind the scenes, posing as a university professor of mathematics and using the name Michael Oikonomous. He shared his time between an apartment in an Athens suburb and at a home on the island of Lipsi in the Aegean Sea. Under his leadership, 17 November committed at least 23 assassinations, and numerous bombings and bank robberies.

Giotopoulos's career as head of 17 November came to an end in July 2002. Two events caused attention to center on 17 November: the Olympic games and the death of British Brigadier Stephen Saunders in 2000. Greece was under international pressure to assure that the 2004 Athens Olympics would be peaceful. The assassination of the British brigadier caused the Greek government to invite Scotland Yard to investigate the activities of 17 November. These factors and the accidental explosion of a bomb on June 29, 2002, by Savas Xiros, a member of 17 November, combined to expose the group. Within weeks 12 members of 17 November were identified and several members of the Xiros family confessed to assassinations. Fingerprints of Giotopoulos left at a safe house led police to identify him. On July 17, Giotopoulos and his French wife were arrested on the island of Lipsi. On July 19, 2002, a Greek court charged Giotopoulos with 963 crimes, including 13 murders and several attempted murders. Trial for the 19 suspected members of the 17 November group before a three-judge panel opened on March 3, 2003. This trial lasted until December 18, 2003, with Giotopoulos receiving 21 life terms for instigating every murder, bomb attack, and robbery committed by the 17 November group. He escaped punishment for the first 4 of the group's 23 killings because of a 20-year statue of limitations. **See also** Revolutionary Organization 17 November (Epanastaiki Organoisi 17 Noemvri).

Suggested readings: Paul Anast et al., "Terror Group's House of Cards," *Daily Telegraph* (London) (July 19, 2002), p. 4; Elena Becatoros, "Alleged Terrorist Leader Charged in Greece," *Montreal Gazette* (July 20, 2002), p. A23; Daniel Howden, "World's Most Elusive Terrorists Go on Trial," *Independent* (London) (March 4, 2003), p. 10; Patricia Kushlis, "The Rise and Fall of the November 17 Terrorist Group," *Santa Fe New Mexican* (September 1, 2002), p. F4; Helena Smith,

"After 27 Years of Secrecy and Murder, November 17 Is Exposed," *Guardian* (London) (July 19, 2002), p. 3; Damian Whitworth, "The Urbane Guerrilla," *Times* [London] (July 26, 2002), Features, p. 2.

Goldstein, Benjamin (Baruch) Carl (1957–1994) (Israel)

Dr. Benjamin Goldstein, a member of the orthodox and nationalistic **Kach** party, carried out a terrorist attack against Palestinians in Hebron's Tomb of the Patriarchs. He was born in 1957 in the Bensonhurst section of Brooklyn, New York. His father was a truant officer with the New York City Board of Education and his mother a bookkeeper in Manhattan. Goldstein was raised as an Orthodox Jew. His high school education was at Yeshiva Flatbush School, where he earned a National Merit Scholarship. He attended Yeshiva University in Manhattan and received a pre-med degree in 1977. His work at the medical school of the Albert Einstein College of Medicine earned him his medical degree in 1981. His internship was at the Brookdale Hospital in Brooklyn during the years 1981–1982.

In the early 1980s, Goldstein became a follower of Rabbi **Meir Kahane**. In 1983, he decided to move to Israel, where he became a close personal friend of Kahane. Goldstein met his wife, a Sephardic Jew, at a Kach meeting in Jerusalem, and Kahane later married them. Goldstein campaigned for Kach in 1984, helping Kahane win a seat in the Knesset. In the meantime, Goldstein and his growing family of children moved to the Kiryat Arba settlement in the Israeli-occupied West Bank. At this settlement, he set up his medical practice, specializing in emergency medicine. Goldstein was highly respected for his medical expertise and he treated Palestinians as well as Jews. He also served as the Kach representative on the Kiryat Arba local council for two years before resigning over a dispute. Goldstein shared Kahane's belief that Palestinians should be forcibly removed from all of biblical Israel. He also believed that the Palestinians were plotting to massacre the Jewish settlers on the West Bank. Goldstein wanted to derail the Israeli-Palestinian peace process and in the process avenge Israeli deaths by Palestinian terrorists.

On February 25, 1994, Goldstein dressed in the uniform of a captain in the Israel Defense Forces (IDF), took his Galil machine gun, and systematically killed 29 Palestinians and wounded over 100 at an evening prayer at Hebron's Tomb of the Patriarchs. An enraged crowd of survivors beat Goldstein to death before Jewish settlers could rescue him. His action polarized public opinion in Israel; some right-wingers eulogized him but the Israeli government and the majority of Israeli citizens were outraged. His supporters made it public that Goldstein was a holy man for his actions. Goldstein is buried in Hebron in a cemetery dedicated to Meir Kahane. **See also** Kach (Only Thus); Kahane, Meir.

Suggested readings: Carole Agus, et al., "Consumed by Outrage," *Newsday* (New York City) (February 26, 1994), p. 5; Mark Juergensmeyer, *Terror in the Mind of God: The Global Rise of Religious Violence* (Berkeley: University of California Press, 1999); Israel Shahak and Norton Mezvinsky, *Jewish Fundamentalism in Israel* (London: Pluto Press, 1999); Colin Smith, "Legacy of a 'Caring' Jew Who Killed," *Sunday Times* (London) (April 3, 1994), p. 1; Ehud Spinzak, *Brother Against Brother: Violence and Extremism in Israeli Politics from Altalena to the Rabin Assassination* (New York: Free Press, 1999).

Graaf, Volkert van der (1970–) (The Netherlands)

Volkert van der Graaf is a militant animal rights activist whose claim to fame is the assassination of the Dutch right-wing populist leader **Pim Fortuyn**. He was born in 1970 and raised in Harderwijk, a town 30 miles east of Amsterdam. He grew up an animal lover and began volunteering at a bird shelter in the coastal province of Zeeland at age 15. As a teenager, Graaf decided to become a vegetarian, but his family insisted that he eat meat. After local schooling, he attended an agricultural college in Wageningen. At school, he became a vegan, eschewing meat, dairy products, eggs, and honey. Graaf also protested the use of animals for laboratory experimentation.

After graduation, Graaf directed his energies to animal rights. He worked briefly for the anti-meat trade group Lekker Dier. In 1992, he was one of the founders of Environment Offensive (Milieu Offensief), a group that used Dutch law to combat large-scale farming. He wanted to prevent pollution of the environment and end animal suffering. Peter Wilson, in an article in *The Weekend Australian,* claimed that this group initiated 2,000 lawsuits against farmers. One of Graaf's targets was a local farmer form Harderwijk, Peter Olofson. Olofson wanted to expand his farming to include large-scale cattle raising, but it took two years of legal wrangling before he won permission. Another of Graaf's opponents was a pig farmer by the name of Wien van den Brink. Brink was a vocal supporter of Fortuyn.

Partly because of his animosity toward Brink, and also because Fortuyn had announced that his party would advocate lifting a ban on the farming of animals for fur in the forthcoming elections, Graaf decided to assassinate Fortuyn. Although Graaf had married, and he and his wife had a six-month-old son, he meticulously planned the assassination of Fortuyn. On May 6, 2002, Graaf shot Fortuyn six times shortly after Fortuyn left the radio station at Hilversum. Police arrested him only blocks from the shooting with his weapon still on him and later found detailed maps of the radio and television complex at Graaf's flat in Harderwijk. Graaf's trial started on March 27, 2003, and it ended on April 16, 2003, with Graaf receiving a prison term of 18 years. The judges refused to give Graaf a life sentence because they had been persuaded that Graaf was not likely to repeat his crime. Graaf's lawyers appealed the verdict, but a Dutch appeals court confirmed the sentence on July 18, 2003. This ruling held even though Graaf is under suspicion for a 1996 unsolved murder of a council farming advisor near Nunspeet. Environmental groups have condemned the murder, but these denials have not helped them avoid hostility from Fortuyn's supporters. See also Fortuyn, Pim.

Suggested readings: Martin Fletcher, "Accused Vegan Was 'a Fanatic Who Cared Only for Animals,'" *Times* (London) (May 9, 2002), p. 1; David Graves, "Animal Activist 'Meticulously Planned Killing,'" *Daily Telegraph* (London) (May 9, 2002); David Graves, "Fortuyn's Killer 'Is Militant Activist,'" *Daily Telegraph* (London) (May 8, 2002), p. 7; Peter Wilson, "The Assassin Who Loved Animals," *Weekend Australian* (Sydney) (May 11, 2002), p. 1.

Grey Wolves (Turkey)

The Grey Wolves, a Turkish nationalist, right-wing group, was formed in the early 1970s to fight communism and democratic institutions. Colonel **Alparslan Turkes** founded the Grey Wolves as the paramilitary and terrorist wing of his Nationalist Action Party and used the group to fight what he perceived to be his left-wing enemies. In 1975, Turkes became head of Turkey's state security, and he took the opportunity to place members of the Grey Wolves in key positions in the state security apparatus. This infiltration lasted even after the 1980 military coup that landed Turkes in prison for four and a half years. He still controlled the Grey Wolves from prison, but operational control resided in the hand of his second in command, Abdullah Catli.

Catli retained operational control of the Grey Wolves even after Turkes was released from prison. By the early 1980s, William Drozdiak, in a 1983 article in *The Washington Post*, estimated that the group had around 18,000 members both in Turkey and in Europe. Members received training in guerrilla warfare from a variety of sources, including in the Middle East. Funding for the group came from membership dues of $4 per month per member, currency transactions, and drug smuggling. Leaders of the Grey Wolves built an army by trading drugs for military equipment, ranging from assault helicopters to tanks. These drugs were transported to Italy, where organized crime processed them during the 1970s and 1980s.

Most of the political activities of the Grey Wolves remained in the background until a member attempted the assassinations of Pope John Paul II and the Turkish prime minister. On May 13, 1981, Mehmet Ali Agca shot and wounded Pope Paul II in St. Peter's Square in the Vatican. Catli had helped Agca escape from a Turkish prison and he had provided him with the gun that Agca used to shoot the Pope. However, the U.S. government advanced the theory that it was a Bulgarian plot to kill the Pope, but little evidence was produced to support this thesis. Later evidence surfaced that the leadership of the Grey Wolves had planned the assassination attempt.

Publicity about the Grey Wolves' involvement in the international drug trade attracted negative attention from both American and European drug agencies. The extent of the smuggling and the support from Turkish authorities came to light after an auto crash in November 1996 killed Catli, a top Turkish police official, and Catli's girlfriend. Documents found in the crash proved that Turkish authorities had given diplomatic credentials to Catli and that Catli had been working for the Turkish police despite his status as an international criminal wanted in Western Europe. He also had worked with the Turkish Counter-Guerrilla Organization in its campaign against the Kurds. **See also** Turkes, Alparslan.

Suggested readings: Wolfgang Achtner and Tony Barber, "Search for a Plot to Kill the Pope," *Independent* (London) (May 19, 1991), p. 18; William Drozdiak, "The 'Grey Wolves': Decade of Crime Attributed to Turkish Rightists," *Washington Post* (July 3, 1983), A1; Jonathan Gorvett, "Turkey Dances with 'Grey Wolves' Party," *Boston Globe* (May 23, 1999), p. A7; Martin A. Lee, "The Cop, the Gangster and the Beauty Queen," *In These Times,* vol. 21 (April 28/May 11, 1997), p. 18; Martin A. Lee, "Turkish Dirty War Revealed, but Papal Shooting Still Obscured," *Los Angeles Times* (April 12, 1998), p. M2; Haluk Sahin, "Did Ozal Gunman Run with the Wolf Pack?" *Times* (London) (June 26, 1988), p. 1.

Griffin, Nick (1959–) (Great Britain)

Nick Griffin is the head of the neo-fascist **British National Party** (BNP). He was born in 1959 in Barnet in north London, but he grew up in rural Suffolk, England. His father, a veteran of the Royal Air Force (RAF) during World War II, and his mother live on a farm, but they run an electrical business in St. John's Wood. Both his mother and father have always been politically active in right-wing politics. Griffin was educated at a minor public school of St. Felix in Southwold. While a teenager, Griffin attended a meeting of the neo-Nazi National Front and was attracted to its program. He joined the National Front in 1974 at age 14. In 1977, he attended Cambridge University, where he studied history and law. Griffin was also a boxer. He graduated with an honors degree in law. After graduation, Griffin turned his attention to **British National Front** (BNF) politics. He spent the next 18 years in various positions in the British National Front. In 1980, he and Joe Pearce, a leading British racist and editor of *Bulldog,* founded *Nationalism Today,* and Griffin became its editor. In 1983, he participated in a political coup that overthrew the head of the British National Front, Martin Webster. In 1988, Griffin was the victim of another power struggle in the British National Front and he left the party at the beginning of 1989.

After leaving the British National Front, Griffin found a home in the British National Party. He also flirted briefly with International Third Position, a group founded by the Italian Fascist Roberto Fiore to advance international fascism. Less than a year after he joined this group, a hostile faction assumed control of the organization and Griffin left it. In the meantime, Griffin lost an eye in a firearms accident, which caused him to spend much of 1989 in the hospital. In the early 1990s, though, he became editor of the anti-Semitic quarterly *The Rune.*

In 1995, Griffin joined the British National Party and soon he became one of its leading figures. John Tyndall, the head of the BNP, had recruited him. Griffin's initial position was that the BNP needed to retain its neo-Nazi roots and emphasis on **Holocaust denial.** He carried this position over to the editorship of *Spearhead,* the BNP's magazine. Griffin ran into trouble with the law over giving out racist literature. He and Paul Ballard, a fellow member of the BNP, were convicted of violating a 1986 law on inciting racial hatred, and a British court gave them a nine-month prison sentence and a £2,300 fine. This sentence was suspended for two years. In 1999, Griffin won a power struggle with Tyndall and replaced him as head of the BNP. Since then, Griffin has been busy trying to turn the BNP into a more moderate British party that has a chance to win elections. This electoral campaign, however, has not muted his advocacy of Holocaust denial.

Griffin's efforts to build the British National Party have been hampered by internal disputes within the party. His standing in the party has been hurt by charges that he used party funds for personal reasons, including adding an extension to his house. Griffin has managed to withstand these challenges by purging the dissidents from the BNP, but both the charges and purges have hurt Griffin's chances of turning the BNP into a national force in British politics. **See also** British National Front (BNF); British National Party (BNP); Holocaust Denial.

Suggested readings: Andrew Anthony, "Flying the Flag: He's the Cambridge Law Graduate and Father of Four Who Is Transforming the British Far Right," *Observer* (London) (September 1, 2002), p. 22; Steve Boggan, "March of the Far-Right," *Evening Standard* (London) (February 3, 2003), p. 16; Paul Gallagher, "Lessons in the Language of Hate," *Scotsman* (Edinburgh) (July 17, 2001), p. 2; Nick Ryan, "Racial Pride and Prejudice," *Independent* (London) (January 7, 1999), p. 8; Michael Seamark, "The Family Whose Middle Name Is Hate," *Daily Mail* (London) (August 25, 2001), p. 5.

Grivas, George (1898–1974) (Cyprus)

George Grivas was the leader of **EOKA** in its war against the British control of Cyprus in the 1950s. He was born on May 23, 1898, in the village of Trikomo in the district of Famagusta, Cyprus. His father was a prosperous corn merchant. After an education in local schools, he was sent at age 11 to the Pancyprian Gymnasium in Nicosia. After graduation in 1916, Grivas traveled to Greece and he earned admittance into the Athens Military Academy. He graduated in time to join a division in the Greek army fighting against Turkey in 1921. In 1924, Grivas reached the rank of captain and he attended both the Athens Staff College and the War School (Ecole de Guerre) in France. Both his military experience and right-wing political orientation turned him into a proponent of the Greater Greece movement. When the Italian army invaded Greece in 1940, Grivas was a lieutenant colonel and he was soon attached to the 2nd Army Division and serving as its chief of staff. After the German invasion of Greece in April 1941, Grivas returned to Athens. There he formed the right-wing paramilitary group Xhi (named after the Greek letter χ, which means "the unknown"). Grivas served as the military leader of Xhi during the Greek civil war against the Communist ELAS (People's National Liberation Army) in the period from 1944 to 1945. He dissolved the Xhi military organization in February 1945 and turned it into a political party, the Party of National Resistance. Despite high hopes, this party failed to win any seats in the 1946 Greek elections.

Grivas's goal of a Greater Greece included the demand for Cyprus's union (Enosis) with Greece. Beginning in 1948, Grivas began making contacts with key figures in Greece for a guerrilla war against the British in Cyprus. In July 1948, Grivas traveled to Cyprus to study the possibility of military operations. Although his contacts in Cyprus were lukewarm to the idea of an uprising, Grivas was more optimistic, basing his strategy not on defeating the British in the field but on mobilizing international public opinion for an independent Cyprus. Once Cyprus was independent, then steps would be taken for a union with Greece. Both Archbishop Makarios (Michael Mouskos), the Greek

Orthodox religious leader in Cyprus, and Field Marshal Papagos, the head of the Greek government, had reservations.

On November 10, 1954, Grivas launched the guerrilla war in Cyprus by landing there in secret. In early January 1955, he formed EOKA as the central organization to carry out guerrilla operations. By this time, he had concluded a tenuous political alliance with Archbishop Makarios. Organizational problems and lack of resources made Grivas wait until April 1, 1955, to launch his campaign. Seizure of a ship carrying weapons and explosives on January 25, 1955, was a setback. The group recovered and managed to set off a series of explosions at different sites around Cyprus on April 1 to announce the existence of EOKA. Most of these attacks were ineffectual, revealing the amateur nature of the bombings. Grivas devoted most of his energies on recruitment and training of new members of EOKA. On June 19, 1955, a second wave of terrorism targeted the administrative structure and the police.

For the next four years Grivas led a guerrilla war against the British in Cyprus. At the peak of the guerrilla campaign the British had 40,000 soldiers fighting Grivas's forces. He concentrated his efforts in attacking British soldiers, civilians, and Cypriot collaborators. This warfare continued until Grivas okayed a truce in August 1958. This truce led to the signing of the London agreement on Cyrpus independence on February 19, 1959. This agreement ended the fighting in Cyprus, but Grivas was still dissatisfied because he had been fighting for the union of Cyprus with Greece. Grivas returned to Greece, where he received a promotion to general in the Greek army.

Grivas's career in Cyprus was less successful after 1959. He was in command of Greek forces in Cyprus and in charge of the Cypriot national guard when fighting broke out between Greek and Turkish Cypriots in August 1964. In November 1967 he was forced to leave Cyprus in the aftermath of fighting between Grivas's national guard and Turkish Cypriots. In 1971, he opened a guerrilla campaign against the government of President Makarios. This campaign weakened the Greek Cypriot forces so that when he defeated the Makarios government in 1974 the Turkish forces seized a northern third of Cyprus, starting the partition of Cyprus. By this time Grivas was seriously ill with cancer and he died later in 1974. **See also** EOKA (Ethniki Organosis Kyrion Agoniston) (National Organization of Cypriot Fighters); Sampson, Nicos Giorgiades.

Suggested readings: Dudley Barker, *Grivas: Portrait of a Terrorist* (New York: Harcourt, Brace, 1959); Nancy Crawshaw, *The Cyprus Revolt: An Account of the Struggle for Union with Greece* (London: Allen & Unwin, 1978); Charles Foley (ed.), *The Memoirs of General Grivas* (New York: Praeger, 1964).

Guillén Vicente, Rafael Sebastián (1957–) (Mexico)

Operating under the codename Subcommandant Marcos, Rafael Sebastián Guillén is one of the leaders and chief spokesperson for the Mexican **Zapatista Army of National Liberation** (Ejercito Zapatista de Liberación, or EZLN). Guillén was born on June 19, 1957, in Tampico, Mexico, into a prosperous family. His father was a furniture retailer in Tampico. His grades at the local Jesuit school were excellent, and he attended the Autonomous Metropolitan University (Universidad Autónoma Metropolitana, or UAM) in Mexico City, where he studied philosophy. This school was famous for its sponsorship of social activism, and Guillén was a leftist activist. After Guillén graduated, he continued his studies, becoming a professor in the Department of Theory and Analysis at the Autonomous Metropolitan University.

Guillén's interest in leftist social activism led him to become active in Chiapas. He joined the National Liberation Forces (Fuerzas de Liberación Nacional, or FLN) sometime in the early 1980s. The FLN was a small Marxist guerrilla group that had formed in 1969 in Mexico City, but by the mid-1970s it had suffered severe military losses from the Mexican army, almost destroying it as a guerrilla force. In August 1983 Guillén arrived in Chiapas convinced that the indigenous population of that region were ripe for revolution. On November 17, 1983, three Indians and three Mestizos organized the Zapatista Army of National Liberation. Guillén and other leaders of the FLN merged it into the EZLN. Most of the rank and file of the EZLN were poorly educated, so the leaders of the EZLN looked to Guillén to serve as a spokesperson for the new movement.

Guillén developed the persona of Subcommander Marcos as the symbol of the Zapatista movement. Subcommander Marcos appeared soon after the launching of the Zapatista military action in Chiapas on January 1, 1994. Supposedly the name Marcos comes from the first letters of the towns in Chiapas that the Zapatistas occupied on January 1—Margaritas, Altamirano, La Realidad, Chanal, Ocosingo, and San Cristóbal. Although Guillén wore a ski mask to disguise his identity, it was obvious from his manners and speech that he was highly educated. Soon after his appearance, speculation about his identity became almost as intense as the interest in the Zapatista movement in Chiapas. His identity surfaced on February 9, 1995, when President Ernesto Zedillo Ponce de León announced his name while issuing an arrest warrant for Guillén. This outing did not prevent Guillén from continuing to serve as the spokesperson for the Zapatista movement, but it did make him a target for Mexican right-wing paramilitary groups.

Despite his unmasking, Guillén as Subcommander Marcos became a national idol. His fame transcended Mexico and even made it to Europe and the United States. Besides political appearances, Guillén has effectively used the Internet to communicate with allies and even opponents. His larger than life image only intensified in March 1999 when Guillén's children's book *The Story of Colors* was translated into English and appeared in the United States. Then on March 11, 2001, Guillén and 23 EZLN marched into Mexico City and before 100,000 supporters he addressed them in the Plaza Zócalo

in the middle of Mexico City. This march had the approval of the new president of Mexico, Vicente Fox, but the march proved to be a political diappointment. Guillén still serves as the spokesperson for the EZLN, but he is no longer as active as before. As the EZLN consolidate their control over the remote areas of Chiapas, Guillén only makes the news when he says something controversial. His most recent controversial statements were over his support for the Basque separatist group **ETA**. **See also** ETA (Euskadi ta Askatasuna) (Basque Fatherland and Liberty); Zapatista Army of National Liberation (Ejercito Zapatista de Liberación).

Suggested readings: Alam Guillermoprieto, "The Unmasking," in Tom Hayden, ed., *The Zapatista Reader* (New York: Thunder's Mouth Press, 2002); Naomi Klein, "The Unknown Icon," in Tom Hayden, ed., *The Zapatista Reader* (New York: Thunder's Mouth Press, 2002); Andres Oppenheimer, "Guerrillas in the Mist," in Tom Hayden, ed., *The Zapatista Reader* (New York: Thunder's Mouth Press, 2002); Ignacio Ramonet, "Marcos Marches on Mexico City," in Tom Hayden, ed., *The Zapatista Reader* (New York: Thunder's Mouth Press, 2002); Jaime Sanchez Susarrey, "Subcommander Marcos's Support for ETZ Seen as Predictable," *World News Connection* (December 14, 2002), p. 1.

Gush Emunim (Bloc of the Faithful) (Israel)

The Gush Emunim (Bloc of the Faithful) is a radical Israeli religious group that espouses the doctrine of Greater Israel. An earlier group, the Movement for the Whole Land of Israel, had been formed a couple of months after the 1967 Six-Day War to lobby for an expanded Israel to include the West Bank and the Gaza Strip. Members of this group were secular Zionist intellectuals, generals, and politicians. A group of Orthodox Israelis held an exploratory meeting in February 1974 to discuss the formation of a new political bloc. Then in March 1974, the founding meeting of Gush Emunim took place at Kfar Etzion, a West Bank settlement. Gush Emunim adopted the program of the Movement for the Whole Land of Israel and absorbed many of its members. Adherents of Gush Emunim came from the National Religious Party (NRP), the Land of Israel Movements, Orthodox students of the Yeshiva Merkaz Harav, and members of the B'nai Akiva movement. Unlike a political party, the Gush Emunim never had an elected leader, or a formal organization with dues-paying members, but it had an effective network of leaders coming out of the settlement movement. Uniting these groups was the ideology of Rabbi Zvi Yehuda Kook, the head of the Yeshiva Merkaz Harav in Jerusalem. He had always believed in the incorporation of the lands of Judea and Samaria into the state of Israel. The victory of Israel in the 1967 Arab-Israeli War was a fulfillment of his dream of a Greater Israel. His followers organized to oppose territorial concessions to the Palestinians and they pursued a policy of acquisition of territory in the West Bank, either by military action or by settlements. After Rabbi Kook's death, Rabbi **Moshe Levinger** became the most important leader in Gush Emunim.

The Gush Emunim found itself in opposition to the policies of the Labor government. In the mid-1970s adherents of the Gush Emunim began establishing settlements in the occupied territories of the West Bank. This action brought these settlers into conflict with the Labor government of Prime Minister Yitzhak Rabin. By 1977, the Gush Emunim had become a close political ally of the right-wing Likud Party. The victory of the Likud Party in 1977 allowed new Prime Minister Menachem Begin to sanction the widespread building of new settlements. Israelis flocked to the settlements not only for new land but also to gain government financial subsidies. Members of the Gush Emunim dominated the settlers' lobby, and they have continued to push for more settlements. This is in support of their view that the occupied West Bank and Gaza Strip should be permanently incorporated into the state of Israel. Jewish vigilante groups formed to drive Palestinians off the land and Israeli authorities did little to curb the violence.

The radical wing of the Gush Emunim formed a terrorist group. Beginning in 1980, 27 members of the Gush Emunim agreed to form the Gush Emunim Underground under the leadership of Yehudah Etzion. Over the next four years, this group exploded several bombs and engaged in shootings. Their most ambitious plan, to blow up the Muslim Dome of the Rock on the Temple Mount in Jerusalem, was thwarted. Members of the Gush Emunim Underground were arrested, and they received prison sentences ranging from 7 to 10 years. An extensive lobbying campaign by the Likud and the National Religious Party led to their early pardon by President Chaim Herzog.

The main goal of the Gush Emunim was to sabotage any attempts at an Israeli-Palestinian peace agreement that creates a Palestinian state. Its leaders opposed the Camp David Accords in 1977 because the agreement gave Palestinians self-rule in the West Bank and Gaza. They lobbied against the agreement and soon actions by both the Israelis and Palestinians insured that the agreement was only a temporary improvement in relations between the two camps.

The next major threat to the Gush Eminim was the September 1993 Oslo Accords. Various Israeli governments had encouraged further settlements in the occupied territories. As these settlements increased in number and size, tensions increased with the Palestinians. The outbreak of the Palestinian **Intifada** in 1987 was the result. Civil disobedience and violence made it impossible for the Israel Defense Forces (IDF) to control the Palestinians. Vigilante actions by members of the Gush Emunim only made the crisis worse. In 1992, a new Labor government won office with Yitzhak Rabin as prime minister. Rabin had a history of opposing the Gush Emunim and its settlement program. Rabin's negotiations leading to the Oslo Agreements infuriated them, because it recognized a Palestinian state. Leaders of the Gush Emunim declared war on Rabin, and members participated with elements in the Likud Party to attack him. This campaign of vilification led to

Rabin's assassination on November 4, 1995, by **Yigal Amir**, a religious fanatic and an adherent of the Greater Israel movement. **See also** Amir, Yigal; Levinger, Moshe.

Suggested readings: William Claiborne, "Rightist Israeli Faction Attacks Accord," *Washington Post* (September 20, 1978), p. A10; Robert I. Friedman, *Zealots for Zion: Inside Israel's West Bank Settlement Movement* (New York: Random House, 1992); Ian S. Lustick, *For the Land and the Lord* (New York: Council on Foreign Relations, 1988); Ehud Sprinzak, *Brother against Brother: Violence and Extremism in Israeli Politics from Altalena to the Rabin Assassination* (New York: Free Press, 1999); Ehud Sprinzak, "From Messianic Pioneering to Vigilante Terrorism: The Case of the Gush Emunim Underground," in David C. Rapoport, *Inside Terrorist Organizations* (London: Frank Cass, 2001), 2nd ed.

Guzman, Abimael (1934–) (Peru)

Abimael Guzman is the founder and leader of Peru's **Shining Path** (Sendero Luminoso) guerrilla group. He was born on December 3, 1934, in the village of Tambo near the port of Mollendo, Peru. His father was a prosperous wholesaler of imported products, but he never married Guzman's mother. She died when Guzman was five years old and he went to live with his uncles. Later he went to live with his father at the Lima port of Callao. Several years later, Guzman moved with his father to the city of Arequipa. He attended the Jesuit La Salle College, where he was an outstanding student. After high school, Guzman studied at the National University of San Agustin in Arequipa where he majored in law and philosophy under the philosopher Miguel Angel Rodriguez Rivas. While still a student, Guzman joined the Peruvian Communist Party. In 1961, he wrote two doctoral dissertations: one on Kantian philosophy and the other on the necessity for revolution. After completing his degree, Guzman was offered a teaching position as head of the philosophy department at the University of San Cristobal de Huamanga in Ayachucho, Peru. He became a popular and influential teacher at the university, attracting students from all over Peru.

Guzman found the Peruvian Communist Party in disarray and he began efforts to revitalize it. His first effort was the formation of the Revolutionary Student Movement, which later became the People's Student Front. In 1965, Guzman made a trip to Mao Tse-tung's People's Republic of China. After returning to Peru, Guzman made an alliance with the Maoist Red Flag group. Soon after joining, Guzman overthrew the local leadership of the Red Flag and he became its regional leader. He was able to advance the communist cause in Ayacucho after the Peruvian military dictatorship of General Juan Valasco passed a law restricting free high school education. In the demonstrations and the military's brutal response, Guzman was able to win new recruits, but he was also briefly arrested for inciting the riots. Guzman was blocked from a national leadership role in the Red Flag, so in February 1970 he formed the Communist Party of Peru by the **Shining Path** of Jose Carlos Mariategui, or in short Shining Path.

Guzman made the Shining Path an authoritarian and hierarchical organization designed to impose its communist ideals on the Peruvian masses. He adopted the codename Gonzolao for official communiqués. Most of the Red Flag's most dedicated Communists followed Guzman into the Shining Path. The pro–Shining Path newspaper *El Diario* provided a forum for Guzman to communicate his message. From the beginning, Guzman directed his recruiting toward university students and peasants in the countryside. By the mid-1970s, these recruiting efforts had brought the student bodies and faculties of several leading Peruvian university into the ranks of the Shining Path. Even more success was made recruiting among the peasants. Guzman transferred his base of operations to Lima in the late 1970s to be better able to coordinate political activities. Guzman began at this time to arm members of the Shining Path and conduct military training. Peruvian police arrested him on January 7, 1979, but his family was able to mobilize its political influence to have him released four days later.

Shining Path leader Abimael Guzman is transferred, under heavy security, to a new maximum security prison in Callao, Peru, April 3, 1993. (AP Photo/Vera Lentz)

In February 1979, Guzman decided to go to war with the Peruvian state. He persuaded the central committee in a meeting that lasted from March 17 to March 25 to opt for open guerrilla warfare. He had those opposing him expelled. Guzman also made it clear that his strategy called for total war against all opponents. The first military operation took place on May 17, 1980, in the Ayacuco village of Chuschi, where five members burned the ballot boxes on the eve of the presidential election. Despite Guzman's adherence to total war, guerrilla activities for the remainder of 1980 remained low because of a lack of trained personnel and weapons. Guzman did have to withstand internal criticism be-cause most of the early operations were urban rather than rural, thus violating Shining Path ideology of concentrating efforts in rural areas. He countered this criticism by noting that urban acts received more publicity than rural ones.

Guzman's career as head of the Shining Path ended abruptly in 1992. A special police intelligence unit captured Guzman on Sept. 13, 1992, in Lima, Peru. His capture was a serious blow to the Shining Path organization since he was not only the political leader but its spiritual leader. His successor was **Oscar Ramirez Durand**. After his capture, Guzman made an appeal to his followers to suspend the Shining Path's war against the Peruvian state. This appeal had no impact on his followers and only hurt his reputation among his former colleagues. A military court sentenced him to life imprisonment at a naval base. In March 2003, a Peruvian court annulled the sentence of Guzman on the grounds that the secret military courts of a decade ago were unconstitutional. The prospect of a free Guzman has delayed a new trial. **See also** Shining Path (Sendero Luminoso).

Suggested readings: Gustavo Gorriti, *The Shining Path: A History of the Millenarian War in Peru* (Chapel Hill: University of North Carolina Press, 1999); Simon Strong, *Shining Path: The World's Deadliest Revolutionary Force* (London: HarperCollins, 1992); Scott Wilson, "Peruvian Guerrillas Fight New Battle in Court," *Washington Post* (March 23, 2003), p. A16.

H

Habash, George (1926–) (Lebanon)

George Habash was the leader of the militant **Popular Front for the Liberation of Palestine** (PFLP) and the main rival to **Yasser Arafat** and the **Palestine Liberation Organization** (PLO). He was born in Lod, Palestine, in 1926. His father was a Greek Orthodox grain merchant. He was a brilliant student and studied medicine at the American University in Beirut, Lebanon. After receiving his medical degree, he entered Arab politics. In 1953, Habash and Wadi Haddad formed the Arab Nationalist Movement (ANM). This group of Arab nationalists looked to Gamal Abdel Nasser to unite the Arab world against the Western powers and Israel. The ANM continued this pro-Nasser policy until 1967. It took the 1967 Arab-Israeli War to convince Habash and his followers that a new direction was necessary.

Habash joined his ANM with **Ahmad Jabril's Palestine Liberation Front** (PLF) in 1967 to form the PFLP. Habash founded the group as a way to continue the struggle against Israel and established its operations in Jordan. Elements in the PFLP decided to pressure the Jordanian government and this led to the **Black September** uprising in 1971, which ended with the expulsion of the Palestinians from Jordan. As a result, Habash moved his headquarters from Jordan to Damascus in 1971 and then to Beirut, Lebanon.

Habash's movement attracted Marxist-Leninist radicals into a group that combined class warfare with hatred of Israel as a colonial power. His group was one of the more active in military and terrorist operations against Israel, specializing in high-profile airliner hijackings. This campaign of hijackings helped overcome the resentment against Habash and the PFLP for refusing help for the Palestinians at the battle of Karameh, Jordan, in March 1968. His chief of operations was Haddad, a doctor with a reputation for violence. In 1972, Habash developed a heart condition and Haddad assumed most of his duties. This lasted until Haddad's death.

Habash has always had a mixed attitude toward the PLO and Arafat, often charging that both are too moderate. His hostility toward both Israel and the United States has never changed, and he was among the most outspoken in his opposition to the Oslo Accords. His health has been an issue ever since a brain operation in 1980. In 1992, Habash traveled to Paris for medical treatment for a stroke. This treatment caused a political controversy and he was sent to Tunisia for further medical care. Habash continued his intransigence toward Israel until he retired from the PFLP for reasons of health in July 2000. His replacement, Abu Ali Mustafa, lasted only slightly more than a year before the Israelis killed him in August 2001. Habash continues to be regarded by the Palestinians as one of the grand old men of the Palestinian cause. **See also** Arafat, Yasser; Palestine Liberation Front (PLO); Popular Front for the Liberation of Palestine (PFLP).

Suggested readings: Phil Davison, "PFLP Leader Habash Often Upstaged Arafat," *Ottawa Citizen* (February 1, 1992), p. A8; Christopher Dickey, "Treating a Terrorist," *Newsweek* (February 10, 1992), p. 37; Robert Fisk, "Still Dreaming of His Homeland," *Independent* (London) (October 9, 1993), p. 10; Michael Jansen, "Habash Says PLO Israel Peace Plan Is a Retreat from Long Term Policy," *Irish Times* (February 16, 1994), p. 8; Walid W. Kazziha, *Revolutionary Transformation in the Arab World: Habash and His Comrades from Nationalism to Marxism* (New York: St. Martin's Press, 1975); Ilene R. Prusher, "Fallout from Israeli Assassination," *Christian Science Monitor* (Boston) (October 23, 2001), p. 6; Claude Salhani, "A Retrospective Look at the PFLP," United Press International (August 28, 2001), p. 1; Khaled Abu Toameh, "PFLP Effectively Wiped Out," *Jerusalem Post* (August 30, 2002), p. 16.

Haider, Jörg (1950–) (Austria)

Jörg Haider is the former leader of the Austrian Freedom Party and one of the leading extremists in Europe. He was born on January 26, 1950, in Bad Goisern, Upper Austria. His father was a shoemaker and his mother a teacher. Both parents were early members of the Nazi Party in Austria, joining in early 1929. Later, his father joined the German army. After World War II, his parents were classified as minor Nazi officials. Despite some hardships, they were able to send Haider and his sister to private schools. He was always a good student. At age 18, he served a year in the Austrian army. After his release from military duty, Haider attended the University of Vienna from 1969 to 1973 and studied law. In 1971, while still in school, he joined the small but fiercely nationalistic neo-Nazi Freedom Party. After

graduation, Haider spent several years in pursuit of an academic career at the Institute for State and Administrative Law at the Vienna University.

In 1976, Haider decided to devote the rest of his career to politics. After winning an election to regional party secretary of the Freedom Party in Carinthia, he won a seat in the national parliament in 1979. Utilizing his parliamentary seat, Haider was soon acknowledged as the leader of the extremist wing of the Freedom Party. At a 1986 congress of the Freedom Party in Innsbruck, Austria, Haider led a successful political coup against Norbert Stegen, the party leader. Also in 1986, a great uncle, William Webhofer, left him a 3,500-acre estate in Carinthia that made him financially independent. At the time that Haider took over as head of the Freedom Party, it was only able to attract about 5 percent of the Austrian electorate. By 2000, the Freedom Party had captured 27 percent of the voters. His political success had come from a campaign to reconcile with Austria's Nazi past, anti-immigration sentiment, and attacks on the European Union. These issues and populist attacks against wealth and privilege have made Haider popular among young Austrians. About a third of Austrians less than 30 years of age are his principal supporters.

Haider's defense of Nazism has caused him political difficulties both in Austria and in Europe. In June 1991, he defended the Nazi employment policies in a speech. This speech caused him to have to resign as the governor of Carinthia. Haider followed in 1995 by defending the conduct of members of the Waffen SS in World War II. His defense of Nazism did not prevent his Freedom Party from winning 27.2 percent of the vote in the October 2000 general election. Pressure from European governments made it impossible for him to assume a ministerial office, but it did not prevent six other members of the Freedom Party from taking ministerial posts. Other members of the European Union initiated diplomatic sanctions against Austria. Haider tried to distance himself from the negative publicity by firing the leaders of the

The leader of the right-wing Freedom Party, Jörg Haider, at a press conference after his party's meeting at Vienna's parliment building February 2, 2000. Haider is displaying a Danish newspaper article that accuses Austrian President Thomas Klestil and Chancellor Viktor Klima of instigating the European Union protest against him. (AP Photo/Martin Gnedt)

Freedom Party in favor of his longtime colleague and fellow extremist Susanne Riess-Passer. In the meantime, in April 1999, he was reelected the governor of Carinthia.

Haider remains on the political sidelines of Austrian national politics, but he remains the decision maker for the Freedom Party. An election in March 2001 in Vienna showed that the Freedom Party was losing much of its support, which decreased by 7 percent. Then, in the summer of 2002, Haider forced the Freedom Party's ministers to resign over a tax-cut controversy. This action weakened the Freedom Party and Haider's control over it. Haider has also created a storm of controversy in both Austria and abroad by statements in December 2003 calling Israel a dictatorship and suggesting that the United States's true purpose for going to war in Iraq was to gain control of its oil. He also characterized the capture of Saddam Hussein as a "second-rate comedy by Americans."

Suggested readings: Roger Cohen, "A Haider in Their Future," *New York Times* (April 30, 2000), sec. 6, p. 54; Imre Karacs, "Jörg Haider— A Man for All Seasons," *Independent* (London) (February 5, 2000), p. 5; Dominic Lawson, "I Lead the People; Jörg Haider Is the First Person to Unite Europe—against Himself," *Sunday Telegraph* (London) (February 13, 2000), p. 20; David J. Lynch, "Haider May Not Be Another Hitler, but . . . ," *USA Today* (February 10, 2000), 10A; Louise Potterton, "Haider Craves Admiration, Lusts Power," *Scotland on Sunday* (Edinburgh) (February 13, 2000), p. 22; Angus Roxburgh, *Preachers of Hate: The Rise of the Far Right* (London: Gibson Square Books, 2002).

Hamas (Haarakat al-Muqawama al-Islami) (Islamic Resistance Movement) (Palestine)

Hamas (Islamic Resistance Movement) is the most militant of the Palestinian resistance organizations operating in the Gaza Strip and the West Bank. **Sheikh Ahmed Yassin**, the head of the Palestinian **Muslim Brotherhood**, and seven other members of the Palestinian Muslim Brotherhood started Hamas on December 14, 1987, shortly after the outbreak of the Intifada. The goal of Hamas is the liberation of Palestine from Israeli control and the establishment of an Islamist state. Besides an emphasis on faithful adherence to the Muslim faith, it opposes alcohol, drugs, bribery, corruption, and prostitution. Israeli authorities at first encouraged the growth of Hamas as a counterweight to the **Palestine Liberation Organization** (PLO) and its chief **Yasser Arafat**, but they soon realized that Hamas was more dangerous than the PLO. Leaders of Hamas are determined enemies of the PLO and Arafat and its idea of a secular Palestinian state. By 1993, support for Hamas among the Palestinians in the occupied territories was in the range of 40 percent. Financial support has come from Iran, Saudi Arabia, and wealthy donors, but much of its income comes from *zaka*, which is a 2.5 percent tax on the wages of its followers. It follows the example of the Egyptian Muslim League and supports charities, colleges, kindergartens, medical clinics, mosques, orphanages, schools, and sporting clubs.

The military wing of Hamas carries out special operations against the Israelis. This strike force is the Martyr Sheikh Al Ezz-Edin al-Qassam military unit and it specializes in attacks on Jewish settlers and soldiers. In October 1991, Yassin was arrested and sentenced to life in jail for the death of Palestinians who allegedly collaborated with the Israelis. Yassin's jail term and Israeli reprisals led Hamas to recruit and train members to go on terrorist missions. Many of their militants traveled to Lebanon, where they received instruction from **Hezbollah** trainers. Hezbollah had already adopted suicide bombings as a tactic with some success.

Hamas started using suicide bombings as a weapon in 1993 in protest of the Oslo Accords. Suicide bombings have proven to be effective in destabilizing Israel and have obvious advantages in Hamas's viewpoint because they produce a large number of casualties with little cost or effort. Most of these so-called "martyrs" are males in their late teens and early 20s who are recruited from high schools and colleges. Recruiters seek out idealistic youth with strong religious and nationalistic views. More recently, several of the suicide bombers have been young women. They have responded to the same appeals as the young men. Among the suicide missions were the Jerusalem bus attack on August 21, 1995, that killed 6 persons and injured over 100 others, and the Jerusalem Ben Yehuda shopping mall bombing on September 4, 1997, that killed 8 persons and wounded nearly 200 others.

Hamas has resisted any outside efforts to persuade it to enter into a Palestinian peace agreement with Israel and has continued with its suicide missions. Israel authorities have targeted Hamas leaders after each suicide bombing in Israel by a member of Hamas. Only Yassin has been left alone because the Israeli government is fearful of making him a lasting martyr. These political assassinations have been counterproductive, however, as Hamas has used these deaths as motivation for more attacks. Only in July 2003 was enough pressure placed on the leadership of Hamas by the Palestinian Authority to cease these suicide bombings as part of the effort to conclude a final peace settlement between Israel and the Palestinians. Leaders of Hamas remain skeptical of the American peace process, but they were willing to at least try it. This ceasefire ended when Israel started targeting Hamas leaders for assassination in July 2003. Hamas retaliated with a sucide bombing in Israel on August 19, 2003, that killed 20 people, including 6 children. Since then Israelis have mounted an assassination campaign against the senior leadership of Hamas that has killed 13 Hamas members, including Ismail Abu Shanab, one of the most moderate leaders of Hamas. Among those attacked was Sheik Ahmed Yassin, but he escaped injury. After each of these assassinations, Hamas has sent a suicide bomber into Israel in retaliation. On September 9, 2003, two Hamas suicide bombings in Israel killed 15 Israelis. Abdulaziz Rantisi, one of the top Hamas leaders in Gaza, announced that a shadow leadership was being groomed to take over if the upper echelon of Hamas is wiped out.

Suggested readings: Henry Chu, "Hamas Leaders Keep Low Profile," *Los Angeles Times* (October 9, 2003), p. A8; Adam Dolnik and Anjali Bhattacharjee, "Hamas: Suicide Bombings, Rockets, or WMD?" *Terrorism and Political Violence* 14, no. 3 (Autumn 2002) p. 109–128; Meir Hatina, *Islam and Salvation in Palestine* (Tel Aviv, Israel: Tel Aviv University, 2001); Bob Hepburn, "Hamas Militant Islamic Fundamentalist Movement Has Become More Violent and Popular among Palestinians than Israel Ever Imagined," *Toronto Star* (January 3, 1993), p. F1; Khaled Hroub, *Hamas: Political Thought and Practice* (Washington, DC: Institute for Palestine Studies, 2000) , p. 24; Nomi Morris and Mariam Shahin, "The True Believers," *Maclean's* (March 18, 1996); Edgar O'Balance, *The Palestinian Intifada* (New York: St. Martin's Press, 1998).

Hambali (Riduan Isamuddin) (1964–) (Indonesia)

Hambali is the head of terrorist operations for the Indonesian Islamic extremist group **Jemaah Islamiyah** (Islamic Community, or JI). He was born on April 4, 1964, in the village of Sukamanah, West Java. He was the eldest of 13 children from a poor Muslim family of religious teachers. He attended local Islamic schools at Ciganjur. Hambali became an opponent of the Indonesian dictator Suharto, and in 1985 he went into exile in Malaysia. It was in Malaysia that Hambali met **Abu Bakar Bashir**, and he became one of Bashir's followers. In 1987, Hambali volunteered to fight in Afghanistan. He returned to Malaysia in 1990, where he married a local Malaysian-Chinese woman. By this time, he had become one of the leaders of the Jemaah Islamiyah.

After the collapse of the Suharto regime in 1998, Hambali stayed in Malaysia for a while before returning to Indonesia. His Afghanistan military training helped him in the planning for terrorist operations. He was the mastermind behind the Jemaah Islamiyah's anti-Christian bombing campaign in December 2000. In April 2001, Hambali became the operations chief of Jemaah Islamiyah responsible for operations in Indonesia, Malaysia, Philippines, and Singapore. He succeeded Mahamad Iqbal B. R. Rahman, an Indonesian cleric, who had been arrested by Malaysian authorities. Hambali has always operated in the background, but his involvement in other terrorist activities is suspected. He is now wanted in both Malaysia and Singapore for his terrorist activities. His name surfaced immediately after the Bali bombing on October 12, 2002, as a chief suspect. The arrests of Amrozi, an East Javanese car repairman and a participant in the Bali bombing, and Imam Samudra, a computer engineer, confirmed the involvement of Hambali in planning the bombing. Hambali's role in the Bali bombing, other terrorist acts, and evidence of his contacts with **al-Qaeda** have made him a wanted man both in Indonesia and by Western intelligence agencies. In February 2003, Hambali realized his high profile made him a target and he resigned as operations chief of Jemaah Islamiyah.

The manhunt for Hambali intensified after the bombing of the Marriot Hotel in Jakarta, Indonesia, in early August 2003. His role in this bombing was as a planner. Shortly after the bombing, Hambali was arrested in Ayutthaya, a town about 60 miles north of Bangkok, Thailand, on August 11, 2003. His captors were a joint team of the Central Intelligence Agency (CIA) and the Thai anti-terrorism forces. Hambali ended up in the custody of the CIA and awaits legal proceedings against him. Australian, Indonesian, and Philippine authorities want to question him about the terrorist activities of Jemaah Islamiyah, but for the immediate future U.S. authorities have limited assess to him until they complete their interrogation of his involvement with al-Qaeda and terrorism. **See also** Bashir, Abu Bakar; al-Ghozi, Fathur Rohman; Jemaah Islamiyah (Islamic Community) (JI); Al-Qaeda (The Base).

Suggested readings: Lawrence Bartlett, "Hambali, the 'Osama bin Laden of the East'," *Agence France Presse* (Oct. 17, 2002), p. 1; Rohan Gunaratna, *Inside Al Qaeda: Global Network of Terror* (New York: Columbia University Press, 2002); Trudy Harris, "Fugitive Extremist with His Sights Trained on Soft Targets—Terror in Jakarta," *Australian* (Sydney) (August 7, 2003), p. 8; Andrew Laxon, "Abu Bakar Bashir and Hambali, Indonesia's Masters of War," *New Zealand Herald* (October 16, 2002), p. 1; Ellen Nakashima and Alan Sipress, "Jailed Indonesian Suspect Details Links to Bombings," *Washington Post* (November 9, 2002), p. A15; Ellen Nakashima and Alan Sipress, "Al Qaeda Figure Seized in Thailand," *Washington Post* (August 15, 2003), p. A1; Maria A. Ressa, *Seeds of Terror: An Eyewitness Account of Al-Qaeda's Newest Center of Operations in Southeast Asia* (New York: Free Press, 2003); Cindy Wockner, "Terror Network; Asia's Most Wanted," *Advertiser* (Sydney) (July 18, 2003), p. 19.

Hanson, Pauline (1954–) (Australia)

Pauline Hanson was the leader of the Australian anti-immigrant and anti-Aborigines **One Nation Party**. She was born Pauline Seccombe in 1954 in Brisbane, Australia. Her parents were of English-Irish descent and were recent immigrants at the time of her birth. Hanson attended the Buranda Girls' School and Coorparoo State High School in Brisbane, but she left school early at age 15. After two unsuccessful marriages, she raised four children as a single parent. After work-

ing for years as a barmaid, she moved to Ispwich, Australia, a town in southeast Queensland, where she acquired a fish-and-chips shop. After listening to customer complaints for nine years, Hanson decided to enter politics. In 1994, she was elected a city councilor in Ipswich. Her election to federal parliament in 1996 from Oxley in Ipswich as an independent MP (Member of Parliament) from Queensland was a surprise. The conservative Liberal Party had dropped her as a candidate because of her negative letter to a local newspaper, the *Queensland Times*, on January 6, 1996, in which she complained about privileges accorded to Aborigines. She campaigned against Asian immigrants and Aborigine land rights, and for high tariffs and a People's Bank to loan to farmers at low interest rates. Her views attracted rural and semi-urban dwellers alarmed by threats of globalization and multiculturalism.

After spending almost a year in Parliament, Hanson decided to form the One Nation Party in 1997 to advance her political views. She formed One Nation on April 11, 1997, in Ipswich. The success of her party in winning 10 seats and 23 percent of the vote in the June 1998 Queensland election made her a national celebrity and scared Prime Minister John Howard in Canberra, who was preparing for an upcoming national election. Hanson and her One Nation Party were a threat to the traditional parties because of its appeal to the dispossessed in Australia.

At the height of her political popularity rumors began to spread about election irregularities in the formation of One Nation. Information about possible fraud led to a January 20, 2000, police raid on the Sydney and Queensland offices of One Nation. On July 5, 2001, Hanson and her chief assistant, David Ettridge, received a summons to answer fraud charges. Hanson was already unhappy about the direction of her political career, so on January 14, 2002, she resigned as president of One Nation. This resignation did not prevent an arrest and trial for Hanson and Ettridge that began on May 27, 2002. They were accused of political fraud because not all the 500 signatures on the

Pauline Hanson, as an independent Member of Parliament, November 21, 1996. Hanson, a former barmaid and fish-and-chips restaurant owner created the anti-immigrant and anti-Aborigines One Nation Party on April 11, 1997. The success of Hanson's party in the June 1998 Queensland election made her a national celebrity, but her celebrity status would change dramatically with her conviction on political fraud charges in August 2003. (AP Photo/Bluey Thomson)

petition to establish the One Nation Party were members of the party; some were members of the Pauline Hanson Support Movement. A Brisbane District Court jury convicted both of them of political fraud on August 20, 2003, and they were sentenced to three years in prison. Hanson spent her term in jail at Brisbane Women's Prison before a Queensland Appeals Court overturned her conviction. Since her release from jail, Hanson has been adamant about retiring from politics. **See also** League of Rights; One Nation Party (ONP).

Suggested readings: Brian Donaghy, "Hanson Puts Racism on Agenda for Multicultural Australia," *Irish Times* (July 3, 1998), p. 14; Michael Leach, Geoffrey Stokes, and Ian Ward, *The Rise and Fall of One Nation* (St. Lucia: University of Queensland Press, 2000); Kevin Meade, "The Starter Kit That Paved the Path to Conviction," *The Australian* [Sydney], p. 4; Natalie O'Brien, Belinda Hickman, and Dennis Shanahan, "Western Showdown," *Weekend Australian* (Sydney) (May 26, 2001), p. 21; Luke Slattery, "The Ex-Barmaid Who Is Tearing Australia Apart," *Scotsman* (Edinburgh) (July 8, 1998), p. 12; Martin Woollacott, "The Peril of Pauline," *Guardian* (London) (July 2, 1998), p. 6.

Harakat ul-Mujahidin (HUM) (Pakistan)

Harakat ut-Mujahidin (HUM) is an Islamic militant group based in Pakistan that is fighting for the liberation of Kashmir from Indian rule. Fazlur Rehman Khalil founded the HUM under the name Harakat-ul-Ansar in 1993. He retained control until he resigned in February 2000. His successor was the military commander Farooq Kashimir. Another important leader was Masood Azhar, but, after his release from an Indian prison in 1994, he formed his own group called Jaish-e Mohammad (Army of Mohammad, or JEM). In 1998, the U.S. State Department classified the HUM as a terrorist group. Headquarters for HUM is in Muzaffarabad, Pakistan. In August 2001, the Pakistani government raided the HUM offices in Karachi and arrested the members there. This raid enraged the leadership of HUM, and prominent leaders charged that the Pakistani government was anti-Islamic.

The Harakat ul-Mujahidin has been an active participant in the attempt to free Kashmir from India. A training camp in Afghanistan, Khalid bin Waleed, trained most of its activists until the fall of the Taliban regime. Elements in the HUM fought beside the **Taliban** in resisting the Northern Alliance and American forces before withdrawing back into Pakistan. Training has been relocated to remote areas in northwest Pakistan. In March 2003, the leadership of the HUM changed the group's name to Jamiat-ul Ansar (JuA). This name change has not prevented the group from sponsoring raids in Kashmir against Indian civilians and military. See also Sheikh, Ahmed Omar Saeed.

Suggested readings: *Ausaf* (Pakistani newspaper), "Jihadi Groups Condemn Pakistani Government over Raids, Fund-Raising Ban," BBC Worldwide Monitoring (August 26, 2001), p. 1; *Ausaf* (Pakistani newspaper), "Pakistan Islamic Party Leader Says US to Be Defeated in Afghan Mountain War," BBC Worldwide Monitoring (December 10, 2001), p. 1; Yosri Fouda and Nick Fielding, *Masterminds of Terror: The Truth Behind the Most Devastating Terrorist Attack the World Has Ever Seen* (New York: Arcade Publishing, 2003); Jessica Stern, *Terror in the Name of God: Why Religious Militants Kill* (New York: HarperCollins, 2003).

Hasselbach, Ingo (1966–) (Germany)

Ingo Hasselbach was one of Germany's leading neo-Nazis until he broke with the movement in the early 1990s. He was born in 1966 in then East Berlin, the illegitimate son of parents who both were journalists and supporters of the East German regime. Because his father was already married with five children, his parents never married. Later, his mother married her boss in the East German press, and Hasselbach lived with them. He never adjusted to living with his stepfather. His education was at Oberschule 31 "Hildi Coppi" in Lichtenberg, a suburb of East Berlin.

Hasselbach rebelled against his parents and the East German regime as a teenager. He was arrested at age 15 for theft and placed in the State Social Youth Service juvenile prison. After release, he lived for nine months with his father and his family. In 1986, he married Christine Hasselbach to obtain the East German marriage subsidy, and he adopted her last name of Hasselbach. In 1987 East German authorities arrested him for yelling, "Down with the Berlin Wall" in the midst of German policemen at a celebration in Lichtenberg honoring the Russian liberators. He received a year in jail for his offense. While in prison, he met several old-time Nazis, and their stories of Nazi Germany intrigued him. After release from jail on October 19, 1987, he worked as a bricklayer. Hasselbach returned to jail after a failed attempt to flee Germany. In 1989, he escaped to West Germany shortly before the Berlin Wall was torn down.

Hasselbach became a leader of the neo-Nazi movement in the newly reunified Germany. Shortly after his arrival in West Germany, Hasselbach met with **Michael Kühnen**, the charismatic leader of the German neo-Nazi movement. The older Kühnen served as a role model for Hasselbach. In May 1989, Hasselbach helped Kühnen start the neo-Nazi party **German Alternative**. Within a year, the German Alternative attracted nearly 800 followers. Kühnen's death from complications due to AIDS (Acquired Immune Deficiency Syndrome) in 1991 was a blow to Hasselbach, but it allowed him the opportunity to become a leading figure in the neo-Nazi movement. He made numerous contacts with most of Germany's major right-wing leaders. Hasselbach also made the acquaintance of the American neo-Nazi leader Gary Rex Lauck. As the German Alternative grew, it became a threat to the German state, and the German government banned it in 1991 because of its advocacy of a return to Nazi Germany.

The deeper Hasselbach was drawn into the German neo-Nazi movement, the more he was disillusioned by it. Part of his initial attraction had been the violence and the assault on East German society. By 1992, the violence and his inability to relate to other neo-Nazi leaders made him reexamine his commitment to neo-Nazism. Conversations with the journalist and filmmaker Winfried Bonengel also influenced him to make an ideological change. Finally, the murder of a Turkish woman and two young girls in a fire-bomb attack in the town of Mölln convinced him to leave the neo-Nazi movement. In March 1992, Hasselbach renounced his allegiance to German right-wing politics and he went into hiding. In 1993, he wrote a book, *The Reckoning: A Neo-Nazi Drops Out*, justifying his rejection of neo-Nazism. He also warned of the danger of right-wing movements to Germany. This political rejection earned him the lasting enmity of his former neo-Nazi colleagues. His mother received a mail bomb, but the police were able to disarm it. Because of his six-foot-six-inch height and his distinctive blond features, Hasselbach has had to remain underground. Despite death threats, he still travels around Europe and the United State warning of the dangers of neo-Nazism. See also Kühnen, Michael.

Suggested readings: Rick Atkinson, "Former Neo-Nazi, in Hiding, Warns of 'Potential for Violence,'" *Washington Post* (December 27, 1993), p. A13; Ingo Hasselbach, "Fantasy Fuhrer," *Guardian* (London) (February 10, 1996), p. 12; Ingo Hasselbach and Tom Reiss, *Fuhrer-Ex: Memoirs of a Former Neo-Nazi* (New York: Random House, 1996); Stephen Kinzer, "A Neo-Nazi Whose Ardor Was Cooled by Killings," *New York Times* (February 2, 1994), p. A4; George Rodrigue, "Germany's Young Neo-Nazis," *Gazette* (Montreal) (October 30, 1994), p. F5.

Hekmatyar, Gulbuddin (1947–) (Afghanistan)

Gulbuddin Hekmatyar is a fundamentalist Afghan political leader and a rival of the **Taliban.** He was born in 1947 in Imam Saheb in the northern province of Kunduz, Afghanistan, into a Ghilzai Pushtun family. His initial education was at the Kabul military cadet school of Mahtabqila, but his political activities there caused him to leave school. He returned to Kunduz and attended the Shirkhan High School. He is by training an engineer, but he never received his engineering degree from Kabul University. While at the university, he was instrumental in the founding of the radical Islamist Muslim Youth Organization of Afghanistan. Despite the lack of a degree, Hekmatyar taught engineering at the Kabul University for several years. In 1972, he was accused of killing a Maoist student, and the government of Sardar Muhammad Da'ud imprisoned him for this murder.

Hekmatyar's imprisonment and later his flight to Pakistan in 1973 led him to devote the rest of his life to Afghan politics. He founded the Islamic fundamental group Hizb-i Islami-i Afghanistan in 1974. Ahmed Rashid, a Pakistani journalist, characterized his party as a "secretive, highly centralized, political organization whose cadres were drawn from educated urban Pashtuns." His goal for his party was to form a purified Islamic state in Afghanistan. Hekmatyar directed his group in resistance to the Afghanistan Communists in the late 1970s and against the Soviet forces in the 1980s.

Hekmatyar was a favorite of the Pakistani government because the Pakistani security agencies believed that they could control him. Part of the Pakistani Inter-Services Intelligence (ISI) agency's strategy was to send foreign aid to militant Islamic groups that were

Gulbuddin Hekmatyar, the leader of the Afghanistan Islamic Party, is shown at a news conference in Tehran, Iran, October 9, 2001. In December 2003, Hekmatyar declared a holy war on all coalition forces in Afghanistan. (AP Photo/Hasan Sarbakhshian)

anti-American. As a result, Hekmatyar's forces of nearly 30,000 troops received nearly 70 percent of their assistance in their fight against the Soviet army from the ISI.

Hekmatyar also established a relationship with militant Islamist leader Sheikh Omar Abdul Rahman because they shared a passion for a holy war against the Soviets and for the spread of their version of the Islamic religion. After the withdrawal of Soviet forces in 1992, Hekmatyar challenged other mujahideen leaders for political power in Afghanistan. His rivalry with Ahmed Shah Masood, the military leader of the Jamai-at-i Islami (Islamic Society) was particularly

fierce. In August 1987, Hekmatyar was nearly killed by a car bomb in Peshawar, Pakistan. It was never proven who carried out the attempt.

In 1992, he became prime minister of the Afghanistan government, but his continuous fighting with other mujahideen groups led to a breakdown in civil order. Even during the war with the Soviets, the other mujahideen leaders never trusted him because of his open ambition. His staunchly anti-American posture made sure that no American political backing came to him. Much of Hekmatyar's support continued to come from the ISI. Pakistan ended their special relationship in late

1992 because he had refused to end the feuding with other mujahideen leaders. He became unpopular in Afghanistan because of the casualties caused by the bombardment of Kabul by forces under his command. In June 1996, Hekmatyar was briefly prime minister of another Afghan government shortly before the Taliban seized Kabul. After failing to reach an understanding with the Taliban, he fled to Iran and lived in Tehran. In an interview with a news correspondent in September 2001, Hekmatyar continued to be critical of the United States and to oppose without reservation the restoration of the exiled former Afghan monarch Zahir Shah. In February 2002, Hekmatyar returned to western Afghanistan and began plotting against the Hamid Karzai government. He made contact with senior Taliban and **al-Qaeda** leaders in an effort to conclude an alliance. Hekmatyar has become such a threat that an American rocket attack targeted him in May 2002, but he escaped harm. Since this attack Hekmatyar has become a growing threat to the security of the Karzai government in Afghanistan. In early December 2003, he issued a call for a holy war against coalition forces in Afghanistan in a 22-minute speech contained in a compact disc. **See also** Abdel-Rachman, Sheikh Omar; Taliban (Students of Religious Schools).

Suggested readings: Maziar Bahari, "Warlord-in-Waiting," *Newsweek* (September 28, 2001), p. 35; Gerald Bourke, "Weary Kabul Expects the Worst," *Guardian* (London) (July 5, 1996), p. 17; James Dao, "Afghan Warlord May Team Up with Al Qaeda and Taliban," *New York Times* (May 30, 2002), p. A12; M. J. Gohari, *The Taliban: Ascent to Power* (Oxford: Oxford University Press, 1999); Robert D. Kaplan, *Soldiers of God: With Islamic Warriors in Afghanistan and Pakistan* (New York: Vintage Books, 2001); Ralph H. Magnus and Eden Nasby, *Afghanistan: Mullah, Marx, and Mujahid* (Boulder, CO: Westview Press, 2000); Alexander Nicoll, and Farhan Bokhari, "Pakistan PM Cools towards Hekmatyar," *Financial Times* (London) (August 17, 1992), p. 3; Ahmed Rashid, *Taliban: Militant Islam, Oil and Fundamentalism in Central Asia* (New Haven, CT: Yale University press, 2000); Elizabeth Shogren and Douglas Frantz, "U.S. Aid to Afghan Rebels Proves a Deadly Boomerang," *Los Angeles Times* (August 2, 1993), p. A1.

Herri Batasuna (Popular Unity) (Spain)

The Herri Batasuna (Popular Unity) is a Basque nationalist political party with strong ties to the **ETA** (Euskadi Ta Askatasuna) (Basque Fatherland and Liberty). This party was formed in April 1978 by the uniting of four Basque political parties, including the Stalinist Revolutionary Socialist People's Party (Herriko Alderdi Sozializta Iraultzailea) (HASI). Herri Batasuna represents the ETA by running Basque nationalists for public offices, and it has had considerable success in both national and local elections in the Basque regions of Spain. One of the early leaders of Herri Batasune was Santiago Brouard, a pediatrician in Lekeitia, Spain, with a strong affiliation with HASI. Gunmen of the death squad GAL assassinated him at his medical office on November 20, 1984. His funeral turned into a mass demonstration by Basque nationalists against the Spanish government.

In the 1990s, the party shortened its name to Batasuna. The success of Batasuna among the Basque population attracted the attention of the Spanish government. Spanish authorities accused it of collusion with the ETA and arrested its leadership in 1997. In December 1997, the 23 leaders of the Batasuna were sentenced to seven years imprisonment for collaborating with the ETA. After the collapse of the ETA's 1998–1999 cease-fire, voting support for Batasuna dropped until it averaged about 15 percent in the Basque region. The refusal of the leadership of Batasuna to condemn the terrorist tactics of the ETA infuriated the Spanish government. In June 2002, the Spanish Parliament passed a special law to outlaw political groups that supported terrorism. This law was directed against the Batasuna. Then, in August 2002, the Spanish Parliament met in special session to petition to the Spanish Constitutional Court to outlaw the party. In March 2003, this court banned the political activity of Batasuna. In May 2003 the Constitutional Court extended the ban on Batasuna to a Basque separatist coalition operating under the Basque acronym AuB. **See also** ETA (Euskadi ta Askatasuna) (Basque Fatherland and Liberty).

Suggested readings: Tony Bailie, "Batasuna Ban Could Lead to More Conflict," *Irish Times* (August 28, 2002), p. 6; Leslie Crawford, "Divided by Violence," *Financial Times* (London) (August 24, 2002), p. 8; Cynthia L. Irvin, *Militant Nationalism: Between Movement and Party in Ireland and the Basque Country* (Minneapolis: University of Minnesota Press, 1999); Paddy Woodworth, *Dirty War, Clean Hands: ETA, the GAL, and Spanish Democracy* (Cork, Ireland: Cork University Press, 2001); Paddy Woodworth, "Saving Democracy by Curtailing It?" *Irish Times* (June 18, 2003), p. 16; Paddy Woodworth, "Spanish Ban on Basque Party May End Up Boosting Support for ETA," *Irish Times* (August 27, 2002), p. 14.

Hezbollah (Party of God) (Lebanon)

The Hezbollah (Party of God) group is the leading Shi'ite terrorist organization in Lebanon. Impetus for the founding of the Lebanese Hezbollah came from the Hezbollah Party formed in Iran in 1978 by Hadi Ghaffary, a cleric with close ties to **Ayatollah Khomeini**. This party unified several pro-Khomeini groups eager to support Khomeini and his policies. By the early 1980s, the Iranian Hezbollah had more than a million members. Khomeini decided to export his Islamic revolution and to form a Hezbollah group among the Shi'ites of Lebanon. In the middle of this planning, the Israel Defense Forces (IDF) invaded Lebanon in 1982. This event accelerated plans for a coalition of Shi'ite political groups. Later in 1982, the radical wing of the **Amal** group and the Lebanese Shi'ite Da'wa Party united to form Hezbollah under the leadership of Abbas Musawi and Sheikh Sobhi Tufeili. These leaders established the Committee of Nine to oversee operations of the new group. Sheikh **Sayyid Muhammad Husayn Fadlallah** became the group's spiritual mentor in Lebanon, but the leaders and the rank-and-file of Hezbollah looked to Iran for political and spiritual support.

Hezbollah's goal was to adapt the Iranian model of a revolutionary Islamic state for Lebanon. Hezbollah ideology divides the world into two competing camps: that of the oppressor and that of the oppressed. The oppressors are all those who have power over others, and the oppressed the powerless. Israel and the United States represent the forces of oppression and they are the main enemy of Islam. In this worldview, the Shi'ites of Lebanon and all Muslims are the oppressed, and they have the obligation to fight the oppressor with every weapon possible. Khomeini sent elements of the Iranian Revolutionary Guards to the Bekka Valley in Lebanon to train the Hezbollah in military operations.

This goal of advancing the Shi'ite cause led it into direct competition with the secular **Palestine Liberation Organization** (PLO). Hezbollah's attitude toward Middle East regimes is one of tolerance unless a country has transgressed by cooperating with Israel. Agreements between **Yasser Arafat**, the head of the PLO, and Israel have earned Arafat assassination threats from Hezbollah. In 1983 and 1984, open fighting broke out between the adherents of Hezbollah and the PLO in southern Lebanon. This antipathy toward Arafat and the PLO has resulted in good relations developing between Hezbollah and the Sunni Islamist groups **Hamas** and **Islamic Jihad**.

The military wing of Hezbollah is the Islamic Resistance Movement (IRM), and it is under the command of **Imad Fayez Mugniyah**. It was this military section that planned and executed the October 23, 1983, suicide car bombing of the U.S. Marine barracks in Beirut, Lebanon, and the suicide car bombing of the French military complex on the same date that killed 58 French paratroopers. Mugniyah also led the numerous kidnapping operations in the mid-1980s.

Open warfare broke out in 1988 between the forces of Hezbollah and another Lebanese Shi'ite group, Amal, for political and military supremacy in South Lebanon. Syria intervened on the side of its ally Amal and curbed Hezbollah's expansion. The result was the Damascus Agreement between Syria and Iran, in which Hezbollah agreed to direct its attention to fighting Israel. This agreement also meant that Syria retained control over Lebanon and indirectly over

Hezbollah. Some of Hezbollah's leaders resent Syria's influence over them.

Hezbollah became more moderate in the 1990s after the removal of Israeli forces from southern Lebanon. Israeli occupation of southern Lebanon beginning 1982 had made the leadership of Hezbollah more radical. Clashes with the IDF were frequent until the Israelis evacuated southern Lebanon. After the death of Musawi in February 1992 by an Israeli helicopter attack, Sheikh **Hassan Nasrallah** became the leader of Hezbollah, and he claimed victory against the Israelis for their withdrawal. This claim of victory and a more moderate leadership has resulted in Hezbollah becoming less aggressive in its attacks on Israel. It also allowed Hezbollah to become more active in the Lebanese political process. Hezbollah's leaders have established Hezbollah as a force in civilian life in southern Lebanon by operating 23 schools, 5 hospitals, and numerous businesses and charities. These activities have not disguised the hostility of Hezbollah toward Israel. Artillery and missile duels between Hezbollah forces and the Israel Defense Forces take place periodically, with an occasional Israeli air strike. These hostile actions have not prevented Hezbollah and the Israelis from concluding an exchange of 436 Arab prisoners and the corpses of 59 Hezbollah guerrillas in exchange for a kidnapped Israeli businessman and the bodies of three dead Israeli soldiers in late January 2004. **See also** Amal; Arafat, Yasser; Hamas (Haarakat al-Muqawama al-Islami) (Islamic Resistance Movement); Islamic Jihad; Khomeini, Ayatollah Ruhollah; Mugniyah, Imad Fayez; Palestine Liberation Organization (PLO).

Suggested readings: Robert Collier, "Hezbollah Branches Out to Win Support," *San Francisco Chronicle* (March 13, 2003), p. A8; Jeffrey Goldberg, "In the Party of God: Are Terrorists in Lebanon Preparing for a Larger War?" *New Yorker* (October 14, 2002), p. 180; Fereydoun Hoveyda, *The Broken Crescent: The "Threat" of Militant Islamic Fundamentalism* (New York: Praeger, 1998); Edgar O'Ballance, *Islamic Fundamentalist Terrorism, 1979–95: The Iranian Connection* (New York: New York University Press, 1997); Amal Saad-Ghorayeb, *Hizbu'llah: Politics and Religion* (London: Pluto Press, 2002); Carl Anthony Wege, "Hizbollah Organization," *Studies in Conflict and Terrorism* 17, no. 2 (April–June 1994); Robin Wright, *Sacred Rage: The Wrath of Militant Islam* (New York: Simon & Schuster, 1985).

Hizb ut-Tahrir al-Islami (Islamic Liberation Party) (HT) (Central Asia)

The Hizb ut-Tahrir al-Islami (Islamic Liberation Party) is a radical Islamic movement that advocates the uniting of the Muslim world under the rule of a caliphate modeled after the Rashid Caliphate (A.D. 632–A.D. 661). Sheikh Taqiuddin an-Nabhani Filastyni, a Palestinian schoolteacher and Islamic judge, founded the HT in 1953 in Hebron. In his book *The Islamic State* (1962) he described the world of the prophet Muhammad and the spread of Islam as a model for the modern world. He advocated winning mass support to convert Muslim regimes rather than revolutionary action to overthrow them. He proposed an Islamic council that would elect a caliph who would have dictatorial powers and a highly centralized administrative structure to control political life and foreign policy. Islamic law (Sharia) would be implemented to govern Muslim society. The role of women would be restricted exclusively to the family. Once the Muslim world is united under the caliphate, then the expansion of Islam into the non-Muslim world would commence by means of a holy war (jihad).

Many of the ideas of the Hizb ut-Tahrir al-Islami resemble those of the **Wahhabi** revival, but differences exist. Both adherents of HT and the Wahhabis want to reestablish an idealized Islamic state modeled on the one from the time of the prophet Muhammad. They also consider the Shi'ites as heretics and would expel them from Muslim states. Jews would suffer a similar fate. The major difference between the two is over tactics. Leaders of the HT advocate a peaceful transition to the purified Islamic state based on the view that all other Islamic movements are in error because HT alone has found the true way. They have found Wahhabism too violent and counterproductive.

The Hizb ut-Tahrir al-Islami soon found itself in trouble with authorities in the Muslim states in the Middle East. Governments felt threatened by HT and its adherents were forced to go underground to avoid persecution. In 1974, members of HT attempted to assassinate Egyptian President Anwar Sadat. Leaders moved to Europe and established headquarters in Germany and in Great Britain. Sheikh Zaloom, a Palestinian and former professor at Egypt's **al-Azhar University**, is the current leader of HT. From a secret location in Europe, he runs a secret organization that raises funds and recruits followers. Muslim students at British universities have been attracted to the HT. These recruits return to their native countries and establish secret cells of five to seven men. Only the cell leader knows the next level of organization and receives instructions from it. The growth of HT has been rapid, especially in Central Asia in the former Soviet states of Kazakhstan, Kyrgyzstan, Tajikistan, and Uzbekistan. Authorities in these states have arrested and imprisoned those HT members whom they can identify. Most of those arrested are educated young men from large cities. See also Wahhabism.

Suggested readings: Douglas Davis, "Islamic Fundamentalism with a Sugar Coating," *Jerusalem Post* (August 24, 1995), p. 7; David Harrison, "Battle for Islam's Future," *Observer* (London) (August 13, 1995), p. 12; Ahmed Rashid, *Jihad: The Rise of Militant Islam in Central Asia* (New Haven, CT: Yale University Press, 2002).

Holocaust Denial (Europe and the Middle East)

Holocaust denial is an attempt by apologists for Adolf Hitler and the Nazis, and anti-Semites, to deny the mass extermination of European Jewry during World War II. Despite overwhelming physical evidence and numerous eyewitness accounts, these Holocaust deniers refuse to accept the existence of the Holocaust. Holocaust denial is an international movement that has attracted Americans, Europeans, and Arabs, but the emphasis here will be on European and Arab Holocaust deniers.

Almost as soon as there was verifiable evidence of the Holocaust, there were individuals both on the political left and the right that refused to acknowledge it. Perhaps the earliest Holocaust denier was the Frenchman Paul Rassinier, a former member of the French Communist Party. His political views landed him in the Nazis' Buchenwald concentration camp. An inability to get along with his fellow Communists led him to collaborate with the Nazis. Rassinier's collaboration earned him a transfer to Camp Dora in the Harz Mountains. His good treatment there converted him to Nazism. After the war, he published several writings that defended the Nazis. In one of these writings, Rassinier defended the Nazi SS and denied atrocities in the concentration camps. He refused to credit eyewitness testimony by either the Nazis or survivors. Rassinier accused the Jews of lying about the gas chambers and for starting World War II. His death in 1967 has not muted his charges.

Rassinier's successor in France was **Robert Faurisson**. He was a professor of French literature at the University of Lyons until his controversial views on the Holocaust ended his academic career. His main thesis was that the Nazi gas chambers in the concentration camps never existed. He considered any evidence to the contrary as a Jewish lie. His advocacy of Holocaust denial got him into trouble with the French authorities. He was convicted of willfully distorting history and for incitement to racial hatred. These charges, a brief jail sentence, and a fine have not stopped Faurisson from continuing to deny the Holocaust. He has been appointed to the editorial board of the American Holocaust denial journal *The Journal of Historical Review*.

Another prominent European Holocaust denier is Wilhelm Staeglich. He had good academic credentials from a German university and a law degree. In 1979, he had published *The Auschwitz Myth: Legend or Reality* in which he repudiated evidence that there had been mass exterminations of Jews in Nazi death camps. Staeglich maintained that the postwar trials of Germans for war crimes were unjust. Any document that did not support his thesis was considered a forgery. Staeglich lost his state job, and his university revoked his doctorate. Despite his loss of academic credentials, he, too, was appointed to the editorial board of *The Journal of Historical Review*.

The most celebrated Holocaust denier has been the British historian **David Irving**. Irving built a reputation as a military historian despite a lack of academic credentials. He pursued a degree in science at London University, but he left school without graduating. Irving published 30 controversial books before he fell into the camp of the Holocaust deniers. Sometime around 1988, Irving's writing changed and he began disputing evidence of the Holocaust both in his books and in public. Irving also started associating with known Holocaust deniers, and his participation in the American Holocaust denial Institute for Historical Review's conferences made him a spokesperson for Holocaust denial.

His association with Holocaust deniers had consequences. In 1993, an American historian, Deborah Lipstadt, wrote a book *Denying the Holocaust: The Growing Assault on Truth and Memory*. She charged that Irving had distorted and misused historical data to further his political agenda. In November 1995, Irving demanded that Lipstadt's book be withdrawn from circulation, and he threatened to sue her and her publisher for defamation of character in British courts. He made it plain that he considered Lipstadt part of a conspiracy to discredit him. Irving sued both Lipstadt and her publisher in 1999.

After a lengthy pretrial discovery period, the trial opened in January 2000 to massive publicity. Commentators on both sides interpreted the trial as a judgment on the Holocaust. Each side conceded that the issues were too complex for a jury and therefore presented its case before a single judge, Charles Gray. Irving represented himself. The trial turned into a battle of experts. After a three-month trial, Judge Gray handed down a 350-page judgment against Irving. This judgment concluded that Irving had misused

history and that he was anti-Semitic. Irving was left with a tattered reputation and £2 million in fees. This case hurt him financially, and it also damaged his relationships with his colleagues among the Holocaust deniers, who blame him for the court defeat.

Holocaust denial is an international phenomenon that has reached as far away as New Zealand. In 1993, Joel Hayward produced a master's thesis on the historiography of the Holocaust at Canterbury University that earned him first-class honors. He followed with a dissertation also at Canterbury University. His thesis, entitled *Fate of Jews in German Hands: An Historical Enquiry into the Development and Significance of Holocaust Revisionism*, claimed that most of revisionist literature was academically suspect, but that there were elements of their arguments that had truth. He questioned Hitler's involvement in the Holocaust, the number of Jews killed, and the German use of gas chambers. This obscure thesis remained in the library until the New Zealand Jewish Council denounced it in late 1999. Canterbury University appointed an independent three-person committee to investigate the thesis, and they concluded that the thesis was flawed and the conclusions went beyond the evidence. Haywood resigned his position as senior lecturer in history at Massey University in June 2002, and his defender, Dr. Thomas Fudge, resigned his position at Canterbury University in July 2003.

Despite legal remedies, Holocaust denial remains popular in certain circles. Arab critics of the Jewish presence in Israel have long been supporters of Holocaust denial. Many leading Muslim leaders in Palestine and Egypt had been sympathetic to Germany in World War II. Anti-Semitism and Holocaust denial have bonded together to be used as a weapon against the state of Israel. **See also** Faurisson, Robert; Irving, David John Cawdell.

Suggested readings: Editorial Staff, "Freedom Stops When Denial Starts," *New Zealand Herald* (August 8, 2003), p. 1; Richard J. Evans, *Lying about Hitler: History, Holocaust and the David Irving Trial* (New York: Basic Books, 2001);

Thomas Fudge, "Holocaust, History and Free Speech," *New Zealand Herald* (July 23, 2003), p. 1; D. D. Guttenplan, *The Holocaust on Trial* (New York: Norton, 2001); Deborah Lipstadt, *Denying the Holocaust: The Growing Assault on Truth and Memory* (New York: Plume, 1993); Pierre Vidal-Naquet, *Assassins of Memory* (New York: Columbia University Press, 1992); John C. Zimmerman, *Holocaust Denial: Demographics, Testimonies and Ideologies* (Lanham, MD: University Press of America, 2000).

Horne, Barry (1952–2001) (Great Britain)

Barry Horne was one of the leaders of the British militant **Animal Liberation Front** (ALF). He was born in 1952 in Liverpool, England. His father was a postman, and his mother died when he was young. He left school at age 15 and worked at a variety of menial jobs as a road sweeper and a dustman. His second wife introduced him to the animal rights movement, and he joined the Animal Liberation Front. He soon became notorious within the ALF for his militancy. In 1988, Horne attempted to liberate a 650-pound dolphin, Rocky, from a marine park in Morecambe, Lancashire. He received a six-month suspended sentence and a $750 fine for this attempt.

Horne decided to change tactics and bomb establishments that he considered to promote the suffering of animals. In 1991, he was arrested and sentenced to a three-year jail term for possession of explosive substances. After his release from jail, he was implicated in a 1994 bombing campaign on the Isle of Wight. British police raided his home in Swindon, Wiltshire, and found literature advocating arson attacks, but he was not charged on this occasion. Horne then moved his area of operations to southwest England. In July 1996, police arrested him after he had placed incendiary devices in two stores that sold furs in a Bristol shopping center. Horne received an 18-year prison sentence for this and the Wright bombings.

Horne used his jail term to lobby British legislators to enact animal rights legislation. He used the **Irish Republican Army** (IRA) tactic of a hunger strike to publicize his campaign. Four times he engaged in hunger strikes at Long Lartin high-security prison. His 68-day hunger strike beginning December 1998 was his longest and most dramatic. These strikes endangered his health by weakening his liver. In his last hunger strike that started on October 21, 2001, Horne's health deteriorated so dramatically that he died in a Ronkswood hospital on November 5, 2001. Animal rights activists immediately claimed him as a martyr to their cause. **See also** Animal Liberation Front (ALF); Lee, Ronnie.

Suggested readings: Stephen Farrell and Russell Jenkins, "Hunger Striker's Life in Hands of a Believer," *Times* (London) (December 12, 1998), p. 1; Richard Ford and Valerie Elliott, "Fanatic Who Revelled in His Notoriety," *Times* (London) (November 6, 2001), p. 1; Sarah Hall, "Animal Activists Mourn Their Martyr," *Guardian* (London) (November 6, 2001), p. 3; Kevin Toolis, "To the Death," *Guardian* (London) (November 7, 2001), p. 6.

Huber, Achmed (1927–) (Switzerland)

Achmed Huber is a Swiss extremist with connections to European neo-Nazi movements and to **Osama bin Laden**'s al-Qaeda. He was born in 1927 in Freiburg, Switzerland. His parents were Swiss German Protestants. Little is known about his early life. He worked for years as a government affairs reporter for the Swiss news media firm of Ringier and its *Swiss Illustrated* (*Schweizer Illustriete*) until he was fired on March 1, 1989, for his public support of **Ayatollah Ruhollah Khomeini**'s death decree against Salman Rushdie for writing *The Satanic Verses*. After the abrupt end to his journalistic career, Huber used his right-wing connections to enter the banking world.

Huber first showed his attraction to extremist politics in the late 1950s. It was at this time that he joined the Swiss Socialist Party. Huber shared its support for the Algerian independence movement during the fighting in the early 1960s. His sympathies for the Algerian cause extended to a developing an interest in the study of Islam. Huber established contacts with the **Muslim Brotherhood**, and after further study he professed his belief in Islam. In 1962, he traveled to Egypt, where he made his conversion to Islam official at **al-Azhar University**. This conversion made Huber a determined enemy of Israel and its supporter, the United States. He also became friends with the pro-Nazi Grand Mufti of Jerusalem, Amin al-Husseini, and Johann von Leers, a former Nazi Propaganda Ministry official working in Egypt for Nasser. In Switzerland, he became the protégé of the neo-Nazi Swiss banker François Genoud. Until his suicide in 1996, Genoud bankrolled neo-Nazi and pro-Arab causes by providing legal support for them. In the 1980s, Huber began advocating **Holocaust denial**, and he established a working relationship with the Institute for Historical Review (IHR) in California. Huber developed an affiliation with the Swiss pagan Avalon Society (Avalon Gemeinschaft) shortly after its founding in 1986. This group worshiped the pre-Christian Celtic gods of Europe, and it attracted Swiss Nazis, Holocaust deniers, and right-wing fanatics. He was also involved in the founding in 1987 of Radio Islam, which maintained programs proclaiming anti-Semitic, anti-Israel, Holocaust denial, pro-Arab, and pro-Nazi propaganda. Huber's extremist politics finally led the Swiss Socialist Party to expel him in 1994.

Huber's name hit the international scene following the **September 11, 2001,** terrorist attacks on the United States. His membership on the board of directors of Nada Management brought him to the attention of the Swiss police. Nada Management was part of the international al-Taqwa (Fear of God) group that provided funding for Osama bin Laden's al-Qaeda. When confronted with the charges of aiding al-Qaeda, Huber's response was to praise bin Laden. **See also** Bin Laden, Osama; Al-Qaeda (The Base).

Suggested readings: Kevin Coogan, "Achmed Huber, the Avalon Gemeinschaft, and the Swiss 'New Right,'" *HITLIST* (April/May 2002), p. 1; Marc Erikson, "Islamism, Fascism and Terrorism," *Asia Times Online*, http://www.atimes.com/atimes/Middle_East/ (accessed November 5, 2002); Peter Finn, "Unlikely Allies Bound by a Common Hatred," *Washington Post Foreign Service* (April 29, 2002), p. A13; Daniel Williams, "Swiss Probe Illustrates Difficulties in Tracking Al Qaeda's Cash," *Washington Post* (November 12, 2001), p. A10.

Hussein, Saddam (1937–) (Iraq)

Saddam Hussein was the head of the Iraqi state, and his actions have destabilized the Middle East. He was born on April 28, 1937, in the small Sunni Muslim village of Al-Awja near Tikrit and about 100 miles north of Baghdad, Iraq. His family belonged to the Albu Nasser clan. Members of this clan were Sunni Muslims with a reputation for violence. His father was already deceased before his birth, and his stepfather barely tolerated him. In 1947, Hussein went to live in Tikrit with a maternal uncle, Kharrallah Tulfan, a former Iraqi army officer arrested after the 1941 uprising. After completing local schooling, Hussein moved to Baghdad with his uncle to further his education. He tried to pass the entrance examination to study at a military college, but he failed the exams.

While in Baghdad, Hussein became active in anti-Iraqi government demonstrations and began association with elements of the Ba'ath Party. The Ba'ath Party had been formed in Damascus, Syria, in April 1947 as a pan-Arab party that claimed to be nationalistic, populist, socialist, and revolutionary. After the 1958 military coup against the monarchy, Hussein found himself in legal difficulties over a murder charge. He was briefly imprisoned but let go for lack of evidence. The Ba'ath Party decided to assassinate the new head of the Iraqi government, General Abdel Karim Kassem. Hussein participated in the attempt on October 7, 1959, but Kassem was only wounded. Suffering from a wound in the leg, Hussein had to leave Iraq to avoid arrest by the police. He traveled to Syria, and in Damascus Hussein joined the Ba'ath Party after recruitment by its founder Michel Aflaq. The Syrian government then allowed Hussein and the other Iraqi Ba'athists to go to Egypt. In Egypt Hussein was able to further his education. He attended Qasr Al Nil

High School in Cairo. After graduation in 1961, he studied law briefly at Cairo University. While in Egypt, the Iraqi government sentenced him to death in absentia. Hussein remained in Egypt until the Ba'ath Party's February 8, 1963, coup against Kassem succeeded. Several of his relatives, including General Ahmad Hassan Al Bakr, were leaders in the coup.

Hussein returned to Iraq two weeks after the coup and received an appointment to the Aref government. In the subsequent feuding between the left and right wings of the Ba'ath Party, Hussein supported the right wing. President Aref in November 1963 seized control of the state from the Ba'athists and Hussein had to go underground to escape arrest. On September 4, 1964, the police arrested Hussein in the middle of a plot to assassinate Aref. While in prison, he was appointed Deputy Secretary of the Iraqi Branch of the Ba'ath Party. On July 23, 1966, Hussein escaped during a transfer between prisons.

Hussein was one of the leaders of the July 17, 1968, coup that brought the Ba'ath Party back to power. His reward was control of the government's security forces. He used the authority of his office and his family relationship with President al-Bakr to purge the government of enemies and possible rivals. In January 1969, Hussein became a member of the ruling Revolutionary Command Council (RRC) and its undersecretary-general. He utilized this position to make the Iraqi army a branch of the Ba'ath Party, thereby making it dependent on the party. His next action was to become the leader of the Iraqi delegation to negotiate with foreign oil companies over Iraqi oil. On June 1, 1972, in a highly popular movement among all segments of the Iraqi population, Hussein nationalized Iraq's oil. By opening the supply of oil on the foreign market, Hussein increased Iraqi national income for both an economic development program and an arms buildup. By 1975, he had replaced Bakr as the head of the RCC, but Bakr, as president of Iraq, remained as a figurehead until he tried to arrange a union between Iraq and Syria in 1978. This alliance threatened Hussein, and he undermined the agreement by making unacceptable demands. In early July 1979, Bakr retired under pressure from Hussein. On July 16, 1979, Hussein replaced Bakr as president of Iraq, and his dictatorship was in place. Hussein removed any possible challengers by discovering a supposedly Syrian-sponsored plot against the RCC on July 28, 1979. In the subsequent purge of the RCC, he had members of the government hierarchy, high-ranking officers, trade union officials, and student union leaders arrested and executed.

Hussein's first major challenge as head of state was the Iran-Iraq War. Iraq had territorial claims against Iran that predated Hussein's rule. Hussein was also aware of the **Ayatollah Khomeini**'s anti-Ba'ath feelings and his call for Iraqi Shi'ites to overthrow the Hussein regime. His response to Khomeini's call was to have the veteran Iraqi Shi'ite leader Mohammed Bahr al-Sadr and his sister Amina al-Sadr executed on April 9, 1980. He then decided that the time was ripe in 1980 to advance these territorial claims and rid Iraq of the Khomeini threat by taking military action against Iran.

The Iran-Iraqi War was almost a disaster for Hussein. Early successes soon led to a stalemate as the Iranians turned the war into a jihad, or holy war. Iranians threw ill-trained and ill-equipped troops against the more highly trained and better-equipped Iraqi army. Hussein went into the war with limited objectives to seize the oil-rich western part of Iran, but Khomeini wanted to overthrow the secular government of Iraq and Hussein. The war lasted for eight years, with neither side winning in the end.

Hussein revitalized his war machine and started looking to expand in a different direction. Iraq had always made a claim on Kuwait and its oil, but international borders made Kuwait an independent state. This did not stop Hussein from coveting Kuwait and its oil wealth. He ordered the Iraqi army to invade Kuwait in 1990. Military forces of Kuwait were no match for the Iraqi army, and Iraqi authorities found enough supporters in Kuwait to run the government there. The problem was that the Western powers, led by the United States, were unwilling to allow Hussein to control Kuwait and its oil reserves. In early 1991, the combined military forces of the United States, Great Britain, and France drove Iraqi forces out of Kuwait, almost wiping out the Iraqi army.

The next 12 years found Hussein concentrating on retaining political control of Iraq. United Nations economic sanctions made it impossible for him to rebuild his military forces. He had enough military power to put down a Shi'ite uprising shortly after the Persian Gulf War, but otherwise his military forces rusted. Hussein tried to bluff his way out when the United States, under President George W. Bush, initiated a campaign to oust him. Despite the failure of United Nations inspectors to find weapons of mass destruction, the Bush administration orchestrated a campaign show that Hussein was a future threat to the United States. In the spring of 2003, military forces from the United States and Great Britain invaded Iraq and overthrew Hussein. His obsolete military forces had little chance against American and British forces.

Hussein's fate remained a mystery until his capture in the evening of December 13, 2003. After receiving intelligence information about Hussein's possible whereabouts in Tikrit, elements of the U.S. 4th Infantry Division discovered Hussein hiding in a small man-made hole of about six by eight feet in size. After a physical, Hussein was placed under arrest pending interrogation and a decision on his fate. The next issue is to decide who will try Hussein and what charges will be brought against him. **See also** Khomeini, Ayatollah Ruholla.

Suggested readings: Said K. Arburish, *Saddam Hussein: The Politics of Revenge* (London: Bloomsbury, 2000); Daniel Byman, "Iraq after Saddam," *Washington Quarterly* 24, no. 4 (2001 Autumn), p. 151; Andrew Cockburn and Patrick Cockburn, *Out of the Ashes: The Resurrection of Saddam Hussein* (New York: HarperCollins, 1999); Reuel Marc Gerecht, "Liberate Iraq: Is the Bush Administration Serious about Toppling Saddam Hussein?" *Weekly Standard* (London) (May 14, 2001), p. 23; Hilip Hiro, *The Longest War: The Iran-Iraq Military Conflict* (New York: Routledge, 1991); Joseph A. Kechichian, "The Future of Iraq: Saddam Hussein Has Already Outlasted One President George Bush," *Arabies Trends* (October 1, 2001), p. 1.

Intifada (Palestine)

The Intifada is the uprising of the Palestinians against the Israeli occupation in Gaza and in the West Bank that began in December 1987 and continues in one form or another today. The massive flight of Palestinians during and in the aftermath of the Israeli victory in 1948 produced more than 5 million refugees. Many of these refugees settled in Gaza and in the West Bank of the Jordan River awaiting help from Arab states to reclaim their lands and property. Efforts to mobilize the Palestinians into resistance by the Palestine Liberation Organization (PLO) had only limited success.

The 1967 Arab-Israeli War convinced the Palestinians that the chances of returning to the Palestine of before were remote. Brief hope emerged during the 1973 Yom Kippur War, but Israel was as strong militarily after the war as before. In the meantime, the Israeli government had total executive and legislative control of the occupied territories of Gaza and the West Bank. Efforts by the Israelis to encourage self-government under strict controls in the early 1980s failed.

Resistance to Israel among Palestinians was undertaken in two ways—through paramilitary operations and civil resistance. Israeli military authorities were able to contain most paramilitary activities in Gaza and the West Bank. Civil resistance was much tougher to control as Palestinians conducted strikes, demonstrations, and other public means to publicize their resistance to Israeli rule. Israeli authorities pursued harsh measures to put down resistance by closing schools and arresting participants. These harsh measures backfired on the Israelis as Palestinian nationalism increased among the Palestinian youth and new leaders emerged as the older ones were deported or arrested.

The emergence of the Israeli settlement movement both in Gaza and the West Bank further infuriated and scared the Palestinians. Shortly before the outbreak of the Intifada, Israeli settlements had requisitioned nearly half of the land in the West Bank and nearly a third of the territory in Gaza. Israel controlled the economies in both areas to the benefit of the Israelis. Civil unrest became more serious in the early 1980s as Palestinians protested the policies of the Menachem Begin government. Even the defeat of the PLO in Lebanon in 1982 did not end the civil unrest. Tensions continued to build throughout the 1980s.

The Intifada broke out over a minor incident in Gaza. On December 7, 1987, an Israel Defense Forces (IDF) truck ran into another truck, killing four Palestinians and injuring seven others. Rumors spread among the Palestinians that the accident had been deliberate. During the funeral of three of the dead at the Jabalya refugee camp in Gaza, a mass demonstration formed. Israeli troops intervened, but they were unable to disperse the rioters. Demonstrations spread throughout Gaza and the West Bank. Confrontations between the IDF and Palestinian youth became a daily occurrence. Palestinian leaders then initiated a campaign of civil disobedience against Israel. Israeli authorities responded by use of force, deportation of Intifada leaders, economic sanctions, curfews, school closings, and finally political assassination. A Mossad hit team assassinated PLO leader Khalil al-Wazir (Abu Jihad) in April 1987 in Tunis, Tunisia. This assassination only further intensified the Intifada. During the first year of the Intifada, the Israelis arrested more than 18,000 Palestinians. Slowly, the Israelis came to the realization that the Intifada was a mass uprising and military force alone could not end it.

Soon after the outbreak of the Intifada, the Palestinians formed a coordinating committee in the Unified National Leadership of the Uprising (UNLU). This leadership group had 15 rotating members drawn from five Palestinian groups—al-Fatah, Popular Front for the Liberation of Palestine (PFLP), Democratic Front for the Liberation of Palestine (DFLP), the Palestine Communist Party, and Islamic Jihad. Each of these groups provided three members to the UNLU. Each time a member of the UNLU was arrested, a new member would be appointed to replace him. The relationship between the UNLU and the PLO was loose because of the difficulty of communications between Palestine and Tunisia. The main mission of the UNLC was coordinating the activities of the Intifada. A secondary mission was the neutralization of Palestinian collaborators with Israel.

The Intifada lasted for nearly three years. Israeli authorities found the cost and the intensity of the Intifada unacceptable. Israeli forces always retained military supremacy, but the Palestinians refused to accept it. The notion that the Israelis could permanently occupy Palestinian territory proved illusory. It took negotiations in Oslo between the Israeli government and the Palestine Liberation Organization to end the Intifada. After the Oslo Accords were signed in September 1993, peace was thought to be possible. This accord allowed autonomy for the Palestinians in the West Bank and Gaza and it had the support of the overwhelming majority of the Palestinians. However, this peace also proved to be illusory, and by the late 1990s the Palestinians became convinced that the peace process was dead. **See also** Arafat, Yasser; Al-Fatah; Islamic Jihad; Palestine Liberation Organization (PLO); Popular Front for the Liberation of Palestine (PFLP).

Suggested readings: Ghassan Andoni, "A Comparative Study of Intifada 1987 and Intifada 2000," in Roane Carey (ed.), *The New Intifada: Resisting Israel's Apartheid* (London: Verso, 2001); Don Peretz, *Intifada: The Palestinian Uprising* (Boulder, CO: Westview Press, 1990); Ze'ev Schiff and Ehud Ya'ari, *Intifada: The Palestinian Uprising: Israel's Third Front* (New York: Simon & Schuster, 1990); Khalil Shikaki, "Palestinians Divided," *Foreign Affairs* (January–February 2002), p. 89.

Irgun Zvai Leumi (National Military Organization) (IZL) (Israel)

The Irgun Zvai Leumi (IZL) was the Jewish terrorist group that fought the British in Palestine in the years before the founding of the Israeli state. Vladimir Ze'ev Jabotinsky, the head of the radical Zionist Revisionist Party (ZRP), and a group of dissidents separated from the Haganah, the Jewish defense force, and formed a separate group in 1931. At first this organization was weak and ineffective, but the Arab terrorist campaign of 1936 caused Jabotinsky, Abraham Stern, and David Raziel to form the IZL in 1938. Jabotinsky led the moderate wing and Stern the militant wing. After Jabotinsky's death in August 1940, Stern and around 100 members of the Irgun left to form the **Stern Gang**. The remaining members of the Irgun supported the British in early World War II. Raziel was killed in a 1941 military operation in Iraq. In early 1944, the new leader of the Irgun, Menachem Begin, decided that armed struggle against the British was the only way to establish a Jewish state.

The Irgun launched an offensive against British rule in Palestine in February 1944. Efforts made to recruit Jewish units in the British army failed, and at the outbreak of the uprising, the Irgun had fewer than 600 men and women fighters and only about 200 weapons. Begin devised a strategy to harass the British by attacking administrative and economic targets but avoid unnecessary casualties. Irgun's leadership ignored the Palestinian Arabs, because it also wanted to avoid a war on two fronts. The first operation was an attack on immigration offices in Jerusalem, Jaffa, and Haifa on February 12, 1944. Other operations against tax offices followed. These first attacks had little impact on the British, but Jewish anger about the Holocaust helped Irgun's recruiting efforts. Although the Stern Gang was more violent than the Irgun, British authorities and the Jewish League considered the Irgun the more dangerous of the two because of Irgun's growing popularity among Palestinian Jews. The Jewish community and the Haganah feared the Irgun's popularity so much that they cooperated with the British, leading to a mini-civil war. Jewish cooperation with the British almost destroyed the Irgun between November 1944 and March 1945. Begin avoided a Jewish civil war by ordering Irgun members to go underground. Relations between the Irgun and the Haganah left an animosity between the two organizations that lasted long after the war.

In the fall of 1945, the Haganah decided to undertake an anti-British campaign and it established a working relationship with the Irgun in the United Resistance Movement. This relationship lasted only about a year. On July 22, 1946, members of the Irgun planted a bomb in the King David Hotel in Jerusalem, the British administrative headquarters in Palestine. The explosion killed over 80 civilians and it convinced the leadership of the Haganah that Begin and the Irgun were unreliable partners. This feeling then led to a mini-civil war between the Haganah and the Irgun. A massacre of more than 100 Palestinians at Dir Yassin, an Arab village near Jerusalem, on April 9, 1948, by Begin's forces only intensified feelings between the two organizations. Even after elements of the Irgun were incorporated into the Israel Defense Forces, the incident of the *Altalena*, an Irgun supply ship sunk by the IDF on June 22, 1948, showed the intensity of the feelings between Prime Minister David Ben-Gurion and Begin's Irgun. Although the Stern Gang was the group that assassinated Count Folke Bernadotte in September 1948, the crackdown of Israeli authorities on extremist organizations ended the career of the Irgun as a military/terrorist group. After September 1948, the leadership of the Irgun devoted their energies to Israeli politics. In the final irony, Menachem Begin became prime minister of Israel in 1977.

Suggested readings: J. Bowyer Bell, *Terror Out of Zion: Irgun Zvai Leumi, LEHI, and the Palestine Underground, 1929–1949* (New York: St. Martin's Press, 1977); Amos Perlmutter, *The Life and Times of Menachem Begin* (Garden City, NY: Doubleday, 1987); Ehud Sprinzak, *Brother against Brother: Violence and Extremism in Israeli Politics from Altalena to the Rabin Assassination* (New York: Free Press, 1999); Saul Zadka, *Blood in Zion: How the Jewish Guerrillas Drove the British Out of Palestine* (London: Brassey's, 1995).

Irish National Liberation Army (INLA) (Northern Ireland)

The Irish National Liberation Army (INLA) is one of the leading terrorist groups in Northern Ireland. Most of its members were partisans of the Trotskyite Socialist Irish Republican Socialist Party (IRSP). Bernadette Devlin and Seamus Costello founded the IRSP in 1974. Under the leadership of Seamus Costello, the INLA broke away from the Official Irish Republican Party (OIRA) in 1975, and it engaged in a bloody feud with it. A leader of the IRSP, Hugh Ferguson, was shot and killed on February 20, 1975, by an OIRA gunman. Members of the INLA retaliated by killing an Official IRA leader in Belfast and wounding another in Dublin. Although most members of the INLA had affiliations with the IRSP, they remain separate organizations. They do share, however, the goal of a united Socialist Ireland.

The **Irish National Liberation Army** initiated a terrorist campaign soon after its founding. To finance its operations, the INLA activists robbed banks in both the Republic of Ireland and in Northern Ireland. They have also attacked Protestant loyalist figures, but their most infamous assassination was that of Airey Neave, a member of Parliament and a close advisor of British Prime Minister Margaret Thatcher, on March 30, 1979, in London. The most notorious of INLA's leaders has been Dessie O'Hare, or the "Border Fox." In 1979, he kidnapped John O'Grady, a dentist, and held him for a ransom of two million Euros. To prove his seriousness, O'Hare hacked off two of O'Grady's fingers. The ransom attempt failed and the Irish police captured O'Hare after he was shot 15 times. After a prison sentence of 40 years, O'Hare has spent the remaining years in prison. In December 2002, he was transferred to a low-security prison in preparation for his eventual prison release, but Irish authorities continue to be reluctant to free O'Hare despite agitation by his followers.

Another major operation was the murder of the Loyalist Volunteer Force chief, **Billy "King Rat" Wright.** Three INLA hitmen, John Glennon, John Kennaway, and Christopher "Crip" McWilliams, carried out the assassination. They and Wright were prisoners in Northern Ireland's high-security Maze Prison. Somebody smuggled into prison a semi-automatic pistol and a Derringer pistol for the INLA prisoners. They then moved through a precut hole in a metal fence into the Loyalist area. There they intercepted a prison van carrying Wright. Four shots were fired into Wright, killing him.

Relations with the **Provisional IRA** (Provos) have always been shaky, but they have improved since the 1998 cease-fire. Many Provisional IRA members left to join the INLA because the INLA had a more militant stance. Later, when the Provos began to toy with the idea of a truce or cease-fire, other members defected to the INLA. Often violent operations by the INLA reflected on the Provos and feuds developed. This adversarial position has lessened since the leadership of the INLA has accepted the cease-fire negotiated by the **Gerry Adams** and **Martin McGuinness**. In February 2002, leaders of the INLA also initiated peace initiatives with the Loyalists. **See also** Adams, Gerry; Irish Republican Army; McGuinness, Martin; Provisional Irish Republican Army (IRA); Wright, Billy "King Rat."

Suggested readings: Stephen Breen, "INLA's Summit Offer to Loyalists," *Sunday Life* (London)) (February 10, 2002), p. 1; Tim Pat Coogan, *The IRA: A History* (Niwot, CO: Robert Rinehart, 1993); Jim Cusack, "IRA Dissidents Co-Operate in Campaign to Unravel North Settlement," *Irish Times* (May 25, 1998), p. 5; Pat Flanagan, "Dessie Will Get His Own House," *Mirror* (London)) (December 9, 2002), p. 10; Audrey Gillan, "Terror Group Says Ulster War Is Over," *Guardian* (London) (August 9, 1999), p. 2; Niall Moonan, "INLA Chief's Bid for Freedom," *Mirror* (London) (October 12, 2002), p. 4; David Wright, "Fresh Doubt Cast on Killer's Bloody End," *Sunday Life* (London) (October 6, 2002), p. 1.

Irish Republican Army (IRA)
(Ireland and Northern Ireland)

The Irish Republican Army (IRA) is the oldest extremist group in Europe. Irish republican nationalists established the IRA under the name Irish Republican Brotherhood (IRB) on February 15, 1858. Goal of this organization was to fight the British occupation of Ireland. Members of the IRB developed a close association with the **Sinn Fein** (Ourselves Alone) after it was founded in 1905. The extremist wing of the IRB planned and carried out the 1916 Easter Uprising under the banner of the Irish Republican Army, and its leaders were executed in the aftermath of the uprising. Leaders of the IRA fought first against the British and later, after the conclusion of peace with the British, in a civil war against the new Irish government. Only after the cease-fire on May 23, 1923, did the Irish Republican Army stop fighting. Despite this cease-fire, the leaders of the IRA never reconciled to the idea that the Irish government represented the legal government of Ireland. They claimed that the

Second Dail Eireann was still the legal government of Ireland. In 1925, the IRA broke with the Sinn Fein after deciding to abandon politics.

The Irish Republican Army instead organized itself as a secret army. Governance for the IRA came from its seven-officer Army Council constituted from a 12-man executive committee. Delegates from IRA units voted for the membership of the Executive Committee. Members of the Army Council appointed a chief of staff whose job was to oversee the operations of the IRA. An administrative staff assisted the chief of staff in the carrying out of his duties.

Throughout the 1930s and 1940s, the Irish Republican Army was in a state of flux, unable to define its mission. In 1931, the Irish government outlawed the Irish Republican Army making it more diffucult for the IRA to operate in the Republic of Ireland. In the late 1930s, elements in the IRA conducted a bombing campaign in England, but, except for a few bombings and light casualties, the campaign was unsuccessful. This terrorism alienated both the British and Irish general public. Throughout the war years, the IRA's activities against the Irish government continued, again with little success.

Only toward the end of the 1940s did new leadership decide to reorient the IRA. In 1948, the new chief of staff, Tony Magan, decided to direct the energies of the IRA toward freeing the six counties that constitute Northern Ireland. To help this campaign, the IRA and the Sinn Fein renewed their alliance in 1949. Operations against Northern Ireland commenced in 1951. Over the next 11 years, until 1962, IRA members made raids against British military arsenals to obtain weapons and ammunition for a military campaign. These raids garnered few arms and lead to the arrests and deaths of key operatives.

Leadership disputes within the Irish Republican Army led to several schisms. Cathal Goulding, a house painter by trade and a veteran IRA activist, became chief of staff of the Army Council in 1962. He decided to recast the IRA into a Marxist mode with the help of Roy Johnson, a young computer scientist and self-educated Marxist. Most of the mainline republican leaders opposed this leftward drift. By the mid-1960s, the IRA lacked arms and money, and it had a divided leadership. Sinn Fein, the political wing of the IRA, occupied most of the attention of the IRA leadership.

The outbreak of violence between Catholics and Protestants in Northern Ireland provided the catalyst for rebellion within the ranks of the Irish Republican Army. Lack of preparation by IRA leadership for armed struggle in Northern Ireland led to a rejection of IRA leadership. Younger members were the most upset with the leadership of Goulding and Johnson. Their attempt to turn the IRA into a political party rather than retain its goal of a united Ireland alienated both the traditionalist and militant wings of the movement. This discontent resulted in the creation of the Provisional IRA in late December 1969. A group of IRA members met in Belfast and they approved the creation of a seven-member Provisional Army Council. Most prominent of the new group were **Sean MacStiofain**, Ruairi O'Bradaigh, and Diathi O'Conaill. The new Army Council selected MacStiofain to be chief of staff. A mass flight of dissidents into the ranks of the Provisional IRA hurt the IRA. Old-line republicans stayed in the IRA and it was soon designated as the Official IRA. Enough pressure was placed on the leadership of Sinn Fein that it also split with the Provisional IRA. Despite the defections and the resulting feud that threatened to turn into a civil war, the Official IRA remained the larger of the two groups until the spring of 1972.

At first, the Official IRA competed with the Provisional IRA in terrorist operations in Northern Ireland. A botched bombing that killed five cleaning women, a Catholic chaplain, and a gardener in February 1972 and the execution of a British soldier in May 1972 led the leadership of the Official IRA to issue a cease-fire on May 29, 1972. Neither Goulding nor Johnston cared for the use of violence. Since this cease-fire, the Official IRA has played a secondary role to the Provisional IRA in both Northern Ireland and the Republic of Ireland. This cease-fire led Seamus Costello to break from the Official IRA in late 1974 and form the Irish Republican Socialist Party (IRSP). Its military wing was the Irish National Liberation Army (INLA). The Official IRA was further weakened when many of its members in Northern Ireland left to join the IRSP. **See also** MacStiofain, Sean; Provisional Irish Republican Army (Provos) (PIRA); Sinn Fein (Ourselves Alone).

Suggested readings: Patrick Bishop and Eamonn Mallie, *The Provisional IRA* (London: Corgi Books, 1988); J. Bowyer Bell, *The IRA, 1968–2000: Analysis of a Secret Army* (London: Frank Cass, 2000); Tim Pat Coogan, *The IRA: A History* (Niwot, CO: Roberts Rinehart, 1993); Ed Moloney, *A Secret History of the IRA* (New York: Norton, 2002); Brendan O'Brien, *The Long War: The IRA and Sinn Féin*, 2nd ed. (Ithaca, NY: Syracuse University Press, 1999); Kevin Toolis, *Rebel Hearts: Journeys within the IRA's Soul* (London: Picador, 1995).

Irving, David John Cawdell (1938–) (Great Britain)

David Irving is a British historian with strong connections to **Holocaust denial** and extremist groups. He was born in 1938 in Essex, England. His father was a Royal Navy Commander. After a short stay at the Imperial College of London University, Irving traveled to the Ruhr area in Germany and worked in a German steel mill. After a year, Irving returned to London University to complete his education. He decided to become a professional historian. His first book, *The Destruction of Dresden*, appeared in 1963. A number of books followed in the next two decades, including *The Mare's Nest* (1964), *Destruction of Convoy PQ.17* (1968), *The German Atomic Bomb* (1968), *The Rise and Fall of the Luftwaffe* (1974), *Hitler's War* (1977), *The Trail of the Fox* (1978), and *The War between the Generals* (1981). By the early 1980s, Irving had established a fair reputation as a popular military historian until his contention in *Hitler's War* that Adolf Hitler had not ordered the extermina-tion of Europe's Jews. Following these works, Irving published another book, *Churchill's War*, which attacked the career of Winston Churchill.

Irving moved from a defense of Hitler to an outright denial of the existence of the Holocaust in the 1980s. He started speaking at right-wing parties and organizations. In 1982, he made speeches at the German right-wing political party **German People's Union** (Deutsche Volksunion, or DVU) political gatherings. His association with Willis Carto and the Institute for Historical Review, a California-based organization that advocated Holocaust denial, became closer after he became affiliated with the group in 1983. Then in 1988, Irving participated in the trial of Ernst Zundel, a Canadian Holocaust denial advocate, supporting him and the *Leuchter Report*, which maintained the Nazis had not used gas chambers to kill Jews at concentration camps. Later, German authorities fined him 10,000 marks (about $7,000) after he violated a German federal law against pro-Nazi statements about the gas chambers. Several countries, including Australia, Canada, and Germany, have banned his entry because of his political views. Because of the controversy over his views, book publishers started rejecting his manuscripts. Irving depended heavily on the income from his publications so these rejections caused him financial distress.

Irving decided to defend his reputation by suing a British publisher and an American historian. In 1993, Deborah Lipstadt, a professor at Emory University, had written the book *Denying the Holocaust: The Growing Assault on Truth and Memory*. In this book, she had characterized Irving's misuse of historical sources for political reasons. Penguin Books republished this work in Great Britain. Irving waited until the book appeared so that he could take advantage the more liberal British libel law. He also decided to argue the case himself before a judge, and not a jury.

The trial proved to be disappointing to Irving and his cause. A series of historians testified in the trial, which lasted from January 11 through March 15, 2000. Justice

British historian David Irving arrives at the London high court January 12, 2000, to attend the second day of his libel case against Penguin Books and U.S. academic Deborah Lipstadt, professor of Modern Jewish, and Holocaust studies at Emory University, Atlanta, GA. Irving, the 62-year-old author of *Hitler's War* and *Goebbels: Mastermind of the Third Reich*, claims that Professor Lipstadt's 1994 book *Denying the Holocaust: The Growing Assault on Truth and Memory*, alleges that he has denied the Holocaust, consorted with extremists, and distorted statistics and documents to serve his own ideological purposes. (AP Photo/Max Nash)

Charles Gray presided over the court. Irving attempted to refute the charges of sloppy and misleading scholarship by a team of historians without success. Gray issued his verdict that Irving was both an anti-Semite and a Holocaust denier. He also concluded that Irving had misstated historical evidence to support his political views. Irving was ordered to pay the legal fees of the defense or nearly £2 million. After an appeals court denied his request for a new trial, Irving avoided paying the fees by threatening bankruptcy. He also tried to intimidate publishers from publishing books attacking his research by threatening them with libel suits. This defeat has not lessened his image among the advocates of Holocaust denial, and he remains in much demand as a speaker in these circles. **See also** German People's Union (Deutsche Volksunion) (DVU); Holocaust Denial.

Suggested readings: Tim Adams, "Memoires of Made of This: David Irving Lost the Libel Trial That Saw Him Branded a Racist," *Observer* (London) (February 24, 2002), p. 1; Ian Buruma, "Blood Libel: Hitler and History in the Dock," *New Yorker* (April 16, 2001), p. 82; Richard J. Evans, *Lying about Hitler: History, Holocaust, and the David Irving Trial* (New York: Basic Books, 2001); D. D. Guttenplan, *The Holocaust on Trial* (New York: Norton, 2001); Robert Jan van Pelt, *The Case for Auschwitz: Evidence from the Irving Trial* (Bloomington: Indiana University Press, 2002).

Islamic Fundamentalism (Middle East)

Islamic fundamentalism of today is part of an Islamic revival that has been going on for more than a century. Both political and religious thinkers found the economic, political, and social backwardness of Muslim countries unacceptable and blamed the colonial powers for these shortcomings. Their solution was an Islamic revival that would make the Koran the basis of all human conduct. Modernization would be accepted, but secularism and political domination by outsiders would not. A number of groups formed in various Middle Eastern countries to bring about this revival. The most famous of these groups was the **Muslim Brotherhood** in Egypt. Since its founding in 1928, members of the Muslim Brotherhood have campaigned for a society based exclusively on the Koran. This organization has had success in converting Egypt's professional classes and because of its concentration among doctors, engineers, teachers, and clerics it has influence out of proportion to its relatively few members. Total membership in Egypt has never exceeded more than 50,000 activists. The principles of the Muslim Brotherhood have been exported to other countries and form the basis of several organizations, including the Palestinian **Hamas**. Until the 1960s, Islamic fundamentalism had only a few converts.

The Israeli victory in 1967 in the Arab-Israeli War caused many Muslims to reexamine their identity and look for solutions. Loss of Jerusalem was a blow to Arab and Muslim pride and self-esteem. Political and religious leaders looked for reasons for the defeat and ways to revive Islam. These leaders found capitalism's preoccupation with conspicuous consumption incompatible with Islam. Marxism and its atheism was even more a threat to the religion. Even modernization was challenged as many Muslim intellectuals and religious leaders came to view it as a type of colonialism. Moreover, the mass of poor in the Middle East, both in the countryside and the city, found Western ideas uncomfortable and dangerous. Islamic organizations were able to focus the discontent and channel it into opposition against governments. Finally, the United States's support for the state of Israel, the Shah of Iran, and Christians in Lebanon made it a natural enemy of the Islamic world. This anti-Americanism has gone so far today that Iraq's **Saddam Hussein** is considered by Muslims to be a victim of America's anti-Islamic policies. The success of the Iranian Revolution and the prestige of the **Ayatollah Khomeini** launched an Islamic fundamentalist revival in the Islamic world that continues.

A return to the laws of the Koran is the foundation of the Islamic revival. Behind this theory is the belief that the Muslim world is in a state of decline and that only by a return to the laws of the Koran can this decline be checked. Islamic fundamentalists want to return to God's revealed law, the Sharia. Two enemies of the revival are westernization and secularism. Modernization is accepted but only as a tool of advancement. These fundamentalists also believe that Islam and the West are engaged in a war of over a thousand years' duration and that it is the duty of all Muslims to be participations in the ageless jihad because it is God's command. Those governments or individuals that refuse to participate in the jihad are no longer considered Muslims and are instead enemies of God. Fereydoun Hoveyda, the former Iran ambassador to the United Nations (1971–1978) and a foreign policy expert, maintains, "Fundamentalism has given Muslims confidence in their future."

Underlying this drive for a return to original Islam is the belief in the need for a charismatic leader to unite behind. This leader would reestablish the Caliphate that was abolished by Turkey in 1922. The closest incarnation of this charismatic leader was Iran's Ayatollah Khomeini. His triumph in Iran served as a model, but he suffered from the disadvantage of being a Shi'ite. Eighty percent of the Muslim world is Sunni and these Sunnis consider Shi'ites as apostates. The search for a charismatic leader to lead the Muslim world continues with no strong candidate apparent. **See also** Khomeini, Ayatollah Ruhollah; Muslim Brotherhood (al-Ikhwan al-Muslimun).

Suggested readings: Lawrence Davidson, *Islamic Fundamentalism* (Westport, CT: Greenwood Press, 1998); John L. Esposito, *The Islamic Threat: Myth or Reality?* rev. ed. (New York: Oxford University Press, 1997); Roxanne L Euben, *Enemy in the Mirror: Islamic Fundamentalism and the Limits of Modern Rationalism: A Work of Comparative Political Theory* (Princeton, NJ: Princeton University Press, 1999); Fereydoun Hoveyda, *The Broken Crescent: The "Threat" of Militant Islamic Fundamentalism* (Westport, CT: Praeger, 1998).

Islamic Group (al-Gama'a al-Islamiyya) (Egypt)

The Islamic Group is a radical Egyptian terrorist group. It was formed in the late 1970s from the radical wing of the **Muslim Brotherhood. Sheikh Omar Abdel-Rahman** has been the spiritual leader of the Islamic Group. Much of its membership came from the ranks of the government—civil servants and the army. President Anwar Sadat's assassin, Lieutenant Khaled Shawky al-Islambouli, was a member of the Islamic Group. Sheikh Omar Abdel-Rahman was arrested after Sadat's assassination, but he was acquitted in a subsequent trial. However, Al-Islambouli and accomplices were executed by a firing squad after a jury convicted them of the assassination.

Police repression made most of the leadership of the Islamic Group move to other countries. Abdel-Rahman's involvement in the bombing of the World Trade Center in New York in 1993 landed him in a U.S. prison. He is now serving a life sentence for conspiracy, but this has not hindered him from issuing political and religious opinions.

Even after the immigration of Abdel-Rahman to the United States, members of the Islamic Group have engaged in terrorist operations in Egypt. Leadership of the Islamic Group claimed responsibility for the 1992 assassination of Egyptian writer Farag Fouda, but this claim was also made by the Egyptian Islamic Jihad. Those Islamic Group activists captured by Egyptian authorities after engaging in terrorist acts have been executed with few exceptions.

The Luxor massacre at the Temple of Hatshepsut was the bloodiest terrorist act of the Islamic Group. New leaders, Rifai Ahmed Taha and Mustafa Hamza, both former students of Abdel-Rahman, had assumed control of the Islamic Group operating from Afghanistan. They decided to strike against the Egyptian government by attacking a primary source of Egyptian income—tourism. A secondary motive may have been to seize hostages for the release of Abdel-Rahman and other imprisoned leaders of the Islamic Group. Under the leadership of Medhat Abdel Rahman, six members arrived at the temple early in the morning of November 17, 1997, dressed in black and systematically hunted down and killed everyone present. Fifty-eight of the victims were Europeans from Britain, Germany, and Switzerland and Japanese men, women, and children. Four of the other victims were security guards. After the murders at the temple, the gunmen seized a bus and went looking for more victims. One of the gunmen was killed in a shootout with police at a checkpoint. The five others escaped to a deep cave in the Valley of the Queens. Police reported finding the bodies of the five with gunshot wounds.

The Islamic Group announced a cease-fire in March 1999, but there has been opposition to this action. Several of the jailed leaders, Karam Zuhdi and Nagih Ibrahim, have supported more the more moderate position. In contrast, in June 2000, Abdel-Rahman issued a call from his prison cell to resume terrorist activities. Mustafa Hamza is the current head of the Islamic Group, but he has been reluctant to break the cease-fire. He has come under pressure from other leaders, especially Taha, to launch new operations. Taha's extradition to Egypt by the Syrian government in November 2001, however, has silenced him. **See also** Abdel-Rahman, Sheikh Omar.

Suggested readings: Jon B. Alterman, "The Luxor Shootout and Egypt's Armed Islamist Opposition," *Policywatch* (November 17, 1997), no. 279; J. Bowyer Bell, *Murders on the Nile: The World Trade Center and Global Terror* (San Francisco: Encounter Books, 2003); Clare Goldwin, "Suicide Squad That Wiped Out My Family Was Linked to Bin Laden but Warning Was Ignored," *Mirror* (London) (December 7, 2002), p. 30; Anthony Shadid, "Egyptian Militants Express Regret 'Islam Never Condones Evil,'" *Boston Globe* (July 21, 2002), p. A1; Anthony Shadid, "Syria Is Said to Hand Egypt Suspect Tied to Bin Laden," *Boston Globe* (November 20, 2001), p. A1.

Islamic Jihad (Egypt)

The Egyptian Islamic Jihad is a militant fundamentalist terrorist group. This group was another of the many spin-offs of the **Muslim Brotherhood** and many of its leaders had also been members of the radical wing of the **Islamic Group**. It was founded in the late 1970s; Colonel Abbud al-Zumur was the original military leader of Islamic Jihad, and Mohammed al-Farag, an electrical engineer, was its spiritual head. These leaders were active in the assassination of Anwar Sadat in 1981, and most of them were arrested. This loss of leadership allowed **Ayman al-Zawahiri**, a medical doctor, to become the political leader of the Islamic Jihad, and **Mohammad Atef**, a former policeman, its military strategist.

The goal of Islamic Jihad is to overthrow the Egyptian government and institute an Islamic state. Most of its operations have been directed toward assassinating key governmental leaders to destabilize the Mubarak regime. Because this group undertakes high-risk operations, absolute secrecy is encouraged among its members. Small cells of 15 to 30 activists carry out operations.

In June 1992, members of the Islamic Jihad claimed to have assassinated Farag Fouda, an Egyptian author who had voiced support for the Israeli-Egyptian peace treaty. Then, in 1993, attempts were made to assassinate Prime Minister Atef Sedky and Minister of Interior Hassan Al-Alfi. Egyptian security forces cracked down on Islamic Jihad activists and both al-Zawahiri and Atef fled from Egypt.

The loss of a political base in Egypt caused al-Zawahiri to look for an ally. **Osama bin Laden** was a natural ally and in the mid-1990s, Islamic Jihad merged with **al-Qaeda**. Both al-Zawahiri and Atef moved to Afghanistan, where they received financial and moral support from the **Taliban** government. The Islamic Jihad still exists but it has merged so many of its operations into al-Qaeda that it has lost its identity. In the meantime al-Zawahiri has emerged as the number-two man behind bin Laden in al-Qaeda. The invasion of Afghanistan and the the loss of Atef in a bombing raid has impacted the operational potential of what is left of the Islamic Jihad. **See also** Bin Laden, Osama; Islamic Group (al-Gama'a al-Islamiyya); Muslim Brotherhood (al-Ikhwan al-Muslimun); Al-Qaeda (The Base).

Suggested readings: Neil MacFarquhar, "Atef Had Been Leader in Egyptian Islamic Jihad," *Houston Chronicle* (November 16, 2001), p. A12; Neil MacFarquhar, "Islamic Jihad, Forged in Egypt, Is Seen as Bin Laden's Backbone," *New York Times* (October 4, 2001), p. B4; Judith Miller, *God Has Ninety-Nine Names: Reporting from a Militant Middle East* (New York: Touchstone Books, 1996); Susan Sachs, "An Investigation in Egypt Illustrates Al Qaeda's Web," *New York Times* (November 21, 2001), p. A1.

Islamic Movement of Uzbekistan (IMU) (Uzbekistan)

The Islamic Movement of Uzbekistan (IMU) is an Islamist guerrilla group with the goal to overthrow the government of the Republic of Uzbekistan and establish an Islamic state. Uzbekistan is one of the new republics formed after the collapse of the Soviet Union in December 1991. Earlier, in June 1990, Tajik Muslim intellectuals had founded the Islamic Renaissance Party (IRP) to establish an Islamic society in Muslim areas. Members of the IRP demanded that the new regime in Uzbekistan allow them to build an Islamist mosque. After the new government refused to allow this mosque and the authorities proclaimed a secular state, a rebellion broke out led by Tahkir Yuldeshev, an Uzbek religious leader, and Juma Namangani, a Soviet army veteran and guerrilla leader. Yuldeshev and Namangani started an organization, Adolat

(Justice), to build an Islamic state, but the government of President Islam Karimov soon suppressed this group.

In response to this opposition from the Uzbekistan state, Yuldeshev and Namangani founded the Islamic Movement of Uzbekistan in Kabul, Afghanistan, during the summer of 1998. Takhir Yuldashev remained the head of the IMU, and, until the overthrow of the Taliban, his headquarters was in Kandahar, Afghanistan. Namangani was the military leader of the IMU until 2001. He was able to recruit Muslim fighters from all of Central Asia's ethnic groups into the IMU. Another important leader was Muhammad Solikh, a former Uzbekistan presidential candidate in the 1991 elections.

Each year since 1998, IMU forces have launched guerrilla attacks from Tajikistan into the economically and politically strategic Fergana Valley, which is shared by the states of Uzbekistan, Kyrgyzstan, and Tajikistan. On February 16, 1999, members of the IMU attempted to assassinate Uzbekistan President Islam Karimov in Tashkent by exploding a bomb that killed 16 bystanders. Material and moral support from the **Taliban** in Afghanistan has helped the IMU in its guerrilla war. Additional financial support has come from Saudi Arabia and other Islamic states and from ransom money collected from kidnappings of Japanese and American citizens. Evidence exists that the IMU has engaged in drug trafficking by moving drugs grown in Afghanistan through Central Asia. On September 15, 2000, the U.S. State Department placed the IMU on its list of terrorist organizations. IMU forces were sent to Afghanistan in the summer of 2000 to fight alongside the Taliban against the Northern Alliance army of Ahmad Shah Masood. This action allowed the IMU to expand its size through the recruitment of various Central Asian nationalities.

The intervention of American forces following the **September 11**, 2001, attacks in the United States has transformed the future of the IMU. Namandani had been able to launch attacks from Tajikistan against Uzbekistan and then retreat into Afghani-

stan. He had established a base camp in the northern Afghan city of Kunduz. When Northern Alliance forces attacked Kunduz in the middle of November 2001, Namandani and his guerrillas fought against them. Namandani was reportedly killed at Kunduz on November 17, 2001. Rumors still circulate that Namandani is still alive, but his wife has attested to his death in the Russian press. His loss is catastrophic to the IMU because there is no military leader of his capabilities ready to replace him. The political wing of the IMU is still active, but the military wing is much less active.

Suggested readings: C. J. Chivers, "Kunduz; Alliance Says It Found School Run by a Titan of Terrorism," *New York Times* (December 1, 2001), p. B1; Svante E. Cornell and Regine A. Spector, "Central Asia: More Than Islamic Extremists," *Washington Quarterly* 25, no. 1 (2002 Winter), p. 193; Ahmed Rashid, *Jihad: The Rise of Militant Islam in Central Asia* (New Haven, CT: Yale University Press, 2002); Joshua Sinai, "Islamist Terrorism and Narcotrafficking in Uzbekistan," *Defense and Foreign Affairs' Strategic Policy* (May, 2000), p. 7; Doug Struck, "Uzbek Taliban Chief Feared in Homeland," *Washington Post* (November 10, 2001), p. A17.

Islamic Party of Turkestan (See Islamic Movement of Uzbekistan)

Islamic Salvation Front (Front Islamique du Salut) (FIS) (Algeria)

The Islamic Salvation Front (FIS) is the Islamic fundamentalist opposition party that has fought a civil war against the Algerian government since 1992. In the mid-1980s, the worsening economic conditions and widespread unemployment in Algeria created an Islamic fundamentalist revival. The Chadli government unveiled a new Algerian constitution in early February 1989 that allowed political parties to vie for power. Some of the leading Islamists had earlier formed the Rabitat Dawa (League of the Islamic Call) to unify Islamic fundamentalists against the regime. **Abassi Madani**, a sociology professor and veteran of the Algerian War; Ali Belhadj,

Portrait of former leader of Islamic Salvation Front Abassi Madani taken in Algiers in 1991, who was freed by an Algerian military court July 15, 1997. Madani was sentenced to 12 years in prison in 1992 with another Front leader for calling a general strike. No reason for Madani's surprise release was given. (AP Photo/REMY DE LA MAUVINIERE)

a popular Islamic preacher; and 13 others founded the Islamic Salvation Front on February 18, 1989. Madani became the president of the party with Belhadj serving as second-in-command. Several of the older Islamic leaders either refused to join the FIS or remained neutral. Soon members of the FIS began to think that it was more than a political party and a militia was formed. Despite some reservations, the Algerian government recognized the FIS as a legal party on September 16, 1989.

The Islamic Salvation Front started a massive recruitment campaign to win political power in Algeria. A four-man executive committee—Madani, Belhadj, Benazouz Zebda, and Hachemi Sahnouni—made the major decisions. Mandani was the chief spokesperson for the FIS. Party leaders built a hierarchical structure that extended down to the local level. Partisans of the FIS utilized the 9,000 mosques under their control to spread the message about winning the local elections scheduled for June 1990. A newspaper, *El Mounqid*, was started to help in the FIS's political campaign. Party activists mobilized huge street demonstrations and rallies in support of FIS issues and candidates.

Soon the Armed Salvation Front and its leaders had become the most popular and influential Islamists in Algeria and a threat to the Algerian state. The Algerian government alternated between a policy of neutrality and support. Results from the June 1990 local elections showed that the FIS candidates received nearly 34 percent of the votes to the government party's 28 percent. Once in control of these governments, FIS supporters started implementing restrictions on secularism and women. They wanted to Arabize Algerian society by controlling the educational system and instituting restrictions against women's role in society. Belhadj also made statements rejecting the idea of democracy and made it plain that there was no place in Algerian society for those who did not share his religious beliefs about the exclusive truth of Islam. The FIS also showed its independence by supporting Iraq's **Saddam Hussein** in the Persian Gulf War.

Envisaging victory in the next election, the leadership of the FIS declared war on the Algerian government. The goal was to overthrow the ministry of Mouloud Hamrouche. In May 1991, the FIS declared a general strike against the Algerian government. Although the strike was only partially successful in attracting supporters, the Algerian military intervened after the first week and deposed the ministry of Hamrouche. A state of siege was declared by the military and the FIS called off the strike. Later in late June 1991, the Algerian government arrested both Madani and Belhadj. New leadership, Abdelkader Hachani and Mohammed Said, assumed control of FIS. On December 26, 1991, in the first round of the election, the FIS received 47 percent of the votes and was guaranteed a majority in the assembly after the results of the second round of voting. This result led to the Algerian military to depose President Benjedid Chadli, cancel the January 1992 election, and ban the FIS. The revolutionary hero Mohammed Boudiaf became the new head of state, but his assassination in June 1992 ended this experiment.

Once the Islamic Salvation Front decided to resort to armed conflict, it formed the Islamic Army of Salvation (Armée Islamique du Salut, or AIS). Later, more radical elements in the FIS formed the **Armed Islamic Group** (Groupes Islamiques Armés, or GIA). This new group operated out of Algiers and recruited violent elements with the city. The AIS cooperated with the Armed Islamic Group for a couple of years, but the more militant GIA soon alienated the FIS leadership. Both the AIS and the GIA conducted bloody campaigns against the government and the Algerian populace. Between 1992 and 1998, William B. Quandt, a student of Algerian politics, estimated that 200 Algerians died weekly from the violence.

Most of the Islamic Salvation Front leaders were in prison or in exile, but negotiations between the Algerian government and FIS representatives opened in January 1995. A position paper compromising the differences between the two positions, the Sant'Egidio Platform, received the blessing of the FIS leadership, but the Algerian government rejected it. Madani was in favor of ending the violence, but Belhadj refused to go along with him. By this time, the FIS had lost all control over the GIA. The government refused to allow the FIS to participate in the parliamentary elections in June 1997, but it did release Madani from prison in July 1997. On September 21, 1997, the AIS declared a unilateral truce with the Algerian government in an attempt to distance itself from the actions of the GIA. Madani has been attempting in January 2004 to broker an end to the violence in Algeria that includes a general presidential amnesty of all participants in the civil war and would include the release of prisoners and guarantees of security for returning exiles. **See also** Armed Islamic Group (Groupes Islamiques Armés) (GIA); Madani, Cheikh Abassi.

Suggested readings: Lahouari Addi, "Algeria's Army, Algeria's Agony," *Foreign Affairs* (July/August 1998), p. 44; Ed Blanche, "Violence and Discontent Worsens as Algeria Goes from Crisis to Crisis," *Jane's Intelligence Review* 13, no. 8 (August 1, 2001); Paul Harris, "Algerian Election Pits Democracy against Terrorism," *Jane's Intelligence Review* 9, no. 9 (September 1, 1997); William B. Quandt, *Between Ballots and Bullets: Algeria's Transition from Authoritarianism* (Washington, DC: Brookings Institution Press,

1998); Milton Viorst, "Algeria's Long Night," *Foreign Affairs* (November/December 1997), p. 86; Michael Willis, *The Islamist Challenge in Algeria: A Political History* (New York: New York University Press, 1996).

Italian Social Movement (Movimento Sociale Italiano) (MSI) (Italy)

The Italian Social Movement (Movimento Sociale Italiano, or MSI) was the leading neo-fascist movement in postwar Italy. Benito Mussolini's Fascism had been discredited by its association with World War II, but a number of Mussolini's former associates still believed in the future of fascism. Guglielmo Giannini, a famous writer, formed the Movement of the Ordinary Man (Uomo Qualungue) in 1946 to serve as a right-wing counterbalance to the strong Communist Party in Italy. Within a year, the extremist wing of the Movement of the Ordinary Man split off to form a new fascist party. Giorgio Almirante, a journalist under Mussolini's regime, and five associates gathered in Rome on December 26, 1946, to form the Italian Social Movement, or MSI. This new party had three goals: to revive Mussolini's brand of fascism, to attack Italian democracy, and to fight communism. The new party selected Almirante to be its first leader. Because the new Italian constitution and agreements with the Allied forces against the reestablishment of fascism, any party advocating a return to fascism had to be discreet about its agenda. An early important convert of the MIS was Prince Valerio Borghese, an Italian war hero and violently anti-American and anti-British. He had served four years in prison after the war for collaboration with the Nazis and anti-partisan activities.

Financial support for the MSI came from wealthy Italian businessmen and landowners scared about the prospect of a communist Italy. Vatican support for the MSI also was forthcoming for the same reason. In January 1950, Almirante was replaced as leader because of his intransigence over political alliances and his anti-NATO (North Atlantic Treaty Organization) stance. This ouster was the result of a growing division within the

MSI between conservatives eager for political alliances and radical fascists ready to take on the Italian state. Electoral advances helped the conservatives retain control of the MSI under the leadership of Augusto De Marsanich. He lasted four years before giving way to Arturo Michelini.

Because fascism was still popular in certain areas of Italy, the Italian Social Movement became a force in Italian politics. This was despite the defection of the radical wing of the party at the 1956 National Conference at Milan. Giuseppe "Pino" Rauti, Clemente Graziani, Stefano Delle Chiaie, and Paolo Signrelli left and formed the radical neo-fascist party **New Order** (Ordine Nuovo). By the late 1950s, the MSI was Italy's fourth-most-powerful party. The growth of this neo-Fascist party produced a backlash and riots between the supporters of the MSI, and its enemies became commonplace in the early 1960s. In October 1965, Italian authorities seized a cache of heavy weapons hidden in a Rome villa by a wealthy supporter of the MSI. Elements within the MSI had become restless with its emphasis on parliamentarism and some of the more radical neo-fascists left the MSI to found other groups. Among these were Pino Rauti of the New Order and Stefano Della Chiaie of the National Vanguard (Vanguardia Nationale).

In 1969, Almirante regained control of the MSI after Michelini's death. His first effort was to revitalize the MSI by pursuing an aggressive policy against the left-wing uprising among Italian students. Almirante remained in control of the MSI until his replacement by **Gianfranco Fini** in 1987.

Fini assumed control of the Italian Social Movement and remodeled it to fit his image. Except for a short period in 1990–1991 he retained the leadership position of the MSI until he transformed it into the National Alliance (Alleanza Nationale) in January 1994. Fini decided to downplay the neo-fascist origins of the MSI and lead the National Alliance into a political coalition with Silvio Berlusconi, the wealthy media magnate.

Remnants of the Italian Social Movement refused to follow Fini into the National

Alliance. Pino Rauti and fellow right-wingers attempted to reconstitute the MSI. This effort had only modest success. In contrast, under Fini's leadership, the National Alliance partnered with the Berlusconi government in 1994 and 2001. Fini's popularity among the Italian voters has made the National Alliance an important part of the Italian political scene. See also Fini, Gianfranco.

Suggested readings: Dennis Eisenberg, *The Emergence of Fascism* (South Brunswick, NJ: Barnes, 1967); Franco Ferraresi, *Threats to Democracy* (Princeton, NJ: Princeton University Press, 1996); Bernard D. Kaplan, "Fascism on the March," *Ottawa Citizen* (February 3, 1995), p. A9; Angus Roxburgh, *Preachers of Hate: The Rise of the Far Right* (London: Gibson Square Books, 2002); Leonard B. Weinberg, *After Mussolini: Italian Neo-Fascism and the Nature of the Fascism* (Washington, DC: University of Press of America, 1979; Leonard B. Weinberg and William Lee Eubank, *The Rise and Fall of Italian Terrorism* (Boulder, CO: Westview Press, 1987).

Ivanov-Sukharevsky, Alexander Kuzmich (1950–) (Russia)

Alexander Ivanov-Sukharevsky is the leader of the neo-Nazi skinhead **People's National Party**. He was born on July 26, 1950, in Rostov-on-Don, Russia. His father was a career army officer from Belarus, and his mother was a pharmacist. She was from the famous Don Cossack Sukharev family. Ivan-Sukharevsky's early life was spent in East Germany where his father had a military command. Later, he moved back to Rostov where he received his elementary and high school education. After graduation, he considered a military career and entered a military school, Rostov High Command Engineering School, in 1967. In 1970, he decided to transfer to Rostov State University to study economics. His interest in economics also was fleeting, so in 1974 he entered the All-Union State Institute of Cinematography. By 1979, Ivanov-Sukharevsky was qualified as a film director and he started work at Mosfilm (Moscow Film Studio). His specialty became historical documentaries. Several of these documentaries contained patriotic and anti-Semitic themes

that invited criticism from Jewish groups. Ivanov-Sukharevsky responded to these criticisms by becoming more extreme in his political views.

Ivano-Sukharevsky examined several extremist groups before forming the People's National Party. Among the groups that he joined was the **Russian National Unity** and the Russian All-People's Union. None of these groups allowed room for him to obtain a leadership post. In January 1994, he gathered a small group of adherents and decided to establish a new political party. Despite this decision, it took until December 1994 before the People's National Party appeared in its final form. His goal was to reestablish a purified Russian empire by ridding Russia of foreigners and members of ethnic groups. He wanted a white brotherhood in Russia that could be expanded to an international movement. To accomplish this task, Ivanov-Sukharevsky built a paramilitary organization of true believers and skinheads. His second-in-command was Semyon Tokmakov.

Several times Ivanov-Sukharevsky landed into legal difficulties with Russian authorities. In 1997, he spent nine months in Butyrka Prison for the charge of incitement of ethnic discord. Then in the fall of 1998, Ivanov-Sukarevsky was charged again with the same crime. He underwent a psychiatric examination for his erratic behavior during the trial and was released after a short time in jail. In May 2002, Ivanov-Sukharevsky was handed a suspended three-year sentence for incitement to violence in the aftermath of the People's National Party's involvement in the November 2001 riots in the Tsaritsyno area of south Moscow. Despite his calculated use of violence, Ivanov-Sukharevsky has publicly announced that his party's only chance to power is through legal means.

Ivanov-Sukharevsky's relationship with other Russian extremist parties is checkered. His biggest rival is **Alexander Barkashov** and his **Russian National Unity** (RNE). The groups vie for the same recruits, and their goals for Russia seem similar. There is less rivalry with **Eduard Limonov** and the **National Bolshevik Party**, but they still compete.

Ivanov-Sukharevsky's closest ally is Yuri Belyaev and his National-Republican Party of Russia (NRPR). Both Belyaev and Ivanov-Sukharevsky share a common worldview and they briefly combined their parties in 1997. However, this alliance ended in 1998 after Ivanov-Sukharevsky experienced legal difficulties. Ivanov-Sukharevsky is only one of many extremists operating in Russia's troubled political environment and his chances of gaining political power are as remote as his rivals. See also Barkashov, Alexander Petrovich; Limonov, Eduard; National Bolshevik Party; Russian National Unity (Russkoje Nationalnoje Edinstv) (RNE).

Suggested readings: Nick Paton, "Russian 'Hitler' Targets Foreigners," *Observer* (London) (June 9, 2002), p. 22; Grigory Punanov, "Portrait of a 'Skinhead Party' and Its Leader," *Current Digest of the Post-Soviet Press* (June 5, 2002), p. 1; Stephen D. Shenfield, *Russian Fascism: Traditions, Tendencies, Movements* (Armonk, NY: M. E. Sharpe, 2001).

J

Jama'at-i Islami (Islamic Party) (Pakistan)

The Jam'at-i Islami (Islamic Party) is the leading Islamist party in Pakistan. **Mawlana Sayyid Abu'l-A'la Mawdudi** founded the Jama'at-i Islami on August 26, 1941, at Lahore, India, with the assistance of 75 followers. His intent was for this party to serve as an opposition party to Muhammad Ali Jinnah's Muslim League. Earlier, Mawdudi had campaigned in favor of a Muslim India, but by the late 1930s he had modified his views and realized the necessity for a Muslim state. His view of the nature of the proposed Muslim state differed significantly from the more secular state advocated by Jinnah and the supporters of the Muslim League. Mawdudi envisaged Pakistan as an Islamic state with himself as its political-religious leader. His new party was to serve as the vehicle for this transformation. The members of the new party voted to make him the head of the party.

The Jama'at-i Islami grew slowly until the creation of Pakistan in 1948. First efforts of party members were devoted to education and propaganda rather than political agitation. Mawdudi wanted to recruit Muslims to his view of Islamic society more than he wanted to win political contests. He and his principal followers traveled the length of India converting Muslims to his version of an Islamic state and attacking Jinnah and the Muslim League. Mawdudi attracted new adherents to his party, but he also had to withstand challenges to his leadership. He survived these challenges and in the process increased his control over the party. At the time of partition, Mawdudi split the party into a Pakistan and an India branch, but he opted for leadership of the Pakistan Jama'at-i Islami. Then Mawdudi moved the party to Lahore, Pakistan. Later there would also be a Bangladesh branch.

Mawdudi expected that the Jama'at-i Islami would become the dominant political party in the new Pakistan, replacing the Muslim League. He considered the leaders of the Muslim League as failures for not installing an Islamic state. In the 1951 Pakistani national elections, the leadership of the Jama'at-i Islami attempted to influence the elections, but without success. Mawdudi spent parts of nearly two years in prison in 1953 and 1954 for attacking the Pakistani government. He returned in time for a scandal over abuse of power and financial irregularities by the leaders of the party. At first Mawdudi took the side of the critics, but, once he determined that the reformers would weaken his control of the party, he changed his mind. He and his chief supporters purged the reformers out of the Jama'at-i Islami and reoriented the party more to politics than religion. This strategy had no

Qazi Hussain Ahmed, chief of the Pakistani religious party Jama'at-i-Islami (Islamic Party), addresses religious students at a mosque July 17, 2002, in Peshawar, Pakistan. Ahmed condemned the government's new laws designed to curtail the teaching of religious extremism in the Islamic schools. He also condemned American action in Pakistan. (AP Photo/Ghaffar Beg)

more success than earlier attempts to gain political power.

Despite the failure to win political power, his followers developed a cult of personality around Mawdudi. This continued until his resignation as its leader in February 1972, following a mild heart attack. His successor was the less charismatic Mian Tufay Muhammad. Muhammad lasted until his retirement in October 1987. Qazi Hussain Ahmed replaced him and is still the party's leader.

Part of the reason that the Jama'at-i Islami has remained a fixture on the religious right in Pakistan has been its ability to attract financial support. Income comes from a variety of sources both internal and external. Internal sources are the dues of members and income from its publishing business. External sources are heavy contributions from Saudi Arabia. Because the religious position of the Jama'at-i Islami resembles that of

Wahhabism, the Saudis have lavished huge sums on the Jama'at-i Islami.

The leadership of the Jama'at-i Islami has frequently been at odds with Pakistani governments. At first, they resisted the more secular Muslim League. Later, in the 1960s, the party opposed the government of Ayub Khan. This opposition continued against the Ali Bhutto regime in the 1970s. General Zia's coup of July 1977 and his fundamentalist government confronted the Jama'at-i Islami with a regime that it could coexist with. Even with General Zia's regime, militants caused the leadership difficulty. Student activities came under the student organization Islami Jami'at-i Tulabah (IJT). Only when student agitation started marring relations with the Zia regime did the Jama'at-i Islami leadership crack down.

Mawdudi had retired from leadership but he still influenced the policies of the Jama'at-i Islami until his death in 1979. Hostility toward the Pakistani government did not cease with the end of the Zia regime. Leaders still campaigned for an Islamic republic, but subsequent governments have paid little attention to them. At the same time other Islamic groups formed, and some of these espoused the violent overthrow of the Pakistani government. Many of the supporters of Jama'at-i Islami left the party to join these direct action groups reducing the influence of the Jama'at-i Islami. **See also** Mawdudi, Mawlana Sayyid Abu'l-A'la.

Suggested readings: Emma Duncan, "Living on the Edge; Governing with God," *Economist* (January 17, 1987), p. 8; Anwar Iqbal, "Militant Devotees Would Die for the Party," United Press International (July 9, 2002), p. 1; Seyyed Vali Reza Nasr, *Vanguard of the Islamic Revolution: The Jama'at-i Islami of Pakistan* (Berkeley: University of California Press, 1994); Tariq Ali, *The Clash of Fundamentalism: Crusades, Jihads, and Modernity* (London: Verso, 2002).

Jammu Kashmir Liberation Front (JKLF) (Pakistan)

The Jammu Kashmir Liberation Front (JKLF) is the leading Pakistani organization conducting a guerrilla war against India's control of Pakistan. Maqbool Bhat founded the JKLF in 1966, and he remained its head until the Indian government hanged him in 1984. Indian government convicted him of murder and conspiring to overthrow the Indian government. Operations of the JKLF continued with a succession of leaders until Hashim Qureshi and Yaseen Malik assumed contol of the JKLF in 1989, but shortly afterwards, the Pakistani Intelligence Service (ISI) intervened against it. When Qureshi showed reluctance to be subservient to the ISI, Amanullah Khan replaced him as its head. Qureshi fled Pakistan and found political asylum in Western Europe. Malik, the commander in chief of military operations, soon replaced Khan as the head of JKLF and Malik has retained that post until today.

Malik made the Jammu Kashmir Liberation Front as Kashmir's largest separatist party. His record of fighting Indian forces in 1989–1990 reinforced his position as leader. In 1990, in a gun battle in Srinagar, he jumped from a fifth-floor building rather than surrender to Indian forces. He survived the jump and became the political leaders of the JKLF.

Although Malik still has not renounced violence, he has announced his willingness to negotiate with Indian authorities for an independent Kashmir state. He has assumed a prominent role in the All Parties Hurriyat Conference, the main Kashmiri separatist alliance attempting to negotiate with India. In March 2001, Malik was arrested by the Kashmir state government on charges of smuggling $100,000 to finance a terrorist war against India. Kashmiri authorities held him in custody for eight months until November 2002. Malik has been arrested several times since his release more often for harassment than for serious crimes.

The Jammu Kashmir Liberation Front has been caught in the middle of negotiations between the Pakistan government and India. At first, the leadership of the JKLF criticized the Pakistan government for what it called the "Talibanization" of Kashmir by unleashing a holy war, or jihad, in Kashmir. More recently, peace overtures from General Pervez Musharraf toward India has made the JKLF fearful of a sell-out to India. The JKLF still fights for a Muslim Kashmir, but its leadership is aware that it lacks the power to impose a solution on Kashmir.

Suggested readings: S. B. Ahmed, "India Frees Top Kashmiri Separatist Leader Yasin Malik," Associated Press (November 11, 2002), p. 1; Scott Baldauf, "As Spring Arrives, Kashmir Braces for Fresh Fighting," *Christian Science Monitor* (Boston) (April 9, 2002), p. 7; Scott Baldauf, "Kashmiri Separatists Vow to Determine Their Future," *Christian Science Monitor* (Boston) (March 14, 2002), p. 7; Vernon Hewitt, "An Area of Darkness, Still? The Political Evolution of Ethnic Identities in Jammu and Kashmir, 1947–2001," in Rajat Ganguly and Ian Macduff," *Ethnic Conflict and Secessionism in South and Southeast Asia* (New Delhi, India: Sage Publications, 2003); Susan Milligan, "Senators Hopeful after Meeting Musharraf but Kashmiri Chief Threatens to Re-arm," *Boston Globe* (January 9, 2002), p. A3.

Janjalani, Ustadz Abdurajak Abubakar (1961–1998) (Philippines)

Abdurajak Janjalani was the founder of the Philippine Islamist terrorist organization the **Abu Sayyaf Group** (Bearer of the Sword, or ASG). He was born in 1961. His father was a fisherman. His early education was in a Catholic school where he excelled as a student. After discovering his Muslim roots, sponsors from the **Moro National Liberation Front** (MNLF) bankrolled him to study military operations in Libya and Islamic jurisprudence in Saudi Arabia. Janjalani became a convert to the Wahhabi school of Islam and he disapproved of television, movies, dancing, and radio music. By 1988, he was in Peshawar, Pakistan, training as a mujahideen to fight against Soviet forces in Afghanistan. In 1990, he returned to the Philippines eager to establish an Islamist state in the southern Philippines. Janjalani found the Moro National Liberation Front unable or unwilling to carry the fight forward, so he broke with the MNLF.

Janjalani gathered other Filipino Afghans in 1991 and formed the Abu Sayyaf to spearhead the war for an Islamist state. His first action was to take his recruits into the hills of Basilan to train for military operations. In organizing for rural and urban guerrilla war, Janjalani divided his forces into cells and small combat groups. Janjalani received financial support from Mohammed Jamal Khalifa, a brother-in-law and supporter of **Osama bin Laden**. The first operation of Abu Sayyaf was in a 1991 grenade attack that killed two young women from New Zealand and Sweden during a cultural performance by Christian missionaries in Zamboanga.

Janjalani original intent was to avoid killing innocent civilians, but by the mid-1990s the Abu Sayyaf Group specialized in atrocities against civilians. In 1995, members of the Abu Sayyaf killed 53 residents of the Christian village of Ipil in Mindanao and razed the town. Janjalani had begun Abu Sayyaf with only 60 members, but by 1998 the group had more than 300 fighters. Bombings of churches and kidnappings of Christian mis-

sionaries attracted the attention of the Philippine government. Military forces trapped Janjalani with a small force in the village of Lamitan on the southern island of Basilan on December 18, 1998. In the ensuing firefight, Janjalani was killed along with two other Abu Sayyaf members. His loss paralyzed the Abu Sayyaf for several months until his younger brother, Khadafy Janjalani, was selected to succeed him. **See also** Abu Sayyaf Group (Bearer of the Sword) (ASG); Bin Laden, Osama.

Suggested readings: Alan Dawson, "Don't Underestimate Abu Sayyaf," *Bangkok Post* (February 19, 2002), p. 1; Dan Murphy, "The Philippine Branch of Terror," *Christian Science Monitor* (October 26, 2001), p. 6; Richard Lloyd Parry, "Treasure Island," *Independent* (London) (March 4, 2001), p. 18.

Japanese Red Army (Sekigun-ha) (JRA) (Japan)

The Japanese Red Army (Sekigun-ha) (JRA) was one of the most violent terrorism groups of the 1970s. Takaya Shiomi, a former student at Kyoto University, and others radicals founded the Red Army Faction in 1969. Most of the supporters of the Red Army Faction were university students with connections to the Japanese Communist Party. These students had become increasing dissatisfied with what they perceived as the failure of the Japanese Communist Party to take revolutionary action. Most of the early activities of the Red Army Faction were at demonstrations in Japan. The exception was the March 31, 1970, hijacking of a Japan Airlines (JAL) aircraft that it redirected to Pyongyang, North Korea. This hijacking attracted attention, but it also cost the Red Army Faction to lose access to the nine hijackers because they were interned in North Korea. Even at its height of activity, the Red Army Faction never had more than 70 members, and it depended on sympathizers among the Japanese student body. In 1970, Shiomi was arrested and imprisoned for his political activities. In 1971, the Red Army Faction and the Keihin Anti-Treaty Joint

Struggle combined to form the United Red Army. This group, under the leadership of Mori Tsuneo and Nagata Hiroko, conducted a series of purges of members that crippled the organization. Fourteen members were killed in the purge. After the arrest of Mori and Nagata, the United Red Army disappeared.

Replacing the United Red Army was the Japanese Red Army. Fusako Shigenobu, a former student at Meiji University in Tokyo, assumed the leadership of the JRA in 1971. She decided to expand its operations to include terrorism and extend JRA operations into the Middle East. To accomplish this she flew to Beirut, Lebanon, in 1971 to establish an international base for the newly named Japanese Red Army. Shigenobu transferred all the loyalists to Lebanon, where members of the **Popular Front for the Liberation of Palestine** (PFLP) trained them for terrorist operations in the Bekka Valley. She was attracted to the PFLP more for its reputation for action than for ideological reasons.

The Japanese Red Army undertook a series of violent terrorist acts in the 1970s. The most famous of these was the suicide terrorist attack on Lod Airport, Tel Aviv, Israel, on May 30, 1972. Three Japanese Red Army members opened fire with small arms and threw grenades in the arrivals terminal, killing 24 people and injuring another 80. Although two of the terrorists were killed, the JRA considered this operation a success. Only Kozo Okamoto survived the attack, and he was arrested by Israeli security forces. This operation was followed by the hijacking of a Japan Airlines aircraft in Amsterdam in July 1974. This aircraft was flown to Libya, where it was blown up. Another operation was the seizure of the French Embassy at The Hague in 1974. The French ambassador and 11 staff members were held hostage for five days until France released a jailed colleague. In September 1977, five members hijacked a Japanese Airliner in Bombay, India, and flew it to Dhaka, Bangladesh. The hostages and plane were released in exchange for $6 million in ransom and the release of six imprisoned criminals in Japan.

Operations of the Japanese Red Army slowed after 1977. Because of the small size of the Japanese Red Army, fewer than 20 operatives, losses were hard to replace. Anti-terrorism organizations also had been able to identify most of the members of the JRA. The last major operation of the JRA was in April 1988 when operatives bombed the USO club in Naples, Italy, killing five. One of the victims was an American.

By the mid-1990s, the activity level of the Japanese Red Army was so low that the U.S. State Department no longer considered it a terrorist threat. This did not mean that members of the JRA were not wanted by Western authorities. These governments placed pressure on the Lebanese government to extradite members of the JRP. In May 2000, the Lebanese government responded by extraditing four members of the JRP to Japan. They had been serving prison terms in Lebanese prisons for their terrorist activities. Then on November 8, 2000, Japanese police arrested Shigenobu in Osaka, Japan. She had left Lebanon in July 2000 and stayed in a hotel in Osaka before her arrest. On April 14, 2001, Shigenobu announced that she was disbanding the JRA, much to the displeasure of two jailed senior members of the group, Haruo Wako and Yikiko Ekita. **See also** Popular Front for the Liberation of Palestine (PFLP).

Suggested readings: William R. Farrell, *Blood and Rage: The Story of the Japanese Red Army* (Lexington, Mass.: Lexington Books, 1990); Mayo Issobe, "Becoming a Mother on the Run," Asahi News Service (April 24, 2001), p. 1; Harumi Ozawa, "The Japanese Red Army's Turbulent Past," *Daily Yomiuri* (Tokyo) (July 21, 2001), p. 7.

Jemaah Islamiyah (Islamic Community) (JI) (Indonesia)

The Jemaah Islamiyah (Islamic Community) (JI) is Indonesia's leading Islamic extremist group. Abdullah Sungkar and **Abu Bakar Bashir** founded the JI in 1973. Their intent was to build as an Islamic self-governing commune to advance their goal for a strict

Islamic society. Sungkar was always the political leader while Bashir provided the ideological and religious doctrine. Although they started out with only 30 students, their activities soon attracted the attention of the authorities of the repressive Suharto regime. Both Sungkar and Bashir were arrested in 1978, and they spent nearly four years in jail for passing literature advocating an Islamic state for Indonesia. In 1985, Sungkar and Bashir fled Indonesia and set up the JI in Malaysia. Malaysia was by this time a self-styled Islamic state, so the Jemaah Islamiyah prospered. Sungkar and Bashir were able to recruit younger Islamic leaders, such as the Afghan veteran **Hambali**. These new leaders were sent to Afghanistan for military training and to fight the Soviet Union. By the mid-1990s the organizational structure of the JI was complete, with its operations controlled by a leadership council headed by Hambali and five division chiefs reporting to him.

The goal of the Jemaah Islamiyah was for a theocratic Islamic state to include Indonesia, Brunei, Malaysia, Singapore, and the southern Philippine island of Mindanao. Because of this goal, leaders of the JI formed working alliances with Islamic groups from the Malaysia Mujahideen Group (KMM) to the **Moro Islamic Liberation Front** (MILF) in Mindanao. Sungkar also established a firm working alliance with **al-Qaeda** after meeting with **Osama bin Laden**.

In 1998, Sungkar and Bashir moved the Jemaah Islamiyah's main organization back to Indonesia. The fall of the Suharto regime gave the JI a chance to expand. Sungkar and Bashir headed the group in Indonesia, but Hambali remained in Malaysia. Hambali had already developed closer ties with al-Qaeda, and, in the late 1990s, JI formed a loose affiliation with it. In 1999, Sungkar died, leaving Bashir in complete control of JI. Bashir recruited members at his religious school in Ngruki village in Solo, Central Java. He continued to serve as the ideological and spiritual head of the JI, and Hambali the leader of the operational wing. JI is organized into operation cells, and its cell leaders carry out operations independent of central decision-making, thus leaving its leaders deniability. Hambali always operated underground planning and directed large-scale operations against non-Muslims. Training for JI operatives came from a Qaeda training camp in Poso, Central Sulawesi, Indonesia. Fruits of this training came in a bombing campaign against Christian churches on December 24, 2000. Thirty churches throughout Indonesia were bombed.

The bombing of the Sari Club on Bali's Kuta Beach on October 12, 2002, directed international attention to the Jemaah Islamiyah. Foreign tourists, mostly Australians, were the targets, and 188 were killed and hundreds more wounded in the bombing. For several years, foreign governments, especially the United States, had been pressuring the Indonesian government of Megawati Sukarnoputri to act against the JI. The Indonesian government had been reluctant, because a crackdown on the JI might stir up Islamic opposition to the government. Other governments, however, in Malaysia, the Philippines, and Singapore had arrested JI operatives throughout 2001. Although Bashir continued to deny JI's involvement in the Bali bombing, anti-terrorist experts around the world believed that Hambali and the JI were behind it. In October 2002, the United Stated formally declared it a terrorist organization subject to sanctions.

The Jemaah Islamiyah has been hurt by the arrests of key leaders. Abu Bakar Bashir has been under arrest since 2001, and a jury convicted him on September 4, 2003, of treasonous activity but not that he headed the Jemaah Islamiyah terrorist network. This verdict included a four-year jail term, but a December 2003 appeal reduced his sentence to three years. His imprisonment did not prevent the JI from launching a suicide bombing attack on the Marriott Hotel in Jakarta, Indonesia, in early August 2003. Increased publicity and police investigations led to the arrest of Hambali on August 12, 2003, in Thailand. The loss of both the spiritual head,

Bashir, and the operations expert, Hambali, has seriously weakened the JI, but there are still enough activists left to undertake terrorist operations. From his prison cell Bahir warned in November 2003 that all Muslim countries with close ties to the United States were subject to attack. **See also** Bashir, Abu Bakar; al-Ghozi, Fathur Rohman; Hambali (Riduan Isamuddin); al-Qaeda (The Base).

Suggested readings: Sharon Behn, "Cleric Warns Muslims Linked to the U.S.," *Washington Times* (November 17. 2003), p. A1; John Burton, "Islamic Network 'Is on a Mission' Terror Group," *Financial Times* (London) (Oct. 16, 2002), p. 12; Rohan Gunaratna, *Inside Al Qaeda: Global Network of Terror* (New York: Columbia University Press, 2002); Rohan Gunaratna, "The Links That Bind Terror Groups," *Guardian* (London) (October 15, 2002), p. 1; Ellen Nakashima and Alan Sipress, "Al Qaeda Figure Seized in Thailand," *Washington Post* (August 15, 2003), p. A1; Jane Perlez, "U.S. Labels Indonesian Faction as Terrorist," *New York Times* (October 24, 2002), p. sec. A, p. 15; Maria A. Ressa, *Seeds of Terror: An Eyewitness Account of Al-Qaeda's Newest Center of Operations in Southeast Asia* (New York: Free Press, 2003).

Jibril, Ahmed (1937–)
(Lebanon and Syria)

Ahmed Jibril is the head of the terrorist group **Popular Front for the Liberation of Palestine—General Command**. He was born in 1937 in Yazur, Palestine (now Azur, Israel) south of Tel Aviv. Little is known about his family's background, but in 1948 his family moved to Quneitra, Syria, on the Golan Heights. In 1956, he joined the Syrian army and reached the rank of captain in the engineers. His skills as a demolitions expert were acquired in the army. In 1958, the army expelled Jibril for his radical politics. He moved to Cairo, Egypt, where he and five compatriots founded the **Palestine Liberation Front** (PLF). In 1961, he returned to Syria and re-entered the Syrian army. Jibril remained head of the PLF and recruited Palestinians for operations against Israel. Jibril came into contact with **Yasser Arafat** and **al-Fatah**, but he has never been an admirer of Arafat. In

1966, Jibril tried to negotiate a merger of the PLF with al-Fatah, but the negotiations floundered over Jibril's insistence on supreme military command. Jibril reacted by participating in a failed attempt to assassinate Arafat on May 5, 1966. Two members of al-Fatah were killed in the attempt, but Arafat escaped harm by not showing up to the meeting. Jibril's rivalry with Arafat has continued, with Jibril ordering of the assassination of several al-Fatah members. His hatred of Egypt goes back to his arrest and torture by Egyptian security officials for his anti-Nasser activities

Despite reservations about other Palestinian groups, Jibril took his Palestine Liberation Front into **George Habash**'s **Popular Front for the Liberation of Palestine** (PFLP) in 1967. This alliance with the PFLP only lasted a little more than a year because Jibril became increasingly dissatisfied with Habash's leadership. In October 1968, Jibril ordered the PLF group out of the PFLP and formed the Popular Front for the Liberation of Palestine—General Command (PFLP-GC). Headquarters for the PFLP-CG was in Damascus, Syria, and the organization had the sponsorship of the Syrian government. Jibril's goal for this group was the destruction of the Israeli state by any means possible. His two chief lieutenants were Abu Abbas, a Palestinian who served as the operations officer for the PFLP-GC, and Marwan Kreeshat, a Jordanian who was his chief bomb-maker. Jibril formed an international section using Sofia, Bulgaria, as his operational base in Europe. Jibril's PFLP-GC specialized in two types of operations—self-trained and coordinated military raids against Israel and bombings of civilian aircraft serving Israel. Kreeshat developed a barometric altimeter bomb that was used twice in February 1970, destroying one of the planes. It was the aircraft bombings and the destruction of an Israeli school bus, which killed the eleven children and three teachers on board on May 20, 1970, that directed world attention to Jibril and the PFLP-GC. Throughout the early and mid-1970s, Jibril continued to send assault teams into Israel. His army was the best organized and most professional of the Palestinian armies. One raid, on Kiryat Shmoneh on April 11, 1974, resulted in the deaths of 18 (eight children, seven men and three women), and 20 were seriously wounded. He also became one of the leaders of the Rejectionist Front that opposed any negotiations between the Palestinians and Israel.

Jibril played an active role in the Lebanese civil war. Civil war broke out on April 13, 1975, after a carload of PFLP-GC gunmen opened fire on Christian Phalangists. Palestinians united to fight the Christian militias, and in the following 10 months the Christian forces steadily lost ground. Jibril had his PFLP-GC in the forefront of the fighting, always with the backing of the Syrian government. Then President Hafiz al-Asad of Syria became fearful of a Palestinian state in Lebanon and intervened with the Syrian army on the Christian side. Jibril remained loyal to Syria, but his chief lieutenant, Abu Abbas, broke with the PFLP-GC and formed the Palestine Liberation Front (PLF) on April 24, 1977. Abbas took with him many former PFLP-GC cadres dissatisfied with Jibril's pro-Syria stance. A mini–civil war ensued between the PFLP-GC and the PLF. On August 13, 1978, PFLP-GC operatives exploded a bomb in the West Beirut headquarters of the PLF, killing hundreds of PLF officers and fighters. After this incident, a lukewarm truce was negotiated between the PFLP-GC and the PLF.

Jibril and the PFLP-GC were ineffective during the 1982 invasion of Lebanon by the Israeli army. His forces fled before the Israelis and found protection with the Syrian army. Jibril proved to be a poor field commander. This debacle hurt his prestige in the Palestinian movement and made him even more determined to fight Israel. An opportunity was soon realized when the PFLP-GC captured three Israeli prisoners. Jibril negotiated the release of 1,150 captive Palestinian terrorists for the three Israelis in May 1985.

Despite this success, Jibril was still not a popular figure among the Palestinians fighting Israel. Even his successful hang glider attack on November 25, 1987, during which one of his operatives killed six Israeli soldiers and wounded seven, did not change this attitude. Jibril was, however, able to conclude an alliance between the PFLP-GC and the Lebanese Shi'ite group **Hezbollah**. This alliance allowed Jibril to develop a good working relationship with Iran. Both the Hezbollah and Jibril were anti-Arafat and anti-PLO, and they allied to free Palestine without the PLO.

Several times the Israelis launched operations to assassinate Jibril. An attack on his base camp by an Israeli gunship on May 12, 1988, killed several of his soldiers, but Jibril escaped unharmed. A more serious attempt was an Israeli commando raid at Jibril's al-Na'ameh facility in southern Lebanon on December 8, 1988. Again Jibril escaped unscathed, but this time he was shaken.

Jibril and the PFLP-GC have had financial problems that have hindered terrorist activities. After Syria cut its financial support in 1987, Jibril courted both Iran and Libya for financial support. He offered help in carrying out terrorist operations. His role in the bombing of Pan-Am flight 103 over Lockerbie, Scotland, on December 21, 1988, is unclear, but the bomb used was one in the PFLP-GC's weapons inventory. Israeli intelligence sources maintain that Jibril and his organization played a role in the bombing.

Jibril is still considered a dangerous enemy by Israel, but the number of operations by the PFLP-GC has lessened over the years. Financial problems are one explanation, but Jibril has also had health problems. Reports have surfaced that Jibril has also converted to Islamist religious views. The loss of his son, Mohammed Jihad Ahmed Jibril, in a bomb blast in Beirut on May 20, 2002, was a serious blow because he had become the number-two man in the PFLP-CG organization. Jibril blamed Israeli intelligence agents for the death of his son.

Even more damaging to the fortunes of Jibril than the loss of his son has been the deterioration of his relationship with Syria. For nearly 40 years Syria sponsored Jibril and the PFLP-CG. This support continued even after the death of its patron, President Asad. However, pressure on states supporting terrorism increased dramatically after the attacks on the United States on **September 11**, 2001. As a result, Syria distanced itself from the PFLP-CG without renouncing Jibril or its operations. **See also** Arafat, Mohammed Yasser; Habash, George; Popular Front for the Liberation of Palestine (PFLP).

Suggested readings: Douglas Jehl, "United in Cause, Syria Allows Foes of Israel in Its Midst," *Washington Times* (October 9, 2001), p. A8; Samuel M. Katz, *Israel versus Jibril: The Thirty-Years War against a Master Terrorist* (New York: Paragon House, 1993); Betsy Pisik, "Car Bomb Kills Son of Palestinian Guerrilla," *Washington Times* (May 21, 2002), p. A1.

Jordan, Colin (1923–) (Great Britain)

Colin Jordan was one of the leading British neo-Nazis in the 1960s and 1970s. He was born in 1923 in Birmingham, England. His father was a university tutor. He served in the Royal Air Force in World War II, first in the Royal Army Medical Corps and later as an instructor in the Education Corps. After the war, he studied history at Cambridge University and graduated with second-class honors in 1949. Jordan worked as a soap salesman in Scotland before becoming a teacher in a Leeds, England, school. Later, he moved to Coventry to take a teaching position. Until the late 1950s, Jordan remained a teacher of English and mathematics in the Coventry Secondary Modern School.

As early as 1938, Jordan displayed a fascination for Adolf Hitler and Nazism. He became a follower of Arnold Leese, a former head of the Imperial Fascist League (IFL) and a fervent anti-Semite. Jordan joined the neo-fascist League of Empire Loyalists (LEL) and became an organizer for it in the Midlands in the mid-1950s. In 1956, Jordan decided to start his own neo-Nazi organization and founded the White Defence League (WDL), an organization with a strong antiblack and antiforeigner orientation. Much of the financial support for the WDL came from Mary Leese, the widow of the founder of the pre-war Imperial Fascist League. Jordan merged the WDL into the **British National Party** (BNP) in 1960 and assumed a leadership role in the new organization.

Jordan's open admiration of Hitler and his attempt to turn the BNP into a Nazi movement soon estranged him from the other leaders of the British National Party. Within months of entering the BNP, Jordan began building a new organization, the British National Socialist Movement (BNSM), within the BNP. His neo-Nazi activities earned him a nine-month prison sentence in Wormwood Scrubs Prison in October 1962. Because of his political activities, he was dismissed from his teaching job in Coventry, and later he was expelled from the National Union of Teachers. In May 1963, he was released from prison. Likewise, his refusals to conform to the leadership of the BNP caused them to expel him from the British National Party in early summer 1963.

After his expulsion, Jordan resumed building the British National Socialist Movement (BNSM). From his headquarters on Princedale Road in London, Jordan launched a pro-Nazi and anti-Semitic campaign in Great Britain. He wanted to expel Jews and nonwhite immigrants from Great Britain. His chief assistant in this campaign was John Tyndall. Together they formed an elite para-military unit, the Spearhead, to serve both as a defense and a strike force. Members of the Spearhead were men between the ages of 16 and 45 with Nordic racial characteristics, who were to become the storm troopers of a National Socialist revolution in Great Britain. Jordan also initiated contact with other prominent neo-Nazis in other countries, including George Lincoln Rockwell of the United States. In the summer of 1963, Jordan hosted the first meeting of the World Union of National Socialists (WUNS) in Cottswold, England. Delegates at the meeting appointed Rockwell and Jordan to be the heads of the WUNS.

In the late 1960s and early 1970s, Jordan was the leading neo-Nazi in Great Britain. For a time he had an unlimited source of funding because of his marriage to Françoise Dior, heir to the Christian Dior fortune. This marriage collapsed in 1967, leaving Jordan's finances in a precarious situation. He also began feuding with John Tyndall, who left the party in 1964 to form the Greater Britain Movement (GBM). This split weakened the neo-Nazi movement because there was little room for three right-wing extremist movements— **Oswald Mosley's British Union of Fascists** (BUF), Jordan's British National Socialist Movement, and Tyndall's Greater Britain Movement.

Jordan used his position as head of the British National Socialist Party and the WUNS to spread Nazi propaganda. His expectations for the growth of his party proved disappointing, as the British populace was not ready for Na-

zism. In the mid-1970s, Jordan's position as head of the British National Socialist Party deteriorated. Other neo-Nazi parties began to make inroads on Jordan's party. Jordan decided to withdraw from politics and retired to the small village of Diabaig in Scotland. However, he continues to finance neo-Nazi literature, and his name makes the national news from time to time.

Suggested readings: Dennis Eisenberg, *The Re-Emergence of Fascism* (New York: Barnes, 1967); Gerard Seenan, "Neo-Fascist Fights to Stop Multifaith Centre in Village," *Guardian* (London) (April 22, 2002), p. 9; Richard Thurlow, *Fascism in Britain: From Oswald Mosley's Blackshirts to the National Front* (London: Tauris, 1998).

K

Kach (Only Thus) (Israel)

Kach (Only Thus) is the political party that Rabbi **Meir Kahane** founded in Israel to continue the anti-Palestinian policies of the American Jewish Defense League (JDL). Kahane founded Kach in 1977 to provide a forum to propagate his ideas on a Greater Israel. He expected to build Kach into a national party and increase his public exposure. In the 1984 election, Kahane won a seat in the Knesset. The Central Election Committee tried to outlaw Kach because of its promotion of racist and anti-democratic activities, but the Israeli Supreme Court overturned the attempt. In 1988, the Israeli government succeeded in banning Kach.

Kach also had a terrorist wing. Terror Against Terror (TNT) was formed in early 1984 by Kach members to carry out terrorist activities against Palestinians. Members of TNT attacked a bus in Jerusalem, killing four Palestinians. Israeli authorities soon caused this group to disband, but elements of Kach continued to undertake vigilante actions against Palestinians.

The murder of Meir Kahane in November 1990 in New York City by a Muslim gunman was a crushing blow to Kach. The central question that faced Kach was whether it could survive without a charismatic leader like Kahane. Many Kach members had settled in the West Bank Jewish settlement Kiryat Arba. They continued the Kach policy of confronting the Palestinian political agitation with force. Kahane's successor was Rabbi Abraham Toledano, a Moroccan computer engineer by training. New leadership attempted to moderate Kach policies to enable the party to evade the Israeli law barring racist and nondemocratic parties running candidates for national office. This change in policy led Kahane's youngest son, Binyamin Kahane, to break with Kach and form **Kahane Chai** (Kahane Lives). Toledano's attempt to reenter the Israeli political process was a failure and he resigned as head of Kach in 1991.

New leadership for Kach came from Baruch Marzel, Tiran Pollack, and Noam Federman. All three were residents of Kiryat Arba and they represented the most extreme wing of Kach. They sponsored vigilante action by forming the Committee for Road Safety, supposedly to protect Jewish drivers. Soon Kach members were promoting violence in Palestinian areas of the West Bank. The outbreak of Palestinian terrorism in 1993 only intensified Kach operations. Kach operatives were always careful to avoid contact with the Israel Defense Forces (IDF). A key platform for Kach became opposition to the 1993 Oslo Accords that granted Palestinians rights in Gaza and the West Bank.

Kach vigilantism culminated in the massacre at the 1994 Tomb of the Patriarchs in Hebron by Dr. **Baruch Goldstein**. Goldstein was a devoted follower of Meir Kahane and a member of Kach. He lived and served as its medical doctor at the Jewish settlement of Kiryat Arba. On February 25, 1994, Goldstein entered the Tomb of the Patriarchs and opened fire, killing 29 Muslims at prayer. He was mobbed by the survivors and killed. Kach members celebrated Goldstein's action; however, the Israeli government did not share their reaction and Kach was banned as a political organization. Members of Kach retreated underground and joined other organizations that shared their ideology of a Greater Israel and anti-Palestinian sentiment. See also Kahane, Meir.

Suggested readings: Mark Juergensmeyer, *Terror in the Mind of God: The Global Rise of Religious Violence* (Berkeley: University of California Press, 2000; Michael Karpin and Ina Friedman, *Murder in the Name of God: The Plot to Kill Yitzhak Rabin* (New York: Metropolitan Books, 1998); Ehud Sprinzak, *Brother against Brother: Violence and Extremism in Israeli Politics from Altalena to the Rabin Assassination* (New York: Free Press, 1999); Elli Wohlgelernter, "The Kahane Legacy," *Jerusalem Post* (November 17, 2000), p. 5B.

Kahane, Meir (1932–1990)
(Israel and United States)

Rabbi Meir Kahane was the leader of the most fanatical wing of the Zionist movement and the founder of both the Jewish Defense League (JDL) in the United States and **Kach** in Israel. He was born on August 1, 1932, in Brooklyn, New York. Both his father and grandfather had been prominent rabbis. At an early age of 14, Kahane joined the Zionist youth organization Betar. His first political action was at the age of 15, when he physically attacked Ernest Bevin, the British foreign minister, who was visiting New York City, by throwing tomatoes at him. Then in 1952, Kahane joined the youth movement of the Orthodox Zionist Federation of Labor, B'nai Akivah. He was ordained as a rabbi in 1955 after studying at the Orthodox Mir

Yeshiva Academy in New York City, and for a time served as a rabbi for Howard Beach in Queens, New York, until he was expelled in 1957 for excessive religious zeal. Furthering his education, Kahane attended New York University Law School, where he earned a master's degree in international law, but he failed to qualify for the New York bar. Among other jobs, Kahane worked briefly for *The Brooklyn Daily* and then became the editor of the *Jewish Press*. In the mid-1960s, Kahane served as an undercover agent for the Federal Bureau of Investigation (FBI) in its efforts to undermine the Black Panther Party in New York City. He also infiltrated the John Birch Society under the name Michael King.

Kahane assumed the leadership of the extreme wing of the American Orthodox Zionist movement soon after he founded the Jewish Defense League. In June 1968, he started the JDL as a civilian protection group whose mission was to protect Jews from physical attacks on the streets of New York City. Soon, however, Kahane turned the JDL into an organization that attacked perceived enemies of Jews using all tactics, including violence. Among these perceived enemies were the Palestinians and the Soviet Union. By 1971, the JDL claimed to have 14,000 members. In 1971, U.S. government authorities imprisoned him briefly on an illegal possession of arms charges. Eager to carry his ideas to Israel and in order to stay one step ahead of a federal indictment for his attacks on Soviet diplomats, Kahane immigrated to Israel in 1971, along with a number of supporters.

In Israel, Kahane soon earned himself the reputation as the most radical exponent of extreme Zionism. Many of the leaders of right-wing Israeli parties welcomed him as an ally until it became apparent that Kahane would be impossible to control. He advocated the removal of all Palestinians from all territories occupied by Israel and the settlement of these lands by Jewish settlers, including the West Bank. Kahane based his anti-Palestinian policy on the belief that violence is justified in the name of Jewish survival. To carry out this program, Kahane formed the Kach (Only Thus) Party in 1977. After several unsuccessful attempts to win a seat in the Knesset, Kahane won a seat in 1984. His harsh anti-Palestinian program won him supporters, but it alienated many Israeli politicians. Despite Kahane's status as a member of the Knesset, Kach was banned from the 1988 election as being racist and undemocratic. Israeli authorities were able to pass a racial incitement law in August 1986, and this law was used against Kahane in December 1989 for his actions in Jerusalem after a Palestinian attack on an Israeli bus. The actions and statements of Kahane and his supporters embarrassed the Israeli government, and various government agencies attempted to curtail his political activities.

Much of Kahane's financial support came from Jewish followers in the United States. In an interview in the late 1980s, Kahane stated that he spent one out of every five weeks in the United States. In November 1990, Kahane made one of his frequent trips back to the United States to raise funds to revitalize his anti-Palestinian campaign. On November 5, 1990, a gunman assassinated Kahane on a street in New York City. An Egyptian-born Moslem, El Sayyid Nosair, was charged with the murder of Kahane, but Nosair was convicted and sentenced to a 15-year jail term for only assault, coercion, and weapons charges. Followers of Kahane protested the murder acquittal. Kahane's funeral attracted most of the significant leaders of the Israeli radical right. He became a martyr to the Israeli extreme right and the religious wings of the Zionist movement. His son, Binyamin Kahane, founded the group **Kahane Chai** (Kahane Lives) to continue his father's political agenda. **See also** Kach (Only Thus); Kahane Chai (Kahane Lives).

Suggested readings: Robert I. Friedman, *The False Prophet: Rabbi Meir Kahane—From FBI Informant to Knesset Member* (London: Faber & Faber, 1990); Mark Juergensmeyer, *Terror in the Mind of God: The Global Rise of Religious Violence* (Berkeley: University of California Press, 1999); Raphael Mergui and Philippe Simonnot, *Israel's Ayatollahs: Meir Kahane and the Far Right in Israel* (London: Saqi Books, 1987; John

Miller and Michael Stone, *The Cell: Inside the 9/11 Plot, and Why the FBI and CIA Failed to Stop It* (New York: Hyperion, 2003); Ehud Sprinzak, *Brother against Brother: Violence and Extremism in Israeli Politics from Altalena to the Rabin Assassination* (New York: Free Press, 1999).

Kahane Chai (Kahane Lives) (Israel)

Kahane Chai (Kahane Lives) is a small group of supporters of the policies of the late Rabbi **Meir Kahane** with membership in both Israel and the United States. Binyamin Kahane, the son of Meir Kahane, founded Kahane Chai shortly after the assassination of his father in New York City on November 5, 1990. He had become dissatisfied with the new leadership of **Kach**. Kahane Chai was set up with dual leadership—Binyamin Kahane was the group's leader in Israel and Mike Guzofshy, a long-time backer of Meir Kahane, is the associate director and chief spokesperson in the United States. The exact size of the group in Israel is uncertain because the Israeli government banned it and arrested Binyamin Kahane. Although leaders have claimed that thousands of American Jews support Kahane Chai, actual membership ranges between 100 and 150. The Clinton administration supported the Israeli crackdown on Kahane Chai by designating it as a risk to peace in the Middle East. In November 1995, the U.S. Treasury Department used an executive order to block a Kahane Chai bank account in New York City.

The future of Kahane Chai remains uncertain. It was always much smaller and less important than Kach. Binyamin Kahane's assassination by Palestinian gunmen on January 1, 2000, left a leadership void in Kahane Chai that has not been replaced. Members of Kahane Chai still conduct demonstrations and an occasional terrorist act. Despite its apparent weakness, the United States Department of State added it to a list of organizations accused of terrorism in November 2001. The Israeli government protested this inclusion because Kahane Chai was classified in the same light as the Palestinian terrorist organizations **Hamas** and **Islamic Jihad**. **See also** Kach (Only Thus); Kahane, Meir.

Suggested readings: Sandro Contenta, "Israeli Police Foil Jewish Extremists," *Toronto Star* (May 13, 2002), p. A10; Michael Karpin and Ina Friedman, *Murder in the Name of God: The Plot to Kill Yitzhak Rabin* (New York: Metropolitan Books, 1998); Ehud Sprinzak, *Brother against Brother: Violence and Extremism in Israeli Politics from Altalena to the Rabin Assassination* (New York: Free Press, 1999).

Al-Khattab, Ibn (1970–2002) (Chechnya)

Ibn al-Khattab was one of the military leaders of the Chechen rebels. He was born in 1970 in northern Saudi Arabia into a wealthy family. His father was from an old Saudi family, but his mother was Turkish. While his birth name is in some dispute, the best sources indicate that it was Habib Abdel Rahman Khattab. Khattab was one of eight brothers. He attended religious schools in Saudi Arabia, but when his family decided to send him to the United States for further schooling, he rebelled. Instead, in 1987, he joined other Saudis and traveled to Afghanistan to fight Soviet military forces. He soon became celebrated among the mujahideen for his fighting ability. When Soviet forces left Afghanistan in 1989, Khattab returned to Saudi Arabia before he went back to Afghanistan. He was a fervent follower of the **Wahhabi** brand of Islam and he felt comfortable in Afghanistan. Sometime during his stay there, Khattab made the acquaintance of fellow Saudi **Osama bin Laden**.

In the spring of 1995, Khattab decided to join the war in Chechnya. His military experience and his connections to financial resources in the Arab world made him a valuable addition to Chechen forces. Khattab was the commander of the Islamic International Brigade, fighting alongside the Chechen army. President Maskhadov, the head of the Chechnya regime, appointed him the chief of the military training center of the central front of the armed forces of the Chechen Republic of Ichkeria in 1996.

Khattab conducted several operations under the command of General **Shamil Basayev** both in Chechnya and in Dagestan, his wife's homeland Khattab and Basayev were the two most respected and feared of the Chechen military commanders. Khattab also served as the chief financial conduit for money from the Arab world to Chechyna, and his ties to **al-Qaeda** were invaluable.

Khattab was such a charismatic figure that Soviet intelligence services targeted him for assassination. On March 19, 2002, a messenger brought a letter addressed to Khattab at the Chechen mujahideen headquarters. This letter had poison on it and Khattab died shortly after touching it. Chechen authorities kept his death secret until April 27, 2002, despite rumors that something had happened to Khattab. Various reports indicate that he was buried in the mountains of Chechnya, and only a few Chechen officials know the whereabouts of his grave. **See also** Basayev, Shamil.

Suggested readings: Marie Colvin, "Deadly Eye of the Believer," *Sunday Times* (London) (September 30, 2001), p. 1; John Daniszewski, "Poison Hidden in a Letter May Have Killed Rebel in Chechnya," *Los Angeles Times* (May 1, 2002), p. 3; Tom De Waal, "Khattab: Bloody Career," *Independent* (London) (May 1, 2002), p. 18; Christopher D. Kondaki, "Chechnya's Vicious War Re-Ignites," *Defense and Foreign Affairs' Strategic Policy* (September 2001), p. 20; Dave Montgomery, "Islamic Fighter Is Link between Chechnya Guerrilla, Bin Laden Network," Knight Ridder/Tribune News Service (December 6, 2001), p. 1.

Khomeini, Ayatollah Ruholla (1900–1989) (Iran)

Ayatollah Khomeini was the leader of the fundamentalist revolution in Iran. He was born on September 24, 1902, in the small village of Khomein in central Iran. His family traced his lineage back to the prophet Muhammad through Muhammad's daughter's line and the line of the seventh Imam of the Shi'a, Musal al-Kazem. His family was wealthy, with extensive land holdings. His father was killed by political rivals when Khomeini was not even five months old. His mother and aunt's death of cholera when he was 16 left him an orphan. Until 17, he studied at the local Shi'ite religious school and afterward attended the religious school of Sheikh Abdulkarim Ha'eri at Sultanabad-Arak. There he studied Islamic law (Sharia), Arabic grammar and rhetoric, logic, theology, and jurisprudence. In 1922, when Ha'eri moved his school to Qom, 90 miles south of Tehran, Khomeini followed. By the early 1930s, Khomeini had become recognized as a *mojtahedi*, or interpreter of Islamic law. He had also studied several of the mystical Shi'ite writers. After forming a religious school, Khomeini began attracting students eager to learn his interpretation of Islam.

Khomeini was an early critic of the Western orientation of the Shah of Iran's regime. In 1941, he wrote *Secrets Exposed*, in which he expressed his opposition to the secularization of Iranian society under the deposed Reza Shah. In the early 1960s, Khomeini became the militant leader of the Shi'ite opposition to the Pahlavi Shahs. In June 1963, Khomeini was arrested for an anti–Shah of Iran speech and imprisoned for 10 months in first the Qasr prison and then in a house in the Davudiya section of Tehran. This arrest only increased his reputation among the Iranian clergy. Then, on November 4, 1964, the Iranian government deported him to Turkey. Before his exile, however, he had trained a generation of religious leaders in his views, and nearly 12,000 students had attended his lectures. His stay was first in Istanbul and then Bursa. Next Khomeini traveled to the Shi'ite religious center of Najaf, Iraq, where he stayed for the next 13 years. An unsettled political and religious climate in Iraq forced Khomeini to settle in Paris, France. In his writings, Khomeini divided the world into two groups—the oppressors and the oppressed. The United States, European countries, Israel, and the Soviet Union were the oppressors. Listed among the oppressed were the Muslim world and the Third World. Khomeini's answer to fighting oppression was a return to the Islamic society of the seventh century, when the prophet lived. His attack on the government of the Shah of Iran

included an indictment of monarchy. He wanted a government ruled or guided by a vice-regent for the prophet, or, if no such person were to exist, by the Islamic clergy, or ulama. He required the Islamic clergy to also be expert jurists. His views were contained in a series of 1960s lectures entitled "Mandate of the Jurist: Islamic Government" ("Velayat-e Faqih: Hukumat-e Eslami") that was published in 1978.

The overthrow of the Shah of Iran on January 6, 1979, allowed Khomeini the opportunity to carry out his religious-political agenda. Khomeini returned to Iran as a national hero, but his views on a clergy-dominated government were relatively unknown. On January 12, 1979, Khomeini established the Council of Islamic Revolution to set up a transitional government. Khomeini returned to Iran on February 1, 1979, and assumed a privileged position in the Iranian state. The assassination of Ayatollah Motahhari, chair of the Council of Islamic Revolution, on May 1, 1979, made Khomeini more determined than ever to purge his enemies. Khomeini made it plain at this time that he wanted the establishment of an Islamic theocracy and the compete eradication of Western cultural influences. In the subsequent power struggle with the provisional government of Mehdi Bazargan that ended by November 1979, Khomeini and his followers were able to reestablish a system in which clergy controlled the political, economic, and social life in Iran. Even those supporters who had backed Khomeini in exile had to conform to his views or suffer the consequences. Revolutionary tribunals began executing former officials of the Shah's government. Former political supporters Bazargan and Abolhassau Bani-Sadr fled Iran, and Sadeq Gobtzadeh was executed. Clerics who disagreed with Khomeini's master plan had to conform or be isolated.

Khomeini played no role in the planning or execution of the November 4, 1979, occupation of the American Embassy in Tehran. Student groups had planned the operation to protest the American decision to give safe haven to the Shah of Iran. The seizure of 63 hostages at the U.S. Embassy surprised Khomeini and the new government. Only after the fact did Khomeini bless the taking of what he then classified as a den of spies. This event marked a more violent phase of the revolution and it started an orgy of anti-Americanism.

The greatest crisis during Khomeini's control of Iran was the Iran-Iraq War. **Saddam Hussein** of Iraq had participated in the deporting of Khomeini from Baghdad in 1978. Khomeini had launched a propaganda war in the spring and summer of 1980 against the secular government of Iraq. He encouraged the Shi'ites of southern Iraq to rebel against Hussein. Hussein had retaliated with anti-Khomeini radio broadcasts encouraging Iran's ethnic minorities to revolt. A series of border skirmishes between Iranian and Iraqi forces took place in late summer. On September 22, 1980, Iraqi military forces invaded the western border of Iran. Saddam Hussein believed that the Iranian government of Khomeini was so weak that he could impose territorial demands on Iran. After initial Iraqi successes, the Iranian army was able to regain territory lost in the first days of the war. Khomeini decided that continuation of the war would allow him to export his religious revolution. After a lengthy stalemate, other Iranian leaders were finally able to convince him that the war was unwinnable, and a truce was concluded on August 20, 1988.

Khomeini's last controversy was over Salman Rushdie's novel *The Satanic Verses*. This book had appeared in early 1989 and its treatment of the prophet Muhammad provoked Muslim anger around the world. On February 14, 1989, Khomeini issued a fatwa, a religious ruling, sentencing Rushdie and all those involved in the book's publication to death. He exhorted all Muslims to carry out this sentence. The Iranian government offered a reward of $2.5 million for Rushdie's death and another $1 million if the killer was an Iranian. Iran broke diplomatic relations with Great Britain over the British protection of Rushdie. This event gave Khomeini an excuse to slow liberalization of Iranian politics and, at the same time, to show his leadership in the Muslim world.

The Khomeini revolution in Iran served as a model for Islamic fundamentalists throughout the Middle East. Khomeini believed that his revolution should be exported and called on Muslims throughout the Middle East to rise up against their governments. The Iranian Ministry of Religious Guidance was in charge of spreading the revolution by providing preachers, sending publications, and setting up conferences. Groups that worked to undermine non-Islamic governments were supported, including those that resorted to violence or terrorism. Both the United States and Israel were high-priority targets, but Khomeini also directed efforts against Egypt and Saudi Arabia. Khomeini continued to agitate for a Muslim revolution in the Middle East until his death on June 3, 1989. He was buried in Behesht-e Zahra (Paradise of Zahra) on the outskirts of Tehran.

Suggested readings: Fouad Ajami, "Iran: The Impossible Revolution," *Foreign Affairs* (1988/1989), p. 135; Said Amir Arjomand, *The Turban for the Crown: The Islamic Revolution in Iran* (New York: Oxford University Press, 1988); Dilip Hiro, *The Longest War: The Iran-Iraq Military Conflict* (New York: Routledge, 1991); Elie Kedourie, "Khomeini's Political Heresy," *Policy Review*, no. 12 (Spring 1980), p. 133; Baqer Moin, *Khomeini: Life of the Ayatollah* (New York: St. Martin's Press, 1999); Amir Taheri, *The Spirit of Allah: Khomeini and the Islamic Revolution* (London: Hutchinson, 1985); Robin Wright, *In the Name of God: The Khomeini Decade* (New York: Simon & Schuster, 1989).

Kühnen, Michael (1955–1991) (Germany)

Michael Kühnen was one of Germany's leading neo-Nazis and the founder of the **German Alternative** party. He was born in 1955 into a middle-class Catholic family. Kühnen worked for a number of years in the Hamburg shipyards. After a brief political flirtation with Maoism, Kühnen became active in various illegal neo-Nazi movements in Germany. He joined the youth group in Adolf von Thadden's National Democratic Party (NPD), but he soon left the NPD because it was too moderate for his tastes. Kühnen then joined the German army, but in 1977 he was dishonorably discharged for his neo-Nazi agitation. Next, he started the neo-Nazi National Socialist Action Front (Aktionsfront Nationaler Sozialisten) (ANS). The ANS was a paramilitary organization that flagrantly displayed its Nazi orientation. West German authorities banned it in December 1983.

Kühnen spent nearly eight years in the 1970s and 1980s in and out of German jails for his affiliations with groups that glorified Adolf Hitler and Nazism. In February 1987, members of the ANS and another neo-Nazi group, Viking Youth, carried out a series of bank robberies and arms thefts. In a September 1979 trial, Kühnen received a three-and-one-half-year prison sentence. His book, *The Second Revolution (Die Zweite Revolution)*, was written during his stay in prison. Kühnen's disdain for democracy included all of the German political parties except those on the extreme right. Kühnen was active in German right-wing politics because it was among these groups that he was able to come into contact with Germans who shared his political views. He started the National Assembly (Nationale Sammlung) in the mid-1980s to appeal to neo-Nazis, but he was only able to attract about 180 members. Much of his financial support and propaganda materials for his recruiting efforts came from abroad, with the best source being Gary Lauck's National Socialist German Workers Party—Overseas Operations, or NSDAP-AO in Lincoln, Nebraska. In March 1984, Kühnen fled to Paris to avoid another term in jail for subversive activities. French authorities deported Kühnen back to Germany, where he was sentenced to a four-year term in prison.

Kühnen decided in the late 1980s to form a new neo-Nazi political party shortly after the banning of his National Assembly group on February 9, 1989. In May 1989, he founded the German Alternative (Deutsche Alternative) party. His goal was to unite German neo-Nazis into a single party and have enough political success to come to power in Germany legally. His model was Hitler's le-

gal accession to power in 1933. Kühnen had the most success in attracting discontented elements in the former East Germany. He was active in anti-immigrant agitation and in the formation of "foreign-free zones" in Germany. His leadership made the German Alternative a force in German politics.

Sometime in the late 1980s, Kühnen contracted AIDS (Acquired Immune Deficiency Syndrome), and this disease began to curtail his political activities in the early 1990s. Kühnen made it public in the mid-1950s that he was a homosexual, and although it had caused a scandal in the neo-Nazi movement, he weathered the political fallout. He died of complications from AIDS on April 25, 1991, in the municipal hospital in Kassel, Germany. His death proved to be a serious blow to the German neo-Nazi movement. His successor in the German Alternative has been less successful in making it a mainstream German political party. **See also** German Alternative (Deutsche Alternative) (DA).

Suggested readings: Martin A. Lee, *The Beast Reawakens* (Boston: Little, Brown, 1997); Ferdinand Protzman, "West German Neo-Nazi Speaks of a Revival," *New York Times* (March 12, 1989), Sec. 1, p. 21; Michael Schmidt, *The New Reich: Violent Extremism in Unified Germany and Beyond* (New York: Pantheon Books, 1993).

Kumplan Militan Malaysia (KMM) (Malaysia)

The Kumplan Militan Malaysia (KMM) is Malaysia's leading terrorist group. Zainon Ismail, an Afghan veteran, founded the KMM on October 12, 1995. Since Malaysia was already in theory at least an Islamic state, the goal of the KMM was to unite with other Islamist groups and build a regional Islamic state from Indonesia, Malaysia, Singapore, and the southern part of the Philippines. Consequently, leaders of the KMM developed close ties with the **Abu Sayyaf Group** of the Philippines and the **Jemaah Islamiyah** of Indonesia. The KMM membership has never exceeded more than a hundred, but it has always had a large number of sympathizers, most of whom belong to the Islamist political party Parti Islam

SeMalaysia (PAS). Soon after the KMM's founding, Nik Adli Nik Aziz, son of a prominent PAS leader, assumed operational control. He retained control until the Malaysian police arrested him on August 4, 2001.

The Kumplan Militan Malaysia also has developed a working relationship with **al-Qaeda**. Many of the leaders of the KMM were veterans of the Afghan war against the Soviets in the 1980s. They retained ties to Afghanistan and sent contingents of KMM supporters in al-Qaeda and **Taliban** training camps in the late 1990s. Others were sent to Mindanao for training with the Abu Sayyaf Group and the **Moro National Liberation Front** (MNLF). KMM members applied their training in a terrorist campaign against Christians, Hindus, and government officials in Indonesia and Malaysia. KMM operatives also conducted a series of bank robberies in May 2001 in Malaysia with mixed results. These operatives intended funds from these robberies to finance further operations.

The political fallout from the **September 11, 2001**, terrorist attacks in the United States caused the Malaysian government to crack down on the KMM and its allies. Malaysian security forces had been monitoring KMM activity for several years, but the association of the KMM with al-Qaeda led to mass arrests of KMM members in December 2001 and again in January 2002. Remaining members of the KMM have gone underground or left Malaysia for safer political climates. In May 2003, the United States placed the KMM on the list of terrorist groups because of its goal of overthrowing the government of Malaysia. **See also** Abu Sayyaf Group; Jemaah Islamiyah (Islamic Community) (JI); Moro National Liberation Front (MNLF); Al-Qaeda (The Base).

Suggested readings: Eddie Chua, Parveen Gill, and Timothy Leonard, "On the Run," *Malay Mail* (September 28, 2002), p. 1; John Gershman, "Is Southeast Asia the Second Front?" *Foreign Affairs* (July 2002/August 2002) p. 60; Rohan Gunaratna, *Inside Al Qaeda: Global Network of Terror* (New York: Columbia University Press, 2002); Salmy Hashim, "KMM, Jemaah Islamiah in US Global Terrorism List," *Malaysia General News* (May 1, 2003), p. 1; Maria A. Ressa, *Seeds of Terror: An Eyewitness Account of Al-Qaeda's Newest Center of Operations in Southeast Asia* (New York: Free Press, 2003).

Kurdistan Worker's Party (Partiya Karkaren Kurdistan) (PKK) (Turkey)

The Kurdistan Worker's Party (PKK) is a guerrilla movement that is fighting to establish an independent Kurdish state in southeastern Turkey. This group, originally called the National Liberation Army (Ulusal Kurtulus Ordusu) (UKO), was founded in 1974 in Ankara by a small group of Kurdish nationalists. Many of the members had been active in the Ankara Higher Education Association (AYOD). Its most prominent early leaders were **Abdullah (Apo) Ocalan**, Cemil (Cuma) Bayik, and Ali Haydar (Fuat) Kaytan. In 1975, the UKO left Ankara and it established itself in the Kurdish areas of eastern Turkey. By this time, Ocalan had become its most dominant leader. The identification with Ocalan became so close that the followers of the UKO were soon called Apocular, or followers of Apo.

On November 27, 1978, the leadership of the UKO met in the Kurdish village of Fis near Lice in Diyarbakir Province, and they proclaimed the formation of the Kurdistan Workers Party, which soon became Ocalan's personal guerrilla organization. At that meeting, the leadership formed a seven-person Central Committee made up of Ocalan, Kesire Yildirim (Ocalan's wife), Cemil Bayik, Mahsun Dogan, Sahin Donmez, Mehmet Hayri Durmus, and Mehmet Karasungar. Later, the larger Central Executive Committee of 30 members was established with seven of its members appointed to the party's Leadership Council. Party congresses were also held in 1981, 1982, 1986, 1990, and 1995. Three national conferences in 1988, 1990, and 1994 provided more guidance for the PPK. Because of deaths and arrests, the leadership changed over the years with only Ocalan remaining in a leadership post.

Two organizations have been formed to carry out the policies of the PKK. The

Kurdistan Peoples Liberation Army (Artes-I Rizgariye Geli Kurdistan) (ARGK) is the professional guerrilla army of the PKK. Members of the Third Congress of the PKK established the ARGK in October 1986. At one time in 1993, the ARGK had as many as 10,000 frontline fighting troops. The other organization is the Kurdistan National Liberation Front (Eniye Rizgariye Nevata Kurdistan) (ERNK). Members of the ERNK serve as both the political front for the PKK and a militia of around 50,000 part-time fighters.

Ocalan left Turkey in May 1979, and he moved to Syria where he arranged for Palestinians to train PKK volunteers for guerrilla warfare in Turkey. Later, Ocalan developed close ties with Syria, and the Syrian government also trained PKK activists. He also established working relationships with other Kurdish liberation groups in Iraq. Ocalan directed its operations against the Turkish government and security forces in a no-quarter-asked-or-given campaign. Somewhere in the neighborhood of 10,000 Turkish casualties have resulted from terrorist acts by the PKK since 1985. Because the Turkish government depended heavily on the revenue from the tourist trade, the PKK targeted tourists in Istanbul and in the Turkish countryside.

In the early 1990s, the Turkish military broke up the military organization of the PKK. Ocalan lost his protection in Syria and moved to Nairobi, Kenya. His seizure by the Kenyan government and subsequent deportation to Turkey was a severe blow to the PKK. His trial and death sentence further weakened the Kurdish movement. While the remaining PKK leaders promised further war against Turkey, the PKK lacked the military strength and leadership to carry out this promise. Only in early 2003 did it seem that the PKK was back in action with several gun battles between Kurds and Turkish forces. **See also** Ocalan, Abdullah (Apo).

Suggested readings: Nur Bilge Criss, "The Nature of PKK Terrorism in Turkey," *Studies in Conflict and Terrorism* 18, no. 1 (January–March 1995); Michael M. Gunter, *The Kurds and the Future of Turkey* (New York: St. Martin's Press, 1997); Ali M. Koknar, "The PKK after Ocalan," *Journal of Counterterrorism and Security International* 6, no. 1 (Fall 1999); Matthew McAllester, "Turkey's Renewed Conflict: After Years of Inactivity, a Kurdish Guerrilla Group Is Back," *Newsday* (New York) (February 5, 2003), p. A33; Roddy Scott, "PKK Is Down but Not Out as Leaders Talk of Three-Front War," *Jane's Intelligence Review* 11, no. 5 (May 1, 1999), p. 1; Paul White, *Primitive Rebels or Revolutionary Modernizers? The Kurdish National Movement in Turkey* (London: Zed Books, 2000); Amberin Zaman, "For Turkish Rebel, Kurds, Disillusionment Replaces Passion for Battle," *Los Angeles Times* (February 11, 2001), p. A7.

L

Lashkar-e-Taiba (Army of the Pure) (Pakistan)

The Lashkar-e-Taiba (Army of the Pure) is one of the leading Pakistani Islamist groups fighting a war for Kashmir. This group was founded in 1987 with funding provided by the Saudi Islamist **Osama bin Laden.** Both financial and material support for the Lashkar-e-Taiba has also come from the Pakistan security forces Inter-Services Intelligence (ISI). Hafiz Mohammed Saeed is the leader of this group. His headquarters is on a 200-acre estate about 20 miles north of Lahore. This estate, a gift from Middle Eastern backers, has six mosques, a hospital, a playground, and a shopping center. By 1999, the Lashkar-e-Taiba had more than 2,000 recruitment centers in Pakistan and three training centers in the Pakistan area of Kashmir. Many of its fighters in Kashmir have been recruited from other Middle Eastern countries.

Followers of Lashkar-e-Taiba have certain core beliefs, one of which is that they are at war against the enemies of Islam. These enemies are Christians, Hindus, Jews, liberal Pakistanis, and Shi'ite Muslims. Leaders of Lashkar-e-Taiba also want to transform Pakistan into an Islamic state and away from democratic institutions because democracy is un-Islamic.

Political events outside Pakistan have resulted in the Pakistani government trying to restrain the activities of Lashkar-e-Taiba. After the terrorist attacks against the United States on **September 11**, 2001, the American government pressured Pakistani President Pervez Musharraf to crack down on the radical Islamist supporters of bin Laden's **Taliban** of Afghanistan. In turn, Musharraf placed pressure on the leaders of the Lashkar-e-Taiba to restrain its attacks in Kashmir. Then the complicity of the Lashkar-e-Taiba leadership in the December 13, 2001, attack on the Indian Parliament and the death of nine Indians caused political complications for the Pakistan government. With the threat of a war with India apparent, the Pakistan government froze the financial assets of Lashkar-e-Taiba and arrested Saeed and 11 of his key officials on January 2, 2002. These arrests have slowed the activities of the Lashkar-e-Taiba, but its followers are still actively fighting in Kashmir and continue to threaten the stability of the Pakistani state.

Suggested readings: Suzanne Goldenberg, "Finishing School for Fanatics," *Guardian* (London) (August 28, 1998), p. 14; Zahid Hussain, and Surinder Singh Oberoi, "Pakistan: New Face of Terror," *India Today* (February 26, 2001), p. 42; David Orr, "Mujahideen Reject Kashmir Deal," *Scotsman* (Edinburgh) (July 6, 1999), p. 10; Paul Watson, "Kashmir Rebel Group Vows to

Escalate War," *Los Angeles Times* (July 18, 2001) p. A1; Nicholas Watt, "Militants Arrest Raises Hopes of New Talks in Kashmir Crisis," *Guardian* (London) (January 1, 2002), p. 2.

Laskar Jihad (Militia of the Holy War) (Indonesia)

The Laskar Jihad (Militia of the Holy War) was an Indonesian Muslim paramilitary group that specialized in fighting against Christians in the Moluccan Islands. **Jaffar Umar Thalib** founded the Laskar Jihad on November 14, 1999. Thalib fought in the anti-Soviet jihad Afghanistan in the late 1980s. Later, in 1987, he met **Osama bin Laden** in Pakistan. Despite his open rejection of bin Laden as a leader, Thalib's goal was to establish an Islamic state in Indonesia and to do it with force if necessary. He opened a network of Koranic schools that preached that the Indonesian state should be governed by strict Islamic law. These schools attracted numerous students, many of whom were then recruited into the Laskar Jihad. Total membership has been estimated at from between 6,000 and 10,000 active supporters. Headquarters for the Laskar Jihad was established in Kebon Cengkih, a village in the hills above Ambon. Simon Montlake estimated in an April 2002 article in *The Christian Science Monitor* that Laskar Jihad's military strength was between 500 and 800 men, but later it had nearly 10,000 fighters. Training for its fighters was on the island of Bogor. Much of the military training and financial support for the Laskar Jihad came from the Indonesian military.

Shortly after its founding, the Laskar Jihad became involved in a dispute between Christians and Muslims in the Moluccan Islands of Indonesia. Sparks for the conflict grew out of a fight between a Christian and a Muslim over a bus ticket, but it soon escalated into widespread rioting. Thalib sent the Laskar Jihad to intervene on the side of the Muslims in a region with a Christian majority. The newsletter *Counterterrorism & Security Reports* reported that the fighting killed more than 6,000 people and forced over 750,000

to seek sanctuary from the conflict. Laskar Jihad and Christian forces signed a peace accord on February 12, 2002, but it was soon ignored.

Thalib disbanded the Laskar Jihad in October 2002. He decided to disband his group in the aftermath of the Bali bombing on October 12, 2002, which killed 188 and wounded hundreds more. Most of the suspicion for the bombing fell on Abu Bakar Bashir's **Jemaah Islamiyah**, but other extremist groups shared in the responsibility. A shift in public opinion following the bombing among moderate Muslims was a key factor, but the possibility of a government crackdown on Muslim extremists was also a consideration. In February 2003, Thalib threatened to revive the Laskar Jihad if Christians attack Muslims in Indonesia. **See also** Thalib, Jaffar Umar.

Suggested readings: Robert Go, "Laskar Jihad Disbands in Face of Blast Outrage," *Straits Times* (Singapore) (October 6, 2002), p. 1; IACSP Staff, "Who Are These Guys?" *Counterterrorism & Security Reports* 9, no. 6 (November/December 2002); Andrew Marshall, "The Threat of Jaffar," *New York Times* (March 10, 2002), sec. 6, p. 45; Simon Montlake, "Militant Group Threatens Indonesian Peace," *Christian Science Monitor* (April 4, 2002), p. 7.

League of Rights (Australia)

The League of Rights is Australia's leading racist organization. Eric Butler founded the League of Rights in 1946. His goal was to build an organization that promoted anticommunism and worked against what he considered to be the Jewish world conspiracy. Butler is a follower of the social credit theories of C. H. Douglas, an anti-Semitic British economic theorist. In 1946, Butler published the book *The International Jew: The Truth about the Protocols of Zion*. In this work, Butler argued that Jews controlled international finance. For most of its lengthy career, the League of Rights has been a small lobbying organization that has publicized its views in publications like *The Strategy*. It also has a publishing company, Veritas, which has published the historical works of

David Irving and promotes **Holocaust denial** and anti-Semitism.

Butler decided to make the League of Rights a national organization in 1960. A rural recession in Australia during the 1960s allowed the League of Rights to increase its membership. Butler never intended to turn the League of Rights into a political party, but he wanted to influence Australian politics toward his political views. His special favorite among Australian politicians has been Graeme Campbell, a former Labor Member of Parliament (MP) and the leader of the racist Australia First Party. Besides its avowed anti-Semitism, the League of Rights has been active in campaigns against Aborigine rights, restriction of immigration, Holocaust denial, and opposition to the "New World Order" of globalization.

Members of the League of Rights became active in **Pauline Hanson's One Nation Party** in Queensland, which has had a history of supporting right-wing or populist causes. Butler endorsed the platform of the One Nation Party despite its failure to promote an anti-Semitic agenda. Members of the League of Rights operated behind the scenes helping the electoral chances of Hanson's party, but the collapse of One Nation as a significant political force has allowed the adherents of the League of Rights to seize complete control of the organization.

Members of the League of Rights have also been linked to a group that calls itself the Independent Sovereign State of Australia (ISSA). This group is led by Donald Cameron, a career criminal having spent 24 years in prison for 20 convictions from crimes since 1961. Adherents argue that they have seceded from the state of Australia, and they challenge elections and legislation at both the national and local level. Federal courts have consistently overruled their litigation against the state and the provinces, but this has not discouraged the members of the ISSA from filing civil suits. **See also** Hanson, Pauline; One Nation (ONP).

Suggested readings: Dennis Eisenberg, *The Re-Emergence of Fascism* (South Brunswick, NJ: Barnes, 1967); Alan Gold and Benseon Apple,

"Shadowy Racist Group Is Still in a League of Its Own," *Sydney Morning Herald* (June 15, 2001), p. 14; Kevin Meade, "Warning on Right-Wing Sect," *Australian* [Sydney] (January 2, 2004), p. 5; Natalie O'Brien, Belinda Hickman, and Dennis Shanahan, "Western Showdown," *Weekend Australian* (Sydney) (May 26, 2001), p. 21; Rae Wear, "One Nation and the Queensland Right," in Michael Leach, Geoffrey Stokes, and Ian Ward (eds.), *The Rise and Fall of One Nation* (St. Lucia: University of Queensland Press, 2000).

Lee, Ronnie (1951–2001) (Great Britain)

Ronnie Lee was the founder of Great Britain's **Animal Liberation Front** and a leading animal rights terrorist. He was born in 1951 in Liverpool and raised in Stevenage, England. His sister's boyfriend introduced him to vegetarianism when Lee was 19. Soon afterward, he became a vegan, a person who adheres to the philosophy that prohibits the use of any animal products, whether for food or clothing. After high school, Lee became a trainee legal clerk. He also joined the anti-hunting group Hunt Saboteurs. In 1972, Lee and others founded the Band of Mercy, an anti-hunting group that specialized in sabotaging British hunters. In 1974, Lee received a three-year jail sentence for various offenses, including the burning of sealing boats.

After an early release from jail, Lee decided to expand his animal rights campaign, and in 1976 he founded the Animal Liberation Front. Under his guidance, the ALF specialized in the use of violent tactics, including incendiary bombs, against targeted businesses. Lee was quoted in a 1988 article in the *Financial Times* (London) that he advocated direct action by "sabotage of the animal abuse industries by causing damage to property." He was adamant, however, about not injuring people or animals. He avoided human casualties by firebombing shops at midnight or early in the morning.

In February 1987, a Sheffield court sentenced Lee to 10 years in prison for conspiracy to commit criminal damage. After his release, Lee returned to the struggle for animal rights. In the early 1990s, he undertook a firebombing campaign on the Isle of Wight.

And in 1996, British police caught Lee in the act of firebombing a store in Bristol, England. A Bristol court sentenced him to a term of 18 years for four charges of arson, five of attempted arson, and one of possessing bomb-making equipment. Lee served his prison sentence at the Long Lartin high-security prison. After losing an appeal for his sentence in October 1999, Lee initiated a hunger strike that lasted until December 1999. Then on October 21, 2001, Lee started another hunger strike to protest mistreatment of animals. This hunger strike lasted until Lee died of liver failure on November 5, 2001. Many animal right activists consider Lee a martyr to the cause. **See also** Animal Liberation Front (ALF); Horne, Barry.

Suggested readings: Richard Donkin, "Animal Rights Advocate Who Urges Sabotage," *Financial Times* (London) (December 24, 1988), p. 6; Sarah Hall, "Animal Activists Mourn Their Martyr," *Guardian* (London) (November 6, 2001), p. 3; Kevin Toolis, "In for the Kill," *Guardian* (London) (December 4, 1998), p. 8; Kevin Toolis, "To the Death," *Guardian* (London) (November 7, 2001), p. 6.

Le Pen, Jean-Marie (1928–) (France)

Jean-Marie Le Pen is the leader of the French extremist party **Front National** (FN). He was born on June 28, 1928, in La Trinité-sur-Mer in Brittany. His father was a fisherman, who was drowned after his fishing boat hit a mine in 1942. Le Pen went to live with his maternal grandfather, who was also a fisherman. He graduated from a Jesuit high school in Brittany before attending law school in Paris in 1947. His right-wing views and strong personality led him to become president of the right-wing Law Student Corporation (Union National d'Etudiants Francais). His student activities prompted some former supporters of the World War II Vichy regime to recruit him for the extreme right-wing group National Union of Independent Republicans (National Union de Independent Republicains) in 1951. Le Pen devoted so much of his energies to politics that he failed to complete his law degree. In 1953, he enlisted in the French Foreign Legion and was attached

to the Third Paratroop Regiment. Le Pen served in Vietnam, but his arrival in Vietnam was too late for him to join the other paratroopers at the Battle of Dien Bien Phu. This French defeat and his experiences in Vietnam reinforced his anti-communism and made him bitter toward those Frenchmen who opposed the war.

After leaving the Foreign Legion in 1955, Le Pen joined the right-wing populist movement led by Pierre Poujade protesting French modernization. Le Pen won a seat to the National Assembly in the January 1956 election as a Poujadist. Soon afterward, Le Pen left the Poujadist movement because of a disagreement with Poujade over Poujade's lack of support for the Algerian cause. In September 1956, Le Pen joined the First Paratroop Regiment of the French Foreign Legion to fight for a French Algeria. His unit was sent to Suez with the French invasion forces during the Suez crisis of 1956. After Suez, Le Pen arrived in Algeria, where he served as an intelligence officer with the Tenth Airborne Division. His job was to interrogate prisoners, and it has been an ongoing controversy of whether or not he tortured prisoners.

In 1957, Le Pen returned to French politics by retaking his seat in the National Assembly. He formed a veteran's organization, the Fighters National Front (Front National des Combattants) to lobby for support for the Algerian War. Le Pen voted against Charles de Gaulle becoming premier in 1958 because he distrusted de Gaulle and his attitude toward Algeria. However, in the 1958 election to the National Assembly, Le Pen won reelection on a pro-Gaullist ticket. Then in 1960, he was invited by military leaders to join the conspiracy to overthrow the Gaullist government. Although he sympathized with them, Le Pen refused to join the conspiracy because he believed that it would fail. In the November 1962 elections to the National Assembly, Le Pen ran on an anti-Gaullist platform and lost his parliamentary seat.

Le Pen retired from active politics for several years. He joined with a friend in forming a public relations and research company.

Chairman of the National Front of France Jean-Marie Le Pen, right, shakes hands with Russian ultranationalist Vladimir Zhirinovsky, left, leader of the Liberal Democratic Party, as they smile during a joint news conference in Moscow, February 10, 1996. Le Pen was specially invited by Zhirinovsky for his church wedding, as Zhirinovsky and his wife renewed their civil marriage vows in a church ceremony celebrating their 25th anniversary. (AP Photo/ Misha Japaridze)

Later he turned this company into a record publishing company specializing in historic recordings. One such historical recording was on Adolf Hitler and the Nazis. This recording led to his arrest in 1968 and the imposition of an eighteen-month suspended sentence and a heavy fine. Le Pen returned briefly to politics by serving as the campaign manager for Jean-Louis Tixier-Vignancour, a veteran right-wing lawyer, who ran for the French presidency in 1965. Le Pen became disillusioned by Tixier-Vignancour and his moderate stances on the issues and withdrew before the election. In 1968, Le Pen lost again for a bid to return to the National Assembly.

Le Pen decided that France needed a unified right-wing party that could win political power. He also wanted to attract support from the neo-fascist group **The New Order** (L'Ordre Nouveau). This group had a violent reputation that Le Pen wanted to tame for his purposes. Le Pen and five veteran right-wing leaders formed the Front National (FN) on October 5, 1972. Three days later, he was elected its national leader. His first task was to make the Front National respectable and bring the wilder elements of the Ordre Nouveau under control. As Le Pen asserted his authority, he expelled some of the more militant members. In 1976, Le Pen became wealthy after a French businessman, Hubert

Lambert, left him 20 million francs and a large estate in the Saint Cloud suburb of Paris. This inheritance allowed Le Pen financial independence to carry out his party's activities.

The initial promise of the Front National was slow to be fulfilled. Le Pen failed to win a place on the ballot for the 1981 presidential election because of his inability to obtain the necessary 500 signatures from political notables. However, bad economic conditions in the early 1980s gave Le Pen an opening. His group gained electoral strength by blaming immigration for French unemployment, street crime, drugs, and AIDS (Acquired Immune Deficiency Syndrome). Le Pen was able to capitalize on these issues and form electoral alliances with the mainstream right. He was also able to capitalize on the Front National's anti-communist stance. As a result of this electoral success, Le Pen and 34 members of the National Front won election to the National Assembly in 1986. In the 1988 presidential election, Le Pen did exceptionally well, garnering 4.3 million votes, or 14.4 percent of the vote. However, his declaration of neutrality in the runoff election allowed the Socialist Francois Mitterand to win the presidency. When the French right retaliated by refusing to form alliances with the FN in the subsequent elections for the National Assembly, Le Pen lost his seat.

Lack of political success made Le Pen look for other enemies. Other political parties were adopting his anti-immigrant position, making it difficult for Le Pen to separate his views from the others. A television interview in September 1987 belittling the Nazi gas chambers led to charges of anti-Semitism. In 1990, he was convicted of incitement to racial hatred for his supportive remarks about Nazis and the persecution of Jews and Gypsies, but he only received a small fine. The Front National's anti-Semitism led members to easily identity Israel, as well as the United States as Israel's main supporter, as an enemy. Anti-Americanism became one of the Front National's key planks. Le Pen's anti-Americanism led him to condemn the American role in the Persian Gulf War.

Le Pen's policies of attacking immigrants and his anti-Americanism brought the Front National to the forefront of French politics. Throughout the 1990s, Le Pen's strategy resulted in voting support of between 12 and 16 percent of the French voters. Le Pen had a setback in 1997 when he was banned from politics for a year after he assaulted a female politician. Le Pen became uneasy about the political ambitions of his number-two man in the party, **Bruno Mégret**. In January 1999, Mégret broke away from Le Pen and the Front National and formed the National Republican Movement (Mouvement national républicain). Two of Le Pen's daughters broke with their father and joined Mégret's party. This split hurt both Le Pen and the party, but it did not prevent Le Pen from springing a surprise in the 2002 presidential election when he finished second in the first round. Le Pen was crushed in the subsequent second round, winning only 17.8 percent of the votes. His initial success, though, has scared French voters enough that Le Pen has become the political bogeyman of France. It has also led to the revival of the charges that Le Pen had engaged in torture during the Algerian War.

Age and ill health caused Le Pen to look for a successor as head of the Front National. Mégret was no longer an option because the break with him was complete. Therefore, Le Pen decided to look closer to home. He is busy grooming his youngest daughter, Marine Le Pen, to replace him, but until that day Le Pen is determined to remain the head of the Front National. **See also** Front National (FN); Mégret, Bruno.

Suggested readings: Owen Bowcott, "The Rise of Le Pen," *Guardian* (London) (April 24, 2002), p. 5; Angus Roxburgh, *Preachers of Hate: The Rise of the Far Right* (London: Gibson Square Books, 2002); Harvey G. Simmons, *The French National Front: The Extremist Challenge to Democracy* (Boulder, CO: Westview Press, 1996); Giles Tremlett, "Battle of Algiers Returns to Haunt Le Pen," *Guardian* (London) (June 4, 2002), p. 3; Stuart Wavell, "I'm Right with You, Papa Le Pen," *Sunday Times* (London) (April 27, 2003), p. 9.

Levinger, Moshe (1935–) (Israel)

Rabbi Moshe Levinger is one of the leaders of the extremist settlers' movement in Israel. He was born in 1935 in the German-Jewish neighborhood of Rehavia, Jerusalem. His father was a neurologist from Munich, Germany, and was from a Hasidic family. Levinger was a sickly child and he spent some time in a Swiss sanatorium. He studied at the B'nai Akiva (Zionist religious youth movement) Yeshiva. After volunteering for military service, he served in the Israel Defense Forces (IDF) in a reconnaissance unit. Levinger then attended Rabbi Zvi Yehuda Kook's Merkaz Harav, where he became a rabbi. Kook's teachings also converted him to the Greater Israel movement. After becoming a rabbi, he worked as a shepherd at the religious kibbutz near the Golan Heights on the Israeli-Syrian border.

The victory of Israel in the 1967 Six-Day War convinced Levinger and other Jewish religious extremists that biblical prophecy was coming true and the ancient Jewish state was in the process of being reborn. Levinger had remained devoted to Rabbi Kook, and Kook commanded him to regain the ancient Jewish city of Hebron. On April 12, 1968, Levinger and a group of Greater Israel activists moved into Hebron claiming it as a Jewish city. Then, in 1970, Levinger received permission from the Israeli government to found the settlement of Kiryat Arba on the outskirts of Hebron. Levinger wanted to reestablish a Jewish presence in the heart of Hebron to reinforce his contention that Hebron was a Jewish city. He remains there with his wife and some of his children.

Levinger was one of the founding members of the **Gush Emunim** (Bloc of the Faithful). Fallout from the 1973 Yom Kippur War had spawned an uncertain political situation. Activists from several organizations came together under the leadership of Kook and Levinger to form an organization in 1974 whose sole purpose was building settlements in the occupied territories. In March 1979, his wife, Miriam Levinger, led a group of Jewish women and children into the center of Hebron and occupied a building. This occupation became permanent.

Members of Gush Emunim formed the terrorist underground group Makhteret in May 1980. Levinger's role in this underground has never been clear, but he never denounced it, either before or after its demise. After a series of terrorist operations, Israeli authorities arrested the members of Makhteret in April 1984. Levinger was also arrested for his role in this terrorist campaign, but he was held for only 10 days before the authorities released him.

Several times, Israeli authorities arrested Levinger for violence against Palestinians. On September 30, 1988, Levinger was driving members of his family through downtown Hebron when a group of Palestinians threw stones at his car. He retaliated by stopping his car and firing a pistol into the crowd. Two bystanders, an Arab textile salesman and a shopkeeper, were wounded, and the salesman died later in a hospital. It took Israeli authorities seven months before charging Levinger with manslaughter, but he was able to plea-bargain to a lesser charge of criminally negligent homicide. Although he was sentenced to five months in prison, he only served 10 weeks. Then in January 1991, Levinger was convicted of a 1988 assault on a Palestinian family in Hebron and sentenced to four months in jail.

Levinger attempted to capitalize on his popularity among members of the settlement movement by running for the Knesset in 1992. His aggressive anti-Palestinian campaign caused concern even among right-wing politicians. Levinger garnered low voting support, receiving only 3,700 votes. This defeat did not discourage either Levinger or his followers. He remains one of the most important leaders of the settlers' movement in Israel. **See also** Gush Emunim (Bloc of the Faithful).

Suggested readings: Robert I. Friedman, *Zealots for Zion: Inside Israel's West Bank Settlement Movement* (New York: Random House, 1992); Ian S. Lustick, *For the Land and the Lord* (New York: Council on Foreign Relations, 1988); Ehud Sprinzak, *Brother against*

Brother: Valence and Extremism in Israeli Politics from Altalena to the Rabin Assassination (New York: Free Press, 1999).

Liberation Tigers of Tamil Eelam (LTTE) (Sri Lanka)

The Liberation Tigers of Tamil Eelam (LTTE) is the largest Tamil guerrilla group fighting for an independent Tamil state in Sri Lanka. In 1970, a Tamil student group formed the Tamil Students Movement to protest discrimination against Tamils in higher education. A new Sri Lanka constitution was promulgated in 1972 that the Tamil students interpreted as anti-Tamil. Soon afterward, three Tamil guerrilla groups appeared ready to fight for Tamil rights. The Liberation Tigers of Eelam was one of these groups. **Vellupillai Prabhakaran** assumed the leadership post for the LTTE. Prabhakaran spent the first few years building the LTTE's guerrilla forces and engaging in small-scale military operations. In July 1983, widespread rioting between the majority Sinalese and the Tamils led the LTTE to commence full-scale guerrilla operations. Fighting was heavy between Sri Lankan government forces and the LTTE for the next two years. The large population of Tamils in southern India helped the Tamil guerrilla forces. Among the terrorist action of the LTTE were the bombing of an Air Lanka Tristar aircraft in Colombo, Sri Lanka, on May 3, 1986, that killed 17 people. Another terrorist act was the explosion of a bomb in a bus station in Colombo, Sir Lanka, on April 21, 1987, that killed 105 people and wounded 200 others.

India intervened and tried to negotiate a peace between the Sri Lankan government and the LTTE. In 1987, Indian Prime Minister Rajiv Gandhi and the Sri Lankan president signed the Indo–Sri Lanka Accord. The leadership of the LTTE relinquished arms and ammunition as its contribution to the accord. Indian peacekeeping forces (IPKF) were placed in disputed areas to keep peace.

Peace lasted until October 1987, when the LTTE declared war on both the Sri Lankan government and the IPKF. This war continued until April 1989, when another cease-fire was negotiated. One of the terms was the withdrawal of the IPKF, which was accomplished by March 1990. Due to the bitterness of LTTE leaders over India's role, they sent a female suicide bomber to Sriperambudur near Madras, India, on May 21, 1991, and Gandhi was killed. The Indian government retaliated by banning all LTTE activities in India.

The Sri Lankan government reacted to the failure of negotiations with the LTTE by initiating major military offenses in 1990 and again in 1995 in which LTTE-controlled areas in northern Sri Lanka were seized. The most notable success was the taking of the city of Jaffna in December 1995 after a 50-day siege. These military operations had only limited success, though, and the LTTE retained control of northern Sri Lanka. Over the years, the LTTE established an authoritarian military government with separate laws, judiciary systems, tax systems, and social systems.

The leadership of LTTE reacted to battlefield losses by reengaging in terrorism. Tactics included assassination of political leaders, security forces, and military leaders. Suicide and truck bombings were other tactics used by the LTTE. Two of the most spectacular operations were the truck bombings of the Sri Lanka Central Bank on December 31, 1996, that killed 100 and wounded 1,400, and the Colombo World Trade Center in October 15, 1997, that killed 18 people. In other operations, the LTTE's naval forces, the Sea Tigers, led attacks against foreign ships in Sri Lankan waters. A special suicide unit, the Black Tigers, specialized in operations that led to the assassination of one Sri Lankan president, the wounding of another president, and the elimination of numerous government ministers and mayors.

Sri Lanka government officials and the leadership of the Liberation Tigers of Tamil Eelam negotiated a formal cease-fire on February 22, 2002. Peace talks began in September 2002 under the auspices of the Norwegian government, but progress has been slow. Prabhakaran and the other leaders of the

LTTE abandoned their demand for a separate state for the Tamil population, but they insist on regional autonomy for areas with a Tamil majority. Sri Lanka's government rejects this position and insists on one country and one central government policy. Elements on both sides remain hostile to the negotiations and any possible settlement, but there is enough pressure on the need for a peaceful solution that the cease-fire holds and peace talks continue. Sri Lankan government has been in turmoil because of an ongoing power struggle between President Chandrika Kumaratunga and Prime Minister Ranil Wickremesinghe over the issue of a federal state for the Tamils in northern Sri Lanka. In late November 2003 Prabhakaran tried to stimulate progress on the final settlement by threatening secession if the Sri Lankan government continued to deny rights to the Tamil people. **See also** Prabhakaran, Vellupillai.

Suggested readings: Peter Chalk, "The Liberation Tigers of Tamil Eelam Insurgency in Sir Lanka," in Rajat Ganguly and Ian Macduff, *Ethnic Conflict and Secessionism in South and Southeast Asia: Causes, Dynamics, Solutions* (New Delhi, India: Sage Publications, 2003); Nick Cumming-Bruce, "Bloodlust Again Grips Tigers," *Observer* (London) (June 4, 1995), p. 14; Manoj Joshi, "On the Razor's Edge: The Liberation Tigers of Tamil Eelam," *Studies in Conflict and Terrorism*, no. 1 (January–March 1996); William McGowan, *Only Man Is Vile: The Tragedy of Sri Lanka* (New York: Farrar, Straus & Giroux, 1992); Sinha Ratnatunga, "The First Step Taken in a Lankan Minefield," *Gulf News* [Dubai, United Arab Emirates](February 26, 2002), p. 1; Amy Waldman, "Masters of Suicide Bombing: Tamil Guerrillas of Sri Lanka," *New York Times* (January 14, 2003), p. A1.

Limonov, Eduard (1943–) (Russia)

Eduard Limonov is a controversial Russian writer and the head of the **National Bolshevik Party**. He was born on February 22, 1943, in the town of Dzerzhinsk, Gorky Province, Russia. His birth name was Eduard Savenko, but later he adopted the pseudonym Liminov. His father was a Ukrainian NKVD (secret police) officer and his mother a Russian. During his youth, the family lived in Kharkov. Despite strict discipline at home, Limonov was a juvenile delinquent as a teenager and was frequently in trouble with the police. He left school at the age of 16 and became a welder. By this time, Limonov discovered the Soviet underground literary world. A brief visit to Moscow in 1966 provoked him to settle there on September 30. He lived in the Moscow literary world and survived by obtaining part-time work.

Limonov became a novelist writing nationalistic books. His anti-Soviet views led to his exile from the Soviet Union in 1974. Soviet authorities were dissatisfied with his bohemian lifestyle and offered him the choice of leaving Moscow or emigrating. Limonov decided to emigrate. He settled first in New York City for six years before moving briefly to Los Angeles, where he married the poet, writer, and musician Natalia Medvedeva. They tired of American culture and moved to Paris in 1982. Limonov despised American democracy and what he saw as corporate domination of the political process. During his stay in Paris, Limonov met with several prominent extremists, from Alain de Benoist, the French right-wing theorist, to **Jean-François Thiriart**, the Belgian pan-Europe advocate. Soon after the collapse of the Soviet Union Limonov returned to Russia. He wrote a series of novels that became popular, but they were never critically acclaimed.

Soon after his return to Russia, Limonov turned to right-wing politics. Russian authorities reinstated his Russian citizenship in 1991. He founded the National Bolshevik Party in September 1992 to unify half a dozen groups from both the extreme left and extreme right. His goal was to revive Russian culture, create a socialist economy, and rebuild the Russian empire. In September 1993, Limonov thought that the time was ripe for a coup d'état against the Yeltsin government. Yeltsin had just disbanded the Russian parliament when Limonov and members of the National Bolshevik Party participated with other groups, including the neo-fascists following **Aleksandr Barkashov**, in an assault on the Russian parliamentary building. After the assault failed and several hundreds were killed, Limonov was arrested. He was freed in the February 1994 amnesty passed by the Russian parliament.

Limonov was an early patron of **Vladimir Volfovich Zhirinovsky**. He recognized the political potential of Zhirinovsky, noting that Zhirinovsky's only drawback was his father's Jewish background. Zhirinovsky also realized the importance of Limonov's backing. He appointed Limonov to the post of head of the Intelligence Department of the Liberal-Democratic Party of Russia (LDPR). Limonov escorted Zhirinovsky on his Paris visit in September 1992 and introduced him to the French extremist and head of the **National Front**, Jean-Marie Le Pen.

Limonov's goal of turning the National Bolshevik Front into a viable political party was stymied by the emergence of Russian President Vladimir Putin. He tried, with limited success, to take advantage of the economic dislocation in Russia. Limonov tried to speed the disintegration process by political demonstration, but when he tried to stockpile weapons, Russian authorities arrested him. Federal Security Service (FSB) agents arrested him in 2001 on charges of forming illegal armed units in preparation of overthrowing the government. After two years of incarceration in Lefortovo Prison, Limonov finally came to trial in May 2003 and received a four-year prison sentence. His sentence lasted less than three months before he received a conditional early release by court order. Limonov returned as head of the National Bolshevik Party, with the goal of returning to an active role in politics. His most recent campaign has been the sponsorship of the Russia Without Putin movement in an effort to unseat Russian President Vladmir Putin by boycotting the March 14, 2004, presidential election. Limonov attacks Putin over the war in Chechnya, widespread terrorism in Russia, Russian ethnic troubles in the Baltic states, and American penetration into former Soviet republics of Central Asia. **See also** Barkashov, Aleksandr Petrovich; National Bolshevik Party; Thiriart, Jean-François; Zhirinovsky, Vladimir Volfovich.

Suggested readings: Martin A. Lee, *The Beast Reawakens* (Boston: Little, Brown, 1997); NTV Mir, "Leader of Russian National Bolsheviks Returns to Moscow after Prison Term," BBC Worldwide Monitoring (July 1, 2003), p. 1; Stephen D. Shenfield, *Russian Fascism: Traditions, Tendencies, Movements* (Armonk, NY: M. E. Sharpe, 2001); Anna Ushakova and Viktor Paukov, "So Long for Now, Edichka," *Current Digest of the Post-Soviet Press*, vol. 55, no. 15 (May 14, 2003); Natalia Yefimova, "Ultranationalist Gets His Say in Court," *St. Petersburg Times* (Russia) (December 6, 2002), p. 1.

Lotta Continua (Continuous Struggle) (Italy)

Lotta Continua (Continuous Struggle) was an Italian anarchist Maoist group. Dissident members of the Communist Party of Italy (PCI) led by Adriano Sofri, a journalist, formed Lotta Continua on May 27, 1969, to prepare the way for a Socialist revolution. They were unhappy with the moderate revisionist policies of the PCI. Leaders decided to recruit supporters among the working classes in the industrialized north of Italy. After 1969, Lotta Continua was influential in labor agitation for higher wages and better working conditions. To defend the group during labor unrest, Lotta Continua formed a security unit of young toughs eager to mix with those they termed neo-fascists. A publication, *Lotta Continua* appeared as a recruiting tool. Leaders of Lotta Continua avoided terrorist activities, but its revolutionary rhetoric established the intellectual background for other groups to engage in terrorism. Both leaders and rank-and-file members gave backing to the early terrorism of the **Red Brigades**, but in the end they found the Red Brigades too extreme. Gradually, the leaders of the Lotta Continua drifted away to other causes and the group withered away by the mid-1970s.

The one instance when members of the Lotta Continua may have engaged in terrorism was the assassination of Luigi Calabresi, a Milan police commissioner, on May 17, 1972. Calabresi had been implicated in the death of Guiseppe Pinelli, an anarchist railroad worker, from a fall from Calabresi's office in 1969. Calabresi was charged with Pinelli's murder, but the case had been dropped. Calabresi's murder outside his home was never solved until Leonardo Marino came forward on July 19, 1988, and claimed that he had driven the getaway car for three members of the Lotta Continua. Sofri, Ovidio Bompressi and Giorgio Pietrostefani were arrested and, after seven lengthy trials, sentenced to 22 years in prison in January 1997. This might have ended the case except for the intervention of two unlikely persons. Dario Fo, winner of the Nobel Prize for literature, wrote a play entitled *Accidental Death of an Anarchist*. Next, the prominent Italian historian Carlo Ginzburg examined the case in his book *The Judge and the Historian: Marginal Notes on a Late 20th Century Miscarriage of Justice* (1998) and proclaimed that there had been a miscarriage of justice. This book led the Italian courts to reexamine the case, but, in January 2000, a Venice court upheld the conviction of the three members of the Lotta Continua. **See also** Red Brigades.

Suggested readings: Carl Bromley, "A Modern Inquisition," *In These Times* (October 21, 1999), p. 21; Richard Drake, *The Revolutionary Mystique and Terrorism in Contemporary Italy* (Bloomington, IN: Indiana University Press, 1989); John Hooper, "Leaning Tower of Justice," *Guardian* (London) (December 3, 1997), p. 4; Frances Kennedy, "'Anarchist' Three Get Sentences for Killings Confirmed," *Independent* (London) (January 25, 2000), p. 12.

Loyalist Volunteer Force (LVF) (Northern Ireland)

The Loyalist Volunteer Force (LVF) is a militant Protestant terrorist group in Northern Ireland. Dissidents from the **Ulster Volunteer Force** (UVF) decided to split from their group in July 1996 after a disagreement over a cease-fire with the **Provisional Irish Republican Army** (PIRA). They intended to undermine the cease-fire by attacking Catholics and Protestant leaders who supported the Northern Ireland peace process. **Billy "King Rat" Wright,** an active brigade commander in the UVF, was the founder of LVF, and he remained its leader until his murder by members of the **Irish National Liberation Army** (INLA) on December 27, 1997, while in prison. Under Wright's leadership, the LVF engaged in a terror campaign against Catholics. Wright promoted drug dealing to provide finances for the group. Wright developed a close friendship and alliance with **Johnny "Mad Dog" Adair,** the leader of the UVF. For a time, it looked as if the LVF and UVF might reunite, but the death of Wright ended this initiative. Mark "Swinger" Fulton succeeded Wright as the leader of the LVF.

Fulton's leadership of the Loyalist Volunteer Force was short and violent. He had been a close associate of Wright. After Wright's death, members of LVF launched a murder spree against Catholics in Northern Ireland. In May 1998, the leadership of the LVF announced a cease-fire as part of a strategy to obtain release of LVF's prisoners under the Good Friday Agreement. In a subterfuge, the militants in the LVF adopted the name Red Hand Defenders and continued their war against the Catholics. On March 15, 1999, a car bomb killed Rosemary Nelson, a Catholic solicitor from Lurgan, Northern Ireland. Her death followed the death of Frankie Millar, a constable. Martin O'Hagan, a journalist for the *Sunday World*, exposed complicity of the LVF in these deaths. His reward was a bullet from a member of the LVF on September 28, 2001. Public outcry led to the arrest of Fulton and his imprisonment in Maghaberry Prison. While Fulton awaited trial, efforts were made by prison authorities to turn him into an informer. Once news got out of these contacts with prison authorities, Fulton feared retribution from former colleagues in the LVF. Fulton committed suicide on June 10, 2002, by hang-

Masked armed members of the Loyalist Volunteer Force (LVF) stand by as one of their colleagues reads out a statement announcing their cease-fire in Portadown, 30 miles southwest of Belfast, in this image from television May 15, 1998. The ruthless pro-British gang, responsible for killing more than a dozen Catholic civilians in recent months, announced their cease-fire in the hope that the open-ended gesture would encourage Protestant voters to reject Northern Ireland's peace accord in a referendum the following week. Flag of Ulster is shown in the background. (AP Photo/APTV)

ing himself. His death further weakened the LVF, but its present leaders have reorganized it to carry on operations against Catholics. **See also** Provisional Irish Republican Army (Provos) (PIRA); Ulster Volunteer Force (UVF).

Suggested readings: Rosie Cowan, "Vengeance Threat by Loyalist Chief," *Guardian* (London) (May 15, 2002), p. 6; Jim Cusack, "Non-Existent Organization a Convenient Cover," *Irish Times* (October 1, 2001), p. 7; Lindsay Fergus, "The Fulton Files," *Mirror* (London) (June 28, 2002), p. 16; Joe Gorrod and Maurice Fitzmaurice, "Swinger's Cell Suicide," *Mirror* (London) (June 11, 2002), p. 4; Gary Kelly, "Trimble Condemns 'Cowardly' Murder of Journalist," Press Association (September 29, 2001), p. 1; Sinead King, "Net Is Closing on LVF," *People* (London) (October 7, 2001), p. 2; Neil Mackay, "Killer of Rosemary Nelson Named," *Sunday Herald* (London) (June 16, 2002), p. 8; Susan McKay, "Blood Brothers' Love Consummated in Death," *Sunday Tribune* (Ireland) (June 16, 2002), p. 12; Gerry Moriarty, "NI Sectarian Hatred Still Has Upper Hand," *Irish Times* (October 2, 2001), p. 6.

M

M-19 (Colombia)

The M-19 was one of Colombia's guerrilla groups that operated in the late 1970s and 1980s. Jaime Bateman, a former member of the **Revolutionary Armed Forces of Colombia** (FARC), and 22 supporters founded M-19 in January 1974. Many of the founders had been disillusioned members of the political party National Popular Alliance (ANAPO) of the early 1960s. They picked the name "M" for the "movement" and "19" to commemorate the stolen election of April 19, 1970, when a populist presidential candidate had been bought off to allow the election of a conservative president. Supporters of the M-19 came from a variety of ideologies, and they agreed only about the overthrow of what they considered the corrupt Colombian state. Bateman remained the head of M-19 until his untimely death in a 1983 plane crash over Panama.

Leadership of M-19 believed in guerrilla theater. The National Directorate of the M-19 Superior Command directed guerrilla operations, most of which had maximum publicity value. First of these symbolic operations was the 1974 theft of the sword of the national hero of Colombia independence, Simón Bolivar. Also in 1974, the theft of hundreds of tons of weapons from the elite XIIIth Brigade Bogata alienated the Colom-bian army. Other operations had similar media value.

The most spectacular operation was the seizure of the Dominican Embassy in Bogota on February 27, 1980. Louis Otero, a former anthropologist and a leader in the M-19, planned the operation. An assault team occupied the embassy during a diplomatic reception in honor of Dominican Independence Day. Among the guests was the American ambassador to Colombia. This occupation lasted more than a month, until the M-19 released the hostages in exchange for $1 million. Besides money, the M-19 gained considerable positive publicity.

Despite its popularity as a foil against the Colombian state, the M-19 was never a serious candidate to overthrow the Colombian government. After Bateman's death, the leadership of the M-19 entered into negotiations with the Betancur government in 1984. A truce of sorts was established, but negotiations collapsed in early 1985. During the truce, right-wing death squads operated with impunity, killing both M-19 leaders and supporters. This unsuccessful truce diminished the popularity of the M-19, and the group's return to guerrilla warfare made it even less popular. Leaders of the M-19 decided that the movement needed a grand spectacle to revitalize it.

This grand spectacle was achieved on November 6, 1985, when an M-19 assault force occupied the Palace of Justice in Bogota. Alvaro Fayad, the head of the M-19, had approved the National Directorate's plans. Fayad wanted to present to the judges in the Palace of Justice charges that the Betancur government had acted with criminal intent during the truce. He hoped that a criminal trial would bring down the Betancur government and that an M-19–affiliated government would replace it. Luis Otero was made the military chief, and Andres Almarales and Alfonso Jaquin the political and legal heads. Both Almarales and Jaquin were senior members of the National Directorate.

Forty-one members of the M-19 seized control of the Palace of Justice. Almost from the beginning things went wrong. Unbeknownst to the M-19 leadership, the Colombian army had learned of a possible attack on the Palace of Justice three weeks earlier. Preparations had been made for such an eventuality. Military leaders had little love for the Colombian judiciary because of charges that military leaders were in league with the Colombian drug lords. This ploy by the M-19 gave the military an opportunity to rid the country of two of its foes—the judiciary and the M-19. In a 27-hour siege, the army used massive firepower to retake the Palace of Justice. This firepower produced heavy casualties among the guerrillas and the hostages. Eleven Supreme Court justices and all the M-19 died in the assault. The military had orders to take no M-19 prisoners. No accurate account of the number of people killed at the Palace of Justice has ever been established, but several hundred died.

The Palace of Justice debacle ended the M-19 as a guerrilla force. In 1989, the surviving M-19 leaders agreed to a political amnesty with the government of President Virgilio Barco. This amnesty included those who planned the assault on the Palace of Justice. Leaders of the M-19 revamped it as a new political party renamed the M-19 Democratic Alliance. This new party's first presidential candidate, Carlos Pizarro, was assassinated in 1990. This loss did not prevent the new leader of the party, Alfonso Navarro, from entering the government of President César Gaviria as minister for heath in 1991. In November 1992, the M-19 Democratic Alliance left the government and it went into political opposition. After it repudiated its insurrectionary past, the M-19 Democratic Alliance is now one of several opposition parties in Colombia. **See also** Revolutionary Armed Forces of Colombia (FARC).

Suggested readings: Diego Asencio, *Our Man Is Inside* (Boston: Little, Brown, 1983); Ana Carrigan, *The Palace of Justice: A Colombian Tragedy* (New York: Four Walls Eight Windows, 1993); Garry M. Leech, *Killing Peace: Colombia's Conflict and the Failure of U.S. Intervention* (New York: Information Network of the Americas, 2002).

MacStiofain, Sean (1928–2001) (Ireland)

Sean MacStiofain was one of the founders of the **Provisional Irish Republican Army**. He was born on February 17, 1928, in South Leyton, Essex. His father was a freelance solicitor's clerk. His mother was pro-Irish, but she was born at Bethnal Green, east London. She died when MacStiofain was only 10. His birth name was John Edward Drayton Stephenson. His family was Protestant, but he joined the Catholic Church as a child to attend St. John the Evangelist's school. After leaving school at 16, he joined the building trade. In 1945, he was drafted into the Royal Air Force (RAF) and he served as a supply clerk in Jamaica. MacStiofain worked for the railroad after leaving the RAF.

MacStiofain became enamored with the republican cause and he joined the **Irish Republican Army**. He married an Irish woman in London, and then traveled to Dublin, where he received permission from the IRA's Army Council to form a London IRA unit. In 1951, Cathal Goulding, chief of staff of the IRA, arrived in England looking for arms, and he recruited MacStiofain to help him. They raided an armory at Felsted School, but the police arrested them. MacStiofain received an eight-year prison sentence, but he served only five years. One of his cellmates was Goulding. While in prison, he learned guerrilla tactics from Greek-Cypriot EOKA prisoners. After his release from prison, MacStiofain moved to Ireland. There he worked closely with Goulding, and in 1966, he became the IRA Army Council director of intelligence. Later, he broke with Goulding over the reorientation of the IRA into a political party. MacStiofain allied with Daithi O'Conaill and Ruairi O'Bradaigh in opposition to Goulding and his increasing Marxist leanings. Violence was breaking out in Northern Ireland and MacStiofain wanted to involve the IRA in a militant campaign against the Ulster Protestants.

MacStiofain's opposition to the leadership of the IRA led to the schism between the Official IRA and the Provisional IRA in December 1969. MacStiofain emerged as the leader of the Provisional IRA and a prominent member of the Army Council. His orchestration of the Provisional IRA's campaign resulted in heavy casualties and led to Prime Minister Edward Heath's suspension of Protestant rule in the Stormont Parliament. MacStiofain claimed this suspension as a victory, and he offered a truce to negotiate a settlement with the British government in 1972. This truce came to nothing, and its failure cost MacStiofain prestige in Northern Ireland. In 1973, MacStiofain was arrested and sentenced to prison for membership in the IRA. While in the Mountjoy jail, he went on a hunger strike that lasted 57 days until he was ordered to end the ordeal by the Army Council. He was released from prison in April 1973, but during his absence other leaders had emerged. MacStiofain had never been a popular leader and his autocratic style alienated him from his colleagues. He received a reprimand for his conduct and the Army Council removed him as chief of staff. MacStiofain never held a responsible position in the Provisional IRA after 1973.

After his retirement from an active role in the Provisional IRA, MacStiofain remained in Ireland and on occasion offered advice to Provisional IRA leadership. He lived in Navan, County Meath, and worked as a salesperson. In 1975, he published his memoirs, *Memoirs of a Revolutionary*, and in it he gave his reasons for becoming a member of the IRA. Then in 1981, he resigned from **Sinn Fein**, the political wing of the Provisional IRA. In 1994, he lent his support for the peace initiative of the Provisional IRA by calling for an end to violence. MacStiofain suffered a stroke in 2000 and he died on May 18, 2001. While he was replaced by younger Provisional IRA leaders, they adopted many of his ideas and tactics. **See also** Irish Republican Army (IRA); Provisional Irish Republican Army (Provos) (PIRA).

Suggested readings: Patrick Bishop and Eamonn Mallie, *The Provisional IRA* (London: Corgie Books, 1987; Anne McHardy, "Sean MacStiofain," *Guardian* (London) (May 21, 2001), p. 22; Ed Moloney, *A Secret History of the IRA* (New York: Norton, 2002); David Sharrock, "Time to End Violence, Says Ex-IRA Leader," *Guardian* (London) (August 30, 1994), p. 2.

Madani, Cheikh Abassi (1931–) (Algeria)

Abassi Madani is the leader of the Islamic fundamentalist political party **Islamic Salvation Front**, which aims to seize political power in Algeria. He was born in 1931 at Sidi Okba in southern Algeria. His father was a devout Muslim, so he sent Madani to a religious school before allowing him to go to French schools. He joined Algeria's National Liberation Front (FLN) in its fight against France. He was captured by French forces and spent seven years in prison. Madani then studied at Algiers University before traveling in the 1970s to Great Britain to work on a doctorate on educational problems in Islamic countries at London University. After receiving a doctorate in philosophy, he became a professor of educational sociology, conducting research on Islamic education.

Madani was active in Islamic political activity in the 1980s. His first political involvement was a 1982 protest in a controversy at Algiers University over the replacement of

French by Arabic. Later in 1982, an Algerian court sentenced him to a two-year sentence for organizing a protest against the FLN for its adoption of socialism over Islam. He joined with Ali Belhadj, a popular Islamic preacher, in forming the militant Islamic Salvation Front (FIS). He became the first president of the four-man Executive Committee of the FIS and led it in its political campaigns in the early 1990s to win political power away from the more secular FLN. His successful strategy in the 1991 elections led the Algerian government to arrest him.

Madani spent the next six years in prison, but his influence over the Islamic Salvation Front continued to be strong. Madani never lost his determination for the FIS to become the leading party in Algeria, but the sometimes senseless violence by the FIS and the GIS distressed him. His opposition to violence led him to oppose his longtime ally Belhadj. In an effort to woo him, the Algerian government released him from prison in July 1997. However, he was placed under house arrest a short time later for anti-government activities. Despite efforts to have him released, Madani remained under house arrest to fulfill his 12-year sentence originally imposed in 1992. In July 2003, Algerian authorities released from custody both Madani and Belhadj. Since then, Madani has been active in trying to settle Algeria's civil war. Although hampered by ill health, he has proposed several initiatives that have included amnesty for all participants in the civil war and protection for those returning from exile. **See also** Armed Islamic Group (Groupes Islamiques Armés) (GIA); Islamic Salvation Front (Front Islamique du Salut) (FIS).

Suggested readings: John Daniszewski, "Algeria Puts New Limits on Top Islamist," *Los Angeles Times* (September 2, 1997), p. A6; Fereydoun Hoveyda, *The Broken Crescent: The "Threat" of Militant Islamic Fundamentalism* (Westport, CT: Praeger, 1998; Jane Kokan, "Fires of Islamic Revolt Kindle in Algerian Cellars," *Sunday Times* (London) (June 21, 1992), p. 1; Kim Murphy, "Islam Fundamentalism Sweeps over Algeria Like Desert Wind," *Los Angeles Times* (June 16, 1990), p. A18; Michael Willis, *The*

Islamist Challenge in Algeria: A Political History (New York: New York University Press, 1996).

Mahler, Horst (1936–) (West Germany)

Horst Mahler was the legal brain behind the West German terrorist group **Red Army Faction**. He was born on January 23, 1936, in Silesia, Germany. His father was a dentist. In 1945, his family moved to Naumburge an der Saale, then to Dassau, and finally, in 1949, to West Berlin. Mahler attended school in Wilmersdorf, Berlin. After leaving school in 1955, he studied law at the Free University of Berlin. Mahler joined the Social Democratic Student group (SDS), the student wing of the Social Democratic Party (SPD). In 1960, the SPD expelled him from the party for his radical activities as a member of the SDS. His advocacy of revolutionary change and violence alienated the more moderate leaders of the SDS. Mahler then established a financially successful law practice in West Berlin, specializing in industrial law. In 1966, Mahler was one of the founders of the Republican Club, an organization that developed a reputation for defending left-wing students in court cases.

In 1967, Mahler left his lucrative law practice to devote himself full-time to radical left-wing causes. He joined with two other lawyers to form the Socialist Lawyers' Collective. He also became a fixture at left-wing demonstrations. In 1968, Mahler began associating with **Andreas Baader** and **Gudrun Ensslin**. This involvement led to his traveling to Jordan in June 1970 to receive training from the Palestinians in terrorist tactics from the Palestinians. Although Mahler was much smarter than Baader, Baader's strong personality made Mahler subservient to him. After training in Jordan terminated, Mahler returned to West Berlin with the others. Although Mahler was never a man of action, he was one of the bank robbers in the September 28, 1970, heist at one of the three banks robbed that day.

Mahler's active career with the Red Army Faction ended abruptly with his arrest on

October 8, 1970. Acting on a tip, the Berlin police raided a safe house. Later that evening, Mahler appeared at the apartment, where he was recognized and arrested. In the spring of 1971, Mahler was placed on trial, but he was found not guilty of the charge of participation in the escape of Baader on May 14, 1970. In a second trial in early 1972, Mahler was accused of forming a criminal association with the RAF and taking part in the three bank robberies. While in prison, Mahler resisted Baader's calls for hunger strikes, calling them unnecessary and counterproductive. He also did not participate in the suicide pact on October 18, 1977.

After his release from prison after serving nearly a decade of his 12-year sentence, Mahler made a complete ideological turn and became a leader of the neo-Nazi movement. He used his left-wing political contacts to regain his right to practice law and he practiced commercial law in Berlin. In the summer of 2000, Mahler shocked his contemporaries by announcing that he had joined the neo-Nazi National Democratic Party of Germany (NPD). Mahler soon became the spokesman for the creation of a Fourth Reich to succeed Adolf Hitler's Third Reich. His view is that the Federal Republic was an illegitimate state imposed on Germany by the Allied powers. Mahler proposes racial laws that would discriminate against Jews and foreigners. His anti-Americanism is so strong that he defended the **September 11, 2001,** terrorist attacks against the United States as a legitimate tactic of war. This stance landed him with legal problems in Germany, forcing him to defend himself against the charges of approving crimes and inciting violence. In 2002 a German court fined Mahler 7,200 euros for his remarks about September 11. Efforts have been made by German authorities to charge him with other crimes. **See also** Baader, Andreas; Ensslin, Gudrun; Meinhof, Ulrike; Raspe, Jan-Carl; Red Army Faction (RAF).

Suggested readings: Stefan Aust, *The Baader-Meinhof Group: The Inside Story of a Phenomenon* (London: Bodley Head, 1985); Desmond Butler, "Marxist to Rightist, and Back to Court," *New York Times* (January 25, 2003), p. A6; Melissa Eddy, "German Far-Right Leader to Defend in Court Comments That Sept. 11 Attacks Were Legitimate as Act of War," Associated Press Worldstream (February 28, 2003), p. 1; Hans Kundnani, "From One Extreme to Another," *Times* (London) (March 22, 2003), p. 35; Derek Scally, "Far-Right Rally Had Welcome for Irish," *Irish Times* (October 11, 2002), p. 11.

Marighela, Carlos (1911–1969) (Brazil)

Carlos Marighela was the ideological theorist for the urban guerrilla movement. He was born on December 5, 1911, in El Salvador (Bahia province), Brazil. His father was an Italian immigrant and his mother was black. He joined the Brazilian Communist Party (Partido Comunista Brasileiro, or PCB) as a youth sometime in 1927. For a while he studied engineering, but he left school to engaged in PCB activities. Marighela spent a year in jail in 1936 for distributing party literature. Several other times the police arrested him for political activities. In 1943, his zeal was rewarded with his selection to the party's Central Committee. After the end of World War II, Marighela won election as a deputy to parliament on the Communist Party ticket. Most of his political support came from São Paulo. After the Communist Party was outlawed in 1947, he left Brazil. He returned to Brazil and was editor of the Communist journal *Problemas*. Due to his prestige in the party, he was elevated to the Executive Committee. The right-wing military coup of 1964 placed him in danger. After leading a protest, Marighela was arrested in a Rio de Janeiro movie house, where the police shot him three times. A few days later he escaped from a medical facility.

Marighela's experiences after the 1964 coup caused him to break with the Brazilian Communist Party. He interpreted the coup as the result of the moderate constitutional policies of the PCB. By 1966, Marighela and Mario Alves had formed the Revolutionary Communist Party of Brazil. They then established an action group, Action for National Liberation (Acao Libertadora Nacional, or

ALN), to carry out the policies of the new party. In 1967 at a conference in Havana, Cuba, his break with the PCB became public. By this time, Marighela had become a student of the revolutionary theories of Che Guevara. Guevara's tactic of rural guerrilla insurrection appealed to him.

After studying the failure of Che Guevara's rural guerrilla movement in Bolivia, Marighela decided that the best way to promote a revolution was through an urban guerrilla movement. In June 1969, he wrote a manual, *Minimanual of the Urban Guerrilla*, outlining his formula for guerrilla warfare. He proposed that the path to revolution would come from destabilizing the state by means of an urban terrorist campaign. Small groups of terrorists, the revolutionary vanguard, would have the mission to carry out assassinations, bombings, and kidnappings, but mass action groups of students and workers would support their activities by providing intelligence, sanctuary, and money. These small groups would have to be mobile and always on the offensive. Members would have to be highly motivated and indoctrinated with the goals of the revolution. His goal was to create an atmosphere of terror that would force the state into political repression, and, in turn, polarize the population into taking the side of the revolutionaries.

Marighela modeled his strategy on his personal experiences and the example of the Uruguayan urban guerrilla organization Tupamaros. In contrast to Marighela, whose rural guerrilla movement launched in 1964 had failed by 1966, the Tupamaros were in the process of threatening the existence of the Uruguayan state. Raul Sendic, a law student, had founded the Tupamaros in 1962. By 1969, the Tupamaros operated mostly in the capital city of Montevideo. This group had formed three levels of operatives: commandos, activists, and supporters. Most of the militants belonged to the commandos and they carried out the majority of the terrorist operations from assassinations to kidnappings. Activists provided the material support, including arms, ammunitions, food,

sanctuary, and medical help. Supporters were part-timers who produced intelligence, documents, and propaganda. Both the organization and tactics of the Tupamoros attracted Marighela's attention.

Marighela's manual became the blueprint for urban guerrillas in Latin American and elsewhere. He attempted to carry out its precepts in a series of holdups of banks, firebombings, and seizures of radio stations. Marighela did not live long enough to enjoy his fame because Brazilian security forces killed him in an ambush in São Paulo on November 4, 1969.

Maoist and Guevaraist doctrine provided the way for rural guerrillas to succeed in Third World countries, but Marighela added the path to success in more industrialized and urban societies. Among the revolutionary groups that adopted his tactics have been the **Armed Islamic Group** in Algeria, the **Irish Republican Army** (IRA) in Northern Ireland, **Montoneros** in Argentina, and the **Red Brigades** in Italy. **See also** Armed Islamic Group (Groupes Islamiques Armés) (GIA); Irish Republican Army (IRA); Montoneros; Red Brigades.

Suggested readings: Paul H. Lewis, *Guerrillas and Generals: The "Dirty War" in Argentina* (Westport, CT: Praeger, 2002); Carlos Marighela, *For the Liberation of Brazil* (Middlesex, UK: Penguin Books, 1971); John W. Williams, "Carlos Marighela: The Father of Urban Guerrilla Warfare," *Terrorism: An International Journal* 12. no.1 (1989).

Marulanda, Manuel (1930–) (Colombia)

Manuel Marulanda is the leader of the Marxist rebel army **Revolutionary Armed Forces of Colombia** (FARC) . He was born on May 12, 1930, in Genova, Colombia. His birth name was Pedro Antonio Marin. His family had little money so he dropped out of school after the fifth grade. Marulanda held a number of menial jobs before opening a grocery store. In 1948, his store was burned to the ground during the civil war (La Violencia) between liberals and conservatives. His family was considered liberal and supporters of the populist leader Jorge Eliécer

Gaitán. Gaitán's assassination on April 9, 1948, launched the civil war that lasted for nearly a decade. Conservatives killed one of his uncles before Marulanda and his cousins formed a self-defense force in 1949.

Marulanda turned this self-defense force into a rural guerrilla army. His self-defense force controlled the area in Marguetalia, a remote rural area in foothills of the Andes in southern Colombia. Colombian armed forces left Marulanda's forces alone, but the scare about Marxist guerrillas in the aftermath of the 1959 Cuban Revolution galvanized them into a military offensive against Marulanda's army. In May 1964, the Colombian army moved into Marguetalia to regain control of the region. Most of Marulanda's forces escaped the government dragnet, but he decided to revamp his forces to continue the struggle against the Colombian state. It was also in the early 1960s when Marulanda earned the nickname "Sureshot," which he retains to this day.

Marulanda formed the Revolutionary Armed Forces of Colombia as a Marxist revolutionary force. Marulanda allied with Jacobo Arenas, a member of the Colombia Communist Party, to build a revolutionary army to establish a Marxist state. At the time of this transformation, Marulanda had no more than 350 fighters in his military force. His opposition to the upper-class control of Colombia resulted in his army growing so that it soon numbered in the thousands. Marulanda was able to survive numerous government attempts to capture or kill him because of his homegrown intelligence and counterintelligence capabilities. His spies were always able to warn him in time to escape. FARC was able to prosper financially because it taxed the drug traffic in its areas of control.

Always a cautious man, Marulanda only felt safe in areas that the FARC had absolute control of militarily. In 1984, the then president Belisario Betancur persuaded him to conclude a cease-fire with the government. Marulanda watched his supporters join the left-wing Patriotic Union in an attempt to participate in Colombian politics. Through-

out 1985 and 1986, the Colombian military, police, and drug dealers formed death squads that wiped out thousands of Marulanda's allies. Marulanda learned a lesson in trusting the Colombian government. After blaming the Colombian government for the slaughter, he reopened FARC military operations. FARC forces won and lost battles with government forces, but its more formidable foe was the right-wing paramilitary leader **Carlos Castaño** and his **United Self-Defense Forces of Colombia** (Autodefensas Unidas de Colombia, or AUC). Both sides engaged in a bloody war to the death.

By the 1990s Marulanda was no longer an active military chief. By this time the FARC army had around 20,000 fighters and a number of capable military leaders. He kept an oversight role, but his military commanders carried out operations on their own initiatives. Marulanda had little fear of the Colombian army because FARC forces were better trained, led, and paid, and they were more highly motivated than the Colombian military. Because Marulanda had so little fear of the Colombian army, he next attempted to influence Colombian national politics.

Marulanda decided to negotiate with the new government of President Andrés Pastrana in 1998. Pastrana was a Harvard-trained son of a former Colombian president. His goal was to bring peace to Colombia. Marulanda was willing to talk but only on his own terms. One of the preconditions was the establishment of a FARC safe haven that was nearly twice the size of El Salvador. Over the next nearly four years, Marulanda negotiated with Pastrana, but a May 2002 kidnapping of a Colombian senator in February 2002 led Pastrana to break off negotiations. Pastrana left office in August 2002 with almost no popular support.

Marulanda has a more militant foe in President Alvaro Uribe Velez. Uribe promised during his presidential campaign that he would capture and turn over Marulanda to the United States. After Uribe was elected in August 2002, he launched a military offensive against FARC forces. This offensive has been only moderately effective, and

Marulanda has counterattacked with an urban guerrilla campaign in several Colombian cities. Uribe also placed a $1 million bounty on the head of Marulanda. At present, neither side has the strength to win a military victory, but the Uribe government has had some success in killing or capturing FARC's senior military commanders. Marulanda is in his early 70s with good health, but because the FARC has always been his personal instrument, a key question remains: Who will replace Marulanda as leader of FARC once he leaves the scene? **See also** Castaño, Carlos; Revolutionary Armed Forces of Colombia (FARC).

Suggested readings: Karen DeYoung, "For Rebels, It's Not a Drug War," *Washington Post* (April 10, 2000), p. A1; ALMA Guillermo Prieto, "Waiting for War," *New Yorker* (May 13, 2002), p. 48; Garry Leech, *Killing Peace: Colombia's Conflict and the Failure of U.S. Intervention* (New York: Information Network of the Americas, 2002); John Otis, "Rebel Held: Inside Colombia's FARC, Latin America's Oldest, Most Powerful Guerrilla Army," *Houston Chronicle* (August 5, 2001), Special Report, p. 1; Frances Robles, "Significant Changes Happening in Colombia's Civil War," *Miami Herald* (January 10, 2004), p. 1; Larry Rohter, "A Colombian Guerrilla's 50-Year Fight," *New York Times* (July 19, 1999), p. A9; Bert Ruiz, *The Colombian Civil War* (Jefferson, NC: McFarland, 2001).

Mawdudi, Mawlana Sayyid Abu'l-A'la (1903–1979) (Pakistan)

Mawlana Mawdudi was the founder of the Pakistani Islamist party **Jama'at-i Islami** (Islamic Party) and a recognized leader in the modern Islamist revival. He was born in 1903 in Delhi, India, to a prominent Muslim family. His early education was at home because his father wanted to protect him from foreign influences. He then was educated in the legal profession, but he had abandoned law in favor of Islamic studies. His education was both at traditional Muslim schools and at Western-style schools. After finishing his education, Mawdudi became a journalist. In the course of his journalistic work, he was attracted in the early 1920s to the Khilafat

movement, a pro-Muslim movement to restore the religious position of the Caliphate that collapsed in 1924. After a brief flirtation with the Jami'at-i Ulama-Hind (Party of Indian Ulama), the Muslim wing of the pro-Indian independence Congress Party, Mawdudi became devoted to the cause of preserving Islam in Muslim society. In 1929, he wrote the book *Al-Jihad fi'l-Islam* (*Jihad in Islam*), a treatise that advanced the idea of a return to the purified Islam of prophet Muhammad. He rejected the idea of a Hindu state for India and instead wanted to replace it with a Muslim India. Because of his position, he attacked the Muslim League of Muhammad Ali Jinnah for its secular orientation and its negotiations with the Hindu Congress Party.

Only gradually did Mawdudi come to the realization that the creation of a separate Muslim state of Pakistan was a necessity. On August 26, 1941, he founded the Islamist party Jama'at-i Islami to serve as a vehicle for the creation of an Islamic state of Pakistan. Mawdudi believed that he should be the founder and leader of Pakistan. He believed that the Islamic state could have only one ideology, that all the powers of the state must be used to maintain Islam, and that its sole purpose would be to implement God's will as interpreted by prophet Muhammad. Because he believed that politics and religion are inseparable, he maintained that both capitalism and socialism were incompatible with Islam. Mawdudi's views spread rapidly and **Sayyid Qutb**, the Egyptian Islamist writer of the Muslim Brotherhood, read and quoted from his writings.

After the independence of Pakistan, Mawdudi became a major political figure in the new state and the Jama'at-i Islami became a major political party. Several times Mawdudi was arrested for political activities, but it was the banning of his party after the military coup in 1958 that curtailed much of his political influence. After the ban was lifted in 1962, Mawdudi returned to national prominence. His attacks on the Pakistani government resulted in his arrest again and another ban of his party, but a Pakistani court determined that the ban of the Jama'at-i Islami was unconstitutional. Even as his political career fluctuated, Mawdudi's concept of an Islamic state gained in popularity in Pakistan. General Zia adopted Mawdudi's vision of an Islamic state and used it for justification for the military coup against the government of Zulfiqar Ali Bhutto in 1978. Despite Zia's affirmation of support, Mawdudi and his followers refused to accept the Zia regime. Mawdudi had long suffered from ill-health, leading to his retirement as head of the Jama'at-i Islami in 1972. His role after retirement was as a political and religious adviser to the Jama'at-i Islami. He died in 1979, but the popularity of his ideas has remained strong in Pakistan and spread to other Muslim states. See also Jama'at-i Islami (Islamic Party).

Suggested readings: Tariq Ali, *The Clash of Fundamentalisms: Crusades, Jihads and Modernity* (London: Verso, 2002); Fereydoun Hoveyda, *The Broken Crescent: The "Threat" of Militant Islamic Fundamentalism* (Westport, CT: Praeger, 1998); Seyyed Vali Reza Nasr, *Vanguard of the Islamic Revolution: The Jama'at-i Islami of Pakistan* (Berkeley: University of California Press, 1994).

McGuinness, Martin (1950–) (Northern Ireland)

Martin McGuinness is one of the leaders of the **Sinn Fein**, the political wing of the **Provisional Irish Republican Army** (Provos), and a longtime Irish republican militant. He was born on May 25, 1950, in Derry's Waterside General Hospital, and he was raised in the Catholic area of Derry called the Bogside (called Londonderry by the Protestants). His father worked in an iron foundry and his mother in a shirt factory, and both were staunch Catholics. McGuinness was second in a family of seven children. The children were raised as Catholics first and Irish nationalists second. McGuinness was educated at St. Eugene's Convent Primary School and then, beginning in 1957, at Christian Brothers Primary School. After failing his 11-plus examinations that would allow him to continue his academic training, he attended the Christian Brothers Brow of the Hill Techni-

cal College. At age 15, he went to work as a shop assistant in a local store. After six years, McGuinness became an apprentice to a butcher at James Doherty's Butcher Shop.

McGuinness was gradually brought into the Catholic civil disobedience campaign during the Catholic rioting in the Derry Bogside in October 1969. His participation resulted in his arrest for disorderly conduct and a fine of 50 pounds. In early October 1970, he joined the Official Irish Republican Army (OIRA). When elements in this group decided to move to the more militant Provisional IRA, McGuinness went with them. He was soon appointed the Derry Brigade's finance officer. Within a year, he was second-in-command of the Derry Provos brigade, as casualties and arrests had crippled the Derry IRA command staff.

McGuinness was in command of the Derry IRA during the events of Bloody Sunday. On January 30, 1972, British soldiers of the 1st Parachute Regiment opened fire on a Catholic crowd in Derry, killing 13 and wounding 12. An informer claimed later that McGuinness provoked the attack by firing on the British soldier, but McGuinness denied this assertion and other witnesses backed his version. McGuinness ordered retaliation for Bloody Sunday, and the Derry IRA launched a bombing campaign. By this time, McGuinness had earned a reputation as a strategic planner, and he had impressed **Sean MacStiofain**, the head of the Provisional IRA. McGuinness was selected along with Belfast IRA leader **Gerry Adams**, MacStiofain, and four other IRA leaders to negotiate a 1972 cease-fire with William Whitelaw, the secretary of state for Northern Ireland, and his staff, who represented the British government. These talks failed and McGuinness returned to his Derry position. Under pressure from the British army, he moved to Donegal in the Republic of Ireland. On December 31, 1972, authorities in the Republic of Ireland arrested him in Donegal in a car full of explosives and ammunition. A Dublin court sentenced him in January 1973 to six months in prison. He was released on May 16, 1973, with time off for good behavior. After his release from prison, McGuinness was active in the planning of a Provisional IRA bombing campaign in England. On February 11, 1974, Irish authorities again arrested him for IRA activities and he spent most of 1974 in prison while serving a one-year sentence. He made his opposition to a Provisional IRA cease-fire in February 1975 public. In February 1976 in Derry, he was arrested yet again and charged by the British authorities of membership in the illegal IRA, but this time he was released without sentencing.

In 1977, the Provisional IRA's Army Council appointed McGuinness and Ivor Malachy Bell, a close associate of Adams in Belfast, to an internal review commission charged with reorganizing the council. In their report, they acknowledged that the IRA was in danger of military and political defeat. They recommended that the Army Council set up a Northern Command and a Southern Command to oversee operations in both Northern Ireland and the Republic of Ireland. Each command would be organized into brigades. Each brigade would have an area of operations, and operations would be at the cell level. The Army Council adopted the recommendations and it appointed McGuinness as the operational chief of Northern Command.

McGuinness was now one of the Provisional IRA's top leaders. In early 1978, Adams replaced Seamus Twomey as chief of staff of the Army Council after Twomey's arrest. Soon afterward, Adams and McGuinness established a working relationship. When Adams was arrested in late 1978, McGuinness and Brian Keenan, a veteran IRA leader, replaced him as chief of staff in a joint capacity. McGuinness was active in the planning of the 1978–1979 bombing campaign in England. On May 20, 1979, Keenan was arrested, leaving McGuinness as the sole chief of staff. McGuinness spent much of his energies in improving weapons supplies and planning operations. McGuinness was in charge during the 1981 hunger strikes of Bobby Sands and others, but he was always ambivalent about the strikes.

McGuinness had a reputation for incorruptibility that helped him make the transition from IRA terrorist to a Sinn Fein politician. In October 1982, McGuinness won a seat in the first election in Northern Ireland, but his refusal to accept British authority caused him to relinquish his seat. Because he had run for public office, McGuinness resigned his post of chief of staff but continued to be active in Provisional IRA operations. Although he returned to his post as chief of staff and later became operations chief of the Northern Command, he decided that political action might be more effective than force. By working together, Adams and McGuinness ended the control of Sinn Fein by Ruairi O'Bradaigh and Daithi O'Connaill in October 1987. Their revolt made Adams and McGuinness the most influential of the Sinn Fein leaders and ended the prohibition of Sinn Fein's participation in the political affairs of the Republic of Ireland. McGuinness's skills led him to be appointed the chief negotiator in the negotiations with the British government in the early 1990s. Despite his political activities, McGuinness continued to run the Provisional IRA's campaign against the British, but British counterterrorism actions and informers were causing severe losses among IRA operations. As members of Sinn Fein's National Executive, McGuinness and Adams were the architects of the 1994 IRA cease-fire. Adams and McGuinness began talks with the British about a cease-fire after the Army Council approved the policy change on August 29, 1994.

McGuinness spent the next several years in the middle of the complex negotiations for a permanent agreement between the British government and the Provisional IRA. Negotiations were slow and not without incidents. Both Adams and McGuinness had been elected to the Army Council and, from this position of strength, were able to come to a tentative agreement with the British government. The most difficult issue was the decommissioning of the IRA. Decommissioning meant that the IRA would disarm and enter the political process. Sinn Fein representatives ran in the 1997 parliamentary elections in Northern Ireland, and McGuinness won a seat on a peace platform. However, because he refused to take the oath of allegiance to the Queen, McGuinness never assumed his parliamentary seat. Nonetheless, his victory proved to be a propaganda success.

This attitude of nonparticipation ended in 2002. McGuinness entered the political arena this time by becoming Sein Fein's representative in the Northern Ireland's government as minister of education. Decades of distrust between Catholics and Protestants have made his job as minister difficult, but he has kept a high profile in trying to improve education in Northern Ireland. See also Adams, Gerry; Provisional Irish Republican Army (Provos) (PIRA).

Suggested readings: Terrence Blacker, "The Hard Man Talking Soft; Martin McGuinness, Sinn Fein," *Independent* (London) (September 5, 1998), p. 5; Elizabeth Buie, "The Big Test for McGuinness," *Herald* (Glasgow) (December 22, 2001), p. 12; Liam Clarke and Kathryn Johnston, *Martin McGuinness: From Guns to Government* (Edinburgh: Mainstream Publishing, 2001); Catherine Deveney, "Martin McGuinness Charm Offensive," *Scotland on Sunday* (Edinburgh) (March 3, 2002), p. 8; David Mckittrick, "Sunday 30 January 1972; A Bloody Day in the Life of Martin McGuinness," *Independent* (London) (January 24, 2002), p. 1; Delia Smith, "From Derry's 'Boy General' to Education Minister," *Irish Times* (February 9, 2002), p. 10; Kevin Toolis, *Rebel Hearts: Journeys within the IRA's Soul* (New York: St. Martin's Griffin, 1995).

McKevitt, Michael "Mickey" (1950?–) (Northern Ireland)

Michael McKevitt is the leader of the Irish republican terrorist group the **Real Irish Republican Army** (RIRA). He was born in 1950. At a young age, McKevitt joined the **Provisional Irish Republican Army** (Provos). By the early 1990s he had become the quartermaster of the Provos. His job was to procure weapons for the military operations. His marriage to Bernadette Sands, the sister of Bobby Sands, who was the leader of the 1981 hunger strike, improved McKevitt's

position in the Irish republican movement. In October 1997, McKevitt broke with the Provos at an army convention in Donegal, Ireland. He disagreed with **Gerry Adams's** and **Martin McGuinness's** leadership of the Shinn Fein and their decision to abandon armed struggle in Northern Ireland in favor of engagement in the political process.

McKevitt formed the Real Irish Republican Army on October 19, 1997, shortly after the end of the Donegal convention. He attracted the radical wing of the Provos. McKevitt created an executive board of eight members, of which he was the most prominent member. Members of the RIRA concluded an alliance with the **Continuity IRA** to plant a bomb at Omagh, Northern Ireland. This bomb detonated on August 13, 1998, killing 29. Public reaction against this bombing rebounded against the RIRA. McKevitt and his family faced public disapproval. Soon afterward, McKevitt lost control of the RIRA to its more militant members. In March 2001, Irish police arrested him. He faced criminal charges in the Irish Republic for directing the activities of a terrorist organization. His trial was postponed several times before the trial took place in the summer of 2003. On August 6, 2003, McKevitt was convicted in the Special Criminal Court in Dublin of directing the activities of an illegal organization. See also Adams, Gerry; Continuity Irish Republican Army (CIRA); McGuinness, Martin; Provisional Irish Republican Army (Provos) (PIRA).

Suggested readings: Chris Boffey, "Real IRA Gets a Chance to Taste Fear," *Gazette* (Montreal) (August 23, 1998), p. A7; Toby Harnden, "Leader of Real IRA Named: McKevitt Broke Away from Sinn Fein over Peace Talks," *Gazette* (Montreal) (August 17, 1998), p. B1; Diarmaid MacDermott and Carol Coulter, "Ormagh Bombing Was 'Joint Operation,'" *Irish Times* (October 9, 2002), p. 4; Dan Mcdougall, "Despite Its Many Failures, the Real IRA Is Still a Determined and Deadly Foe," *Scotsman* (Edinburgh) (August 4, 2001), p. 4; Ian Miller, "Real IRA Terrorists Planned to Murder Politicians," *Mirror* (London) (May 8, 2002), p. 16; Liz Walsh, "McKevitt Found Guilty of Directing Terrorism," *Irish News* (August 7, 2003), p. 2.

Mégret, Bruno (1949–) (France)

Bruno Mégret is one of France's leading right-wing extremists and head of the National Republican Movement. He was born in April 1949 in Paris to affluent parents. His father was a top-ranking civil servant and a member of the Council of State. His upper-class upbringing allowed him to attend the prestigious Lycée Louis-le-Grand in Paris. Mégret's scholarly achievements gained him entry into the elite Ecole Polytechnique. He graduated from there in the top 20 of his class with a civil engineering degree. After graduation, Mégret traveled to the United States to enter the University of California–Berkeley. He graduated in 1975 with a master's of science degree in city planning.

After returning to France, Mégret had the option of a obtaining a high-paying civil service position or pursuing a political career. He chose to go into politics. In 1979, he joined the Gaullist party expecting to rise high in its ranks. At first Mégret was successful and he was elected to the party's central committee in 1980. But after several years and an unsuccessful election campaign, he decided to abandon the Gaullist ranks. Around this time he married his wife Catherine Mégret, a graduate of Cambridge as interested in politics as her husband. Mégret reoriented his political career by becoming one of the cofounders of the Committee for Republican Action. In 1985, he met **Jean-Marie Le Pen**. Mégret used his committee and Le Pen's influence to win a seat as a deputy for the department of Isére in 1986.

Mégret soon realized the political potential of the nationalistic and racial appeal of Le Pen's **Front National** and he joined it. Shortly thereafter, Mégret became one of Le Pen's chief advisors. His role was to broaden Le Pen's appeal to attract French voters. Mégret's success earned him the title of "Le Pen's Goebbels," referring to Adolf Hitler's famous propaganda chief. By the late 1990s, Mégret was seen as number two in the Front National's hierarchy and the heir apparent to Le Pen. He shared Le Pen's racial views on immigrants, but he was careful to make Le Pen's views appear to be more moderate.

Mégret was the author of the Front National's campaign for "national preference" for native-born Frenchmen and Frenchwomen. Jobs, public housing, and university slots were to be reserved for the ethnic French majority. Mégret had a power base as a mayor of Vitrolles, a suburb of Marseilles, to express his views.

By the spring of 1997, Le Pen's leadership of the Front National had so frustrated Mégret that Mégret thought that he could do better. Two events led to Mégret breaking with Le Pen. First was the election of Mégret's wife to mayor of Vitrolles, a suburb of Marseilles, replacing her husband, who was ineligible to run because of past political spending irregularities. Second, Le Pen faced legal difficulties after assaulting a Socialist female candidate running against his eldest daughter, Marie-Caroline Le Pen, in a parliamentary election. His legal difficulties meant that Le Pen was ineligible to run for political office for several months. Mégret believed that his time had come to assume power in the Front National.

Mégret's power play caused a schism in the Front National. He called a convention at Marseille in December 1998 to assume control. Mégret had been contacting potential allies and he attracted more than 2,500 members of the Front National to his convention. Le Pen was not invited to this meeting, but his daughter, Marie-Caroline Le Pen, was one of those supporting Mégret. After being elected president by this convention, Mégret renamed the party Front National-Mouvement National (FN-MN). In a later court battle, a French judge ruled that Le Pen still controlled the Front National and its political apparatus. Mégret responded by forming a new party, the National Republican Movement (MNR).

Mégret's revolt was less successful than Mégret anticipated. Le Pen managed to retain the loyalty of the majority of the membership of the pre-schism Front National. Mégret had lost a bid to become mayor of Marseille in March 2001. Then Le Pen's unexpected strong showing in the 2002 presidential race made Le Pen appear to be a more dominant political figure than he actually was, but it was still a blow against Mégret. In March 2001, Mégret's wife had won her reelection to her mayor's position at Vitrolles, but in July 2002 the Council of State annulled her reelection.

Mégret's strategy appears to be to outlive Le Pen and then absorb his followers into a revitalized Front National, but this strategy has been weakened by Mégret's further political problems. On Bastille Day, July 14, 2002, a neo-Nazi gunman, Maxime Brunerie, with an affiliation to Mégret's National Republican Movement, attempted to assassinate French President Jacques Chirac. Spectators and police officers stopped him after he had fired one shot at Chirac. His association with Mégret's party produced a backlash that even Mégret's condemnation of the assassination attempt could not prevent. Then on January 26, 2004, a Marseilles court barred Mégret from public office for a year and imposed a 10,000 euro fine after he was found guilty of illegal party financing in his 2001 run for the Marseilles mayor office. Mégret is appealing this verdict, but the negative publicity is hurting his image as political leader. **See also** Front National (FN); Le Pen, Jean-Marie.

Suggested readings: John-Thor Dahlburg, "Far-Right Party Splits in France," *Los Angeles Times* (January 25, 1999), p. A9; Christopher Dickey and Judith Warner, "Bruno the Smooth," *Newsweek* (April 20, 1998), p. 15; Robert Graham, "A Right Mess," *Financial Times* (London) (January 26, 1999), p. 18; Jon Henley, "France's New Right: A Pact with the Devil," *Observer* (London) (March 22, 1998), p. 7; John Lichfield, "Internal Feud Devastates French Right," *Independent* (London) (October 23, 1998), p. 18; John Lichfield, "'Mr. Charisma' Takes Up Le Pen's Far-Right Mantle," *Independent* (London) (March 10, 2001), p. 18; Frances Viviano, " From Berkeley to the Extreme Right," *San Francisco Chronicle* (February 18, 1997), p. A1.

Meinhof, Ulrike (1934–1976)
(West Germany)
Ulrike Meinhof was one of the leaders of the violent West German terrorist group the **Red Army Faction.** She was born on October 7, 1934, in Oldenburg, Germany. Her father was the curator of the Jena Municipal Museum. He died when Meinhof was only six. Her mother left Jena after the war and moved to Oldenburg, where she became a teacher. When Meinhof was 15, her mother died in the aftermath of a cancer operation. Meinhof lived with her foster mother, who was an education professor. She was an exceptional and popular student. After final school exams, Meinhof started school at the University of Marburg, studying education and psychology. Later, she moved to the University of Munster, where she became active in the anti–atomic bomb movement. Meinhof joined the student wing of the Social Democratic Party (SDP) in May 1958, and later she joined the German Communist Party (KPD). Her anti–atomic bomb activities attracted the editors of the left-wing political journal *Konkret.* She joined the staff as a writer and in January 1960 she became its editor-in-chief. Meinhof also married one of the founders and former editors of *Konkret* on December 27, 1961.

Meinhof became a celebrity in 1961 when she wrote an article attacking the West German right-wing politician Franz Josef Strauss. He sued Meinhof for libel, but he lost the court case. Then in 1962, Meinhof suffered a brain condition during her pregnancy with her twin daughters, Bettina and Regine. After an early delivery by cesarean section, she underwent brain surgery. An enlarged blood vessel, not a tumor, was the problem, and the only solution was to clamp a silver clip on the blood vessel. Afterward, she returned to her writing and editorial work with *Konkret.* Her paper broke with the KPD over an editorial supporting the Czech literary and political renaissance in 1964. Despite Meinhof's successful journalism career, she was drawn into radical left-wing politics.

The aftermath of the failed assassination attempt of the German radical student leader Rudi Dutschke propelled Meinhof to join the terrorist movement. Most of the radical left blamed the Springer Press for the assassination attempt, and so did Meinhof. She participated in the demonstrations against the Springer Press. In 1968, she divorced her husband and left *Konkret*. Meinhof began attacking her ex-husband and *Konkret* for selling out to the right wing. Her next project was a television file, Bambule, on the treatment of the young in state homes and reform schools. Soon after finishing this project in February 1970, she renewed an earlier acquaintance with **Andreas Baader** and **Gudrun Ensslin**. They persuaded her to join them in the Red Army Faction. After Baader was arrested in early April, Meinhof played a leading role in his escape on May 14, 1970. From this time onward, Meinhof was committed to the revolutionary violence of the Red Army Faction.

Meinhof always ranked behind Baader and Ensslin in the hierarchy of the Red Army Faction. She traveled with them to Jordan to receive terrorist training from the Palestinians. After training terminated, Meinhof returned to West Berlin with the group. She used her extensive contacts in left-wing circles to find safe houses. On September 28, 1970, Meinhof participated in one of three bank robberies. Meinhof continued her activities with the RAF throughout 1971 and 1972, but most of the time she operated independently, arranging logistical support. On June 15, 1972, Meinhof was arrested by the police in Langenhagen, Hanover, at the apartment of a teacher.

Meinhof received special attention from the police as one of the leaders of the Red Army Faction. She was held for nearly six months in Cologne's Ossendorf jail and then transferred to Zeibrucken prison. Receiving word through an informal communication system from Baader, Meinholf followed orders and went on several hunger strikes. In August 1974, Meinhof went to trial in West Berlin for her part in the prison break of Baader on May 14, 1970. She received an eight-year prison sentence in November 1974 for attempted murder of the security guard.

Meinhof's next court appearance was with the co-conspirators Baader, Ensslin, and Raspe in a trial that began on May 21, 1975.

Meinhof had never been close to Baader and by this time her relationship with Ensslin was also strained. During the first half of the trial, they kept a united front attacking the jurisdiction of the court and the judges. In the middle of the trial, Baader and Ensslin's constant belittlement began taking its toll. On May 6, 1976, Meinhof committed suicide by hanging herself. This suicide ended the career of the most talented but troubled member of the RAF. More than a year later, her companions in the RAF also committed suicide. **See also** Baader, Andreas; Ensslin, Gudrun; Raspe, Jan-Carl; Red Army Faction (RAF).

Suggested readings: Stefan Aust, *The Baader-Meinhof Group: The Inside Story of a Phenomenon* (London: Bodley Head, 1985); Jillian Becker, *Hitler's Children: The Story of the Baader-Meinhof Terrorist Gang* (Philadelphia: Lippincott, 1978); Barry Davis, *Terrorism: Inside a World Phenomenon* (London: Virgin Books, 2003); Astrid Proll (ed.), *Baader Meinhof: Pictures on the Run 67–77* (Zurich: Scalo Verlag, 1998).

Misuari, Nur (1932–) (Philippines)

Nur Misuari was the leader of the **Moro National Liberation Front** (MNLF) during its revolt against the Philippine government. He was born in 1932 in Jolo, Philippines, to a poor Tausug fisherman. Despite this background, Misuari was a good student and it allowed him access to a good education. Misuari became a political science professor at the University of the Philippines. In 1972, he formed the Moro National Liberation Front to fight for a separate Islamic state in the southern Philippines. After a cease-fire with the Philippine government in 1977, Misuari left the MNLF and moved to the friendly Muslim countries of Saudi Arabia and Libya until 1986. He then returned to the Philippines and resumed control of the MNLF. Over the next decade the MNLF waged a military war against the Philippine government. In 1986, he negotiated a peace agreement and limited Muslim self-rule. However, the peace agreement failed and he went into exile once again.

In the early 1990s, Misuari returned to Mindanao and he was elected governor of the Autonomous Region of Muslim Mindanao as part of the 1996 peace settlement. Misuari's term as governor proved to be a disappointment. It earned him growing unpopularity among the Muslims in Mindanao because the Philippine government did not fulfill the terms of the peace agreement and because he was accused of a lavish lifestyle. His number-two man in the MNLF, **Hashim Salamat,** became disillusioned and formed a rival group, the **Moro Islamic Liberation Front (MILF).** Even the aftermath of the peace agreement with President Fidel Ramos failed to improve his image. The appearance of an even more radical group, the **Abu Sayyaf,** moved Misuari more to the middle of the political spectrum and left him isolated. Even the Philippine government realized that Misuari was no longer the head of the Moro liberation movement. In 2001 Misuari lost his position as governor as well. He attempted to regain his position in the national liberation movement by allying with the MILF and launching a guerrilla offensive against the Philippine government, but this campaign was ineffective. In May 2001, Misuari was deposed as chairman of the MNLF. Realizing his vulnerability to arrest or assassination, Misuari fled to Malaysia, where he was arrested in November 2001. The Malaysian government then deported him back to the Philippines where he is under arrest and awaiting trial on rebellion charges. The Philippine government is in no hurry to bring him to trial, as the chances of a conviction remain in doubt and while in jail Misuari has little chance of winning the governship back. **See also** Abu Sayyaf Group (Bearer of the Sword) (ASG); Moro Islamic Liberation Front (MILF); Moro National Liberation Front (MNLF).

Suggested readings: Luz Baguioro, "Misuari's downfall," *Straits Times* (Singapore) (November 27, 2001), p. A1; Raissa Espinosa-Robles, "Lone Fighter," *Asiaweek* (November 30, 2001), p. 28; Nirmal Ghosh, "Guerilla Chief Begins New Life as Governor," *Straits Times* (Singapore) (September 15, 1996), P. 20; Ron Gluckman, "Revolutionary with Room Service," *Asiaweek* (September 5, 1997), p. 25; Clayton Jones, "Meet the Moros," *Christian Science Monitor* (September 9, 1986), p. 9; Claire MacDonald and Raissa Espinosa-Robles, "Tribulations of an Ex-Rebel," *Asiaweek* (May 28, 1999), p. 28.

Mohamed, Ali A. (1952–) (Egypt)

Ali Mohamed was the leader of the **Qaeda** network of **Osama bin Laden** in the United States until his arrest in 1998. He was born in 1952 in a town near Alexandria, Egypt, under the name Ali Abu-al-Saud Mustafa. His father was in the Egyptian army. Mohamed graduated from high school in Alexandria. After graduating from the Cairo Military Academy in 1971, he served in the Egyptian army as an intelligence specialist, reaching the rank of major. Mohamed attended the University of Alexandria and received a bachelor of arts degree in 1980. His affiliation with militant Islamic fundamentalism, his membership in **Islamic Jihad,** and his contacts with **Sheikh Omar Abdel-Rahman** caused his removal from the Egyptian army in 1984. After Mohamed found a job as a security advisor to Egypt Airlines, he worked briefly for the U.S. Central Intelligence Agency (CIA) as a probationary agent. It was determined by the CIA leadership that Mohamed was unreliable as an agent because of contacts with a **Hezbollah** cell, and he was dismissed. In 1986, he moved to the United States and married an American woman. After working as a computer technician for a computer company in California, he joined the U.S. Army and served with the Special Forces and Green Berets, reaching the rank of sergeant. Marriage and service in the military gave him U.S. citizenship.

Mohamed took a leave from the U.S. Army in 1988 to join the Afghan resistance against the Soviet forces. He used his leave to take an unauthorized trip to Afghanistan. During his time in Afghanistan, he joined Osama bin Laden and **Ayman al-Zawahiri's** network of Islamists. In November 1989, he left the U.S. Army with an honorable discharge to devote himself full-time to Islamist causes. He started a leather import-export business as a cover to travel and then moved to Santa Clara, California. His first job was to train Islamists in the United States to fight in Afghanistan. In 1990, he traveled to Afghanistan again, but this time to train mujahideen to fight and to recruit candidates to form terrorist cadres in the United States. He delegated most of his organizational responsibilities in the United States to his chief assistant, Khalid al-Sayyid Ali Abu-al-Dahab, during his sojourn overseas. Mohamed then moved to the Sudan, where he advised bin Laden on military matters. His next mission was in planning the strategy to fight the American military forces in Somalia. After this success, Mohamed's next mission was to plan the bombing of the U.S. Embassy in Nairobi, Kenya. In the aftermath of the embassy bombings in Nairobi and Dar-es-Salaam, Tanzania, Mohamed was arrested in September 1998 and charged in the Nairobi bombing. Mohamed pleaded guilty to five federal counts of conspiracy to commit terrorism and has been cooperating with federal authorities investigating the Qaeda network. See also Abdel-Rahman, Sheikh Omar; Bin Laden, Osama; al-Zawahiri, Ayman.

Suggested readings: Yossef Bodansky, *Bin Laden: The Man Who Declared War on America* (New York: Forum, 2001); John J. Goldman, "Ex-Army Sergeant Admits Guilt in '98 Embassy Blasts," *Los Angeles Times* (October 21, 2000), p. A1; John Miller and Michael Stone, *The Cell: Inside the 9/11 Plot, and Why the FBI and CIA Failed to Stop It* (New York: Hyperion, 2003); Kit R. Roane, David E. Kaplan, and Chitra Ragavan, "Putting Terror Inc. on Trial in New York," *U.S. News & World Report* 130 (January 8, 2001), no.1, p. 25; Lance Williams and Erin McCormick, "Al Qaeda Terrorist Worked with FBI," *San Francisco Chronicle* (November 4, 2001), p. A1.

Mohammed, Khalid Sheikh (1965–) (Pakistan)

Khalid Sheikh Mohammed was **al-Qaeda's** chief of military operations until his capture in March 2003. He was born on April 24, 1965, in Kuwait. His father was a cleric from the Pakistani province of Baluchistan and he preached at al-Ahmadi Mosque in Kuwait. Even after his family lost its Kuwaiti citizenship due to a feud over land with a powerful Kuwaiti family, Mohammed grew up in Kuwait amidst the wealth of Kuwaiti society. But Mohammed came to resent his inferior status in Kuwait. Then, in his teens, he joined the **Muslim Brotherhood**. In 1983, he traveled to the United States to study mechanical engineering at Chowan College in Murfreesboro, North Carolina. The following year he transferred to North Carolina Agricultural and Technical State University in Greensboro, North Carolina. At both schools Mohammed remained aloof from American students and was friendly only with other Arab students. After graduation in 1986, Mohammed traveled to Pakistan to join the mujahideen fighting against the Soviets in Afghanistan.

Mohammed's war experiences in Afghanistan changed his life. His three brothers, Abed, Aref, and Zahid, were already in Afghanistan in the middle of the fighting. Both Abed and Aref were later killed in battles against Soviet forces. Mohammed spent the next five years in Peshawar, Pakistan, and in Afghanistan. He became secretary to one of the Afghan warlords, Abdul Rasul Sayyaf. Sayyaf was a former professor of theology and a devotee of **Wahhabism**. Through his association with Sayyaf, Mohammed became acquainted with **Abdullah Azzam** and **Osama bin Laden**. They became his patrons. After Azzam's death, Mohammed's loyalty shifted to bin Laden.

After the end of the Afghan-Soviet war, Mohammed stayed in Pakistan and directed terrorist attacks against the West. His first involvement was with his nephew **Ramzi Ahmed Yousef**. They planned the February 26, 1993, bombing of the World Trade Center in New York City. Mohammed's role was behind the scenes in the planning, a fact that was only discovered during a raid on Yousef's house in Quetta, Pakistan. Mohammed directed his operations under cover as an import-export businessman with a company called Konsonjaya operating out of Kuala Lumpur, Malaysia. One of the members of the board of directors of this company, **Hambali,** was the operational head of the **Jemaah Islamiyah.** Mohammed sponsored Yousef's bombing activities in the Philippines and even visited there on occasion. After Yousef's cover was blown when one of his bombs accidentally exploded in January 1995, Mohammed fled to Qatar.

Mohammed joined al-Qaeda in 1996. After he learned that American authorities were looking for him, Mohammed journeyed to Kandahar, where the Taliban protected him. He also renewed his association with bin Laden. His connections with both the **Abu Sayyaf** and the Jemaah Islamiyah made him a valuable addition to bin Laden's new al-Qaeda organization. He was given responsibility for operations in Europe, the Middle East and Southeast Asia, but his biggest operation was the planning of the **September 11,** 2001, terrorist attacks in New York City and Washington, D.C. In a June 2002 interview with Yosri Fouda, a journalist with the TV station al-Jazeera, Mohammed indicated that the operation in the United States had been in the planning stages for two and a half years. Once the operatives had been selected, Mohammed watched from behind the scenes. American authorities only learned later of his involvement from captured al-Qaeda members. Once it was apparent that Mohammed had played a key role, American authorities posted a reward of $25 million for his capture.

Mohammed eluded capture for several years. He was always elusive and used as many as 27 aliases, but his luck ran out on March 1, 2003. A joint team of Pakistani and American agents arrested Mohammed in the early morning at a safe house in the Saddar neighborhood of Rawalpindi, southwest of Islamabad, Pakistan. Also arrested with him was Ahmed Abdul Qadoos, a member of the Pakistan Islamist political party Jama'at-i Islami. He was immediately sequestered for debriefing of al-Qaeda operations. American authorities indicated that he will be charged as an enemy combatant and held indefinitely at a remote prison site, where he will be interrogated about his role in al-Qaeda. His role as a planner for al-Qaeda is at an end, and he is considered a pivotal source for information on al-Qaeda. **See also** Afghan Arabs; Azzam, Sheikh Abdullah Yussuf; Bin Laden, Osama; Hambali (Riduan Isamuddin); Muslim Brotherhood (al-Ikhwan al-Muslimun); Yousef, Ramzi Ahmed.

Suggested readings: Farhan Bokari, et al., "The CEO of al-Qaeda," *Financial Times* (London) (February 15, 2003), p 1; Jenny Booth, "Dedicated Hater of the West with a Taste for High Living," *Sunday Telegraph* (London) (March 2, 2003), p. 17; Yosri Fouda, "Masterminds of a Massacre—9/11—One Year On," *Australian* (Sydney) (September 9, 2002), p. 8; Yosri Fouda and Nick Fielding, *Masterminds of Terror: The Truth behind the Most Devastating Terrorist Attack the World Has Ever Seen* (New York: Arcade Publishing, 2003); Josh Meyer, "Major Al Qaeda Operative Captured in Pakistani Raid," *Los Angeles Times* (March 2, 2003).

Montoneros (Argentina)

The Montoneros became the leading urban guerrilla group in Argentina in the 1970s. Nelida Esther (Norma) Arrostito, Mario Firmenich, Fernando Abal Medina, Jose Sabino Navarro, and Carlos Gustavo Ramus founded the group in 1968 during the presidency of General Juan Carlos Ongania. Several of these leaders were previously active in the pro-Perón Juventud Peronista (Perónist Youth) and in the earlier right-wing Tacuara movement. They also had been active in attempts to have the former dictator, Juan Domingo Perón, returned to power in Argentina. They believed that peaceful attempts to restore Perón had proven ineffectual and therefore advocated an armed struggle. The name Montoneros was borrowed from a frontier legend about gauchos on the Argentine pampas who had defended the country from enemies. This group also had ties with the Third World Priests' Movement and the Jesuit priest Father Carlos Mugica. Although the leadership members were Perónist, they also had sympathy for the oppressed and identified with struggles for national liberation. This part of the Montoneros ideology attracted supporters from the radical left.

By May 1970, the group decided to launch urban guerrilla warfare. This offensive took place at a time when the group had only 12 members, and it lacked any experience in guerrilla warfare. Only Arrostito and Medina had received any military instruction, and that was during visits to Cuba in 1967–1968. On May 29, 1970, Montoneros activists kidnapped General Pedro Eugenio Aramburu, the former Argentine head of state, and they announced his execution as an enemy of the state on July 1, 1970. The murder of Aramburu made the Montoneros popular among the Perónists. After Argentine authorities killed Abal Medina, and Ramus on September 7, 1970, and Sabino Navarro in late July 1971, Firmenich became the leader of the Montoneros. By this time the Montoneros had organized into a federal structure with groups formed in various localities. Each group had local leaders and the ability to carry out local operations. This compartmentalization of operations had been adopted from a study of the anti–Nazi Resistance movements in World War II and the tactics adopted by the Uruguayan Tupamaros guerrillas.

The Montoneros launched a nationwide terrorist campaign. Many activists moved from other terrorist groups: People's Revolutionary Army (ERP), Revolutionary Armed Forces (FAR), and Perónist Armed Forces (FAP). Activists began robbing banks to obtain funds and attacking military barracks to locate weapons and ammunitions. At times, Montoneros members kidnapped wealthy businessmen and held them for ransom. The also planted bombs in police stations and at foreign businesses. A rivalry developed between the Montoneros and the right-wing Perónists. Open warfare broke out during the expected arrival of Perón at Ezeiza Airport near Buenos Aires on June 2, 1973. Right-wing Perónists opened fire with machine guns on a Montoneros delegation and the Montoneros returned fire.

Soon after Perón returned to the presidency of Argentina in 1973, he supported the right wing against the Montoneros. The leadership of the Montoneros retaliated with a new wave of assassinations of Perónist labor leaders and kidnappings of business leaders. The most important of these assassinations was Jose Rucci, the secretary general of the General Confederation of Labor, in September 1973. Perón then authorized the creation of **death squads** to attack the Montoneros and their sympathizers. However, Perón died on July 1, 1974, in the middle of this campaign.

Perón's successor, Isabel Perón, continued the war against the Montoneros. Jose Lopez Rega, an advisor to both Peróns, formed the **Argentine Anti-Communist Alliance** (Triple A) out of elements of the police and military. This secret organization used the power of the state to attack the Montoneros and any potential opponents of the state. Because it was immune from legal prosecution, the Triple A proceeded to wipe out the Montoneros and other guerrilla groups by murdering or throwing them into concentration camps. This repression did not prevent Montoneros members from exploding a bomb in the dining room of the federal police security building in Buenos Aires on July 2, 1976, that killed 18 and wounded 66. They followed up with a bomb attack on December 15, 1976, in the Defense Ministry building in Buenos Aires that killed 15 and injured 30 military officers and civilians.

Despite these actions, by early 1977 the Montoneros had ceased to operate as an urban guerrilla group. Most of its leaders left the country using false passports. Firmenich went to Brazil, where he stayed under Brazilian government protection. This protection ended in October 1984, when the Brazilian government extradited him to Argentina with the stipulation that the maximum sentence be no more than 30 years. Other important Montoneros leaders have been arrested and sentenced to long terms in prison. See also Argentine Anti-Communist Alliance (Alianza Argentina Anti-Comunista) (Triple A).

Suggested readings: Richard Gillespie, *Soldiers of Peron: Argentina's Montoneros* (Oxford, U.K.: Clarendon Press, 1982); Patricia

Marchak and William Marchak, *God's Assassins: State Terrorism in Argentina in the 1970s* (Montreal: McGill-Queen's University Press, 1999; Michael McCaughan, "Children Confront Hunter of Their Rebel Father as Argentina Faces Its Past," *Irish Times* (July 11, 1998), p. 10; William D. Montalbano, "Life Term Urged for Argentine Terrorist Leader," *Los Angeles Times* (November 8, 1985), p. 36.

Moro Islamic Liberation Front (MILF) (Philippines)

The Moro Islamic Liberation Front (MILF) is the most recent Islamic separatist group in the southern part of the Philippines. It emerged out of rejection of the 1996 peace treaty between the Philippine government and the leadership of the **Moro National Liberation Front** (MNLF). This treaty had established a four-province autonomous region of Muslim Mindanao and mandated the disbandment of the MNLF. Rivals of **Nur Misuari**, the head of the MNLF, rejected this peace treaty because it did not allow a separate Muslim state independent of the Philippines. Most prominent of the dissidents was **Hashim Salamat**, a Moro graduate of **al-Azhar University** in Cairo, Egypt, who had been the number-two man in the MNLF.

These rejectionists decided to continue the struggle for an independent Muslim state in the Mindanao-Sulu region of the Philippines. The goals of the new Moro Islamic Liberation Front were independence from the Philippine state and the creation of an Islamic state. The two most important dissident leaders, Salamat and Amin Cusain, led a force of 12,000 fighters into the Moro Islamic Liberation Front. Soon after launching military operations against the Philippine army in 1997, Cusain was killed, leaving Hashim Salamat in charge of the MILF. Cusan's loss has not prevented the MILF from conducting large-scale military operations in the last five years. Arms shipments from Muslim allies have allowed the MILF to match the Philippine army in firepower.

In 2001, the MILF and the MNLF concluded an alliance. Both sides were unhappy with the terrorist activities of the **Abu Sayyaf** and the possibility of losing control of the Moro national liberation movement. This alliance has been a loose agreement allowing both groups to conduct operations on their on initiative. In August 2001, the leaders of the MILF signed a cease-fire with the Philippine government, ending its participation in the guerrilla warfare. American intervention in the southern Philippines after the **September 11**, 2001, terrorist attacks against the United States has alarmed the leadership of the MILF, but these leaders have been reluctant to renew guerrilla operations. The leader of the MILF, Salamat, had always been reluctant to use terrorism to gain independence and he was quoted in Philippine newspapers as describing terrorism as "anathema to the teachings of Islam," but this did not mean that the MILF ceased building up its military forces.

Negotiations between the Moro Islamic Liberation Front and the Philippine government have been sporadic and shaky. A Febrary 2003 offensive launched by the Philippine government placed pressure on the MILF and it endangered the MILF's control in Mindanao. In late July 2003, both the MILF and the Philippines decared a cease-fire that was a prelude for negotiations. Salamat was the chief sponsor of the negotiations, but he died on July 13, 2003, of natural causes. His successor as head of the MILF is al-Haj Murad Ebrahim. Murah Ebrahim's main problem as leader is that he lacked the moral stature of **Hashim Salamat**. Philippine authorities have blamed the MILF for several terrorist attacks in late 2002 and early 2003. In May 2003, the Philippine army launched a 10-day punitive operation against the MILF in the southern Philippines. At the end of this operation the Philippine government declared a victory and both sides have scheduled negotiation sessions to take place later in 2004. **See also** Abu Sayyaf Group (Bearer of the Sword) (ASG); Misuari, Nur; Moro National Liberation Front (MNLF); Salamat, Hashim.

Suggested readings: Anthony Davis, "Rebels without a Pause," *Asiaweek* (April 3, 1998), p. 30; Raissa Robles, "Philippine Muslim Rebels Confirm

Death of Their Leader," *South China Morning Post* (August 6, 2003), p. 8; Syed Serajul Islam, "Ethno-Communal Conflict in the Philippines: The Case of Mindanao-Sulu Region," in Rajat Ganguly and Ian Macduff (eds.), *Ethnic Conflict and Secessionism in South and Southeast Asia: Causes, Dynamics, Solutions* (New Delhi, India: Sage Publications, 2003); Maria A. Ressa, *Seeds of Terror: An Eyewitness Account of Al-Qaeda's Newest Center of Operations in Southeast Asia* (New York: Free Press, 2003); Carl Yaeger, "Moro National Liberation Front and the Political Terrorists of the Philippines," *Journal of Counterterrorism and Security International* 6, no. 4 (2000 Summer).

Moro National Liberation Front (MNLF) (Philippines)

The Moro National Liberation Front (MNLF) was the largest Islamic separatist group in the Philippines from 1971 to 1996. Its formation was an outgrowth of unrest against the Ferdinand Marcos regime and its anti-Muslim policies. This unrest led to the formation of the Muslim Independence Movement (MIM). After the collapse of the MIM and the founding of the MNLF, **Nur Misuari**, a left-wing political science professor at the University of the Philippines in Manila, assumed control of the group in 1972. He was a staunch Muslim of Tausug extraction from Jolo in the Sulu chain of islands in the southern Philippines. It was in this region that Misuari built the military wing of the MNLF, Bangsa Moro Army (BMA). The Moro National Liberation Front was one of the groups to receive financial and moral support from **Muammar Qaddafi**, the head of Libya. By 1973, the MNLF had a military force of 15,000 combatants, and Misuari launched military operations. During the next two years, the MNLF engaged in a series of successful battles with the Philippine army. In 1974, Misuari formed an MNLF Central Committee, the Committee of Thirteen, with most of its members residing in Tripoli, Libya. This committee was to provide political oversight for the MNLF, but communications between Libya and the Philippines caused problems.

The success of the MNLF led the government of Philippines President Fernando Marcos to negotiate a settlement. In 1976, a 16-point accord was negotiated that included a cease-fire and a degree of political autonomy for the Muslim areas of the southern Philippines. Part of the agreement mandated a referendum that would allow Muslims political control of the thirteen southernmost provinces. A referendum held in April 1977 failed, however, because the Christian majority voted against it.

The failure of the referendum almost destroyed the MNLF because of internal dissension. Elements within the MNLF rejected the original cease-fire and violated it by assassinating Philippine Brigadier General Bautista and 34 soldiers. Then, members of the Committee of Thirteen challenged Misuari's leadership. Misuari responded by attempting to purge the dissidents. In a 1977 meeting in Mecca, Saudi Arabia, Misuari lost the chairmanship of MNLF to one of the dissidents, **Hashim Salamat**. Misuari rejected this vote and went into exile in Tripoli for the next decade, still leading the militant wing of the MNLF.

The absence of Misuari did no prevent the MNLF from carrying out small-scale operations. Elements of the MNLF conducted a series of kidnappings of foreign nationals beginning in 1984 and lasting until 1991. These individuals were held for ransom to be paid to the MNLF. Kidnappings continued even after Misuari returned to the Philippines.

The threat of guerilla warfare caused the Philippine government of President Fidel Ramos to sign a peace treaty with the MNLF in 1996. This treaty established a four-province autonomous region, of Muslim Mindanao to be under the political control of the MNLF. Misuari was elected governor of this autonomous region and the military wing of the MNLF was disbanded. Elements within the MNLF revolted, and Salamat and Amin Cusain took around 12,000 of the group's fighters and formed a new organization, the **Moro Islamic Liberation Front** (MILF).

Misuari remained governor of the autonomous region for five years, but the economic and political life of the region remained unsettled despite his efforts to attract outside resources. Complicating his efforts was the military campaign launched by the Moro Islamic Liberation Front. Misuari's campaign for reelection failed in 2001. Misuari then revolted with support from his former followers in the MNLF against the Philippine government. After his forces were overwhelmed, his colleagues in the MNLF deposed him as chairman of the group in May 2001. Parouk Hussin assumed the chairmanship of the MNLF. Misuari fled the Philippines and attempted to enter Malaysia. However, Malaysian authorities arrested him and in November 2001 turned Misuari and his key advisors over to the Philippine authorities for trial. Since then Philippine authorities have kept Misuari in prison, but they seem reluctant to bring him to trial. **See also** Moro Islamic Liberation Front (MILF); Qaddafi, Muammar.

Suggested readings: Luz Baguioro, "Misuari's Fall," *Straits Times* (Singapore) (November 27, 2001), p. A1; Anthony Davis, "Evolution in the Philippines War," *Jane's Intelligence Review* 12, no. 7 (July 1, 2000); Syed Serajul Islam, "Ethno-Communal Conflict in the Philippines: The Case of the Mindanao-Sulu Region," in Rajat Ganguly and Ian Macduff (eds.), *Ethnic Conflict and Secessionism in South and Southeast Asia: Causes, Dynamics, Solutions* (New Delhi, India: Sage Publications, 2003); Andrew Tan, "Armed Muslim Separatist Rebellion in Southeast Asia: Persistence, Prospects and Implications," *Studies in Conflict and Terrorism* 23, no. 4 (October–December 2000); Carl Yaeger, "Moro National Liberation Front and the Political Terrorists of the Philippines," *Journal of Counterterrorism and Security International* 6, no. 4 (Summer 2000).

Mosley, Oswald (1896–1980)
(Great Britain)

Oswald Mosley was the leading British fascist leader in the period from 1932 to 1980. He was born on November 16, 1896, into a wealthy family in 1896 in Staffordshire, England. His upper-class education was at Winchester School and the Royal Military College

Sandhurst. He served first in a fashionable cavalry regiment before transferring to the Royal Flying Corps during World War I. He was a navigator and he sustained a serious leg injury in a crash. After the war, Mosley became a Tory M.P. for Harrow. In 1920, he married the heiress Cynthia Curzon. His concern about the state of British politics caused him to join the Labor Party in 1924. He remained a member of the Labor Party until 1930 and during that time he made efforts to convince British politicians of the need for reform. The economic theories of John Maynard Keynes and his advocacy of state intervention in economic life convinced him of the need for strong leadership in dealing with economic problems. In 1930, he and six Labor members of Parliament formed the New Party to pursue Keynesian economic policies, but they lost their seats in Parliament in the 1931 general election. This failure turned Mosley to fascism.

In October 1932, Mosley founded the **British Union of Fascists** (BUF). At its peak in 1934, the BUF had 5,000 members and constituted the most extreme political faction in British politics. A combination of violence from the Blackshirts of the BUF and the aggressive actions of Adolf Hitler and Nazi Germany curtailed the growth of the BUF. Soon after the beginning of World War II in late May 1940, the British government invoked Defence Regulation 18b and interned Mosley. Mosley spent most of the war in a four-room flat at Holloway Jail with his second wife. His first wife had died in 1933 and he had married Lady Diana Mitford of the famous Mitford family in 1936. The British government released Mosley and his wife from internment in November 1943.

Mosley returned to building a fascist movement soon after his release from internment. In February 1948, he established the Union Movement as a new fascist party. His agenda was published in his book *The Alternative*. Mosley continued to agitate for a British fascist state, but electoral success eluded him and his followers. In 1951, he purchased an estate near Galway, Ireland, and briefly retired from British politics. In the late 1950s, Mosley decided to attempt a comeback by opposing the British anti-apartheid boycott of South Africa. Throughout the early 1960s, Mosley was active in the international fascist movement, but more as a father figure than an active fascist. Mosley lived most of the last years of his life in a home at Orsay near Paris, France. He died on December 2, 1980. His legacy was paving the way for a revival of neo-fascism in the late 20th century in Great Britain. **See also** British Union of Fascists (BUF).

Suggested readings: D. S. Lewis, *Illusions of Grandeur: Mosley, Fascism, and British Society, 1931–81* (Manchester, UK: Manchester University Press, 1987; Thomas Linehan, *British Fascism, 1918–39: Parties Ideology and Culture* (Manchester, UK: Manchester University Press, 2001); Suzie Mackenzie, "Beloved Monster," *Guardian* (London) (January 24, 1998), p. 14; Richard Thurlow, *Fascism in Britain: From Oswald Mosley's Blackshirts to the National Front* (London: Tauris, 1998.

Moussaoui, Zacharias (1968–) (France)

Zacharias Moussaoui is the **Qaeda** operative whose arrest prevented him from participating in the **September 11**, 2001, terrorist attacks on New York City and Washington, D.C. He was born on May 30, 1968, in St.-Jean-de-Luz near Narbonne, France, but his parents were from Morocco. His parents divorced when Moussaoui was young, and his mother raised him along with a brother and two sisters. His mother brought the children up as a modern French family. He was a happy, carefree child until a female cousin visited the family from Morocco and disturbed him with her Muslim views. Moussaoui and his brother then moved to Montpellier. In 1992, he traveled to London, England, where he spent a disillusioning six-month stay. Moussaoui found British society intolerant and class-ridden. He returned to France, and shortly afterward he began to espouse radical Islamist views. Despite his earlier experience, Moussaoui went back to England and enrolled at the South Bank University in London, where he studied international business. After obtaining a degree in 1995, Moussaoui traveled back to Montpellier.

By 1995, Moussaoui's political and religious views resembled those of the radical Algerian Islamist group **Armed Islamic Group** (Groupes Islamiques Armés, or GIA). The GIA was in the midst of a violent terrorist campaign in Algeria, with wholesale massacres of Algerian civilians. In 1997, Moussaoui traveled to Pakistan and then to Afghanistan for military and terrorist training. He was at al-Qaeda's Khaldan training camp in the spring of 1998 when the recruiting for the suicide mission to the United States took place. **Mohamed Atta**, the future head of the September 11 operation, was at the same camp at that time. Atta and Moussaoui were both selected for future suicide missions.

Moussaoui's terrorist career was cut short because he became too conspicuous. He had not been selected to be part of the original Mohamed Atta cell, but he was substituted after another member had visa problems that prevented his entry into the United States. Because of his English-language expertise and his British passport, Moussaoui was a natural substitute. After arriving in the United States, he enrolled in a flying school in Norman, Oklahoma. His tenure at this school was unsuccessful, with the flight instructor refusing to allow him to fly solo. Moussaoui's mistake was then to enroll at the Pan Am International Flight Academy in Minneapolis, Minnesota, in August 2001. His lack of flying skills and his belligerence made the flying instructors suspicious. They reported their suspicions to the Federal Bureau of Investigation (FBI). Moussaoui was arrested in August 2001 and FBI agents found incriminating evidence at his motel residence. Several of the agents wanted to intensify the investigation, but the FBI bureaucracy refused to take the evidence to the Justice Department because they thought the evidence insufficient. Attempts by the agents to bypass the bureaucracy earned them a reprimand. Only after September 11 did the FBI realize how close it had been to breaking the Qaeda cell. **See also** Atta,

Mohamed; Al-Qaeda (The Base); September 11th.

Suggested readings: Eric Boehlert, "The Moussaoui Mess," Edmonton Journal (July 20, 2003), p. D3; Jane Corbin, *Al-Qaeda: The Terror Network That Threatens the World* (New York: Thunder's Mouth Press, 2002); Seymour M. Hersh, "The Twentieth Man: Has the Justice Department Mishandled the Case Against Zacharias?" *New Yorker* (September 30, 2002), p. 56; Rick Linsk and Hannah Allam, "Moussaoui a Study in Contradictions," *Saint Paul Pioneer Press* (September 8, 2002), p. 1; Dahlia Lithwick, "Terrorism on Trial," *Slate Magazine* (June 14, 2002), p. 1.

Mugabe, Robert (1924–) (Zimbabwe)

Robert Mugabe is the former freedom fighter who has become the dictatorial president of Zimbabwe. He was born in 1924 in Kutama Mission in Zvimba about 50 miles west of Harare. His father was a carpenter. Mugabe was raised as a Catholic by his parents, and he retained most of his religious beliefs. He attended the Jesuit Kutama School. His father died when Mugabe was young and his mother raised him and his brothers. Mugabe was a precocious student, and he trained to become a teacher. He graduated with a diploma in teaching in 1945. After teaching at various schools, he won a scholarship to Fort Hare, an all-black university on the Cape in South Africa. Besides training in academic subjects, Mugabe received a political education from the young leaders of the African National Congress (ANC). Shortly before graduation, Mugabe joined the ANC. He returned to Rhodesia and obtained teaching post at various missions. He also renewed a friendship with Leopold Takawira. Takawira was to serve as his political mentor during the early stages of Mugabe's political career. Mugabe moved first to Zambia in 1955 and then to Ghana in 1957. Mugabe found Kwame Nkrumah and Ghana's independence exhilarating. His stay in Ghana garnered Mugabe an ideology, Marxism, and a wife, Sarah "Sally" Francesca Hayfron. She was a schoolteacher and the daughter of parents involved in the Ghanaian liberation movement. Until her death in 1992, Sally Mugabe was a loyal and supportive wife who was active in politics.

Mugabe returned to Rhodesia in 1960 just in time for the revolt against white rule. He was in the crowd and spoke at the "March of the 7000" in Salisbury, Rhodesia. The police repression following this demonstration made Mugabe into a nationalist. Shortly after the government banned Rhodesia's African National Congress, the National Democratic Party (NDP) was founded on January 1, 1960. At the first party congress in October 1960, the delegates elected Mugabe publicity secretary. Mugabe's role was to revitalize the independence movement by appealing to a common African heritage and enthusiasm for change among the young. He did this by organizing the NDP Youth Wing.

Mugabe became more prominent in the NDP after he challenged its leader, Joshua Nkomo. Nkomo had agreed to a controversial constitutional settlement in November 1960. Mugabe and other young leader revolted, accusing Nkomo of a sellout. In 1961, Mugabe and the others began threatening open warfare against the white government of Rhodesia. This agitation led the government to ban the NDP. Less than a week later, the leadership of the NDP formed the Zimbabwe African Peoples Union (ZAPU). In 1962, ZAPU was also banned, and the government placed Mugabe under restrictions for three months. As the political situation deteriorated, Mugabe's unhappiness over the leadership of Nkomo increased. Nkomo wanted to fight a war from exile, whereas Mugabe and his supporters believed that the war must be fought in Rhodesia. Nkomo acted first by suspending Mugabe and the dissidents. These dissidents retaliated by founding the Zimbabwe African National Union (ZANU) with Ndabaningi Sithole at its head. ZANU's goal was to conduct an armed struggle against the Rhodesian government.

Mugabe's stance landed him in prison for the next 11 years. He had gone to Zambia for a party meeting. On his return to

Zimbabwean President Robert Mugabe speaks during a press conference in Pretoria November 23, 1996. For the first time since this former British colony won independence in 1980, people are seriously asking if President Robert Mugabe, the only leader Zimbabwe has ever known, can endure. (AP Photo/Adil Bradlow)

Rhodesia in December 1963 he was arrested for subversive statements. His trial lasted nearly three months, and he was given a 21-month prison sentence. Despite this lenient sentence, authorities kept Mugabe in either jail or a detention center until December 1974. While he was in prison, open warfare broke out between the ZAPU and the ZANU. Mugabe decided to use prison time to educate the political prisoners so that they would be prepared for leadership positions after their release. On his own time, Mugabe pursed a law degree by correspondence from London University. Sithole had become increasingly erratic so, in January 1969,

Mugabe was elected to replace him as head of ZANU. In December 1974, Mugabe and several other leaders were suddenly freed from prison. Mugabe assumed total control of ZANU after he left prison.

Mugabe's leadership led to the overthrow of the Rhodesian government and the conclusion of the 1980 Lancaster House negotiations. An agreement that instituted majority rule led the creation of Zimbabwe. In 1980, Mugabe assumed political power. His first order of business was isolating and destroying the political power of his chief rival, Joshua Nkomo, and his ZAPU party. After crushing an army rebellion, Mugabe forced the submerging of the ZAPU into his Zimbabwe African National Union Patriotic Front (ZANU-PF) party in 1987.

Mugabe soon became the darling of left-wing governments around the world because of his imposition of socialism in Zimbabwe. His rule was dictatorial, crushing potential political rivals whenever they appeared. Mugabe's hatred of the white settlers was also apparent. His regime prospered with international support from leftist governments until the collapse of the communist regimes in 1989. Since then, the Zimbabwe economy also has collapsed. Mugabe reacted by confiscating the property and lands of white settlers, and he used the lands to reward political cronies and war veterans. This policy caused an international uproar. His marriage in 1996 to his former mistress, Grace Marufu, also produced complications. Mugabe became increasingly unstable in the late 1990s, which led to rumors that he was seriously ill.

Efforts to replace him by democratic means have been ineffective. In the March 2002 election, a viable opposition formed in the Movement for Democratic Change (MDC) under the leadership of Morgan Tsvangirai. There were enough election irregularities to question the outcome of the election that returned Mugabe to power. Tsvangirai's challenge earned him a high treason charge for plotting the assassination of Mugabe. Later, Tsvangirai was also charged with treason for organizing work stoppages and demonstrations in June 2003 to persuade Mugabe to resign. Mugabe has been under pressure to resign, but he has been reluctant to acquiesce. The problem of a successor is one of the major problems.

Suggested readings: Rebecca Fowler, "Last Days of a Despot," *Daily Mail* (London) (May 10, 2003), p. 12; Philip Gourevitch, "Comrade Mugabe Is Clinging to Power, and Taking His Country Down with Him," *New Yorker* (June 3, 2002), p. 1; David Ignatius, "New Doubts Cast on Mugabe Victory," *International Herald Tribune* (April 3, 2002), p. 3; Andrew Meldrum, "From Joy and Hope to Corruption, Tyranny and the Misery of Poverty," *Guardian* (London) (May 19, 2003),

p. 16; Alex Dubal Smith and Basildon Peta, "This Land Is My Land," *Independent on Sunday* (London) (February 17, 2002), p. 22; David Smith and Colin Simpson, *Mugabe* (Salisbury, UK: Pioneer Head, 1981); Gary Younge, "Comrade Bob," *Guardian* (London) (September 4, 2001), p. 2.

Mugniyah, Imad Fayez (1962–) (Lebanon)

Imad Mugniyah is the head of the terrorist group **Hezbollah**'s security service and its planner for terrorist operations. He was born on July 12, 1962, in Tayr Dibba near Tyre in southern Lebanon. He studied engineering at the American University of Beirut before joining **Yasser Arafat's al-Fatah** faction of the **Palestine Liberation Organization** (PLO). He fought in Lebanon's civil war and at one time was a member of Arafat's personal bodyguard unit, Force 17. After the PLO was forced out of Lebanon by Israel's June 1982 invasion, Mugniyah joined the new Shi'ite organization Hezbollah.

Mugniyah's military experience and abilities permitted him to advance to a high position in Hezbollah. Leaders of Hezbollah assigned him to the security section to plan terrorist operations. His first major operation was the April 18, 1983, car bombing at the U.S. Embassy in Beirut that claimed 63 lives and wounded 120. Later, on October 23, 1983, he planned the truck bombing at the U.S. Marine compound in Beirut that killed 241 American troops. This action caused President Ronald Reagan to withdraw American troops from Lebanon. Two of his men also assassinated Malcolm Kerr, president of the American University of Beirut, because Mugniyah considered him a bad influence on Lebanese students. On June 14, 1985, Mugniyah initiated the hijacking of a Trans-World Airline (TWA) aircraft, which lasted 17 days and resulted in the death of an American.

Mugniyah was in charge of a series of kidnappings in Beirut of American personnel. William Buckley, the Central Intelligence Agency (CIA) station chief in Beirut, was the first victim, on March 16, 1984. Peter

Kilburn, a librarian at the American University of Beirut, was the next victim, on December 3, 1984. Neither Buckley nor Kilburn survived his kidnapping. Other prominent kidnap victims were Terry Anderson, an American journalist, who was kidnapped on March 16, 1985, and Terry Waite, an Anglican layman who was negotiating the release of other hostages, on January 20, 1987. These later hostages were kept for more than five years. Mugniyah was able to keep security because he used members of the Mugniyah clan as the kidnappers.

Mugniyah continued his activities with Hezbollah, but he also formed the Lebanese Islamic Jihad. These groups kept a separate existence, but Mugniyah was able to conduct independent operations under the auspices of **Islamic Jihad**. This dual identity has caused problems to anti-terrorism specialists. Regardless of the group, Mugniyah participated in the planning of two anti-Israel bombings in Buenos Aires, Argentina. He organized a March 17, 1992, bombing of the Israeli Embassy in Buenos Aires, which killed 25 people and wounded 252 others. Also attributed to him was an attack on July 18, 1994, when a car bomb destroyed the building housing two Argentine-Israel organizations, killing 85 people and injuring 300.

Mugniyah's success as a terrorist has made him a public enemy with Western states. He has an American price tag of $25 million for his capture or death. He is public enemy number three behind **Osama bin Laden** and **Ayman al-Zawahiri**. Despite the publicity, Mugniyah has been successful in avoiding capture by frequent moves between Iran and Lebanon. In October 2001, the government of Mohammad Khatami announced that Mugniyah had been expelled from Iran as an undesirable. Mugniyah has returned to Beirut, Lebanon, and he is the alleged head of Hezbollah's security service and reports directly to the head of Hezbollah, **Hassan Nasrallah**.

Mugniyah's name hit the national headlines in April 2003 when Canadian authorities broke up a Hezbollah cell in Canada. This cell had the mission to plan and execute the assassination of Israel's prime minister,

Ariel Sharon. Mugniyah has long been suspected of planning operations against the United States and Israel in retaliation for U.S. policies in the Middle East. **See also** Hezbollah (Party of God).

Suggested readings: J. Bowyer Bell, *Murders on the Nile: The World Trade Center and Global Terror* (San Francisco: Encounter Books, 2003); Steward Bell, "Canadian a Suspect in Plot to Kill Israeli PM," *National Post* (Toronto) (April 5, 2003), p. A1; Kevin G. Hall, "Trial in Argentina Illustrates Difficulty in Pursuing Terrorists," Knight Ridder Washington Bureau (September 21, 2001), p. 1; Justin Huggler, "Iran Says It Threw Out One of FBI's Terror Suspects," *Independent* (London) (October 16, 2001), p. 7; Magnus Ranstorp, *Hizb'Allah in Lebanon: The Politics of the Western Hostage Crisis* (London: Palgrave, 1997); James Risen, "U.S. Traces Iran's Ties to Terror through a Lebanese," *New York Times* (January 17, 2002), p. A17.

Al-Muhajiroun (The Emigrants) (AM) (Middle East)

Al-Muhajiroun (The Emigrants) is an Islamist group that campaigns for a world Islamic state. Sheikh Omar Bakri Mohammed, the current leader, claims to have founded this organization in 1983 in Jeddah, Saudi Arabia, but first notice of this group came after it broke from the **Hizb ut-Tahrir al-Islami** (Islamic Liberation Party) (HT) in February 1996. He had been a vocal advocate for HT before its leadership became concerned about his confrontational tactics and high media profile. The goal of Bakri Mohammed and his co-leader Muhammed al-Masari, the former head of the Saudi opposition group Campaign for the Defence of Legitimate Rights (CDLR), is to reestablish the Caliphate, a central Islamic religious authority that the Turkish government abolished in 1924. Mohammed blames the abolition of the Caliphate on Western imperialist states. His activities on behalf of a caliphate in Saudi Arabia led to his expulsion in 1986. Since then, Mohammed has lived in London, where he has established al-Muhajiroun's headquarters. His chief spokesperson claimed in an October 2001 interview in *The Daily Telegraph* that the al-Muhajiroun had 30 offices scattered throughout the Muslim world and in Great Britain, France, and South Africa.

Mohammed has been active in the last decade exhorting Muslims to join a holy war against Islam's enemies in Bosnia, Chechnya, Israel, and Kashmir. Despite attacks, British authorities have tolerated the activities of al-Muhajiroun and Mohammed because they consider their acts as more of a bother than a threat. Jewish groups, however, have protested the anti-Jewish propaganda published by this group. More attention has been paid to al-Muhajiroun since the terrorist attacks in the United States on **September 11**, 2001. Leaders of al-Muhajiroun celebrated the Muslim attack on the United States. Members of the group volunteered to fight in Afghanistan to support the **Taliban** and **Osama bin Laden**. Both **Richard Reid**, the shoe bomber, and **Zacharias Moussaoui**, the so-called "20th member" of the September 11 attack, had connections to al-Muhajiroun. Two members, Asif Mohammed Hanif and Omar Khan Sharif, plotted a suicide bombing against Israel. In early May 2003, Hanif blew himself up in Tel Aviv, Israel, killing three Israelis and injuring dozens. British authorities have been investigating the activities of al-Muhajiroun and its leader Omar Bakri Mohammed, but no charges have been forthcoming. Since the passage of the Terrorism Act 2000 by the British Parliament, Omar Bakri Mohammed has been careful by only giving his seal of approval of terrorist incidents after the fact while just stopping short in public of calling for more terrorist acts. The most provocative act has been the public celebration on September 11, 2003, of martyrdom of the "The Magnificent Nineteen" suicide hijackers. **See also** Bin Laden, Osama; Moussaoui, Zacharias; Reid, Richard; September 11th; Taliban (Students of Religious Schools).

Suggested readings: Martin Bright and Fareena Alam, "Britain's Suicide Bomber," *Observer* (London) (May 4, 2003), p. 18; Rosie DiManno, "For Some, 9/11 Isn't for Mourning," *Toronto Star* (September 11, 2003), p. A2; Peter Foster, "Militants of al-Muhajiroun Seek World Islamic State," *Daily Telegraph* (London) (October 21, 2001), p. 6; Ori Golan, "One Day the Black Flag of Islam Will Be Flying over Downing Street." *Jerusalem Post* (June 27, 2003), p. 5B; Paul Harris, Burhan Wazir, and Jason Burke, "War on Terror: The British Recruits," *Observer* (London) (November 4, 2001), p. 20; Neil Mackay, "On the March with Allah's Army," *Sunday Herald* (London) (November 4, 2001), p. 20; Olivia War, "Britain's Terror Connection," *Toronto Star* (November 18, 2001), p. B4; Burhan Wazir, "The Talibanizing of Britain Proceeds," *New Statesman* (February 11, 2002), p. 1.

Mujahedin-e Khalq Organization (People's Holy Warriors) (MEK or MKO) (Iran)

The Mujahedin-e Khalq Organization (People's Holy Warriors, or MEK) is an Iranian dissident group that is at war with the Iranian government. Three engineering graduates of Tehran University, Mohammad Hanifnezhad, Said Mohsen, and Ali-Asghar Badizadegan, formed the Mujahedin-e Khalq on September 6, 1965, in response to what they perceived as the excessive Western orientation and political repression of the Shah of Iran's regime. These engineers had earlier been affiliated with the Liberation Movement of Iran of Mehdi Bazargan, but they left this group because they considered it too reformist. The failed June 1963 student uprisings in Tehran served as a catalyst for them to build an organization to carry out armed struggle against the Shah's regime. These leaders of MEK attracted others to organize a Central Committee of 15 members to work out both an ideology and a revolutionary strategy. This process of study took three years. These intellectuals decided on an ideology that combined Marxist economic analysis with the religious fervor of Islam. Their desire for a socialist Islamic regime followed the Islamic modernist ideas of the Iranian theorist Ali Shariati.

MEK remained a secret organization until 1972. This seven-year period allowed the leaders of MEK to recruit members without harassment from the Iranian police or secret service. The original members of the Central Committee were young, and a majority of them were engineering graduates. Only two clerics, two social scientists, and one dentist belonged to the Central Committee. Massoud Rajavi, a political science major and a member of the Central Committee, had become its operational leader by the time that the MEK went public. Members of MEK engaged in terrorist activities in the 1970s against foreign targets, mostly U.S. civilian and military personnel.

The leaders of the MEK welcomed the Iranian Revolution of 1979. They viewed the new regime as a golden opportunity to build a socialist Islamic state. Within months of the new regime of **Ayatollah Ruhollah Khomeini,** the MEK leaders found out that they had no role in the new regime. Khomeini's cleric state tolerated neither opposition nor socialistic ideas.

In response, supporters launched a terror campaign against Khomeini's regime. On June 28, 1981, two bombs killed 74 members of the pro-Khomeini Islamic Republic Party (IRP) at a party conference in Tehran. An earlier bomb attack at Qom had killed 8 and wounded 23. Ali Khameinei, a close supporter of Khomeini, a member of the Supreme Defense Council, and his future successor, was severely injured at a prayer service in Tehran. On August 30, 1981, the MEK assassinated President Mohammad Ali Raja'i, Prime Minister Ayatollah Mohammad Javad Bahanor, and three security officials at Bahanor's home in Tehran. These attacks led to a brutal crackdown on all dissidents. Throughout 1981 a mini–civil war existed between the Khomeini regime and the MEK. By the end of 1982, most MEK operatives in Iran had been eradicated.

By this time, most MEK leaders left Iran for refuge in France. While in France, the MEK organization reorganized and began a propaganda war against Khomeini's regime. Limited terrorist activities commenced against the Iranian government, but the MEK needed a location closer to Iran. Iranian government had also placed pressure on the French government to banish the MEK. By 1987, most MEK leaders and most of its activists had relocated in Iraq and under **Saddam Hussein**'s sponsorship. Rajavi married Maryam Rajavi in 1988 and

he raised her to be equal to him in the MEK hierarchy.

In April 1992, MEK launched attacks against Iranian embassies in 13 countries. By this time the MEK forces numbered between 4,000 and 5,000 with about half of the fighters being women. Periodic attacks were conducted and followed by intervals of little activity. In February 2000, the MEK initiated its most serious operation with a series of terrorist attacks in Iran. These operations included mortar attacks and raids against the Iranian military and police. Periodic attacks on Iranian targets continued until May 2003.

The activities of the MEK ended abruptly during the American/British invasion of Iraq. Despite efforts to minimize its vulnerability with the lobby of the American Congress, the MEK became a victim of the overthrow of the Saddam Hussein regime in Iraq. American lack of tolerance toward terrorist groups included the MEK. After all, the American State Department had designated the MEK as a terrorist organization in 1997. Early in the war, the leadership of the MEK agreed to a cease-fire and assumed neutrality. Then in early May 2003, U.S. military commanders disarmed the MEK and transported its troops away from its military base camp. This action has ended the effectiveness of the MEK as a military weapon directed against the Iranian government. **See also** Khomeini, Ayatollah Ruholla.

Suggested readings: Ervand Abrahamian, *The Iranian Mojahedin* (New Haven, CT: Yale University Press, 1989); Sam Dealey, "MEK Mounting Charm Offensive to Generate Support on Capitol Hill," *Hill* (Washington, DC) (April 23, 2003), p. 8; Elizabeth Rubin, "The Cult of Rajavi," *New York Times* (July 13, 2003), sec. 6, p. 26; Robin Wright, *In the Name of God: The Khomeini Decade* (New York: Simon & Schuster, 1989).

Munich Olympic Massacre (See Black September)

Murphy, Thomas "Slab" (1949–) (Northern Ireland)

Tom "Slab" Murphy is the leader of the **Provisional Irish Republican Army** (Provos, or

PIRA) in South Armagh, Northern Ireland. He was born on August 26, 1949, and raised on a farm in Ireland that straddles the border between the Republic of Ireland and Northern Ireland. He attended Blasdrumman School, but he left school at age 14 to work on the family farm. As a schoolboy and young man, Murphy was most noted for his proficiency as a player of Gaelic football. He played for Roche Emmets and then for the Noamh Malachi Football Club. Sometime in the mid-1960s, Murphy joined the **Irish Republican Army** (IRA), and he was listed as a member of the Inniskeen unit in County Monaghan in 1968.

Murphy steadily advanced up the ranks of the Provisional Irish Republican Army's leadership ranks because of his efficiency and ruthlessness. By the mid-1970s, Murphy had become a senior intelligence operative planning military operations and was sent to Libya to receive weapons training. British intelligence sources attribute the development of the IRA's homemade Mark 10 mortars in the 1970s to Murphy and his weapon designers. Among the operations that he planned was the Narrow Water Castle bombing that killed 18 British soldiers on August 27, 1979. He also served as the intelligence officer for the Lord Mountbatten assassination on August 27, 1979. Because of his training in Libya, he was placed in charge of the four arms shipments that the Provisional IRA received from Libya in 1985 and 1986. His success in these operations led to Murphy's appointment to the PIRA's Army Council. In 1996, he replaced Kevin McKenna as the Provisional Irish Republican Army's chief of staff.

Murphy's area of operation is in the South Armagh area of Northern Ireland. This area is heavily Catholic and anti-British army. Murphy assumed leadership of the ongoing battle in South Armagh against the British army and he has conducted an aggressive campaign of bombings and shootings. On his farm at Bellybinaby, Murphy raises cattle and pigs, and he has made a fortune smuggling grain, cattle, and pigs to Northern Ireland. He has also gone into the oil smuggling business, allowing him to raise money for the

Provisional Irish Republican Army in South Armagh. Murphy uses his farm as a staging area both for smuggling and for military operations against the British army.

Murphy has always been a hard-liner and his relationship with the leadership of **Sinn Fein** has never been close. Murphy's forces have been more successful than their brethren in Belfast in military operations and in financial matters in South Armagh, and these successes have led to some resentment on both sides. Murphy and his compatriots were unhappy with the PIRA's 1994 cease-fire. He was a reluctant adherent to the October 10, 1997, Falcarragh Convention that approved the **Gerry Adams** and **Martin McGuinness** strategy of a moderate policy and negotiations. Some of his South Armagh supporters broke with the new policy and joined the Real IRA of **Micky McKevitt** and Bernadette Sands-McKevitt. Murphy pursued a policy of neutrality, but the disastrous bombing at Omagh on August 15, 1998, by the Real IRA hurt his prestige because he was accused of tolerating the activities of the Real IRA. Murphy also had a setback when he lost a libel case against the British newspaper *Sunday Times* for an article identifying him as an IRA terrorist leader. He lost the case on appeal in 1996 and he had to pay legal bills totaling 1 million pounds. The principle witness against him, a former IRA activist, was found murdered in January 1999.

Murphy remains the dominant Irish nationalist in the South Armagh area, but this doesn't necessarily mean that he is safe. In March 2003 members of the Real IRA targeted him for murder. Murphy is the head of the Provisional IRA's fuel and tobacco smuggling operation that produces big profits. Leaders of the Real IRA wanted to kill Murphy in revenge for the murder of Real IRA member Jo Jo O'Connor in Belfast, and at the same time take over his smuggling operations. This plot failed and the Real IRA killed another Provisional IRA member.

Suggested readings: Liam Clarke, and Kathryn Johnston, *Martin McGuinness: From Guns to Government* (Edinburgh: Mainstream Publishing, 2001); Toby Harnden, *"Bandit*

Country": The IRA and South Armagh (London: Hodder and Stoughton, 1999); John Kelly, "`Slab' Was Target of Real IRA Border Gang," *Sunday Mirror* [London] (March 16, 2003), p. 5.

Muslim Brotherhood (al-Ikhwan al-Muslimun) (Egypt)

The Muslim Brotherhood has long been the leading Islamic fundamentalist organization in Egypt. In 1928, **Hassan al-Banna,** a schoolteacher and a follower of the Sufi school of Islam, founded the Muslim Brothers in Ismaila, Egypt. His original intent was for this organization to become a leader in the anti-colonial movement against the British. From the beginning, the leadership of the Muslim Brotherhood denounced both capitalism and Marxism as failures and looked toward a revival of Islam. This involvement in politics found the Muslim Brotherhood in direct opposition to the British. During World War II, a secret organization with the Muslim Brothers, the Special Order, was formed to carry out violent attacks against the British authorities. British authorities arrested al-Banna for anti-British activities. After the war, al-Banna launched a terrorist campaign against what he considered to be enemies of Islam. On December 8, 1948, the Egyptian government banned the Muslim Brotherhood. Leadership of the Muslim Brother retaliated with the assassination of the Egyptian Prime Minister Mahmoud Fahmy el-Nokrashy Pasha on December 28, 1948. On February 12, 1949, the Egyptian secret police killed al-Banna on a Cairo street. Despite the banning of the Muslim Brotherhood and the assassination of al-Banna, the Egyptian government allowed the Muslim Brotherhood to reconstitute itself because King Farouk and his advisors wanted to use it as a buffer between the Egyptian nationalists and the Communists. Sheikh Hassan al-Hodeibi, a moderate cleric, assumed the leadership post of the Muslim Brotherhood, but his chief rival, Saleh al-Ashmawy, a radical cleric, attracted support from the more radical elements in the Muslim Brotherhood.

The leadership of the Muslim Brotherhood supported the new government of Gamal Abdel Nasser until it became apparent that he had no intention of founding an Islamic government. Both Nasser and his chief assistant, Anwar Sadat, had made contact with the Muslim Brotherhood before their seizure of power in July 1952. By the early 1950s, the Muslim Brotherhood had two million members scattered throughout the Muslim world, but most of its political strength remained in Egypt. The leadership formed a terrorist branch, the Secret Organ, to carry out assassinations against political leaders opposing its policies. Nasser's settlement in 1954 of a Suez Canal dispute caused the leaders of the Muslim Brotherhood to attempt an assassination of Nasser in Alexandria, Egypt, on October 26, 1954, but they failed. The Egyptian government arrested Hodeibi and other leaders. Several of the leaders of the Muslim Brotherhood were executed and over 4,000 were arrested and imprisoned. After the Nasser government banned the Muslim Brotherhood, both leaders and members went underground. It was at this time that the influence of **Sayyid Qutb** became the dominant philosophy in the Muslim Brotherhood. In his book, *Signposts Along the Road,* and other writings, he declared perpetual religious war (jihad) against all religions other than Islam and against the Nasser government. Qutb and other leaders of the Muslim Brotherhood were arrested, tortured, and executed in 1965.

After Nasser's death in 1970, the government of Sadat was more tolerant of the Muslim Brotherhood. Members still in prison since a crackdown in 1965–1966 were released. By 1977, the Muslim Brotherhood had been revitalized and used the government's tolerance to attack it. Leaders of the Muslim Brotherhood considered the Sadat government to be oppressive, anti-Islamic, and a puppet of the Western governments. They were particularly unhappy about Sadat's close association with the United States and his efforts to separate religion and politics. Members of another group carried out Sadat's assassination on October 6, 1981, but the membership of the Muslim Brotherhood applauded the deed.

The Muslim Brotherhood has become the major opposition to the subsequent Hosni Mubarak government. Mubarak's government has been less oppressive than Sadat's and the Muslim Brotherhood has prospered in this environment. Financial support from Saudi Arabia has allowed the Muslim Brotherhood to provide medical clinics, social welfare centers, and clubs. These mosque-based support services have been popular among the Egyptian lower middle classes. The strength of the Muslim Brotherhood is in the Egyptian professional classes—doctors, engineers, lawyers, and journalists. Recruitment of members takes place among the students in the universities. Inability of the Egyptian government to solve chronic economic problems has helped the recruitment of Muslim Brotherhood members. The success of the Muslim Brotherhood in Egypt has led to its export to other Muslim countries.

The most dynamic and deadly of the spin-offs of the Muslim Brotherhood is **Hamas**. Only after the outbreak of the Intifada in 1987 was the Muslim Brotherhood transformed into the political entity Hamas that carries out a terrorism war against Israel. At the same time that Hamas was launching its war with Israel it was also establishing schools, hospitals, mosques, and other social services in the Gaza Strip and in the West Bank. Hamas's popularity among Palestinians comes from a combination of its Islamist orientation, war against Israel, and the social services that it provides. **See also** Al-Banna, Hassan; Hamas (Haarakat al-Muqawama al-Islami) (Islamic Resistance Movement).

Suggested readings: J. Bowyer Bell, *Murders on the Nile: The World Trade Center and Global Terror* (San Francisco: Encounter Books, 2003); John L. Esposito, *The Islamic Threat: Myth or Reality?* (New York: Oxford University Press, 1992); Fereydoun Hoveyda, *The Broken Crescent: The "Threat" of Militant Islamic Fundamentalism* (Westport, CT: Praeger, 1998); Richard Mitchell,

The Society of the Muslim Brothers (London: Oxford University Press, 1966); Harold Schneider, "Fundamentalists Gain Small Voice in Egypt" *Washington Post* (December 7, 2000), p. A27.

Mustafa, Shukri Ahmed (1942–1977) (Egypt)

Shukri Mustafa was the leader of Egypt's most extreme Islamist group, the Society of Muslims. Shukri was born on June 1, 1942, in the village of Abu Khurus near Asyut, Egypt. When Mustafa was young, his father, the mayor of the village, divorced his mother. He grew up in Asyut where he received his education at Islamic schools. Always an indifferent student, he enrolled at the University of Asyut in the school of agriculture. During his college days, Shukri joined the **Muslim Brotherhood**. He was arrested during Gamal Abdel Nasser's crackdown on the Muslim Brotherhood in 1965. While in prison, Mustafa read the writings of **Sayyid Qutb**. Soon afterward, he joined the Society of Muslims, which preached complete separation from civil society. This group threatened to disintegrate after the defection of its leader, Sheikh 'Ali 'Abduh Isma'il in 1969. After six years in prison, however, Mustafa was released in October 1971, and he assumed the leadership of the Society of Muslims.

As leader, Mustafa started advancing the group's goals of separation from Egyptian society. By 1976, he was leading another group that had 2,000 members. This group, Unbelief and Migration (Takfir wal Hijara) attracted engineering and scientific students from Egyptian universities. These recruits formed communities in the Egyptian desert where harsh military discipline was imposed. Because this group rejected modern life and wanted to return to primitive Islam, they condemned both Muslims and non-Muslims that opposed them. Even after the death of Mustafa in 1997, his followers continued to carry out violent attacks on what they considered unbelievers. Later, al-Qaeda was able to recruit former members of Unbelief and

Migration. **See also** Muslim Brotherhood (al-Ikhwan al-Muslimun); Qutb, Sayyid.

Suggested readings: J. Bowyer Bell, *Murders on the Nile: The World Trade Center and Global Terror* (San Francisco: Encounter Books, 2003); Jane Corbin, *Al Qaeda: In Search of the Terror Network That Threatens the World* (New York: Thunder's Mouth Press, 2002); Wilhelm Dietl, *Holy War* (New York: Macmillan, 1984); Christina Phelps Harris, *Nationalism and Revolution in Egypt: The Role of the Muslim Brotherhood* (The Hague, The Netherlands: Mouton, 1964); Gilles Kepel, *Muslim Extremism in Egypt: The Prophet and Pharaoh* (Berkeley: University of California Press, 1986.

N

Namangani, Juma (1969–2001) (Uzbekistan)

Juma Namangani was the military leader of the radical Islamist guerrilla group **Islamic Movement of Uzbekistan** (IMU). He was born in 1969 in the village of Namangan in the Fergana Valley of Uzbekistan. His birth name was Jumaboi Ahmadzhanovitch Khojaev. In 1987, when he was 18, he was drafted into the Soviet army. His career in the Soviet army as a paratrooper was successful and he reached the rank of sergeant. Numangani was sent to Afghanistan during the Soviet-Afghan war to fight against the mujahideen. He came to respect the Afghans as fighters, and this admiration made him reexamine his Muslim roots. After leaving the army, Namangani became a follower of Tahkir Abdouhalilovitch Yuldeshev, a religious leader in Namangan, and shared his vision of an Islamic state in Uzbekistan. At first the Uzbekistan government tolerated agitation from Islamic advocates, but in 1992 it cracked down on radical Islamists. Both Namangani and Yuldeshev fled to neighboring Tajikistan, where Namangani became a guerrilla leader in the Tajik civil war on the side of the Islamic Renaissance Party (IRP). He was a successful military commander and his reputation grew to almost mythical proportions. His opposition to a cease-fire and the peace settlement in Tajikistan proved to be embarrassing to the leadership of the IRP, but the leaders were able to persuade him to accept the final settlement.

Namangani settled down to be a farmer and businessman. He purchased a large farm in the village of Hoit northeast of Garm in Tajikistan. His wife and daughter lived with him and he worked as a farmer. Later, Namangani purchased several trucks and entered the transportation business. His reputation soon attracted Islamic radicals, and they attempted to recruit him as a military leader to fight against the Uzbekistan government. After Yuldeshev visited and conversed with him in Hoit in 1997, Namangani traveled to Kabul, Afghanistan, in the summer of 1998 for further talks with Yuldeshev, **Osama bin Laden,** and representatives of the **Taliban** government. As a result of these talks, Namangani and Yuldeshev founded the Islamic Movement of Uzbekistan with the goal to overthrow the Uzbekistan government of Islam Karimov and establish an Islamic state.

Namangani returned to Tajikistan and began organizing a guerrilla army. In August 1999, Namangani's forces made a raid into Kyrgyzstan. Then, on August 25, 1999, the IMU declared a holy war (jihad) against the Uzbekistan government. From a fortified base camp in the Tavildara Valley of Tajikistan, Namangani launched a series of military operations against Uzbekistan. Between military offenses, Namangani traveled to Afghanistan where Yuldeshev, bin Laden, and the Taliban government gave him support. He was able to recruit new fighters for the IMU and find places to train them at Afghan training camps. Some of the financial aid came from bin Laden and the Taliban government, but most of the money came from IMU's growing involvement in the Afghan opium trade. These sources of funding allowed Namangani to supply his fighters with modern weapons and pay them monthly salaries of between $100 and $500.

Namangani had striking successes in his military campaigns against Uzbekistan until the American intervention into Central Asia in the aftermath of **September 11, 2001,** terrorist attacks in the United States. Although Namangani never commanded more than 2,000 troops, his offenses in 1999, 2000, and 2001 were effective guerrilla campaigns and helped destabilize the Uzbekistan government. The Uzbekistan government tried Namangani in absentia and condemned him to death, but capturing him was another matter. When pressure on the Tajikistan government was too intense, Namangani and his soldiers slipped across the border and lived in Kunduz. This sanctuary ended in the fall of 2001 when the alliance of the anti-Taliban Northern Alliance and the United States overthrew the Taliban regime. Reports surfaced that Namangani died in the fighting at Kunduz against coalition forces on November 17, 2001. He is reportedly buried near Kabul. In 2002, his wife confirmed his death in the Russian press, and his loss is a blow to the IMU. **See also** Islamic Movement of Uzbekistan (IMU).

Suggested readings: Christian Caryl, "In the Hot Zone," *Newsweek* (October 8, 2001), p. 30; Lynne O'Donnell, "Al-Qa'ida Military Strongman Killed," *Australian* (Sydney) (November 20, 2001), p. 9; David Filipov, "Battle-Tested Commander," *Boston Globe* (October 26, 2001), p. A18; Ahmed Rashid, *Jihad: The Rise of Militant Islam in Central Asia* (New Haven, CT: Yale University Press, 2002); Doug Struck, "Uzbek Taliban Chief Feared in Homeland," *Washington Post* (November 10, 2001), p. A17.

Nasrallah, Hassan (1960–) (Lebanon)

Hassan Nasrallah is the leader of **Hezbollah** (Party of God) in Lebanon. He was born in 1960 in Beirut, Lebanon. His father was a Shi'ite vegetable seller, but his family traced its descent to the prophet Muhammad. He studied at the Baalbek Theological School in the Bekka Valley. The civil war in Beirut caused him to leave and travel in 1976 to the Iraqi holy city of Najaf to study Shi'ite theology. After an expulsion from Iraq by **Saddam Hussein** in 1978, Nasrallah traveled to Iran and met the **Ayatollah Ruholla Khomeini**. Returning to Lebanon, he joined the **Amal**, a Shi'ite terrorist organization, and became a follower of the Amal leader Abbas Musawi. His area of operation was in the Bekka valley of Lebanon.

Nasrallah joined the Hezbollah soon after its founding in 1982. Musawi and Sobhi Tufeili started the Hezbollah with the blessing of Khomeini and Iran's intelligence services. Tufeili was the first leader of Hezbollah, but he was replaced as its secretary-general in 1990. Nasrallah's mentor Musawi became the new chief of Hezbollah. Nasrallah acted as the organization's military leader until an Israeli helicopter attack killed Musawi, his family, and his bodyguards on February 16, 1992. Nasrallah was on the 11-member ruling council of the Hezbollah and this council elected him as secretary-general on February 18, 1992. His main rival for leadership remained Tufeili.

Nasrallah's first action was to launch military attacks against the Israeli occupation of southern Lebanon. These attacks involved rocket attacks and later suicide bombers. Military pressure by Hezbollah led to Israel withdrawing from southern Lebanon in May 2000. This retreat made Nasrallah popular both among the Shi'ites in Lebanon and in the Arab world. He has been able to translate this popularity into a role as a national leader in

Lebanon. Nasrallah has never forgotten nor forgiven the United States for its abandonment of the Iraqi Shi'ites in the aftermath of the Persian Gulf War. His hatred of Hussein rivals his distrust of the United States. Despite his feelings toward Hussein, he opposes the 2003 military occupation of Iraq by American military forces and he has threatened operations against the Americans. But Nasrallah has hinted that he would be willing to disband Hezbollah's military wing in the event of a comprehensive Middle East peace. He has also warned about renewed military operations if the United States attempts to attack Hezbollah. At the same time, he negotiated an exchange with Israel that took place on January 30, 2004, that freed more than 400 Palestinians and allowed the return of the remains of 60 Lebanese fighters in exchange for the return of a Jewish businessman and the remains of 3 Israeli soldiers. **See also** Hezbollah (Party of God).

Suggested readings: Nicholas Blanford, "Hezbollah Chief Offers Carrot, Stick," *Christian Science Monitor* (July 31, 2003), p. 1; Hugh Dellios, "Lebanon's Guerrilla 'Hero,'" *Ottawa Citizen* (May 27, 2000), p. B1; Dan Ephron, "Israel, Hezbollah Exchange Prisoners," *Boston Globe* (January 30, 2004), p. A18; Robert Fisk, "Hezbollah's New Face," *Ottawa Citizen* (June 15, 1992), p. D13; Hala Jaber, *Hezbollah: Born with a Vengeance* (New York: Columbia University Press, 1997); Roula Khalaf, "A Guerrilla with Charm: Man in the News Sheikh Hassan Nasrallah," *Financial Times* (London) (May 27, 2000), p. 15; Neil MacFarquhar, "Hezbollah Becomes Potent Anti-U.S. Force," *New York Times* (December 24, 2002), sec. A, p. 1; Josh Meyer, "Hezbollah Vows Anew to Target Americans," *Los Angeles Times* (April 17, 2003), p. 1; Thomas O'Dwyer, "Nasrallah: Hezbollah's Ruthless Realist," *Jerusalem Post* (September 19, 1997), p. 8.

National Bolshevik Party (NBP) (Russia)

The National Bolshevik Party is one of the leading extremist parties in Russia. **Eduard Limonov,** the novelist and former associate of **Vladimir Zhirinovsky,** and **Alexander Dugin,** an extremist philosopher and political theorist, founded the National Bolshevik Party in May 1993. Both had been associated with other extremist groups, including the anti-Semitic Pamyat, but were dissatisfied with them. The alliance of Limonov and Dugin lasted until 1998 when Dugin decided to leave the party. Since then, the National Bolshevik Party has been under the exclusive control of Limonov, who suffers no opposition to his policies.

The founders of the National Bolshevik Party created the party to serve as the catalyst for a new conservative social revolution that rejects liberalism, democracy, and capitalism. Because it embraces an amalgamation of ideas from both the communist left and the fascist right, the group's only constant is a commitment for extreme change in Russian society. Leaders welcome extremists from all spectrums—anarchists, Christians, Islamists, neo-fascists, neo-Nazis, and Stalinists.

The goal of the National Bolshevik Party is to gain control of the state. Russia would then be divided into 45 districts to be governed from a center. Leadership of this center would come from the head of the National Bolshevik Party. A limited parliament would be allowed with two chambers, the Chamber of Deputies and the Chamber of Representatives. State socialism would be reintroduced, with all economic activity controlled by the state. Foreign policy would be anti-American and anti–North Atlantic Treaty Organization (NATO).

The drive for political power by the National Bolshevik Party has been restricted by its failure to gain registration from the Russian government. This lack of registration prevents the party from running a slate of candidates, but individual members can run for political office. Efforts to do so, however, have had limited success. Other members participate in marches and demonstrations, and they sometimes engage in violent and illegal activities. Other actions include boycotts of foreign goods and demonstrations against foreign companies operating in Russia.

Limonov's legal problems threatened to short-circuit his control of the National Bolshevik Party. Limonov and Sergei Aksenov, a deputy in the party, decided in early 2001 to form a paramilitary force named the National Bolshevik Army. Several members of the party began to acquire arms in March 2001. Special services police arrested these individuals. Later in March, a company of special troops arrested Limonov and the leadership of the National Bolshevik Party. They charged Limonov and his colleagues with criminal conspiracy to acquire arms. On January 31, 2003, a court found Limonov and five other party members guilty of forming an illegal armed formation and the purchase of weapons. He was sentenced to four years in prison, but he was released on June 30, 2003 after serving 25 months of his sentence. While in prison, Liminov wrote eight books and numerous articles. During his absence, the party languished without its leader. A Moscow court closed the party's newspaper *Limonov* (Russian slang for hand grenade) for inciting ethnic conflict and for advocating the violent overthrow of the Russian government.

Since his return, Limonov has revitalized the National Bolshevik Party, but he has not been able to persuade the Justice Ministry to register the NBP as a political party. This setback has not prevented the NBP from publishing a new newspaper *Generalynaya Linia* with the same editorial line as the former newspaper. Limonov's most recent tactic to destablize the Russian political system is to have his followers boycott the March 14, 2004, presidential elections. His goal is for Russia to have a weak executive and a strong parliament that would allow the BNP to play a prominent role in national politics.

See also Dugin, Alexander Gelevich; Limonov, Eduard.

Suggested readings: Nabi Abdullaev, "Limonov Set Free, Vows to Fight On," *Moscow Times* (July 1, 2003), p. 1; Maksim Glikin, "Security Forces vs. Fringe Youth Groups," *Current Digest of the Post-Soviet Press* (July 18, 2001), p. 1; NTV Mir, "Leader of the Russian National Bolsheviks Returns to Moscow after Prison Term, "BBC Worldwide Monitoring (July 1, 2003), p. 1; Shagen Ogandzhanyan, "A Party That Isn't a Party," *Current Digest of the Post-Soviet Press* (September 3, 2003), p. 1; Stephen D. Shenfield, *Russian Fascism: Traditions, Tendencies, Movement* (Armonk, NY: M. E. Sharpe, 2001).

National Front (See British National Front)

National Front (See Front National)

National Front for the Liberation of Corsica (See Front de la Liberation Nationale De la Corse) (FLNC)

National Liberation Army (See ELN Ejército de Liberación) (National Army of Liberation) (Colombia)

National Religious Party (NRP) (Mafdal) (Israel)

The National Religious Party (NRP) is one of Israel's most extreme right-wing political parties. Members of several religious Zionist groups came together in 1956 and formed the National Religious Party. The goal of the NRP was to make Israeli law consistent with Jewish religious law. Many of the followers of the new NRP were followers of Rabbi Zvi Yehuda Kook and the Greater Israel movement. Over the years the party has had three central beliefs: sanctity of the Torah, sponsorship of Greater Israel and Jewish settlements, and the refusal to recognize a Palestinian state. They have been a determined enemy of the 1993 Oslo Accords that gave the Palestinians limited autonomy in the West Bank and Gaza Strip. This hostility was also aimed Yitzhak Rabin, and his assassination was greeted with considerable satisfaction by the leadership and rank-and-file members of the NRP.

The National Religious Party has been active in an alliance with the right-wing Likud.

In 2002, the party selected right-wing ex-Israel Defense Forces (IDF) general Effie Eitam to head it. Eitam has bargained into the Likud ministry of Ariel Sharon and the party has received two cabinet posts, including the important post of Housing. The Housing agency oversees the growth of settlements on the West Bank and Gaza. Leaders of the party have made it public that the only reason that they joined the Sharon government was to continue to move away from the Oslo Accords and the idea of a Palestinian state.

The debate over the use of IDF soldiers to remove the illegal outposts in Judea and Samaria has complicated relations between the settler movement and the National Religious Party. An appeal from the Council of Jewish Settlement Rabbis for Israeli soldiers to ask for release from the army, or to refuse to carry out orders for the removal of illegal outposts, has caused Eitam to break with the council. He has rejected the idea of soldiers disobeying orders, and he has had a similar lukewarm reaction to the idea of the National Religious Party leaving the Sharon coalition over this issue.

Suggested readings: Netty C. Gross, "The New Face of the National Religious Party," *Jerusalem Post* (December 30, 2002), p. 22; Peter Hermann, "New Israeli Government Presents Unlikely Alliance," *Baltimore Sun* (February 25, 2003), p. 9A; Charles S. Liebman and Eliezer Don-Yehiya, *Religion and Politics in Israel* (Bloomington, IN: Indiana University Press, 1984); Yoram Peri (ed.), *The Assassination of Yitzhak Rabin* (Stanford, CA: Stanford University Press, 2000); Israel Shahak and Norton Mezvinsky, *Jewish Fundamentalism in Israel* (London: Pluto Books, 1999).

Naval Mechanics School (La Escuela Superior Mecánica de la Armada) (ESMA) (Argentina)

The Naval Mechanics School (ESMA) was the prison and torture camp of the Argentina generals' war on dissidents in the mid-1970s and early 1980s. Rear-Admiral Ruben Chamorro, the commander of ESMA, had close ties to the military junta that had overthrown President Isabel Perón. This prison camp was established in 1975 to hold and dispose of enemies of the Argentine government. Most of the prisoners did not survive the rigors of the camp, but those that did referred to it as a concentration camp. They considered the camp to be modeled after the Nazi "Night and Fog" system, or in Spanish, "Noche y Niebla." Those individuals that disappeared into this camp and others who never reappeared were called *desaperecidos*, or people who disappeared without a trace.

The Naval Mechanics School was particularly inhumane. Authorities picked up prisoners in Ford Falcons, thus identifying this car with terror. Each prisoner was then interrogated by torture to identify other dissidents. Prisoners that had broken under torture were used to identify and pick up new prisoners. The capturers seized personal property of those arrested. Those prisoners that survived torture were hooded, cuffed, shackled, and blindfolded except when they were given jobs or tasks. Special attention was given to pregnant women, because the babies were made available for adoption after the mother's death. When prison authorities decided to dispose of prisoners, they were loaded on trucks, taken to airplanes, and thrown alive from the air into the sea. At other camps, the prisoners were shot and buried.

Since the return to civilian government in 1983, information about the torture and deaths at the Naval Mechanics Schools has become public. Estimates have placed the number arrested and kidnapped at around 30,000. ESMA handled more than a quarter of these victims, but it was the most notorious death camp. In July 1985, nine former military commanders, including Lieutenant Alfredon Astiz, were put on trial for crimes commited by the ESMA. President Carlos Menem gave a general amnesty in October 1989, ending official charges against those who had perpetrated the crimes at these camps. The defense of those implicated in torture and murder was in the military principle of "Due Obedience." Due Obedience doctrine allows the "just following orders" defense that is contrary to the Nuremberg Trial of Nazi precedent. Regardless of the amnesty, a number of staff at the Naval Mechanics School have made public confessions of torture and murder, and they have identified many of the victims. The most significant lobby group to continue the inquiry about the missing is the Mothers of the Plaza de Mayo. These mothers of the missing and dead demonstrate and demand the Argentinean government provide information about the missing and punish the guilty. Families of victims that have been unable to find justice in Argentina have resorted to courts in other countries.

Suggested readings: Marguerite Feitlowitz, *A Lexicon of Terror: Argentina and the Legacies of Torture* (New York: Oxford University Press, 1998); Christina Lamb, "Give Me Back My Past," *Sunday Telegraph* (London) (September 17, 2000), p. 1; Patrick Marchak, *God's Assassins: State Terrorism in Argentina in the 1970s* (Montreal, Canada: McGill-Queen's University Press, 1999); Calvin Sims, "Argentines Fight Razing of a Place of Horror," *New York Times* (January 18, 1998), sec. 1, p. 15; Douglas Tweedale, "1,000 Witnesses Uncalled at Astiz Terror Trial," *Times* (London) (July 23, 1985), issue 62197; Tim Weiner and Ginger Thompson, "Wide Net in Argentine Torture Case," *New York Times* (September 11, 2000), p. A6.

Naxalite Movement (India)

The Naxalite movement is a Maoist communist insurrection against the Indian state that has lasted for more than 35 years. It began on May 25, 1967, as a guerrilla movement under the leadership of Charu Mazumdar in West Bengal in the village of Naxalbari among lower-caste peasants. A civil war developed between rural landlords and police on one side and a mass movement of landless peasants and laborers on the other. Atrocities have been committed on both sides. Naxalites targeted landlords and rural police for assassination. Police retaliated with repressive tactics and mass arrests. By 1977, a newspaper reporter for *The Washington Post* reported that the Indian government had arrested more than 1,000 Naxalites and none of them was ever brought to trial.

The Naxalite movement has changed over time. Soon after the uprising, Indian adherents of Mao Tse-tung, the Chinese Communist leader, and his revolutionary theories began organizing the discontented peasants and laborers into a mass movement. On April 22, 1969, the Naxalites organized into a political party, the Communist Party of India (Marxist-Leninist) (CPI-ML) to promote the revolution. Mazumdar was elected secretary of the Central Organizing Committee. The Indian government outlawed this party, and the Naxalites went underground. In July 1972, Mazumdar was captured, and he died in captivity on July 28, 1972. A leadership crisis ensued after his capture. Because the Naxalites no longer had a centralized organization, the movement became decentralized with each part forced to have its own leaders and strategies. In July 1974, Subrata Dutt (also called Jaukar) became the leader of the CPI-ML, but he was killed in November 1975. The movement flourished in India's most depressed rural areas, especially in the state of Bihar.

The most successful group in the Naxalite movement has been the People's War Group (PWG). It was formed in the late 1970s under the leadership of Kondapalli Seetharamaik. Most of the PWG's earliest operations were in the rural areas of the central and southeastern state of Andhra Pradesh. Later the PWG expanded its area of operations to other Indian states. At the time of expansion the People's War Group allied with the CPI-ML and formed the CPI-ML (People's War).

Other Naxalite groups have been active. Other important Naxalite groups have been the CPI-ML (Party Unity) and the Maoist Communist Centre (MCC). The impoverished state of Bihar has become the main battleground for these groups. In August 1998, the CPI-ML (People's War) and the CPI-ML (Party Unity) united their forces in Andhra Pradesh and Bihar to fight the common enemy. It had taken nearly five years of negotiations before these two groups agreed to unite. This marriage of competing groups has been rocky.

Naxalite activities continue to plague the states of Andhra Pradesh, Bihar, and Jharkhand. Indian state police have conducted extensive operations in these states and have arrested several hundreds of suspects. Despite these operations, Naxalite violence has not abated. Its most notable victim was Madhava Reddy, the state minister for Andhra Pradesh and a leading critic of the Naxalites, who was assassinated in March 2000. In 2002, Naxalites in Bihar killed 117 people in comparison with 111 people in 2001. More ominous to the Indian authorities is the increasing demand of the Naxalite movement to establish a separate state from India in Bihar.

Suggested readings: Samarpita Chakravorty, "Destined to Stay a Blot on Democracy," *Statesman* (India) (March 2, 2000), p. 1; Pamela Constable, "Violent Extremes," *Washington Post* (May 1, 1999), p. A9; Dipak Mishra, "Naxalite Violence on the Rise: Report," *Economic Times* (India) (February 14, 2003), p. 1; Amarnath K. Menon, "Striking on the Run," *India Today* (March 20, 2000), p. 36; Surnit Mitra, "West Bengal: A Deeper Shade of Red," *India Today* (July 22, 2002), p. 36; Jairam Ramesh, "Why Bihar Is Aflame," *India Today* (April 12, 1999), p. 44; Lewis M. Simons, "Rebels in India Forswear Violence for Time Being," *Washington Post* (June 10, 1977), p. A18.; Stanley Theodore, "Bizarre War, Cold Tactics," *Statesman* (India) (May 10, 2000), p. 1.

Ne Win (1911–2002) (Myanmar)

Ne Win was the president and former dictator of Myanmar. He was born on May 24, 1911, in Paungdale, in central Burma. His birth name was Shu Maung (Apple of One's Eye). His father was a district revenue surveyor. He attended Rangoon University, but he left school to become a postal clerk. Ne Win then joined the Burmese nationalist Our Burma Association (Dobama Asiayone). Leaders of this movement, Aung San and U Nu, wanted independence from the colonial empire of Great Britain. Ne Win was an emerging leader in the Our Burma Association so he was sent in 1940 to Japan for military training. It was at this name that he changed his name to Ne Win (Brilliant as the

Sun). While in Japan, Ne Win was appointed commander in the Japanese-sponsored Burma National Army. He also served as an aide and advisor to Aung San. Shortly after the Japanese army invaded Burma in December 1941, Ne Win returned to Burma. Ne Win worked for three years with the Japanese, and he was appointed commander–in chief of the Burmese army in August 1943. By the end of 1943, he had become convinced that the Japanese wanted to replace the British as the colonial masters of Burma. His response was to launch guerrilla warfare against the Japanese army beginning in December 1944.

After the war, Ne Win controlled the military power behind the two Burmese political leaders Aung San and U Nu. After the assassination of Aung San in 1947, Ne Win became closer to U Nu as his deputy and defense minister. In 1948, Burma received its independence from Great Britain, and Burmese politics was complicated by the threat of civil war. Ne Win was a loyal supporter of U Nu until 1958 when he deposed him. After serving as prime minister in an interim military administration, Ne Win led a military coup in 1962.

Ne Win was the military dictator of Burma until 1988. His goal was to build a monolithic system of government under what he called the "Burmese Way of Socialism." Ne Win attempted to build a system of government under the Socialist Programme Party that combined nationalism, Buddhism, and Marxism. To accomplish this task, he closed Burma to outsiders, and his refusal to open the country to the rest of the world caused severe economic problems during his dictatorship. His other preoccupation was quelling the various ethnic separatists movements, from the Karens Separatists to the Mons. Ne Win was more successful in crushing political opposition than he was in defeating the separatists. His behavior became more erratic and superstitious. Ne Win finally resigned in July 1988, shortly before Burma was renamed Myanmar.

Even after his resignation Ne Win was influential in Burmese politics. He had left office estimated worth of around $4 billion.

He lived on an estate and became increasingly absorbed in Buddhist studies. In 2001, he was accused of sponsoring a military coup by members of his family and was placed under house arrest by the military junta. He died in Rangoon on December 5, 2002.

Suggested readings: Derek Davies, "General Ne Win: Ruthless Ruler of Burma over Three Baleful Decades," *Independent* (London) (December 6, 2002), p. 22; Richard S. Ehrlich, "Ne Win's Legacy: Burma in Shambles," *Washington Times* (December 21, 2002), p. A8; Christina Fink, *Living Silence: Burma Under Military Rule* (Bangkok, Thailand: White Lotus, 2001); Martin Smith, *Burma: Insurgency and the Politics of Ethnicity*, rev. ed. (Dhaka, Bangladesh: University Press, 1999); Martin Smith, "General Ne Win: Burmese Military Strongman Whose Increasingly Obtuse Dictatorship Reduced His Country to Poverty," *Guardian* (London) (December 6, 2002), p. 26.

Negri, Antonio (1933–) (Italy)

Antonio Negri is Italy's leading postmodern Marxist philosopher whose revolutionary ideas were adopted by the **Red Brigades**. He was born in 1933 in Padua, Italy. Negri was always a brilliant student and he entered the University of Padua. After earning a doctorate degree in philosophy in 1955, he became the assistant to the university rector. In the years 1957–1958 Negri studied at the Benedetto Croce Institute for Historical Studies in Naples. Then in 1959, he obtained a professorship in Philosophy of Law at the University of Padua. Negri remained in this position until 1967 when he was awarded the professorship in Doctrine of the State also at the University of Padua. During these years, Negri helped make the Institute for Political Sciences an international center for radical thought.

Negri had become one of Italy's leading Marxist thinkers. Despite his growing involvement in Marxist studies, Negri remained a staunch Catholic until the late 1950s, when the conservative politics of Pope Pius XII alienated him from the church. His interest in Marxism led him to join the Italian Communist Party (Partito Comunista Italiano, or PCI) in 1955, but he soon left the

PCI because it was too conservative for him. Negri then moved to the Italian Socialist Party, serving as a municipal councilman for Padua in 1959. He was also active in the Socialist Party journal *Il Progresso Veneto* from 1959 to 1963. His writings in this journal attacked working class unions and left wing parties for their lack of revolutionary zeal. Negri also became close to the noted Italian radical Marxist Raniero Panzieri. They would have a parting of the ways over the role of the Italian working class in the projected revolution shortly before Panzieri's untimely death in October 1964.

Negri's writings made him the spokesperson for the workers autonomy movement. His writings in the *Workers' Power* (*Potere Operaio*) attracted both workers in northern Italy and university students. Negri declared war on the capitalist system, seeking to have it destroyed. While Negri did not recommend the use of terror, he never argued against it, maintaining that it was one of several ways to promote the workers revolution against the state. Among the many worker and student groups that formed in the years 1967–1969 was the Antonomia Operaio (Workers' Autonomy). This group was in the middle of the agitation that led to the creation of radical leftist revolutionary terrorist groups such as Red Brigades and **Lotta Continua** (Struggle Continues). Negri followed the exploits of the Red Brigades in the 1970s only occasionally criticizing it for its tactics but not for its ultimate goal of overthrowing the Italian state.

Negri's sponsorship of Marxist revolution ideology attracted the attention of Italian authorities and led to criminal action against him. Police used the rioting around the University of Padua to lodge charges against him of inciting to riot in March 1977. Eventually he was cleared of this charge, but not before he spent from November 1977 to June 1978 in Paris, France, teaching at the École Normale Supérieure. In April 1979, Negri returned to Milan just in time to be arrested on April 7, 1979, charged in the complicity of the Red Brigades's killing of Aldo Moro, the Italian Christian Democrat politician and former prime minister. He was accused of being the secret brains behind the Red Brigades, because many members of the Red Brigades had formerly belonged to the Potere Operaio.

Negri spent 1979 to 1983 in preventative detention awaiting trial. While in prison in 1979, Negri's most famous work, *Marx Beyond Marx,* appeared in print. This work marked Negri's ascendancy into the forefront of the modern interpreters of the revolutionary theories of Karl Marx. Negri remained in prison until the summer of 1983 when the Italian Radical Party ran him as a candidate for the Italian Parliament. After winning a seat, Negri had parliamentary immunity until a September 1983 vote in the Italian parliament withdrew his immunity. Negri aware of the impending vote fled Italy and return to Paris where he continued to teach until he decided to return to Italy in 1997. In the meantime, on June 13, 1984, Negri received a 30-year prison sentence that was overturned by another court. Appeal after appeal ended up with Negri's sentence of 30 years confirmed.

Negri spent the next six years in the Italian prison before his release in April 2003. While in prison, Negri continued to write books and articles on his interpretations of Marxist theory. His fame as the postmodern interpreter of Marxism continued to grow. An international movement to free Negri appeared soon after his 1997 imprisonment that culminated in his April 2003 release.

Suggested readings: Katharine Ainger, "Great Thinkers of Our Time—Antonio Negri," *New Statesman* (July 14, 2003), p. 1; Richard Drake, *The Revolutionary Mystique and Terrorism in Contemporary Italy* (Bloomington, IN: Indiana University Press, 1989); George Katsiaficas, *The Subversion of Politics: European Autonomous Social Movements and the Decolonization of Everyday Life* (Atlantic Highlands, NJ: Humanities Press International, 1997); Conor McCarthy, "The Blinding Rhetoric of Rights," *Irish Times* [Dublin] (May 17, 2003); Antonio Negri, *Marx Beyond Marx: Lessons on the Grundrisse* (South Hadley, MA: Bergin & Garvey Publishers, 1984).

New Order, The (L'Ordine Nuovo) (ON) (Italy)

The New Order has been one of the most militant of Italian right-wing extremist groups. Many of its members are former supporters of the neo-fascist **Italian Social Movement** (MSI). They left the MSI because they found it too moderate politically. German Nazism appealed to them more than Mussolini's Fascism. Pino Rauti formed the New Order in 1956 ostensibly to study Fascism and National Socialism, but it soon became more than a study group. Members of the ON were attracted to the philosophy of Italian philosopher **Julius Evola**. Evola rejected both Marxism-Leninism and Western capitalism. In the place of these ideologies, he advocated an aristocratic elitism that would lead easily to a neo-fascist society.

From its beginning, the New Order avoided national politics and turned to direct action. Summer camps were established to train young recruits and to indoctrinate them. Underground cells were established throughout Italy to carry out terrorist activities. A relationship was also developed with the Italian military intelligence in a alliance against Italian leftists. Because of its neo-fascist orientation, the leaders of the New Order formed alliances with foreign neo-Nazi groups. A Rome court sentenced 30 members of the New Order to various prison terms on November 21, 1973, for reconstituting the banned Fascist Party. New Order members in this case later assassinated the judge, Vittorio Occorsio, in July 1976. Throughout the 1970s and early 1980s, members of the New Order engaged in terrorist acts. Its chief rival among right-wing terrorism groups was Stefano Delle Chiaie's National Vanguard (Avanguardia Nazionale). Both groups engaged in disinformation campaigns by blaming their terrorist acts on leftist groups, including the **Red Brigades**. Only after investigations in the early 1980s that proved that the New Order had participated in terrorist incidents with the collusion of Italian intelligence services did the group whither away. **See also** Evola, Julius Cesare Andrea; Italian

Social Movement (Movimento Sociale Italiano) (MSI); Red Brigades.

Suggested readings: Franco Ferraresi, *Threats to Democracy: The Radical Right in Italy After the War* (Princeton, NJ: Princeton University Press, 1996); Leonard B. Weinberg, *After Mussolini: Italian Neo-Fascism and the Nature of Fascism* (Washington, DC: University Press of America, 1979); Leonard B. Weinberg and William Lee Eubank, *The Rise and Fall of Italian Terrorism* (Boulder, CO: Westview Press, 1987); Philip Willan, *Puppetmasters: The Political Use of Terrorism in Italy* (London: Constable, 1991.

New Peoples Army (NPA) (Philippines)

The New Peoples Army (NPA) is a Maoist communist insurgency movement that has been waging an armed struggle against the Philippine state since early 1969. José María Sison, the former head of the youth movement of the Communist Party of the Philippines (CPP), and 11 supporters founded the NPA on December 26, 1968. This is the official date, but the first meeting of the NPA was on January 3, 1969. Sison and the other leaders of the NPA had earlier broken away from the established Communist Party of the Philippines. Sison was the acknowledge leader of the NPA, but operations were run by the group's Central Committee. These leaders intended the NPA to serve as the military wing of a new Maoist mass movement. Lacking a military force, Sison concluded a military alliance with one of the leaders of the Communist agrarian reform HUK rebellion in Luzon. This leader, Bernabe Buscayno (his codename was Commander Dante), became the military commander of the NPA. The Hukbalahap (HUK) guerrilla movement had been in existence since World War II, but the movement was failing until the appearance of the NPA.

Starting out with a force of only 50 fighters and a limited number of weapons, the NPA developed an army of nearly 32,000 at its peak of strength in 1985. Sison was a devoted follower of the military strategy of Mao Tse-tung, the Chinese Communist leader. This strategy depended on forming disciplined guerrilla forces, auxiliaries in the civilian population for information and material support, and an underground political organization. The NPA built all three, but it lacked the support in the countryside to move to the fourth requirement of success: a regular army able to defeat the Philippine army in the field. NPA forces were able to win local victories over the Philippine army, but they were never able to garner enough fighters or civilian support to form a regular army. What success the NPA had was the result of the failure of the Philippine state to raise the standard of living of its rural inhabitants. Three American observers noted in a 1986 *Newsweek* article that "for every armed clash, NPA operatives are now pulling off three political operations—collecting taxes, holding trials or staging their own brand of teach-ins." NPA's successes were notable enough that they attracted the attention of American authorities. U.S. aid in the form of military advisors and supplies have been made available to the Philippine army since the 1970s.

The growth of the NPA fluctuated according to the strength of the Philippine government. After a slow start, widespread opposition to the regime of President Ferdinand Marcos in the 1970s and 1980s allowed the NPA the opportunity to build a large guerrilla force to fight his government. Leadership of the NPA was willing to assist anti-Marcos agitation by staging terrorist acts, such as the attack on Marcos's liberal opposition at Manila's Miranda Plaza on August 21, 1971. A further stimulus to NPA's growth was the assassination of opposition leader Benigno Aquino in August 1983. Philippine intellectuals and peasants joined the NPA to fight the Marcos regime. A serious setback to the NEP was the arrest of Sison by Philippine authorities on November 8, 1977. Rodolfo Salas, a protégé of Sison, succeeded Sison as head of the NEP. Membership on the Central Committee constantly changed because of arrests and deaths. New leaders emerged to continue the struggle. By December 1985, reporters from *Maclean's*

Jailed New Peoples Army leader Amado Payot talks inside the Davao City jail, located in southern Philippines, February 20, 1999. The military said the rebels holding hostage Brigadier General Victor Obillo and Captain Eduardo Montealto asked for the release of Payot in exchange for the two military officials. Payot was on trial for the alleged murder of 19 persons. (AP Photo)

claimed that NPA leaders controlled a full-time guerrilla force of 12,000, with another 20,000 reserves operating in 58 of the country's 73 provinces. Sources from the Philippine army confirmed that the NPA had a military force exceeding 28,000.

Political blunders and the collapse of the Marcos regime severely damaged the New Peoples Army. Leadership of the NPA concluded a political alliance with the opposition to the Marcos government, but its policy to boycott the 1985 election rebounded to its discredit when a popular revolution overthrew Marcos. This failure in strategy led to

the resignation of Salas as head of the NPA. It also left the NPA facing the popular government of President Corazon Aquino. A temporary truce between the Aquino government and the NPA was negotiated in November 1986, but it ended in January 1987 with both sides blaming each other. In August 1987, the Central Committee reaffirmed its commitment to revolutionary struggle and launched a guerrilla war against the Aquino regime. At the same time, the NPA began a land reform policy of distributing land to landless peasants in various provinces. These lands had been confiscated from existing landholders, some of whom had been supporters of Marcos. Those landlords opposing the transfers were assassinated.

The New Peoples Army continued to be a threat to the Philippine state in the 1990s. Its strategy was to conduct a guerrilla war using the tactic of fighting only on its own terms and only when it had superior force. Whole areas in remote rural areas were under control of the NPA. Efforts by the Philippine army to overcome the NPA were sporadic. Every three or four months, the Philippine army would launch sweeps into NPA areas of operation, but these sweeps rarely found NPA units.

The leadership of the New Peoples Army started looking for allies. After a hiatus of several years during which the Philippine government attempted to conclude an amnesty, the leadership of the NPA resumed its hit-and-run guerrilla tactics in late 2002. Among the victims of this new offensive were a governor, a congressman, mayors, judges, and police chiefs. The arrival of American military advisors caused the NPA's leadership to seek a military alliance with the Abu Sayyaf and the **Moro Islamic Liberation Front** (MILF). This alliance between Islamist Muslims and hard-line communists is a tactical one and does not indicate an acceptance of the other's viewpoint. **See also** Abu Sayyaf Group (Bearer of the Sword) (ASG); Alex Boncayao Brigade; Moro Islamic Liberation Front (MILF).

Suggested readings: Cameron W. Barr, "Philippines' Communists, Losing Enemies, Keep the Faith," *Christian Science Monitor* (March 21, 1995), p. 7; William Branigan, "In Philippines, Communist Party Slowly Self-Destructs," *Washington Post* (January 15, 1993), p. A30; Angus Deming, Richard Vokey, and John Walcott, "Targeting the NPA," *Newsweek* (February 17, 1986), p. 20; Ann Finlayson, Marci McDonald, and Lin Neumann, "A Growing Fury on the Left," *Maclean's* (December 16, 1985), p. 26; Gregg R. Jones, *Red Revolution: Inside the Philippine Guerrilla Movement* (Boulder, CO: Westview Press, 1989; Melinga Liu, "Inside the Rebel Ranks," *Newsweek* (April 4, 1988), p. 28; Anastasia Stanmeyer and Antonio Lopez, "Final Showdown Ahead?" *Asiaweek* (August 13, 1999), p. 26.

Nidal, Abu (1937–2002) (Palestine)

Abu Nidal is the militant leader of the terrorist group **Abu Nidal Organization** (ANO). He was born in May 1937 in Jaffa, Palestine, under the name Sabri al-Banna. His father was elderly when he married a young Alawite Shi'ite woman. His family was wealthy and owned an orange grove plantation in Jaffa, but the family lost its wealth in the aftermath of the 1948 Arab-Israeli War. He was raised in Nablus in the West Bank, but he dropped out of school after the third grade. Nidal survived by working on a number of menial jobs, including a job as an electrician's assistant in Amman, Jordan. In 1955, he joined Jordan's Baath Party. After the Baath Party ran afoul of Jordanian authorities in 1957, Nidal moved in 1958 to Riyadh, Saudi Arabia. He built up an electrical and house painting business in Riyadh. His interest in politics continued and he formed the Palestine Secret Organization. In the mid-1960s, Nidal joined **al-Fatah** and his political activities led Saudi authorities to expel him from Saudi Arabia in 1967. He moved back Amman, Jordan, and established a new business there. His trading company, Impex, served both as both a legitimate business and a front for his al-Fatah connections. About this time he adopted the name Abu Nidal (Father of the Revolution) as his war name.

Nidal's activities in al-Fatah earned him various promotions. Leaders of al-Fatah appreciated his organizational skills and dedication to the Palestinian cause. His friendship with **Salah Khalaf**, one of the founders of al-Fatah, helped in his advancement. By 1969, he had become a member of al-Fatah's Revolutionary Council. After briefly serving as al-Fatah's representative in Sudan, he was assigned in 1970 to Baghdad, Iraq. Despite his promotions, Nidal began questioning the policies of **Yasser Arafat** and al-Fatah. Leaders in al-Fatah tried to retain him for the PLO, but he was increasingly belligerent toward them. In March–April 1972, he traveled to China and North Korea and his reception there was positive.

In 1973, Nidal broke with the Palestine Liberation Organization (PLO) and Arafat over a moratorium on terrorism. Nidal had already been found to be unreliable and probably had been recruited by Iraqi intelligence to work with them. He was also unhappy about Syrian intervention in Lebanon. On October 26, 1973, al-Fatah expelled him and sentenced him to death in absentia for a plot to kill a PLO leader. Nidal then created another group on November 22, 1974, that he named al-Fatah—Revolutionary Council and moved it to Iraq. Soon this group became more famous as the Abu Nidal Organization (ANO).

Nidal earned a reputation for ruthlessness. He declared open war on Arafat and the PLO. Over the years, his agents have killed more than a dozen PLO officials. Using Iraq as a safe base camp, Nidal carried out a series of terrorist acts in the 1970s and 1980s. In November 1983, **Saddam Hussein** expelled Nidal from Iraq in an attempt to distance himself from the charge that he was sponsoring terrorism. Hussein needed help from the West in his war with Iran. Nidal transferred his operations to Syria and continued conducting terrorist acts. In 1987, Syria reconsidered his status and expelled Nidal. Nidal then moved his operations to Libya. He established a base camp outside of Tripoli and trained operatives for the Abu Nidal Organization. Besides Israeli and PLO targets, Abu Nidal began operations against Saudi Arabia and its regime. **Muammar Qaddafi** supported Nidal until bad publicity about Nidal's purge of the ANO caused him to abandon Nidal. Alex Blair in a 1998 article in *The Scotsman* estimated that Nidal killed 150 out of his 800 followers in a purge to rid the ANO of infiltrators and spies. Nidal moved briefly to Egypt, but Egyptian authorities arrested him.

In December 1998, Nidal relocated to Iraq. He took with him less than 300 fighters. Pressure from Western and Middle Eastern countries resulted in a reduction in terrorist opportunities for Nidal. His followers have a presence in the Bekka Valley in Lebanon, but there are far fewer than in the 1970s and 1980s. Nidal also maintained a much lower profile than in the past. Unconfirmed reports suggested that Nidal was in ill heath with a heart condition or skin cancer. Nidal retained a big reputation in terrorist circles, but nothing of significance came out of the Abu Nidal Organization since 1994.

Even in death Nidal is controversial. First reports came from Baghdad that he had committed suicide on August 14, 2002. He was living in a villa in al-Masbah, a wealthy neighborhood of Baghdad, and his presence was known to Iraqi police. Then, news surfaced that agents of the Iraqi intelligence service, the Mukhabarat, had attempted to arrest Nidal, and in the attempt he had been shot or had shot himself to evade arrest. Nidal was rushed to a nearby hospital, where he died. **See also** Abu Nidal Organization (ANO); Arafat, Yasser; Palestine Liberation Organization (PLO).

Suggested readings: Alex Blair, "Mystery Still Surrounding Abu Nidal, Once the World's Deadliest Terrorist," *Scotsman* (Edinburgh) (August 27, 1998), p. 13; Marie Colvin and Sonya Mura, "Executed," *Sunday Times* (London) (August 25, 2002), p. 13; Con Coughlin, "He Who Lives by Terrorism," *Sunday Telegraph* (London) (August 25, 2002), p. 19; Ann LoLordo, "Once-Feared Terrorist Seen as 'Has-Been,'" *Sun* (Baltimore) (August 30, 1998), p. 1A; Yossi Melman, *The Master Terrorist: The True Story behind Abu Nidal* (New York: Adama Books, 1986); James Risen, "A Much-Shunned Terrorist Is Said to Find Haven in Iraq," *New York Times* (January 27, 1999), p. A1; Patrick Seale, *Abu Nidal: A Gun for Hire* (New York: Random House, 1992).

Northern League (Lega Nord) (Italy)

The Northern League is an extremist Italian political party that first advocated the separation of northern Italy from the Italian state and then adopted an anti-immigration platform. Two friends, **Umberto Bossi** and Roberto Maroni, believed in the early 1980s that the Lombardy region of northern Italy was being exploited by Rome politicians and the less prosperous southern Italy. They were both natives of Varese, near Milan. Lombardy was in the midst of an economic expansion that was attracting the migration of workers from southern Italy in the early 1980s. High taxation and political corruption among Italian politicians was causing disquiet in northern Italy. Bossi began campaigning for political separation by forming the Lombard League (Lega Lombard) in 1982. At the time it was one of several separatist groups—Venetian League and Union Valdotaine among others—but Bossi's attacks on the Italian state soon attracted the attention of the alienated voters of northern Italy. Bossi used his charismatic personality and personal contacts to expand the political base of the Lombard League, but political progress was slow in both the 1983 and 1985 elections.

The first breakthrough for the Lombard League was in 1987. Electoral successes resulted in a seat in Parliament and a Senate seat. Bossi continued his attacks on political corruption and high taxation, but a new facet of his campaign was an anti-immigrant stance. Slowly the Italian national media began to pay attention to the new movement. This publicity and the prospect of political success allowed Bossi to conclude political alliances with other Northern Italian separatist movements and form the Northern League in 1990.

Bossi had been the dominant leader of the Lombard League and this carried over to the Northern League. He moved the headquarters of the Northern League to Milan in 1992. Much of the Northern League's appeal was to the Italian voters alienated from the political process. His authoritarian leadership style caused elements in the other separatist parties to leave them. These defections did not prevent Bossi from utilizing the newfound electoral clout to form an alliance with Silvio Berlusconi, the wealthiest man in Italy due to his media empire and an emerging political figure. Bossi believed that the Northern League had to make a political al-

liance with Berlusconi or else suffer political defeat at the next election. Berlusconi had also concluded a political alliance with **Gianfranco Fini** and the National Alliance, an offshoot of the neo-fascist **Italian Social Movement** (MSI). These political alliances allowed Berlusconi to win the March 1994 national election under the banner of the Pole of Liberty. To participate in this alliance Bossi had to reorient the Northern League away from attacks on southern Italy to target immigration from the Third World. To the surprise of political analysts, the Northern League won 117 seats in the Chamber of Deputies and 60 seats in the Senate.

Electoral success presented new problems for the leadership of the Northern League. The alliance with Berlusconi and the neo-fascist National Alliance of Gianfranco Fini was unpopular with the militant wing of the Northern League. Bossi made it plain at a post-election conference that he would only allow the Northern League to participate in the new Berlusconi government as a way to continue the battle for federalism and to control Berlusconi. Soon after entering the coalition, infighting began between Berlusconi's Italian Force (Forza Italia) and the Northern League. Bossi's dissatisfaction led him to leave the government in December 1994. His defection caused the Berlusconi government to fall on December 22, 1995. See also Bossi, Umberto; Fini, Gianfranco.

Suggested readings: Elizabeth Neuffer, "Italy's Angry North Dreams of Breakup," *Boston Globe* (October 25, 1997), p. A1; Francis X. Rocca, "Out of Their League," *American Spectator* (March 1999), p. 1; Peter Semier, "A Sword Over Europe," *New Statesman* (May 14, 2001), p. 1; Damian Tambini, *Nationalism in Italian Politics: The Stories of the Northern League, 1980–2000* (London: Routledge, 2001); Ed Vulliamy, "Northern League Goes from Hard to Soft as It Finds New Supporters," *Guardian* (London) (January 30, 1993), p. 11.

O

Ocalan, Abdullah (Apo) (1948–) (Turkey)
Abdullah (Apo) Ocalan was the leader of the
Kurdistan Worker's Party (Partiya Karkaren
Kurdistan, or PKK) until his capture by the
Turkish government. Even Ocalan is uncertain about his date of birth or the year stating on several occasions that he was born in
either 1946 or 1947. Best evidence suggests
that he was born on April 4, 1948, but at
least one source claims that it was April 4,
1949. His parents were poor Kurdish farmers living in the village of Omerli in Urfa
Province of Eastern Turkey. Ocalan was the
eldest of seven children. His early education
was in local schools where he showed a religious aptitude. During the early 1960s,
Ocalan worked in temporary jobs in the cot-
ton fields around Adana. In 1966, he traveled
to Ankara, Turkey's capital, to take his university entrance examinations. His goal was
to win admittance to the Turkish War Academy and pursue a military career. After failing to gain admittance to the Turkish War
Academy, Ocalan entered Ankara University.
While there he studied political science and
economics, and, in the process, he replaced
his early Muslim beliefs with Marxism. His
involvement in the student politics led to his
imprisonment in 1970 for participation in an
illegal student demonstration. Ocalan also at
this time was converted to Kurdish nationalism. He was also instrumental in the formation of the student organization Ankara
Higher Education Association (AYOD) in
1974. Later, the membership of the AYOD
constituted the main body of the Kurdistan
Worker's Party.

Ocalan and associates formed the
Kurdistan Worker's Party to serve as the vanguard for the armed struggle for a Kurdish
state. Before Ocalan organized the PKK, he
married Kesire Yildirim, a leftist leader in the
AYOD. Together they served as two of the
original seven members of the Central Committee of the PKK when it was formed in
1978. From the beginning, Ocalan dominated the PKK. Ocalan tolerated no opposition to his policies and several times
dissidents were executed on his orders. His
intolerance to opposing views caused his wife
to flee to Sweden in 1987 after a divorce.

Ocalan directed the Kurdistan Worker's
Party's operations against Turkey from
Damacus, Syria, during most of the 1980s
and the 1990s. He traveled considerably,
sometimes to Kurdish areas in southeastern
Turkey. Besides directing guerrilla operations
in Turkey, Ocalan wrote several books justifying his leadership of the PKK: *Popular War
and the Guerrilla in Kurdistan* (1991), *12th
September Fascism and the PKK Rebellion*
(1992), and *Kurdish Reality since the 19th*

Abdullah Ocalan, leader of the Kurdistan Worker's Party (PKK), looks toward Turkish prosecutors May 31, 1999, in a courtroom at Imrali Prison Island in northwestern Turkey. In June 1999, the court sentenced Ocalan to death for treason and terrorism, but in October 2002 his sentence was commuted to life imprisonment in accordance with a new Turkish law that abolished capital punishment in peacetime. (AP Photo/Mustafa Abadan, Anatolia/File)

Century and the PKK Movement (1994). His activities in Turkey caused the Turkish government to declare him enemy number one. Several times Ocalan had to escape assassination attempts from Turkish security forces and other Kurdish groups.

Ocalan's career ended in February 1999. The Turkish government had instituted an international manhunt to find Ocalan. He had no place to go except sanctuary in the Greek ambassador's compound in Nairobi, Kenya. Finally, the Kenyan government intervened and delivered him to the Turkish government. In June 1999, a Turkish court sentenced him to death for treason and terrorism. This sentence became controversial, especially since Turkey wanted to join the European Union, whose member states have no capital punishment. In October 2002, the Ankara State Security Court followed a new Turkish law that abolished capital punishment in peacetime and commuted Ocalan's sentence to life imprisonment without chance of an amnesty or parole. Ocalan remains imprisoned in solitary confinement at Imrali Prison Island in northwestern Turkey. His imprisonment did not prevent Ocalan from appealing his capture and trial to the European Court for Human Rights. In a May 2003 decision, this court ruled that Turkish authorities had violated Ocalan's right to a fair trial. **See also** Kurdistan Worker's Party (Partiya Karkaren Kurdistan) (PKK).

Suggested readings: Mark Dennis and Sam Seibert, "A Kurdish Inferno," *Newsweek* (March 1, 1999), p. 12; Robert Fisk, "Psychopathic Killer Who Is Great Hope of a Nation," *Independent* (London) (February 17, 1999), p. 3; Michel M. Gunter, *The Kurds and the Future of Turkey* (New York: St. Martin's Press, 1997); Florian Hauswiesner, "What Is the Legal Fight against Terrorism?: The Case of Ocalan v. Turkey Decided by the European Court for Human Rights," *International Enforcement Law Reporter*, 19, no. 6 (June 2003), p. 1; Paul White, *Primitive Rebels or Revolutionary Modernizers? The Kurdish National Movement in Turkey* (London: Zed Books, 2000).

Omar, Mohammed (1959–) (Afghanistan)

Mohammed Omar is the founder and the leader of the **Taliban** movement in Afghanistan. He was born in 1959 into a poor Pashtun family in the small village of Nodeh (Noudi), near Kandahar, Afghanistan. His father was a landless peasant of the Pashtun Hotak tribe of the Ghilzia branch of Pashtuns and his death left Omar to be brought up by his relatives. For a time, he and his family lived in Tarinkot in Urozgan province. Omar studied at an Islamic school in Kandahar, but he never graduated. After leaving school, he opened a religious school in Singhesar, a village near Kandahar. In the 1980s, Omar joined the mujahideen to fight against the Soviet forces in the Afghan War. Serving in the ranks of Younis Khalis' brigade of the Islamic Party (Hizb e Islami), Omar suffered four wounds in the fighting, including a shrapnel wound that caused the loss of his right eye. This wound increased his influence with the Afghan Islamists because it proved that he had suffered for the Muslim cause. After the war, Omar returned

to his religious studies. He entered Afghan politics soon after he had a religious dream to avenge the rapes of two young women by troops of a former mujahideen commander. He gathered a group of religious students (talibs) in the spring of 1994 and they hanged one of the rapists from the barrel of a tank. Omar then began serving as an advisor to Pashtuns in distress. Pakistan authorities noted his growing popularity and decided to give military aid to Omar and his Taliban forces. Saudi intelligence also gave Omar financial support. A council of religious leaders at Kandahar in March 1996 selected him to become the leader of the Taliban by proclaiming him the Commander of the Faithful (Amir-ul-Mumineen). On April 4, 1996, Omar appeared with the Cloak of the Prophet Muhammad and proclaimed a jihad (holy war) against the Afghanistan government.

Using this support, Omar and his Taliban forces were strong enough militarily in 1996 to seize Kabul and control most of Afghanistan. Omar was uncomfortable as a leader and he remained in seclusion in Kandahar while his Taliban forces fought and won battles. During his five years in power, he rarely traveled outside of Kandahar and only twice briefly visited Kabul. Because of his shyness, he has remained a poor public speaker and has never has allowed himself to be photographed. His knowledge of the world is limited because he refused to talk to foreigners. All contact with Omar during his control of the Taliban was through a personal secretary, Mullah Wakil Ahmad. He is tall for an Afghan standing at six feet four inches, and his strength as a leader is because of his piety rather his political acumen. He married three women and has five sons and one daughter. Despite his apparent popularity, the opposition to Omar rule attempted to assassinate him on August 24, 1999, by exploding a bomb that killed 10 people and wounded many others in Kandahar.

Omar's strict interpretation of the Koran led him to institute the most severe religious restrictions on the Afghan population. Following the precepts of the Hanafi

Sunni religious sect that believes the duty of a Muslim is to create an ideal society that existed under the Prophet, sports, dancing, and the shaving of beards were deemed blasphemous. The most active ministry in the Taliban government was the Department for the Suppression of Vice and Promotion of Virtue. Women were not allowed to hold jobs outside the home and were forced to wear burkas. Religious praying was enforced by corporal punishment. Schooling for boys was allowed, but not for girls.

Omar had his regime firmly established in Afghanistan, but his association with **Osama bin Laden** and **al-Qaeda** proved his undoing. Little evidence exists that Omar was anti-American, but his association with bin Laden put him into the anti-American camp. Omar extended an invitation to bin Laden to find refuge in Afghanistan in 1997 after bin Laden had to leave Sudan. Bin Laden used this sanctuary to build his al-Qaeda network of terrorist organizations. Omar protected bin Laden until the **September 11**, 2001, attack on the Twin Towers of the World Trade Center in New York City and the Pentagon in Washington, D.C. Even after pressure was placed on his regime, Omar refused to hand over bin Laden to the United States. In response, America and its allies joined with the Northern Alliance to overthrow the Taliban regime. On October 22, 2001, an air strike mortally wounded Omar's 10-year-old son. Omar reluctantly left Kandahar on October 7, 2001, and escaped capture by moving from one location to another. His disappearance has been disappointing, because the United States wanted to capture him and place him on trial. American authorities believe Omar is hiding in the tribal lands of northwest Pakistan, but they have had no sightings of him. See also Bin Laden, Osama; Taliban (Students of Religious Schools).

Suggested readings: Jeffrey Bartholet, "Inside the Mullah's Mind," *Newsweek* (October 1, 2001), p. 30; Martin Regg Cohn, "Commander of the Faithful," *Toronto Star* (April 29, 2001), p. 1; Robert Fisk, "Campaign against Terrorism," *Inde-pendent* (London) (December 7, 2001), p. 3; Suzanne Goldenberg, "Heart of Darkness," *Guardian* (London) (October 13, 1998), p. 2; John Otis, "Mystery Shrouds Taliban Leader," *Houston Chronicle* (December 16, 2001); Ahmed Rashid, "The Mysterious Man behind the Taliban," *The Ottawa Citizen* (September 17, 2001); Ahmed Rashid, *Taliban: Militant Islam, Oil and Fundamentalism in Central Asia* (New Haven, CT: Yale University Press, 2000); Ralph H. Magnus and Eden, *Afghanistan: Mullah, Marx, and Mujahid* (Boulder, CO: Westview Press, 2000).

One Nation Party (ONP) (Australia)

The One Nation Party (ONP) is Australia's leading anti-immigrant and anti-Aborigine party. **Pauline Hanson** formed this party in 1997 shortly after she was elected to the Australian Parliament from Oxley in Ipswich, Queensland. After her maiden speech in the House of Representatives during which she attacked taxpayer support for minority groups, a spontaneous group of backers formed to give her political support. In April 1997, Hanson launched the One Nation Party. Her advisors David Ettridge and David Oldfield advised her to divide One Nation into two separate entities. The first, One Nation Limited, was incorporated so that Hanson, Ettridge, and Oldfield could control it. The other, One Nation Party, had a membership and operated as a political party. Within months One Nation Party had 200 local branches across Australia. Appeal of the ONP was to Australians feeling alienated from a society experiencing rapid social and economic change. These alienated Australians directed their anger against Aborigines, Asians, and other ethnic minorities. Hanson articulated their viewpoint by emphasizing the positive legacy of white Australians in the building of Australia. Her attacks on the governing elites also attracted attention from the alienated.

The political stronghold of the One Nation Party was in Queensland. The first indication of the drawing power of the One National Party was in the 1998 Queensland election. Adherents of the ONP won 11 of the 89 seats. Almost as soon as the ONP deputies assumed their seats, dissension broke out within the party. Dissidents claimed that the ONP had been fraudulently registered in the 1998 Queensland election. In August 1999, the Supreme Court of Queensland ruled that the registration had indeed been fraudulent. Even before this ruling Hanson, Ettridge, and Oldfield began purging the party of dissidents.

Internal dissension and failure in the 1998 federal elections weakened the One Nation Party. Many of its deputies in the Queensland Parliament broke away from the party and became independents. Despite the populist rhetoric emanating from Hanson, the leadership in the ONP was autocratic and it became less popular over time. Charges of election irregularities also appeared involving the registration of the party in 1997. In January 2003 Pauline Hanson resigned as head of the One Nation Party to face the fraud charges along with her chief aide, David Ettridge. Their later conviction of election fraud and prison sentences have had a further negative impact on the party. After an appeals court quashed their sentences, Hanson and Ettridge gained an early release from prison in December 2003. Hanson has since retired from politics. **See also** Hanson, Pauline; League of Rights.

Suggested readings: Dennis Atkins, "How the West Has Won," *Courier Mail* (January 19, 2002), p. 28; Paul Kelly, *Paradise Divided: The Changes, the Challenges, the Choices for Australia* (St. Leonards, NSW: Allen & Unwin, 2000); Michael Leach, Geoffrey Stokes, and Ian Ward, *The Rise and Fall of One Nation* (St. Lucia: University of Queensland Press, 2000); Gerald McManus, "Why They Vote for Hanson," *Sunday Herald Sun* (Melbourne) (February 18, 2001), p. 38; Natalie O'Brien, Belinda Hickman, and Dennis Shanahan, "Western Showdown," *Weekend Australian* (Sydney) (May 26, 2001), p. 21; Greg Roberts, "Tactical Withdrawal," *Sydney Morning Herald* (January 19, 2002), p. 27.

Ortega Saavedra, Daniel (1946–) (Nicaragua)

Daniel Ortega Saavedra was the leading figure in the Sandinista government of Nicaragua in the 1980s and he is now the leader of the Sandinista opposition to the Nicaraguan government. He was born on November 11, 1946, in the mining town of La Libertad, Chontales, Nicaragua. His father was an accountant for a mining concern, but later he ran a small import-export business in Managua. His father also was a supporter of Augusto César Sandino, and he served time in jail for protesting Sandino's assassination. The family left La Libertad for Juigalpa when Ortega was only two months old and later moved to Managua. Ortega went to the Catholic school Colegio Pedagógico in Managua, but his political activities caused the school to refuse to readmit him or his brother, Humberto. Next, Ortega and his brother went to Masay to study at the Salesian school. After graduation from the Maestro Valdivieso, he attended the Universidad Católica for a short time.

Ortega had always been active in political demonstrations, and his first arrest was in 1960. In 1963, he joined the **Sandinista National Liberation Front** (Frente Sandinista de Liberación Nacional, or FSLN) in its struggle against the regime of Anastasio Somoza. He soon became the head of the FSLN underground organization in Managua. In 1967, Ortega was arrested and he served a seven-year prison term in La Modelo Prison in Managua. While in prison, he participated in a hunger strike that lasted for more than 30 days. Ortega won release when the Sandinistas raided the home of "Chem" Castillo, the minister of agriculture, during a Christmas party. After release, Ortega flew to Cuba where he stayed from 1974 to 1976. In 1976, Ortega reappeared in Nicaragua to fight for the Sandinista cause.

The overthrow of the Somoza regime in 1979 made Ortega a national hero. His first role was as a member of the five-person Junta of National Reconstruction. Ortega soon became the leading figure on the Junta. It also made him the number-one target for the administration of President Ronald Reagan. Ortega served as the president of Nicaragua from 1984 until he lost the presidency to Violeta Barrios de Chamorro in

1990. In the meantime, his government had to face an insurgency led by the Contras. The United States armed and provided logistical support for the Contra rebels, some of whom had formerly been supporters of the Sandinista revolution. Ortega's one accomplishment as president was bringing an end to the seven-year Contra War by agreeing to a national election in 1990. It was the combination of civil war, runaway inflation, and an economic collapse that doomed the Ortega election.

After failing to win the presidency in 1990, Ortega went into opposition to the government. His election to the National Assembly and head of the FSLN allowed him a political base. He remained a popular figure in Nicaragua, but the legacy of the Sandinista regime haunted him. Ortega consolidated his control of the FSLN by purging the party of what he perceived as dissidents even though the dissidents claimed they were reformers. Even a 1994 heart attack did little to slow him down in his efforts to regain political power. In 1996, he lost another presidential race, this time to Arnoldo Aleman. This loss paled in comparison to the March 1998 charge by his stepdaughter, Zoilamerica Narvaez Murillo, that Ortega had sexually abused her as a child. Although he denied the charge, she initiated criminal charges against him. Ortega survived the scandal, but it hurt him politically.

Ortega reinvented his image for the 2001 presidential race. He ran a campaign during which he apologized for mistakes of the past and promoted a moderate image. Critics had relegated his chances to the dustbin, but early polls indicated that he had a chance of success. His opponent was Enrique Bolanos, an anti-Sandinista businessman and vice-president in the Alaman government. Ortega ran such a strong campaign that the George W. Bush administration intervened to lobby against him. Bolanos won the election in November 2001. Ortega was re-elected head of the FSLN in 2002 and he has vowed to run for the presidency in 2006. **See also** Sandinista National Liberation Front (Frente Sandinista de Liberación Nacional) (FSLN).

Suggested readings: Duncan Campbell, "Getting the Right Result: Nicaragua's Election Showed the US Still Won't Allow a Free Vote," *Guardian* (London) (November 7, 2001), p. 17; Lynn Daly, *Life Stories of the Nicaraguan Revolution* (New York: Routledge, 1990); Francisco Goldman, "The Autumn of the Revolutionary," *New York Times* (August 23, 1998), sec. 6, p. 38; David Gonzalez, "Nicaragua Votes Reject Ortega's Bid for the Presidency," *New York Times* (November 6, 2001), sec. A, p. 6; David Nolan, *The Ideology of the Sandinistas and the Nicaraguan Revolution* (Coral Gables, FL: Institute of Interamerican Studies, 1984); John Otis, "Daniel Ortega Attempts Clinton-Style Comeback," *Insight on the News* (October 21, 1996), p. 22; Ed Vuiliarny, "Daniel Ortega: In the Lion's Den Again," *Observer* (London) (September 2, 2001), p. 21; Alan Zarembo, "Return of the Rebel," *Newsweek* (August 6, 2001), p. 26.

P

Paisley, Ian Kyle (1926–)
(Northern Ireland)

Ian Paisley is the leading Protestant loyalist politician in Northern Ireland. He was born on April 6, 1926, in Armagh, Northern Ireland. His father was an evangelical Baptist minister and his mother was from a Reformed Presbyterian, or Covenanter, background. Soon after his birth, the family moved to a new church in Ballymena in County Antrim. His father adhered to the fundamentalist side of Protestantism and Paisley accepted his religious outlook. Paisley had a normal childhood and education. He spent a year in 1942 at the Barry School of Evangelism in South Wales. Returning to Northern Ireland in 1943, he studied at the Reformed Presbyterian Church in Belfast for three years. In early 1946, Paisley became the minister at Ravenhill Evangelical Mission Church in a working-class East Belfast neighborhood. He joined the National Union of Protestants (NUP), an English organization that had been formed to defend the Protestant religion, serving as its treasurer. In 1951, Paisley became embroiled in a Presbyterian church dispute that resulted in his assuming the leadership of the Free Presbyterian Church. By 1965, the Free Presbyterian Church had 12 congregations and they served as Paisley's religious base for his entry into Ulster politics.

Paisley is an Ulster Unionist both from family background and personal conviction. Through the late 1940s to the 1950s, he had been on the fringe of Protestant Unionist politics, supporting Protestant candidates for the Stormont Parliament. His anti-Catholicism and opposition to the moderate government of Captain Terence O'Neill infuriated him. In the autumn of 1964, Paisley gained national prominence by his protest against the presence of an Irish Tricolor flag on Divis Street in Belfast. After garnering publicity for his flag protest, Paisley began attacks on what he considered the pro-Catholic stance of the Terrence O'Neill government. By mid-1965, Paisley was in the forefront of the Ulster Protestant movement to overthrow the O'Neill government. In 1966, he formed the Ulster Constitution Defence Committee (UCDC) to defend the Protestant cause in Ulster. Paisley also supported the formation of the Ulster Protestant Volunteers (UPV). His associate Noel Docherty formed the UPV as a paramilitary organization with secret cells for military operations against the **Irish Republican Army** (IRA). The extent of Paisley's involvement in this mission of the UPV has never been adequately explained, but he did expel Docherty from further associa-

Northern Ireland's Ian Paisley speaks to reporters in Belfast, Northern Ireland, February 15, 1999. Paisley, who is opposed to the Irish peace process, joined other politicians at Stormont to debate the joint Protestant-Catholic government. (AP Photo/ Peter Morrison)

tion with him after Docherty was caught with explosives.

Paisley's public campaign against Catholics in Northern Ireland led him to trouble with Ulster authorities. In June 1966, Paisley led a Protestant march to picket the Irish Presbyterians' General Assembly, and, in the subsequent riot with Catholic bystanders of the march, he earned a brief jail sentence. This jail term only enhanced his standing among Ulster Protestants. His intervention in Armagh in November 1968 to counter a Catholic civil rights demonstration resulted in a January 1969 sentence of three months in jail for unlawful assembly. His church bailed him out of jail so he could run for

public office after only three days. After losing his election, Paisley served the remainder of his sentence.

Paisley decided to launch a political movement to save Protestant Ulster. In May 1969, Paisley won election to the Stormont Parliament from Bannside in a by-election by gaining the rural Protestant vote. Then in June 1969, he was elected to the British Parliament from North Antrim. These successes encouraged Paisley to believe that he could form a major political party. On October 30, 1971, Paisley and his supporters founded the Ulster Democratic Unionist Party (DUP) to challenge the established Official Unionist Party (OUP). The DUP has always operated as Paisley's private party and from the beginning it experienced considerable success in elections. His success as a party leader was because of his commitment to Protestantism and Ulster. He garnered enough loyalist votes for the 1979 European Parliament election to win a seat. Several times in Paisley's political career he has taken stands on issues that have produced a political backlash. Steve Bruce, in his study of the politics of Paisleyism, claims that for Paisley religion comes before politics.

Paisley's anti-Catholicism and fear for Protestant Ulster led him to oppose the peace process in Northern Ireland. He has always articulated a no-compromise policy with the Irish nationalists. Although Paisley has been careful not to advocate violence, he has supported the militancy of Ulster Protestant groups. The Good Friday Peace Accord negotiated by **Sinn Fein** and Ulster political groups on April 10, 1998, found Paisley outside in opposition. He has savagely attacked the agreement as a Catholic Trojan Horse and he has traveled around Northern Ireland attacking it as hostile to Protestant interests.

Suggested readings: Steve Bruce, *God Save Ulster!: The Religion and Politics of Paisleyism* (Oxford, U.K.: Oxford University Press, 1986); Gavin Jennings, "The Legendary Face of Ulster's Political Landscape," *Belfast News Letter* (Northern Ireland) (September 27, 2001), p. 22; Patrick Marrinan, *Paisley, Man of Wrath* (Tralee, Ireland: Anvil Books, 1973); Peter Taylor, *Loyalists: War and Peace in Northern Ireland* (New York: TV Books, 1999).

Palestine Islamic Jihad (PIJ) (Palestine)

The Palestine Islamic Jihad is one of the most violent of the Palestinian groups that has engaged in terrorist acts against Israel. Zaid al-Husseini and other activists from the Gaza Strip formed the precursor of this group in 1964. They originally called their group the Palestine Liberation Force before changing their name to the Palestine Islamic Jihad. This group became the predominant Palestinian terrorist organization in the Gaza Strip and it was often in opposition to **Yasser Arafat**'s **al-Fatah**. In 1971, Israeli forces

killed al-Husseini and arrested most of his followers. While in prison, members of the Palestine Islamic Jihad converted to the fundamentalist creed of the Islamists.

The Palestine Islamic Jihad reestablished itself after most of its members were released from prison in the early 1980s. In 1981, **Fathi Shikaki**, a Palestinian medical doctor, revived the Palestine Islamic Jihad and associated it with the ideology of the **Muslim Brotherhood**. He was also able to recruit the ex-prisoners when they returned to the Gaza Strip. Most of these members were still hostile toward al-Fatah, but a truce was arranged between the two groups. Shikaki was also able to recruit Sheikh Abdul al-Aziz Odeh, a popular lecturer in Islamic law and a strong Islamist preacher, at a large mosque in the Gaza Strip to the Palestine Islamic Jihad. Shikaki's philosophy was to recruit a small group of hard-core militants to carry out operations against Israel regardless of the cost in lives and property. Because of Shikaki's favorable impression of the **Ayatollah Komeini**'s regime, he sought and received financial aid from the Iranian government.

Leaders of the Palestine Islamic Jihad spent the first three years organizing the group before launching military operations against Israel. These operations commenced in late 1983. Besides conducting terror attacks against Israeli targets, the group mobilized Palestinian youth. In the early 1980s, the leadership of the Palestine Islamic Jihad turned its attention to recruiting promising students at Bir Zeit University. Student recruits organized a series of student demonstrations. During one of these demonstrations on April 13, 1987, Israeli forces opened fire, killing a student and wounding several others. By the early 1990s, the leadership decided to adopt the tactic of suicide bombing. Both **Hamas** and the Palestine Islamic Jihad have specialized in suicide bombings, mostly inside Israel.

Israeli authorities believed that the Palestine Islamic Jihad posed a serious threat to the security of Israel and decided to repress it. Raids against the leadership of the Palestine Islamic Jihad resulted in more than 50 arrests. Odeh was one of the arrested and he was deported along with several his colleagues. These losses were serious, but Shikaki was able to escape Israeli pressure until 1986, When he received a four-year prison sentence for smuggling arms into Gaza. Rather than keep him imprisoned, Israeli authorities deported him to Lebanon in August 1988. Shikaki's presence in Lebanon meant ties between the Palestine Islamic Jihad and **Hezbollah** became closer. He then moved to Damascus, Syria, in 1990. He continued to provide leadership for the Palestine Islamic Jihad. Then on October 26, 1996, an Israeli hit team assassinated Shikaki in Valetta on the island of Malta. Ramadan Abdullah Shallah, a former professor of Middle Eastern politics at the University of South Florida, replaced him as head of the Palestine Islamic Jihad.

Palestine Islamic Jihad has always been a small group, and that has been both its strength and weakness. Its strength is that it has been difficult for the Israeli authorities to penetrate the group and destroy it. Israelis have made numerous assassination attempts at leaders of the Palestine Islamic Jihad, but new leaders emerge from the ranks. Suicide bombers have been recruited and have produced civilian and military casualties in Israel. The weakness is that its small size makes it difficult to compete with Hamas as the leaders of a mass movement for an independent state. Leaders of the Palestine Islamic Jihad have always had a better working relationship with the Palestinian Authority (PA) than has Hamas. This relationship made it easier for the leadership of the Palestine Islamic Jihad to accept the truce with Israel in the summer of 2003. **See also** Al-Fatah; Hamas (Haarakat al-Muqawama al-Islami) (Islamic Resistance Movement); Intifada.

Suggested readings: Mary Curtius, "Founder of Islamic Jihad Reported Slain," *Los Angeles Times* (October 29, 1995), p. A1; Michael Fechter, "Ex-USF Prof Leads Jihad," *Tampa Tribune* (October 31, 1995), p. 1; Richard Harwood, "The Riddle of Islamic Jihad," *Washington Post* (September 21, 1984), p. A27; Meir Hatina, *Islam and Salvation in Palestine* (Tel Aviv, Israel: Tel Aviv University, 2001); Gustav Niebuhr, "Professor Talked of Understanding but Now Reveals Ties to Terrorists," *New York Times* (November 19, 1995), sec. A, p. 12; Edgar O'Balance, *The Palestine Intifada* (New York: St. Martin's Press, 1998); Susan Sachs, "Terrorism Inc.; Islamic Jihad Founder Admits Funding by Iran," *Newsday* (New York City) (April 11, 1993), p. 7; Ze'ev Schiff and Ehud Ya'ari, *Intifada: The Palestinian Uprising—Israel's Third Front* (New York: Simon and Schuster, 1990).

Palestine Liberation Front (PLF) (See Jibril, Ahmed)

Palestine Liberation Organization (PLO) (Palestine)

The Palestine Liberation Organization (PLO) has been the leading organization in the struggle for a Palestinian state. Gamal Abdel Nasser, the Egyptian head of state, was afraid that the Palestinians would drag Egypt into a war with Israel. He wanted a Palestinian organization that would provide the Palestinian people a forum for self-expression and self-importance but also one that he could control. The PLO made its appearance at a meeting of Arab countries at Cairo in January 1964. Ahmed Shuquiri was its first leader. The Palestinian National Congress of 422 Palestinian representatives met in East Jerusalem on May 22, 1964, and it approved the Palestinian National Charter and a basic constitution for the PLO. Headquarters for the PLO was established in Cairo, Egypt. A military wing, the Palestine Liberation Army (PLA), was also formed, but it was under the control of the Arab states because they provided the military units.

The defeat suffered by Arab forces in the 1967 Arab-Israeli War transformed the Palestine Liberation Organization. Nasser decided that the PLO needed to play a more active role on the military side of the struggle against Israel. After extensive internal debate and much soul-searching, the PLO's National Council (PNC) elected **Yasser Arafat** as the head of the PLO on April 15, 1968. Arafat's action was to bring the various Palestinian groups into the PLO, but this was a difficult task. Arafat finally brought **al-Fatah** into the PLO in February 1969.

Arafat had two tasks confronting him. His first major crisis was dealing with George **Habash**'s **Popular Front for the Liberation of Palestine** (PFLP). This group's violent attacks on Israeli targets both in Israel and abroad were garnering unfavorable publicity around the world. The next problem was financial. Diplomatic efforts gained financial and military support from King Feisal of Saudi Arabia. Controlling the PFLP proved more difficult than gaining support from Saudi Arabia

The PLO has had two complementary roles to fulfill. In 1974, the United Nations recognized the PLO as the representative of the Palestinian people. Arafat has recognized this function and has spoken on the international stage for the Palestinian cause. The second function has been to unify the various groups within the PLO and speak as one voice. This function has been more difficult to achieve and Arafat has been unable to accomplish this except on rare occasions. His acceptance of the right of Israel to exist and the renunciation of terrorism had alienated the radical segments of the PLO.

Arafat had difficulty finding a home for the PLO. He had moved most PLO operations to Jordan by early 1970. The Jordanian government tolerated the PLO until its behavior threatened the Jordanian state. Open warfare broke out in 1970–1971 between PLO groups and the Jordanian military, with the PLO groups suffering a major defeat. The PLO was able to reestablish itself in Lebanon and carry out operations against Israel by 1971. Defeat of Arab military forces in the Arab-Israeli War of 1973 was a major blow to the PLO. This defeat did not prevent PLO military units from continuing operations against Israeli targets. PLO units operated with impunity in Lebanon until the June 1982 Israeli invasion of Lebanon. On the brink of total defeat, international pressure allowed Arafat to move PLO headquarters to Tunis, Tunisia. Arafat had to withstand a threat to his leadership from dissident groups

that had the support of Syria's President Hafiz al-Asad.

Arafat survived the attacks on his leadership by his diplomatic efforts on the international scene. In 1974, he proclaimed the PLO's opposition to terrorist operations outside Israel and the occupied territories. Arafat followed this statement in November 1985 with the Cairo Declaration, which proclaimed that the PLO opposed all forms of terrorism. These declarations and the moderation of the PLO caused many of those opposed to Arafat's policies to leave the PLO. These defections from the PLO hurt the Palestinian cause, so, in April 1987, a reunification session that was able to reunite most of the dissident groups was held in Algiers, Algeria. Only **Abu Nidal** and his **Abu Nidal Organization** (ANO) refused to rejoin the PLO.

The next crisis of the PLO was the outbreak of the **Intifada**. This spontaneous rebellion by Palestinians against Israeli rule in the occupied territories broke out on December 9, 1987, in response to an accident on December 8 near the Jebaliya refugee camp in the Gaza Strip in which four Palestinians died. Impromptu demonstrations led to a violent Israeli response with Palestinian casualties. PLO leaders had been caught by surprise, but within a week they had assumed leadership of the Intifada. Palestinians engaged in a series of demonstrations and strikes that garnered considerable international attention.

The leadership of the Palestine Liberation Organization was able to channel the Intifada into the Oslo Accords. Representatives of the PLO concluded an agreement that allowed the Palestinians autonomy in the West Bank and Gaza Strip. This autonomy meant that the PLO turned over jurisdiction to the Palestinian Authority (PA), but because the PA absorbed the PLO's infrastructure, there was no substantial change of leadership. Arafat remained the head of the PLO and the PA. As disillusionment grew over failure of the Oslo Accords, elements within the PLO began to question the leadership. Charges of corruption and high living started circulating. Efforts by the Israeli government to discredit and then to ignore Arafat weakened the PLO even further. By the early 2000s, both the PLO and the PA were under increasing attacks internally and externally. Arafat still has retained control of the Palestinian movement, but the question of his successor or replacement is often posed. **See also** Arafat, Mohammed Yasser; Intifada.

Suggested readings: Jillian Becker, *The PLO: The Rise and Fall of the Palestine Liberation Organization* (London: Weidenfeld and Nicolson, 1984); Kemal Kirisci, *The PLO and World Politics: A Study of the Mobilization of Support for the Palestinian Cause* (New York: St. Martin's Press, 1986); Jamal R. Nassar, *The Palestine Liberation Organization: From Armed Struggle to the Declaration of Independence* (New York: Praeger, 1991); Edgar O'Balance, *The Palestinian Intifada* (New York: St. Martin's Press, 1998); Barry Rubin, *The Transformation of Palestinian Politics: From Revolution to State-Building* (Cambridge, MA: Harvard University Press, 1999); Avraham Sela and Moshe Ma'oz, *The PLO and Israel: From Armed Conflict to Political Solution, 1964–1994* (New York: St. Martin's Press, 1997).

Panthic Committee (India)

The Panthic Committee is the umbrella group for Sikh terrorist groups that want to establish an independent Sikh state from the Indian state of Punjab. This organization appeared on January 26, 1986, in the aftermath of the Indian army's assault on the Golden Temple complex of Amritsar in 1984 under the codename of Operation Blue Star. Sikhs had been outraged by the Indian army's attacks on the Golden Temple. The assassination of Indira Gandhi on October 31, 1984, by her Sikh bodyguards was one response. The Hindu massacre of nearly 10,000 Sikhs in the aftermath of Gandhi's assassination only further alienated Sikh militants. In response, five prominent Sikhs were elected to guide the Sikh community. These Sikhs were Arur Singh, Gurbachan Singh Manochal, Wesson Singh Zaffarwal, Gurdev Singh Usmanwala, and Dhanna Singh. Manochal was considered the head of the

original Panthic Committee, but he was considered first among equals. The goal of the Panthic Committee was to prepare for armed struggle against India. In April 1986, the Panthic Committee declared Khalistan (Land of the Pure) an independent state. Since India designated the Panthic Committee as an illegal organization, its leadership has remained hidden. Despite precautions, only two of the original members have survived; the others were killed by Indian authorities.

The military wing of the Panthic Committee was the Khalistan Commando Force (KCF). The original commander of the KCF was General Manbir Singh Chaheru, who assumed the name Hari Singh. Under the authority of the Panthic Committee, the KCF launched a guerrilla war beginning in the summer of 1986. The main problem of this campaign was that the Punjab area of India does not easily lend itself to guerrilla warfare. Hari Singh set up a military hierarchy, but ad hoc groups conducted most operations at the local level. However, after Indian forces captured Hari Singh, he disappeared. General Labh Singh replaced him, but he was killed soon afterward. KCF retaliated to these losses by assassinating the Indian commander of Operation Blue Star General Vaidya.

The leadership of the Panthic Committee came to support other guerrilla groups. Among these were the Bhindranwale Tiger Force of Khalistan (BTFK), Khalistan Liberation Force (KLF), and several smaller groups. Another group, the Babbar Khalsa International (BKI), remained independent of the Panthic Committee. The goal of all these groups affiliated with the Panthic Committee has been to establish a Sikh state and to extract revenge for what they perceive to be discrimination by a Hindu state against Sikhs. Each group responsible to the Panthic Committee has its own leader and carries out terrorist operations independently. In 1988, the Panthic Committee selected Bhai Jasbir Singh Rode, the nephew of Jarnail Singh Bhindranwale, to become the Akal Takht's high priest, the highest religious position in the Sikh religion. The leadership of the Panthic Committee has always had close ties with the radical All India Sikh Students' Federation, and although they share some of the same members, they are independent of each other.

Members of the groups represented in the Panthic Committee have engaged in a lengthy terrorist campaign against India and moderate Sikhs militants. This war has been fought with little regard to niceties. Complicating the war was the schism within the Panthic Committee in the summer of 1988 when three separate Panthic committees appeared. Manochal retained control of the original Panthic committee until his death. His death narrowed the number of Panthic committees to two. Zaffarwal gathered remnants of the original Panthic Committee (Zaffarwal Panthic Committee) with his committee, and Sohan Singh (Sohan Singh Panthic Committee) headed the second. Each represented a different facet of the Sikh movement: Zaffarwal Panthic Committee had a strong political base and Sohan Singh constituted the military wing. These divisions and Indian repression of the Sikhs led to widespread immigration to Canada and the United States. From these remote sites, the Panthic Committee still retains control of the Sikh separatist movement. **See also** Sikh Separatism.

Suggested readings: Cynthia Keppley Mahmood, *Fighting for Faith and Nation: Dialogues with Sikh Militants* (Philadelphia: University of Pennsylvania Press, 1996); Vipul Mudgal, "Roots of Violence in Indian Punjab," *Asian Journal of Internationals Terrorism and Conflict* 2, no. 3 (April 2001); Joyce Pettigrew, *Sikhs of the Punjab: Unheard Voices of State and Guerilla Violence* (London: Zed Books, 1995); Sarab Jit Singh, *Operation Black Thunder: An Eyewitness Account of Terrorism in Punjab* (New Delhi, India: Sage Publications, 2002).

Pastora Gomez, Edén (1937–) (Nicaragua)

Edén Pastora Gomez remains one of the most famous guerrilla leaders in Nicaragua because of his role first as a Sandinista military commander and then as a Contra leader. His fame as a guerrilla leader led him to be nicknamed "Commander Zero." He was born in 1937 in Nicaragua. His family had emigrated from Sicily. After studying at Jesuit schools in Nicaragua, Pastora traveled to Guadalajara, Mexico, to study medicine. His opposition to the Somoza regime caused him to leave his medical studies without a degree and return to Nicaragua. In the early 1960s, he joined the **Sandinista National Liberation Front** in its guerrilla war against the Somoza regime and the Nicaraguan National Guard. He spent the next decade and a half as a guerrilla fighter. His abilities as a guerrilla fighter led to his promotion to a commander of a guerrilla unit operating out of Costa Rica. On August 22, 1978, Pastora commanded the unit that seized the Nicaraguan legislative palace and captured 1,500 hostages. Pastora was able to trade these hostages for Sandinistas being held in prison and $500,000. Tomas Borge Martinez, one of the founders of the Sandinista National Liberation Front, was among those of the 50 Sandinista prisoners released.

After the collapse of the regime of Anatasio Somoza Debayle in July 1979, Pastora soon was at odds with the new Sandinista regime. He never received a high position in the new government serving only as deputy defense minister. Pastora came to distrust the Marxist-Leninist orientation of the leaders of the Sandinista government and its dependence on financial and military aid from Cuba and the Soviet Union. Lack of freedom of the press and democratic institutions also bothered him. In July 1981, Pastora resigned his post as deputy defense minister and he left Nicaragua. On April 15, 1982, Pastora went into active opposition to the Sandinista ruling party by joining opposition leaders Alfonso Robelo Callejas and Arturo Cruz. His relations with other opposition leaders were always strained because so many of them had formerly been members of the hated Nicaraguan National Guard. Pastora traveled to Europe and the United States seeking military and political support.

Pastora was one of the key leaders of the Contras in the struggle to overthrow the Sandinistas. In September 1982, four opposition groups united to form the Democratic

Revolutionary Alliance (ARDE). Pastora assumed the military leadership of ARDE and, on April 15, 1983, announced the opening of military operations against the Sandinistas. Soon he was in command of nearly 2,000 soldiers. For the next six years he fought with the Contras to defeat the Sandinista regime, but he also kept communications open with the Sandinistas. News of these contacts alienated American advisors and other Contra leaders. In early 1984, he survived an assassination attempt at La Penca. By then all sides wanted to be rid of him. Forces under his command controlled the area along the border of Nicaragua and Costa Rica, and he retained this control until the end of the civil war. Pastora also survived more than a dozen assassination attempts.

After the agreement between the Contras and the Sandinista government for elections, Pastora lost all his political connections. By alienating both sides of the war, Pastora had no allies or political base. Both the new Violetta Chamorro government and the Sandinista opposition ignored him. He moved to Costa Rica and became a Costa Rican citizen. After returning to Nicaragua, Pastora suffered financial reverses until he had to sell his Managua home. In 1996, he thought about running for political office, but his Costa Rican citizenship prevented this. His most recent activity has been to become one of the leaders of an anti-corruption campaign against former Nicaraguan President Arnoldo Aleman leading to judicial proceedings against Aleman. Pastora has lobbied heavily for the Nicaraguan parliament to pull Aleman's parliamentary immunity. After Nicaragua's Supreme Court ruled in late January 2003 that he could run for political office in Nicaragua, Pastora proclaimed his intention to run for the presidency of Nicaragua in 2006. **See also** Sandinista National Liberation Front (Frente Sandinista de Liberación Nacional) (FSLN).

Suggested readings: Filadelfo Aleman, "Famed Nicaraguan Rebel Leaders Says He's Heading Back to Fish for Sharks," Associated Press (January 16, 2002), p. 1; Karen DeYoung, "Exiled Nicaraguan Guerrilla Pledges to Depose Somoza," *Washington Post* (October 19, 1978), p. A21;

James Nelson Goodsell, "'Commander Zero' Tells Sandinistas to Shape Up . . . or Else," *Christian Science Monitor* (April 20, 1982), p. 4; Stephen Kinzer, *Blood of Brothers: Life and War in Nicaragua* (New York: Putnam's, 1991); R. Pardo-Maurer, *The Contras, 1980–1989: A Special Kind of Politics* (New York: Praeger, 1990); Alan Riding, "Disenchanted Hero of Sandinistas Emerges as Leader of Their Foes," *New York Times* (July 2, 1982), p. A1.

People's National Party (PNP) (Russia)

The People's National Party (PNP) is Russia's leading neo-Nazi **skinhead** political group. In December 1994, Alexander Kuzmich Ivanov-Sukharevsky, a former soldier and filmmaker, founded the People's National Party. He and his deputy, Semyon Tokmakov, organized the People's National Party into a paramilitary organization. Members are divided into five-man squads with the sixth man serving as the commander. Each commander is subordinate to Ivanov-Sukharevsky or to Tokmakov. Headquarters for the party is in a one-room apartment in Moscow. Funding for the party comes from mandatory membership dues. Ivanov-Sukharevsky has tried to arm his paramilitary squads, but Russian authorities have denied permission for weapons. Leadership has given recruitment of new members high priority and much of the recruiting is done at soccer games or rock concerts. Members can be recognized by shaven heads, heavy army boots, black jackets, and armbands with the Celtic cross. A reporter for the Russian newspaper *Izvestia* claims that the People's National Party has a membership of 10,000 nationwide and around 1,500 members in Moscow. Much of the appeal of the People's National Party is to young Russian nationalists, who were raised by parents from the former Soviet middle class and whose standards of living have deteriorated since the collapse of the Soviet Union.

The goal of the People's National Party is to rid Russia of foreigners and members of ethnic groups and reestablish the Russian empire. Ivanov-Sukharevsky has made plans to deport people—Asians, Jews, and other ethnic groups—but this will only come to pass when his party comes to power. In the meantime, members of the People's National Party engage in the bashing of foreigners. An emphasis on violence has brought Ivanov-Sukharevsky and Tokmakov to the attention of the police. In 1997, Ivanov-Sukharevsky spent nine months in Butyrka Prison for the incitement of ethnic discord. Tokmakov received a year-and-a-half prison sentence in 2000 for beating up a black American U.S. Marine in Moscow.

The most famous of the People's National Party's attacks on foreigners was in the Tsaritsyno area of south Moscow in November 2001. This area was selected because there were lots of immigrants living there. Riots left three dead and dozens wounded. In May 2002, Moscow authorities placed Ivanov-Sukharevsky on a suspended three-year sentence for incitement to violence. Despite these efforts by the authorities, the People's National Party continues to recruit Russian youth between the ages of 15 and 18 for the next round of ethnic violence. **See also** Skinhead Movement.

Suggested readings: Alexander Bogomolov, "The Tsaritsyno Riot Was Not the Last," *What the Papers Say* (Moscow) (November 13, 2001), p.1; Grigory Punanov, "Portrait of a 'Skinhead Party' and Its Leader," *Current Digest of the Post-Soviet Press* 54, no. 19 (June 5, 2002); Anatoly Sautin, "Russian TV Shows Skinheads Undergoing Initiation Rites," BBC Monitoring International Reports (October 15, 2002), p.1; Stephen D. Shenfield, *Russian Fascism: Traditions, Tendencies, Movements* (Armonk, NY: M. E. Sharpe, 2001); Alexander Tarasov, "Russian Skinheads: A Social Portrait," *What the Papers Say* (Moscow) (August 13, 2002), p. 4.

People's Revolutionary Army (Ejercito Revolucionario del Pueblo) (ERP)/ Revolutionary Workers' Party (Partido Revolucionario de los Trabajadores) (PRT) (Argentina)

Both the People's Revolutionary Army (ERP) and the Revolutionary Workers' party (PRT) had separate existences, but they cooperated in the battle for revolutionary change in Argentina in the 1970s. Mario Roberto Santucho formed the Popular Front for Intra-American Revolution (Frente Revolucionario Indoamericano Popular) (FRIP) in 1960 in the province of Tucuman. In 1962, he traveled to Cuba, and it was there that he was converted to Marxism and Che Guevara's brand of revolutionary guerrilla warfare. Also in 1962, Angel Bengochea, a Trotskyite, founded the Workers' Word (Palabra Obrera) (PO) in Buenos Aires. After Bengochea died in an explosion accident, his group allied with Santucho's FRIP to form the Revolutionary Workers' Party in 1965. Santucho also adopted the Trotskyite program of the PO and started building a political party to support the strategy of guerrilla warfare. The People's Revolutionary Army came out of the proceedings of the Fifth Congress of the Revolutionary Workers' Party in 1970 to serve as the armed wing of the PRT. Despite this alliance, the PRT and the ERP had a different leadership structure and membership. Both groups remained Marxist and anti-Perón. They developed a working relationship with the Perónist **Montoneros**, but the difference in ideology never allowed a formal alliance.

The People's Revolutionary Army and the Revolutionary Workers' Party engaged in a terrorist campaign in the early 1970s. On April 10, 1972, members of the ERP-PRT assassinated General Juan Carlos Sanchez, commander of the 2nd Army Corps in Rosario. They continued their attacks on the Argentine government even after Juan Domingo Perón returned to power in 1973. The appearance of the **Argentine Anti-Communist Alliance** (Triple A) formed in part to combat the activities of the ERP-PRT. In 1973, ERP-PRT activists kidnapped 170 businessmen in Argentina and held them for ransom. Leadership of both groups believed that the rich should finance the revolution. Military facilities were also raided to gather arms and ammunition.

In 1975, leaders of the ERP decided to seize control of the province of Tucuman. Tucuman was one of Argentina's poorest provinces and the ERP believed that its population would rally to the revolution. Only about 140 members of the ERP participated in this campaign. President Isabel Perón sent 1,500 army troops to Tucuman to fight the rebels. Over the next few weeks, the army wiped out the ERP forces and instituted a period of repression in Tucuman.

The last major operation of the ERP was in December 1975. A force of 150 ERP guerrillas attacked a military arsenal in the Buenos Aires suburb of Monte Chingolo. This attack failed and the ERP suffered heavy casualties. These losses following the defeat at Tucuman ended the ERP as a fighting guerrilla army. ERP leaders decided to end the separate identities of the ERP and PRT and a formal merger took place in 1976. By this time the Argentine government's repression started taking its total of the leaders and the rank-and-file. By 1979, most of the leaders of the ERP/PRT were either dead or in concentration camps. A few rank-and-file members were able to flee abroad. **See also** Argentine Anti-Communist Alliance (Alianza Argentina Anti-Comunista) (Triple A); Montoneros.

Suggested readings: Richard Gillespie, *Soldiers of Peron: Argentina's Montoneros* (Oxford, UK: Clarendon Press, 1982); Patricia Marchak and William Marchak, *God's Assassins: State Terrorism in Argentina in the 1970s* (Montreal: McGill-Queen's University Press, 1999).

Polay Campos, Victor (1952–) (Peru)

Victor Polay Campos is the founder and leader of the leftist guerrilla group **Tupac Amaru Revolutionary Movement** (Movimiento Revolucionario Tupac Amaru) (MRTA). He was born in 1952. His parents were leftist political reformers who had been active in the creation of the left-wing anti-imperialist party American Popular Revolutionary Alliance (APRA). He received a first-class education and was sent to study law abroad in Madrid, Spain, and in Paris, France. In Paris, his roommate had been Alan Garcia, the future president of Peru and head of the APRA. In 1982, Polay Campos returned to Peru and promptly became engaged in left-wing politics. In 1984, Polay Campos founded the Tupac Amaru Revolu-

tionary Movement. He named his group after the Indian leader Tupac Amaru, who had led a 17th-century insurrection against the Spanish before being executed in Cuzco. His friend Garcia became president of Peru in 1985, but Polay Campos put him on notice, giving Garcia's administration a year to produce radical reforms.

Polay Campos unleashed a guerrilla campaign to overthrow the Peruvian government in 1986. His model was the guerrilla tactics of the Cuban guerrilla leader Che Guevara. He also found the MRTA in competition with the Maoist **Shining Path** guerrillas. Unable to coexist because of ideological differences, these groups clashed in armed battles, but Shining Path's superior size gave it an advantage. Polay Campos was careful to avoid indiscriminate attacks, and so he targeted high profile targets such as Kentucky Fried Chicken franchises. These targets were bombed and political leaders assassinated.

Polay Campos became the subject of a national search by Peruvian authorities. On February 3, 1989, police arrested Polay Campos in a raid on a tourist hotel in Huancayo. He was sentenced to life imprisonment at Canto Grande prison in Lima. Polay Campos and 46 inmates escaped from prison by digging a long tunnel with outside help. After the escape, Polay Campos resumed control of the operations of the MRTA. However, on June 10, 1992, Polay Campos was arrested again, this time at a sidewalk café in Lima. Peruvian authorities took no chances this time and imprisoned him in solitary confinement in the maximum-security facility in the Callao naval base.

Several attempts have been made to free Polay Campos and other MRTA leaders. In November 1995, Nestor Cerpa Cartolini organized 30 MRTA activists into a plot to occupy the Peruvian Congress and hold the deputies hostage until Polay Campos and the others were freed. Police arrested the plotters before this plan could be implemented. The next attempt was the seizure of the Japanese ambassador's residence in Lima at a reception honoring Japan's emperor on December 17, 1996. Fourteen MRTA guerrillas under the command of **Cerpa Cartolini** captured nearly 500 guests. After releasing all but 72 hostages, Cerpa Cartolini bargained to free the more than 450 MRTA prisoners, including his wife. The Peruvian government placed considerable pressure on Polay Campos to denounce the attack, but he refused to cooperate with the government. Negotiations lasted until April 22, 1997, when Peruvian commandos freed the hostages and killed all of the MRTA guerrillas. After this operation, only a handful of MRTA activists remained free. Polay Campos remains imprisoned in solitary confinement at the naval base with little hope of being released. He is allowed to read novels but not books that are in any way political. **See also** Cerpa Cartolini, Nestor; Tupac Amaru Revolutionary Movement (Movimiento Revolucionario Tupac Amaru) (MRTA).

Suggested readings: Sally Bowen, "Terrorist Jail-Break Embarrasses Garcia," *Financial Times* (London) (July 11, 1990), p. 6; Yutaka Ishiguro, "Jailed Guerrilla Leader Refuses to Denounce Attack," *Daily Yomiuri* (Japan) (December 23, 1996), p. 2; Diana Jean Schemo, "A Born Revolutionary's Path to a Living 'Tomb' in Peru," *New York Times* (January 4, 1997), sec. 1, p. 1; Simon Strong, "Peru's Civil War Fought by Former Comrades," *Newsday* (February 26, 1989), p. 15.

Polisario Front (Frente Popular para la Liberación de Saguia el-Hamra y Rio de Oro) (Morocco)

The Polisario Front is a Saharawi national liberation movement that seeks to build a state in what is now southern Morocco. Morocco was a Spanish colony until it received its independence from Spain in 1975. Southern Morocco had a population of around 100,000 Saharawis in the early 1970s. In 1973, the Polisario Front formed from the leadership of the Saharawis to fight against Spanish colonialism. Spain had promised a referendum for southern Morocco, but in late 1975 Francisco Franco, the Spanish head of state, signed over rights to the Spanish Sahara to Morocco and Mauritania. Shortly afterward, Morocco occupied most of the former Spanish Sahara.

Guerrillas of the Polisario Front responded with a guerrilla campaign against both Morocco and Mauritania. Initial results were disastrous for the Polisario Front as a two-pronged Moroccan and Mauritanian offensive forced the rebels to seek safe haven in southern Algeria. Headquarters of the Polisario Front is in Tindouf, Algeria. A longtime leader has been Mohamed Abdelaziz, but collective leadership comes from the seven-member executive committee. Throughout the late 1970s, Polisario Front guerrillas made forays into Morocco and Mauritania. These attacks on Mauritania forced the Mauritanian government to sign an armistice with the Polisario Front in 1979, giving up its claims to Western Sahara. This guerrilla campaign has been less successful with Morocco. King Hassan of Morocco decided to limit access to the richest area of the disputed territory by building a wall hundreds of miles long and stationing 160,000 soldiers behind it. The combination of this wall and military defeats led the Polisario Front to conclude a truce in 1991.

This truce has lasted over a decade, but it has not solved the problem of a Saharawi state. Efforts to legitimize the struggle by proclaiming the Saharawi Arab Democratic Republic (SADR) occurred in February 1976. In 1982, the Organization of African Unity (OAU) recognized the SADR by admitting into membership. More than 70 countries have accepted the existence of the SADR. Then, in April 1991, the United Nations set up a UN Mission for the Referendum in Western Sahara (MINURSO) to administer a referendum on self-determination. Lengthy debates over the eligibility of voters in the referendum have prevented the referendum from taking place. Leaders of Polisario Front have threatened to restart guerrilla warfare unless the referendum takes place. On July 30, 2002, the UN Security Council extended the peacekeeping mission in Western Sahara, but the issue of a referendum is still up in the air. In July 2003 the leaders of the Polisario Front accepted the Baker Plan II that provides for two referendums to decide the fate of the territory in the Western Sahara in dispute between the Polisario Front and Morocco, but Morocco has declined acceptance.

Suggested readings: Nizar Al-Aly, "Politics-Western Sahara: Weary Annan Recommends U.N. Pull-Out," Inter Press Service (February 21, 2002), p. 1; Jon Lee Anderson, *Guerrillas: The Men and Women Fighting Today's Wars* (New York: Times Books, 1992); Katherine Butler, "In Africa's Last Colony," *Independent* (London) (May 18, 2002), p. 15; Katherine Butler, "War Drums Beat Again for Polisario Front Guerrillas," *Independent* (London) (May 1, 2002), p. 13; Paul Laverty, "Reach for the Sky," *Guardian* (London) (December 19, 2003), p. 4.

Popular Front for the Liberation of Palestine (PFLP) (Palestine)

The Popular Front for the Liberation of Palestine (PFLP) has long been one of the leading Palestinian terrorist groups. **George Habash**, a Lebanese medical doctor, founded the PFLP in 1967 shortly after the 1967 Arab-Israeli War. He was able to unite his Arab Nationalist Movement (ANM) and **Ahmed Jibril's Palestine Liberation Front** to form the PFLP. This group had a Marxist-Leninist political orientation toward revolutionary action. Unlike **al-Fatah's** approach to restrict anti-Israeli operations in Palestine, Habash launched operations against Israeli targets worldwide. Members of the PFLP became specialists in airplane hijackings, beginning with the first skyjacking on July 28, 1968. Dr. Wadi Haddad headed the terrorist operations until his death.

The most famous operative of the PFLP was Leila Khaled. She gained international fame for her skyjacking of the TWA B-707 flight from Rome to Tel Aviv on August 29, 1969. Khaled followed another skyjacking of an El Al flight from Amsterdam to New York in 1970. This time the operation failed and onboard security agents arrested her and killed her companion. British police arrested her when the aircraft landed in London, but less than a month later she was released in exchange for hostages from another skyjacking. After her release, she retired from terrorism, but her actions and a 1973 autobiography, *My People Shall Live: The Auto-*

biography of a Revolutionary, made her famous among the Palestinians.

Habash and the other leaders of the PFLP decided to overthrow King Hussein of Jordan. Numerous Palestinian base camps existed in Jordan, making the Palestinians a state within a state. Limited fighting between the PFLP and the Jordanian army flared up in early June 1970. This friction led to **Black September**, when outright warfare broke out between the Jordanian army and the Palestinians. Activists of the PFLP were in the middle of the fighting, but the Palestinians were unable to overcome the Jordanian army. Surviving elements of the PFLP fled to Lebanon, where relations with the **Palestine Liberation Organization** (PLO) remained shaky.

The Popular Front for the Liberation of Palestine has conducted some of the most violent terrorist operations in the Middle East. Leaders of the PFLP popularized the skyjacking of airliners, beginning in 1969. Other individuals and groups had skyjacked aircraft before, but the PFLP used the hostages as leverage to free its members imprisoned for other crimes. Particularly in the 1970s, leaders of the PFLP conducted joint operations with other terrorist groups and individuals, such as the **Japanese Red Army** (JRA) and the German **Red Army Faction** (RAF), German **Revolutionary Cells** (RZ), and **Ilich Ramirez Sànchez** (Carlos the Jackal). Among the most famous terrorist acts by members of the PFLP were the assault on the OPEC Conference in Vienna, Austria, on December 21, 1975, and the skyjacking of the airliner on June 24, 1976 that led to the Entebbe Raid by the Israelis; seizure of the Italian cruise ship Achille Lauro on October 7, 1985.

The Popular Front for the Liberation of Palestine continued operations against Israel, but over the years it began to lose its popular appeal as other non-Marxist groups formed. Habash retained the top leadership position, but his health had deteriorated after a brain operation in 1980s and a stroke in 1990. In July 2000, Habash's longtime colleague Abu Ali Mustafa succeeded him as head of the PFLP. Mustafa's control of the

PFLP lasted just over a year until an Israeli helicopter gunship killed him in his office in Ramallah on August 27, 2001. His successor was Ahmed Saadat.

Saadat continued the intransigent policies of his predecessors. In revenge for the assassination of Mustafa, a PFLP hit team killed the Israeli hard-liner Tourism Minister Rehavam Ze'evi on October 17, 2001. This action enraged the Israeli government and led the Palestinian Authority (PA) to outlaw the PFLP. Yasser Arafat, the head of the PA, also authorized the arrest of 20 members of the PFLP. On January 15, 2002, the PA police arrested Saadet, and he has been incarcerated since then. The PFLP reacted by going underground and it has allowed other groups to take the offensive against Israel in its place. **See also** Habash, George; Palestine Liberation Organization (PLO).

Suggested readings: Alef Publishing, "After Mustafa's Assassination," *Mideast Mirror* (London) (August 29, 2001), p. 1; Jonathan Curiel, "Ex-Hijacker Condemns Terror," *San Francisco Chronicle* (October 30, 2001), p. A2; Christopher Dobson, and Ronald Payne, *The Terrorists: Their Weapons, Leaders, and Tactics*, rev. ed. (New York: Facts on File, 1982); Michael Jensen, "Assassination of Revolutionary Has Resonance for Palestinians," *Irish Times* (August 28, 2001), p. 12; Ilene R. Prusher, "Fallout from Israeli Assassination," *Christian Science Monitor* (October 23, 2001), p. 6; David Rudge, "Back in the Terror Business," *Jerusalem Post* (August 31, 2001), p. 2B.

Popular Front for the Liberation of Palestine—General Command (PFLP-GC) (See Jibril, Ahmed)

Pot, Pol (Saloth Sar) (1925–1998) (Cambodia)

Pol Pot was the leader of the Khmer Rouge and, as head of the Cambodian state in the 1970s, instigated one of the most repressive regimes in recorded history. He was born in 1925 in the village of Prek Sbauv about 90 miles north of Cambodia's capital of Phnom Penh. His parents were ethnic Khmers and his birth name was Saloth Sar. Pot's father

was a prosperous farmer. In the mid-1930s, Pot was sent to live with relatives in Phnom Penh and spent several months as a novice at a Buddhist monastery. Between 1936 and 1942, Pot attended a Catholic primary school where most of the students were French or Vietnamese. In 1942, Pot was selected to attend the brand-new College Nordom Sihanouk. Because he was a mediocre student but good in sports, his next schooling was as a carpentry student at the Ecole Technique. Using family connections with the royal family, he won a government scholarship to study in France in 1948. He also became friends with Ieng Sary.

Pot's stay in France was eventful because he became a member of the French Communist Party. At first he studied technical subjects at Paris's Cité Universitaire. In the summer of 1950, he volunteered to work in Yugoslavia. After returning to Paris, Pot joined other Cambodian students in a Marxist-Leninist discussion group. Political turmoil in Cambodia and the foundation of the Communist Khmer People's Revolutionary Movement attracted their attention. In 1952, Pot joined the French Communist Party. Because he was neglecting his studies, Pot lost his scholarship and returned to Cambodia in December 1952.

Pot joined the communist movement in Cambodia soon after his return. In August 1953, he joined the Indochina Communist Party. Vietnamese Communists dominated this party, but Pot was considered a valuable member because of his contacts with Cambodian dissidents, the Cambodian elite, and the French Communist Party. His mentor in the party was Tou Samouth, a veteran Cambodian Communist. After the Geneva settlement in 1954, Pot returned to Phnom Penh to teach French, history, geography, and civics in a private college, Chamraon Vickea (Progressive Knowledge). Pot was a popular teacher, but most of his out-of-school activities involved working under cover for the Indochina Communist Party.

The outbreak of the Vietnam War gave Pot the opportunity to move up the Communist Party hierarchy. Cambodian Communists

In a 1983 snapshot, believed to be taken in Pyongyang, North Korea, former Khmer Rouge leader Pol Pot, center, is shown with fellow Khmer Rouge leaders Ieng Sary, left, and Son Sen. Pol Pot is believed to have gone to North Korea to solicit support. The photo was obtained from a Cambodian soldier. (AP Photo)

supported their Vietnamese colleagues by attacking the Cambodian government. The disappearance and probable murder of Tou Samouth led to Pot's promotion in the party. In 1962, he replaced Samouth and became the acting secretary of the party's Central Committee. After this position was confirmed in early 1963, a government crackdown forced Pot and the party leadership to flee Phnom Phenh for the countryside.

For the next seven years, Pol Pot remained in the Cambodian countryside in the east and northeast organizing the party. In isolation

and relatively safe, Pot began to develop his ideas for a Communist utopia. Pot studied Mao Tse-tung's Cultural Revolution and in 1966 traveled to China to witness its early stages. He was impressed with what he considered its ideal version of communism and incorporated many facets of Chinese Communism into his utopian plan for Cambodia. American intervention into the Vietnam War caused the Cambodian head of state, Prince Sihanouk, to conclude an alliance with the North Vietnamese that gave the growing communist movement popular support in

Cambodia. Pot made several trips to North Vietnam, but relations began to cool because of the insistence of the North Vietnamese that the struggle in Cambodia be subordinated to the one in South Vietnam. In 1966, Pot and the Central Committee renamed the party the Communist Party of Kampuchea (CPK).

Throughout the late 1960s, Pol Pot remained in hiding with little chance to overthrow the Sihanouk regime. Helping his cause, however, was the growing political and economic weaknesses of the Cambodian government. Popular unrest in the form of peasant rebellions gave Pot a chance to regroup his forces. Pot concluded an agreement with the North Vietnamese for a campaign to overthrow the Lon Nol regime after Lon Nol had engineered the ouster of Sihanouk. Pot joined his forces with Sihanouk in a National Front to liberate Cambodia. Sihanouk was a figurehead, but he allowed Pot to build the military forces of the Khmer Rouge.

Civil war broke out in Cambodia in the early 1970s with the Pot's Khmer Rouge in the middle. Most of the fighting in the early 1970s was by the North Vietnamese army or by Cambodians under Vietnamese leadership. Gradually this changed and the Cambodians assumed control of military operations. Between January 1973 and April 1975, the Khmer Rouge attacked Phnom Penh three times. By 1975, the Khmer Rouge had an army of 60,000. The final assault on Phnom Penh was successful on April 17, 1975.

Pol Pot instituted a regime that ensured a complete regeneration of Cambodian society. He believed that the victory belonged to the party, the army, workers, and peasants, and all other segments of the Cambodian population were enemies. These enemies were called April 17 people. Pot undertook no attempts at reconciliation, because in his view enemies had no rights. All inhabitants of Phnom Penh were forced into the countryside at gunpoint. The sick, malnourished, or exhausted were allowed to die or were killed. Soldiers in the former regime were rounded up and shot. Since Pot and his followers had little experience setting up a government, it took nearly a year before the administrative apparatus could function. Cambodia was renamed Democratic Kampuchea.

Soon after Pol Pot achieved supreme power he began purging his enemies both in and outside the party. He announced on August 21, 1976, his Four Year Plan to reconstruct Cambodia and purge it of enemies. His first step was to abolish money. An effort was made to increase rice production by the wholesale use of April 17 people, whom Pot considered expendable. He also began to purge key members of the Khmer Rouge. These former leaders were unable to believe the charges against them before being executed. Most of the party's intellectuals were purged. So many of these leaders were executed that the government administrative structure began to collapse.

By 1977, Pol Pot's hostility toward Vietnam began to lead to open warfare and then disaster. Cambodia was the initial aggressor, because Vietnam wanted to avoid another war. After Cambodian authorities started rounding up, imprisoning, and then killing Vietnamese and after a number of border incursions into Vietnam, the Vietnamese retaliated with armed forces. After the Vietnamese army's penetration 15 miles into Cambodia in December 1977, Pol Pot had the Cambodian army in the Eastern Zone purged, executing around 100,000 soldiers and family members. Vietnam followed with a massive invasion of Cambodia on December 25, 1979, that overthrew the Pot regime. On January 7, 1980, Pol Pot went into exile in Thailand.

Pot's regime had a tragic legacy. Somewhere between 800,000 to 1 million men, women, and children died as a direct consequence of Pot's policies. Pot's government executed as many as 100,000, declaring them to be political enemies of the state. Around 14,000 men, women, and children passed through the interrogation center of Tuol Sleng, S-21, in a suburb of Phnom Phenh, and few of them survived. Efforts were made in the 1980s to bring Pot to trial at the International Court of Justice in the Netherlands, but his protectors—China, Thailand,

and the United States—shielded him as part of their anti-Vietnam policy.

Pol Pot continued a guerrilla movement against the Vietnam-sponsored Cambodian government. He remained the military leader of the Khmer Rouge until 1985, but he continued as the secretary of the Communist Party until 1997. In 1989, Vietnamese troops left Cambodia and military action by Pot's Khmer Rouge intensified. Pot opposed efforts to end the Cambodian civil war by the United Nations Transitional Authority in Cambodia (UNTAC) in the early 1990s. In 1994, Pot tried to reimpose strict political and social controls in the areas under Khmer Rouge authority, but these plans backfired so severely that the Khmer Rouge began to disintegrate. Then in late 1955, Pot suffered a major stroke that affected the left side of his body. In August 1996, his lifelong associate **Ieng Sary** deserted him by seeking a pardon from the Cambodian government. Pot became desperate and ordered the assassination of another longtime colleague, Son Sen, and his family on June 9, 1997. This assassination outraged Khmer Rouge leaders and the rank-and-file and within days Pot had to flee from his headquarters. He was captured and placed on trial in July 1998 for the murder of Son Sen and crimes against the Khmer Rouge. His sentence was life house arrest. Pot died on April 16, 1998, shortly after it was announced that the Khmer Rouge leaders were going to turn him over to a tribunal to try him for crimes against humanity. His body was cremated without ceremony and with nobody in attendance. **See also** Sary, Ieng.

Suggested readings: Jerry Adler, Ron Moreau, and Melinda Liu, "Pol Pot's Last Days," *Newsweek* (April 27, 1998), p. 38; John Barron and Anthony Paul, *Murder of a Gentle Land: The Untold Story of Communist Genocide in Cambodia* (New York: Reader's Digest Press, 1977); David P. Chandler, *Brother Number One: A Political Biography of Pol Pot* (Boulder, CO: Westview Press, 1999); Ben Kiernan, *How Pol Pot Came to Power: A History of Communism in Kampuchea, 1930–1975* (London: Verso, 1985); John Pilger, "How Thatcher Gave Pol Pot a Hand," *New Statesman* (April 17, 2000), p. 1; Konstantin Richter, "Losing Pol Pot," *Columbia Journalism Review* (July–August 1998), p. 48.

Prabhakaran, Vellupillai (1954–) (Sri Lanka)

Vellupillai Prabhakaran is the leader of the Tamil separatist group **Liberation Tigers of Tamil Eelam** (LTTE) and its war against the Sri Lanka government. He was born in 1954 in village of Valvedditturai into the fishermen caste (Karaiar). His father was a Tamil civil servant. Prabhakaran grew up hearing the tales of anti-Tamil riots and atrocities conducted by the Sinhalese majority in Sri Lanka. He left school during the equivalent of high school at 16 and joined the revolutionary organization Tamil New Tigers (TNT). His revolutionary mentor was V. Navaratum, a Tamil activist preaching war against the Sinhalese. Much of his experience in the TNT was in India, where he received training from Indian intelligence (Research and Analysis Wing, or RAW) and from retired Indian servicemen sympathetic to the Tamil cause. Prabhakaran attracted attention when he murdered the Tamil mayor of Jaffna, A. Duraippa, a leader of the Tamil opposition, on July 27, 1973. His leadership in the operation against the mayor of Jaffna led to his taking command of the Liberation Tigers of Tamil Eelam. He became the chairperson of the Central Committee of the LTTE and the commander-in-chief of its military wing.

Prabhakaran spent the next decade building the LTTE. He demanded strict discipline and obedience from his followers and threatened to kill any Tamil that opposed him. His refusal to use tobacco and alcohol was extended to the members of LTTE. Illicit sex was also banned. Each member of the LTTE carried a cyanide capsule and was ordered to use it if captured. Prabhakaran organized the LTTE into small commando groups with little hierarchical structure to carry out operations, but he retained overall dictatorial control in part by suppressing dissenters by having them executed. Because of LTTE contacts with the Indian army, Prabhakaran was

Vellupillai Prabhakaran, the Tamil Tiger leader, addresses a news conference in Kilinochchi, Sri Lanka, April 10, 2002. Prabhakaran said conditions were not right for giving up his group's independence demand. The Liberation Tigers of Tamil Eelam have been fighting Sri Lankan forces to create a separate homeland in northern and eastern Sri Lanka since 1983, claiming more than 64,000 lives. (AP Photo/ Gemunu Amarasinghe)

able to equip his guerrillas with better weapons than the Sri Lankan forces. Besides conventional weapons, the LTTE specialized in the use of land mines.

Prabhakaran's strategy was to drive Sri Lankan military forces and the Sinhalese population out of northern and eastern Sri Lanka. Intimidation and sporadic attacks on the Sinhalese population caused this part of his strategy to be successful. The campaign to force Sri Lankan military forces outside these areas has been more problematic. Prabhakaran made the city of Jaffna the de facto seat of government of the separatist state of Eelam.

Prabhakaran's success as the leader of LTTE was helped by Indian military and popular support and recruits following the Sinhalese-Tamil riots in Colombo in July 1983. India provided both sanctuary in times of trouble and financial and military assistance. Hostility between the Sinhalese-controlled government and the Tamil minority culminated in the July riots in 1983. Even Tamil citizens formerly lukewarm toward the LTTE rallied to it as a defender of Tamil rights. Government crackdowns on Tamils only further alienated the Tamil population and made them sympathetic to Prabhakaran and the LTTE.

Prabhakaran was a reluctant supporter of the 1987 peace accord negotiated by India and the Sri Lankan government. Sri Lankan military forces had made gains against the LTTE in northern Sri Lanka when India decided to intervene. A peace accord was negotiated with an Indian Peace-Keeping Force (IPKF) occupying key Tamil areas. This force was to ensure peace, but soon the IPKF and the LTTE began having difficulties. Prabhakaran retaliated against what he perceived as anti-Tamil actions by Indian forces and ordered attacks against them. The IPKF invaded the north and in heavy fighting captured Jaffna. Prabhakaran then ordered the LTTE into the countryside to continue harassing both the IPKF and the Sri Lankan forces. This guerrilla warfare and the new government of Ranasinghe Premadasa's pressure caused India to recall Indian forces from Sri Lanka.

Prabhakaran has retained control of the LTTE and kept it as a threat to the Sri Lankan state throughout the 1990s and early 2000s. Sri Lankan military campaigns in the mid-1990s threatened the areas under LTTE control, but each time Prabhakaran was able command LTTE forces to regain lost territory. Throughout the fighting Prabhakaran never deviated from his demand for a separate Tamil state in northern Sri Lanka. Recent negotiations undertaken by the Norwegian government for a peaceful settlement have allowed Prabhakaran to moderate his stance to a demand for a federated state under the control of the Tamils. This stance has not been accepted by the Sri Lankan government and there has been dissidence between the president and the prime minister over this demand. Prabhakaran has threatened to resume military operations unless progress is made in the negotiations. See also Liberation Tigers of Tamil Eelam (LTTE).

Suggested readings: Peter Goodspeed, "Leader of Tamil Tigers Known for Ruthless Warfare," *Toronto Star* (August 21, 1994), p. E5; Indira A. R. Lakshamanan, "A Ruthless Tiger Leads Long Battle against Sri Lanka," *Boston Globe* (June 22, 2000), p. A1; William McGowan, *Only Man Is Vile: The Tragedy of Sri Lanka* (New York: Farrar, Straus & Giroux, 1992); Peter Popham, "Tamil Tiger's Triumph Caps a Lifetime of War and Murder," *Financial Times* (London) (May 28, 2000), p. 1; Edgar O'Balance, *The Cyanide "War: Tamil Insurrection in Sri Lanka 1973–88* (London: Brassey's, 1989); Sinha Ratnatunga, "The First Step Taken in a Lankan Minefield," *Gulf News* (Dubai, United Arab Emirates) (February 26, 2002), p. 1; Ravi Velloor, "The Mind of a Guerrilla," *Strait Times* (Singapore) (June 25, 1995), p. 7; Paul Watson, "A Tamil Rebel Leader Vows: No Surrender," *Toronto Star* (November 16, 1995), p. A1.

Provisional Irish Republican Army (Provos) (PIRA) (Northern Ireland)

The Provisional Irish Republican Army (Provos, or PIRA) has been the leading Catholic republican extremist group in Northern Ireland. Most of the Provos leaders had been active members of the **Irish Republican Army (IRA)**, but, in late December 1969, they split from the IRA over whether or not to concentrate energies on freeing the six countries of Northern Ireland from British rule. Catholics had started a civil rights movement in Northern Ireland in January 1967, which produced a violent response from Protestant loyalists. Those bolting the IRA adopted the name of Provisional IRA and those staying in the original IRA earned the name Official IRA. Key leaders of the Provos were **Sean MacStiofain**, who became the chief of staff of the Provisional IRA, Ruairi O'Bradaigh, and Daithi O'Conaill. After splitting from the Official IRA, the Provisional IRA established its headquarter in Dublin, but most of its operations were in Northern Ireland. The IRA had not been active in the Catholic civil rights campaign, but there was a demand from IRA leaders in Belfast for the IRA to intervene. Up until 1972, the Official IRA was larger in Northern Ireland than the Provisional IRA. Throughout 1970 and early in 1971, the rival IRA groups spent as much energy fighting against each other than they did against the British and Protestants in Northern Ireland. After several attempts by each group to assassinate the other group's leadership, both groups concluded an unofficial truce in early 1971.

As the Provos became more engaged, the leadership devised a strategy of terrorism that would make the situation in Northern Ireland so inoperable that the British army would have to withdraw and Northern Ireland would be able to unite into one country. They devised a variety of tactics. Younger members resorted to rioting and stone throwing. More senior member bombed and shot British security forces, Protestants, and followers of the Ulster loyalist groups. Recruitment was most successful among young, working-class Catholics, and these recruits were necessary because of heavy losses in deaths and captures. Recruitment became easier after a British military unit opened fire on a Catholic crowd in Derry, Northern Ireland, on January 30, 1972, killing 13 Catholic civilians. This incident earned the name "Bloody Sunday." After May 1972, the Official IRA withdrew its participation in the terrorist campaign in Northern Ireland by proclaiming a cease-fire. This cease-fire meant that the Provisional IRA bore the responsibility for the militant campaign in Northern Ireland. Even the leadership of the Provos participated in talks in July 1972 with the British government for a settlement, but these talks broke down over the insistence of the Provos representatives that the British withdraw from Northern Ireland. This breakdown and tension still present in Catholic circles about Bloody Sunday resulted in Provisional IRA activists planting 22 bombs around Belfast that exploded on July 21, 1972, killing 11 and wounding more than 100.

During the course of 1971 and 1972, most of the veteran leaders had been arrested and imprisoned. Republic of Ireland police arrested MacStiofain in November 1972. He engaged in a hunger strike, but he gave in after 57 days. His inability to win concessions with his hunger strike hurt his prestige in the Provisional IRA movement and he was removed as chief of staff after he was released from prison. He was replaced by a series of appointments, but none of them lasted long. After 1973, operations in Northern Ireland became less successful and more dangerous. This lack of success in Northern Ireland led to the Army Council in 1973 to approve a bombing campaign in England. This bombing campaign and a subsequent February 1975 cease-fire proved to be failures.

Failures on the part of the leadership of the Provisional IRA led to a crisis of confidence in the older leaders. Two critics of the Army Council were **Gerry Adams** and **Martin McGuinness**. In 1977, the Army Council commissioned McGuinness, the head of the Derry Provisional IRA, and Ivor Malachy Bell, a leader of the Belfast Provisional IRA and a close associate of Belfast leader Adams, to study its operations and propose changes in the Army Council's administrative structure. They concluded in a report that the IRA was on the verge of defeat unless it reorganized. Their proposal was that a Northern Command and a Southern Command be established. The Northern Command would have administrative control of the six Northern Ireland counties of Antrim, Armagh, Down, Derry, Fermanagh, and Tyrone, and the five border counties of the Republic of Ireland (Cavan, Donegal, Leitrim, Louth, and Monaghan). This Northern Command would then be divided into five operational brigades operating out of Armagh, Belfast, Derry, Donegal, and Tyrone/Monaghan. Each brigade would be further divided into self-contained operational cells. Cells would have 5 to 10 members and each cell would carry out operations with a minimum of oversight. In contrast, the Southern Command would serve as a quartermaster service providing finances, weapons, training, and transportation for the Northern Command. It would have one brigade in Dublin, but it would have operatives throughout the rural areas. Both the Northern and Southern Command would be accountable to the Chief of Staff and the Army Council.

In 1978, the Army Council implemented the recommends of the McGuinness-Bell report. This system made it more difficult to identify IRA activists and provided more security. At the same time senior IRA leaders were placed in figurehead positions while younger leaders assumed operational responsibilities. Ranks of active fighters dropped from around 3,000 to slightly more than 300. Operations became more efficient and casualties lessened.

The first test of the reforms was in a series of spectacular terrorist operations. Most famous of these was the August 27, 1979, bomb blast on a boat skippered by Earl Mountbatten, which killed him, several members of his family, and family friends. The same day, two bombs exploded near Narrow Water Castle, killing 18 British paratroopers of the Second Parachute Regiment. These actions had been planned and executed by the Army Council under the leadership of Adams.

British reaction and former crackdowns had filled Northern Ireland prisons with Provisional IRA members. Previous to March 1, 1976, Provisional IRA prisoners were classified as de facto prisoners of war. After that date, prisoners would be treated as regular convicts. On October 27, 1980, seven prisoners began a hunger strike to win concessions from the British government. After this attempt failed, Bobby Sands initiated his 65-day hunger strike on March 1, 1981, which led to his death on May 5. During the hunger strike, he was elected to the House of Commons from Fermanagh and South Tyrone. Three others died with Sands. These hunger strikes were a propaganda coup for the Provisional IRA.

After the hunger strikes, Adams and McGuinness transferred their attention from the Army Council to Sinn Fein. Sinn Fein had little role previously, but now it became the way to reorient the struggle and turn to politics. This conversion away from a military strategy to a political one resulted in several defections. Among these were former members of the Provisional IRA, who formed the Real IRA and the **Continuity IRA.**

Militants within the Provisional IRA still carried out terrorist acts. These acts took place mostly in Northern Ireland, but sometimes operations extended into England. One of these was the bombing in London on July 20, 1982, during the military changing of the guard ceremonies that killed 9 soldiers and wounded 49 soldiers and civilians. Another such act was the November 8, 1987, bombing in Enniskillen that killed 11 and wounded another 63. But it was the car bomb assassination of Ian Gow, Conservative member of the British Parliament and a harsh critic of the Provisional IRA, that infuriated the British government.

It was the Sinn Fein under the leadership of Adams and McGuinness that negotiated the 1994 cease-fire and the 1998 Good Friday Accord. These political initiatives always had the specter of the Provisional IRA behind it. Several times its militants conducted terrorist operations, including ending the 1994 cease-fire with a bombing at Canary Wharf in London on February 9, 1996. Despite these incidents, the main political initiative belonged to Sinn Fein leaders. Adams and McGuinness used the disarming of the Provisional IRA as a bargaining ploy to win concessions and allow McGuinness to enter the Northern Ireland government. Now the Provisional IRA is a partner in the peace process, but progress has been slow because of the need to disarm the warring parties. **See also** Adams, Gerry; Irish Republican Army (IRA); MacStiofain, Sean; McGuinness, Martin; Sinn Fein (Ourselves Alone).

Suggested readings: Patrick Bishop, and Eamonn Mallie, *The Provisional IRA* (London: Corgi Books, 1988); Liam Clarke, and Kathryn Johnston, *Martin McGuinness: From Guns to Government* (Edinburgh: Mainstream Publishing, 2001); Tim Pat Coogan, *The IRA: A History* (Niwot, CO: Robert Rinehart, 1993); Ed Moloney, *A Secret History of the IRA* (New York: Norton, 2002).

Q

Qaddafi, Muammar (1942–) (Libya)

Muammar Qaddafi is the head of the Libyan state and is the advocate of a form of socialist Islam. He came to power in 1969 by overthrowing the conservative monarchy of King Idris. His goal has been to unify pan-Arabism, socialism, and Islam. In his three volumes, *The Green Book* (1977–1979), Qaddafi provided a blueprint for Libyan society and a revolutionary goal to create a populist-socialist world order. He formed the Green Revolutionary Guard to carry out his agenda in Libya. During the late 1970s, Qaddafi undertook a cultural revolution in Libya to carry out his ideas. Libya became a people's state with a decentralized, participatory government of people's committees overseeing all aspects of economic, political, and social life.

Although Qaddafi proclaimed Libya an Islamic fundamentalist state, Islamic fundamentalists throughout the Middle East condemned Qaddafi and Libya. To these Muslim leaders Qaddafi had subordinated Islam to another ideology. Qaddafi interpreted the Koran to justify his views and produced a radical Islam that was unacceptable to Islamic fundamentalist. His rejection of Islamic law, the Sharia, in favor of his personal interpretation was troubling to them. Qaddafi's rejection of traditional religious authority and his radical interpretation of Islam made him enemies in the Islamic world. His seizure of the mosques in Libya only intensified the hostility. Both the **Muslim Brotherhood** and the Islamic Liberation Organization (ILO) campaigned against Qaddafi and thus earned his enmity. Members of both organizations have been arrested and executed in Libya.

Qaddafi has been active in exporting his brand of Islamic revolution. Using the oil wealth of Libya, Qaddafi has tried to replace Gamal Abdel Nasser as the leading figure in the Arab world. He believes that Western colonialism is the main enemy that the Arabs face and that Israel is a product of this colonialism. His policy has been to strike at the Western world by advancing a twofold strategy—economic development of Third World countries and strategic terrorism. Economic development has been channeled through the Islamic Call Society that Qaddafi established in 1972. Qaddafi has supported various terrorist groups, including the **Abu Nidal Organization** (ANO), the **Irish Republican Army** (IRA), and the **Moro National Liberation Front** (MNLF). Support has been in the form of money and sanctuary for its leaders.

Qaddafi's nemesis was President Ronald Reagan. Reagan and his advisors decided that Qaddafi's sponsorship of terrorism made him a worthy target. Confrontation led to an

American bombing attack that targeted Qaddafi. Qaddafi escaped unharmed but an adopted member of his family died. Qaddafi retaliated by sponsoring the terrorism that resulted in the December 21, 1988, bombing of Pan American Flight 103 over Lockerbie, Scotland. This bombing killed 270 people and it marked the final step in his support of terrorism.

Qaddafi has tried to revamp his image and become more moderate. No longer does he sponsor armed struggle against Western imperialism and the destruction of Israel. He has accepted the responsibility for the Lockerbie bombing and agreed to pay $2.7 billion to the families of the 270 victims. In the 1990s, he toyed with supporting neo-Nazi movements in Europe and North America, but recently he has turned his attention to other matters. He was one of the first Muslim leaders to decry the **September 11, 2001,** terrorist attacks on the United States. His efforts have been directed at ending United Nations sanctions against Libya for its former support of terrorism. At present he is working on a plan to support a pan-African movement. Qaddafi has turned from his Arab roots to his African ones. Although the George W. Bush administration has sent out signals that it is willing to discuss a change of status with Libya, Qaddafi continued to make American policymakers nervous. This nervousness increased when Qaddafi confessed that Libya had a nuclear program capable of making weapons of mass destruction (WMD).

Despite Libya's oil reserves, the Libya economy had deteriorated enough in the 1990s that Qaddafi has been more receptive to overtures from the West. In early 1999 representatives from the United States met with a representative from the Libyan government to study ways that Libya could reestablish good relations with the United States and its allies. These requirements were an end to Qaddafi's sponsorship of terrorism, cooperate with the United States in fighting terrorism, and accept full responsibility for the Lockerbie crash victims. In return, the United States would work to remove the United Nations sanctions against Libya. These sanctions ended in 1999. Qaddafi repaid this return to international respectability by condemnation of the September 11, 2001, attacks on the United States, and by the agreement by Qaddafi in early 2004 to end his development of nuclear weapons. **See also** Abu Nidal Organization (ANO); Irish Republican Army (IRA); Moro National Liberation Front (MNLF).

Suggested readings: Edward Alden and Roula Khalaf, "Dealing with Gadaffi: How the US Negotiated Libya's Rehabilitation," *Financial Times* [London] (October 28, 2003), p. 21; Scott Anderson, "The Makeover," *New York Times* (January 19, 2003), sec. 6, p. 29; David Blundy and Andrew Lycett, *Qaddafi and the Libyan Revolution* (Boston: Little, Brown, 1987); Stephen Fidler, Mark Huband, and Roula Khalaf, "Return to the Fold: How Gadaffi Was Persuaded to Give Up His Nuclear Goals," *Financial Times* [London] (January 27, 2004), p. 17; Lillian Craig Harris, *Libya: Qadhafi's Revolution and the Modern State* (Boulder, CO: Westview Press, 1986); Judith Miller, *God Has Ninety-Nine Names* (New York: Touchstone, 1996); Rosemary Righter, "Mad, or Just Bad? The Man Who Would Be King of Africa," *Times* (London) (January 22, 2003), p. 2; Ray Takeyh, "Has Gaddafi Reformed?" *Washington Post* (August 19, 2003), p. A19; George Tremlett, *Gadaffi: The Desert Mystic* (New York: Carroll & Graf, 1993).

Al-Qaeda (The Base) (Afghanistan)

Al-Qaeda is the international terrorist network led by **Osama bin Laden**. Bin Laden formed this umbrella network in 1988 out of an Afghan resistance group, the Mujahideen Services Bureau (MAK). Al-Qaeda has a variety of terrorist organizations affiliated with it including the **Armed Islamic Group** (GIA) (Algeria), **Hezbollah** (Lebanon), **Islamic Group** (Egypt), **Hamas** (Palestine), **Islamic Jihad** (Egypt), **Moro Islamic Liberation Front** (Philippines), and **Abu Sayyaf** (Philippines) along with at least 24 others. Some confusion exists among Western analysts over the extent of al-Qaeda's control over these groups, but it has been able to establish a degree of coordination among them. Rohan Gunaratna, a research fellow at the Centre for the Study of Terrorism and Political Violence at the University of St. Andrews in Scotland, has described al-Qaeda as "a secret, almost virtual, organization, one that denies its own existence in order to remain in the shadows." **Mohammad Atef,** a former Egyptian policeman, was its operational leader until his death in 2001, and **Ayman al-Zawahiri,** an Egyptian medical doctor and the leader of the Islamic Jihad, remains bin Laden's closest associate.

Osama bin Laden is both its political leader and its chief financial supporter. He has used his personal fortune of between $30 million and $35 million to support many of al-Qaeda's operations. Other significant sources of funding have been Islamic nongovernment organizations (NGOs), such as Islamic charities and foundations and state sponsors (Afghanistan, Sudan, and Iran). Gunaratna suggests that the annual budget for al-Qaeda is in the neighborhood of $50 million, but for all of its operations it needs about $100 million a year.

Al-Qaeda is a selective organization that tightly oversees the selection of its members to carry out operations. Al-Qaeda only recruits the most highly motivated and talented candidates. These candidates consider it an honor to be allowed into al-Qaeda, and they are highly motivated to carry out operations, even suicide missions. It has trained more than 5,000 operatives in a dozen training camps in Afghanistan to carry out terrorist operations. Because of its prestige, there is a reservoir of those trained in Afghanistan, probably as many as 100,000, who are willing to join al-Qaeda, if invited. Al-Qaeda uses cells of from 2 to 15 members to carry out operations. This system is used to make operations resistant to intelligence services penetration. Internal security is tight, and suspected agents trying to penetrate al-Qaeda are killed. At last count in 2002 al-Qaeda had operatives in 55 countries.

Bin Laden has shifted the headquarters of al-Qaeda several times. The original base camp was near the city of Peshawar, Pakistan. In 1991, bin Laden transferred the headquarters to Sudan, where the friendly regime of **Hasan al-Turabi** allowed his organization complete freedom. Pressure by the Western powers on the Sudanese government caused bin Laden to move al-Qaeda's headquarters again in 1996. This time the move was back to Afghanistan to a base camp near Farmihadda. Over the next five years, bin Laden's close ties to the **Taliban** government allowed him to establish a dozen al-Qaeda training centers.

Al-Qaeda's first terrorist operation occurred in 1992. Operatives exploded a bomb in a hotel in Aden, Yemen, on December 29, 1992. The target was U.S. troops embarking from Aden to Somalia, but the only casualties in this attempt were two Austrian tourists. In their next operation, a Qaeda operative, **Ramzi Yousef,** made the bomb that detonated in the basement of the World Trade Center in New York City on February 26, 1993, killing 6 and injuring more than 1,000. On June 26, 1995, an al-Qaeda-affiliated group tried to assassinate Egyptian President Hosni Mubarak in Addis Ababa, Ethiopia. Another major operation was the truck bombing that killed 19 U.S. servicemen and wounded 500 others outside the Khobar Towers in Dhahran, Saudi Arabia, on June 25, 1996. Next, al-Qaeda members planned and carried out the bombings of the U.S. embassies in Nairobi, Kenya, and Dar es Salaam, Tanzania, on August 7, 1998, killing 234 people. Finally, on October 5, 2000, suspected members of al-Qaeda conducted on October 12, 2000, a suicide bombing of the American warship the USS *Cole,* which killed 17 sailors and wounded 39 others.

These terrorist actions paled in comparison to the **September 11,** 2001, suicide attacks on the World Trade Center Towers in New York City and on the Pentagon in Arlington, Virginia. Nineteen members of the Qaeda network seized control of four commercial airliners and used them as suicide missiles against selected targets. Two of the airliners crashed into the towers of the World Trade Center, causing both towers to collapse. Casualties of this attack numbered nearly 3,000 people. A third airliner crashed into a wing of the Pentagon, killing nearly 200. A fourth aircraft never made it to its target and went down in a field in Pennsylvania, killing everyone aboard.

The collapse of the Taliban in Afghanistan in 2001 was a serious blow to al-Qaeda's operations. Al-Qaeda lost its main base for the training of its members and a secure planning area. Al-Qaeda's guerrilla organization, 055 Brigade, was also seriously damaged. This military force had around 2,000 non–Afghan Arab fighters, but more than 500 were lost in the fighting. Because of its decentralized command structure, al-Qaeda has been able to recover much of its strike capability by entrusting operations to subordinate groups. The survival of bin Laden and al-Zawahiri has also helped it reestablish operations. Great Britain and Yemen have been important centers for al-Qaeda operations since the late 1990s and they are still centers of activity.

Attacks by security agencies in the United States, Europe, and in the Middle East have been partially successful in hindering al-Qaeda's terrorist campaign. Al-Qaeda has been put on the defensive, with the alternatives being advancing operations before they are ready, or making operatives go underground as sleepers for operations in the future. Western security forces continue to consider al-Qaeda a major threat posed to strike at any time and anywhere with any type of weapon, from biological to nuclear. **See also** Abu Sayyaf Group (Bearer of the Sword) (ASG); Armed Islamic Group (Groupes Islamiques Armés) (GIA); Bin Laden, Osama; Hamas (Haarakat al-Muqawama al-Islami) (Islamic Resistance Movement); Hezbollah (Party of God); Islamic Group (al-Gama'a al-Islamiyya); Islamic Jihad; Moro Islamic Liberation Front (MILF).

Suggested readings: Yonah Alexander, and Michael S. Swetnam, *Usama bin Laden's al-Qaida: Profile of a Terrorist Network* (Ardsley, NY: Transnational Publishers, 2001); Jason Burke, *Al-Qaeda: Casting a Shadow of Terror* (London: I. B. Tauris, 2003); Jane Corbin, *Al-Qaeda: The Terror Network That Threatens the World* (New York: Thunder's Mouth Press, 2002); John Gray, *Al-Qaeda: Casting a Shadow of Terror* (London: I. B. Tauris, 2003); Rohan Gunaratna, *Inside Al Qaeda: Global Network of Terror* (New York: Columbia University Press, 2002); Jessica Stern, "The Protean Enemy," *Foreign Affairs* (July/August 2003), p. 27; Olivia Ward, "Al Qaeda Mutating Like a Virus," *Toronto Star* (June 22, 2003), p. F3.

Qutb, Sayyid (1906–1966) (Egypt)

Sayyid Qutb was the chief theoretician of the **Muslim Brotherhood** and remains the ideological leader of the modern Islamist movement. He was born on October 8, 1906, in Musha, Egypt. His family members were rural notables, but no longer prosperous. Qutb's father was an Egyptian nationalist who belonged to Mustafa Kamil's National Party. Always a good student, he was educated in the government schools in Musha. His education was interrupted because of political troubles in Egypt and he lived in Cairo for four years before enrolling in a teachers college. In 1930, he obtained more schooling at the House of Sciences in Cairo. After graduation in 1933, Qutb found a job in the Ministry of Public Instruction as a teacher. He was a teacher at a variety of posts from 1933 to 1940, ending up at Helwan near Cairo. In 1940, he became an inspector for the Ministry of Public Instruction. Besides teaching, Qutb worked as a journalist-literary critic for newspapers. His interests fluctuated between political writings and the literary subjects of poetry, short stories and novels. He published three autobiographical novels in the 1930s and 1940s along with numerous poems. After 1945, he turned most of his attention to politics and social problems.

Qutb's increasing hostile attitude toward political and social trends in Egypt earned him the enmity of the government of King Farouk. His critical writings on Egyptian politics and society led King Farouk to demand his arrest. Qutb avoided arrest by traveling to the United States in 1948 on an educational inspection tour. Everything about the United States disgusted him, from its secularism to what he considered the looseness of American women. His anti-Americanism was so strong that it led to his resignation from the Ministry of Public Instruction after his return to Egypt in 1951. While in the United States, two of his books, *Social Justice* (1949) and *The Battle of Islam and Capitalism* (1950), appeared in print in Egypt.

Soon after his return to Egypt, Qutb joined the Muslim Brotherhood. His rebellion against Americanism made him return to his religious upbringing. Within a year of his joining the Muslim Brotherhood in 1951 he was elected to the Muslim Brotherhood's leadership council. Qutb began in 1952 his 30-volume commentary of the Koran entitled *In the Shade of the Qur'an*. Before and after the 1952 military coup, Qutb met frequently with Gamal Abdel Nasser and was on friendly terms with him. This friendship ended when Qutb supported the leadership of the Muslim Brotherhood in its dispute with Nasser over the lack of movement to an Islamic state. His anti-Nasser position landed him a three-month prison term in early 1954. After his release, he became editor-in-chief of the newspaper of the Muslim Brotherhood, *The Muslim Brethren*. After the failed assassination of Nasser by a member of the Muslim Brotherhood on October 26, 1954, Qutb was arrested and tortured. In a July 1955 trial, he was sentenced to 25 years of hard labor.

Even before Qutb was imprisoned, he had already become the leading ideologue of the Muslim Brotherhood. Three of his eight works on Islamist doctrine appeared before 1955. In prison, however, Qutb finished the last five works, including finishing his *In the Shade of the Qur'an (1952–1964)*. The most significant of his writing, however, was his *Signposts Along the Road* (1964). In his book on Muslim extremism in Egypt, Gilles Kepel traced the outline of Qutb's theology. Qutb renounced

Western capitalism and socialism as ideologies that were morally bankrupt. He turned instead to Islam as a way to regenerate society. His interpretation meant that no regime was legitimate unless it ruled in God's name. Any legislation that did not rest in Islamic religious law, or the Sharia, would not be considered Muslim. In his interpretation, Nasser's government in Egypt was non-Islamic as was that of Egypt's future president, Anwar Sadat. He also advocated the need for a vanguard that would have the duty to reestablish the ideal Islamic society of the Prophet and his first four righteous successors. Only by a rigorous adherence to the Koran and the rejection of non-Muslim culture could the ideal Islamic society be formed. This book and his other writings became the cornerstone of the Islamist movement.

Qutb was not fated to witness the triumph of his ideology. After release from prison in 1964, he retained his leadership position in the Muslim Brotherhood for a brief time. In 1965, Nasser instituted another attack on the Muslim Brotherhood by charging it with a conspiracy against him and the state. Qutb was arrested along with two other Muslim Brotherhood leaders. After a short trial, Qutb was sentenced to death. He was hanged on August 29, 1966. His martyrdom only increased the popularity of his writings and his theological views. Qutb's theology has been particularly popular in Saudi Arabia and Afghanistan, but Islamists in all Middle Eastern countries study it. See also Muslim Brotherhood (al-Ikhwan al-Muslimun).

Suggested readings: Roxanne L. Euben, *Enemy in the Mirror: Islamic Fundamentalism and the Limits of Modern Rationalism: A Work of Modern Rationalism* (Princeton, NJ: Princeton University Press, 1999); Robert Irwin, "After September 11: Is This the Man Who Inspired Bin Laden?" *Guardian* (London) (November 1, 2001); Gilles Kepel, *Muslim Extremism in Egypt: The Prophet and Pharaoh* (Berkeley: University of California Press, 1986.

R

Rael (1946–) (France)

Rael is the founder of the **Raelian Movement**. He was born on September 30, 1946, in France. His birth name was Claude Vorilhon. After a career as a singer-songwriter and part-time race car driver, he pursued a career as a sports car journalist for his own publication *Autopop*. Vorilhon claimed that on December 13, 1973, he was contacted by extraterrestrial creatures at a volcano near Auvergne in the Clermont-Ferrand mountain range in France. In honor of this contact, Vorilhon changed his name to Rael. In 1978, his two earlier works describing his contacts with these extraterrestrials were combined into *Space Aliens Took Me to Their Planet: The Most Important Revelations in the History of Mankind*. He continues to write books to explain the principles and ideas of the Raelian Movement.

Rael began to attract adherents. Neil Mackay in *The Sunday Herald* in December 2002 estimated his following to be "55,000 followers in 84 countries." The only requirement to join the Raelian Movement is that members give the Raelians 3 percent of their income annually. Rael established his headquarters near Quebec, Canada, at his theme park, UFOland.

Rael would have been relegated to the head of a weird UFO (unidentified flying object) sect except that he landed in the middle of the cloning controversy. Cloning had been a part of Rael's religious vision and the way for immortality of his followers. Soon after the news about the scientific viability of cloning, Rael recruited a French biochemist, Brigitte Boisselier, to set up a company, Clonaid, and a laboratory to study the possibility of cloning a human. On December 26, 2002, Boisselier announced at a press conference that she had successfully cloned a seven-pound baby girl that she named Eve. Since then, Boisselier has announced the existence of two other cloned babies. Despite these announcements, Rael or his associates have produced no proof beyond photographs. Scientists around the world have been skeptical about the clonings, but the international media has had a feeding frenzy covering this story. Rael continues to assert his theories of immortality and cloning to his followers around the world. **See also** Raelian Movement.

Suggested readings: DeNeen L. Brown, "The Leader of UFO Land," *Newsbytes* (January 17, 2003), p. 1; James R. Lewis, *Peculiar Prophets: A Biographical Dictionary of New Religions* (St. Paul, MN: Paragon House, 1999; John Preston, "The Rael Thing," *Sunday Telegraph* (London) (April 13, 2003), p. 1.

Raelian Movement (France)

The Raelian Movement is an international millenarian UFO cult. Claude Vorilhon, a former French race car driver and journalist, founded the movement in December 1973 after having an alleged encounter with space aliens. Shortly after this alleged incident, Vorilhon adopted the name Rael. Rael's interpretation of his interaction with space aliens included the story that extraterrestrial scientists, the "Elohim," had placed humans on Earth. Rael has maintained that he is the last of a series of 40 prophets who have been crossbred in unions between the Elohim and human women. Among the other 39 prophets are Jesus, Buddha, Muhammad, Joseph Smith, and other great religious and scientific leaders. According to him, humanity has entered the apocalyptic phase of history, and the Elohim will save only 4 percent of the humans to populate other planets. In this scenario, the Elohim will select those to be saved from the list of Raelian believers. Raelians are those who acknowledge the Elohim as their fathers. Immortality for the chosen is promised through cloning. A company, Valiant Venture Ltd., has been set up in the Bahamas to offer human cloning for interested partners willing to invest in the process.

The Raelian Movement has an international membership. Strongholds of members exist in France, Japan, and in French-speaking Canada. Although the leaders have claimed that there are as many as 55,000 members, the active membership is much smaller, probably numbering in the hundreds. Members are encouraged to give 11 percent of their net income to the movement and leave their estates to local Raelian leaders. Because salvation is achieved through cloning, Rael has discouraged marriages. Instead, he advises his followers to explore their sexuality with members of the opposite or same sex. This open sexuality message has earned the Raelian Movement notoriety in the media. Rael's advocacy of abortion to end unwanted pregnancies is another controversial aspect of this movement. In August 1997, Rael opened a center called UFOland in Quebec, Canada, showing his interpretation of an alien spaceship. Other exhibits explain Raelian cloning and other Raelian teachings.

The Raelian Movement was a quaint cult

with little political impact until scientific breakthroughs made human cloning possible. Suddenly, human cloning became a fervent ethical, political, and religious issue. As soon as Rael learned of the scientific possibilities from the cloning of the sheep Dolly in 1997, he established a corporation in the Bahamas, Clonaid, to conduct research on cloning. Rael placed Brigitte Boisselier, a French scientist, in charge of cloning experiments. On December 26, 2002, Boisselier claimed that a baby girl, Eve, had been cloned at Clonaid. This news produced an animated discussion among American political and religious leaders on the ethical implications of cloning.

By late 2003, the Raelians had claimed to have cloned five babies, but the cult made even more sensation news by saying that it had found the secret of eternal youth. Dr. Boisselier maintains that the use of stem cells can turn back the clock on any part of the body. Again the medical community wants proof of the procedures before accepting any of the claims. See also Rael.

Suggested readings: William M. Alnor, *UFO Cults and the New Millennium* (Grand Rapids, MI: Baker Books, 1998); Ben Hills, "It's The Rael Thing," *Sydney Morning Herald* (February 1, 2003), p. 29; James Langton, "Now Cloning Cult Says It Has Found the Secret of Eternal Youth," *Evening Standard* [London] (November 14, 2003), p. 5; James R. Lewis (ed.), *The Gods Have Landed: New Religions from Other Worlds* (Albany: State University of New York Press, 1995); Neil Mackay, "First Dolly, Then Eve: Now My Aim Is to Use Cloning to Change Humankind," *Sunday Herald* (Edinburgh) (December 29, 2002), p.3.

Ranvir Sena (India)

The Ranvir Sena is an upper-caste army established by landlords in the eastern province of Bihar of India to fight the Maoist Communist **Naxalite** rebels. On October 8, 1994, landlords formed a private army at the village of Belaur to defend their land and property against the threat of lower-caste Naxalites. Bihar is one of India's poorest states and it has a long history of lawlessness. Upper-caste landlords recruited an army from their retainers and trained them to conduct military and terrorist operations against lower-class Dalits (formerly called "untouchables"). The first leader of the Ranvir Sena, Brahmeshwar Singh, retained control until his arrest on August 29, 2002. Replacing him in September 2002 was Shamsher Bahadur Singh. In August 1995, the state government banned Ranvir Sena after the Sarathna massacre of six Dalits in late July 1995.

Despite the banning, the Ranvir Sena decided to launch a terrorist campaign in the mid-1990s. On December 2, 1997, hundreds of Ranvir Sena adherents massacred 61 persons, including 22 women and 17 children, at Laxmanpu Bathe in Jehanabad district in Bihar. Ranvir Sena leaders identified 14 houses filled with what they perceived to be Naxalite supporters and directed its military forces against the inhabitants. On June 16, 2000, a Ranvir Sena army of 500 slaughtered 34 lower-caste peasants at the village of Miapur. Indian authorities have been reluctant to investigate these crimes in depth because the political influence of the sponsors of the Ranvir Sena. Except for an occasional arrest of minor operatives, the operations of the Ranvir Sena continue unmolested. This changed in August 2003, when Indian police captured Bishewhwar Roy, the alleged area commander of Ranvir Sena. His capture, however, has not curtailed the terrorist activities of the Ranvir Sena. **See also** Naxalite Movement.

Suggested readings: Pamela Constable, "Violent Extremes; Intensifying Conflict Over Land, Labor and Caste Claims Hundreds of Victims in Poor Indian State," *Washington Post* (May 1, 1999), p. A9; Bharat Desai, "Bihar: Primed to Kill," *India Today* (August 31, 1998), p. 40; Bharat Desai and Sanjay Kumar Jha, "Bihar: Savage Reprisal," *India Today* (December 15, 1997), p. 52; Hema Shukla, "Indian Militants Promise Revenge Slayings," *Ottawa Citizen* (June 20, 2000); Nalin Verma, "And Now, a Temple to Ranvir Baba," *Statesman* (India) (July 6, 2000), p. 1.

Rashtriya Swayamsevak Sangh (National Volunteer Organization) (RSS) (India)

The Rashtriya Swayamsevak Sangh (National Volunteer Organization) (RSS) is India's leading Hindu supremacist organization. It was founded in 1925 to fight British colonial rule and Muslim separatists. Inspiration for the new group came from the Italian Fascist Party with its uniforms and mass demonstrations. British authorities soon banned the RSS because of its militant activities, and the group went underground. During World War II, leaders of the RSS were open admirers of Adolf Hitler. The group reappeared at the time of the partition of India. Members were active in organizing relief for Hindus fleeing from Pakistan. A member of the RSS assassinated Mohandas K. Gandhi in 1948. This assassination led the new Indian government to ban the RSS once again.

The Rashtriya Swayamsevak Sangh became the leading Hindu nationalist organization in India. Besides openly espousing Hindu nationalism, the RSS opened charities and schools to propagate its ideology. By the early 1990s, there were 6,000 RSS schools and 26,000 clubs. The most militant wing of the RSS has been the **Bajrang Dal**. At first the RSS directed most of the militancy toward Muslims, but this hostility was extended to Buddhists and Christians in the 1990s. The RSS was banned a third time in 1992 after RSS and **Shiv Sena** activists destroyed a sixteenth-century mosque in the northern Indian town of Ayodhya, claiming that it had been built on the birth site of the Hindu god Ram. This ban lasted only until 1993.

The Rashtriya Swayamsevak Sangh has become more politically influential since the victory of the Bharati Janata Party (BJP) in 1998. Both the Prime Minister Atal Bihari Vajpayee and Home Minister **Lal Krishna Advani** came out of the ranks of the RSS. Current leader of the RSS Kuppahalli Sitaramayya Sudershan has advocated that all foreign churches and missionaries be expelled and that India have a state-controlled indigenous church. Much of the grassroots political campaign for the BJP comes from the RSS. Peace overtures between the Vajpayee government and Pakistan in 2003 have been unpopular among the RSS rank-and-file because of their desire for direct military action. Despite dissatisfaction, the

RSS has no choice but to support the BJP because the opposition Congress Party will have nothing to do with it. **See also** Advani, Lal Krishna; Bajrang Dal; Shiv Sena (Sword of Shiva).

Suggested readings: Farzand Ahmed, "RSS: Missionary Imposition," *India Today* (October 23, 2000), p. 37; Tony Clifton, "Hindustan for the Hindus," *Newsweek* (October 18, 1999), p. 42; Swapan Dasgupta and Farzand Ahmed, "RSS: Hawkish Postures," *India Today* (March 27, 2000), p. 24; Uday Mahurkar, "RSS: Crouching Tiger," *India Today* (August 13, 2001), p. 28; Robert Marquand, "Anti-Christian Violence in India Builds on Fear of Conversions," *Christian Science Monitor* (October 5, 1998), p. 7; Tim McGirk, "Hindu 'Stormtroopers' Fuel Religious Revival," *Independent* (London) (February 22, 1993), p. 8.

Raspe, Jan-Carl (1944–1977) (West Germany)

Jan-Carl Raspe became one of the leaders of the West German terrorist group **Red Army Faction** (RAF). He was born in 1944 in Berlin, Germany. His father, who was a businessman, died before Raspe was born. His mother raised him in East Berlin. He received his primary education in East Berlin, but East German educational authorities refused him admittance into secondary school because of his class background. Raspe instead commuted to West Berlin to the Bertha von Suttner High School until the Berlin Wall went up in August 1961. Raspe decided to stay in West Berlin and he lived there with an uncle and aunt. He attended the Free University in West Berlin, studying first chemistry and then sociology. His involvement in student demonstrations led to his joining the Social Democratic Party's youth group Social Democratic Students (SDS). In August 1967, Raspe was one of the founders of Commune II. This commune of four men, three women, and two children had the goal of building a new society. Members of the commune wrote a book on the experiment. Soon after he left the commune with his girlfriend, he met **Ulrike Meinhof**, a leader of the Red Army Faction.

Raspe decided to join the RAF, and in the late 1970s he was one of its key operatives. He was active in bank robberies and in the May 1972 bombing campaign. On June 1, 1972, Raspe was arrested with **Andreas Baader** outside the garage where the RAF was manufacturing bombs. On May 21, 1975, he was placed on trial with Baader, **Gudrun Ensslin**, and Meinhof. Raspe was not as aggressive as the others in his attacks on the trial and the judges, but he showed solidarity with his compatriots. On April 28, 1977, Raspe was sentenced to life imprisonment for his participation in murder and attempted murder and for forming a criminal association. German authorities sent him to the special section of Stammheim prison with other members of the RAF. Raspe never challenged Baader for leadership of the RAF, but he was an active supporter of Baader. He served as the communications expert for the prisoners. In the early morning of October 18, Raspe learned that the RAF skyjacking of a German Lufthansa aircraft had failed after a successful assault on the aircraft. He informed the other prisoners, and they decided on a suicide pact. Raspe used a pistol that he had smuggled past the guards to commit suicide sometime later on the morning of October 18. Raspe never had the notoriety of Baader, Ensslin, or Meinhof, but many of the operations of the RAF would have never been possible without his technical expertise. **See also** Baader, Andreas; Ensslin, Gudrun; Meinhof, Ulrike; Red Army Faction (RAF).

Suggested readings: Stefan Aust, *The Baader-Meinhof Group: The Inside Story of a Phenomenon* (London: Bodley Head, 1985); Jillian Becker, *Hitler's Children: The Baader-Meinhof Terrorist Gang* (Philadelphia: Lippincott, 1978); Tome Vague, *Televisionaries: The Red Army Faction* (London: AK Press, 1994).

Real Irish Republican Army (RIRA) (Northern Ireland)

The Real Irish Republican Army (RIRA) is a small group of dissidents from the **Irish Republican Army** (IRA) that has rejected the Northern Ireland peace process. **Michael**

"Mickey" McKevitt, the former quarter-master-general of the IRA, led a body of dissidents to form the Real IRA in November 1997. They share the belief that the **Provisional IRA** of **Gerry Adams** has sold out the cause of uniting Northern Ireland with the Republic of Ireland. Estimates from various sources place the RIRA at between 70 to 175 activists.

The Real IRA has launched a terrorist campaign in Northern Ireland. Several of the recruits from the IRA were explosives experts. This expertise has been used to build car bombs and mortars. Most of the bombings and mortar attacks between January 1998 and August 1998 were made after warning the British authorities in an attempt to lessen casualties. An exception was on August 15, 1998, when a car bomb detonated 500 pounds of explosives in Omagh, Northern Ireland, and killed 28 people and wounded hundreds of others. The casualties were so heavy and public outrage so high that the leaders of the RIRA decided to cease operations on August 18, 1998. Police on both sides of the Irish border have increased pressure on the RIRA and arrested several of its members.

The 32 County Sovereignty Committee is the political wing of the Real Irish Republican Army. Its goal is the political reunification of Ireland. Bernadette Sands McKevitt, the sister of the leader of the 1981 hunger strike and the wife of Michael McKevitt, founded this group in November 1997 and remains its leader. Although the committee denies its affiliation with the RIRA, members have been arrested trying to smuggle arms and bomb materials to the RIRA.

The leaders of the 32 County Sovereignty Committee have been active in trying to raise funds for the Real Irish Republican Army. In 1998, Bernadette Sands McKevitt traveled to the United States to persuade Irish Americans to redirect their financial support away from the Provisional IRA and toward the RIRA. This effort had some success with the Chicago Irish, but the designation of the RIRA as a terrorist organization in the spring of 2001 has limited its fund-raising in the United States.

The arrest and trial of McKevitt ended the career of the Real IRA. A Federal Bureau of Investigation (FBI) and MI5 (British intelligence) agent, David Rupert, had penetrated the Real IRA and informed on its activities. Based on his evidence, a Special Criminal Court in Dublin sentenced McKevitt on August 6, 2003, to a 20-year prison term for directing the activities and being a member of the Real IRA. Earlier, in October 2002, the leaders of the Real IRA had disbanded the group by announcing its demise in the *Sunday Independent* (Dublin). This declaration and the conviction of McKevitt ended the career of the Real IRA. See also Adams, Gerry; McKevitt, Michael "Mickey"; Provisional Irish Republican Army (Provos) (PIRA).

Suggested readings: Kevin Cullen, "IRA Splinter Group Poses New Threat," *Boston Globe* (May 10, 1998), p. A1; James Dingley, "The Bombing of Omagh, 15 August 1998: The Bombers, Their Tactics, Strategy and Purpose behind the Incident," *Studies in Conflict and Terrorism* 24, no. 6 (November–December 2001); Ian Mather, "The End of the Road?" *Scotland on Sunday* (Edinburgh) (August 10, 2003), p. 15; Chris Parkin, "Real IRA Plans to Disband," Press Association (October 20, 2002), p. 1; Maeve Sheehan, Liam Clarke, and David Leppard, "Tracking Down the Bombers," *Sunday Times* (London) (August 23, 1998), p. 1; Liz Walsh, "McKevitt Found Guilty of Directing Terrorism," *Irish News* (August 7, 2003), p. 2; Jamie Wilson, "How the Real IRA Recruits Boys into a Life of Terrorism," *Guardian* (London), p. 1.

Red Army Faction (RAF) (West Germany)

The Red Army Faction (RAF) was the most violent terrorist group in West Germany in the 1970s and 1980s. **Andreas Baader, Gudrun Ensslin,** and **Ulrike Meinhof** founded the Red Army Faction on May 14, 1970, in the aftermath of Baader's successful escape from prison. They soon adopted the symbol of the RAF—a red five-pointed star ornamented with a Kalashnikov rifle and the acronym RAF. Earlier, Baader and Ensslin had firebombed two Frankfurt department stores on April 3, 1968, but their actions were independent of any type of organization. In the summer of 1970, members of the RAF traveled to Jordan for terrorist training with Palestinian instructors. Both Baader and Ensslin rebelled against restrictions in the training. Palestinian instructors responded by terminating the training and arranging the return of RAF members to West Germany. The first operation back in West Berlin was the planning and carrying out of three bank robberies on September 28, 1970. These bank robberies were intended to raise fund for further terrorist operations.

In the next two years, Baader, with the support of Ensslin, masterminded the terrorist activities of the Red Army Faction. He initiated a bombing campaign that included U.S. Army and West German targets. The most deadly of these bombing attacks was at the U.S. Army headquarters in Heidelburg on May 24, 1972, which killed three U.S. soldiers. These bombings and bank robberies attracted attention from the West German police. By the spring of 1971, numerous arrests had weakened the ranks of the RAF. Members of the RAF began recruiting members from the Socialist Patients Collective (SPK). Dr. Wolfgang Huber had found this collective in February 1970 and its goal was to cure mental problems by overthrowing the perceived source of the problems: the capitalist system. Several recruits came out of this collective.

Two highly publicized deaths transformed the Red Army Faction. The first was the killing of RAF member Petra Schelm in a gunfight with police on July 15, 1971. Next was the shooting death of policeman Norbert Schmid on October 22, 1971. Both deaths intensified hostility between the German police and the RAF. More shootings and deaths on both sides in 1972 followed. On December 22, 1971, four members of the RAF robbed a bank in Kaiserslauten, and in the process they killed a policeman. By this time the RAF, also known as the Baader-Meinhof Gang, had become so famous that a media frenzy broke out. Several times police arrested innocent individuals on suspicion of being terrorists.

The capture of the major leaders of the Red Army Faction curtailed most of its activities during the period from 1973 to 1975. In the space several weeks in the summer of 1972, the leaders of the RAF were captured at various places. West German police captured Baader and **Jan-Carl Raspe** on June 1, 1972, in Frankfurt, and Ensslin on June 8, 1972, in Hamburg. Meinhof remained free until June 15, 1972, when police arrested her in Hannover. West German authorities housed these leaders in a variety of prisons to keep them separate. A special courthouse was constructed to try the RAF leadership. Before the trial, Baader called for three hunger strikes. During the last of these hunger strikes, Holgar Meins died of complications from starvation. By the time of the trial in May 1975, new recruits to the RAF and sympathizers began to rejuvenate the RAF.

On April 24, 1975, sympathizers of the Red Army Faction seized the West German Embassy in Stockholm, Sweden. Six of them occupied the embassy and held 12 hostages. They broadcasted demands for the release of 26 political prisoners to include Baader, Ensslin, Meinhof, and Jan-Carl Raspe. They shot the West German military attaché to illustrate their determination. After the West German government refused to concede to their demands, the terrorists executed the West German economic attaché. Shortly before the Swedish police were to storm the building, the terrorists accidentally exploded bombs in the building. Altogether four died in the affair; the two West German attachés and two terrorists in the explosion and in the aftermath.

The trial opened for Baader, Ensslin, Meinhof, and Raspe on May 21, 1975. The prisoners from the beginning used the trial as political theater to attack the West German political and judicial system. This tactic led the presiding judge to banish the prisoners from the courtroom much of the time. During the course of the trial, Meinhof committed suicide by hanging herself in her cell on May 8, 1976. Toward the end of the trial, the federal prosecutor General Siegfried Buback, his driver, and a passenger were shot and killed on April 7, 1977 by the self-styled Ulrike Meinhof Commando group. The trial finally came to an end on April 28, 1977. Baader, Ensslin, and Raspe received life sentences for murder and attempted murder and for having formed a criminal association. German prison authorities devoted a special section of the Stammheim prison to house the RAF prisoners.

A second generation of Red Army Faction members assumed control. Siegfried Haag, Baader's lawyer, was the principal leader of the RAF until his arrest in November 1976. Brigitte Mohnhaupt, a longtime RAF activist, and Christian Klar, who worked in Haag's law firm, replaced him as the new leaders of the RAF. They remained in control until November 1982 when German police arrested them. Around 10 activists planned to kidnap the banker Jurgen Ponto on July 30, 1977, but the kidnapping was bungled and Ponto was killed. After a rocket launcher attack in August 1977, the next operation was the kidnapping of Hanns Martin Schleyer, president of the Employers' Association of the Federal Republic of Germany and of the Federation of German Industry, on September 5, 1977. Kidnappers killed three police officers and Schleyer's driver at the scene of the kidnapping in Cologne. A letter demanding the release of all RAF leaders in prison soon followed, but the government of Helmut Schmidt refused to negotiate with the kidnappers and the government stalled.

In the meantime four Middle East terrorists from the **Popular Front for the Liberation of Palestine** (PFLP) seized a Lufthansa aircraft on October 13, 1977. This aircraft carried 86 passengers and five crew members and was scheduled to fly from Palma de Mallorca, Spain, to Frankfurt, West Germany. After several stops, including Rome, Larnaca Airport in Cyprus, and stops in the Middle East, the aircraft was flown to Mogadishu, Somalia. A communiqué on October 14, 1977, from Schleyer's kidnappers indicated that his kidnapping and the skyjacking were part of the same plot to free the RAF prisoners. Demands were increased

to the release of the RAF prisoners, two Palestinians imprisoned in Turkey, and a ransom of $15 million. The German government decided in a cabinet session that everything be done to save the hostages but without releasing the prisoners. German authorities sent the crack anti-terrorist unit of the Federal Border Police (GSG9) to Mogadishu. On the evening of October 17, 1977, elements of the GSG9 stormed the aircraft and, within minutes, three of the kidnappers were dead and one was seriously wounded, but no hostages were injured.

News of the hijacking failure reached West Germany in the early morning of October 18. Raspe had a small transistor radio in his cell, and he passed the bad news to the others. Baader, Ensslin, Raspe, and Irmgard Moller agreed to a suicide pact. Both Baader and Raspe had been able to obtain pistols and they used them to commit suicide. Ensslin used loudspeaker cable to hang herself. Moller had stolen a prison issue table knife, and she stabbed herself near the heart four times. Only Moller survived the suicide pact.

The German government conducted an investigation because the deaths looked suspicious in the most closely guarded prison in Europe. This inquest never determined how the weapons were smuggled into prison, but it concluded that the deaths were by suicide. Followers of the RAF never accepted this explanation, and they charged that the German government had killed them. In response, Schleyer's RAF kidnappers killed him sometime on October 19, 1977. His body was found in a green Audi in Mulhouse. Several of the kidnappers were arrested later and given life sentences.

The Red Army Faction continued to function but without the notoriety of the original leaders. This second wave proved to be more violent than the original group. They spent several years acquiring explosives, money, and weapons before launching operations again in 1982. After the arrests of Mohnhaupt and Klar in November 1982, the RAF went through nearly two years of rebuilding. Special attention in a new terrorist campaign was against American and NATO

(North Atlantic Treaty Organization) targets and pro-American German industrialists. Then on February 1, 1985, members of the RAF murdered a prominent German industrialist, Ernst Zimmerman, in Munich, Germany. Then on August 8, 1985, RAF exploded a car bomb on the U.S. Air Force base at Rhein-Main, killing 2 Americans and injuring 20 others. This attack was followed on July 9, 1986, by the assassination of Siemens executive Karl Heinz Beckurts and his driver near Munich. A hiatus of three years ended on November 30, 1989, when a bomb killed Alfred Herrhausen, the head of Deutsche Bank. Finally, in April 1991, a sniper killed the director of the Treuhand (Public Trustee of Eastern German Lands), Detlev Karsten Rohwedder.

The Red Army Faction's war against the German state ended in 1998. Throughout the 1990s, the members of the RAF carried out fewer operations. Key leaders had been caught or killed by the German police. East Germany had always been a sanctuary for those RAF activists on the run, but this had ended in 1989. West German police started shifting through the records of the East German government and found clues on the whereabouts of RAF members. Surviving leaders began to argue over strategy and tactics. The RAF's last major operation was a meaningless bombing in 1993. In the middle of April 1998, the leadership of the RAF issued an eight-page statement announcing the end of their struggle to overthrow the German state. **See also** Baader, Andreas; Ensslin, Gudrun; Mahler, Horst; Meinhof, Ulrike.

Suggested readings: Yonah Alexander and Dennis Pluchinsky, *Europe's Red Terrorists: The Fighting Communist Organizations* (London: Frank Cass, 1992); Stefan Aust, *The Baader-Meinhof Group: The Inside Story of a Phenomenon* (London: Bodley Head, 1985); Rupert Cornwell and David Marsh, "Red Army Faction Aims Its Lethal Fire at a New Target," *Financial Times* (London) (July 18, 1986), p. 2; William Drozdiak, "West German Terrorists Shift Tactics," *Washington Post* (August 18, 1985), p. A1; Richard Ellis and David Brierley, "Germany's Lethal New Breed of Terrorist—They Just Like Killing," *Times* (London) (December 3, 1989), issue 8625;

Dennis A. Pluchinsky, "An Organizational and Operational Analysis of Germany's Red Army Faction Terrorist Group (1972–91), in Yonah Alexander, and Dennis A. Pluchinsky (eds.), *European Terrorism: Today & Tomorrow* (Washington, D.C.: Brassey's, 1992); Denis Stanton, "Red Brigades Announce End of Their Struggle to Overthrow German State," *Irish Times* (April 22, 1998), p. 11; John Vinocur, "German Terrorists Pursue Fresh Targets with Old Strategy," *New York Times* (September 20, 1981), sec. 4, p. 3.

Red Brigades (Brigate Rosse) (Italy)

The Red Brigades have been the leading left-wing terrorist group in postwar Italy. Former university students **Renato Curcio, Margherita Cagol**, and Alberto Franceschini formed the Red Brigades out of a Milan study group in the summer of 1970. They also designed the red five-pointed star enclosed in a circle as the Red Brigades' revolutionary symbol. Members of the study group, the Metropolitan Political Collective (MPC), researched the possibility of a Communist revolution in Italy. Most of the radical members of the MPC joined the Red Brigades.

In September 1970, the Red Brigades initiated terrorist operations. At first the main tactic was firebombing automobiles. After each incident, the leadership would publish a lengthy justification for the attack. Needing funds for revolutionary operations, members next turned to robbing banks and kidnappings for ransom. For a time, Italian police officials were slow to adjust to Red Brigades' activities. Throughout the period from 1970 to 1973, the Red Brigades operated with impunity. Even the discovery of hideouts, arsenals, and some arrests by the police in mid-1972 did not damper its activities. On April 18, 1974, Red Brigades operatives kidnapped Mario Sossi, an ultra-conservative magistrate in Genoa, and held him for 35 days until the government released eight captured members of the Red Brigades. These successes ended on September 8, 1974, when Curcio and Franceschini were arrested at Pinkroot near Turin. Cagol was able to hold the organization together until she was able to free Curcio in a prison break in February 1975. Her death in a shootout with the police and the recapture of Curcio in January 1976 seriously weakened the Red Brigades.

The loss of the major leaders of the Red Brigades allowed new leaders to emerge. **Mario Moretti,** a close associate of Curcio and Franceschini, became the chief leader, and he decided to give new direction to the Red Brigades by the forming of a revolutionary council of four members. This committee would only meet once or twice a year to decide on a political line and nominate future candidates for membership on the Executive Committee. Operations would be undertaken by independent groups but under the direction of a centralized leadership. Moretti and the other leaders decided to declare open warfare on the Italian state. The assassination of Francesco Coco, the prosecutor general in Genoa, on June 8, 1976, was the opening salvo in this war. Kneecapping, or a gunshot to the knee, neutralized minor political figures. Then on March 16, 1978, the Red Brigades kidnapped Aldo Moro, a prominent Italian politician in the Christian Democratic Party and five-time former prime minister, and killed his five bodyguards. After negotiations over the release of 13 prisoners for Moro fails with government of Giulio Andreotti, Moro is killed and his body is found in a car on May 9, 1978. This murder earned the Red Brigades the reputation as the most ruthless terrorist organization in Europe.

Next, the idea surfaced among the Red Brigades leaders to attack American interests in Europe by conducting an operation against an American target. In the spring of 1981 Italian police arrested Moretti. Antonio Savasta, the son of a Rome policeman and a former student at the University of Rome, filled his place on the Executive Committee. It was his plan to kidnap a major NATO figure. They proceeded to kidnap General James Dozier, an American general working for the North Atlantic Treaty Organization (NATO) in Italy, on December 17, 1981 in Verona, Italy. He was kept is a safe house in Padua until the Italian National Police unit responsible for high-risk cases found and released him on January 28, 1982. Police arrested Savasta at the scene, and he turned into a state witness against his colleagues in the Red Brigades. With information from Savasta, the police rounded up most of the leaders of the Red Brigades. This roundup did not prevent the Red Brigades from killing General Carlo Alberto Della Chiesa, the former chief of the Italian anti-terrorist war, on September 3, 1982, Leamon R. Hunt, an American diplomat, in Rome on February 15, 1984. In April 1984, imprisoned leaders of the Red Brigades announce the end of the war with the Italian state.

This announcement ended the first phase of the Red Brigades. In 1986 survivors of the original Red Brigades split into two factions: the New Red Brigades/Communist Combatant Party and the Union of Combatant Communists. The New Red Brigades/Communist Combatant Party retained most of the former Red Brigades' activists. This group continued to emphasize armed military struggle and the Marxist-Leninist ideas of the former Red Brigades, but the leaders began to target Americans and those they considered American supporters. First target was Lando Conti, ex-mayor of Florence and a staunch pro-American politician, on February 10, 1986. Then on March 20, 1987, two members of the New Red Brigades/Communist Combatant Party kill General Licio Giorgieri, a pro-NATO Italian military leader, in Rome. On May 20, 1999, members of this assassinated Massimo D'Antona, a Labor Minister advisor to the Italian government in Rome, and they followed with the murder of Professor Marco Biagi, a government labor advisor, on March 19, 2002, in Bologna. This group is still active, but the recent arrest of seven of its members on October 26, 2003, may curtail some of their operations. **See also** Cagol, Margherita; Curcio, Renato.

Suggested readings: John Brecher and Rita Dallas, "Moro's Executioner Falls into a Trap," *Newsweek* (April 20, 1981), p. 54; Laimondo Catanzaro (ed.), *The Red Brigades and Left-Wing Terrorism in Italy* (New York: St. Martin's Press, 1991); Raymond Carroll, et al., "Inside the Red

Brigades," *Newsweek* (May 15, 1978), p. 43; Richard Oliver Collin and Gordon L. Freedman, *Winter of Fire: The Abduction of General Dozier and the Downfall of the Red Brigades* (New York: Dutton, 1990); Richard Drake, *The Revolutionary Mystique and Terrorism in Contemporary Italy* (Bloomington, IN: Indiana University Press, 1989); Anthony A. Lukin, "History in the Headlines: The Return of the Red Brigades?" *Journal of Counterterrorism and Security International* 6, no. 1 (Fall 1999); Robert C. Meade, *Red Brigades: The Story of Italian Terrorism* (New York: St. Martin's Press, 1990); Leonard Weinberg and William Lee Eugank, *The Rise and Fall of Italian Terrorism* (Boulder, CO: Westview Press, 1987).

Red Zoras (Germany)

The Red Zoras is a radical leftist feminist group in Germany that has conducted a terrorist campaign since the 1970s. The all-women group emerged out of the West German **Revolutionary Cells** (Revolutionare Zellen) terrorist group. Members picked the name Red Zoras out of a novel in which women play Robin Hood figures by stealing from the rich and giving to the poor. Red Zoras made its first appearance in 1974, when members bombed the West German Supreme Court building shortly after that court had overturned a pro-abortion law. Targets of the Red Zoras have included the pornography businesses, drug companies, doctors' groups, international corporations, and international traders offering Asian brides for German men. A special target has been the Adler Corporation, Germany's largest clothing retailer, for their exploitation of South Korean female labor. After the Red Zoras firebombed 10 of Adler's stores in Germany, Adler reformed its policies toward South Korean female labor. Public statements from the Red Zoras proclaim their solidarity with women around the world.

Because Red Zoras is a secret and decentralized organization with no recognized leaders, German police have had difficulty combating it. Police tried to isolate the Red Zoras with a crackdown on all female activists. This effort was only partially effective. Members of Red Zoras attacked any business or individual that they perceived as patriarchal institutions, from those engaged in pornography to doctors carrying out forced sterilizations. In the early 1990s the group Red Zoras disappeared as its members moved into other radical and feminist German groups. See also Revolutionary Cells (Revolutionare Zellen) (RZ).

Suggested readings: George Katsiaficas, *The Subversion of Politics: European Autonomous Social Movements and the Decolonization of Everyday Life* (Atlantic Heights, N.J.: Humanities Press International, 1997); Reuter News Service, "Feminist Group Says It Bombed German Stores," *Toronto Star* (August 18, 1987), p. E15.

Reid, Richard (1973–) (Great Britain)

Richard Reid's claim to fame is as **al-Qaeda**'s "shoe bomber." He was born in 1973 in south London, England. His father was half Jamaican and half English and had a lengthy jail record. His mother was English and the daughter of a magistrate. After his parents divorced, Reid lived with his mother and stepfather outside London. He was always an indifferent student at Thomas Tallis and then Lewisham, so he left school at an early age. Reid soon was in trouble with the law for shoplifting and muggings. In 1992, he received a five-year prison sentence for 28 robberies and 22 thefts. After a chance meeting with his father in prison in 1995, Reid converted to Islam. After his release from prison in 1996, Reid started attending the Brixton mosque. **Zacharias Moussaoui**, a member of al-Qaeda, recruited Reid for the more radical Finsbury Park mosque. There he fell under the influence of Abu Qatada, one of al-Qaeda's religious leaders.

By 1998, Reid was a full-fledged member of al-Qaeda. He made a trip first to Pakistan and then to Afghanistan. Al-Qaeda leaders sent him to the Khaldan training camp to study explosives. In June 2001, he traveled to Israel and disappeared into the Palestinian-controlled Gaza Strip. Reid returned to Europe and settled in Amsterdam, Holland. It was in Amsterdam that he received instructions and the explosives for his one-man suicide mission.

Reid's mission was to blow up an American airliner with the explosives hidden in his shoes. Each sole of his shoes was filled with a hundred grams of the explosive PETN and mixed with TATP. These explosives are both powerful and unstable. A cord came out of each of the shoes, and each cord had been filled with gunpowder. Reid's first attempt to board an American airliner on December 21, 2001, in Paris, France, failed because his one-way ticket and lack of luggage aroused suspicion. Reid's interrogation made him miss the flight. The next day he tried again and this time he boarded American Airlines Flight 63. Once airborne, Reid attempted to light his shoes, but his shoes were damp from an overnight rain in Paris. A flight attendant noticed the burning smell. As soon as she screamed for help, passengers overpowered him and a doctor injected him with a sedative. A stewardess suffered a severe bite on the hand but that was the only injury sustained by anyone.

Reid has denied any affiliation with al-Qaeda, but evidence exists that he had contact with it. A captured al-Qaeda computer in Kabul, Afghanistan, provided the evidence that Reid was an al-Qaeda operative on a suicide mission. These files took weeks to decode, but one of them described Reid's activities and the nature of his mission. Reid pleaded guilty of trying to blow up Flight 63 in October 2002. On January 30, 2003, a Boston judge sentenced him to life imprisonment for the bombing attempt and an additional 110 years for other charges. This sentence rules out any chance of parole. See also Moussaoui, Zacharias; al-Qaeda (The Base).

Suggested readings: Jane Corbin, *Al-Qaeda: The Terror Network That Threatens the World* (New York: Thunder's Mouth Press, 2002); Jack Gee and Mark Watts, "Stewardess Hurt as She Helps Overpower Arab with 'Shoe Bomb,'" *Sunday Express* (London) (December 23, 2001), p. 2; Audrey Gillan and Julian Borger, "Shoe Bomb Briton Named as Key Agent in Bin Laden's Network," *Guardian* (London) (January 17, 2002), p. 1; Alfons Luna, "'Shoe Bomber' Richard Reid Sentenced to Life in Prison," Agence France Presse (January 31, 2003), p. 1; Keme Nzerem, "At

School with the Shoe Bomber," *Guardian* (London) (February 28, 2002), p. 2.

Remer, Otto Ernst (1912–1997) (Germany)

Ernst Remer served as the godfather of the German neo-Nazi movement since World War II. He was born on December 18, 1912, in Neubrandenburg, Mecklenburg, Germany. He attended a military academy and became an officer in the German army. Remer had a distinguished record in the German army in World War II and was wounded nine times in combat. His claim to fame, however, was his role in suppressing the officers' revolt against Adolf Hitler on July 20, 1944. At the time, he was a major in charge of a guard battalion in Berlin. In response to Hitler's orders, Remer took charge of the German army in Berlin and arrested the conspirators. His reward was a promotion to major general and the post of Hitler's chief bodyguard for the remainder of the war. Although Remer never officially joined the Nazi Party, he became a fanatical Nazi.

Remer's career in postwar Germany was devoted to rebuilding the image of Hitler and Nazi Germany. He was held in an internment camp from the end of the war until February 1948. Most of this time Remer worked for the U.S. Army on a German account of the Battle of the Bulge. After his release, Remer entered an apprentice bricklaying program in Oldenburg, Germany. In October 1949, he relinquished this trade to enter German politics and was a founding member of the neo-Nazi Socialist Reich Party (Sozialistische Reichs-Partei) (SRP). Remer became the deputy director of the SRP. This party was modeled closely on Hitler's National Socialist German Workers Party (NSDAP) and campaigned for the reestablishment of the Nazi state.

Remer served the chief spokesperson for the Socialist Reich Party. He attacked the German government of Konrad Adenauer for being a puppet of the United States. Remer also dismissed reports of Nazi atrocities of the Holocaust by denying the Holocaust's existence. The SRP under Remer wanted Germany to be an independent third force in Europe opposed to both the Soviet Union and the United States. Remer and the other leaders of the SRP even toyed with the idea of an alliance with the Soviet Union and received funding from the Soviets. After the SRP started garnering some success in local elections in the early 1950s, the German government in Bonn began to apply political pressure on the SRP. In 1951, Remer received a four-month prison term for slandering Adenauer and the German government. Then he was tried and convicted for making defamatory remarks about German officers in the assassination plot against Hitler in his book *July 20th, 1944*. On October 23, 1952, the West German Constitutional Court outlawed the SRP, citing it as a successor to the Nazi Party. Facing another jail term, Remer escaped the jurisdiction of the court by fleeing to Cairo, Egypt. In Egypt, Remer worked with other former Nazis selling German technology and weapons to Arab countries. He also served for a couple years as a political-military advisor to Egyptian President Gamal Abdel Nasser. In 1956, Remer moved his operations to Damascus, Syria, where he remained active in the weapons trade. One of his best customers was the Algerian resistance group FLN in its struggle against France.

In the early 1980s, Remer returned to Germany and renewed his contacts with German neo-Nazis. In 1983, he founded the German Freedom Movement (Die Deutsche Freihheitsbewegung) that united 23 right-wing or neo-Nazi groups. Remer used this organization to campaign against the North Atlantic Treaty Organization (NATO) and for an independent and reunified Germany. This organization had a combined membership of only about 1,500, but it trained a generation of neo-Nazis. His friendship with **Michael Kühnen**, a young neo-Nazi leader, gave him access to a new generation of German neo-Nazis. Remer left the German Freedom Movement in 1989, but he retained his influence in the neo-Nazi movement by publishing first the *Remer Dispatch* (Remer Depesche), and then the *Deutschland Report*. He continued to publish writings and to make speeches denying the Holocaust. In 1994, Remer fled to Spain to avoid a lengthy prison sentence for inciting hatred, violence, and racism. He lived in a rented villa outside Marbella, Spain, where he was considered a leading figure in the European neo-Nazi movement. Germany tried to have him extradited to Germany in 1996, but a Spanish court overturned a lower court order to have him transferred to Germany. He died in Marbella on October 5, 1997, and his ashes were taken to an undisclosed place in Germany for burial.

Suggested readings: David Childs, "Obituary: Otto Ernst Remer," *Independent* (London) (October 9, 1997); Phil Davison, "Nazi Who Saved Hitler Is in Spain," *Independent* (London) (July 20, 1994); Lee, Martin A., *The Beast Reawakens* (Boston: Little, Brown, 1997).

Republican Party (Die Republikaner) (REP) (Germany)

The Republican Party (Die Republikaner, or REP) is an extreme nationalist party in Germany. Franz Schönhuber, a former radio journalist and former member of the Waffen SS in World War II; Franz Handlos, a German member of the Bundestag; and Ekkehard Voigt, a member of the Bundestag, formed the Republican Party in a Bavarian tavern on November 17, 1983. A divergence of political viewpoints between Schönhuber and both Handlos and Voigt led to Handlos and Voigt leaving the party. In June 1985, Schönhuber was elected chairperson. His goal was to make this Bavarian party into a political force that could win elections across the Federal Republic. Despite this effort, most of its early voting strength came from Baden-Württemberg and Bavaria.

Schönhuber's intent was to build a party that would attract German nationalists by not repudiating its Nazi past. Among his platform points were the abolition of trade unions, curtailment of the welfare state, expulsion of all foreigners, and a return to Germany's 1937 borders. This party has been successful in appealing to traditional German nationalistic value by combining it with condemnations of foreign workers. Schönhuber's campaign to overthrow the German Democratic Republic and replace it with a unified Germany also became popular in the late 1980s. Since the enactment of the Maastricht Treaty establishing the European Union (EU), the REP has consistently attacked the EU as an infringement on German sovereignty.

The Republican Party began enjoying political success as the drive for German unification became more realistic. In January 1989, the REP won 7.5 percent of the vote in the West Berlin municipal elections, attracting heavy support from working-class districts. Support also came from elements of the German neo-Nazi movement. In June of the same year, the party garnered enough votes to send Schönhuber and five colleagues to the European Parliament in Strassburg. Electoral support for the NEP has come from small-business owners, workers, and government workers fearful for the future. Many of his supporters also belong to other extreme nationalistic or neo-Nazi groups—**German Alternative** (Deutsche Alternative, or DA), **German National Democratic Party** (Nationaldemokratische Partei Deutschlands, or NPD), **German People's Union** (Deutsche Volksunion, or DVU), and Liberal German Workers Party (Freiheitliche Deutsche Arbeiterpartei, or FAP)—many of which have been banned by the German government. Schönhuber has been able to position his party in the mainstream of the German extreme right in an effort to achieve political power in Germany. By December 1989, the REP had around 25,000 members.

The Republican Party lost most of its political gains in the 1990s. Dissension among the leadership between the moderates and the extremists caused rifts in the party. Schönhuber wanted to mainstream the party and win elections, but his chief deputy, Harald Neubauer, a former member of the National Democratic Party, desired to make the party more extreme. This rivalry led to a purge of the extremists from the party. A further factor was the failure of the REP to attract East German extremists after reunification. This failure threatened to marginalize the party and left its membership open to

recruitment by more extreme political groups. Then in 1994, the German Federal Government declared the REP a right-wing extremist group.

Schönhuber tried to revitalize the Republican Party in August 1994. He concluded an electoral alliance with Gerhard Frey and the German People's Union (DVU). Because the REP had a lengthy history of opposition to Frey and the DVU, this alliance caused a backlash in the REP. In a subsequent meeting of the leadership of the REP in October 1994, Schönhuber was dismissed as party leader. Rolf Schlierer, a lawyer and the leader of the moderate wing of the REP, replaced him. Schönhuber and his adherents opened political warfare on Schlierer and his supporters. In 1995, Schönhuber finally resigned from the REP that he had helped found. Schlierer won this battle, but, in the process, the party has become further marginalized in German politics. **See also** German Alternative (Deutsche Alternative) (DA); German National Democratic Party (Nationaldemokratische Partei Deutschlands) (NPD); German People's Union (Deutsche Volksunion) (DVU).

Suggested readings: Adrian Bridge, "A Far Cry That Sounds Just Like Hitler," *Independent* (London) (March 21, 1993), p. 14; Paul Hockenos, *Free to Hate: The Rise of the Right in Post-Communist Eastern Europe* (New York: Routledge, 1993); Martin A. Lee, *The Beast Awakens* (Boston: Little, Brown, 1997); Cas Mudde, *The Ideology of the Extreme Right* (Manchester, UK: Manchester University Press, 2000); Angus Roxburgh, *Preachers of Hate: The Rise of the Far Right* (London: Gibson Square Books, 2002); Serge Schmemann, "Is Extremist or Opportunist behind Bonn Rightist's Tempered Slogans?" *New York Times* (June 27, 1989), p. A1.

Revolutionary Armed Forces of Colombia (Fuerzas Armada Revolucionarias de Colombia) (FARC) (Colombia)

The Revolutionary Armed Forces of Colombia (FARC) is the oldest and largest left-wing rural guerrilla group in Latin America. **Manuel Marulanda** formed the FARC out of a rural self-defense force that he founded in

The founder and top leader of the Revolutionary Armed Forces of Colombia, Manuel Marulanda, right, stands alongside FARC's second commander, Jorge Briceno, at a ranch near San Vicente del Caguan, 185 miles (300 km) south of Bogotá, January 8, 1999. Colombians have never seen Marulanda in public and his presence would have lent credibility to FARC claims that they are serious about ending the long conflict that claims thousands of lives every year. (AP Photo/ Joaquin Gomez)

1949. Colombian conservatives had attacked his family during a civil war between conservatives and liberals. After an uncle was killed, Marulanda and 14 cousins formed a militia group. By 1955, this militia group had migrated into the Marquetalia, a remote area in the Andes in the southern Tolima state. Out of the mainstream of Colombian politics, Marulanda and his followers established an independent society. His militia group avoided contact with the Colombian army until the military invaded Marquetalia in May 1964. Marulanda and most of the members of the militia escaped from the invasion, and he decided to regroup. His next step was to ally with Jacobo Arenas, a leader

in the Colombian Communist Party. Marulanda recast his militia into a rural guerrilla movement intent on establishing a Marxist regime in Colombia. He selected the name of Southern Bloc for his revolutionary army, but, in May 1966, he recast it as the Revolutionary Armed Forces of Colombia, or FARC.

The Revolutionary Armed Forces of Colombia has pursued a war against the Colombian state for nearly 40 years. At the beginning of the guerrilla war, FARC had only about 350 fighters. Most of these fighters were peasants and malcontents, and they lacked modern weapons. From this modest beginning, FARC military forces have grown to as many as 18,000 fighters. Although FARC has been able to gain control of huge slices of Colombian territory, there has never been an occasion when the FARC could defeat the Colombian army in open combat. FARC forces are divided into small guerrilla groups that function independently in hit-and-run operations.

FARC's leadership tried to turn it into a political force in the 1980s. Leaders formed the Patriotic Union in 1980. During this political effort, FARC military forces maintained a truce for three years. This political initiative failed because right-wing paramilitary groups killed off the Patriotic Union's leaders and supporters. More than 4,000 FARC supporters were killed in this three-year period. Marulanda learned his lesson and FARC returned to its guerrilla warfare. In the 1990s, FARC has established a secret group called the Pacoclan (Clandestine Communist Party) to infiltrate Colombian society and prepare for an eventual Communist revolution.

The Revolutionary Armed Forces of Colombia has been able to prosper financially. Sources of income include taxes on the drug trade, extortion, and ransom from kidnappings. Taxes on the drug trade have been particularly lucrative. This affiliation with the drug trade has made the FARC doubly suspect by the American government. In 1977, the U.S. State Department classified FARC as a terrorist organization. Several of the FARC kidnappings have involved American citizens and on at least one occasion the Americans were killed. Massive financial and military aid has been given to the Colombian government by various U.S. administrations.

The best chance for peace between FARC and the Colombian state was in the late 1990s and early 2000s. President Andrés Pastrana engaged in negotiations for nearly four years attempting to conclude a peace. He established a 16,000-square-mile demilitarized zone in Colombia in December 1998 where the FARC could exist without government military pressure. This conclave provided the FARC with a safe haven. FARC

leaders also concluded an alliance with the **Irish Republican Army** (IRA) to have trainers sent over to train FARC fighters. Demands from the FARC leadership that all FARC prisoners be freed and a series of kidnappings led to Pastrana ending negotiations in February 2002. Shortly afterward, the FARC launched three major military offenses.

The new presidency of Alvaro Uribe Velez ensures that the war between the FARC and the Colombian state will continue. He won the presidency with the support of the Colombian right-wing paramilitary groups and on the platform to defeat the guerrillas. FARC celebrated his inauguration in Bogotá on August 7, 2002, with a mortar attack that killed 21 people. A subsequent military crackdown has hurt the FARC in Bogotá and Medellin, but the government has been less successful in the countryside. FARC forces have counterattacked by raiding rural communities and deposing municipal governments. FARC's control of the countryside and inroads into urban areas make it uncertain whether the Colombian state can defeat it in the field. A state of civil war between the FARC and the right-wing paramilitary forces of **Carlos Castaño** and his **United Self-Defense Forces of Colombia** (AUC) exists with heavy casualties on both sides. Negotiations between FARC and the Colombian government have been difficult, but, without a truce between the FARC and the AUC, there will be no peace.

The Uribe government has received increasing financial and military support from the United States to fight the FARC during the latter half of 2003 and early 2004. These resources have been used to target FARC leaders. This tactic uses special squads to be sent out to capture or kill senior guerrilla leaders. Five FARC commanders have been killed since October 2003. In early January Colombian agents seized Simon Trinidad, a high-ranking FARC leader, in Quito, Ecuador, and they have brought him to Bogata, Colombia for trial. These actions threaten FARC's initiative on military operations and it remains to be seen how Marulanda and the other FARC leaders respond. **See also** Castaño, Carlos; Marulanda, Manuel.

Suggested readings: Ana Arana, "Colombia's Growing Nightmare," http://salon.com/ (accessed February 23, 2002), p.1; Yadira Ferrer, "Families Demand Accord on Captives," Inter Press Service (May 6, 2003), p. 1; John Otis, "Inside Colombia's FARC, Latin America's Oldest, Most Powerful Guerrilla Army," *Houston Chronicle* (August 5, 2001), p. 1; John Otis, "Rebel Held; The Future: Peace or War," *Houston Chronicle* (August 5, 2001), p. 11; Dick J. Reavis, "FARC Guerrillas Are Rebels without a Clear Cause," *San Antonio Express News* (January 16, 2001), p. 1A; Frances Robles, "Significan Changes Happening in Colombia's Civil War," *Miami Herald* (January 10, 2004), p. 1; Bert Ruiz, *The Colombian Civil War* (Jefferson, NC: McFarland, 2001); Scott Wilson, "Colombian Rebels Use Refuge to Expand Their Power Base, *Washington Post* (October 3, 2001), p. A25; Scott Wilson, "Guerrilla Strategy Perplexes Colombians," *Washington Post* (February 26, 2002), p. A14.

Revolutionary Cells (Revolutionare Zellen) (RZ) (West Germany)

Revolutionary Cells (Revolutionare Zellen, or RZ) was a West German terrorist group that participated in a number of terrorist acts in the 1970s and 1980s. Johannes Weinrich, a former radical student leader at the University of Frankfurt and the owner of a racial Frankfurt bookstore, and Wilfried Bose, a former radical student at the University of Frankfurt, organized the Revolutionary Cells in 1973. This group served as an umbrella organization for a number of West German leftist groups. Anti-Americanism and opposition to the Vietnam War tied these groups together. The Revolutionary Cells also published a journal, *Revolutionary Wrath* (Revolutionare Zorn), whose writers expressed a commitment to armed struggle to destabilize governmental institutions. The feminist wing of the Revolutionary Cells was the **Red Zoras**, and the members of this cell pursued independent tactics.

Soon after its founding, the Revolutionary Cells began to specialize in firebombing American and American international companies in West Germany. This group never had more than a hundred activists, but these activists were hard to detect because they conducted their terrorist operations on an ad hoc basis in their own localities. The leadership of the Revolutionary Cells was more ambitious. Both Weinrich and Bose also made contacts with **George Habash's Popular Front for the Liberation of Palestine** (PFLP) and conducted special operations with it. Among these were the attempt to shoot down Israeli El Al airliners outside Paris in January 1975 and the kidnapping of the Organization of Petroleum Exporting Countries (OPEC) oil ministers in Vienna, Austria, in December 1975. Seven members of the Revolutionary Cells placed themselves under the operational control of **Ilich Ramirez Sánchez** (Carlos the Jackal) and provided weaponry to carry out this mission.

Members of the Revolutionary Cells also participated in other PFLP operations. Bose was the leader of the hijacking of the Air France Airbus in July 1976. His orders were to kill the Jewish hostages at Entebbe Airport in Uganda, but an Israeli assault team prevented the executions. Israeli soldiers killed Bose in a gunfight. Weinrich later joined with Sánchez and his Organisation of Arab Armed Struggle. He continued in this group until his capture by German authorities in June 1995. The career of Revolutionary Cells ended with the defection and deaths of its leaders. **See also** Habash, George; Popular Front for the Liberation of Palestine (PFLP); Red Zoras; Sánchez, Ilich Ramirez.

Suggested readings: Yonah Alexander and Dennis Pluchinsky, *Europe's Red Terrorists: The Fighting Communist Organizations* (London: Frank Cass, 1992); John Follain, *Jackal: The Complete Story of the Legendary Terrorist, Carlos the Jackal* (New York: Arcade Publishing, 1998); George Katsiaficas, *The Subversion of Politics: European Autonomous Social Movements and the Decolonization of Everyday Life* (Atlantic Highlands, NJ: 1997).

Revolutionary Organization 17 November (Epanastaiki Organoisi 17 Noemvri) (Greece)

The Revolutionary Organization 17 November Greek terrorist group was one of the longest lasting of the radical Marxist-Leninist terrorist organizations in Europe. This group was a small, secret, urban terrorist organization that was named after a failed student riot against the Greek government at the Athens Polytechnic Institute on November 17, 1973. Operations of 17 November started soon after the police brutally crushed the demonstration. The terrorists' tightly closed cell structure made it difficulty for Greek authorities to learn more about it. Police estimated at the time that the group had no more than a dozen active members. Leaders of 17 November issued statements that showed it to be violently anti-American, anti-NATO, anti-Turkey, and anti-Greek establishment.

Most of November 17th's operations were targeted against high-profile American, British and Greek industrialists. In the late 1980s, however, it also started targeting Turkish citizens. Members of the group specialized in assassinations and avoided the more dangerous bank robberies and kidnappings. Most attacks were made by three-member teams riding on motor scooters. The first murder victim of the 17 November was Richard Welch, the CIA station chief in Athens, on December 23, 1975. Next targets were prominent Greeks. On January 16, 1980, a 17 November hit team killed Major General Pantelis Petrou, deputy commander of the Athens Riot Police, in Athens. The next important Greek figure to be assassinated was Nikos Momferatos, publisher of Greece's largest conservative newspaper *Afternooner*, on February 21, 1985, in Athens. Then on March 1, Greek industrialist Alexandros Athanasiadis was shot and killed by a gunman on a motorcyle in Athens. Among the more spectacular assassinations was that of U.S. Navy Captain William Nordeen in June 28, 1988, when a car bomb exploded next to him in Athens. This operation was uncharacteristic of 17 November,

because earlier assassinations had been hit-and-run and the murder weapon was a .45-caliber handgun. The assassination of British Brigadier Stephen Saunders in June 2000 for what the 17 November characterized as crimes of NATO in Yugoslavia was its last major terrorist act. At the scene of each assassination the group left pamphlets justifying the killing in literary language. By 2001, 17 November had claimed 23 deaths, including U.S. officials, NATO officials, Greek politicians, magistrates, newspaper publishers, industrialists, and ship owners.

Various attempts made to identify members of 17 November were unsuccessful. Critics suggested that members of the 17 November may have been protected by elements in Greek security forces. A CIA operation in 1994 ended disastrously when two CIA agents were arrested in Athens in the so-called "Men-in-Wigs" affair. After massive publicity in Greece, the agents were expelled as an embarrassment to the Greek government. The American government posted rewards, which began at $500,000 and ultimately reached $10 million, for the capture and conviction of 17 November terrorists, but there were no takers. Charges of ineptness and collusion were levied against the Greek government. In 2000, the Greek government invited assistance from the British police, Scotland Yard, to help them apprehend the group.

The career of 17 November ended abruptly in June 2002. Savas Xiros, a religious icon painter, had an accident on June 29, 2002, with a bomb that he was carrying. He was severely wounded and the police began to investigate him and his brothers. One of these brothers, Christodoulos Xiros, confessed to participation in terrorist acts that had killed nine, including two U.S. military officers. The other brother, Vassilis Xiros, confessed to the murder of Brigadier Saunders. These confessions and fingerprints found at one of the safehouses of 17 November led to the arrest on July 17, 2002, of its ideological leader, Alexandros Giotopoulos, a former university economics professor on the Aegean island of Lipsi. Slowly throughout the summer the Greek authorities managed to capture leaders and the major operatives of 17 November.

Greek authorities placed the 19 alleged members of the Revolutionary Organization 17 November on trial in April 2003. This trial in an Athens court lasted for nine months, ending with a guilty verdict on 15 of the defendants on December 17, 2003. Giotopoulos had been charged with 963 offenses and as the leader of the group he received 21 life sentences. Dimitris Koufodinas, the group's chief assassin, got 15 life sentences. Twelve other members were jailed for from eight years to life. The fifteenth received a suspended 25-year sentence. Four other defendants were acquitted. Because of a 20-year statute of limitations, the defendants were not prosecuted for four of the earliest crimes, including the murder of CIA chief Richard Welch in 1975.

Suggested readings: Yonah Alexander and Dennis Pluchinsky, *Europe's Red Terrorists: The Fighting Communist Organizations* (London: Frank Cass, 1992); Hugh Barnes, "Remember, Remember 17 November," *Observer* [London] (March 13, 1994), p. 40; John Carr, "British Diplomat Was Killed 'For War Crimes,'" *Times* (London) (December 14, 2000); Andrew Corsun, "Group Profile: The Revolutionary Organization 17 November in Greece (1975–91), in Yonah Alexander and Dennis A. Pluchinsky, eds., *European Terrorism: Today & Tomorrow* (Washington, D.C.: Brassey's, 1992); George Kassimeris, "17N: 25 Years and Still at Large," *Jane's Intelligence Review* 12, no. 12 (December 1, 2000); Daniel McGrory and John Carr, "Greek Clan Confess to Killing British Envoy," *Times* (London) (July 19, 2002), p. 16; Helena Smith, "Leaders of Greek Terrorist Group Jailed for Life," *Guardian* [London] (December 18, 2003), p. 14; Theodore Stanger, "The Elusive Assassins of Athens," *Newsweek* (July 11, 1988), p. 37.

Revolutionary Workers' Party (See People's Revolutionary Army) (Ejercito Revolucionario del Pueblo) (ERP)/ Revolutionary Workers' Party (Partido Revolucionario de los Trabajadores) (PRT)

Roche, Jack (1953–) (Australia)

Jack Roche is a British convert to the Indonesian terrorist group **Jemaah Islamiyah** (JI). He was born in 1953 in England. After an undistinguished educational record, he served in the British army. After leaving the army, he settled in Sydney, Australia, with his wife and several children. He worked at various jobs, but his excessive drinking caused him problems. After a divorce, Roche converted to Islam in 1989. In a 2002 interview on Australian radio, Roche claimed that his reason for converting was that "I was looking for something to motivate my life."

Soon after his conversion to Islam, Roche traveled to Indonesia, where he contacted Islamic militants. After learning the local language, he married an Indonesian woman in 1994. In the mid-1990s, Roche joined the Jemaah Islamiyah. On a trip to Indonesia he was introduced to **Abu Bakar Bashir**, the head of the Jemaah Islamiyah, and **Hambali**, its operational chief. He was then sent to Perth, Australia, where he joined the Australian branch of the Jemaah Islamiyah. Leaders of this branch were the Indonesian twins, Abdul Rahman Ayub and Abdul Rahim Ayub. Roche was a prize recruit because of his Western appearance and mannerisms. In 2000, Roche traveled to Afghanistan to receive training in the operation of explosives from al-Qaeda insructors. While in Afghanistan, Roche briefly met but did not talk to **Osama bin Laden**.

Roche never received operational orders for a mission before his November 2002 arrest by the Australian Federal Police. The Australian branch of the Jemaah Islamiyah had never been effective because of the lack of leadership. Neither Roche nor his wife trusted the Ayub brothers. Hambali wanted this branch to target Israeli or American interests in Australia, but no action was taken. Roche began to feel ostracized by other members of the group. Roche's uncertainty ended on November 18, 2002, when the Australian Federal Police raided his home in Perth. Authorities charged Roche with conspiring with others to bomb Israeli missions in Canberra and Sydney. Even after his arrest, Roche continued to support bin Laden and the JI. He has denied both bin Laden's complicity in the **September 11, 2001**, attacks against the United States and JI's role in the October 2002 Bali bombings. Roche is in prison awaiting a trial scheduled for May 2004. **See also** Bashir, Abu Bakar; Bin Laden, Osama; Hambali; Jemaah Islamiyah (Islamic Community) (JI); September 11th.

Suggested readings: Raymond Bonner and Jane Perlez, "Australia Comes to Terms with a New Sense of Vulnerability," *New York Times* (December 16, 2002), sec. A, p. 16; Philip Cornford, "Terrorist Wannabe Who Decided Staying Asleep Was Better Option," *Sydney Morning Herald* (November 27, 2002), p. 8; Colleen Egan, "The Insider," *Weekend Australian* (Sydney) (November 23, 2002), p. 19; Mark Russell and Nicolette Casella, "I'm Not a Terrorist, Says Man Who Likes Bin Laden," *Advertizer* (Sydney) (November 30, 2002), p. 48.

Russian National Unity (Russkoje Nationalnoje Edinstv) (RNE) (Russia)

The Russian National Unity (Russkoje Nationalnoje Edinstv, or RNE) is Russia's leading neo-fascist party. **Aleksandr Petrovich Barkashov** had been active in the anti-Semitic Russian party Pamyat (Memory) until he had a fight with its leader Dmitry Vasilyev. Barkashov gathered several fellow dissidents and formed the Russian National Unity in Moscow on October 16, 1990. His goal was to start an organization that promoted Russian nationalism and at the same time would lead the struggle against what he believed to be the Jewish world conspiracy. This meant that Russia's hegemony extended to the boundaries of the former Soviet Union. In this new Russian empire, the economic system would be closed to all outsiders and Russia's natural resources preserved for native Russians.

Barkashov organized the Russian National Unity into an organization that resembled the Nazi Party. He idealized Adolf Hitler and the Nazi state. A Central Council had an oversight role in the RNE, but Barkashov was the leader. RNE's symbols combined Russian patriotic ones with the Russian left-handed swastika (*kolovrat*). Members also wore black shirts and clothes resembling a uniform. Membership had three levels: supporters, associate members, and comrades-in-arms. Each level required a different kind of commitment with the comrades-in-arms required to devote most of their time to the cause. Leaders have targeted young teenagers for recruitment. After recruitment, these youthful members receive military training. Stephen D. Shenfield, an independent research on Russian politics, estimates that the RNE had an active membership in mid-2000 of between 20,000 and 25,000. Many of the RNE's important followers were in the army, Ministry of Internal Affairs, certain regional administrative bodies, and the police.

The Russian National Unity came to national prominence during the October 1993 assault on the Russian Parliament. Barkashov was an active participant, but he escaped arrest and went into hiding. The RNE was also briefly banned by the Russian government. Several months later, Barkashov was arrested, but he was freed in the general amnesty of February 1994. During each election in the late 1990s, the RNE put up a slate of candidates with unspectacular results. Voting totals averaged less than 5 percent. Barkashov was more conciliatory towards the Russian government of Boris Yeltsin after the outbreak of the war in Chechnya. This alliance ended as the Yeltsin government started an anti-Fascism campaign.

Elements in the RNE have become disillusioned by Barkashov's leadership. By December 2000, 26 local groups had seceded from the RNE. These defections and unhappiness with Barkashov's autocratic behavior caused Oleg Kassin, Andrei Dudinov and Yuri Vasin to leave the RNE and form a new neo-fascist party, Russian Renaissance (Russkoje Vozrozhdenije). Remnants of the old RNE still remain, but defections by dissidents have weakened it as a political force. Barkashov has been able to conclude an unofficial alliance with the Russian communists, but this alliance has to produce electoral results for it to continue. **See also** Barkashov, Aleksandr Petrovich.

Suggested readings: Alexei Pankin, "Under the Surface of the Skinhead Threat," *Moscow Times* (April 23, 2002), no. 2429; Stephen D. Shenfield, *Russian Fascism: Traditions, Tendencies, Movements* (Armonk, NY: M. E. Sharpe, 2001); Yury Vasilyev, "Who's Behind Latest Ethnic Violence in Moscow?" *Current Digest of the Post-Soviet Press*, vol. 53, no. 45 (December 5, 2001).

S

Sabaya, Abu (1962–2002) (Philippines)

Abu Sabaya was one of the leaders of the Philippine terrorist group **Abu Sayyaf**. He was born on July 18, 1962, in Barangay Carbon on Malamarvi Island in Isabela, Basilan, Philippines. His family was of Tausog extraction and his birth name was Aldam Tilao. Sabaya received his elementary and secondary education in Basilan. After graduation, he attended AE College's College of Criminology in Zamboanga City from 1982 to 1985. Sabaya was only an average student and he failed to graduate. He trained to become a policeman in the southern Philippines before he turned to religion. Sayaba then traveled to Saudi Arabia, where he worked as a contact worker. After awhile, Sabaya moved to Libya, and there he received military training under the sponsorship of the **Moro National Liberation Front** (MNLF). Some evidence exits that he fought in the Chad wars in Central Africa.

Sabaya returned to Basilan in 1999. By this time the Moro National Liberation Front had concluded a peace agreement with the Philippine government. The Abu Sayyaf group had replaced the MNLF as the principal Islamist guerrilla group in the southern Philippines. This was despite the 1998 death in action of Abu Sayyaf's leader, **Ustadz Abdurajak Janjalani**. Khadafy Janjalani replaced his brother as the head of the group, filling a power vacuum in the Abu Sayyaf. Sabaya returned to the Philippines just in time for the renewal of Abu Sayyaf operations. He commanded one of the terrorist groups that specialized in kidnappings. Among his victims were Jeffrey Schilling, who escaped, and Guillermo Sobero, whom Sabaya executed by beheading. On May 27, 2001, his unit kidnapped two American missionaries, Martin Burnham and Gracia Burnham, and a Filipino nurse, Edibora Yap. Sabayo used these hostages to negotiate with the Philippine government. On June 7, 2002, Philippine troops attacked Sabaya's unit, rescuing Gracia Burnham, but Martin Burnham and Yap were killed. Sabaya decided to leave Sibuco, Zamboanga del Norte, and travel to Basilan by boat. Unknown to him was that Philippine government agents had planted a bug in a backpack that Sabaya had purchased in May 2002. This bug alerted the agents to Sabaya's request for a boat for the morning of June 21, 2002, to pick him up at Parang Parang. His boat was intercepted almost immediately after he boarded. In the ensuing firefight, Sabaya disappeared into the water. Some uncertainty remains about his fate, with the Philippine government claiming his death and others less sure. Sabaya has always been a flamboyant personality and his silence since that morning indicates that he is probably dead. **See also** Abu Sayyaf Group

(Bearer of the Sword) (ASG); Janjalani, Ustadz Abdurajak Abubakar; Moro National Liberation Front (MNLF).

Suggested readings: Julie S. Alipala and Nico Alconaba, "Pa Says He Was Playful; Neighbor Says a Joker," *Philippine Daily Inquirer* (Manila) (June 22, 2002), p. 1; Raymond Bonner and Eric Schmitt, "Philippine Officials Detail the Trap, Set with U.S. Help, That Snared a Rebel Leader," *New York Times* (September 22, 2002), p. 22; Carlito Pablo and Arlyn de la Cruz, "2 Videos Do Not Show Sabaya Killed," *Philippine Daily Inquirer* (August 28, 2002), p. 1; Alexander Young, Julie Alipala-Inot, and Carlito Pablo, "Sabaya Threatens to Behead US Captive," *Philippine Daily Inquirer* (June 8, 2001), p. 1.

Al-Sadr, Musa (1928–1978) (Lebanon)

Musa al-Sadr was the founder and head of the Lebanonese Shi'ite group **Amal**. He was born in 1928 in Qom, Iran. His father, Ayatollah Sadr al-Din al-Sadr, was one of the leading Shi'ite religious leaders in Iran. Al-Sadr was educated in schools in Qom. He attended college at the Tehran Faculty of Law and Political Economy. At the urging of his father, al-Sadr changed his plans for a secular career and became a religious scholar. After studying at a religious school in Qom, he moved to Najaf to study religious law under Muhsin al-Hakim. While in Qom, he edited a religious magazine titled *Makatib Islami* (Schools of Islam).

Al-Sadr's family had originally been from Lebanon and in 1957 he traveled to Lebanon to visit Shi'ite leaders there. He made such a good impression on these religious leaders that he was invited to replace the deceased al-Asyyid Abd al-Husain Sharaf al-Din, as the Shi'ite religious leader in Lebanon. In early 1960, al-Sadr moved to Lebanon and assumed this position. He became so popular among the Shi'ites that they bestowed on him the religious title "Imam" (leader of the faith and trust in Allah).

Al-Sadr used his position as religious leader to improve the status of Lebanese Shi'ites. Shi'ites in Lebanon occupied the lowest economic and social status among the various confessional groups. They also had the highest birth rate of the other groups and, by the early 1960s, constituted around 30 percent of the Lebanese population. Shi'ites were also the least politically conscious segment of the population. Al-Sadr started working on ways to improve the economic and social status of the Shi'ites by establishing a vocational institute in the southern Lebanese town of Burj al-Shimali. His next task was to build a political group to make the Shi'ites a political force in Lebanon. It helped that in 1963 he was made a citizen of Lebanon. Early in his career, al-Sadr was on good terms with the Shah of Iran and accepted aid from the Iranian government. In the aftermath of the 1973 Arab-Israeli War, however, he became estranged from the Shah and accused him of persecuting Iranian Shi'ites.

Next, Al-Sadr founded a Shi'ite political and military group. The political wing was formed in 1974 and named Harakat al-Mahrumin (Movement of the Deprived). A military wing called the Afwaj al-Mahrumin al-Lubnaniya (Lebanese Resistance Detachment), or better known as the Amal (Harakat Amal) (Movement of Hope), emerged in July 1975. At first al-Sadr allied with Kamal al-Jumblatt's Lebanese National Movement (LNM), but in May 1976 he broke with the LNM because he believed that it was prolonging the 1975 Lebanese civil war. Because al-Sadr held strong anti-communist views, he was reluctant to cooperate with any of the radical Palestinian groups. His relationship was also shaky with the **Palestine Liberation Organization** (PLO), but he did conclude an agreement for PLO operatives to train Amal fighters. While he supported the Palestine resistance movement, al-Sadr was fearful about the impact of PLO raids on Israel from southern Lebanon. He was able to use his position as chairman of the prestigious Supreme Shi'ite Council to make his views known on the national scene.

Al-Sadr's leadership of Amal and his championing of Shi'ite rights made him many enemies. His most determined enemy among the Shi'ites was the veteran parliamentary leader Kamil al-Asad. His independent stand on the growing disenchantment among Shi'ites with the PLO and other Palestinian groups after the 1978 Israeli invasion of Lebanon made him even more enemies. Al-Sadr was distantly related by marriage to **Ayatollah Ruholla Khomeini,** but their relationship was not close because al-Sadr was a rival to Khomeini among Shi'ites. Despite their critical relationship, al-Sadr tolerated Khomeini's ideas among Lebanon's Shi'ites. In August 1978, al-Sadr made visits to Algeria, Kuwait, and Saudi Arabia seeking support for Amal. The last state of this tour was a visit with **Muammar Qaddafi** in Libya. He arrived on August 25, 1978, in Libya with two associates. They were to have left on August 31, 1978, but none of them has ever been seen again. Various theories abound, but most of them having to do with a dispute with Qaddafi that led to their murders.

Elements in Amal went on a terrorist binge. Hamza Hamiel led a three-month campaign during which six airliners were hijacked. Gradually, Nabih Berri, the political head of Amal, gained control and ended the terrorist campaign. Al-Sadr's death left a void in the leadership of the Amal, but he is recognized in Lebanon as a martyr to the Shi'ite cause. *See also* Amal; Khomeini, Ayatollah Ruholla.

Suggested readings: Fouad Ajami, *The Vanished Iman: Musa al Sadr and the Shia of Lebanon* (Ithaca, NY: Cornell University Press, 1986); Majed Halawi, *A Lebanon Defied: Musa al-Sadr and the Shi'a Community* (Boulder, CO: Westview Press, 1992); Fereydoun Hoveyda, *The Broken Crescent: The "Threat" of Militant Islamic Fundamentalism* (Westport, CT: Praeger, 1998); Hala Jaber, *Hezbollah: Born with a Vengeance* (New York: Columbia University Press, 1997); Peter Theroux, *The Strange Disappearance of Iman Moussa Sadr* (London: Weidenfeld and Nicolson, 1987).

Salamat, Hashim (1942–2003) (Philippines)

Hashim Salamat was the head of the Moro Islamist group **Moro Islamic Liberation Front** (MILF). He was born on July 7, 1942, into a religious Muslim family in Pag-alungan, Maguindano, Philippines. After finishing at the local high school with high academic honors, Salamat went on a pilgrimage to Mecca in 1958. This religious experience convinced him to stay in Saudi Arabia and study at a religious fundamentalist school Madrasat as-Sulatiyah ad-Diniyah. Then in 1959, he attended **al-Azhar University** in Cairo, Egypt, where he studied at the university's Institute of Islamic Research. After graduation from this school in 1963, Salamat then pursued a second bachelor's degree at al-Azhar's College of Theology, majoring in philosophy and fundamental religious beliefs. Soon after graduating in 1967 with this second degree, Salamat worked on a master's degree also at al-Azhar's College of Theology. Next, Salamat completed coursework for a doctorate, and he was on the verge of starting research to complete his dissertation when he received news that the Moro independence movement had been launched.

Salamat returned to the Philippines to take an active role in the Moro independence movement. While in Egypt, he had been a student activist leader and this role led to his election as the president of the Philippine Muslim Student Association. Salamat has also been exposed to the Islamist ideas of Sayyid Qutb and Sayyid Abul A'la Mawdudi. Before his return to the Philippines Salamat helped organize military training camps for the **Moro National Liberation Front** (MNLF). After his return to the Philippines in 1972, he was soon number two leader in the leadership hierarchy of the MNLF after **Nur Misuari.**

Salamat broke with Misuari and the MNLF in 1978. He formed the Moro Islamic Liberation Front and a number of the fighters from the MNLF joined the new group. His reasons for forming the new group were dissatisfaction over Misuari's leadership and the lack of progress towards the creation of an Islamic state. In 1980, Salamat sent 1,000 of his followers to Afghanistan for military training to fight against the Soviet forces there. Casualties among the Filipino Muslims was heavy, but the combat experience helped them fight against the Philippine government when hostilities broke out between the MILF and the Philippine military in the 1990s. Despite his break with the MNLF, Salamat still had a working relationship with Misuari and the other leaders of the MNLF until 1982 when Salamat decided to go completely alone with his group. Salamat and the MILF established a parallel Muslim state alongside the Philippine state with Islamic committees and its own security forces, Bangsamoro Internal Security Force (BISF), and military force, Bangsamoro Islamic Armed Forces (BIAF). Salamat used his military forces to fight against the efforts of the Philippine army to reestablish military and political control of Muslim areas of the southern Philippines. He was able to use his association with first **Osama bin Laden** and later various **al-Qaeda** groups to build training camps for his forces to continue the war and provide training for other terrorist groups in southeast Asia, including the **Jemaah Islamiyah.**

Salamat was slow to end the war against the Philippine state and he only accepted peace negotiations under duress. He was hostile towards MNLF's negotiations with the Philippine government in the mid-1990s. Later, when Misuari signed a peace accord with the Philippine government, Salamat refused to go along and continued the fighting against the Philippine government. Slowly under Philippine army pressure, the MILF began to lose ground and Salamat had to go on the run moving from one base to another. This life style began to affect his health. In 2002, this pressure and the prospect of defeat led him to reconsider accepting peace negotiations with the Philippine government. Salamat was in the midst of these negotiations when his health broke and he died on July 13, 2003, of complications of acute ulcer and heart ailments. The MILF replaced him with Al Haj Murad Ebrahim, a veteran MILF leader, but Salamat was more than a revolutionary leader. He was the spiritual leader of the Muslim population in the southern Philippines. **See also** Bin Laden, Osama; Jemaah Islamiyah; Misuari, Nur;

Moro Islamic Liberation Front (MILF); Moro National Liberation Front (MNLF); al-Qaeda.

Suggested readings: Maria A. Ressa, *Seeds of Terror: An Eyewitness Account of Al-Qaeda's Newest Center of Operations in Southeast Asia* (New York: Free Press, 2003); Raissa Robles, "Philippine Muslim Rebels Confirm Death of Their Leader," *South China Morning Post* (Hong Kong, China) (August 6, 2003), p. 8; Felipe F. Salvosa II and Karen L. Lema, "MILF Chief Denies Terror Links," *BusinessWorld* (London) (June 23, 2003), p. 12; Mynardo Macaraig, "Philippine Muslim Rebel Chief: From Librarian to Warrior to Peacemaker," *Agence France Presse* (August 5, 2003), p. 1; Aquiles S. Zonio, "Goodbye, Ustadz Salamat," *Philippine Daily Inquirer* (Manila) (August 10, 2003), p. 14.

Sampson, Nicos Georgiades (1934–2001) (Cyprus)

Nicos Sampson was a right-wing journalist who was one of the most ruthless assassins for Cyprus's terrorist group **EOKA** (National Organization of Cypriot Fighters). He was born on December 16, 1935, in Famagusta, Cyprus. His family was in the publishing business. He attended journalism school in Athens, Greece. After leaving school, Sampson found a position in Nicosia with the English-language *Times of Cyprus* as a photojournalist. His birth name was Nicos Georgiades, but shortly after he became a journalist he changed his name to Nicos Sampson.

Sampson was able to use his position as a journalist to become an assassin for the EOKA. Colonel George Grivas had founded the EOKA in 1954 to drive the British out of Cyprus and unite Cyprus with Greece. In 1955, Sampson joined the EOKA. He became one of the leaders of an assassination squad on Ledra Street, an area that earned the name the "Murder Mile." His job was organizing riots protesting British policies and throwing grenades. British authorities realized that Sampson's journalist scoops about terrorist attacks meant that he had inside information. They arrested Sampson in 1957 and charged him with the murder of two British soldiers. Sampson was able to convince the British judge that his confession had been induced by torture and he was acquitted. He was convicted in a later trial of carrying a gun and this offense carried with it the death sentence. The governor of Cyprus, Field Marshal Sir John Harding, commuted the sentence to life imprisonment. He was sent to Great Britain to serve his sentence at Wormwood Scrubs. In 1960, he regained his freedom when a general amnesty was granted at the time of Cyprus's independence from the British. Sampson arrived in Cyprus a national hero.

After his arrival, Sampson returned to journalism and Cypriot politics. He became editor of the newspaper *Combat* (Makhi). In his newspaper, he confessed to the killing of more than 20 British soldiers and civilians. Sampson also was one of the leading political figures demanding that Cyprus unify with Greece. His attacks on the government of President Makarios and on Turkish-speaking Cypriots in his newspaper increased political tensions in Cyprus. Several times Sampson traveled to Greece to confer with the Greek government to intervene in Cyprus. He helped increase inter-ethnic tension by leading Greek paramilitary group in fighting with Turkish Cypriots. In 1970, he was elected to the Cypriot Parliament from Famagusta on a right-wing platform.

Sampson was a participant in the political coup in 1974 against the Makarios government. His reward for the July 15, 1974, coup sponsored by the Greek military junta was appointment as the head of the Cypriot government. His term of office, however, lasted only eight days. Despite his assurances that the rights of the Turkish minority would be protected, Turkey invaded Cyprus to prevent the union of Cyprus with Greece. The result was a partition of Cyprus that has lasted until today. President Makarios was restored as president, and one of his first actions was to arrest Sampson. In subsequent court proceedings in August 1976, Sampson received a sentence of 20 years for his role in the coup. In 1991, Sampson was released from prison. In the last decade of his life, Sampson became

a newspaper publisher. He died of cancer on May 9, 2001. Many Greek Cypriots blame him for the partition of Cyprus, and the Turkish Cypriots hated him for his anti-Turkish policies.

Suggested readings: Gerald Butt, "Nicos Sampson," *Independent* (London) (May 11, 2001), p. 6; Nancy Crawshaw, *The Cyprus Revolt: An Account of the Struggle for Union with Greece* (London: Allen & Unwin, 1978); Kosta Pavlowitch, "Nicos Sampson; The Executioner of Murder Mile Who Twice Escaped the British Death Sentence," *Guardian* (London) (May 21, 2001), p. 22.

Samudra, Imam (1967–) (Indonesia)

Imam Samudra is the mastermind behind Indonesia's **Jemaah Islamiyah**'s bombing in Bali in the summer of 2002. He was born in 1967 in the poor rural village of Serang, West Java, Indonesia, under the name of Abdul Aziz. His mother raised him and 11 other children. Samudra attended the local Muslim school, where he was a gifted student. After graduation in 1990, he left for Malaysia, where he remained until 1993. In 1993, he traveled to Afghanistan, where he continued his religious studies. Samudra stayed in Afghanistan from 1993 to 1996. He then returned to Malaysia, where he studied computer engineering at a university. While in Malaysia, he found a job at a religious school operated by the members of Jemaah Islamiyah (JI). He established permanent residency in Malaysia after marrying and settling in Banting, a coastal town south of Kuala Lumpur.

Samudra had become a key operative for the Jemaah Islamiyah by the end of 1996. He returned to Afghanistan several times and there he received bomb training by the **Taliban** government and **al-Qaeda**. In the late 1990s, Samudra made several trips to Indonesia. He received access to a quarry in Banten, on the island of Java, where he had bomb-making materials at his disposal. By this time, the leaders of Jemaah Islamiyah, **Abu Bakar Bashir** and **Hambali**, had returned to Indonesia. Samudra reported to the leaders of JI and he received the go-ahead to begin a bombing campaign. He was one of the leaders of the church bombing campaign on December 24, 2000, that destroyed numerous churches and killed 18. In August 2002, Samudra organized a jewelry story robbery in Bandung, Java, Indonesia, to raise funds to carry out terrorist acts.

Samudra was the operational leader of the Bali bombing on October 12, 2002. After consulting with JI leaders, he joined with Amrozi bin Nurhasyim, a car mechanic; Iqbal, and two bodyguards to plan the bombings at two nightclubs, Paddy's and Sari Club, on Bali. These targets had been selected because foreigners frequented them. Iqbal initiated the bombings by setting off a suicide bomb in a backpack that he was caring. Another bomb also exploded soon after. These explosions killed 188 with most of the dead Australians. Samudra stayed in the vicinity of the bombings for four days examining the results. The arrest of bin Nurhasyim in early November 2002 and his interrogation led Indonesian authorities to identify Samudra as the leader of the bombings. Australian police also began tracking Samudra from his mobile phone calls and from a network of informers. On November 22, 2002, Indonesian authorities arrested Samudra on a passenger bus aboard a ferry bound for Pekanbaru, Sumatra.

Samudra's trial took place in the summer of 2003. At this trial Samudra made little pretense about his guilt and admitted involvement in the Bali attack. However, he denied being the mastermind of the operation. His response to the death sentence of fellow conspirator bin Nurhasyim was that he would welcome a death sentence. **See also** Bashir, Abu Bakar; Hambali (Riduan Isamuddin); Jemaah Islamiyah (Islamic Community) (JI).

Suggested readings: Martin Chulov, "The Plot to Blast Bali—The Verdict," *Australian* (Sydney) (August 8, 2003), p. 8; Peter Lalor, "Master MindBeloved Son Who Plotted Acts of Barbarity," *Daily Telegraph* (Sydney) (November 23, 2002), p. 23; Dan Murphy, "A Classic Al Qaeda Field Operative," *Christian Science Monitor* (November 27, 2002), p. 6; Jane Perlez, "Defiant Suspect Says He Planned Bali Blast, Police Say," *New York Times* (November 23, 2002), p. A11; Cindy Wockner and David Murray, "A Life on Run Ends in Confession," *Herald Sun* (Melbourne) (November 23, 2002), p. 5.

Sánchez, Ilich Ramirez (Carlos the Jackal) (1949–) (Venezuela)

Ilich Sánchez, codenamed Carlos, was the leading international terrorist in the 1970s and 1980s. He was born on October 12, 1949, in Caracas, Venezuela. His father was a prosperous lawyer and a dedicated Marxist-Leninist who named his other two sons Lenin and Vladimir. In contrast, his mother was a staunch Catholic and tried to convert him unsuccessfully to the church. Sánchez received a private education from tutors. After his parents divorced in 1961, his father sent him to the radical Fermin Toro Lycee in Caracas, Venezuela. In January 1964, Sánchez joined the outlawed Venezuelan Communist Youth organization. Then in August 1966, Sanchez traveled to London, England, to study at the Stafford House Tutorial College and then at the Earls Court Tutorial College. After plans to attend the Sorbonne in Paris fell through, Sánchez's father sent him and one of his brothers in September 1968 to the Patrice Lumumba University in Moscow. Sánchez was more interested in being a playboy than in his studies and was expelled from school in 1970. His refusal to acquiesce to the policies of Soviet authorities and his dislike of Soviet Communism made it impossible for the Soviet KGB to recruit him as an agent.

Sánchez turned his search for a cause toward the Palestinian struggle with Israel. His role model was Wadi Haddad of the **Popular Front for the Liberation of Palestine** (PFLP). Haddad's goal of the destruction of Israel with a revolutionary Palestine appealed to Sánchez. In July 1970, he traveled to Beirut, Lebanon, to join the PFLP. Abu-Sharif, the recruiting officer for the PFLP, accepted him and gave him the codename of Carlos. Sánchez was sent to a training camp in Jordan about the same time as the Jordanian crackdown on the Palestinians in September 1970. Carlos gained a good reputation as a fighter and was slightly wounded in a gunfight with the Jordanian army. George Habash, the head of the PFLP, decided to use Carlos as a terrorist and sent him to Beirut, Lebanon, for specialized training in terrorism.

Sánchez's first mission was undercover in London. His contact was Mohamed Boudia, the head of terrorist operations in Europe for the PFLP and a veteran of the Algerian-French War. Sanchez's cover was as a student at the University of London. He was also active in London nightlife. Boudia's assassination on June 28, 1973, by an Israeli hit team, Wrath of God, in revenge for his role in the Munich Olympics massacre of Israeli athletes allowed Sanchez to become the chief assistant to Boudia's replacement, Michel Moukharbal.

For the next several years, Sánchez conducted terrorist operations in Europe. His first effort was the unsuccessful assassination attempt on a prominent Jewish businessman, Joseph Edward Sieff, on December 30, 1973, in London. He failed again in a bombing of the Hapoalim Bank in London, but Sánchez was more successful in the bombing of three pro-Israel newspapers in the summer of 1974. Next, he worked with the **Japanese Red Army** in the kidnapping of the French ambassador in The Hague, The Netherlands, in September 1974. In support of the kidnappers, Sánchez exploded a grenade in a drugstore in Paris that killed 2 and wounded 34. His next two operations were attempts to shoot down El Al airliners at Orly airport in January 1975 using RPGs (Rocket Propelled Grenade launchers), but both attempts failed.

Sánchez was still unknown as a terrorist until he killed two French counterintelligence agents and Moukharbal on June 27, 1975. Three French agents cornered Sánchez in a Paris apartment and tried to question him. Sánchez responded by opening fire on the unarmed French agents, killing two of them and wounding the other after Moukharbal identified him as his contact with the PFLP. Sánchez fled France and returned to Beirut, where the PFLP proclaimed him a hero.

Sánchez earned worldwide fame for his leadership in the kidnapping of the Organization of Petroleum Exporting Countries (OPEC) oil ministers from their meeting in Vienna, Austria, in December 1975. The leaders of the PFLP gave him command of this mission. Sánchez recruited seven members of the West German radical group Revolutionary Cells and three members of the PFLP and planned the operation. On December 21, 1975, the team seized the OPEC ministers after killing two of the security guards and a Libyan economist. With 62 hostages, Sánchez began negotiations for save haven in return for the release of the hostages. Within 24 hours the Austrian government provided an aircraft for Sánchez, his team, and the hostages to fly to Algeria. All but the Arab delegations were released in Algeria. He released more delegates in Libya, but authorities there forced him to return to Algeria where the remaining delegates were released. His orders from the PFLP leadership had been to kill the Saudi delegate, Sheikh Ahmed Yamani, and the Iran delegate, Jamshid Amouzegar, but Sánchez spared them in exchange for a large sum of money.

Sánchez's failure to kill Yamani and Amouzegar caused Haddad to end his relationship with the PFLP. Haddad did not wish to associate with an unreliable agent. Without an organization to support him, Sánchez went looking for allies. He was briefly arrested in Yugoslavia, but Marshal Tito ordered his release. He ended up in South Yemen under the protection of **Muammar Qaddafi** of Libya. Haddad's death in March 1978 left the field open to Sánchez to build his own terrorist organization that he called the Organisation of Arab Armed Struggle (OAAS). He recruited former associates in the Revolutionary Cells, PFLP, and any others who would enlist with him. Sánchez offered his new group to the highest bidder. Among his new contacts was the East German state security (Stasi), and with its help set up operations in Budapest, Hungary. His chief sponsor in the Middle East by the end of the 1970s was Syria, but he still had good relations with Qaddafi.

Sánchez allowed his personal relationships to determine his strategy. In February 1982, Sanchez's wife, Magdalena Kopp, and Bruno Breguet, a Swiss member of the OAAS, were arrested in Paris. He launched a bombing campaign to have them released. This strategy failed, however, because both received jail terms of from four to five years. In late December 1983, two bombs exploded on French trains, killing 5 and wounding 46 others. French authorities released both Kopp and Breguet after they served only a portion of their sentences.

Political pressure from the United States made the Eastern European countries break ties with Sánchez and his organization. He settled in Damascus, Syria, but the Syrian government had little for him to do. By the late 1980s, he was considered retired and foreign intelligence agencies were no longer interested in him. In September 1991, Sánchez and his family were expelled from Syria because the Syrian government wanted to improve relations with the United States. After trying to gain entry into several Middle Eastern countries, Sánchez ended up in the Sudan. Al-Turabi, the Islamist leader in Sudan, welcomed Sánchez as a warrior fighting for Palestine. Sánchez spent the next few years partying, drinking, and engaging in frequent love affairs. Al-Turabi decided to bow to American and French pressure and turn him over to French authorities. On August 14, 1994, Sánchez was kidnapped by French security agents and flown to France.

After nearly three years in prison, Sánchez went on trial in Paris on December 12, 1997. Five years before, Sánchez had been given a life sentence in absentia for the three murders in June 1995. In an eight-day trial, a jury of six women and three men declared Sánchez guilty of murder and he was sentenced to life imprisonment. Overall, Sánchez was responsible for the deaths of 24 people and the wounding of 257 others, but his arrest and conviction ended both his career and his terrorist organization. **See also** Habash, George;

Popular Front for the Liberation of Palestine (PFLP).

Suggested readings: Jon Follain, *Jackal: The Complete Story of the Legendary Terrorist, Carlos the Jackal* (New York: Arcade Publishing, 1998); Colin Smith, *Carlos: Portrait of a Terrorist* (New York: Hold, Rinehart, & Winston, 1976); David A. Yallop, *Tracking the Jackal: The Search for Carlos, the World's Most Wanted Man* (New York: Random House, 1993).

Sandinista National Liberation Front (Frente Sandinista de Liberación Nacional) (FSLN) (Nicaragua)

The Sandinista National Liberation Front (Frente Sandinista de Liberación Nacional, or FSLN) is the leading leftist political group in Nicaragua. This group was named after General Augusto Cesar Sandino (1895–1934), who had led a rebellion against the U.S.-sponsored Nicaraguan government from 1927 to 1933. The head of the Nicaraguan National Guard under the leadership of General Anastasio Somoza Garcia had Sandino and his key associates assassinated on February 23, 1934. In 1936, Somoza became president of Nicaragua and he established a dictatorship that lasted until his assassination on September 29, 1956. Political power in Nicaragua passed to his two sons, Luis Somoza Debayle and Anastasio Somoza Debayle. They shared power until Luis Somoza died of a heart attack in 1967. Growing discontent with the Somoza regime led to the formation of the Sandinista National Liberation Front in 1961. Founders of the FSLN were Carlos Fonseca Amador, a Marxist student leader; Tomas Borge Martinez, a former activist in the Independent Liberal Party; and Silvio Mayorga, a Marxist student leader and friend of Fonseca. They had all been active in the student rebellions of 1959–1961. Fonseca had also traveled to Cuba in 1959 and he had studied the guerrilla movement of Fidel Castro.

The Sandinista National Liberation Front's military operations started slowly. At first the FSLN had only 20 members. Initial operations in the northern part of Nicaragua in

1963 ended with heavy casualties as the FSLN was badly outgunned by the Nicaraguan National Guard units. Another attempt an offensive in 1967 met with little more success. By 1970, the guerrillas of the FSLN were better trained and armed than before, and they were able to recruit more effectively. This enabled the guerrillas to match the National Guard in the field. Recruitment increased after the failure of the Somoza government to respond effectively to the 1972 Managua earthquake. Both among the peasants and students, the FSLN was seen as an ally against the corrupt Somoza regime. In 1974, the FSLN launched yet another offensive, starting with the assault on a party celebrating the U.S. ambassador, Turner B. Shelton, at the home of Jose Maria Castillo Quant on December 24, 1974.

As the Sandinista National Liberation Front began to have military success, it started dividing into competing factions. The Prolonged Popular War Tendency was the heir to the legacy of Fonseca and its leaders were Borge, Bayardo Arce, and Henry Ruiz. A faction that had a more Marxist orientation was the Proletarian Tendency led by Jaime Wheelock, Carlos Nunez, and Luis Carrion. The most recent faction was the Insurrectional Tendency under the leadership of Daniel Ortega, Humberto Ortega, and Victor Tirado. On December 9, 1978, the three factions decided to unite. Then on March 7, 1979, a nine-member Sandinista National Directorate was formed with three representatives from each faction. On June 16, 1979, the Sandinistas announced the creation of a five-member provisional government, the Government of National Reconstruction (GRN), with Daniel Ortega, Moises Hassan, Sergio Ramirez, Alfonso Robelo, and Violeta Chamorro as members. With the resignation of Anastasio Somoza Debayle and his leaving of the country on July 17, 1979, the GRN assumed control of the Nicaraguan government. Over the next six months the Sandinistas consolidated their control over Nicaragua, and, in December 1979, the GRN was restructured to place

Sandinistas in key ministerial positions. In April 1980, both Chamorro and Robelo resigned from the GRN, implying opposition to the increasing leftward leanings of the Sandinistas.

The policy of the Sandinista government in its support for the insurgents in El Salvador led to political difficulties with the United States. President Jimmy Carter had supported the overthrow of Somoza, but he was uncomfortable with the Sandinistas' close association with Cuba and their support of the rebels in El Salvador. Election of President Ronald Reagan turned this discomfort into outright hostility. Published reports from Daniel and Humberto Ortega proclaiming the Marxist-Leninist orientation of the Sandinista National Liberation Front made it more difficult for the U.S. government to negotiate with the Sandinista government. Sandinista's policies caused the Miskito Indians located along the Atlantic Coast to revolt. Former Sandinista leader Edén Pastora Gomez also turned against the Sandinista government and he concluded a political alliance with Robelo. With the direct support of the Reagan administration, opposition to the Sandinista formed under the banner of the Contras. A civil war developed between the Sandinista government and the Contras. This civil war lasted almost a decade, with more than 30,000 deaths and a complete breakdown of the Nicaraguan economy. In an effort to end the civil war, the head of the Sandinista government, **Daniel Ortega Saavedra**, negotiated an agreement to allow free elections for a new president.

Contrary to the expectations of the Sandinista government, the candidate of the Sandinistas, Ortega, lost the 1990 election to Chamorro. There was widespread anxiety that the Sandinistas would not honor the election, but they did. Leaders of the FSLN went into opposition to await the next presidential election. In the meantime, they constituted a strong opposition to any party in power. In succeeding presidential elections, the FSLN has run Ortega and lost. Each time the American government has intervened with propaganda and funds on the anti-Sandinista side to help defeat the FSLN. The FSLN has a solid base of about 45 percent of the Nicaraguan populace, but it is having difficulty overcoming its past and the opposition of the United States. **See also** Fonseca Amador, Carlos; Ortega, Daniel Saavedra.

Suggested readings: John A. Booth, *The End and the Beginning: The Nicaraguan Revolution* (Boulder, CO: Westview Press, 1985); Timothy C. Brown (ed.), *When the AK-47s Fall Silent: Revolutionaries, Guerrillas, and the Dangers of Peace* (Stanford, CA: Hoover Institution Press, 2000); Stephen Kinzer, *Blood of Brothers: Life and War in Nicaragua* (New York: Putnam's, 1991; Rick Rockwell, Noreene Janus, and Kristin Neubauer, "Sandinista Salvation? Old Adversaries Make a Bid for Power in the New Nicaragua," *In These Times* (November 12, 2001), p. 10.

Sary, Ieng (1929?–) (Cambodia)

Ieng Sary was one of the leaders of the Khmer Rouge before becoming a leader in the Cambodian government. He was born around 1929 in Tra Vinh province, Vietnam. His father was a prosperous landowner. Sary was a good student, but he devoted much of his energy to agitating against French authorities. In 1945, he was awarded a scholarship to the Lycée Sisowath. Then in 1950, the Cambodian government awarded him a scholarship to study in France. His studies in France allowed him to renew his friendship with **Pol Pot**, the future leader of the Khmer Rouge. While in France, he joined the French Communist Party. On his return to Cambodia, he found a teaching position at Kambuj'bot (Sons of Kampuchea) College. Sary resumed his association with Pot and worked with him in underground agitation against the Cambodian government. He also married a sister of Pot's wife. In 1963, Sary joined Pot on the Central Committee of the Cambodian branch of the Indochina Communist Party and was number three in the party hierarchy behind Pot and Nuon Chea. He fled with Pot into the Cambodian jungles to avoid arrest by the Sihanouk regime.

Sary's job in the early 1970s was to shadow the activities of the party's new ally, Prince Norodom Sihanouk, until the Khmer Rouge seized power in 1975.

During the Khmer Rouge regime, Sary held the positions of deputy prime minister and foreign minister. He advocated wiping out the enemies of the Khmer Rouge revolution. His wife, Ieng Thirith, was minister of social affairs. Sary fled Cambodia when the Vietnamese invaded in January 1979 and the Chinese government granted him asylum. Later in 1979, the Cambodian government convicted Sary for genocide against the Cambodian people and sentenced him to death. This sentence was never carried out because after Sary had returned to Cambodia he remained in hiding in areas controlled by the Khmer Rouge. He brokered financial and military aid from China in the Khmer Rouge war against the Vietnamese-controlled Cambodian regime.

In August 1996, Sary broke away from Pot and the Khmer Rouge. After the 1991 Paris Peace Accords and the end of Chinese support, Sary's role in the Khmer Rouge became less secure. He started negotiations with the Cambodian government to repeal his death sentence, restore his property rights, and issue a general pardon. His terms were a royal pardon for past crimes and the freedom to remain in the area under his political and military control in Pailin, Cambodia. King Sihanouk pardoned him and Sary brought with him 10,000 Khmer Rouge fighters. His former colleagues accused him of stealing $25 million worth of Chinese aid and teak and gem revenues. Since the pardon, Sary has lived in a mansion in the Cambodian capital of Phnom Penh with his wife. He has become wealthy by smuggling rubies, sapphires, and logs from Cambodia to Thailand. International pressure to prosecute the leaders of the Khmer Rouge for the crime of genocide has included Sary. Cambodian Prime Minister Hun Sen has resisted efforts to include Sary in a trial, because Sen fears the outbreak of a civil war. United Nation representatives became so frustrated that they left Cambodia after years of trying to set up trials against the Khmer Rouge leaders. Sary maintains that he was ignorant of the mass murders of the Khmer Rouge regime, but it is well known that he was both aware of and participated in the crimes. **See also** Pot, Pol (Saloth Sar).

Suggested readings: Robin Ajello and Dominic Faulder, "The Rehabilitation of Ieng Sary," *Asiaweek* (December 27, 1996/January 3, 1997), p. 39; Mark Baker, "Called to Account," *Age* (Melbourne) (July 17, 2001), p. 11; David P. Chandler, *Brother Number One: A Political Biography of Pol Pot* (Boulder, CO: Westview Press, 1999); Tom Fawthrop, "Pol Pot Minister Lives it Up in Phnom Penh," *Straits Times* (Singapore) (January 7, 2002), p. A6; Puy Kea, "Khmer Rouge Leaders Relieved as U.N. Abandons Trial Plans," Japan Economic Newswire (February 9, 2002), p. 1; David Roberts, "Machiavelli: Alive and Well and Living in Cambodia?" *Jane's Intelligence Review* 10, no. 4(April 1, 1998), p. 37.

Savimbi, Jonas Malheiro (1934–2002) (Angola)

Jonas Savimbi was the founder and leader of the Angolan guerrilla group National Union for the Total Independence of Angola (Uniao Nacional para a Independencia Total de Angola, or UNITA). He was born on August 3, 1934, in the small village of Munhango beside the Benguela Railway in Angola's central highlands. His father was a stationmaster on the Benguela Railroad and a part-time Protestant minister. The family belonged to the Ovimbundu Tribe that constitutes nearly half of the Angolan population. After attending missionary schools and high school at the Marist Brothers College in Silva Porto, he traveled to Lisbon, Portugal, in May 1958, to study medicine. Savimbi spent almost as much time on Angolan liberation politics as he did his medical studies. Because his activities started attracting attention from Portuguese officials, Savimbi fled to Switzerland in February 1960. In Switzerland, Savimbi changed his major to political science and enrolled at the Social Science Institute of the Legal Faculty of Lausanne University. In

1964, he received a doctorate in political science from Lausanne University.

Savimbi's involvement in Angolan liberation politics became a personal crusade. Angola's war of liberation began in 1961 and Savimbi became involved in exile politics. He joined the Union of the Peoples of Angola (UPA) in 1961 and was appointed its secretary-general. When the UPA merged with another group to form the Front for the National Liberation of Angola (FNLA), Savimbi followed along. Holden Roberto was the leader of the FNLA and he appointed Savimbi to be the foreign minister of its government-in-exile. On July 15, 1964, Savimbi left the FNLA after concluding it had no future under the leadership of Roberto. He then tried unsuccessfully to join the Marxist Popular Movement for the Liberation of Angola (MPLA).

Next, Savimbi decided to found his own guerrilla group. In 1965, he traveled to the People's Republic of China and met Mao Tse-tung, who advised him on the conduct of a guerrilla campaign in Angola. On March 13, 1966, he formed the National Union for the Total Independence of Angola (UNITA). Savimbi set up UNITA as a rival to MPLA. Since the MPLA received most of its financial and military assistance from the Soviet Union, Savimbi sought similar assistance from the People's Republic of China (PRC). Savimbi established base camps in Zambia from which he launched guerrilla attacks against Portuguese-controlled Angola. His attacks were so successful that the government of Zambia forced him in July 1967 to leave Zambia for Cairo, Egypt. On July 1968, Savimbi returned to Angola and he moved into remote areas, where his forces spent almost as much time fighting the forces of the MPLA as it did those of the Portuguese.

The decision of the Portuguese government in 1974 to grant Angola its independence gave Savimbi an opportunity to participate in the new Angolan government. Three Angolan leaders, Savimbi, Agostinho Neto, and Roberto hold a meeting in Mombassa,

Angolan UNITA leader Dr. Jonas Savimbi is shown in Umtata, South Africa, on January 7, 1997. Savimbi's thirty-plus-year leadership came to an abrupt end on February 22, 2002, when an Angolan patrol ambushed and killed him near the town of Lucuse. (AP Photo/ Sasa Kralj)

Kenya, on January 3, 1975, and they decided to make Angola a democratic country. After the political situation deteriorated in Angola, Savimbi led the UNITA in February 1976 into a civil war with the MPLA that lasted more than 25 years. The MPLA gained the support of the Soviet Union and had more than 30,000 Cuban soldiers on its side. Savimbi countered with support from the United States and the South African government. In 1986, President Ronald Reagan declared Savimbi a "Freedom Fighter." By 1990, the Soviet Union had collapsed and Cuban troops had left Angola. In May 1991,

Savimbi signed a peace accord with the MPLA Angolan government. He ran in the 1992 Angolan presidential election, but electoral fraud led to Savimbi denouncing the election. Despite these charges, the Clinton administration pressured him to make peace with the Angola government. Savimbi retired from Angolan politics and returned to the bush guerrilla war. Without external financial or military support, Savimbi depended on raids on the diamond trade to finance operations, but over the years he had to downscale his military campaign. By the late 1990s, Savimbi was directing a small-scale guerrilla war.

Savimbi was always a controversial figure. He considered himself as the natural leader of Angola. His leadership of the UNITA was authoritarian as he brooked no dissension. In 1987, he purged UNITA by executing several of its leaders and killing their families. His power base was among the Ovimbundu who supported him as their leader. Several times he was offered posts in the Angolan government, but Savimbi refused because he wanted to be the sole head of government. His career ended abruptly on February 22, 2002, when an Angolan patrol ambushed and killed him near the town of Lucuse. General Antonio Dembo replaced Savimbi as head of UNITA, but his reported death from complications due to diabetes transferred control to the group's current leader, General Paulo Gato Lukamba.

Suggested readings: Fred Bridgland, "New Blow for Angolan Rebels," *Scotsman (Edinburgh)* (March 6, 2002), p. 10; Gregory Copley, "Where Lion Roam No More," *Defense and Foreign Affairs* (September 1984), p. 8; Jon Jeter, "Angolan Rebels' Hit-and-Run Strategy," *Washington Post* (November 20, 2001), p. A16; Richard Dowden Savimbi, "Jonas Savimbi," *Independent* (London) (February 25, 2002), p. 6; Nicholas D. Kristof, "Our Own Terrorist," *New York Times* (March 5, 2002), p. A23; John W. Turner, *Continent Ablaze: The Insurgency Wars in Africa 1960 to the Present* (London: Arms and Armour Press, 1998).

Sendic, Raul (1926–1989) (Uruguay)

Raul Sendic was the leader of the Uruguayan urban guerrilla group the Tupamaros in their battle with the government of Uruguay in the late 1960s and early 1970s. He was born in 1926 into a farm family. He attended law school in the late 1950s, but he left school to join the Uruguayan Socialist Party. Sendic became a trade union activist working with sugarcane workers and he led them in a series of strikes in 1960 and 1961. After the failure of these strikes, Sendic studied the Cuban Revolution of 1959 and the rural guerrilla strategy of Che Guevara. He decided that because Uruguay was mostly an urban environment, urban guerrillas could function much as the Cubans had done in the countryside.

As a result, Sendic founded the Tupamaros in 1962 to conduct an urban guerilla campaign in Uruguay. The group's name came from the name of an Inca chief, Tupac Amaro, who had rebelled against Spanish control of Peru in the eighteenth century. The first action of the Tupamaros was an arms raid on a gun club in a rural town 80 miles from Montevideo in 1964. These weapons and others acquired allowed the Tupamaros to battle the Uruguayan army and police from 1967 to 1972. Soon the Tupamaros became famous for their championing of the underdog. Among the operations undertaken under Sendic's leadership were assassinations, bombings, robberies, and kidnappings. A key feature of their operations was kidnappings for ransom. The most famous kidnappings were of Dan Mitrione, an American police advisor, on July 31, 1970, and Sir Geoffrey Jackson, the British ambassador to Uruguay, on January 8, 1971. Jackson was released after lengthy negotiations, but Mitrione was murdered after the Tupamaros demand for the release of 150 Tupamaros prisoners was refused. Another famous kidnapping was that of Aloisio Gomide, a Brazilian diplomat also kidnapped on July 31, 1970, but the Brazilian government negotiated his release.

Sendic became public enemy number one in Uruguay. Police captured him in 1970, but he escaped in a mass jailbreak in 1971. Sendic resumed control of the Tupamaros, but less than a year later he was recaptured.

This time he was seriously wounded in the face during the gunfight. He was sentenced to 45 years in prison. Uruguayan officials made certain that Sendic would not escape. He was kept in solitary confinement off and on from 1972 to 1984. Due to his wounds and torture, Sendic's health deteriorated. During his absence, the Uruguayan army and police crushed the Tupamaros with the assistance of funds and training from the U.S. government. The Uruguayan government released Sendic in 1985 as part of a general amnesty of prisoners. His health failing, Sendic founded an organization to promote rural land reform, but otherwise stayed out of politics. He spent much of his time writing a column for the Tupamaros biweekly newspaper admitting mistakes in the Tupamaros armed struggle. Sendic was in Paris seeking medical attention for a neurological ailment when he died on April 28, 1989. His early successes as head of the Tupamaros served as the model for **Carlos Marighela**, the Brazilian revolutionary leader, to develop his theory of urban guerrilla warfare. **See also** Marighela, Carlos.

Suggested readings: Richard Gott, "Obituary of Raul Sendic; El Bebe Robin Hood," *Guardian* (London) (May 2, 1989), p. 1; Isabel Hilston, "Raul Sendic," *Independent* (London) (May 3, 1989), p. 20; Alfonso A. Narvaez, "Raul Sendic, 64, Founder of Uruguay Rebel Group," *New York Times* (April 29, 1989), p. 10; Alan Riding, "For Freed Leftists in Uruguay, Hidden Terrors," *New York Times* (March 7, 1985), p. A2; Carla Ann Robbins and Juan de Onis, "Guerrillas Who Came in From the Cold," *U.S. News & World Report* (May 11, 1987), p. 33.

September 11th (United States and Middle East)

The September 11, 2001 attacks on the United States by **al-Qaeda** operatives were the culmination of a decade-long war declared by **Osama bin Laden** and al-Qaeda. Bin Laden had opened hostilities against the United States and the West by the issuing of a series of anti-American fatwas, or religious rulings, by al-Qaeda's religious committee. These fatwas were followed by a series of attacks against American targets in Kenya, Saudi Arabia, Tanzania, and Yemen. American intelligence soon identified the Qaeda connection in these attacks, but the U.S. intelligence community was unable to penetrate al-Qaeda. Afghanistan's **Taliban** government protected bin Laden, and accurate intelligence was hard to find. Even Pakistani sources had been corrupted by pro-Taliban supporters. Despite the weakness of intelligence, the Clinton administration tried to retaliate against bin Laden by launching a cruise missile attack, but it only killed a few Qaeda recruits.

Al-Qaeda had been planning a terrorist operation in the United States for several years. **Khalid Sheikh Mohammed**, the head of al-Qaeda's military committee, came up with the plan under the codename "Holy Tuesday." Mohammed proposed the operation to the military committee about two and a half years before September 11. In June 2002, Mohammed explained to Yosri Fouda, a journalist of the Arab TV channel al-Jazeera, that "the attacks were designed to cause as many deaths as possible and havoc and to be a big slap for America on American soil."

Al-Qaeda had no difficulty finding candidates for a suicide mission. Mohammed turned to al-Qaeda's Department of Martyrs for volunteers. The five well-educated and highly motivated members of al-Qaeda who were chosen entered the United States by legal means. The leader of these students was **Mohamed Atta**, an Egyptian city planner. His chief assistant was Nawaf al-Hazmi. All five enrolled in flying schools in California, Florida, Minnesota, and Texas. Some of these students were more capable than others, but they all became competent to fly a large aircraft already in flight. In May and June 2001, the rest of the Qaeda operatives, mostly Saudis, arrived in the United States. Four teams of four or five operatives were trained to seize control of four commercial airliners and fly them into four designated targets—both World Trade Center towers in New York City and the Pentagon and the White

House in Washington, D.C. One of the pilots, **Zacharias Moussaoui**, missed the operation because he had been arrested in August in Minneapolis, Minnesota, for suspicious activities. This left 19 hijackers available for the mission.

In a coordinated effort, the four highjacking teams were able to seize control of four commercial airliners. The first was American Airlines Flight 11 flying out of Boston's Logan Airport with a destination of Los Angeles, California. Shortly after takeoff, the hijackers gained control of the aircraft and flew it into the North Tower of the World Trade Center at 8:45 A.M. EST. Less than 30 minutes later, a second team of hijackers seized control of United Airlines Flight 175, also flying out of Logan Airport to Los Angeles. This aircraft crashed into the South Tower of the World Trade Center shortly after 9:00 A.M. EST. A third aircraft, American Airlines Flight 77, bound from Dulles Airport just outside Washington, D.C., to Los Angeles, was seized by the third team of hijackers. This aircraft crashed into the western face of the Pentagon shortly after 9:40 A.M. EST.

By the time of the third hijacking, the U.S. government had realized the enormity of the attacks and it ordered the Federal Aviation Authority to ground all the 4,546 aircraft in the air on September 11. Presidential orders were issued to shoot down any civilian airliner known to be under the control of hijackers. In the meantime, the fourth team had gained control of United Airlines Flight 93 flying out of Newark Airport bound for San Francisco, California. Because this aircraft had been over 40 minutes late leaving Newark, the pilot and crew had been warned about a possible attempt. Passengers had also heard about the fates of the earlier airliners from mobile-phone calls. Soon after the hijackers gained control of the aircraft, the passengers revolted and the aircraft crashed at 10:03 A.M. EST in a field southeast of Pittsburgh. The probable destination of this airliner was the White House and the Capitol complex.

The impact of September 11 on the American polity cannot be overstated. It has transformed both American politics and foreign policy. Americans seemed to be able to tolerate terrorist activities directed against diplomatic, military, and foreign targets, but a terrorist strike at the American homeland produced a trauma. Besides the 3,000 or so deaths at the World Trade Center and the Pentagon, the thought of American civilians at risk prodded Congress to pass the USA PATRIOT Act, full of restrictions on American civil liberties that otherwise would have never been considered. An American administration launched two military interventions in Afghanistan and Iraq that otherwise also would never have happened. Only two other events have rivaled September 11th's revolutionary impact on the American society in the 20th and 21st centuries: Pearl Harbor and the assassination of President John F. Kennedy. **See also** Atta, Mohamed al-Amir Awad al-Sayed; Bin Laden, Osama; Mohammed, Khalid Sheikh; Al-Qaeda (The Base).

Suggested readings: J. Bowyer Bell, *Murders on the Nile: The World Trade Center and Global Terror* (San Francisco: Encounter Books, 2003); Richard Bernstein, *Out of the Blue: The Story of September 11, 2001 from Jihad to Ground Zero* (New York: Times Books, 2002); Jane Corbin, *Al-Qaeda: The Terror Network That Threatens the World* (New York: Thunder's Mouth Press, 2002); Yosri Fouda, "Masterminds of a Massacre—9/11—One Year On," *Australian* (Sydney) (September 9, 2002), p. 8; Yosri Fouda and Nick Fielding, *Masterminds of Terror: The Truth Behind the Most Devastating Terrorist Attack the World Has Ever Seen* (New York: Arcade Publishing, 2003); John Miller and Michael Stone, *The Cell: Inside the 9/11 Plot, and Why the FBI and CIA Failed to Stop It* (New York: Hyperion 2003).

17 November (See Revolutionary Organization 17 November)

SHAC (See Stop Huntingdon Animal Cruelty)

Shankill Butchers (Northern Ireland)

The Shankill Butchers, a small group of Ulster **Volunteer Force** (UVF) members, conducted a murderous campaign against Catholics in Northern Ireland in the 1970s. The leader of the Shankill Butchers was Lenny Murphy, a high school dropout and small-time hoodlum. Protestants were reeling in the early 1970s from attacks by the **Provisional Irish Republican Army** (Provos) and by the feeling that the British government was abandoning them. Leaders of the UVF began public discussions on the need for Protestant vigilante groups to defend Ulster's Protestants against the Catholic republican Provos. Murphy attended trials of Provos members, studying the legal issues involved in their capture and conviction. He participated in at least three murders in 1972 and for the last murder was arrested by Ulster police. While in prison awaiting trial, Murphy poisoned and killed the only witness against him. Murphy was acquitted of the murder charge, but he remained in prison for two attempts at escape. Gusty Spence was the leader of the UVF in his prison, but Murphy showed him little respect or loyalty. Murphy was finally released in May 1975.

After leaving prison, Murphy decided to form a vigilante group of the UVF under his leadership. By this time Murphy had a violent reputation and this reputation attracted many of the younger UVF members. He recruited Robert "Basher" Bates, Samuel "Big Sam" McAllister, and William "Billy" Moore to provide the leadership cadre for the Shankill Butchers. Moore was important to the group because he owned a taxicab and, as a former meat packer, he had access to butcher knives and a meat cleaver. By September 1975, this group had grown to 20 members. Headquarters was in a room above the Brown Bear pub in Shankill, Belfast.

Although Murphy reported to no superiors in the UVF, he received an unofficial go-ahead from UVF leadership to launch a terrorist campaign against the Provos and Catholics. On October 2, 1975, Murphy and accomplices murdered two Catholic men and two Catholic women in a bungled robbery of a liquor establishment. In the early morning of November 25, 1975, Murphy and three others killed and mutilated a young Catholic man in the first of the savage killings that the media named the Shankill Butchers. This was the beginning of the mutilation campaign.

This campaign of terror against Catholics lasted less than a year. After several brutal murders, Murphy was arrested on March 13, 1976, and he was sentenced to 12 years on firearms and ammunition possession charges. His leadership of the Shankill Butchers was unknown to the police. Murphy continued to direct the operations of the group from prison. Northern Ireland authorities finally arrested Bates, Moore, and others in 1977. Bates and Moore received sentences of life imprisonment. Murphy escaped the murder charges, but a relative of one of his victims gunned him down shortly after Murphy's release from prison in 1982. **See also** Ulster Volunteer Force (UVF).

Suggested readings: Martin Dillon, *The Shankill Butchers: The Real Story of Cold-Blooded Mass Murder* (New York: Routledge, 1989); Peter Taylor, *Loyalists: War and Peace in Northern Ireland* (New York: TV Books, 1999).

Shariati, Ali (1933–1977) (Iran)

Ali Shariati provided the philosophy behind the idea of reconciling Islam and socialism that was adopted after his death by the Mujahadin-e Khalq and other Iranian revolutionaries. He was born on November 24, 1933, in the small village of Kahak, about 50 miles from Sabzevar, Iran. His father was a prominent religious teacher at Mashhad High School and later at the Center for the Propagation of Islamic Truths (CPIT), and he supported the anti-British government of Mohammad Mosaddegh. Shariati was educated in the elementary school of Ibn Yamin and later at Ferdowsi High School in Mashhad. After the ninth grade, he attended the Teachers' Training College. In 1952, Shariati graduated from this school, but not before some difficulty at school over his pro-Mosaddegh political views. His first job was at the Ketabpur primary school at Ahmadabad. Deciding to earn his high school diploma, he passed comprehensive examinations in June 1954. After receiving a scholarship, Shariati started graduate work at the University of Paris–Sorbonne. In 1964, he received his doctorate in sociology.

Shariat's first exposure to politics had been father's Center for the Propagation of Islamic Truths. At the center, he was an active participant in the discussions on the political issues of the day. Shariati joined the High School Students' Islamic Association (HSIA), an offshoot of the CPIT, in 1952. In 1953, he joined the League for the Freedom of the Iranian People (Jam'iyat-e Azadi-ye Mardom-e Iran). Shariati continued to be active in the pro-Mosaddegh movement until a U.S. Central Intelligence Agency (CIA) coup overthrew Mosaddegh. In response, Shariati joined the anti–Shah of Iran group, the National Resistance Movement of Iran (Nehzat-e Mogavemat-e Melli, or NRM). He became one of its leaders in Mashhad. When the various anti-Shah groups formed the political party the Iranian People's Party (Hezb-e Mardom-e Iran, or IPP), Shariati became a member of the party's Central Committee of Mashhad.

In the midst of his active involvement in politics, Shariati began writing on ways to reconcile Islam with socialism. In one of his early writings, he championed the ideas of Abu Zarr, a contemporary of the Companions of the Prophet and an advocate of social justice for the downtrodden. Next, he advanced the idea of the Islamic countries serving as the third way between the communist and capitalist blocs. Shariati called this approach the "Median School of Islam." Several of his other writing also promoted Iranian nationalism. These and other writings in Mashhad's prestigious daily *Khorasan* in 1954 and 1955 made Shariati a national figure.

Iranian authorities considered Shariati and his growing reputation to be dangerous. When Shariati returned to Iran in 1965, the Iranian police arrested him. After six months in protective custody, the authorities allowed

him to return to Mashhad University to teach sociology. His courses reconciling sociological theory and Islam became popular with the students. In 1967 the Monthly Religious Society invited him to become a lecturer at the Husainiyeh Ershad institution in Tehran. Again his lectures made him a national figure and again Shariati attracted the attention of the Shah of Iran's police. In 1973 police shut down the Husainiyeh Ershad institution and arrested Shariati. This time Shariati spent 2 years in jail and following the jail term the authorities exiled him to the remote Khurasan Province. Finally, in 1977, Shariati left Iran and settled in England. His stay in England was brief because he died on June 19, 1977, under mysterious circumstances. It was widely believed then and now that the Iranian Security Agency (SAVAK) had killed him.

Shariati's death did not end his influence in Iran. Many of the participants of the Iranian Revolution of 1978 were inspired by his ideas. Even the fundamentalist clerics used his name and his writings to inspire their followers. This ended after the **Ayatollah Khomeini** consolidated his regime. These same clerics decided that Shariati's views were too extreme and dangerous and his works were banned by the Khomeini government. His views still have adherents in Iran and among the enemies clerical regime in Iran, including the MEK.

Suggested readings: Ervand Abrahamian, *The Iranian Mojahedin* (New Haven, CT: Yale University Press, 1989); Lawrence Davidson, *Islamic Fundamentalism* (Westport, CT: Greenwood Press, 1998); Ali Rahnema, *An Islamic Utopian: A Political Biography of Ali Shari'ati* (London: I. B. Tauris, 1998).

Sheikh, Ahmed Omar Saeed (1973–) (Pakistan)

Omar Saeed Sheikh is one of the leaders of the Pakistani terrorist group Army of Muhammad (Jaish-e-Muhammad) and the architect of the murder of American journalist Daniel Pearl. He was born on December 23, 1973, at Whipps Cross Hospital in Wanstead, East London, England. His father is a wealthy clothing wholesaler, who had immigrated with his family to England in 1968. Sheikh's first schooling was at Nightingale Primary School at Wanstead. Sheikh then attended Forest School, a small but prestigious private school, in East London. He was considered a good student but his classmates considered him a bully. His parents became so concerned about his drinking, smoking, and chasing women that they decided to move back to Pakistan. They placed him in the prestigious Aitchison College in Lahore, but he was expelled for beating up fellow students. In 1990, Sheikh returned to the Forest School. After a trip to Lahore, Pakistan, Sheikh enrolled at the London School of Economics to study mathematics and statistics. He began spending more time with Muslim politics in the London School of Economics' Islamic Society than he did with his studies. His political activities, however, did not prevent him from conducting a stock exchange business on the side. In 1993, he traveled to Bosnia to work for the Convoy of Mercy, a Muslim charity. After this experience in a war zone, he left school and returned to Pakistan. By this time, his political attitude had hardened and he no longer believed that Muslims could be friends with Christians and Jews.

Sheikh's zeal for the Muslim cause turned him into a terrorist. After returning to Pakistan, he joined the Islamist Harakat ul-Mujahidin (HUM). In early 1994, he received training at a Qaeda camp in Afghanistan. His first mission for HUM was to travel to India and arrange a series of kidnapping. In July 1994, he kidnapped three British backpackers and an American backpacker near Delphi and tried to exchange them for the release of 10 jailed Muslim activists, including Maulana Masood Azhar. On October 30, 1994, Indian police freed the kidnapped victims and wounded Sheikh in the process. Sheikh spent the next five years in a Delhi's Tihar prison despite an attempt by HUM operatives to free him and Azhar by kidnapping six western tourists in Kashmir, India, in July 1995. This attempt failed and five of the six tourists were murdered. Sheikh

was released on December 30, 1999, after members of the Army of Muhammad hijacked an Indian airliner.

Sheikh became an important figure in the Islamist movement in Pakistan. The Pakistani intelligence service, Inter-Services Intelligence (ISI), was the sponsor of many of the groups that Sheikh belonged to after his return from India. He became second-in-command to Azhar in the Jaish-e-Muhammad (Army of Muhammad or JEM), a breakaway faction of HUM. Later, he broke with Azhar over Azhar's support for an anti-Shi'ite group. Sheikh then joined **al-Qaeda** and he soon developed close ties with **Osama bin Laden** and other al-Qaeda leaders. His ties with the Army of Muhammad led him into fighting in Kashmir. Sheikh also played a role in the October 1, 2001, attack on the Srinagar legislature in Kashmir that killed 38 people. Then he helped plan the assault on India's parliament on December 13, 2001, that caused 15 deaths. His distress over the collapse of the **Taliban** government in Afghanistan made him eager to strike back at the United States.

Sheikh planned the operation to kidnap and then murder Daniel Pearl. Pearl was a journalist with the *Wall Street Journal* who was following a story about the attempted terrorist bombing by the "shoe bomber" Richard Reid in the United States. An e-mail message informed Pearl of a possible meeting with the Muslim cleric Sheik Mubarik Ali Gilani. On January 23, 2002, Pearl entered a Karachi restaurant and was never seen alive again. His murder on January 31, 2002, was recorded on tape. ISI agents arrested Sheikh on February 5, 2002, in Lahore, but he was not turned over to law enforcement officers until February 12. Soon after his arrest, Sheikh confirmed his participation in the kidnapping of Pearl. After a trial, Sheikh was sentenced to death on July 15, 2002, along with three others. He reacted to the sentence by threatening to kill the judge, and he called for a jihad against non-Muslims. **See also** Bin Laden, Osama; Al-Qaeda (The Base).

Suggested readings: John Ward Anderson, and Peter Baker, "Killers Likely Never Intended to

Free Pearl," *Washington Post* (February 23, 2002), p. A16; Yosri Fouda and Nick Fielding, *Masterminds of Terror: The Truth behind the Most Devastating Terrorist Attack the World Has Ever Seen* (New York: Arcade Publishing, 2003); Susan B. Glasser, "Prominent Militant Key Suspect in Pearl Kidnapping," *Washington Post* (February 7, 2002), p. A10; Rohan Gunaratna, *Inside Al Qaeda: Global Network of Terror* (New York: Columbia University Press, 2002); Charles Hymas, "LSE Student Is Held Over India Kidnap," *Sunday Times* (London) (November 6, 1994), p. 1; Stephen Mcginty, "The Very Model of an English Islamic Terrorist," *Scotsman* (Edinburgh) (July 16, 2002), p. 2; Daniel McGrory and Zahid Hussain, "Briton's Path from School Bully to 'Terror Chief,'" *Times* (London) (March 23, 2002), p. 1.

Shigenobu, Fusako (1945–) (Japan)

Fusako Shigenobu was the leader of the **Japanese Red Army** (JRA) until her capture in 2000. She was born on September 20, 1945. Her father had been a teacher on the island of Kyushu before entering the Imperial Japanese Army and serving in the military police (Kempeitai). He had belonged to the notorious Blood Brotherhood League that conducted assassinations of liberal government leaders in prewar Japan. Military defeat in World War II destroyed his world, but not his rightist views. Shigenobu grew up poor with two brothers and a sister. She came to resent the lack of status that her family's poverty inspired. Her attendance at a commercial high school in Tokyo did not diminish her bitterness. After graduation in 1964, Shigenobu found a job as an office worker at the Kikkoman Soy Sauce factory. Unhappy with the male-dominated company, she decided to become a science teacher by studying at Meiji University in Tokyo. She then joined the radical student movement. Later she worked as a hostess at a bar in the Ginza area of Tokyo. Her combination of student, revolutionary, and worker left her little time for anything else. Police arrested her in 1969 for assembling without a permit, but she was soon released.

Shigenobu decided that the Japanese Red Army needed to align with existing terrorist groups rather than try to build a new movement. This strategy placed her in opposition to the leadership of Mori Tsuneo in the group. Her idea was to align the Japanese Red Army with Palestinian groups in the Middle East. After receiving Mori's reluctant permission, Shigenobu and her new husband, Okudaira Takeshi, a former engineering student at Kyoto University and an activist in the Japanese Red Army, moved to the Middle East in February 1971. She decided to attach the Japanese Red Army to **George Habash**'s **Popular Front for the Liberation of Palestine** (PFLP).

After receiving training from the Popular Front for the Liberation of Palestine, the first operation of the Japanese Red Army was the attack on Lod Airport. On May 30, 1972, three members of the JRA attacked passengers at the Lod Airport in Tel Aviv, Israel. This operation was a suicide mission, so none of the three expected to survive. Twenty-six people died and 86 were wounded. Two of the three JRA members died, including Shigenobu's husband, but one, Kozo Okamoto, was captured.

Shigenobu continued to lead the Japanese Red Army and plan its operations throughout the 1970s and 1980s. Two of the operations in July 1973 and September 1977 were hijackings of Japan Airlines aircraft. In both cases casualties were kept at a minimum. Then, in September 1974 and in August 1975, members of the JRA assaulted embassies and held hostages. The last major operation was on April 14, 1988, when the JRA bombed an American military recreational club in Naples, Italy, and killed five. After this terrorist attack and an abortive attack on the Imperial palaces in Kyoto and Tokyo in January 1990, Shigenobu ordered the JRA to maintain a low profile.

This low profile encouraged Shigenobu to take the chance to return to Japan. In July 2000, she used forged Japanese passports to return to Japan. She remained hidden in a hotel in Osaka Prefecture, Japan, but she began to make contact with Japanese Red Army sympathizers. Japanese police acting on a tip arrested her outside her hotel on

November 8, 2000. Since then she has been held for trial scheduled for sometime in 2004. While in prison, she wrote a book, *Under the Apple Tree, I Decided to Give Birth to You, Gentosha*. This book described the trials of raising a daughter in the Arab world. Her daughter, Mei Shigenobu, has traveled around the Middle East and Europe defending her mother and attempting to reconcile Israelis and Palestinians. **See also** Japanese Red Army (JRA); Popular Front for the Liberation of Palestine (PFLP).

Suggested readings: William R. Farrell, *Blood and Rage: The Story of the Japanese Red Army* (Lexington, MA: Lexington Books, 1990); Mayo Issobe, "Becoming a Mother on the Run," Asahi News Service (April 24, 2001), p. 1; Harumi Ozawa, "New World Daughter: Shigenobu's Child Sees Emergence of French Viewpoints," *Daily Yomiuri* (Tokyo) (July 21, 2001), p. 7.

Shikaki, Fathi (1951–1995) (Palestine)

Fathi Shikaki was one of the founders and the head of the Palestinian terrorist group **Palestine Islamic Jihad**. He was born in 1951 in the Gaza slum of Shubeira. His parents were both Palestinians who had been expelled from their home near Ramlah. Most of his early education was at the local United Nations school, where he became interested in the study of science. When he was fifteen, his mother died. Shikaki attended Bir Zeit University on the West Bank, where he studied physics and mathematics. There he became an admirer and follower of **Sheikh Ahmed Yassin**, a leader in the **Muslim Brotherhood** and later the founder of the Islamist group **Hamas**. After graduation from Bir Zeit University, he was a teacher in a school in East Jerusalem. In 1974, he decided to study medicine at the Mansoura University in Egypt.

Shikaki became further attracted to the philosophy and religious views of the Muslim Brotherhood during his study of medicine in Egypt. Among his contacts in Egypt were Sheikh Omar Abdel-Rahman, the religious leader of the Egyptian Islamic Jihad, and Salah Sariya, the radical Palestinian who was later executed in 1976 for a plot against President Anwar Sadat. He also became a convert to the political and religious views of **Sayyid Qutb**. Qutb had been executed in 1966 for his political opposition to the Egyptian government, but his writings were popular among young Muslim intellectuals. Shortly after the Iranian revolution of 1979, Shikaki wrote a book, *Khomeini: The Islamic Solution and the Alternative*, that praised the **Ayatollah Khomeini** and his approach to an Islamist state. The Egyptian government banned the book and briefly arrested him. After receiving his medical degree and feeling the hostility of the Egyptian authorities, Shikaki began work in a general practice at the Augusta Victoria Hospital in Jerusalem. Then Shikaki moved to the Gaza Strip, where he opened a medical clinic.

By the early 1980s, Shikaki had turned away from medicine to head the newly revitalized Palestine Islamic Jihad. A variant of this organization had been formed in 1964, but Israeli security had almost wiped it out. Shikaki and six others were able to reconstitute it in 1981 by attracting former members of earlier groups with his militant Islamist views and his ambition to attack Israel. He decided to keep his new organization small and capable of initiating operations against Israel in secret. At first, most of the operations were small-scale attacks by bombings and random shootings. This changed when the tactic of suicide bombings was adopted. Young Palestinians were recruited for suicide missions within Israel. The purpose of these attacks was to bring home the Palestinian struggle to the average Israeli.

Despite his precautions for secrecy, Israeli security forces soon learned of his leadership and took steps to curtail his influence. Israeli security captured Shikaki in 1986 and sentenced him to four years in prison. In August 1988, Israel decided to deport him to Lebanon. Shikaki took this opportunity to reestablish his authority in the Palestine Islamic Jihad. Then in 1990, he moved his headquarters to Damascus, Syria, where he had the protection of the president of Syria, Hafiz al-Asad. Shikaki continued to travel around the Middle East making contacts and recruiting support for the Palestine Islamic Jihad. On one of these trips he stopped in Valetta, Malta. On October 26, 1995, an Israeli hit team found him outside of a Valletta hotel and shot him five times in the back. His death was a blow to the Palestine Islamic Jihad, but his friend Ramadan Abdullah Shallah was appointed to replace him within days. **See also** Abdel-Rahman, Sheikh Omar; Islamic Jihad; Muslim Brotherhood (al-Ikhwan al-Muslimun); Qutb, Sayyid.

Suggested readings: Patrick Cockburn, "Arafat Murder Was Foiled by Malta Killing," *Independent* (London) (December 7, 1995), p. 13; Patrick Cockburn, "Jihad Leader Took Just One Risk Too Many," *Independent* (London) (October 31, 1995), p. 12; Robert Fisk, "The Doctor Who Finds Death a Laughing Matter," *Independent* (London) (January 30, 1995), p. 11; Robert Fisk, "Obituary: Dr Fathi Shkaki," *Independent* (London) (October 31, 1995), p. 14; Robert Fisk, "Ugly End for Man Who Laughed at Death," *Independent* (London) (October 30, 1995), p. 12; Meir Hatina, *Islam and Salvation in Palestine* (Tel Aviv, Israel: Tel Aviv University, 2001); Charles Richards, "Intifada's Gentle Man of War," *Independent* (London) (December 15, 1992), p. 10.

Shining Path (Sendero Luminoso) (Peru)

The Shining Path is a Peruvian Maoist guerrilla organization that has carried out since 1980 the most bloody guerrilla war in Latin America. **Abimael Guzman**, a philosophy professor at the University of San Christobal de Huamanga in Ayachucho, Peru, founded the Shining Path in February 1970. The official name of the group is the Communist Party of Peru by the Shining Path of Jose Carlos Marrategui, but it was soon called by the shorter name of the Shining Path, or Sendero Luminoso. Guzman created the Shining Path in the image of a Marxist-Leninist party with an authoritarian and hierarchical organizational structure. The party had a central committee that had overall responsibility for the party, but Guzman was the dominant personality. For the first decade of its existence, Guzman built the party along Maoist lines by recruiting peasants and stu-

dents to fight a guerrilla war against the Peruvian state.

In February 1980, Guzman led the Shining Path into open conflict with the government of Peru. At a meeting of the central committee beginning on March 17 and lasting until March 25, Guzman persuaded the central committee to launch a military campaign. Those that opposed his position were expelled from the party. Guzman made it understood that the Shining Path was to engage in total war against the state and anybody who stood in its way. Following the committee meeting, a military school was set up to train and indoctrinate the Shining Path's future military leaders. This school lasted from April 2 to April 19.

The initial operation, the burning of the ballot boxes in the Ayacuco village of Chuschi on May 17, 1980, gave no indication of how fierce the war would become in the next decade. Operations were slow to develop as the Shining Path lacked trained personnel and weapons. Over the course of the first year, the leadership organized the Shining Path into three operational forces: local guerrilla forces, regional guerrilla forces, and the main force. Local guerrilla forces remained in one area and these units were composed of part-time fighters. Regional forces were full-time units able to conduct operations over several provinces. Finally, the main force was a full-scale insurgent army able to match the Peruvian army in the field.

Throughout the 1980s and early 1990s, the Shining Path carried out terrorist attacks against the Peruvian government. Peruvian forces were unable to stop the Shining Path in the field so intelligence targeted its leadership. Guzman's capture on September 13, 1992, was a severe blow to the Shining Path. He was not only the political leader of the movement but also its spiritual leader. His life sentence and imprisonment in a cage demoralized him, and his appeals to his followers to suspend the war hurt his image. His successor was **Oscar Ramirez Durand** (codenamed Feliciano) until his capture in

July 1999. In the years from 1993 to 1995 it appeared to outside observers that the Shining Path was a spent force. President Fujimori led a campaign that combined authoritarian and police state tactics to attack the Shining Path and this campaign was working until he ran into political trouble because of these tactics.

The discrediting of President Fujimori allowed the Shining Path to reconstitute itself as an insurrectionary force. Human rights abuses of Fujimori's government were highlighted and he fled Peru for asylum in Japan. President Alejandro Toledo assumed the presidency of Peru in July 2001, and he attempted to continue the campaign against the Shining Path. By December 2001, it had become apparent that the Shining Path was reviving. This resurgence led to a March 20, 2002, bombing in Lima three days before the arrival of President George W. Bush for a state visit. Despite the claims that the Shining Path has only 500 or 600 activists and no recognizable leader, the guerillas still constitute a continuing threat against the Peruvian state. A series of March 2003 court opinions have annulled the sentences of 2,000 members of the Shining Path, including Guzman, on the grounds that the secret military courts of a decade ago were unconstitutional. President Toledo is fighting the release of these prisoners, and new trials are scheduled in the next year or so. See also Durand, Oscar Ramirez; Guzman, Abimael.

Suggested readings: James Brooke, "Leader's New Image Saps Shining Path's Strength," *New York Times* (November 27, 1993), sec.1, p.3; Gabriel Escobar, "Peru's Shining Path Maoists: Leaderless, Decimated, Divided," *Washington Post* (November 21, 1994), p. A1; Anthony Faiola and Lucien Chauvin, "Peru Rebels Suspected in Bombing," *Washington Post* (March 22, 2002), p. A1; Gustavo Gorriti, *The Shining Path: A History of the Millenarian War in Peru* (Chapel Hill: University of North Carolina Press, 1999); Simon Strong, *Shining Path: The World's Deadliest Revolutionary Force* (London: HarperCollins, 1992); Scott Wilson, "Peru Fears Reemergence of Violent Rebels," *Washington Post* (December 10, 2001), p. A18; Scott Wilson, "Peruvian Guerrillas Fight New Battle in Court," *Washington Post* (March 23, 2003), p. A16.

Shiv Sena (Sword of Shiva) (India)

The Shiv Sena is a Hindu extremist group that operates in Bombay and in the province of Maharashtra, India. Bal Thackeray, a former political cartoonist, founded this group in 1966 to rid Bombay of what he considered foreign elements—Muslims and southern Indians. He was able to mobilized the lower and working classes in Bombay and by the late 1960s the Shiv Sena was a potent political force in the city. Active members received the name Shiv Sainiks and they followed the party line as dictated by Thackeray. Thackeray preferred to operate behind the scenes so he appointed members of his family to leadership posts in the Shiv Sena. Despite his behind-the-scenes posture, his views appeared in the party newspaper *Saamna* (Confrontation). Thackeray directed the Shiv Sena into a militant program against Buddhists, Christians, Muslims, and Dalits (formerly called Untouchables) in the name of Hinduism. His attacks on the Dalits were because many of them had converted from Hinduism to Buddhism. An attempt to block the publication of a book attacking Hinduism by the Dalit political leader B. R. Ambedkar, *Riddles of Hinduism* (1987), failed, and it led to widespread Shiv Sena rioting.

In 1992, Thackeray exhorted followers to rid Bombay of Muslim influences, and, in the riots that followed in Bombay, more than 800 Muslims were killed. A Bombay judge made a report that charged Thackeray and his Shiv Sainiks were responsible for the riots and deaths. Indian authorities refused to prosecute either Thackeray or the Shiv Sena until 2000, but a judge dismissed the charge on a statute of limitations ruling.

The voters of Bombay voted the Shiv Sena into political power in 1995. Leaders of the party took the opportunity to punish its enemies and enrich themshelves. They used their political clout to take over the city's criminal rackets and nightclubs. Bombay police were used to protect the property of the Shiv Sena. Land speculation in Bombay also made the leaders rich. These activities were so flagrant that the Shiva Sena party was voted out of office in September 1999.

The Shiv Sena's political power was revitalized in 1989 by an electoral alliance with the Hindu nationalist party the Bharatiya Janata Party (BJP). In the late 1980s, the BJP's leadership concluded an alliance with the Shiv Sena to gain national political power. This strategy proved successful and the Shiv Sena provided votes for the BJP's victory in 1996. The alliance between the BJP and the Shiv Sena became rocky in the summer of 2003 because of the peaceful overtures of the Vajaypee government toward Pakistan.

Suggested readings: V. Shankar Aiyer and Lakshmi Iyer, "Bal Thackeray: Threatening Tiger," *India Today* (July 31, 2000), p. 16; Bernard Imhasly, "Shivas Tigers in the Jungle of Bombay," *Swiss Review of World Affairs* (March 1993), p. 1; Robert Marquand, "A Charming Extremist Defies Moderate India," *Christian Science Monitor* (July 28, 2000), p. 1; Gail Omvedt, "Hinduism, Social Inequality, and the State," in Douglas Allen (ed.), *Religion and Political Conflict in South Asia: India, Pakistan, and Sri Lanka* (Westport, CT: Greenwood Press, 1992); Sheela Raval and Harish Gupta, "BJP: Muzzling the Tiger," *India Today* (February 1, 1999), p. 18.

Sikh Separatism (India)

Sikh separatism is an outgrowth of the activities of a number of dissident Sikh groups that desire an independent Sikh state carved out of northwest India. These groups want to form an independent state that they would call Khalistan (Land of the Pure). Most of the members of these groups belonged as students to the All-India Sikh Students Federation. This organization had been founded on September 13, 1944, and it had become more radical in the 1970s. Bhai Amrik Singh reorganized the organization on July 2, 1978, to make it a more radical Sikh group. As the All-India Sikh Students Federation became more radicalized, the Indian government cracked down on it by arresting its leaders and attempting to suppress it. Shortly before a showdown with Sikh separatists, the Indian government finally banned the All-India Sikh Students Federation on March 19, 1984.

The leader of the most militant wing of the Sikh separatist movement was **Jarnail Singh Bhindranwale.** He had become the most recognized leader of Sikh separatism until his death in the siege of the Golden Temple complex at Amritsar on July 5–6, 1984. His death in Operation Blue Star made him a martyr to the Sikh cause. Most of his followers escaped and they began forming groups to advance the cause of Sikh separatism. Even those Sikhs not in sympathy with the idea of an independent Sikh state opposed the military operation against the Golden Temple Complex. The assassination of Indira Gandhi by her Sikh bodyguard on October 31, 1984, and the resulting riots by Hindu attacking Sikhs only intensified tension between the Sikhs and the Indian government. The riots resulted in more than 6,000 deaths, most of them Sikhs, and left another 50,000 homeless. At least seven major Sikh groups—All-India Sikh Student Federation, Babbar Khalsa, Bhindranwale Tiger Force, Bhindranwale Tiger Force of Khalistan, Khalistan Commando Force, Khalistan Liberation Force, and Sikh Student Federation—coalesced to carry out terrorist operations against India. The most violent of these groups was the Babbar Khalsa under the leadership of Talwinder Singh Parmar. This group's terrorist campaign involved a series of spectacular operations, including the bombing of the Air India airliner Boeing 747 Flight 182 off the coast of Ireland on June 21, 1985, which killed 329 people. The leader of the moderate Sikh party Akali Dal (Army of the Immortals), Harchand Singh Longowal, negotiated an agreement with the Indian government, but he was assassinated in August 1985 by Sikh separatists.

On April 29, 1986, the **Panthic Committee**, a Sikh umbrella group, proclaimed the independence of Khalistan. Five Sikh leaders were elected to the Panthic Committee to organize and lead a Sikh military campaign against India for Sikh independence. This unity ended in 1988 when the Panthic Committee split into three committees. After the leader of one of the committees, Gurbachan Singh Manochal, died, the Zaffarwal Panthic Committee of Wasson Singh Zaffarwal and the Sohan Singh Panthic Committee of Sohan Singh competed with each other for leadership of the Sikh separatist movement. Each carved its niche in the Sikh movement—Zaffarwal Panthic Committee in politics and the Sohan Singh Panthic Committee in military operations. The present leader of the Khalistan political movement is Dr. Jagjit Singh Chohan, a former physician, and a member of the Zaffarwal Panthic Committee.

Attempts to establish a Sikh state have had little impact as the Indian government launched an anti-terrorism campaign directed against the Sikhs. State government in Punjab was replaced by President's Rule in 1987. In May 1988, the Indian authorities again stormed the Golden Temple Complex in Operation Black Thunder II and killed at least 40 Sikh extremists. This crackdown did not stop the various Sikh terrorist groups from conducting assassinations of Indian businessmen, civil servants, journalists, and businessmen. Terrorist leaders devoted special attention to the assassination of Sikh politicians and police who cooperated with the Indian government. On August 31, 1995, Beant Singh, chief minister of Punjab and a Sikh, was killed by a car bomb in Chandigarh along with 15 security men and aides.

Despite the high profile of Khalistan activists, the Indian government has been able to curtail Sikh extremists in Punjab. Most of the terrorist groups have lost key leaders to either arrest or death. Parmar's controversial death by the Indian police in October 1992 was the most significant loss. Remaining leaders and activists have emigrated abroad. Canada has become a haven for a majority of the Sikh extremists. Canadian authorities are aware of Sikh activities and have arrested Sikh activists for terrorist crimes. The most important catches have been those charged with the bombing of Air India Boeing Flight 747, Ajalb Singh Bagri and Ripudaman Singh Malik. **See also** Bhindranwale, Jarnail Singh; Panthic Committee.

Suggested readings: Ivan B. Armstrong, "Turmoil in India's Punjab; Why Sikhs' Zeal Has Turned Violent," *Christian Science Monitor* (May 1, 1984), p. 20; Kim Bolan, "How Did Talwinder Parmar Really Die?" *Vancouver Sun* (October 14, 2002), p. A1; Kim Bolan, "Sikh Separatist Groups Use Clout to Lobby Britain to Lift Ban," *Vancouver Sun* (April 21, 2001), p. A15; Pratap Chakravaty, "India's Most-Wanted Sikh Separatist Leader Returns Home from Britain," *Agence France Presse* (June 27, 2001), p. 1; Mark Juergensmeyer, *Terror in the Mind of God: The Global Rise of Religious Violence* (Berkeley: University of California Press, 2000); Cynthia Keppley Mahmood, *Fighting for Faith and Nation: Dialogues with Sikh Militants* (Philadelphia: University of Pennsylvania Press, 1996); Joyce J. M. Pettigrew, *The Sikhs of the Punjab: The Unheard Voices of State and Guerrilla Violence* (London: Zed Books, 1995); Sarab Jit Singh, *Operation Black Thunder: An Eyewitness Account of Terrorism in Punjab* (New Delhi, India: Sage Publications, 2002).

Sinn Fein (Ourselves Alone) (Ireland)

Sinn Fein (Ourselves Alone) is the political party affiliated with the **Irish Republican Army** (IRA). Arthur Griffith, a printer and Irish nationalist, founded Sinn Fein in 1905 and he became its first president. His program of total political and economic independence from Great Britain was published in his newspaper the *United Irishman*. Many members of the Irish Republican Brotherhood, the precursor of the Irish Republican Army, also belonged to the Sinn Fein. A number of Sinn Fein members participated in the 1916 Easter Uprising in Dublin, and the British executed or imprisoned them for their rebellion. Sinn Fein as an organization avoided the 1916 uprising, and it ran candidates for the 1917 by-elections in Ireland. Eamonn de Valera, a participant in the 1916 Easter Uprising who was saved from execution by his American citizenship, replaced Griffith as president of Sinn Fein in 1917. After winning a landslide victory in the 1918 Westminster general election, the leadership of the Sinn Fein established a separatist parliament (Dail Eireann) and proclaimed an Irish republic. The Irish Republican Army had been reconstituted out of the 1916 Easter Uprising. In the aftermath of the Irish civil war in the early 1920s, members of the Sinn Fein and the IRA refused to recognize Irish governments after the end of the Second Dail Eireann and the separation of the six countries into an independent Northern Ireland. The resulting civil war over this issue only ended on May 24, 1923 when a cease-fire was declared, but both the leaders of the Sinn Fein and the IRA have never recognized the Republic of Ireland as the rightful government of Ireland.

In November 1925, the IRA separated from the Sinn Fein. On December 8, 1938, the last member of the old Dail Eireann bequeathed the government of the republican state to the Army Council of the IRA. In 1949, the Sinn Fein reconstituted an alliance with the IRA and pledged allegiance to the IRA Army Council. That same year the Irish government constituted itself into the Republic of Ireland, but the merged IRA and Sinn Fein refused to recognize the new state as the lawful government of Ireland.

Sinn Fein remained as the political wing of the Irish Republican Army until the schism in December 1969. At that time, the IRA broke into the Official IRA and Provisional IRA groups. Under pressure from both sides, the Sinn Fein also split, with elements of the Sinn Fein forming the Provisional Sinn Fein in February 1970. Once the Official IRA ended operations in Northern Ireland in 1972, the Provisional Sinn Fein assumed the mantle of the original Sinn Fein.

In the early 1970s efforts of the British government to effect a settlement in Northern Ireland made Sinn Fein more moderate. The chief political rival to Sinn Fein was John Hume's Social Democratic Labour Party (SDLP). Hume had founded this party in 1970 as a Catholic nationalist party whose goal was a unification of Ireland by peaceful means. Both the Sinn Fein and the SDLP have contested for the same constituency for more than 30 years. The British government started to attract the SDLP by negotiating a political settlement that would be a compromise between the Protestant Loyalists and the Catholic republicans. Ultimately this compromise failed in the 1970s, but it did cause Sinn Fein to recognize there was another way besides violence to reach a potential settlement.

The Sinn Fein has assumed more importance as an organization since the 1994 cease-fire. Once **Gerry Adams** and **Martin McGuinness** decided to pursue a political settlement rather than a violent approach, they became public figures. Adams has always denied association with the Provisional IRA, but this assertion has never been believed. It was Adams and McGuinness that provided the momentum on the republican side for the Good Friday Accords in 1998. Adams continues to be the chief spokesperson for the Sinn Fein in the controversy over the disarming of the Provisional IRA. McGuinness has entered the Northern Ireland government as the minister of education. **See also** Adams, Gerry; Irish Republican Army (IRA); McGuinness, Martin; Provisional Irish Republican Army (Provos) (PIRA).

Suggested readings: Patrick Bishop and Eamonn Mallie, *The Provisional IRA* (London: Corgi Books, 1988); Susan McKay, "Republican Old Guard Unites," *Sunday Tribune* (Ireland) (April 20, 2003), p. 14; Susan McKay, "'Stormontgate' Likely to Bring Down Northern Government," *Sunday Tribune* (Ireland) (October 6, 2002), p. 10; Ed Moloney, *A Secret History of the IRA* (New York: Norton, 2002); Brendan O'Brien, *The Long War: The IRA and Sinn Fein*, 2nd ed. (Syracuse, NY: Syracuse University Press, 1999); Peter Taylor, *Behind the Mask: The IRA and Sinn Fein* (New York: TV Books, 1999).

Sison, José María (1939?–) (Philippines)

José María Sison was the founder of the Philippine Maoist Communist **New Peoples Army** (NPA) and its ideological leader. He was probably born around 1939 in the northwestern Luzon's Ilocos Sur province. He came from a family of wealthy landowners who had a history of political opposition to both Spanish and American rule. He was sent to school in Manila where he proved to be an excellent student. Sison attended the University of the Philippines in Manila where he studied English literature.

By this time, Sison had become a Philippine nationalist and he had begun a serious study of Marxism. While as a graduate student assistant at the University of the Philippines, he had become a student leader. In 1959, he formed the Student Cultural Association of the University of the Philippines (SCAUP). This student group soon started participating in student demonstrations. After forming secret Marxist study groups within SCAUP, Sison joined the Philippine Communist Party (Parido Komunista ng Philipines, or PKP) in 1963. Party leaders appointed him to head the PKP's youth department. One of his first acts was to start a new Marxist student youth group Patriotic Youth (Kabataan Makabay, or KM). This group attempted to extend communist indoctrination to the rural population by combining nationalism and Marxism. Two events—the Vietnam War and China's Cultural Revolution—turned Sison toward the Maoism of Mao Tse-tung. This new orientation brought him into conflict with the Stalinist leaders of the PKP. In April 1967, this conflict led the PKP to expel Sison and his followers from the party. Sison responded by gathering a number of his student and worker supporters and began planning for a new Maoist Communist party.

Sison had established the New Peoples Army and its program of revolutionary struggle by December 1968. His blueprint for a communist state borrowed heavily from the Chinese example of Tse-tung and its emphasis on rural guerrilla warfare. Officially, the NPA was formed on December 26, 1968, but the first organizational meeting was held on January 3, 1969. From the beginning, Sison was the ideological head of the NPA, but he was not a military leader. He set up the Central Committee of 12 to oversee operations. This committee selected Sison as its chair. He realized his inability to lead a military insurrection so his first action was to recruit a

military leader. Sison recruited the young Hukbalahap (HUK) guerrilla leader Bernabe Buscayno, or Commander Dante, to organize and lead military operations of the NPA. Buscayno had joined the HUK movement because of its goal of agrarian reform so it was easy for Sison to appeal to him.

Sison left military operations to his commanders, but he retained tight ideological control of the New Peoples Army. Political opposition to the authoritarian and corrupt government of President Ferdinand Marcos helped the NPA. Military fortunes of the NPA fluctuated, but the recruiting efforts among students and peasants remained strong. In 1979, Sison published a book, *Philippine Society and Revolution*. In this book, Sison characterized the Philippines as a semi-colonial state oppressed by foreign imperialists, domestic capitalists, and domestic landlords. He argued that the only cure for the Philippines was a communist revolution that would free the Filipino people. This could only be accomplished by building a peasant army that could defeat the forces of oppression. This book became the bible of the NPA.

Sison realized that the key to the success of the revolution was foreign material support. He began looking for allies. The most obvious source was the People's Republic of China. China was only 400 miles away from the Philippines. Sison sent a delegation to China to procure arms and ammunition. This delegation had only limited success; most of the equipment sent by China to the NPA never reached its destinations. This inability to find dependable sources of arms remained a weakness of the NPA.

Sison retained his leadership of the New Peoples Army until his capture in 1977. He had organized the NPA with a hierarchical administrative structure for tight control of the movement. Military and political setbacks had made this structure impractical so Sison had to relinquish some of his control. His decision to allow the August 21, 1971, bombing of Marcos's liberal opposition at Manila's Plaza Miranda also proved to be a mistake. This incident caused several of the other NPA leaders to question Sison's leadership. Later in the mid-1970s, NPA leaders in Manila began questioning Sison's political leadership and his strategy not to ally electorally with the liberal opponents of Marcos. Sison's leadership of the NPA ended with his capture by Philippine government agents on November 8, 1977.

Sison's capture changed the political command structure of the New Peoples Army. He spent the next nine years in a Philippine prison. He was able to communicate with his colleagues in the NPA, but his influence diminished. In late 1986, the government of President Corazon Aquino released him from prison in an effort to conclude a peace with the NPA. Aquino tried to win him over by promising reforms, but Sison refused to go along with her. Sison and his wife left the Philippines and settled in Utrecht, The Netherlands. Close contacts with the NPA have been reestablished by Sison though the National Democratic Front of the Philippines (NDF). His self-exile prevents effective control of NPA's operations. His prestige within the NPA has remained enormous because his writings serve as the ideological base of the movement. Sison was active in peace negotiations with the Philippine government in early 2001. His hard-line position resulted in the collapse of these peace talks. He then ordered in 2002 a resumption of military operations of the NPA to bring down the Arroyo government.

Sison's stay in the Netherlands has been threatened in the anti-terrorism drive by the United States after **September 11, 2001**. In August 2002, the U.S. State Department declared the Communist Party of the Philippines and the New Peoples Army as terrorist organizations. This label of "terrorist" also fell on Sison. His personal bank account has been frozen. Both the American and Dutch governments are pressuring the European Union to take further action against Sison. See also New Peoples Army (NPA).

Suggested readings: Gregg R. Jones, *Red Revolution: Inside the Philippine Guerrilla Movement* (Boulder, CO: Westview Press, 1989); Dona Z. Pazzibugan and Juliet L. Javellana, "Kalaw Blames Reds for '71 Blast," *Philippine Daily In-quirer* (Manila) (June 20, 2001), p. 1; Jovito Salonga, "Front Page Politburo Denounces Sison as Mad Killer," *Philippine Daily Inquirer* (Manila) (June 19, 2001), p. 1; Oscar S. Villadolid, "Fight, Talk, Fight, Talk," *BusinessWorld* (August 13, 2002), p. 5.

Skinhead Movement (International)

The Skinhead movement began in Great Britain in the early 1970s, but by the 1980s it had become a worldwide phenomenom. It started among young British working-class elements as a protest against the hippie movement, the barriers of the English class structure, and the lack of job opportunities. These young Brits substituted traditional British society with their own version of a society. This society featured shaved heads, suspenders on blue jeans, and Doc Marten boots. Three factors united them: music, soccer, and beer. Of the three, music became the most important, with the development of white power, or "Oi" (Hey) music. This music gloried white supremacy and the virtues of violence. Much of their glorification of violence came from the racism of the anti-immigration movement. Skinheads gained an early reputation for beating up minorities and gays. Almost as important as music was skinhead loyalty to their local soccer team. Members of skinhead groups have always been willing to fight supporters of other teams. Heavy drinking has been another characteristic. British fascists and neo-Nazis have been intrigued by the nihilism of the Skinhead movement and the **British National Party** has been active in recruiting them. **Ian Stuart Donaldson** used his influence as the lead singer in the neo-Nazi band Skrewdriver to form the skinhead group **Blood and Honor**.

The British Skinhead movement began to branch to other countries in the late 1970s. Skinheads in certain countries—Germany, Russia, and the United States—adopted most of the characteristics of the British movement, including dress and political views. Violence against immigrants and minorities became endemic in the areas of former East Germany and in Russia. Most the attacks on foreigners in those countries have come from members of skinhead groups. The Anti-Defamation League reported in 1995 that the neo-Nazi Skinheads were active in at least 33 countries on six continents, and its adherents numbered around 70,000. Among the political parties that have recruited skinheads have been: Vlaams Blok (VB) (Belgium), **German National Democratic Party** (NPD) (Germany), **Italian Social Movement** (MSI) (Italy), **National Bolshevik Party** (NBP) (Russia), British National Party (BNP) (Great Britain), and the Populist Party (United States). Skinhead activity has also been growing in Eastern Europe, including the Czech Republic, Hungary, and Poland. What makes the Skinhead movement so appealing to neofascist and neo-Nazi movements is a common attitude toward violence and a nihilistic attitude toward democratic states. **See also** Blood and Honor; British National Party (BNP); German National Democratic Party (NPD); Italian Social Movement (MSI); National Bolshevik Party (NBP).

Suggested readings: Anti-Defamation League, *The Skinhead International: A Worldwide Survey of Neo-Nazi Skinheads* (New York: Anti-Defamation League, 1995); Hugh Barnes, "Black in the USSR: Xenophobia Is on the Increase in Russia, Propelled by Groups of Violent Extremists," *Financial Times* (London) (June 14, 2003), p. 24; Mark S. Hamm, *American Skinheads: The Criminology and Control of Hate* (New York: Praeger, 1994); Milton Kleg, *Hate Prejudice and Racism* (Albany: State University of New York Press, 1993); Alexander Tarasov, "Russian Skinheads: A Social Portrait," *What the Papers Say* (Russia) (August 13, 2020), p. 4.

Spence, Augustus "Gusty" (1933–) (Northern Ireland)

Gusty Spence is one of the leaders of the Progressive Unionist Party (PUP) and a former leader of the **Ulster Volunteer Force** (UVF). He was born in 1933 in the working-class district of Shankill, Belfast, Northern Ireland. His family was from the Protestant lower working class. His father had been a member of the original Ulster Volunteer Force and he had fought in World War I as an Ulster

Volunteer. Spence did well in school, but he had to leave school early to work in the mills to help his family. In 1957, he joined the British army serving in the Royal Ulster Rifles. His tour of duty took him to West Germany and then to Cyprus where he fought against Cyriot terrorists. After completing his military duty, Spence returned to Belfast and worked in the shipyards. He also joined the Ulster loyalist Orange Order.

Ulster Protestant loyalists recruited Spence to help launch in 1966 a revival of the Ulster Volunteer Force. Under his leadership, the UVF initiated a terrorist campaign against Catholics in Northern Ireland. Spence was arrested for the murder of Peter Ward, a Catholic barman, in 1966 and sentence to life imprisonment. In prison, he assumed command of the UVF prisoners, installing military discipline and a self-education regime. In July 1972, Spence spent four months free when members of the UVF helped him escape after he had attended his daughter's wedding. Spence was needed because at the time the UVF was losing out among Ulster Loyalists to the **Ulster Defence Association** (UDA). During this free time, he reorganized and retrained the UVF along military lines. A British army unit recaptured him on November 4, 1972, and he returned to prison. Spence then began a personal study of Irish history and politics. His readings led him to become a Marxist socialist, but they also made him reexamine his hostility toward the **Irish Republican Army** and Catholics. He decided that violence was not the answer to Northern Ireland's problems and in 1974 he resigned as commanding officer of the UVF. Then in 1977, he resigned from the UVF altogether. After 18 years in prison, he was released on December 13, 1984.

Spence has devoted his energies to reconciling Catholic and Protestant interests in Northern Ireland. His followers had formed the Volunteer Political Party (VPP) while he was still in prison. After the VPP had little electoral success, it was disbanded. In the early 1990s, Spence became an important figure in the Progressive Unionist Party. This party has a loose affiliation with the UVF. He is acknowledged to have been the architect of the UVF's cease-fire in 1995. He remains the elder statesman of the loyalist cause. **See also** Ulster Volunteer Force (UVF).

Suggested readings: Steve Bruce, *The Red Hand: Protestant Paramilitaries in Northern Ireland* (Oxford, U.K.: Oxford University Press, 1992); Roy Garland, *Out of Shankill: Gusty Spence* (London: Blackstaff Press, 2001); David Sharrock, "Gusty Wind of Change," *Observer* (London) (December 15, 1996), p. T6; Peter Taylor, *Loyalists: War and Peace in Northern Ireland* (New York: TV Books, 1999).

Stern Gang (Israel)

The Stern Gang was the most violent of the Jewish terrorist organizations in the 1940s. Abraham Stern had been a leader in the **Irgun Zvai Leumi**, a radical offshoot of the Jewish army group Haganah, in the late 1930s, but he broke away from the Irgun along with 100 members in 1940 to form the Freedom Fighters of Israel (FFI). The FFI soon earned the name the Stern Gang. Members of the Irgun supported the British early in World War II, but those in the Stern Gang refused to go along with the British. Stern led his small organization into open hostilities with British forces in Palestine. Members of the Stern Gang specialized in selective assassinations and soon developed a reputation for terrorism. The British killed Stern on February 12, 1942, but three leaders—Natan Yellin-Mor, Yisrael Eldad, and Yitzhak Shamir, replaced him.

The Stern Gang carried out a series of spectacular assassinations. On September 29, 1944, its first notable victim was the British Constable T. Wilkin, who was assassinated on a street in Jerusalem. Then on November 6, 1944, two members of the Stern Gang killed Lord Moyne, the British minister for the Middle East, in Cairo, Egypt. Both assassins were apprehended and hanged after a short trial, but their deeds had a profound influence on British policies toward Palestine. Winston Churchill had been receptive to Jewish interest in Palestine, but he changed his mind after the assassination of Lord Moyne,

who had been a close personal friend. The entry of the Irgun into the terrorism war in late 1944 had little impact on the operations of the Stern Gang, but it did distract the British authorities. More deadly was the hostility of the Haganah, the Jewish military armed forces, and its campaign in late 1944 against the Stern Gang.

Leadership of the Stern Gang pursued an anti-British campaign after the war. In 1945, the Stern Gang joined with the Haganah and the Irgun in attacking British targets. But by 1946, the Haganah had concluded that the Stern Gang was too violent to remain in an alliance. In 1948, Yellin-Mor, Eldad, and Shamir decided to assassinate the United Nations representative in Palestine, Count Folke Bernadotte of Sweden, because they believed him to be pro-Palestinian. On September 17, 1948, assassins shot and killed Bernadotte and Colonel Andre Serot, the French senior UN peacekeeping observer. The new Israeli government reacted by declaring the Stern Gang a terrorist organization and rounding up its members. Eldad and Shamir escaped capture, but Yellin-Mor was arrested for his membership in the Stern Gang. No member of the Stern Gang was arrested and charged for the murder of Bernadotte, but his murder was the last military operation of the Stern Gang. Leaders of the Stern Gang instead devoted themselves to right-wing politics, and Shamir was the Israeli prime minister from 1983–1984 and 1986–1992. **See also** Irgun Zvai Leumi (IZL).

Suggested readings: J. Bowyer Bell, *Terror out of Zion: Irgun Zvai Leumi, LEHI and the Palestine Underground, 1929–1949* (New York: St. Martin's Press, 1977); Ehud Sprinzak, *Brother against Brother: Violence and Extremism in Israeli Politics from Altalena to the Rabin Assassination* (New York: Free Press, 1999); Saul Zadka, *Blood in Zion: How the Jewish Guerrillas Drove the British Out of Palestine* (London: Brassey's, 1995).

Stop Huntingdon Animal Cruelty (SHAC) (Great Britain)

The Stop Huntingdon Animal Cruelty (SHAC) is one of Great Britain's leading animal rights extremist groups. **Greg Avery** started this group in 1999 to target the drug-testing company Huntingdon Life Sciences for animal rights abuses in its testing program. Avery and his wife, Heather James Avery, had been active in the animal rights movement starting with the Save the Hill Grove Cats campaign to protest against cat breeding for research at Hill Grove Farm in Oxfordshire, and then against dog breeding at the Consort Kennels near Ross-on-Wye, in Herefordshire. These campaigns led to both operations closing down.

The main focus of the Stop Huntingdon Animal Cruelty was an attack on the financial base of Huntingdon Life Sciences. This corporation, Europe's largest contract animal testing laboratory, was using beagle puppies in research on the effects of drugs. Instead of depending on sympathy for the dogs, SHAC began a harassment campaign against the executives, scientists, shareholders, and creditors of Huntingdon Life Sciences. The Internet has allowed SHAC the capability to reach around the world to supporters. In early 2002, it had 12,000 people on its mailing list in Great Britain and another 3,000 people who signed up on the Internet. When the American bank Stephens, Inc. assumed financial control of the company, the supporters of SHAC started harassing the employees of the bank at its headquarters in Little Rock, Arkansas. In January 2002, Stephens found a secret buyer for its credit line to end the harassment. Shares of Huntingdon Life Sciences still trade on NASDAQ, but only one marker manager handles the shares and the controversy had hurt its stock prices. **See also** Avery, Greg.

Suggested readings: Chris Fontaine, "Animal Rights Campaigners Raise Pressure on British Lab, Financiers," Associated Press State & Local Wire (April 11, 2001), p. 1; Patrick Jenkins, "A Ruthless Hunter; Man in the News Greg Avery," *Financial Times* (London) (January 12, 2002), p. 9; Lauren Mills, "Shac's Attack Goes Multinational," *Sunday Telegraph* (London) (October 20, 2002), p. 7; Giles Trendle, "Anti-Corporate Activism," *Enterprise* (October 1, 2002), p. 18.

Sufaat, Yazid (1965–) (Malaysia)

Yazid Sufaat was one of the leaders in the Malaysia branch of the **Jemaal Islamiyah** (JI) and a collaborator of those planning the **September 11**, 2001, terrorists attacks on the United States. He was born in 1965 and raised in Paloh, Malaysia. His father was a subsistence rubber tapper. Sufaat showed early promise as a science student and his potential earned him a spot in state-funded schools. Scholastic success allowed him to win a scholarship to the prestigious Royal Military College in preparation for a military career. The Malaysian army granted him a government scholarship to study medical technology and biochemistry at California State University in Sacramento. After earning his degree in 1987, he returned to Malaysia to resume his military career. Soon after obtaining the rank of captain, Sufaat left the army in 1991. He then founded a laboratory analysis company that specialized in medical testing for the Malaysian government.

Up until the early 1990s, Sufaat had avoided both politics and religion. His lack of interest in religion changed in 1993 when he enrolled in private religious lesson. In the course of his studies, Sufaat made contact with Mohamed Iqbal, an Islamism cleric, and he soon became one of Iqbal's disciples. Iqbal preached holy war against Christians in Indonesia, and he introduced Sufaat to two leaders of Jemaah Islamiyah—**Abu Bakar Bashir** and **Hambali**. Under the growing influence of the leaders of Jemaah Islamiyah, Sufaat became hostile to the Malaysian government of Prime Minister Mahathir Mohamad. By 1998, Sufaat had joined the inner circle of Jemaah Islamiyah in Malaysia and he was their chief bomb maker.

Leaders of the Jemaah Islamiyah cultivated Sufaat for a leadership role in Malaysia. One of his chief tasks was to serve as a contact between the JI and **al-Qaeda**. Several times, key al-Qaeda operatives, including at least two members of the operation on September 11, visited Sufaat in Malaysia. He also provided hospitality to **Zacharias Moussaoui** in October 2000 before providing him with fake papers to enter the United States. At this time, Sufaat also bought four tons of ammonium nitrate for use in making bombs. After the September 11, 2001, attacks, Sufaat received orders to go to Afghanistan to assist the **Taliban** repulse the American invasion. While in Kandahar, Afghanistan, Sufaat served in a Taliban medical unit.

In November 2001, al-Qaeda leaders ordered Sufaat to return to Malaysia to assume a leadership role in the Jemaah Islamiyah there. Throughout the summer and fall of 2001, Malaysian and Singapore authorities were busy breaking up Jemaah Islamiyah terrorist operations in both countries. Malaysian authorities arrested Sufaat in December 2001 while he was trying to enter Malaysia from Thailand. The American government has tried to have Sufaat extradited to the United States to face charges in the conspiracy for September 11, but so far the Malaysian government has refused to extradite Sufaat. **See also** Bashir, Abu Bakar; Hambali (Riduan Isamuddin); Jemaah Islamiyah (Islamic Community) (JI); al-Qaeda (The Base); Taliban (Students of Religious Schools).

Suggested readings: Marhalim Abas, "Just How Deeply Involved Was Yazid in KMM?" *Malay Mail* (December 21, 2002), p. 1; Raymond Bonner, "How Qaeda Linked Up with Malaysian Groups, *New York Times* (February 7, 2002), sec. A, p. 15; Leslie Lopez, "A Experiment Gone Radically Wrong," *Ottawa Citizen* (January 19, 2003), p. A13; Philip Shenon and David Johnston, "Suspect Calls Malaysia a Staging Area for Terror Attacks," *New York Times* (January 31, 2002), sec. A, p. 13; John Solomon, "Growing Evidence Links Moussaoui to 2nd Wave Attack, Officials Contend," Associated Press (March 29, 2002), p. 1.

T

Taliban (Students of Religious Schools) (Afghanistan)

The Taliban is a radical Islamist movement that ruled Afghanistan from 1996 until 2001. **Mulawi Mohammed Omar**, a veteran Pushtun mujahideen commander from Kandahar, Afghanistan, founded the Taliban in the spring of 1994. He claims that the prophet Muhammad came to him in a dream and told him to kill an oppressive warlord who had raped two young women and to cleanse his tribe spiritually. After killing the warlord, Omar formed the Taliban from former mujahideen and students from religious schools in Kandahar. His reputation for piety and good works attracted supporters, but until the Taliban received backing from the Pakistani government, it remained a local Kandahar movement without much of a future. The Pakistani government was looking for a dependable ally in Afghanistan, because it had lost faith in **Gulbuddin Hekmatyar**. Hekmatyar's constant battles with other Afghanistan warlords over political control of Afghanistan had alienated both the Afghanistan and the Pakistani government. Part of the success of the Taliban in recruiting adherents was the revulsion toward the civil war of the mujahideen warlords.

In early November 1994, Taliban forces captured Kandahar, and this success convinced the Pakistani government to back the Taliban. The adoption of the Taliban by the Pakistani government in late November 1994 gave the Taliban the training and resources to launch an offensive against other Afghan cities. This alliance between the Taliban and the Pakistani government allowed them to overthrow the weak Afghan government. Pakistanis provided weapons and combat support supplies and the Taliban provided the manpower. Recruits began to stream across the Pakistani border and from the Afghan countryside until reports came in that the Taliban had an army large enough to contest for political control of Afghanistan. Although the Hekmatyar government complained about Pakistani support from security forces of the Inter-Services Institute (ISI), aid increased for the Taliban. Support for the Taliban came not only from religious-oriented Afghans but also from an influx of Pakistani religious students. By early 1995, the Taliban had an army of 25,000 with 3,000 to 4,000 of the army being Pakistani religious students. After suffering several battlefield defeats, Taliban forces finally captured the important city of Herat in September 1995. This success enabled the Taliban army to defeat the military forces of the Hekmatyar government and seize control of Kabul and most of Afghanistan by September 1996.

Taliban fighters seen near Kabul, October 3, 1996. The Taliban, an Islamic fundamentalist army, took over Kabul and drove out forces loyal to President Burhanuddin Rabbani a week earlier. The Taliban government had gained control of most of Afghanistan by 2001 but all of this would change after September 11th—in just four months they would be overthrown. (AP Photo/Hurriyet)

Even before victory, the Taliban had established an administrative committee (*shoora*) to oversee affairs. Omar was the supreme authority of the 10-member administrative committee. Pushtuns held five of the major positions—supreme authority, deputy commander, defense, foreign affairs, and security. The other five positions included three Uzbeks and two Tajiks. Later in May 1997, the Taliban formed 20 ministries, which were overseen by the administrative committee, to run its government.

Once in power, the Taliban government began building the Afghan state into its image of an Islamic state. Any behavior that conflicted with their perception of Islam was banned. Men were subjected to compulsory praying and were required to wear beards and turbans. Art, dancing, music, and television were forbidden. Authorities punished harshly those Afghans transgressing these rules. Criminals faced execution or mutilation for their crimes. Women lost all rights to hold jobs outside the home. They could only appear in public completely covered from head to foot and in the company of a male relative.

To ensure complete control over Afghan society the Taliban seized control of education. All secular education ended immediately after the Taliban gained control of the state. Boys had to attend religious schools.

Schooling for girls ended entirely. Girls were to receive religious instruction in the home or none at all. Despite disapproval from Western countries and some in the Middle East, the Taliban intended a complete reform of Afghani society.

The Taliban government had gained control of most of Afghanistan by 2001 except for a limited area in the north, where it was winning a war with its major opposition, the Northern Alliance. Taliban leaders had concluded an alliance with **Osama bin Laden** and **al-Qaeda** soon after bin Laden's arrival in Afghanistan in 1996. Training camps had been established throughout Afghanistan to train both Taliban and al-Qaeda forces. Taliban forces fighting the Northern Alliance received reinforcements from al-Qaeda volunteers. Foreign pressure on the Taliban government to curtail support for al-Qaeda was ignored.

Toleration for the Taliban government ended after al-Qaeda's operation against the United States on **September 11, 2001**. The Northern Alliance was on the brink of defeat until the United States began massive military support. Commitment of air support, equipment, and military advisors rejuvenated the Northern Alliance. In a four-month military campaign, the Taliban was overthrown. Despite military defeats, most of the Taliban leaders and bin Laden escaped into Pakistan where they remain in hiding among supporters. The political situation in Afghanistan remains uncertain; a portion of the Afghan populace is still pro-Taliban, and there is massive support for the Taliban in Pakistan. Periodic fighting between Taliban and Afghani forces continued throughout 2002 and 2003.

Suggested readings: M. J. Gohari, *The Taliban: Ascent to Power* (Oxford, U.K.: Oxford University Press, 1999); Kamal Matinuddin, *The Taliban Phenomenon: Afghanistan, 1994–1997* (Oxford, U.K.: Oxford University Press, 1999); Ralph H. Magnus and Eden Naby, *Afghanistan: Mullah, Marx, and Mujahid* (Boulder, CO: Westview Press, 2000); Ahmed Rashid, *Taliban: Militant Islam, Oil and Fundamentalism in Central Asia* (New Haven, CT: Yale University Press, 2000).

Tamil Tigers (See Liberation Tigers of Tamil Eelam) (LTTE)

Tanzim (Organization) (Palestine)

Tanzim (Organization) is the military wing of **al-Fatah**. **Yasser Arafat** formed Tanzim in 1994 shortly after the Palestinian Authority (PA) had fought a battle with **Hamas** in Gaza. He needed a military force to counter those of his enemies in the Palestinian movement. Because Tanzim is a secular organization, it has been used as a counterweight to Islamist military groups. Funding for Tanzim comes from Arafat, and a modest salary is paid to members. Marwan Barghouthi, a member of the Palestinian Legislative Council, is the current leader of Tanzim. The leadership of Tanzim remains loyal to Arafat and is hawkish about peace with Israel. Barghouthi is a hard-liner on the issues of Jerusalem and the right of return. At times, he has been critical of the Palestinian Authority, charging that its members are corrupt. His capture and imprisonment by the Israelis has hurt Tanzim, but other leaders have replaced him.

Tanzim has become a significant military force in Palestine. Training camps are held each summer for new recruits. The highly disciplined and highly motivated recruits are mostly college-age students, and a significant number of them come from other Palestinian security forces. Estimates have placed Tanzim's strength as high as 50,000, but the number of activists remains much fewer. On several occasions, Tanzim units have clashed with the Israel Defense Forces (IDF) with bloody results. Israeli authorities have also targeted Tanzim leaders for assassination.

In July 2003, leaders of Tanzim started deescalating their military campaign against Israel by restricting its operations against civilians. Israeli soldiers and armed male settlers were still acceptable as targets, but not civilians. Israeli lack of response to this deescalation proved disappointing to Tanzim leaders. Hamas, Palestine Islamic Jihad, and al-Aqsa Martyrs' Brigades also refused to go along. Tanzim leaders then reestablished its policy of all-out war against Israel. **See also** Al-Aqsa Martyrs' Brigades; Hamas; Palestine Islamic Jihad; Palestine Liberation Organization (PLO).

Suggested readings: Ian Bruce, "Arafat's Secret Army of Students," *Herald* (Glasgow) (October 9, 2000), p. 12; Matthew Kalman, "Revolutionaries on the Line," *USA Today* (October 16, 2000), p.1A; Isabel Kershner, "Order in the House," *Jerusalem Report* (February 10, 2003), p. 32; Ewen MacAskill, "Palestine's Napoleon Draws Up Battle Lines," *Guardian* (London) (January 2, 2001), p. 11; David Schenker, "Inside the Fatah Tanzim: A Primer," *Peacewatch,* no. 284 (October 6, 2000).

Tehiya (Renaissance) (Israel)

Tehiya (Renaissance) was one of the most extreme political parties in Israel in the 1980s. Yuval Neeman and **Geula Cohen** formed the Tehiya Party on October 8, 1979. Neeman, a prominent nuclear physicist and former Israel Defense Forces (IDF) officer, and Cohen, a former controversial member of the right-wing Likud Party, gave Tehiya instant recognition. Their goal was to oppose the Camp David Accords and establish a "Greater Israel." Members of the Gush Emunim and the Movement for the Land of Israel also joined this party. Rabbi Uvi Yehuda Kook, the leading rabbi in Israel, gave Tehiya his blessings. Because of this blessing and its policies, this party attracted political support from both religious and secular Israelis unhappy with Menachem Begin and the Likud Party.

Despite its attractiveness as a nationalist party, Tehiya had only marginal success in Israeli elections. It won only three seats to the Knesset in 1981 and only two in 1984. Part of the problem was that its leaders had strong personalities and they often disagreed over strategy and tactics. In 1988, Tehiya lost all of its representatives in the Knesset. This setback caused the party to languish in obscurity as members migrated to other extremist parties that also advocated a Greater Israel. The party regained some momentum

in the next election when it won three seats in the Knesset. As a reward, Neeman became the science minister in the Likud government of Prime Minister Yitzhak Shamir. He was instrumental in the fall of the Shamir ministry in January 1992, when he resigned over an offer of limited autonomy for the Palestinians. In the 1992 election, the Tehiya Party did not gain a single new seat in the Knesset. In 1994, it formed a merger with another right-wing Israeli party, Moledet, but this merger proved only temporary. Tehiya was unable to adapt to the emergence of several single-issue groups, and other parties adopted its platform. Then, in 1999, another electoral defeat led the disbanding of Tehiya. **See also** Cohen, Geula; Gush Emunim (Bloc of the Faithful).

Suggested readings: Ian Black, "The Hard Faces behind Israeli Party's Soft Sell," *Guardian* (London) (July 17, 1984), p. 1; Nina Gilbert, "The Right Stuff," *Jerusalem Post* (March 12, 1999), p. 2b; Sarah Honig, "Elections Likely by June as Tehiya Says; 'We Quit,'" *Jerusalem Post* (January 16, 1992), p. 1a; Raphael Mergui and Philippe Simonnot, *Israel's Ayatollahs: Meir Kahane and the Far Right in Israel* (London: Saqi Books, 1987).

Terre Blanche, Eugene Ney (1941–) (South Africa)

Eugene Terre Blanche is the leader of the South African neo-Nazi organization the **Afrikaner Resistance Movement** (Afrikaner Weerstandsbeweging, or AWB). He was born on January 31, 1941, in Ventersdorp (Transvaal), South Africa. His father was an extreme Afrikaner nationalist. As a schoolboy, Terre Blanche shared his father's nationalist and racist views. In 1963, he joined the South African police force and served as a police bodyguard to Prime Minister John Vorster. Always active in right-wing politics, Terre Blanche ran as a parliamentary candidate in 1969 as a member of the National Party, but he lost. In 1973, he founded the Afrikaner Resistance Movement along with another policeman, Jan Groenewald. Terre Blanche modeled this organization along the Nazi model with a pseudo-swastika flag, a paramilitary force, and a program with anti-Semitic and anti-black platforms. His goal was to establish a white Afrikaner homeland in the territory of the former Boer Republics in Northern Natal and Northern Cape. In June 1983, a South African court sentenced Terre Blanche to a one-year jail term and a 300-rand fine for possession of arms and ammunition. He was also prosecuted later in 1987 for terrorism and received a two- to four-year prison sentence. In the late 1980s, Terre Blanche began to moderate his political demands on the National Party. At the same time, he received considerable negative publicity for his drinking and womanizing.

Terre Blanche's career and the AWB were revitalized in the 1990s by the prospect of the dismantling of apartheid and the acceptance of the African National Congress (ANC) as a legal political party. Afrikaners flocked to the AWB to support Terre Blanche's demand to retain white control of the South African government. His supporters occupied the World Trade Center in the middle of negotiations between the National Party's F. W. de Klerk and the ANC's Nelson Mandela. The murder of Chris Hani, the popular leader of the South African Communist Party, in April 1993 by an assassin with links to the AWB showed the extent of the hostility of Terre Blanche and his supporters toward the ANC. Then, on the eve of the national elections on April 27, 1994, members of the AWB conducted a bombing campaign that killed 20 people and caused $18.8 million in property damage. Nine AWB members were convicted of these bombings in April 1996. Despite these attempts by Terre Blanche and the AWB to influence the election, the ANC won the election and Mandela assumed power as prime minister of the South African government.

Terre Blanche's popularity and prestige fell as the AWB proved unable to prevent the loss of Afrikaner political power. As members left the AWB to join other Afrikaner parties, Terre Blanche has had to refocus the AWB away from violence and toward practical politics. After first refusing to cooperate with the Truth and Reconciliation Commission, Terre Blanche changed his mind, and in May 1999 applied for amnesty for three incidents. The first was the tarring and feathering of Professor Floors van Jaarsvelt at the University of South Africa in Pretoria in 1979 for anti-Boer remarks. Another incident was the possession of illegal weapons and ammunition in Ventersdorp in 1982. Finally, he claimed responsibility for public violence in Ventersdorp in 1991. Terre Blanche continues to campaign for an Afrikaner homeland and for the amnesty of the AWB members convicted of bombings before the 1994 elections. These setbacks were nowhere as devastating as the publicity over his 1989 affair with a journalist from a liberal newspaper, Jani Allan. **See also** Afrikaner Resistance Movement (Afrikaner Weerstandsbeweging) (AWB).

Suggested readings: Alan Cowell, "To Botha's Right, Rattling of Swords," *New York Times* (August 21, 1985), sec. A, p. 4; Alan Cowell, "To the Far Right of Apartheid," *New York Times* (November 23, 1986) sec. 6, p. 63; Scott Kraft, "We Will Kill If . . . ? Far-Right Afrikaners Circling the Wagons," *Los Angeles Times* (October 12, 1987), p. 9; Edward O'Loughlin, "Terre Blanche's AWB Awaits Dawn of Bloodshed," *Irish Times* (August 8, 1995), p. 7; Stephen Ward, "The Journalist, the Neo-Nazi and the Bedroom Farce," *Ottawa Citizen* (August 6, 1992), p. A2.

Thackeray, Balasabeb "Bal" (1927–) (India)

Bal Thackeray is the leader of the extremist Hindu party **Shiv Sena**. He was born on January 23, 1927, in Bombay, India. His father was a journalist and a social reformer in Bombay and he sent his son to middle-class schools. Thackeray found a job on the English-language newspaper the *Free Press Journal* as a cartoonist-journalist. The owner of the newspaper fired him after a political dispute over Thackeray's attacks on southern Indian immigration into Bombay. In 1966, Thackeray founded the party Shiv Sena to oppose southern Indians occupying businesses and white-collar professions in

Hindu nationalist leader Bal Thackeray speaks at a press conference at his residence in Bombay, India, October 18, 2002. A day after police charged him with inciting religious hatred for calling for Hindu suicide squads, Thackeray said he wanted such groups to attack terrorists and Muslims who support Pakistan. Thackeray, leader of the Shiv Sena, a partner in India's coalition government, said that his call for the suicide squads, made in a speech at a party rally earlier that week, was not intended to target India's Muslim minority. (AP Photo/Rajesh Nirgude)

Bombay. He named his party after Shivali, prince of the Mahrattas, who had fought against the Muslim Mogul Empire in the seventeenth century. His party's emblem was a tiger. Thackeray was also an admirer of Adolf Hitler and modeled his organization after Hitler's Brownshirts. His followers were named Shiv Sainiks and they carry out Thackeray's policies with enthusiasm.

By the 1970s, Thackeray had become a political force to reckon with in Bombay and in the state of Maharashtra. He refuses to run for political office and instead prefers to operate behind the scenes directing operations. By appointing relatives to high offices in the Shiv Sena and his political writings in the party organ *Saamna* (Confrontation), he retains dictatorial control over his party. After a campaign against southern Indians, Thackeray turned his attention to Bombay's Muslim population. His newspaper attacks on Muslims led to riots in Bombay in December 1992 and January 1993 that killed over 800 Muslims. Because he was such a powerful political figure, he was able to evade criminal responsibility for inciting these riots.

It helped that the Shiv Sena won a majority in the Bombay municipal elections in 1995. Thackeray used his political influence after the elections to enrich himself and his family. He also masterminded the changing of the name of Bombay to Mumbai. Thackeray considers himself the guardian of Hindu morality, and no movies or art that he deems anti-Hindu appear in Bombay. He has clashed several times with national leaders over his opposition and attacks on cricket matches between India and Pakistan. Salman Rushdie satirized Thackeray in his novel *The Moor's Last Sigh* (1995) in the character Raman Fielding, who heads a party called Mumbai's Axis.

Thackeray's influence started diminishing in the mid-1990s until he concluded an electoral alliance with the Hindu nationalist Bharatiya Janata Party (BJP). In 1999, Shiv Sena lost control of Bombay's municipal government after a series of corruption scandals. Thackeray's alliance with the BJP helped the party to come to national office in 1998 and its leader, Atal Behari, Vaypayee to become prime minister. His Shiv Sena resides among the right-wing parties in the national coalition supporting the BJP. Thackeray's relationship with Vaypayee is uneasy because Thackeray wants the national government to pursue his anti-Muslim policies. He is always threatening to leave the coalition unless the BJP is more aggressive against India's Muslim minority. His ties to the BJP did help Thackeray escape charges levied against him in August 2000 for responsibility for the 1992–1993 Bombay riots. Thackeray has suffered from a heart condition for a number of years, but he has positioned family members in Shiv Sena to replace him. See also Shiv Sena (Sword of Shiva).

Suggested readings: John Ward Anderson, "The Flame That Lit an Inferno; Hindu leader Creates Anti-Muslim Frenzy," *Washington Post* (August 11, 1993), p. A14; V. Shankar Aujer and Lakshimi Iyer, "Bal Thackeray: Threatening Tiger," *India Today* (July 31, 2000), p. 16; Asghar Alki Engineer, "The Politics of Thackeray's Arrest," *Hindu* (August 12, 2000), p. 1; Suzanne Goldenberg, "Master of Mumbai," *Maclean's* (February 26, 1996), p. 32; Krishna Guha, "'Brown-shirts' Take the Gloss Off Brash City of Dreams," *Financial Times* (London) (August 21, 1998), p. 6; Bernard Imhasly, "Shivas Tigers in the Jungle of Bombay," *Swiss Review of World Affairs* (March 1993), p. 1; Tim McGirk, "Rushdie Tackles Improbable Mr. Big," *Independent* (London) (September 3, 1995), p. 15; Robert Marquand, "A Charming Extremist Defies Moderate India," *Christian Science Monitor* (July 29, 2000), p. 1.

Thalib, Jaffar Umar (1961–) (Indonesia)

Jaffar Umar Thalib is the leader of the Indonesian Islamic extremist paramilitary **Laskar Jihad** (Militia of the Holy War). He was born in 1961 in east Java. His father was a veteran of Indonesia's war of independence and a religious scholar who ran a religious school. Thalib received his early education at his father's religious school. At age 19, he moved to Jakarta where he studied Arabic. After a disagreement with the teacher, Thalib left Indonesia to study at a religious school in Lahore, Pakistan. The lure of the war in Afghanistan caused him to neglect his religious studies, and, beginning in 1987, he served with the mujahideen fighting the Soviet military forces. Thalib found the experience enlightening and at the same time he learned how to conduct a guerrilla war that could defeat a superpower. He also met **Osama bin Laden** at Peshawar, Pakistan, in 1987, but he found bin Laden unimpressive and called him a lightweight.

Thalib returned to Indonesia and founded a network of religious schools. In these schools, Thalib advanced the idea of an Islamic state for Indonesia and strict adherence to Islamic law. He sat on an Islamic court in 2001 that sentenced a man to death by stoning for adultery and then he made certain that the sentence was carried out. This verdict was contrary to Indonesian law, but, after a brief arrest, Thalib was released. Thalib has always considered the United States as the main enemy of Muslims because of its support for Israel. Although Thalib has denied any association with **al-Qaeda**, he has defended both the 1993 attack on the World

Trade Center and the events of **September 11, 2001**, as legitimate operations against an enemy of the Muslims. Thalib has attracted a faithful following of between 3,000 and 10,000.

In April 2000, he founded the Laskar Jihad to defend Muslims in a religious war against Christians in the Moluccan Islands. He sent this group to the Moluccan Islands to intervene in fighting between Christians and Muslims. In this bloody war, casualties numbered over 6,000 and nearly 750,000 people were displaced. Despite this intervention by the Laskar Jihad, the Indonesian government was reluctant to arrest Thalib. His followers are fanatical and the Indonesian government wanted to avoid conflict with the Islamists of Thalib. Indonesian police finally detained him on May 4, 2002, after Muslim rioting in Ambon, Indonesia, killed 12 people. Police reluctance to charge him with crimes changed after the October 12, 2002, bombing on Bali that killed 188 and wounded hundreds more. Because many of the victims were foreign nationals, mostly Australians, foreign governments placed pressure on the Indonesian government to crack down on Islamist extremists. Responding to this changing environment, Thalib disbanded the Laskar Jihad in late October 2002. He was fearful of a close association with the Islamist terrorist group **Jemaah Islamiyah**. An Indonesian court acquitted Thalib of the charge of inciting attacks on Christians and attacking the Indonesian government on January 30, 2003. This acquittal was a blow to the government's attempt to control extremism. Thalib still has political ambitions for Indonesia becoming an Islamic state, but he appears at present to be reluctant to challenge the Indonesian government. He has, however, threatened to reestablish the Laskar Jihad in the event that Christians start persecuting Muslims in Indonesia. **See also** Jemaah Islamiyah; Laskar Jihad (Militia of the Holy War)

Suggested readings: Don Greenlees, Militia Boss Cleared of Incitement," *Australian* (Sydney) (January 31, 2003), p. 7; Andrew Marshall, "The Threat of Jaffar," *New York Times* (March 10, 2002), sec. 6, p. 45; Simon Montlake, "Militant Group Threatens Indonesian Peace," *Christian Science Monitor* (April 4, 2002), p. 7; Grace Nirang, "Jihad Chief Held after Attacks in Indonesia," *National Post* (Canada) (May 6, 2002), p. A16; Richard C. Paddock, "Indonesian Extremist Backs Terror," *Los Angeles Times* (September 23, 2001), p. A4.

Thiriart, Jean-François (1922–1992) (Belgium)

Jean-François Thiriart was the leader of the post–World War II pan-European movement. He was born in 1922 in Belgium. While in high school, Thiriart joined the Young Socialist Guards, a leftist student organization. His left-wing viewpoint changed after his mother married a German Jew. Thiriart rebelled by joining the extremist right-wing National Legion in 1939. At about the same time, he also joined the Association of the Friends of the German Reich. During World War II, Thiriart joined the German army and served in a Waffen SS unit. After the war, he was sentenced to a three-year prison term for collaborating with Germany. After his release from prison, Thiriart kept his ties to the neo-Nazi movement, but he retired from active politics.

Thiriart became a successful businessman in Belgium. He opened a chain of optometry stores in several European countries and the stores made him wealthy. Thiriart married and had a stable home life. His only eccentric behavior was the large number of cats that he kept in his home. Thiriart remained out of politics until the early 1960s.

Thiriart reentered politics because he had come to believe that Europe was losing its status as a political and cultural center. The loss of the Belgium colony of the Belgian Congo and France's defeat in Algeria was to him a sign of Europe's decline. In 1964, Thiriart formed the group Jeune Europe (Young Europe). His goal for this organization was for it to provide leadership to create a united European homeland with no ties to either the Soviet Union or the United States. A government of an elite would rule this united Europe, and this elite would pursue an independent foreign policy based on its nuclear arsenal. His vision of Europe appeared in his 1964 book *Europe: An Empire of 400 Million Men*. In his book, Thiriart accused both the Soviet Union and the United States of dominating Europe and turning it into a potential battlefield. Thiriart attempted to distance himself from his Nazi past by repudiating Nazism.

Thiriart's ideas caught on among many European intellectuals on both the left and right of the political spectrum. Within a year, Jeune Europe branches appeared in 13 countries. The most receptive countries, however, were Belgium, France, Italy, and Spain. Although Thiriart had dismissed both neo-Nazism and fascism, Jeune Europe appealed more to Europe's ultra-right than to radical leftists. Despite this success, Thiriart became discouraged about the chances for future success, and he retired from politics in the late 1970s.

In the 1990s, Thiriart reemerged in European politics. He was encouraged enough by the collapse of the Soviet Union to start working with the National European Community Party (Parti Communautaire National-Européen, or PCN). This party of Luc Michel was a small National Communist party with headquarters in Brussels. In August 1992, Thiriart traveled to Russia with a delegation from the PCN to discuss the future with Russian fascists and neo-Nazis. He advanced the theme of a European-Russian alliance to serve as a counter to the influence of the United States. Several of the Russian right-wing groups were attracted to his arguments. Thiriart returned to Brussels, but his plans were short circuited by his death from heart failure on November 23, 1992. His followers set up the European Liberation Front (ELF) to continue Thiriart's pan-European campaign.

Suggested readings: Angelo Del Boca, *Fascism Today* (New York: Heinemann, 1969); Martin A. Lee, *The Beast Reawakens* (Boston: Little, Brown, 1997); Jean Thiriart, *Europe: An Empire of 400 Million Men* (Brussels, Belgium: n.p., 1964).

Tupac Amaru Revolutionary Movement (Movimiento Revolucionario Tupac Amaru) (MRTA) (Peru)

The Tupac Amaru Revolutionary Movement (Movimiento Revolucionario Tupac Amaru, or MRTA) is a Peruvian Marxist-Leninist guerrilla group whose goal is to establish a Marxist regime in Peru. **Victor Polay Campos**, a jurist, formed the MRTA in June 1984 from elements of the Peruvian radical-left in the Revolutionary Socialist Party (PSR). This group is named after the 18th-century rebel leader, Tupac Amaru, who had led an insurrection against Spanish rule. Amaru's execution in Cuzco, Peru, made him a martyr among the Peruvian indignant population. The MRTA used the Tupac Amaru name to appeal to Peru's rural population. Polay Campos and the other leaders believed that capitalism was unsuited for Peru and wanted to institute a democratic socialist regime. For this reason, the MRTA worked closely with the Peruvian peasants and workers. The MRTA was never a large group with less than 600 active fighters, but it had a much larger number of supporters. Relations with the **Shining Path** guerrillas were never close because MRTA leaders believed that the Maoist group was too dogmatic and they accused it of being Stalinist. Part of the rivalry was over control of some of the major drug-producing areas of Peru. The Shining Path controlled these areas after driving the MRTA out.

The Tupac Amaru Revolutionary Movement began its guerrilla campaign against the Peruvian state in 1986. Leaders directed the MRTA in the areas in the northern Amazon region. Guerilla action included assassinations, ambushes, bombings, and kidnappings. In February 1987, the MRTA forces occupied seven radio stations in Lima, Peru's capital, and broadcast a pro-MRTA communiqué. In 1987, MRTA gained control of a provincial capital, Juanji, and held it for several months. Later that year, MRTA elements occupied the Sisa Valley for two weeks. MRTA's guerrilla units were able to seize key real estate, but they lacked the military strength to hold onto it. In February 1989, police captured Polay

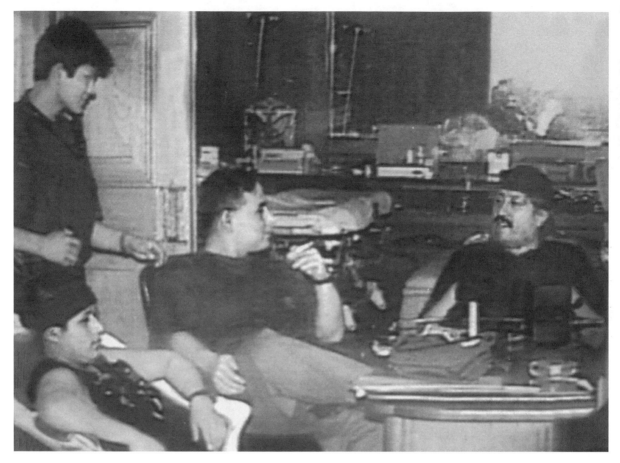

Tupac Amaru rebel leader Nestor Cerpa Cartolini, right, speaks with Roli Rojas, center, holding a cigarette, as other guerrillas look on inside the Japanese ambassador's residence in Lima in this undated photo taken with a secret camera by Peruvian forces. Seventy-one hostages were rescued in a commando assault on April 22, 1997. One hostage, two soliders, and all 14 Tupac Amaru rebels were killed, including Cerpa. Hidden cameras and listening devices gave commandos who stormed the mansion intimate knowledge of the hostage-takers' daily routines. (AP Photo)

Campos and imprisoned him in Lima. This setback only briefly curtailed MRTA operations. In July 1990, Polay Campos and 46 supporters escaped from their prison. He resumed his leadership of MRTA until on June 10, 1992, when the police recaptured him. Since then, Polay Campos has been kept in virtual isolation at a naval base.

Loss of Polay Campos's leadership was a devastating blow to the Tupac Amaru Revolutionary Movement. **Nestor Cerpa Cartolini**, a former union official and longtime second-in-command to Polay Campos, replaced him as leader. MRTA activity de-

creased dramatically after 1992. Peruvian authorities believed that military pressure was paying off. On November 30, 1995, the police broke up a plot to occupy the Peruvian Congress and hold the deputies hostage to bargain for the release of Polay Campos and other members of the MRTA. Thirty MRTA activists were arrested and jailed in the aftermath of this plot. Again, Peruvian political leaders forecasted the end of the MRTA.

The next MRTA operation gained worldwide attention. On December 17, 1996, Cerpa Cartolini and 13 MRTA guerrillas seized the Japanese ambassador's residence in

Lima during a reception in honor of Japan's emperor. More than 450 guests were present, and all but 72 hostages were released in stages from December 18, 1996, to January 1, 1997. The hostages were a combination of politicians, generals, police chiefs, Supreme Court justices, ambassadors of Japan and Bolivia and other guests. For more than five months the MRTA occupied the building with hostages and negotiated with the Peruvian government. The key issue for the guerrillas was the release of 400 MRTA prisoners in Peruvian prisons. These negotiations ended when Peruvian Special Forces assaulted the building on April 22, rescuing the hostages and killing all of the MRTA guerrillas, including Cerpa Cartolini. After this event, MRTA no longer constituted a serious threat to the Peruvian state because most of the guerrillas were either in prison or dead.

The MRTA is still in the news because of the Lori Berenson case. She was a former anthropology student at the Massachusetts Institute of Technology (MIT) in Cambridge, Massachusetts. Her interest in Central American and South American affairs led her to collaborate with radical elements in both regions. Berensen was arrested in Lima, Peru, in November 1995, shortly before a police raid on the house that she rented resulted in a gunfight with MRTA guerillas and the recovery of a large store of ammunition and dynamite. In January 1997, a secret, hooded military court sentenced her to life imprisonment for treason. She was not allowed to testify, present evidence, or call or cross-examine witnesses. On June 20, 2001, Berenson was given a new trial before a three-judge tribunal. This time the court ruled her a collaborator rather than a militant and gave her a 20-year prison sentence and a fine of $28,000. She is serving her sentence at a secure facility with the more than 400 MRTA activists.

Suggested readings: Sally Bowen, "Peru Army Teams Up with Locals to Beat Guerrillas," *Financial Times* (London) (December 11, 1992), p. 8; Barbara Durr, "'Robin Hood' Guerrillas on the Warpath," *Financial Times* (London) (November 27, 1987), p. 5; Clifford Krauss, "20-Year Sentence for New Yorker after 2nd Terrorism Trial in Peru," *New York Times* (June 21, 2001), p. A1; William R. Long, "Isolation, Defeats Push Rebel Movement toward Bitter End," *Los Angeles Times* (August 14, 1993), p. A3; Gordon H. McCormick, *Sharp Dressed Men: Peru's Tupac Amaru Revolutionary Movement* (Santa Monica, Calif.: Rand Corporation, 1993); Julia Preston, "Rescue in Peru: The Guerrillas," *New York Times* (April 24, 1997) p. A1; Sebastian Rotella, "The Face behind the Rebel Mask," *Los Angeles Times* (January 4, 1997), p. A1.

Al-Turabi, Abdallah Hassan (1932–) (Sudan)

Hassan al-Turabi is Sudan's leading Islamic fundamentalist leader. He was born in 1932 in Kassala in eastern Sudan into a merchant family. His father, a judge, was also a scholar of Islam and trained him in Islamic studies. Al-Turabi attended English-language schools in the Sudan before entering the British-run Gordon College in Khartoum. In 1955, he graduated with a degree in law. At the same time that he studied in Western schools, he became a secret member of the Khartoum branch of the Egyptian **Muslim Brotherhood**. In 1955, he won a scholarship to the University of London, where he earned a master's degree in law in 1957. In 1959, he won another scholarship and worked on a dissertation in law at the Sorbonne in Paris. In 1961, al-Turabi traveled to the United States, and he was disturbed by the racial prejudice he encountered. After finishing his dissertation in 1964, al-Turabi traveled extensively in Europe.

Al-Turabi returned to Sudan in 1965 and entered Sudanese politics. He formed the Islamic Charter Front (ICF) as an umbrella group to permit a variety of Islamic fundamentalist groups to influence politics. Winning a seat in the Sudanese parliament, al-Turabi served as attorney general of Gaafar Nimeiri's government. When outside the government, al-Turabi provided political opposition. From his writings and speeches, he soon became one of the leading **Islamic fundamentalist** political thinkers. Al-Turabi also converted the ICF into the National Islamic Front (NIF). His chance for political

Hassan al-Turabi, former parliament speaker and once Sudan's chief Islamic theologian, speaks to a news conference in Khartoum, February, 20, 2001. The next day, the government placed him under house arrest at his home in Khartoum. His detention followed a fiery speech made by the Sorbonne-educated Turabi in which he called on the Sudanese to rise up against President Omar el-Bashir's government and announced that he was in contact with the U.S. government and that he reached an understanding with rebels fighting successive Khartoum governments in the south of Sudan since 1983. (AP Photo/ Abdel Raouf)

power emerged after the June 30, 1989, military coup of General Omar al-Bashir. General Bashir allowed al-Turabi to form an Islamic fundamentalist military dictatorship. In 1991, al-Turabi launched an Islamization program that mandated the Islamic law of the Sharia for Sudan.

After the Persian Gulf War, al-Turabi's outspoken anti-Americanism made him a leader in the Muslim world. His position was that all of the non-Islamic states in the Middle East were puppets of the United States and should be destroyed. He attempted with some success to unite Sunni and Shi'ite Muslims into an international Islamic alliance. His efforts led to the formation of the Armed Islamic Movement (AIM) to carry out a new terrorist campaign against non-Islamic governments. Al-Turabi's close relationship with General Bashir led to Sudan becoming a safe haven for terrorist leaders

and groups. Among those enjoying Sudan hospitality in the early 1990s were **Osama bin Laden** and his supporters. In a conference in April 1991, al-Turabi assumed leadership of the Islamic Arab People's Conference (IAPC). Members of this conference formed the Popular International Organization (PIO) in Khartoum, Sudan, to coordinate the activities of the Islamic liberation struggle. This organization soon became affiliated with the Iranian government. Training camps to education and train terrorists were established in Sudan. Al-Turabi also had connections with **Sheikh Omar Abdel-Rahman** and with the participants in the 1993 plot to bomb the World Trade Center in New York City.

Al-Turabi's relationship with bin Laden had positive benefits for Sudan. Sudan's infrastructure of dams, roads, bridges, and ports needed building. Bin Laden's construction expertise and his financial connections made it easy to start a large public works program. This infrastructure upgrade was necessary because the government's Islamic policies had provoked a military uprising in southern Sudan from non-Muslims.

Al-Turabi's relationship with al-Bashir soured in the late 1990s. Sudan had become a haven for terrorist groups with al-Turabi's blessings. In 1992, a dissident Sudanese national assaulted him in Ottawa, Canada, and al-Turabi blamed the United States for the assault. Pressure from the United States and the civil war in southern Sudan persuaded al-Bashir to declare his independence from al-Turabi. Osama bin Laden had to relocate to Afghanistan and the profile of other terrorist groups tolerated by al-Turabi was lowered. Al-Turabi's influence has been reduced to that of a figurehead and the government has placed him under house arrest at his home in Khartoum in February 2001. The al-Bashir government has been reluctant to bring him before a court on serious changes, because it wants to avoid making him a martyr. President Bashir released Turabi from house arrest on October 14, 2003. Turabi has used his freedom to attack the Bashir government and its handling of the rebellion in southern Sudan. **See also** Bin Laden, Osama; Islamic Fundamentalism.

Suggested readings: Kamal Bakhit, "Turabi Released in Khartoum," *Mideast Mirror* [London] (October 14, 2003), p. 1; David Hirst, "Behind the Veil of Sudan's Theocracy," *Guardian* (London) (May 27, 1997), p. 16; David Hirst, "Dark Times Loom for Visionary Sudan," *Guardian* (London) (May 26, 1997), p. 12; Fereydoun, Hoveyda, *The Broken Crescent; The "Threat" of Militant Islamic Fundamentalism* (Westport, CT: Praeger, 1998); Robert MacLaughlin, "Sudan the Coup de Grace," *Arabies Trends* (May 1, 2001), p. 1; Judith Miller, "Faces of Fundamentalism: Hassan al-Turabi and Muhammed Fadlallah," *Foreign Affairs* (November–December 1994), p. 123; Jonathan C. Randal, "Sudan's Urbane Islamic Leader Sends Shivers from Behind the Scenes," *Washington Post* (May 9, 1995), p. A14; Abdel Salam Sidahmed, *Politics and Islam in Contemporary Sudan* (Richmond, UK: Curzon Press, 1997); Al Venter, "Sudan— Sudan's Spymaster: Hassan al-Turabi," *Jane's Intelligence Review* 5, no. 7 (July 1, 1998), p. 6.

Turkes, Alparslan (1917–1997) (Turkey)

Alparslan Turkes was the Turkish ultranationalist leader. He was born on November 25, 1917, in Nicosia, Cyprus. After schooling in Greek schools on Cyprus, he moved to Istanbul, Turkey, in his late teens and joined the Turkish army, attending Kuleli Military Academy. His first venture into politics was a work attacking the Soviet Union in May 1944 that resulted in his arrest. After an acquittal, he returned to the army, reaching the rank of colonel. In 1960 he was one of the leading participants in the military coup against the Turkish government of Adnam Menderes. Intemperate actions on his part in the new government led to his exile to New Delhi, India. After returning from India in 1963, he became leader of the Republican, Peasants and National Party. Turkes changed the name of the party to Nationalist Action Party (MHP) in 1969. The MHP had a radical right-wing nationalism agenda that included a Greater Turkey with territory from the Soviet Union and other central Asian states. Turkes was reported by William Drozdiak in an article in *The Washington Post* in 1983 to use the slogan "one people, one nation" as justification for the liquidation of all minorities in the pan-Turkish state of Turan. In early 1970s, he formed the **Grey Wolves** as the terrorist wing of the MHP to carry out assassinations and street battles. Twice in the 1970s, Turkes served as deputy prime minister. In 1975, he assumed control of Turkey's state security forces. His Grey Wolves infiltrated the state security forces during his tenure in office, and its members carried out street demonstrations and assassinations against opponents of the regime.

The military coup in 1980 ended Turkes's role in the Turkish government. Turkes and key members of the MHP and the Grey Wolves were arrested in 1985. He received an 11-year prison sentence in April 1987, but he was released from prison in 1990 on medical grounds earlier after serving a total of four and a half years in prison. During his stay in prison, a member of the Grey Wolves, Mehmet Ali Agca, attempted to assassination Pope John Paul II in St. Peter's Square in

1981. In 1988, another member of the Grey Wolves, Kartal Demirag, attempted to assassinate the Turkish Prime Minister Turgut Ozal at a political rally. After his release from prison, Turkes returned to politics. He renamed the Nationalist Action Party as the Nationalist Work Party and continued his radical right-wing nationalist program. In 1991, Turkes returned to the Turkish Parliament and he pursued a more moderate policy in his political party, but the Grey Wolves continued its terrorist activities and members also became involved in the drug trade by dealing with the Turkish smugglers. Turkes died on April 5, 1997. **See also** Grey Wolves.

Suggested readings: David Barchard, "Turkish Far-Right Leader Jailed for 11 Years," *Financial Times* (London) (April 8, 1987), p. 3; William Dorzdiak, "The 'Grey Wolves': Decade of Crime Attributed to Turkish Rightists," *Washington Post* (July 3, 1983), p. A1; Kevin Klose, "Probe of Turkish Right Links Pope Suspect," *Washington Post* (May 19, 1981), p. A10; Mina Toksoz, "Alparslan Turkes: Keeper of the Grey Wolves," *Guardian* (London) (April 8, 1997), p. 20.

U

Uighurs Separatists (China)

Muslim Uighurs from China's far western province of Xinjiang have established groups to fight for an Islamist state. Uighurs have had a lengthy history of independence going back to an independent state in A.D. 744. More recently, there were Uighur states set up in 1933 and 1944, but both lasted only a few years. First outlines of a new independence movement appeared in the mid-1960s during Mao Tse-tung's Cultural Revolution. Nearly 120,000 Uighurs were arrested for anti-Mao activities during the Cultural Revolution. In response to this persecution, a small group of Uighur militants formed the Eastern Turkestan People's Party to begin the process to lead to an independent Uighur state. Later this party was renamed the Eastern Turkestan Islamic Movement (ETIM).

Both the party and political agitation among the Uighurs remained dormant until Chinese authorities decided to use the Muslim Uighurs to weaken the Soviets in Afghanistan. In case of unintended consequences, the Chinese government encouraged Uighurs to fight in Afghanistan against the Soviet army. Uighur recruits received military training in mujahideen camps where they also received indoctrination in Islamic religious teachings. These Uighur veterans returned to China ready to fight for a Uighur separatist Islamic state in Xinjiang. This militancy happened at the same time the Chinese government decided to promote immigration of the ethnic Chinese Han population into Xinjiang. A clash of cultures ensued, leading to the Baren uprising in April 1990. The two days of rioting that took place in Baren resulted in the deaths of at least 30 people, and the government arrested almost 8,000 others. Throughout the 1990s attacks on Chinese police and ethnic Hans resulted in a harsh crackdown by the government on Uighurs in Xinjiang. Uighur militants retaliated with a terrorist campaign of bombings of buildings and buses directed against Chinese officials and Uighurs remaining loyal to the Chinese government.

The Eastern Turkestan Islamic Movement remains the largest and most active of the Uighur separatists. Hasan Mahsum is the current leader of the ETIM and he fled China in 1997 after release from a Chinese reeducation through labor camp. Mahsum directed ETIM operations first in Afghanistan, but later he moved to Pakistan and other Central Asian states. ETIM's relationship to **Osama bin Laden**'s **al-Qaeda** has been close with most of ETIM's fighters receiving training at al-Qaeda training camps. ETIM leaders send graduates of these camps to Xinjiang, China, to form terrorist groups for operations there.

The Eastern Turkestan Islamic Party had been a major participant in the terrorist campaign, but several other Islamist groups have also become active. These groups operate under various names, including Eastern Turkestan Islamic Party of Allah, East Turkestan Opposition Party, Lobnor Tigers, Revolutionary Front of Eastern Turkestan, and Organization for Turkestan Freedom. Sources have identified 15 Uighur extremist groups in operation in Central Asia and China. Most of the leaders of these groups reside outside of Xinjiang. They recruit, organize, and plan operations from safe havens in other Muslim states in the region, including Afghanistan, Kazakhstan, Kyrgyzstan, and Pakistan. Germany has also been a place from which Uighur leaders could operate. These leaders have been able to raise funds to continue their struggle, but they remain isolated from their compatriots in China. Chinese authorities have shown no reluctance in executing captured Uighur activists. This war between a secular state and Islamist Uighurs has little chance of abating because of the no-compromise positions on both sides. China has additional reasons not to permit a separatist state. Xinjiang is rich in natural resources with around 27 percent of China's oil reserves and 22 percent of its natural gas. It is also the site of the Chinese nuclear test program at Lop Nor.

U.S. policy toward Uighur separatism has been cautious. The U.S. State Department has charged that the East Turkestan Islamic Movement has had contacts with al-Qaeda. This charge is enough to discourage any American support. Besides not wanting to antagonize China, any evidence of ties with al-Qaeda cools any enthusiasm to intervene to support another Islamic movement. In September 2002, the U.S. government declared the East Turkestan Islamic Movement a terrorist organization, and the United Nations placed it on the list of global terrorist organizations on **September 11,** 2002.

Suggested readings: Chien-peng Chung, "China's 'War on Terror': September 11 and Uighur Separatism," *Foreign Affairs* (July, 2002/August, 2002), p. 8; Michael Dwyer, "In the Shadow of the Han," *Australian Financial Review* (June 28, 2002), p. 40; Erik Eckhom, "U.S. Labeling of Group in China as Terrorist Is Criticized,"

New York Times (September 13, 2002), p. A6; Rohan Gunaratna, *Inside Al Qaeda: Global Network of Terror* (New York: Columbia University Press, 2002); Mark O'Neill, "A Life in Forgotten Exile," *South China Morning Post* (May 15, 2001), p. 15; Craig S. Smith, "China, in Harsh Crackdown, Executes Muslim Separatists," *New York Times* (December 16, 2001), p. 1A; Russell Working, "China's Own Muslim Nationalists," *Moscow Times* (October 26, 2001), p. 1.

Ulster Defence Association (UDA)/ Ulster Freedom Fighters (UFF) (Northern Ireland)

The Ulster Defence Association (UDA) and its military wing, the Ulster Freedom Fighters (UFF), are Protestant loyalist paramilitary groups that carry out terrorist operations against Catholics and other Protestant loyalist groups in Northern Ireland. Various Protestant vigilante groups merged at a meeting on May 15, 1971, to establish the Ulster Defence Association to coordinate their activities. Early leaders were Billy Hull, a Protestant trade unionist, and Jim Anderson, a glazier. Andy Tyrie, a machinist at Rolls Royce and commander of Company A (Glencairn), became the supreme commander of the UDA for 15 years from 1973 until March 11, 1988. Members considered the UDA to be the defender of Protestantism and the maintainer of the link between Northern Ireland's Protestants and Great Britain. Leadership of the UDA organized it along military lines with members from areas forming seven brigades: North Belfast, East Belfast, South Belfast, West Belfast, Southeast Antrim, Londonderry, and the Border Counties. Brigades included battalions, companies, platoons, and sections. An Inner Council of brigade commanders and their staffs made strategic decisions. Later, Tyrie reformed this unwieldy command structure and replaced it with a more centralized one. At the height of its influence in the 1970s, the leadership claimed a membership in the neighborhood of 50,000. Because of its close association with the British government, the UDA attracted many ex-servicemen and former policemen to its ranks. Corruption became so endemic among the top leadership in the 1980s that it began to discredit the UDA. Younger, more militant leaders began to emerge as the older leadership faced imprisonment for corruption and forced retirements.

Leaders of the Ulster Defence Association became concerned that its use of violence might cause the government of Northern Ireland to ban the organization. They decided to form a military wing, and in 1973, John White organized the **Ulster Freedom Fighters** to carry out the UDA's terrorist campaign and protect the UDA. White organized the UFF following the model of the **Provisional Irish Republican Army** with its small units and cells of five to eight members. Units of this size were difficult for the authorities to penetrate and plant agents. John McMichael became the commander in chief of the UFF and a close associate of Tyrie. His murder in December 1987 by the Provisional IRA was a reprisal for UFF operations. This plan to insolate the UDA from government sanctions by sponsoring another group failed when on August 10, 1992, the Northern Ireland government banned the Ulster Defence Association for its use of violence.

Among the chief targets of the Ulster Freedom Fighters was the Provisional IRA leader **Gerry Adams.** As one of the Provisional IRA's chief leaders, he was a natural target. A UFF three-man hit team shot Adams on April 14, 1984, in downtown Belfast. Four bullets hit Adams, but he survived the assassination attempt. Other attempts were planned and made, but none of them came as close to success as the 1984 operation.

Johnny "Mad Dog" Adair was the acknowledged leader of the Ulster Freedom Fighters. He became the leaders of C Company of the UFF, which was the assassination wing of the UDA. The UFF has retained its affiliation with the Ulster Defence Association, but Adair has displayed considerable independence. A Combined Loyalist Military Command (CLMC) directs the activities of both the UDA and the UFF, and it coordinates operations with the Ulster Volunteer Force. Gary McMichael, the son of John

McMichael, heads the Ulster Democratic Association, the political wing of the UDA.

Both the Ulster Defence Association and the Ulster Freedom Fighters have been weakened by defections. In 1996, **Billy "King Rat" Wright** broke away from the UDA-UFF and he organized the Loyalist Volunteer Force (LUF). However, since Wright's murder in the Maze prison by an IRA hit team in December 1997, the LUF has lacked strong leadership. Adair has been active in trying to win this group back into UFF ranks.

In the late 1990s, a feud broke out between the Ulster Freedom Fighters and the Ulster Volunteer Force over the question of political accommodation with Ulster Catholics. The UVF has adopted a more moderate approach toward the Catholics, but it has had to fight off violence from the UFF and its youthful gangs affiliated with Ulster Young Militants (UYM).

Next, the Ulster Freedom Fighter broke with its parent unit the Ulster Defence Association over the UFF's violent tactics. Almost as importance as the disagreement over tactics was the issue of the control of the drug trade in Northern Ireland. On September 25, 2002, UDA's leadership banished Adair from the UDA, claiming that Adair was no longer acceptable in the organization. Adair's arrest and imprisonment left the field wide open for violence between the UFF and the UDA. On February 2, 2003, UFF assassins killed John "Grug" Gregg, a member of the UDA's ruling council and the failed assassin of Gerry Adams in 1984. On the verge of outright war the UDA and UFF announced a 12-month ceasefire on February 22, 2003. Since this ceasefire, Adair's control of the UVF has deteriorated and the level of violence has decreased. Leadership of both the UDA and UFF continue to be unstable as various individuals jockey for power. **See also** Adair, Johnny "Mad Dog"; Provisional Irish Republican Army (Provos) (PIRA), Ulster Volunteer Force (UVF); Wright, Billy "King Rat."

Suggested readings: Steve Bruce, *The Red Hand: Protestant Parmilitaries in Northern Ireland* (Oxford, U.K.: Oxford University Press, 1992);

Liam Clarke, "Could Mad Dog Be Trying to Re-place the King Rat?" *Sunday Times* (London) (July 9, 2000), p. 1; Martin Dillon, *God and the Gun: The Church and Irish Terrorism* (New York: Routledge, 1990); Henry McDonald, "Loyalists at War," *Observer* (London) (August 27, 2000), p. 14; David McKittrick, "Paramilitaries Feud over Money, Power and Sex as Adair Leaves Behind a Vacuum," *Independent* (October 18, 2003), p. 1; Andrew Silke, "In Defense of the Realm: Financing Loyalist Terrorism in Northern Ireland—Part One: Extortion and Blackmail," *Studies in Conflict and Terrorism* 21, no. 4 (October–December 1998); Peter Taylor, *Loyalists: War and Peace in Northern Ireland* (New York: TV Books, 1999).

Ulster Freedom Fighters (See Ulster Defence Association)

Ulster Volunteer Force (UVF) (Northern Ireland)

The Ulster Volunteer Force (UVF) is the oldest Protestant loyalist paramilitary organization in Northern Ireland. An earlier version of the Ulster Volunteer Force had been formed in 1912 and it was active in fighting before World War I against Irish Home Rule. UVF's opposition to Irish Home Rule led to the creation of a separate Northern Ireland. After this success, the UVF had withered way in the middle 1920s. Catholic agitation for equality in economic and political rights in Northern Ireland in the early 1960s led to the resurrection of the UVF. Ulster's Protestant politicians decided in 1965 to reconstitute the UVF to replace the moderate government of Terence O'Neill and replace it with a more resolute Ulster Protestant government. Gusty Spence and other Protestant leaders plotted the strategy for the UVF in a pub on Shankill Road in Belfast in 1966. The goal of the UVF was to preserve Protestant domination in Northern Ireland and fight against the **Provisional Irish Republican Army**. In 1966, the Ulster government declared the UVF as an illegal organization after its role in the murders of Catholics became known. Leaders of the UVF were willing to achieve this goal by either violence or by negotiations. A cease-fire in 1973 and unsuccessful negotiations with both the Provisional IRA and the Official IRA proved this intent.

Regardless, the Ulster Volunteer Force developed a reputation for violence. Beginning in 1966, members of the UVF carried out a series of terrorist attacks on Catholics. One such attack on December 4, 1971, when UVF activists bombed McGurk's Bar in Belfast, Northern Ireland, killing 15 Catholics. Its most spectacular and bloody operation, however, was the May 17, 1974, car bombings in Dublin and Monaghan, Republic of Ireland, that claimed the lives of 32 people and wounded more than 200 others. In the late 1970s, a subunit of the UVF earned the reputations as the **Shankill Butchers** for their brutal killings of Catholics. Eight members of the Shankill Butchers were arrested and sentenced to life imprisonment on February 20, 1979. Leadership of the UVF decided that these violent acts were counterproductive because they were alienating even Protestant supporters. These activities had also resulted in most of the veteran UVF leaders serving prison time. This exodus of veteran leaders led to a new generation of UVF leadership. In early 1991, the new leadership concluded an alliance with the **Ulster Defence Association** and formed a Combined Loyalist Military Command (CLMC) to coordinate operations between the groups.

Leaders of the Ulster Volunteer Force decided in the mid-1990s to moderate their terrorist image. They implemented a cease-fire in October 1994 and formed the Progressive Unionist Party (PUP) to serve as the political wing of the UVF. Parliamentary leaders of the PUP have been Billy Hutchinson and David Ervine. Both have been elected to the Northern Ireland Assembly. Gusty Spence still retains influence in the PUP, but he has broken most of his ties with the rest of the UVF. Leadership of both the PUP and the UVF has been supportive of the Good Friday Accord. Backing of this peace accord, however, has led to open warfare between the UVF and the Ulster Freedom Fighters. Members of both the UVF and the UFF have been assassinated in an ongoing loyalist feud. This feud has died out since the imprisonment of **Johnny "Mad Dog" Adair**, the head of the Ulster Freedom Fighters. **See also** Adair, Johnny "Mad Dog'; Shankill Butchers; Spence, Augustus "Gusty"; Ulster Defence Association (UDA)/Ulster Freedom Fighters (UFF).

Suggested readings: Steve Bruce, *The Red Hand: Protestant Paramilitaries in Northern Ireland* (Oxford, U.K.: Oxford University press, 1992); Martin Dillon, *God and the Gun: The Church and Irish Terrorism* (New York: Routledge, 1990); Macer Hall and Jenny Mccartney, "Agony and Ecstasy: This Is Why They're Dying in Belfast," *Sunday Telegraph* (London) (August 27, 2000), p. 19; David Pallister, "Quest for Truth Over Dublin Bomb Massacre," *Guardian* (London) (February 26, 2001), p. 10; Andrew Silke, "In Defense of the Realm: Financing Loyalist Terrorism in Northern Ireland—Part One: Extortion and Blackmail," *Studies in Conflict and Terrorism* 21, no. 4 (October–December 1998); Peter Taylor, *Loyalists: War and Peace in Northern Ireland* (New York: TV Books, 1999).

United Self-Defense Forces of Colombia (Autodefensas Unidas de Colombia) (AUC) (Colombia)

The United Self-Defense Forces of Colombia (AUC) is a right-wing paramilitary group in Colombia that is fighting a war with the Marxist guerrilla group **Revolutionary Armed Forces of Colombia** (FARC). The AUC is a successor to the Death to Kidnappers (Muerte a Secuestradores) group formed in December 1981 to fight against leftist and Maoist guerrillas. Death squads were organized to eliminate guerrillas and their sympathizers. Soon other paramilitary groups formed under the sponsorship of the Colombian military, drug lords, large landowners, and wealthy businessmen. Two brothers, Fidel and **Carlos Castaño**, allied with Pablo Escobar, the Medellin drug cartel head, and they founded the Peasant Self-Defense Groups of Córdoba and Urabá (ACCU). These groups and other regional forces engaged in a war of terror against those that they perceived as threats.

These paramilitary groups undermined the attempt of the Colombian government

to conclude peace with leftist guerrillas. In 1985, the Belisario Betancour government negotiated peace with the (FARC) and the M-19. These guerrillas attempted to engage in the political process by forming the Patriotic Union. In a campaign of assassinations by the death squads, most of the leaders and sympathizers of the Patriotic Union were murdered in 1985 and 1986. In May 1989, the Colombian government outlawed paramilitary groups, but the paramilitary groups ignored the government.

Carlos Castaño is the military commander of the United Self-Defense Forces of Colombia, but he reports to an AUC governing committee. In April 1997, Castaño organized rural vigilantes, drug protection gangs, and former members of the Colombian army into an army of about 8,000. His headquarters is a fortified camp in the jungle of Nudo de Paramillo about 325 miles north of Bogatá. Recruits who join the AUC are paid a wage of $350 a month. Financial support for AUC comes from rural landowners and profits from a 20 percent tax on the lucrative drug trade. This tax produces around $1 million a year to finance operations of the AUC.

The AUC has been able to make inroads into FARC-controlled territory using brutal methods to instill terror. A reporter from *The Ottawa Citizen* claims that the AUC kills an average of 1,000 per year, making it more violent than the FARC. These killings are part of a terror strategy to end support for the FARC by making the Colombian population more afraid of the AUC than the FARC. The AUC has considerable support among members of the Colombian army, but the government has made halfhearted attempts to curtail the excesses of the AUC. AUC forces never attack Colombia security forces because they share a common enemy. Castaño and the AUC have opposed the efforts of the Colombian government to conclude a peace with the FARC, and they have threatened to continue the war even if peace is concluded.

The Colombian government became more active in trying to suppress the activities of the AUC, and thus elements within the group wanted to retaliate. However, Castaño was reluctant to pursue an aggressive policy against the state. In response to subsequent opposition to his leadership, Castaño resigned as head of the United Self-Defense Forces of Colombia on June 1, 2001. **See also** Castaño, Carlos; Revolutionary Armed Forces of Colombia (Fuerzas Armada Revolucionarias de Colombia) (FARC).

Suggested readings: Laura Brooks, "Colombian Paramilitaries Gain Strength," *Washington Post* (December 27, 1997); Andres Cala, "Colombia's Most Popular Killer, *Ottawa Citizens* (March 18, 2001), p. D10; Linda Diebal, "Are We Now the Enemy?" *Toronto Star* (July 13, 1997), p. F1; Garry M. Leech, *Killing Peace: Colombia's Conflict and the Failure of U.S. Intervention* (New York: Information Network of the Americas, 2002); Tod Robberson, "Paramilitary Groups Gaining Strength in Colombia," *Times-Picayune* (New Orleans) (July 13, 1997), p. A30; Scott Wilson, "Colombian Right's 'Cleaning' Campaign," *Washington Post* (April 17, 2001), p. A1.

V

Villalobos, Joaquin (1951–) (El Salvador)
Joaquin Villalobos was the military leader of
El Salvador's **Farabundo Martí National Liberation Front** (FMLN). He was born in 1951.
His father was a printer in San Salvador. He
attended Catholic schools in San Salvador.
After graduation from high school, he entered the National University to study economics. While in college, Villalobos became
a follower of Marxist-Leninist ideology and
a student activist. In the early 1970s, he
helped form the **People's Revolutionary
Army** (Ejercito Revolucionario del Pueblo, or
ERP). By 1977, he was the acknowledged
head of the ERP.

Villalobos led the People's Revolutionary
Army into the alliance that culminated in
the creation of the Farabundo Martí National Liberation Front. He became one of
the military leaders of the FMLN. He specialized in economic sabotage, blowing up
roads, structures and bridges to interrupt
coffee bean harvesting. Units under his
command confronted and often defeated
Salvadoran army forces. Villalobos was
famous among the FMLN members, but he
avoided contacts with the foreign media.
Salvadoran death squads were never able
identify him or his location. By the time
that a peace settlement came in December
1992, he was one of the FMLN's chief
spokespersons.

Once peace came to El Salvador, Villalobos
made a move to the middle. He had long
been a doctrinaire Marxist, but he decided
that the Salvadorian left had to move to the
center of the political spectrum. This more
moderate stance did not keep him from serving a short jail term in 1994 for criminal
libel. He publicly accused a wealthy businessman of financing Salvadoran death
squads in 1993. While the charge was probably true, Villalobos was unable to find
witnesses willing to testify against the businessman. In the 1994 presidential election,
the right-wing **ARENA** (Nationalist Republican Alliance) promised better economic
times. In contrast, the factions within the
FMLN refused to compromise over ideology
and lost out to ARENA and its candidate,
Armando Calderón Sol.

Shortly before the 1994 presidential election Villalobos broke with his FMLN colleagues and started to rebuild his guerrilla
group into a political party. He changed the
name of the People's Revolutionary Army to
the People's Renovated Expression. Villalobos's group was able to elect several deputies to the National Assembly in 1994. He
alienated most of his former colleagues by
having the deputies belonging to his party
vote with ARENA on electing the assembly's
directorate. Villalobos decided early on that
the FMLN had little future as a political

party and he has spent the last decade building fences with the Salvadorean right wing for future political office. See also ARENA (Alianza Republicana Nacionalista, or National Republican Alliance); Farabundo Martí National Liberation Front (FMLN).

Suggested readings: Ana Arana, "The Smiling Chameleon," *The Bulletin of the Atomic Scientists* (1994); Hugh Byrne, *El Salvador's Civil War: A Study of Revolution* (Boulder, CO: Lynne Rienner, 1996); Douglas Farah, "Salvadoran Ex-Rebel, Key to Peace Pact," *Washington Post* (November 12. 1992), p. A29; James LeMoyne, "Salvador Rebel Chief: A Militarist Without Doubts," *New York Times* (July 13, 1985) sec. 1, p. 2; Marjorie Miller, "Trading a Mean Streak for the Human Touch," *Los Angeles Times* (September 22, 1992), p. 6.

Vishwa Hindu Parishad (World Hindu Organization) (VHP) (India)

The Vishwa Hindu Parishad (VHP) (World Hindu Organization) is one of the most extreme Hindu nationalist parties in India. Hindu nationalists with Ashok Singhal as the leading activist founded the VHP in 1964. Singhal was the international president of the VHP from its founding until October 2003 when he retired. Its present head is Dr. Pravinbhai Togadipi (sometimes spelled Togadia), a cancer surgeon from Gujarat state. The group's mission is to reconvert of all Buddhist, Christian, and Muslim Indians to Hinduism. Complicating this reconversion is that a significant proportion of new Christian converts, and, in the past, a significant number of Muslims had made inroads among the Dalits (the Oppressed) caste, or what was once called the "Untouchable" caste. Since 2000, mass conversion of Dalits to Buddhism has taken place much to the displeasure of Hindu nationalists. Members of the VHP have been aggressive in their contacts with Muslims and they have been active in much of the Hindu-Muslim rioting since the 1980s.

The most controversial action of the Vishwa Hindu Parishad has been its campaign to build a Hindu temple on the site of a mosque at Ayodhya. This agitation has been named "the Ramjanmabhoomi campaign." Leaders of the VHP claim that the Muslim mosque, the Babri Masjid, was built on the site of the birthplace of the Hindu God Lord Ram, where a Hindu temple had previously existed. They want to tear down the Muslim mosque and build a temple to the Lord Ram. This issue has been so emotionally charged that it has led to rioting between Muslims and Hindus throughout India. An electoral alliance of the VHP with the Hindu nationalist Bharatiya Janata Party (BJP) beginning in 1980 has only increased tensions in India over the temple.

In the late 1990s, members of the Vishwa Hindu Parishad were active in attacks on Indian Christians. The leadership of the VHP justified these attacks by charging that Christians were forcibly converting Hindus to Christianity. India has a Christian population of less than 2 percent, but Christian missionary activity has alarmed militant Hindus. Most of the attacks on Christians have been in Gujarat, an economically prosperous state with a reputation for Hindu extremism. The goal of the VHP is to expel Christians from India.

The issue of the mosque came to a head in December 1992. A mob of Hindu activists tore down the mosque in Ayodhya to make way for a temple of the Hindu god Ram. Since then, the leaders of the Vishwa Hindu Parishad have been agitating for the building of the temple. The advent of the Hindu nationalist Bharatiya Janata Party to power in 1998 gave the leadership of the VHP the expectation that the temple could be built with little opposition. An alliance with the other militant Hindu organization, **Rashtriya Swayamsevak Sangh** (RSS), seemed to ensure success. This political agitation and an increasing number of Hindu pilgrims created intense hostility in the Muslim population, which culminated in the massacre of 58 Hindu pilgrims by a Muslim mob on February 27, 2002. Vajpayee's Indian government has been reluctant to allow the temple to be built with tensions so high with Pakistan. **See also** Rashtriya Swayamsevak Sangh (National Volunteer Organization) (RSS).

Suggested readings: Atul Chandra, "Temple Movement Reaches a Dead End?" *Times of India* (March 19, 2002), p. 1; Rajeev Deshpande and Farzand Ahmed, "Ayodhya: Here They Go Again, Why? *India Today* [New Delhi] (October 27, 2003), p. 24; Ranjit Devraj, "Ruling Party Using Trident as a Sharp-Edged Symbol," Inter Press Service (April 29, 2003), p. 1; Ajay Jha, "Togadia to Take Over as VHP Chief," *Gulf News* [Dubai, United Arab Emirates] (October 25, 2003), p. 1; Robert Marquand, "Anti-Christian Violence in India Builds on Fear of Conversions," *Christian Science Monitor* (October 5, 1998), p. 7; Gail Omvedt, "Hinduism, Social Inequality, and the State," in Douglas Allen (ed.), *Religion and Political Conflict in South Asia: India, Pakistan, and Sir Lanka* (Westport, CT: Greenwood Press, 1992).

Vlaams Blok (Flemish Bloc) (VB) (Belgium)

Vlaams Blok (Flemish Bloc, or VB) is the leading extremist political party in Belgium. Dissidents from two early extremist parties, Flemish National Party (Vlaams Nationale Partif, or VNP) and the Flemish People's Party (Vlaamse Volkspartij, or VVP), merged to form the Vlaams Blok on May 28, 1979. Karel Dillon, formerly a member of the VNP, and Piet Bocken, formerly a member of the VVP, were the principal leaders of the merger. They also became the principal leaders of the new party. Later Roeland Raes, formerly a member of the VVP, replaced Bocken as one of the top leaders.

The original goal of the Vlaams Blok was to unite all factions of the Flemish nationalist movement into a political movement to create an independent Flemish state. Creation of an independent Flemish state separate from the French-speaking areas of southern Belgium has remained its reason for existence, but other issues such an anti-immigrant policy, law and order, and attacks on the political system have also become important. At first, the party attracted mostly members from the radical wing of the Flemish nationalist movement and from former collaborators with Nazi Germany during World War II. Almost all of its voting strength came from the city of Antwerp.

In the mid-1980s, the Vlaams Blok reorganized and transformed its electoral base. Leadership of the party became concerned over Vlaams Blok's narrow political base. Dillon persuaded party leaders to open leadership positions to younger members untainted by charges of collaboration during World War II. After the adoption of an anti-immigration campaign titled "Own People First!" Vlaams Blok began to attract more political support. Successes in the 1987 parliamentary election and in the 1988 local elections made the mainstream Belgian parties take notice. These successes had a price as the radical wing of the Vlaams Blok wanted to emphasize the anti-immigration policy over Flemish nationalism. Dillon opposed this shift and the dissidents left the VB to from the Nationalist Association-Dutch People's Movement (Nationalistisch Verbond-Nederlandse Volksbeweging). These defections did not prevent the VB's triumph in the November 1991 parliamentary election. By winning 10.3 percent of the vote, the VB gained 18 parliamentary seats (12 in the Lower House and 6 in the Senate).

The other Belgian parties reacted by excluding the Vlaams Blok from political power. Internal disputes within the Flemish nationalist movement also had a negative impact on the VB. On June 8, 1996, Dillon retired as head of the party, but he appointed his successor Frank Vanhecke. In the 1999 elections to the Belgian and European parliaments, the Vlaams Blok won over 15 percent of the votes. This made the VB Belgium's third-largest political party. Further successes in the 2000 local elections have encouraged the leadership. Filip Dewinter, the former head of the Vlaams Blok in Antwerp, is now the undisputed leader of the Vlaams Blok. The Vlaams Blok is still a long way from obtaining control of the government of Belgium, but it has been making steady inroads in the political support of the mainstream political parties.

Vlaams Blok's anti-immigrant stance has produced a reaction since 2002. Most of its anti-immigration agitation has been directed against Muslim immigrants. Antwerp has around 30,000 Muslims, most from Morocco. Militant Muslims have formed the Arab European League (AEL) under the leadership of Dyab Abou Jahjah, a former **Hezbollah** guerrilla from Lebanon. Clashes between the members of the VB and AEL have become violent. In November 2002, riots broke out in Antwerp after the murder of a Moroccan schoolteacher by a Belgian citizen. The anti-Israeli rhetoric of the AEL has caused much of Antwerp's Jewish population to become more sympathetic toward the Vlaams Blok and to vote for its candidates.

Vlaams Blok hit the headlines again in early September 2003 over the banning of a VB politician from the Scottish Parliament. Dominiek Lootens-Stael had violated diplomatic protocol by co-writing ill-conceived comments about the Scottish political system to Gavin Hewitt, the British ambassador to Belgium. This action led to the leaders of the Scottish Parliament to ban his scheduled visit to the parliament. Lootens-Stael protested this banning and traveled to Scotland to talk to the Scottish Parliament's Presiding Officer, but he was turned away.

Suggested readings: Corinna Da Fonseca-Wollheim, "Fear and Loathing in Antwerp," *Jerusalem Post* (January 17, 2003), p. 6B; Cas Mudde, *The Ideology of the Extreme Right* (Manchester, UK: Manchester University Press, 2000); Angus Roxburgh, "Belgian Far-Right Parades a New Nationalism That Barely Masks the Same Old Xenophobia," *Sunday Tribune* (London) (October 13, 2002), p. 22; Angus Roxburgh, *Preachers of Hate: The Rise of the Far Right* (London: Gibson Square Books, 2002); Martin Williams, "Belgium Drops Extremist from Delegation; Far-Right Politician Will Now Not Visit Parliament," *Herald* (Glasgow) (September 3, 2003), p. 9.

W

Wahhabism (Saudi Arabia)

Wahhabism is the most extreme form of Islamic fundamentalism prevalent in the Middle East. The inspiration and the theology for this movement came from the writings of Ibn Abdul Wahhab (1703–1792), a religious leader form the Najd area of present-day Saudi Arabia. He believed that the Islam of his day was corrupt and longed to return Islam to the purity of its original form. Wahhab attacked all ostentatious displays, from music to the celebration of Prophet Muhammad's birthday. Leaders of this movement have been intolerant of Islamic practices that do not meet its standards of religious behavior, and they have never been reluctant to use force or invoke the death penalty against those opposing their viewpoint. This puritanical sect had little political influence until the Arab Saud family adopted Wahhabism in the mid-eighteenth century. It became the ideology of Arab nationalism that was employed by Arab leaders to gain independence from the Ottoman Turkish empire. When the founder of Saudi Arabia, Ibn Saud, gained control of the religious centers of Mecca and Medina in the 1920s, he established Wahhabism as the official creed of the new state.

Wahhabism now dominates all aspects of Saudi life, from social relationships to the law. The religious police (*mutawwa*) in Saudi Arabia make certain that all Saudi citizens adhere to Wahhabi practices. Government authorities in Saudi Arabia persecute non-Wahhabi brands of Islam, including other Sunni sects. These officials give special attention to what the Wahhabis consider the "heretical Shi'ites."

Wahhabism has been exported by the Saudi royal government throughout the Middle East and to any place where Muslims reside. Members of the Saudi royal family have given huge sums of money to missions in Arab countries promoting Wahhabism. Stephen Schwartz, a Western critic of Wahhabism, reported in November 2001 that Wahhabism controlled 80 percent of the Muslim mosques in the United States because of Saudi financial support. Other converts to Wahhabism outside the Saudi royal family, and often in opposition to it, have also exported this ideology. Several terrorists, including **Osama bin Laden** and **Ayman al-Zawahiri**, subscribe to Wahhabi beliefs.

Suggested readings: Hamid Algar, *Wahhabism: A Critical Essay* (London: Islamic Publications International, 2002); Andrew Jack, Islamic Sect Made Scapegoat in Dagistan Turmoil," *Financial Times* (London) (September 28, 1999), p. 3; Stephen Schwartz, "This Business All Began in Saudi Arabia," *Sunday Telegraph* (London) (September 23, 2001), p. 20; Stephen

Schwartz, "Wahhabis in America," *Weekly Standard* (London) vol. 7 (November 5, 2001), p. 15; Levon Sevunts, "Saudi Wahhabi Sect Helped Put Taliban in Power," *Gazette* (Montreal) (December 12, 2001), p. B1; Mike Trickey, "Exporting Terror," *Ottawa Citizen* (October 1, 2001), p. A3; Bill Wallace, "Sect Drives Terror Group," *San Francisco Chronicle* (October 14, 2001), p. A18.

Wijeweera, Rohanna (1942–1989) (Sri Lanka)

Rohanna Wijeweera was the leader of the radical Sinhalese Maoist guerrilla group People's Revolutionary Front (Janata Vimukti Peramuna) (JVP) in Sri Lanka. He was born in 1942 in Kotagoda, a seaside fishing village in southern Sri Lanka. His father was a Communist Party activist. He attended school in Sri Lanka until his academic success won him a scholarship to study at Patrice Lumumba University in Moscow in 1961. His intention was to become a medical doctor, but during his stay in Moscow he decided to be a full-time revolutionary. After returning to Sri Lanka, he decided in 1963 to side with the Maoist wing of the Ceylon Communist Party in a doctrinal dispute and therefore was prevented from going back to the Soviet Union.

Wijeweera used the political discontent among the Sinhalese population in the 1960s to start a Maoist communist party. He founded the People's Revolutionary Front in 1967. His intent was to lead a revolution in Sri Lanka that would produce an economic society that would be a rejection of the international capitalist system. In March 1971, Wijeweera planned a revolutionary uprising. Police authorities learned about the uprising and arrested Wijeweera and over 4,000 suspects. The remaining elements of the JVP attempted an uprising on April 5, 1971, but they were brutally suppressed. Nearly 10,000 suspects were killed and another 18,000 arrested. Since best estimates placed the JVP at no more than 2,000 activists, this reaction on the part of the police exceeded the danger. An unrepentant Wijeweera remained in jail until he was paroled in 1977.

Wijeweera resumed leadership of the JVP in 1977. This time he decided to make the JVP into a political party. In 1982, he ran for president of Sri Lanka and made a respectable showing. In the aftermath of the 1983 anti-Tamil rioting in Colombo, the Sri Lanka government made the JVP a scapegoat and banned it as a political party. Wijeweera responded by taking the JVP underground. He began to transform the JVP from a Maoist communist party into a Sinhalese nationalist party with a strong anti-Tamil orientation. To accomplish this radical transformation, Wijeweera had to purge the JVP of hard-liners and old fighters. Once this had been accomplished, Wijeweera cultivated a personality cult identifying him with national Sinhalese heroes. His new goal was a purification of Sinhalese society and a return to a golden age.

Wijeweera directed the JVP in a civil war against the Sri Lankan government. For the next five years, the JVP controlled southern Sri Lanka through a terrorist campaign against the government. JVP's terrorism was becoming a greater threat than the **Liberation Tigers of Tamil Eelam** (LTTE). In a five-week period between August and September 1989, more than 5,000 killings took place. The government responded by employing death squads against known and suspected JVP activists. To ensure total commitment, the government negotiated a truce with the LTTE and turned all of its attention to suppressing the JVP. Government authorities arrested a JVP leader who under torture confessed that Wijeweera was living under an assumed name on a tea plantation near Kandy. Wijeweera was arrested on November 13, 1989, in the village of Ulapane and died shortly thereafter under mysterious circumstances. His death and the decimation of the JVP's leadership ended the group's control of southern Sri Lanka, and it slowly withered away.

Suggested readings: Steve Coll, "Silence in the Killing Zone," *Washington Post* (January 16, 1994), p. W16; William McGowan, *Only Man Is Vile: The Tragedy of Sri Lanka* (New York: Farrar, Straus & Giroux, 1992); Feizal Samath,

"Rebel's Death Fails to End Sri Lankan Violence," *Toronto Star* (December 27, 1989), p. A29; Jon Swain, "Sri Lanka Reels under Terrorist Onslaught," *Times* (London) (November 27, 1988), p. 1.

World Trade Center Bombing (United States)

The World Trade Center bombing on February 26, 1993, was the first major terrorist operation in the United States by Middle East terrorists. This target had been selected because the World Trade Center was a symbol of American economic success. **Ramzi Yousef** was in charge of the operation. He was an explosives expert and he prepared the nitroglycerine to bring down the twin towers of the World Trade Center. His delivery vehicle was a medium-sized Ryder van. By parking the van in the underground garage, Yousef hoped the explosive pressure would be enough to accomplish his mission.

The bombing proved to be deadly but not strong enough to destroy the World Trade Center. The explosion took place at 12:17 P.M. at lunchtime, thereby unintentionally limiting the number of casualties to six but wounding another 1,042. Initially, authorities surmised that it was a transformer explosion, but the massive damage soon convinced the FBI and the New York Police Department (NYPD) that it was a bomb of some kind. The Joint Terrorist Task Force (JTTF) assumed control of the investigation jurisdiction until it was proved that the explosion had been a terrorist bombing, and then the FBI took over the investigation. A search of the garage produced a part of the Ryder bomb vehicle that had a VIN (vehicle identification number). A search of records found that the part came from a Ryder van rented to Muhammad Salameh with a New Jersey address. After arresting Salameh, FBI agents found a bomb-making apparatus at a New Jersey storage unit. From telephone records, FBI agents were able to trace the group that had built and exploded the bomb.

Yousef made his escape, but the remaining members of the conspiracy were caught.

Ahmad Muhammad Ajaj, Nidal Ayyad, Mahmud Abu Halima, and Muhammad Salameh each received prison sentences of 240 years after a March 4, 1994, jury conviction. It was not until February 7, 1995, that American agents were able to apprehend Yousef in Peshawar, Pakistan. His trial in 1996 ended with a conviction and he joined **Sheikh Omar Abdel-Rahman** in a maximum-security prison with a life sentence. **See also** Yousef, Ramzi Ahmed.

Suggested readings: Russ Baker, "I Am a Terrorist and Proud of It," *Weekend Australian* (Sydney) (November 3, 2001), p. M36; J. Bowyer Bell, *Murders on the Nile: The World Trade Center and Global Terror* (San Francisco, CA: Encounter Books, 2003); Peter Caram, *The 1993 World Trade Center Bombing: Foresight and Warning* (London: Janus Publishing, 2001).

Wright, Billy "King Rat" (1960–1997) (Northern Ireland)

Billy "King Rat" Wright was the leader of the **Ulster Freedom Fighters** (UFF) and later the head of the Loyalist Volunteer Force (LUF). He was born in 1960 in Wolverhampton, England, but his family had originally come from Northern Ireland. After his mother left his father, Wright and his four sisters were sent to Northern Ireland while his father remained in England. He was brought up in an orphanage before living with an aunt in Portadown. In 1974, he joined the Young Citizens Volunteer Force, the youth wing of the **Ulster Volunteer Force** (UVF). Wright received training in weapons and explosives. During the following year, Wright joined the UVF as a full-fledged member. His activities in the UVF led to his arrest in 1977 for possession of weapons and hijacking a van. Wright received a six-year prison term, but he was released on parole in 1980. After only a few months out of prison, Wright was arrested again on murder charges. This time he served almost two years in prison, but he was released without a trial in 1982. Wright was arrested again months later on suspicion of weapons possession. He spent 14 months in prison before a trial was held and he was found not guilty.

Wright decided to settle down in Portadown. He married a local girl and opened a grocery store. Despite this business, he remained an active member of the UVF and Ulster police kept a close watch on him. Several times, Provisional Irish Republican Army (Provos) elements tried to assassinate him. These attacks and police raids caused him to close his grocery store and his marriage failed.

Wright then became the militant leader of the Ulster Volunteer Force. His reputation for violence was unequalled among the Protestant loyalists. During his leadership, the UVF killed at least 40 Catholics. Some were Provos, but others were retaliation killings. Wright used the media to build his reputation by his willingness to speak on the record. He believed that the war in Northern Ireland was an ethnic struggle between the Catholics and the Protestants with no moral restraints on either side allowed. His initial response to the Provisional IRA's cease-fire in 1994 was to accept it at face value. Soon, however, he decided that the peace process was only a cover for British disengagement from Northern Ireland. Wright became disillusioned with the UVF's cease-fire and he decided to force the issue by ordering his men to murder a Catholic taxi driver. This action led the UVF to expel him and threatened him with death.

Wright founded the Loyalist Volunteer Front (LVF) in July 1996 as a rival group to the UVF. Leaders of the UVF considered the foundation of this group to be a betrayal and he was given an ultimatum of leaving Northern Ireland or death. He ignored the threat. Wright was arrested in 1996 for an assault on a Catholic woman. He received a six-year prison sentence and was sent to the H-Block 6 of the Maze prison. Wright continued to direct the affairs of the LVF from prison. On December 27, 1997, prison authorities informed him of a visitor at the prison. During the trip to the reception center in a prison van, Wright was shot six times and killed by Christopher McWilliams, a member of the Irish National Liberation Army (INLA) who had escaped from his prison cell. His death led to reprisals against Catholics in Northern Ireland by his loyalist followers. Both Catholic and Protestant leaders, however, were relieved that one of the major obstacles to peace in Northern Ireland had been removed. **See also** Ulster Volunteer Force (UVF).

Suggested readings: Steve Bruce, "In Death, King Rat May Win His Battle," *Herald* (Glasgow) (December 30, 1997), p. 11; Rosie Cowan, "Ceaseless Quest of King Rat's Father," *Guardian* (London) (December 27, 2000), p. 5; Alison Hardie and Denis Campbell, "Security Questions as Assassination Visits H-Blocks," *Herald* (Glasgow) (December 29, 1997), p. 2; Peter Taylor, *Loyalists: War and Peace in Northern Ireland* (New York: TV Books, 1999).

Y

Yassin, Sheikh Ahmed (1936–) (Palestine)

Sheikh Ahmed Yassin is the founder of the militant Palestinian Islamic fundamentalist group Hamas. He was born in the village of Joura near Ashkelon, Israel. His family moved to the Gaza Strip in 1947. His father was a farmer and a strict Muslim. In 1948, Yassin and his family had to flee Joura because of the Arab-Israeli War and they ended up in a Gaza refugee camp. In 1952, an accident left him with a broken back and partially paralyzed. For a number of years, Yassin could walk with the aid of crutches, but since the mid-1980s he has been restricted to a wheelchair. He attended **al-Azhar University** in Cairo, where he earned a bachelor's degree in Arabic literature. While at the university, Yassin became a member of the **Muslim Brotherhood.**

Soon after returning to Palestine, Yassin became one of the leading Islamist leaders among the Palestinians. His first position was as a teacher in an elementary school, but soon he started preaching in a local mosque. Yassin's reputation for piety and his unrelenting hostility toward Israel made him an important figure among the Palestinians. His disabilities, including blindness in one eye, only increased his prestige among the militants. Yassin's militancy led to his arrest by

Israeli authorities in 1984. He was convicted of stockpiling weapons and sentenced by an Israeli military court to 13 years in prison. After only 13 months in prison, Yassin was released along with others who were exchanged in the 1985 swap of Palestinian prisoners for three Israeli soldiers.

Shortly after the outbreak of the **Intifada** in December 1987, Yassin and seven other Palestinian members of the Muslim Brotherhood started **Hamas.** These leaders followed the example of the Egyptian Muslim Brotherhood and sponsored special charities, medical clinics, mosques, and orphanages. This was the only social support system in the Gaza Strip. Israeli authorities saw it at first as an alternative to the **Palestine Liberation Organization** (PLO), but before long they lost control of it.

Yassin has supported the military wing of Hamas as it has carried out terrorist attacks on Israel. Israeli authorities arrested Yassin in 1989 for his complicity in the kidnapping and killing of two Israeli soldiers. He was sentenced to life plus 15 years. His reputation increased among his followers during his imprisonment, and the Israeli government decided to release him on October 6, 1997. The Israeli government was fearful that he would die in prison and his martyrdom would only intensify Palestinian hatred

Iranian president Mohammad Khatami, right, meets with Sheikh Ahmed Yassin, the head of the Palestinian militant group Hamas, in Tehran, May 2, 1998. Hamas and Iran oppose the Israeli-Palestinian peace agreements. They call for the destruction of the Jewish state, which they believe was created on Palestinian land. Hamas has carried out several suicide attacks in Israel since 1994, killing scores of Israelis. (AP Photo/Canadian Press, Mohammad Sayyad)

of the Israelis. Since his release, Yassin has remained implacable in his opposition to Israel and the United States. He has deemed the suicide missions, or what he calls "martyrdom operations," as justified because Israel is a "nation at arms," meaning that there are no civilians. Yassin's opposition to any settlement with Israel has made him a vocal opponent of **Yasser Arafat** and the Palestinian Authority. He has opposed any settlement that does not include the right of Palestinians to return to their villages in Israel. Attempts in the spring of 2003 to end the stalemate between the Israelis and the Palestinians met with his scorn. His opposition to peace overtures with Israel led the Israelis to target him for assassination in August 2003, but all attempts have failed. In a January 2004 statement, Israeli Deputy Defense Minister Zeev Boim made it plain that Yassin is marked for death. **See also** Arafat, Mohammed Yasser; Hamas (Haarakat al-Muqawama al-Islami) (Islamic Resistance Movement); Muslim Brotherhood (al-Ikhwan al-Muslimun); Palestine Liberation Organization (PLO).

Suggested readings: Ken Ellingwood, "Hamas Founder Shrugs Off Israeli Assassination Threats," *Los Angeles Times* [January 17, 2004), p. 3; Nicolas Goldberg, "The Enigmatic Face of Hamas," *Newsday* (New York) (October 14, 1997), p. A3; Michael Parks, "Sheik Ahmed Ismael Yassin," *Los Angeles Times* (March 7, 1995); Fathi Sabbah, "Hamas' Sheikh Yassin: 'Reform According to Israeli Criteria Becomes Corruption.'" *Mideast Mirror* (May 22, 2002), p. 1; Deborah Sontag, "Freed Palestinian Militant Leader Calls for Holy War against Israel," *New York Times* (December 28, 1998), sec. A, p. 1; Khaled Abu Toameh, "Arafat's New Rival," *Jerusalem Report* (October 30, 1997), p. 18.

Yousef, Ramzi Ahmed (1968–) (Pakistan)
Ramzi Ahmed Yousef was the leader of the group of terrorists who exploded a bomb at the World Trade Center in New York City in 1993. He was born Abdul-Basit Mahmud Abdul-Karim on April 27, 1968, in the Kuwaiti oil town of Fuhayhil. His father was an engineer from the Baluchistan region of Pakistan who worked for Kuwaiti Airlines, and his mother was a Kuwaiti of Palestinian origin. The father was a Baluchi nationalist and a Sunni Muslim who hated Shi'ites. Yousef was exposed to his father's puritanical Wahhabi viewpoint at an early age. At school, Yousef was a good student with an aptitude for the study of English and the sciences. In early 1986, Yousef and his family moved to Turbat in the Baluchistan area of Pakistan. Yousef wanted to continue his education, so in November 1986, he traveled to Oxford, England, where he attended the Oxford College of Further Education. In 1987, Yousef enrolled in the Swansea Institute (then the West Glamorgan Institute of Higher Education) in South Wales, where he studied computer-aided electrical engineering. He also made contact with other foreign students, including members of the Egyptian **Muslim Brotherhood**. In the summer of 1988, Youssef left Swansea and traveled to Afghanistan to join the mujahideen fighting against the Soviet forces. His tour of service there was at an **Osama bin Laden** training camp in Peshawar, Pakistan, teaching electronics and learning bomb-making techniques. In September 1988, he returned to Swansea to finish his education. After his graduation in the spring of 1989, with a diploma in computer-aided electrical engineering, he found a job in Kuwait in the Planning Ministry. Yousef was in Kuwait during the Iraqi invasion, but his activities during the Iraqi occupation remain unclear. Kuwait authorities have accused Yousef of collaborating with the Iraqis.

Yousef became a terrorist in the early 1990s. He had Islamist tendencies, but his motivation appears to have been more political than religious. His primary motivation was to support the Palestinian struggle against Israel and the United States. By 1991, Yousef had returned to Pakistan, where he joined Abdul Rasul Sayyaf's Islamic Alliance. He also reestablished contact with bin Laden's group and formed a friendship with **Abdurajak Abubakar Janjalani,** the founder of the Philippine **Abu Sayyaf** terrorist group. He traveled to the Philippines and for three months trained Abu Sayyaf members on making and using explosives.

In September 1992, Yousef entered the United States on a mission. His mission was to build a team of Islamic extremists in the United States to carry out military operations. Yousef made contact with fellow Islamists at the Alkifah Refugee Center in New York City. He renewed his acquaintanceship with Mahmud Abouhalime, an old friend from the Afghan War. He also met with **Sheikh Omar Abdel-Rahman**. Yousef assumed leadership of the conspiracy to bring terrorism to the United States and began to recruit members, but most of them were untrained and made a series of mistakes. These recruits joined the terrorist mission because of their bitter anti-Americanism and their Palestinian militancy. After collecting the chemicals to make a bomb, Yousef and his compatriots rented a Ryder van in late February 1993 and loaded the bomb into it. The bomb exploded in the basement of the World Trade Center on February 26, 1993. His intent was to kill the maximum number of people, but the explosion killed six and injured over one thousand. Shortly after the bomb exploded, Yousef flew out of New York City and back to Pakistan. He was disappointed in the results of the bombing because it failed to bring down the Twin Towers and kill hundreds of thousands of Americans. After the bomb plot was exposed, his co-conspirators implicated Yousef in the bombing and U.S. authorities made his arrest a high priority.

Yousef had developed close ties with members of the Philippines terrorist group **Abu Sayyaf** during his days in Afghanistan. In 1994, he moved to Manila, Philippines, to work with fellow terrorists in a plot to blow up U.S. commercial airliners. His most ambitious scheme was to assassinate Pope John Paul II during his visit to the Philippines on January 15, 1995. Shortly before this plan was to be implemented, on January 6, 1995, a chemical explosion in a Manila apartment frustrated this plot. Yousef fled the apartment, but the plans for the operation were captured. Another scheme captured was a plan to assassinate Pope John Paul II. Yousef returned to Pakistan, staying in Qaeda safe houses. On the evening of February 7, 1995, Pakistani authorities arrested Yousef in Islamabad, Pakistan, after receiving a tip on his location from a former accomplice. Pakistan extradited Yousef to the United States to stand trial of the 1993 World Trade Center bombing.

After he was returned to the United States, Yousef stood trial for his role in the Manila airline conspiracy and the World Trade Center bombing. He decided to defend himself in the trial for the Manila airline conspiracy

even thought the trial judge admonished him to have a lawyer. A jury convicted him on September 5, 1996, and the court sentenced Yousef to life imprisonment in solitary confinement without the possibility of parole. A second trial for the World Trade Center bombing started shortly afterward. This time a lawyer represented Yousef, but the results were the same. A witness testified that Yousef wanted to blow up the World Trade Center to let Americans know that they were at war with Islam and to punish the U.S. government for its support of Israel. A jury convicted him on February 12, 1997, on all counts. The judge sentenced him to 240 years in prison, imposed restrictions on his visitors, and fined him $4.5 million. Yousef was sent to the Federal Maximum Facility in Florence, Colorado, where he is kept in solitary confinement. Despite efforts by U.S. authorities, Yousef has never revealed his associates or those who financed his operations. **See also** Abdel-Rahman, Sheikh Omar; World Trade Center Bombing.

Suggested readings: Russ Baker, "I Am a Terrorist and Proud of It," *The Weekend Australian* (Sydney) (November 2, 2001), p. M36; J. Bowyer Bell, *Murders on the Nile: The World Trade Center and Global Terror* (San Francisco, CA: Encounter Books, 2003); Maria A. Ressa, *Seeds of Terror: An Eyewitness Account of Al-Qaeda's Newest Center of Operations in Southeast Asia* (New York: Free Press, 2003); Simon Reeve, *The New Jackals: Ramzi Yousef, Osama Bin Laden and the Future of Terrorism* (Boston: Northeastern University Press, 1999); Mary Anne Weaver, *A Portrait of Egypt: A Journey through the World of Militant Islam* (New York: Farrar, Straus & Giroux, 1999).

Z

Zapatista Army of National Liberation (Ejercito Zapatista de Liberación) (EZLN) (Mexico)

The Zapatista Army of National Liberation (Ejercito Zapatista de Liberación, or EZLN) is the Indian organization that has led the Chiapas Rebellion in Mexico since 1994. Chiapas is one of Mexico's poorest regions, and the indigenous population of Mayan Indian groups has had a long history of rebellions against the state dating back to colonial times. Land redistribution problems and a combination of a growing population and immigrants from Guatemala are reasons for modern discontent. Open hostilities between the owners of large estates and both Indian landowners of smaller plots and the landless have also caused tensions. Two other factors came together in 1993 that precipitated an uprising in Chiapas—Mexican President Salinas de Gortari's decision to amend Article 27 of the Mexican Constitution to end land redistribution and the passage of the North American Free Trade Agreement (NAFTA). Several Indian organizations had organized in the 1980s to deal with regional economic and social issues.

The most militant of these Indian organizations is the Zapatista Army of National Liberation. Three Indians and three Mestizos founded the EZLN on November 17, 1983. EZLN's name comes from Emiliano Zapata, the peasant leader in the Mexican Revolution of 1910 and advocate of peasant land reform. This group grew slowly and had only about 60 members by 1986. Leaders of the EZLN decided to give military grassroots control to local inhabitants and coordinate these local military units through a centralized committee, the Clandestine Indian Revolutionary Committee (CCRI). The CCRI is composed mostly from representatives from indigenous groups—Chol, Mam, Tzotze, Tzeltal, Tojolabal, and Zoque. This committee selected a non-Indian, who went by the name of Subcommander Marcos, to serve as their spokesperson. Subcommander Marcos was **Rafael Sebastián Guillén Vicente**, a former philosopher professor from Tampico. He and the rest of the EZLN wore black masks to confuse identification. By the early 1990s, large numbers of Indians started arming themselves and training in the use of weapons. A shortage of weapons was always a problem for the EZLN because it lacked the funds and the contacts to buy weapons. Members have had to depend on seizing guns from drug dealers and ranchers. Estimates have placed the number of EZLN troops under arms in 1993 at 8,000. Two-thirds of the troops were men and one-third women. The de facto capital of the EZLN was established at Guadeloupe Tepeyac in eastern Chiapas.

Zapatista military leader Marcos, center, walks with a security detail around the grounds of the meeting site between the Zapatista command and the CONAI, the mediation group involved in the peace talks headed by Samuel Ruiz Garcia Obispo of Chiapas, and the COMCOPA, the government's mediating body in La Realidad, September 30, 1995. This gathering, which laid the foundation for the next round of peace talks on October 2, 1995, was the largest public gathering of Zapatista military and leadership in over a year. (AP Photo/Scott Sady)

The Zapatista Army of National Liberation opened hostilities on January 1, 1994. Armed men and women seized the town of San Cristobal de la Casas and the municipal seats in Ocosingo, Las Margaritas, and Altamirano. Insurgents destroyed land records and released prisoners from jails. Mexican military and police counterattacked throughout the next week and by the second week of January, open combat had ceased in Chiapas. In the meantime, the Mexican army had moved 17,000 troops into Chiapas. Casualties on the government side numbered 159, but on the rebels' side, 500 died, 300 disappeared, 370 were taken prisoners, and 50 were wounded.

The Chiapas Rebellion shook up the Mexican government of President Salinas, which decided to negotiate with the EZLN. Negotiations opened in San Cristobal de la Casas on February 22, 1994. A tentative accord was reached in 10 days with considerable concessions, including amnesty, given by the Mexican government's representative. This accord, however, collapsed after the assassination in Tijuana of the presidential candidate Luis Donaldo Colosio on March 23, 1994, and the resulting backlash by

Chiapas businessmen, ranchers, and politicians. Leaders of the EZLN began to remobilize its army. Landless Indians started appropriating lands from large estates. Ranchers claimed that squatters had occupied 2,157 estates. On April 22, 1994, the leadership of the EZLN formally rejected the February accords stating that 97.88 percent of its followers had voted to reject the accords for not going far enough to promote democracy. At the same time, these leaders declared that the EZLN would maintain the cease-fire. On August 6, 1994, the EZLN held a convention in San Cristobal de la Casas attended by 6,000 delegates with the goal of reforming the Mexican government. After moving to Aguacalientes, the delegates, 40 percent of whom were women, debated revolutionary reforms. On December 19, 1994, the Zapatistas declared the establishment of 38 autonomous municipalities in a direct challenge to the Mexican government. In February 1996, the Mexican government and the EZLN signed the San Andres Accords, which promised autonomy for local communities in Chiapas.

In the 10 years following the Zapatista rebellion, various Mexican governments tried curtail the rebellion by first suppressing it and then negotiating with its leaders. Mexican paramilitary organizations formed in the mid-1990s to fight against the Zapatistas. One such group massacred 45 refugees in Acteal, municipality of Chenalho, on December 22, 1997. A leading spokesperson for the EZLN has remained Subcomandante Marcos. He and the other leaders have been pursuing political rather than military goals. The government of President Vicente Fox conducted the latest attempt at negotiations with the EZLN. Following the lead of a Peace Commission, Fox sent a bill on indigenous rights to the Mexican Congress in 2001 that would allow indigenous people control of natural resources on their lands, local tradition courts, and limited political autonomy. Deputies in the Congress refused to go along and reduced the rights to be granted in the package. This action and a subsequent negative Mexican Supreme Court ruling caused the EZLN to threaten to resume military operations. This shift in tactics, however, did not take place; instead, local communities began to implement the San Andres Accords for local autonomy by setting up local municipal governments independent of the Mexican state. By isolating themselves in Chiapas' mountains and jungles, which border Guatemala, the Zapatistas have been able to isolate their communities from the Mexican government. This tactic has worked against the Mexican government, but it has not eased the low standards of living of the inhabitants of these communities. **See also** Guillén Vicente, Rafael Sebastián.

Suggested readings: Diego Cevallos, "Zapatistas' Subcomandante Marcos—A Fading Star," Inter Press Service (May 17, 2003), p. 1; Linda Diebel, "Inside Mexico's Rebellion," *Ottawa Citizen* (April 10, 1994), p. E1; Susan Ferris, "Broken Promises: How Economic Reforms Have Failed Mexico," *Austin American-Statesman* [Texas] (December 26, 2003), p. A33; Phil Gunson, "Living on the Edge of a Political Volcano," *Guardian* (London) (August 13, 1994), p. 11; Patrick McDonnell, "The Roots of the Rebellion," *Los Angeles Times* (March 6, 1994), p. 30; Matthew MacLean, "Zapatistas Focus on Politics, Not Conflict," *Christian Science Monitor* (August 18, 2003), p. 10; Dan Murphy, "Reforms Falter for Mexican Indians," *Christian Science Monitor* (September 5, 2001), p. 6; Philip L. Russell, *The Chiapas Rebellion* (Austin, TX: Mexico Resource Center, 1995); Bill Weinberg, "Mexico's Dirty War; Six Years after the Zapatists Uprising," *In These Times* (February 21, 2000), p. 14; John Womack, *Rebellion in Chiapas: An Historical Reader* (New York: New Press, 1999).

Al-Zarqawi, Abu Musab (1966–) (Jordan)

Abu Musab al-Zarqawi is one of the leaders of the Iraqi resistance against American occupation forces. He was born in 1966 in Zarqa, Jordan, with the birth name Ahmad Fadeel Nazzal al-Khalayleh. Zarqa is a small village about 25 miles north of Jordan's capital, Amman. His family belongs to the prominent but poor Bedouin tribe Bani Hassan. Al-Zarqawi earned a high school diploma from Zarqa, but he had difficulty finding work in Jordan. Deeply religious, he decided to go to Afghanistan in 1987 and fight the Soviet military forces there. He led a small band of Jordanians to Afghanistan. In the training camps in Afghanistan al-Zarqawi learned to handle explosives and poisons. After the end of the war, al-Zarqawi returned to Jordan in 1992. Soon afterwards, Jordanian police arrested him for working with groups plotting to overthrow the Jordanian monarchy and establishing an Islamic state. Al-Zarqawi spent the period from 1992 to 1997 in a Jordanian prison. After his release, al-Zarqawi resumed his anti-Jordanian activities. Jordanian authorities were about to arrest him for planning a gas attack on American and Israeli tourists in 1999, when al-Zarqawi fled to Afghanistan. Finding the **Taliban** regime to his liking, al-Zarqawi worked in a training camp instructing trainees in explosives and chemicals.

Al-Zarqawi's stay in Afghanistan ended with the fall of the Taliban regime. He was seriously wounded in an American bombing attack in Afghanistan that cost him a leg. In the spring of 2002 al-Zarqawi had a prosthetic leg fitted in Baghdad, Iraq. This handicap did not prevent him from forming a terrorist group, Al Tawhid. His intent was to carry out terrorist activities in Europe and the Middle East. Al-Zarqawi's group has been implicated in bombings in Turkey and Morocco, and with the assassination of Laurence Foley, an administer of U.S. aid programs in Jordan, in Amman, Jordan, on October 28, 2002.

In May 2003, al-Zarqawi moved his operations to Iraq. His whereabouts in Iraq remains a mystery, but he has been able to build a network of terrorists within Iraq that has undertaken guerrilla operations against American and British forces. Among the operations that American intelligence believe that al-Zarqawi is responsible for were the August 19, 2003, truck bombing of the United Nations headquarters in Baghdad that killed Sergio Vieira de Mello, the top UN representative in Iraq, 22 others, and wounded more than 150; the Au-

gust 29, 2003, car bombing outside the Imam Ali Mosque in the Shi'ite Muslim holy city of Najaf that killed the Ayataollah Mohammed Baquir al-Hakim and 85 others; and the November 12, 2003, suicide truck bombing of the Italian police headquarters in Nasiriyah that killed 30, including 19 Italians. In a 17-page document captured in an early February 2004 raid of a Qaeda safe house, al-Zarqawi outlined his strategy to attack Iraq's Shi'ite targets to provoke them into attacking Iraq's Sunnis. This document was also an appeal from al-Zarqawi for help from **al-Qaeda**. On February 5, 2004, U.S. Secretary of State Colin Powell linked al-Zarqawi with **Osama bin Laden** and al-Qaeda. This linkage is controversial, because many Western intelligence agents question whether al-Zarqawi and his terrorist group are part of al-Qaeda or operate independently. Regardless of his affiliations, al-Zarqawi is a wanted man and the United States has placed a $10 million reward for information leading to his capture or death. Al-Zarqawi's expertise in chemical weapons is what worries American intelligence the most. **See also** Bin Laden, Osama; Al-Qaeda.

Suggested readings: Jason Burke, "Crisis in Iraq: Countdown to Conflict: Terror Chief Not Key to 'Iraq Connection,'" *Observer* [London] (February 9, 2003), p. 17; Rosie DiManno, "Family Denies Suspect Is Terror Alchemist," *Toronto Star* (March 7, 2003), p. A1; Dexter Filkins, "Memo Asks Qaeda to Help Wage War in Iraq," *International Herald Tribune* [New York] (February 11, 2004), p. 1; Jamal Halaby, "Abu Musaab al-Zarqawi, a Fanatic Muslim with Poison Gas Expertise," *Associated Press Worldstream* (February 5, 2003), p. 1; James Hider, "Arab Terrorist Blamed by US for Fomenting Iraq Civil War," *Times* [London] (February 12, 2004), p. 1; Kent Kilpatrick, "Extremist Jordanian Suspected in Terror Operations from Iraq to Britain," *Associated Press* (February 11, 2004), p. 1; Shafika Mattar, "Jordanian Terror Suspect Is a Modest Religious Man, Has No Knowledge of Poisons, Explosives, His Mother Says," *Associated Press Worldstream* (February 6, 2003), p. 1; Don Van Natta and David Johston, "A Terror Lieutenant with a Deadly Past," *New York Times* (February 10, 2003).

Al-Zawahiri, Ayman Muhammad Rabi (1951–) (Egypt)

Ayman al-Zawahiri is the second most important member of the **al-Qaeda** network of terrorist organizations. He was born on June 9, 1951, in al-Sharquiyyah, Egypt, into a prominent family. His father was a professor at Cairo University's medical school. At an early age, al-Zawahiri joined the Muslim Brotherhood. His first arrest for political agitation was in 1966 at the age of 15. By that time al-Zawahiri was a disciple of the Islamist thinker **Sayyid Qutb**. After studying medicine at the University of Cairo, he qualified as a physician in 1974. In 1978, he received a master's degree in surgical medicine. In 1984, he assumed the leadership of the militant Islamist group **Islamic Jihad** soon after its head, Lieutenant-Colonel Abbud al-Zumur, had been arrested. He was tried and acquitted for participation in the assassination plot against President Anwar Sadat. Later, he served a three-year prison sentence for illegal possession of arms. Al-Zawahiri fled Egypt in the middle of President Hosni Mubarak's purge of Egyptian dissidents in 1985. After arriving in Pakistan, al-Zawahiri started coordinating activities for the Afghan resistance against the Soviet Union. It was at this time that he became acquainted with and then allied with **Osama bin Laden**. This association continued after the end of the Afghan-Soviet war.

Al-Zawahiri served as the chief advisor to bin Laden in the creation of the al-Qaeda network. He aided the opposition in the Somalian fight against the American intervention. After U.S. forces left Somalia, al-Zawahiri was active in building support for the Bosnian Muslims in their separatist war against Yugoslavia. Next, al-Zawahiri coordinated aid for Albanian Muslims in the Kosovo war. These efforts were part of al-Zawahiri's responsibilities in al-Qaeda, but his main job was to set up terrorist operations in Europe and the United States. Terrorist bases were organized in various European countries and also in the United States, replacing Abdel-Rahman's organization. By the mid-1990s, these terrorist bases were operational.

Al-Zwarahiri visited the United States to inspect operations in 1995. His contacts were **Ali A. Mohamed**, an Egyptian who had served as a sergeant in the U.S. Army, and Khalid al-Sayyid Ali Abu-al-Dahab, an Egyptian-born American citizen. His inspection tour convinced him that major terrorist activities could be undertaken against American targets.

After his American tour, the Islamist movement gave al-Zawahiri the assignment to assassinate President Mubarak of Egypt. The leaders of the Islamist movement believed that because Egypt's strategic position and its size that it was the key to the success of the Islamist movement in the Middle East and Mubarak's death would also destabilize Saudi Arabia. After elaborate plans backfired, Mubarak escaped the deathtrap in Addis Ababa, Ethiopia. Al-Zawahiri returned to Afghanistan to serve as second-in-command to bin Laden. He remained in this position during the planning for the **September 11, 2001,** mission in the United States. American authorities suspected that al-Zawahiri had a role in the September 11th attack and placed a $5 million bounty on him for information that could lead to his capture. After the defeat of the **Taliban** and the fall of Afghanistan, al-Zawahiri disappeared along with bin Laden. He reappeared in May 2003 on an audiotape that called upon Muslims to attack America and the West. Al-Zawahiri then appeared on an audiotape with Osama bin Laden on September 10, 2003, exhorting Iraqi resistance fighters to defeat American forces in Iraq. **See also** Bin Laden, Osama; Islamic Jihad; Al-Qaeda (The Base); Qutb, Sayyid.

Suggested readings: Elise Ackerman, "Zawahiri: Thinker, Poet, Bin Laden's Chief Deputy," *Charleston Gazette* (West Virginia) (December 23, 2001), p. 9A; Mohamad Bazzi, "America's Ordeal; Bin Laden's 'Logistical Mastermind,'" *Newsday* (New York) (September 21, 2001), p. A6; J. Bowyer Bell, *Murders on the Nile: The World Trade Center and Global Terror* (San Francisco, CA: Encounter Books, 2003);

March Erikson, "Islamism, Fascism and Terrorism," *Asia Times Online,* http://www.atimes.com/atimes/Middle East/ (accessed November 8, 2002); Rohan Gunaratna, *Inside Al Qaeda: Global Network of Terror* (New York: Columbia University Press, 2002); Douglas Jehl, "Egyptian Seen as Top Aide and Successor to Bin Laden," *New York Times* (September 24, 2001), p. B1; Anton La Guardia, "Bin Laden Henchman Sends an Ominous Signal," *Daily Telegraph* (London) (May 22, 2003), p. 4.

Zhirinovsky, Vladimir Volfovich (1946–) (Russia)

Vladimir Zhirinovsky is the leading neofascist politician in Russia and the leader of the Liberal Democratic Party of Russia (LDPR). He was born in Alma-Ata, Kazakhstan, on April 25, 1946. His father was Volf Isaakovich Eidelstein, a Polish Jewish lawyer. His mother was a Russian. Shortly after he was born, his father died in an automobile accident. Zhirinovsky attended a school in Almaty and was an active member of the Komsomol, the communist youth organization. He had difficulty coping in school because of his Jewish background. In 1964, he graduated from high school and changed his name from Eidelstein to his mother's name, Zhirinovsky. In the summer of 1964, Zhirinovsky moved to Moscow and attended the Moscow University Institute of Asian and African Studies, where he specialized in studying Turkish affairs. In 1969, he traveled to Turkey to work as a combination interpreter-translator at the Iskenderun Iron and Steel Joint Soviet-Turkish Works. His stay in Turkey was brief, however, as Turkish authorities arrested him for espionage and deported him. Soviet authorities considered him politically unreliable and refused him admittance to membership in the Communist Party. Nevertheless, he graduated from Moscow University in 1971 with honors. Soon after graduation, Zhirinovsky was drafted into the Soviet army. He served as an officer in the Transcaucasian Military District at Tbilisi, Georgia, for two years before being discharged as a captain in 1973. He held a variety of jobs while studying law at Moscow State University night school. In 1977, Zhirinovsky obtained a law degree. He then took a position as vice president at the Higher School of the Trade Union Movement where he remained until 1983. Zhirinovsky's next job was head of the law department at the Mir Publishing House where he stayed until he entered politics.

In 1988, Zhirinovsky decided to enter politics. He founded the Liberal Democratic Party of Russia (LDPR) in December 1989 and became its head at the March 1990 Congress. The LDPR was the second party officially registered in Russia. Zhirinovsky's call to Russian nationalism garnered him almost 8 percent of the vote in the June 1991 presidential elections, finishing third in the election. Help in making Zhirinovsky acceptable to the Russian right wing came from **Eduard Limonov**, the novelist and head of the National Bolshevik Front. Zhirinovsky's position in Russian politics improved in the December 1993 parliamentary elections when the LDPR captured nearly one quarter of the electoral and elected 64 deputies to the Duma. His efforts in the December 1995 elections resulted in a drop in popular appeal, but the LDPR still won 51 seats in the Duma. Zhirinovsky ran for the presidency in the June 1996 elections, but the result was less than 6 percent of the vote. His political strength fell during the late 1990s because of his disqualification and the disqualifications of his running mates for not reporting properly before elections.

Zhirinovsky is still a political force in Russia because of the popularity of his extremist views. He stands for the re-creation of the Russian empire by a large-scale southward expansion. His vision includes includes access to the Indian Ocean and the Mediterranean Ocean. An expansion of this nature means that the Russian army would have be expanded and used in the drive to the south. Russia's sphere of control would have to include Afghanistan, Iran, and Turkey. Central Europe would be divided between Germany and Russia, and Poland would no longer exist. He has supported the war in Chechnya, because it coincides with his drive to the south. Zhirinovsky believes that the United States is too passive to interfere with the creation of a Russian empire.

Besides his geopolitical schemes, Zhirinovsky is also controversial because of his anti-Semitic views and statements. He has charged that Russian Jews have been disloyal to Russia. One of his more extreme demands has been for Jews to be segregated on reservations. He has also refused to honor Holocaust victims. His views have not modified despite his admittance in 2001 that his father was a Polish Jew who had escaped from the Nazis in 1939. His anti-Semitism and other right-wing views have made him popular among other European right-wing leaders, including France's **Jean-Marie Le Pen**. His popularity with other right-wing extremists, however, has deteriorated because of what they consider his erratic behavior. **See also** Le Pen, Jean-Marie; Limonov, Eduard.

Suggested readings: Susan B. Glasser, "Russian Revises His Heritage; Anti-Semitic Politician Zhirinovsky Admits Father Was Jewish," *Washington Post* (July 17, 2001), p. A13; Vladimir Kartsev, *Zhirinovsky!* (New York: Columbia University Press, 1995); Martin A. Lee, *The Beast Reawakens* (Boston: Little, Brown, 1997); Stephen D. Shenfield, *Russian Fascism: Traditions, Tendencies, Movements* (Armonk, NY: M. E. Sharpe, 2001); Mark Smith, "The Last Dash South—The Geopolitics of Vladimir Zhirinovsky," *Jane's Intelligence Review* 6, no. 6 (June 1, 1994), p. 250; Vladimir Solovyov and Elena Klepikova, *Zhirinovsky: Russian Fascism and the Making of a Dictator* (Reading, MA: Addison-Wesley, 1995).

Selected Bibliography

REFERENCE WORKS

Anderson, Sean, and Stephen Sloan. *Historical Dictionary of Terrorism.* 2nd ed. Lanham, MD: Scarecrow Press, 2002.

Anti-Defamation League. *The Skinhead International: A Worldwide Survey of Neo-Nazi Skinheads.* New York: Anti-Defamation League, 1995.

Atkins, Stephen E. *Encyclopedia of Modern American Extremists and Extremist Groups.* Westport, CT: Greenwood Press, 2002.

———. *Terrorism: A Reference Handbook.* Santa Barbara, CA: ABC-CLIO, 1992.

Babkina, A. M. *Terrorism: A Bibliography with Indexes.* 2nd ed. Huntington, NY: Nova Science Publishers, 2001.

Crenshaw, Martha, and John Pimlott, eds. *Encyclopedia of World Terrorism.* 3 vols. Armonk, NY: Sharpe Reference, 1997.

Davidson, Lawrence. *Islamic Fundamentalism.* Westport, CT: Greenwood Press, 1998.

Grover, Verinder, ed. *Encyclopaedia of International Terrorism.* 3 vols. New Delhi, India: Deep and Deep Publications, 2002.

Hamm, Mark S. *American Skinheads: The Criminology and the Control of Hate Crime* Westport, CT: Praeger, 1994.

Henderson, Harry, *Global Terrorism: The Complete Reference Guide.* New York: Checkmark Books, 2001.

Hiro, Dilip. *Dictionary of the Middle East.* New York: St. Martin's Press, 1996.

Kaplan, Jeffrey, ed. *The Encyclopedia of White Power: A Sourcebook on the Radical Racist Right.* Walnut Creek, CA: AltaMira Press, 2000.

Kushner, Harvey W. *Encyclopedia of Terrorism.* Thousand Oaks, CA: Sage Publications, 2003.

Lakos, Amos. *Terrorism, 1980–1990: A Bibliography.* Boulder, CO: Westview Press, 1991.

Lewis, James R. *Peculiar Prophets: A Biographical Dictionary of New Religions.* St. Paul, MN: Paragon House, 1999.

Mickolus, Edward F. *Terrorism, 1980–1987: A Selectively Annotated Bibliography.* New York: Greenwood Press, 1988.

———. *Terrorism, 1988–1991: A Chronology of Events and a Selectively Annotated Bibliography.* Westport, CT: Greenwood Press, 1993.

———. *Terrorism, 1992–1995: A Chronology of Events and a Selectively Annotated Bibliography.* Westport, CT: Greenwood Press, 1997.

Nash, Jay Robert. *Terrorism in the 20th Century: A Narrative Encyclopedia from the Anarchists, through the Weathermen, to the Unabomber.* New York: Evans, 1998.

Prunckun, Henry W. *Shadow of Death: An Analytical Bibliography on Political Violence, Terrorism, and Low-Intensity Conflict.* Lanham, MD: Scarecrow Press, 1995.

Rees, Phillip. *Biographical Dictionary of the Extreme Right since 1890.* New York: Simon & Schuster, 1990.

Ridenour, David, and David Almasi. *Nicaragua's Continuing Revolution: A Chronology for 1977 to 1990.* Washington, DC: Signal Books, 1990.

Rosie, George. *The Directory of International Terrorism.* New York: Paragon House, 1986.

Shafritz, Jay M., E. F. Gibbons, Jr., Gregory E. J. Scott. *Almanac of Modern Terrorism*. New York: Facts on File, 1991.

Thackrah, John Richard. *Encyclopedia of Terrorism and Political Violence*. London: Routledge and Kegan Paul, 1987.

AUTOBIOGRAPHIES AND MEMOIRS

Anderson, Terry A. *Den of Lions: Memoirs of Seven Years*. New York: Crown, 1993.

Begin, Menachem. *The Revolt*. New York: Nash, 1977.

Cabezas, Omar. *Fire from the Mountain: The Making of a Sandinista*. New York: Plume, 1985.

Evola, Julius. *Men among the Ruins: Post-War Reflections of a Radical Traditionalist*. Rochester, VT: Inner Traditions, 2002.

Giorgio. *Memoirs of an Italian Terrorist*. New York: Carroll and Graf, 2003.

Foley, Charles, ed. *The Memoirs of General Grivas*. New York: Praeger, 1964.

Hasselbach, Ingo, and Tom Reiss. *Fuhrer-EX: Memoirs of a Former Neo-Nazi*. New York: Random House, 1996.

Marighella, Carlos. *For the Liberation of Brazil*. Middlesex, UK: Penguin Books, 1971.

Proll, Astrid, ed. *Baader Meinhof: Pictures on the Run 67–77*. Zurich: Scalo Verlag, 1998.

Thiriart, Jean. *Europe: An Empire of 400 Million Men*. Brussels, Belgium, 1964.

BIOGRAPHIES

Ajami, Fouad. *The Vanished Iman: Musa al Sadr and the Shia of Lebanon*. Ithaca, NY: Cornell University Press, 1986.

Arburish, Said K. *Arafat: From Defender to Dictator*. New York: Bloomsbury, 1998.

———. *Saddam Hussein: The Politics of Revenge*. London: Bloomsbury, 2000.

Barker, Dudley. *Grivas: Portrait of a Terrorist*. New York: Harcourt, Brace and Company, 1959.

Bodansky, Yossef. *Bin Laden: The Man Who Declared War on America* New York: Forum, 2001.

Chandler, David P. *Brother Number One: A Political Biography of Pol Pot*. Rev. ed. Boulder, CO: Westview Press, 1999.

Clarke, Liam, and Kathryn Johnston. *Martin McGuinness: From Guns to Government*. Edinburgh, Scotland: Mainstream Publishing, 2001.

Coogan, Kevin. *Dreamer of the Day: Francis Parker Yockey and the Postwar Fascist International*. Brooklyn, NY: Autonomedia, 1999.

Follain, John. *Jackal: The Complete Story of the Legendary Terrorist, Carlos the Jackal*. New York: Arcade Publishing, 1998.

Hart, Alan. *Arafat: Terrorist or Peacemaker?* London: Sidgwick & Jackson, 1984.

Goodrick-Clarke, Nicholas. *Hitler's Priestess: Savitri Devi, the Hindu-Aryan Myth, and Occult Neo-Nazism*. New York: New York University Press, 1998.

Gowers, Andrew, and Tony Walker. *Behind the Myth: Yasser Arafat and the Palestinian Revolution*. New York: Olive Branch Press, 1991.

Kartsev, Vladimir. *Zhirinovsky!* New York: Columbia University Press, 1995.

Kiernan, Thomas. *Arafat, the Man and the Myth*. New York: Norton, 1976.

Marrinan, Patrick. *Paisley, Man of Wrath*. Tralee, Ireland: Anvil Books, 1973.

Melman, Yossi. *The Master Terrorist: The True Story behind Abu Nidal*. New York: Adama Books, 1986.

Moin, Baqer. *Khomeini: Life of the Ayatollah*. New York: St. Martin's Press, 1999.

Perlmutter, Amos. *The Life and Times of Menachem Begin*. Garden City, NY: Doubleday, 1987.

Rahanam, Ali. *An Islamic Utopian: A Political Biography of Ali Shari'ati* London: I. B. Tauris, 1998.

Seale, Patrick. *Abu Nidal: A Gun for Hire*. New York: Random House, 1992.

Sharrock, David, and Mark Devenport. *Man of War, Man of Peace: The Unauthorized Biography of Gerry Adams*. London, U.K.: Pan Books, 1997.

Simonelli, Frederick J. *American Fuehrer: George Lincoln Rockwell and the American Nazi Party*. Urbana: University of Illinois Press, 1999.

Smith, Colin. *Carlos: Portrait of a Terrorist*. New York: Holt, Rinehart, & Winston, 1976.

Smith, David, and Colin Simpson. *Mugabe*. Salisbury, UK: Pioneer Head, 1981.

Tremlett, George. *Gadaffi: The Desert Mystic*. New York: Carroll and Graf, 1993.

Wallach, Janet, and John Wallach. *Arafat: In the Eyes of the Beholder*. Rev. ed. Secaucus, NJ: Carol, 1997.

Zimmermann, Matilde. *Sandinista: Carlos Fonseca and the Nicaraguan Revolution*. Durham, NC: Duke University Press, 2000.

MONOGRAPHS

Abrahamian, Ervand. *The Iranian Mojahedin.* New Haven, CT: Yale University Press, 1989.
———. *Khomeinism: Essays on the Islamic Republic.* Berkeley: University of California Press, 1993.

Abu-Amr, Ziad. *Islamic Fundamentalism in the West Bank and Gaza: Muslim Brotherhood and Islamic Jihad.* Bloomington: Indiana University Press, 1994.

Abu-Khalil, As'ad. *Bin Laden, Islam and America's New "War on Terrorism."* New York: Seven Stories Press, 2002.

Agirre, J. *Operation Ogro: The Execution of Admiral Luis Carrero Blanco.* New York: Quadrangle, 1975.

Ajami, Fouad. *The Vanished Imam: Musa Al Sadr and the Shia of Lebanon.* Ithaca, NY: Cornell University Press, 1986.

Akhavi, Shahrough. *Religion and Politics in Contemporary Iran: Clergy-State Relations in the Pahlavi Period.* Albany: State University of New York Press, 1980.

Alexander, Yonah, and Dennis A. Pluchinsky, *European Terrorism: Today and Tomorrow.* Washington, D.C.: Brassey's, 1992.

Alexander, Yonah, and Dennis Pluchinsky. *Europe's Red Terrorists: The Fighting Communist Organizations.* London: Frank Cass, 1992.

Alexander, Yonah, and Michael S. Swetnam. *Usama bin Laden's al-Qaida: Profile of a Terrorist Network.* Ardsley, NY: Transnational Publishers, 2001.

Alexander, Yonah, Michael S. Swetnam, and Herbert M. Levine. *ETA: Profile of a Terrorist Group.* Ardsley, NY: Transnational Press, 2001.

Algar, Hamid. *Wahhabism: A Critical Essay.* London: Islamic Publications International, 2002.

Allen, Douglas, ed. *Religion and Political Conflict in South Asia: India, Pakistan, and Sri Lanka.* Westport, CT: Greenwood Press, 1992.

Alnor, William M. *UFO Cults and the New Millennium.* Grand Rapids, MI: Baker Books, 1998.

Anderson, Jon Lee. *Guerrillas: The Men and Women Fighting Today's Wars.* New York: Times Books, 1992.

Arjomand, Said Amir. *The Turban for the Crown: The Islamic Revolution in Iran.* New York: Oxford University Press, 1988.

Armstrong, Robert, and Janet Shenk. *El Salvador: The Face of Revolution.* Boston: South End Press, 1982.

Arnold, Guy. *The Maverick State: Gaddafi and the New World Order.* London: Cassell, 1996.

Asencio, Diego. *Our Man Is Inside.* Boston: Little, Brown, 1983.

Aust, Stefan. *The Baader-Meinhof Group: The Inside Story of a Phenomenon.* London: Bodley Head, 1985.

Barreveld, Dirk J. *Terrorism in the Philippines: The Bloody Trial of Abu Sayyaf, Bin Laden's East Asian.* San Jose, CA: Writers Club Press, 2001.

Barron, John, and Anthony Paul. *Murder of a Gentle Land: The Untold Story of Communist Genocide in Cambodia.* New York: Reader's Digest Press, 1977.

Becker, Jillian. *Hitler's Children: The Baader-Meinhof Terrorist Gang.* Philadelphia: Lippincott, 1978.
———. *The PLO: The Rise and Fall of the Palestine Liberation Organization.* London: Widenfeld and Nicolson, 1984.

Bell, J. Bowyer. *The IRA, 1968–2000: Analysis of a Secret Army.* London: Frank Cass, 2000.
———. *Murders on the Nile: The World Trade Center and Global Terror.* San Francisco, California: Encounter Books, 2003.
———. *Terror Out of Zion: Irgun Zvai Leumi, LEHI, and the Palestine Underground: 1929–1949.* New York: St. Martin's Press, 1977.

Benewick, Robert. *The Fascist Movement in Britain.* Rev. ed. London: Allen Lane, 1972.

Benjamin, Daniel, and Steven Simon. *The Age of Sacred Terror.* New York: Random House, 2002.

Bernstein, Richard. *Out of the Blue: The Story of September 11, 2001, from Jihad to Ground Zero.* New York: Times Books, 2002.

Betz, Hans-Georg. *Postmodern Politics in German: the Politics of Resentment.* New York: St. Martin's Press, 1991.
———. *Radical Right-Wing Populism in Western Europe.* New York: St. Martin's Press, 1994.

Bishop, Patrick, and Eamonn Mallie. *The Provisional IRA.* London: Corgi Books, 1988.

Blair, David. *Degrees in Violence: Robert Mugabe and the Struggle for Power in Zimbabwe.* London: Continuum, 2002.

Blundy, David, and Andrew Lycett. *Qaddafi and the Libyan Revolution.* Boston: Little, Brown, 1987.

Selected Bibliography

Booth, John A. *The End and the Beginning: The Nicaraguan Revolution.* Boulder, CO: Westview Press, 1985.

Boulton, David. *The Ulster Volunteer Force, 1966–1973.* Dublin, Ireland: Gill and McMillan, 1973.

Bracamonte, Jose Angel Moroni, and David E. Spencer. *Strategy and Tactics of the Salvadoran FMLN Guerrillas: Last Battle of the Cold War, Blueprint for Future Conflicts.* Westport, CT: Praeger, 1995.

Brackett, D. W. *Holy Terror: Armageddon in Tokyo.* New York: Weatherhill, 1996.

Bronner, Stephen Eric. *A Rumor about the Jews: Reflections on Antisemitism and the Protocols of the Learned Elders of Zion.* New York: St. Martin's Press, 2000.

Brown, Timothy C. *The Real Contra War: Highlander Peasant Resistance in Nicaragua.* Norman: University of Oklahoma, 2001.

———, ed. *When the AK-47s Fall Silent: Revolutionaries, Guerrillas, and the Dangers of Peace.* Stanford, CA: Hoover Institute Press, 2000.

Bruce, Steve. *God Save Ulster! The Religion and Politics of Paisleyism.* Oxford, U.K.: Oxford University Press, 1986.

———. *The Red Hand: Protestant Paramilitaries in Northern Ireland.* Oxford, U.K.: Oxford University Press, 1992.

Burke, Jason. *Al-Qaeda: Casting a Shadow of Terror.* London: I. B. Tauris, 2003.

Byrne, Hugh. *El Salvador's Civil War: A Study of Revolution.* Boulder, CO: Lynne Rienner, 1996.

Campbell, Bruce B., and Arthur D. Brenner, eds. *Death Squads in Global Perspective: Murder with Deniability.* New York: St. Martin's Press, 2000.

Caram, Peter. *The 1993 World Trade Center Bombing: Foresight and Warning.* London: Janus Publishing, 2001.

Carey, Roane, ed. *The New Intifada: Resisting Israel's Apartheid.* London: Verso, 2001.

Carr, Gordon. *The Angry Brigade: The Cause and the Case.* London: Gollanz, 1975.

Carrigan, Ana. *The Palace of Justice: A Colombian Tragedy.* New York: Four Walls Eight Windows, 1993.

Catanzaro, Raimondo, ed. *The Red Brigades and Left-Wing Terrorism in Italy.* New York: St. Martin's Press, 1991.

Clark, Robert P. *The Basque Insurgents.* Madison: University of Wisconsin Press, 1984.

Cockburn, Andrew, and Patrick Cockburn. *Out of the Ashes: The Resurrection of Saddam Hussein.* New York: Harper Perennial, 1999.

Collier, George A. *Basta! Land and the Zapatista Rebellion in Chiapas.* Rev. ed. Oakland, CA: Food First Books, 1999.

Coogan, Tim Pat. *The IRA: A History.* Niwot, CO: Roberts Rinehart, 1993.

Cooley, John K. *Unholy Wars: Afghanistan, America and International Terrorism.* 2nd ed. London: Pluto Press, 2000.

Corbin, Jane. *Al-Qaeda: The Terror Network That Threatens the World.* New York: Thunder's Mouth Press, 2002.

Crawshaw, Nancy. *The Cyprus Revolt: An Account of the Struggle for Union with Greece.* London: Allen & Unwin, 1978.

Cross, Colin. *The Fascists in Britain.* London: Barrie and Rockliff, 1961.

Dartnell, Michael Y. *Action Directe: Ultra-Left Terrorism in France, 1979–1987.* London: Frank Cass, 1995.

Davis, Barry. *Terrorism: Inside a World Phenomenon.* London: Virgin Books, 2003.

DeClair, Edward G. *Politics on the Fringe: The People, Policies, and Organization of the French National Front.* Durham, NC: Duke University Press, 1999.

Del Boca, Angelo. *Fascism Today.* New York: Heinemann, 1969.

Dietl, Wilhelm. *Holy War.* New York: Macmillan, 1984.

Dillon, Martin. *God and Gun: The Church and Irish Terrorism.* New York: Routledge, 1990.

———. *The Shankill Butchers: The Real Story of Cold-Blooded Mass Murder.* New York: Routledge, 1989.

Dobson, Christopher. *Black September: Its Short, Violent History.* New York: Macmillan, 1974.

Dobson, Christopher, and Ronald Payne. *The Terrorists: Their Weapons, Leaders and Tactics.* New York: Facts on File, 1982.

Drake, Richard. *The Aldo Moro Murder Case.* Cambridge, MA: Harvard University Press, 1995

———. *The Revolutionary Mystique and Terrorism in Contemporary Italy.* Bloomington: Indiana University Press, 1989.

Eisenberg, Dennis. *The Re-Emergence of Fascism.* New York: Barnes, 1967.

Esposito, John L. *The Islamic Threat: Myth or Reality?* New York: Oxford University Press, 1992.

Euben, Roxanne L. *Enemy in the Mirror: Islamic Fundamentalism and the Limits of Modern Rationalism: A Work of Comparative Political Theory.* Princeton, NJ: Princeton University Press, 1999.

Evans, Richard J. *Lying about Hitler: History, Holocaust, and the David Irving Trial.* New York: Basic Books, 2001.

Farrell, William R. *Blood and Rage: The Story of the Japanese Red Army.* Lexington, MA: Lexington Books, 1990.

Ferraresi, Franco. *Threats to Democracy: The Radical Right in Italy after the War.* Princeton, NJ: Princeton University Press, 1996.

Fink, Christina. *Living Silence: Burma under Military Rule.* Bangkok, Thailand: White Lotus, 2001.

Foley, Charles, and W. I. Scobie. *The Struggle for Cyprus.* Stanford, CA: Hoover Institution Press, 1975.

Fouda, Yoshi, and Nick Fielding. *Masterminds of Terror: The Truth behind the Most Devastating Terrorist Attack the World Has Ever Seen.* New York: Arcade Publishing, 2003.

Fraser, Nicholas. *The Voice of Modern Hatred: Tracing the Rise of Neo-Fascism in Europe* Woodstock, NY: The Overlook Press, 2000.

Friedman, Robert I. *Zealots for Zion: Inside Israel's West Bank Settlement Movement.* New York: Random House, 1992.

Fuller, Graham E. *Algeria: The Next Fundamentalist State?* Santa Monica, CA: Rand, 1996.

Gall, Carlotta, and Thomas de Waal. *Chechnya: Calamity in the Caucasus.* New York: New York University Press, 1998.

Ganguly, Rajat, and Ian Macduff, eds. *Ethnic Conflict and Secessionism in South and Southeast Asia: Causes, Dynamics, Solutions.* New Delhi, India: Sage Publications, 2003.

Gillespie, Richard. *Soldiers of Peron: Argentina's Montoneros.* Oxford, UK: Clarendon Press, 1982.

Gohari, M. J. *The Taliban: Ascent to Power.* Oxford, UK: Oxford University Press, 1999.

Golsan, Richard J., ed. *Fascism's Return: Scandal, Revision, and Ideology Since 1980.* Lincoln: University of Nebraska Press, 1998.

Gorriti, Gustavo. *The Shining Path: A History of the Millenarian War in Peru.* Chapel Hill: University of North Carolina Press, 1999.

Gowers, Andrew, and Tony Walker. *Behind the Myth: Yasser Arafat and the Palestinian Revolution.* New York: Olive Branch Press, 1992.

Groussard, Serge. *The Blood of Israel: The Massacre of the Israeli Athletes: The Olympics 1972.* New York: Morrow, 1975.

Gunaratna, Rohan. *Indian Intervention in Sir Lanka: The Role of India's Intelligence Agencies.* Colombo, Sri Lanka: South Asian Network on Conflict Research, 1993.

———. *Inside Al Qaeda: Global Network of Terror.* New York: Columbia University Press, 2002.

Gunter, Michael M. *The Kurds and the Future of Turkey.* New York: St. Martin's Press, 1997.

Gupte Pranay. *Vengeance: India and the Assassination of Indira Gandhi.* New York: Norton, 1985.

Guttenplan, D. D. *The Holocaust on Trial.* New York: Norton, 2001.

Halawi, Majed. *A Lebanon Defied: Musa al-Sadr and the Shi'a Community.* Boulder, CO: Westview Press, 1992.

Hamm, Mark S. *American Skinheads: The Criminology and Control of Hate Crime.* Westport, CT: Praeger, 1994.

Harnden, Toby. *"Bandit Country": The IRA and South Armagh.* London: Hodder and Stoughton, 1999.

Harris, Christina Phelps. *Nationalism and Revolution in Egypt: The Role of the Muslim Brotherhood.* The Hague, The Netherlands: Mouton, 1964.

Harris, Geoffrey. *The Dark Side of Europe: The Extreme Right Today.* Edinburgh, Scotland: Edinburgh University Press, 1994.

Harris, Lillian Craig. *Libya: Qadhafi's Revolution and the Modern State.* Boulder, CO: Westview Press, 1986.

Hass, Amira. *Drinking the Sea at Gaza: Days and Nights under Siege.* New York: Henry Holt, 1996.

Hatina, Meir. *Islam and Salvation in Palestine.* Tel Aviv, Israel: Tel Aviv University, 2001.

Hayden, Tom, ed. *The Zapatista Reader.* New York: Thunder's Mouth Press, 2002.

Heyck, Denis Lynn Daly. *Life Stories of the Nicaraguan Revolution.* New York: Routledge, 1990.

Hiro, Dilip. *The Longest War: The Iran-Iraq Military Conflict.* New York: Routledge, 1991.

Hockenos, Paul. *Free to Hate: The Rise of the Right in Post-Communist Eastern Europe.* New York: Routledge, 1993.

Hoffman, Bruce, *Inside Terrorism.* New York: Columbia University Press, 1998.

Selected Bibliography

Hoveyda, Fereydoun. *The Broken Crescent: The "Treat" of Militant Islamic Fundamentalism.* New York: Praeger, 1998.

Hroub, Khaled. *Hamas: Political Thought and Practice.* Washington, DC: Institute for Palestine Studies, 2000.

Huband, Mark. *Warriors of the Prophet: The Struggle for Islam.* Boulder, CO: Westview Press, 1999.

Hunter, R. Robert. *The Palestinian Uprising: A War by Other Means.* Berkeley: University of California Press, 1991.

Irvin, Cynthia L. *Militant Nationalism: Between Movement and Party in Ireland and the Basque Country.* Minneapolis: University of Minnesota Press, 1999.

Jabar, Habar. *Hezbollah: Born with a Vengeance.* New York: Columbia University Press, 1997.

Jacquand, Roland. *In the Name of Osama Bin Laden: Global Terrorism and the Bin Laden Brotherhood.* Durham, NC: Duke University Press, 2002.

Jonas, Susanne. *The Battle for Guatemala: Rebels, Death Squads and U.S. Power.* Boulder, CO: Westview Press, 1991.

Jones, Gregg R. *Red Revolution: Inside the Philippine Guerrilla Movement.* Boulder, CO: Westview Press, 1989.

Kaplan, Jeffrey, and Tore Bjorgo, eds. *Nation and Race: The Developing Euro-American Racist Subculture.* Boston: Northeastern University Press, 1998.

Kaplan, Robert D. *Soldiers of God: With Islamic Warriors in Afghanistan and Pakistan.* New York: Vintage Books, 2001.

Karpin, Michael, and Ina Friedman. *Murder in the Name of God: The Plot to Kill Yitzhak Rabin.* New York: Metropolitan Books, 1998.

Kassimeris, George. *Europe's Last Red Terrorists: The Revolutionary Organization 17 November.* New York: New York University Press, 2001.

Katsiaficas, George. *The Subversion of Politics: European Autonomous Social Movements and the Decolonization of Everyday Life.* Atlantic Heights, NJ: Humanities Press International, 1997.

Katz, Samuel M. *Israel versus Jibril: The Thirty-Year War against a Master Terrorist.* New York: Paragon House, 1993.

Kazziha, Walid W. *Revolutionary Transformation in the Arab World: Habash and His Comrades from Nationalism to Marxism.* New York: St. Martin's Press, 1975.

Kelly, Paul. *Paradise Divided: The Changes, the Challenges, the Choices for Australia.* St. Leonards, NSW: Allen & Unwin, 2000.

Kepel, Gilles. *Muslim Extremism in Egypt: The Prophet and Pharaoh.* Berkeley: University of California Press, 1986.

Kiernan, Ben. *How Pol Pot Came to Power: A History of Communism in Kampuchea, 1930–1975.* London: Verso, 1985.

Kinzer, Stephen. *Blood of Brothers: Life and War in Nicaragua.* New York: Putnam's, 1991.

Kirisci, Kemal. *The PLO and World Politics: A Study of the Mobilization of Support for the Palestinian Cause.* New York: St. Martin's Press, 1986.

Kitschelt, Herbert. *The Radical Right in Western Europe: A Comparative Analysis.* Ann Arbor: University of Michigan Press, 1995.

Kleg, Milton. *Hate Prejudice and Racism.* Albany: State of New York Press, 1993.

Knezys, Stasys, and Romanas Sedickas. *The War in Chechnya.* College Station: Texas A&M University Press, 1999.

Laqueur, Walter. *A History of Terrorism.* New Brunswick, NJ: Transaction Publishers, 2001.

Leach, Michael, Geoffrey Stokes, and Ian Ward, eds. *The Rise and Fall of One Nation.* St. Lucia: University of Queensland Press, 2000.

Lee, Martin A. *The Beast Reawakens.* Boston: Little, Brown, 1997.

Leech, Garry M. *Killing Peace: Colombia's Conflict and the Failure of U.S. Intervention.* New York: Information Network of the Americas, 2002.

Lewis, D. S. *Illusions of Grandeur: Mosley, Fascism, and British Society, 1931–81.* Manchester, UK: Manchester University Press, 1987.

Lewis, James R., ed. *The Gods Have Landed: New Religions from Other Worlds.* Albany: State University of New York Press, 1995.

Lewis, Paul H. *Guerrillas and Generals: The "Dirty War" in Argentina.* Westport, CT: Praeger, 2002.

Liebman, Charles S., and Eliezer Don-Yehiya, *Religion and Politics in Israel.* Bloomington, IN: Indiana University Press, 1984.

Lieven, Anatol. *Chechnya: Tombstone of Russian Power.* New Haven, CT: Yale University Press, 1998.

Linehan, Thomas. *British Fascism, 1918–39: Parties, Ideology and Culture.* Manchester, UK: Manchester University Press, 2001.

Lipstadt, Deborah. *Denying the Holocaust: The Growing Assault on Truth and Memory.* New York: Plume, 1993.

Liss, Sheldon B. *Radical Thought in Central America.* Boulder, CO: Westview Press, 1991.

Long, David E. *The Anatomy of Terrorism.* New York: Free Press, 1990.

Lotringer, Sylvere, and Christian Marazzi, eds. *Autonomia: Post-Political Politics.* New York: Semiotexte), 1980.

Lungo Ucles, Mario. *El Salvador in the Eighties: Counterinsurgency and Revolution.* Philadelphia, PA: Temple University Press, 1996.

Lustick, Ian S. *For the Land and the Lord.* New York: Council on Foreign Relations, 1988.

Magnus, Ralph H., and Eden Naby. *Afghanistan: Mullah, Marx, and Mujahid.* Boulder, CO: Westview Press, 2000.

Mahmood, Cynthia Keppley. *Fighting for Faith and Nation: Dialogues with Sikh Militants.* Philadelphia: University of Pennsylvania Press, 1996.

Marchak, Patricia, and William Marchak. *God's Assassins: State Terrorism in Argentina in the 1970s.* Montreal, Canada: McGill-Queen's University Press, 1999.

Matinuddin, Kamal. *The Taliban Phenomenon: Afghanistan, 1994–1997.* Oxford, UK: Oxford University Press, 1999.

McCormick Gordon H. *From the Sierra to the Cities: The Urban Campaign of the Shining Path.* Santa Monica, CA: Rand Corporation, 1992.

———. *The Shining Path and the Future of Peru.* Santa Monica, CA: Rand Corporation, 1990.

———. *Sharp Dressed Men: Peru's Tupac Amaru Revolutionary Movement.* Santa Monica, CA: Rand Corporation, 1993.

McGowan, William. *Only Man Is Vile: The Tragedy of Sri Lanka.* New York: Farrar, Straus & Giroux, 1992.

Meade, Robert C. *Red Brigades: The Story of Italian Terrorism.* New York: St. Martin's Press, 1990.

Menzel, Sewall H. *Bullets versus Ballots: Political Violence and Revolutionary War in El Salvador, 1979–1991.* Boulder, CO: Lynne Rienner, 1994.

Meredith, Martin. *Our Votes, Our Guns: Robert Mugabe and the Tragedy of Zimbabwe.* New York: Public Affairs, 2002.

Mergui, Raphael, and Philippe Simonnot. *Israel's Ayatollahs: Meir Kahane and the Far Right in Israel.* London: Saqi Books, 1987.

Miller, John, and Michael Stone. *The Cell: Inside the 9/11 Plot, and Why the FBI and CIA Failed to Stop It.* New York: Hyperion, 2003.

Miller, Judith. *God Has Ninety-Nine Names: Reporting from a Militant Middle East.* New York: Touchstone Books, 1996.

Miranda, Roger, and William Ratliff. *The Civil War in Nicaragua: Inside the Sandinistas.* New Brunswick, NJ: Transaction Publishers, 1993.

Mishal, Shaul. *The PLO under Arafat: Between Gun and Olive Branch.* New Haven, CT: Yale University Press, 1986.

Mishal, Shaul, and Avraham Sela. *The Palestinian Hamas: Vision, Violence, and Coexistence.* New York: Columbia University Press, 2000.

Mitchell, Richard. *The Society of the Muslim Brothers.* London: Oxford University Press, 1966.

Moloney, Ed. *A Secret History of the IRA.* New York: Norton, 2002.

Montgomery, Tommi Sue. *Revolution in El Salvador: From Civil Strife to Civil Peace.* 2nd ed. Boulder, CO: Westview Press, 1995.

Moroni Bracamonte, Jose Angel, and David E. Spencer. *Strategy and Tactics of the Salvadoran FMLN Guerrillas: Last Battle of the Cold War, Blueprint for Future Conflicts.* Westport, CT: Praeger, 1995.

Morrison, James W. *Vladimir Zhirinovskiy: An Assessment of a Russian Ultra-Nationalist.* Washington, DC: National Defense University, 1994.

Moss, Robert. *Urgan Guerrilla Warfare.* London: International Institute for Strategic Studies, 1971.

Najumi, Neamotollah. *The Rise of the Taliban in Afghanistan: Mass Mobilization, Civil War, and the Future of the Region.* New York: Palgrave, 2002.

Nasr, Seyyed Vali Reza. *Vanguard of the Islamic Revolution: The Jama'at-I Islami of Pakistan.* Berkeley: University of California Press, 1994.

Nassar, Jamal R. *The Palestine Liberation Organization: From Armed Struggle to the Declaration of Independence.* New York: Praeger, 1991.

Nolan, David. *The Ideology of the Sandinistas and the Nicaraguan Revolution.* Coral Gables, FL: Institute of Interamerican Studies, 1984.

Norton, Augustus Richard. *Amal and the Shi'a: Struggle for the Soul of Lebanon.* Austin: University of Texas Press, 1987.

O'Ballance, Edgar. *The Cyanide War: Tamil Insurrection in Sri Lanka 1973–88.* London: Brassey's, 1989.

———. *Islamic Fundamentalist Terrorism, 1979–95: The Iranian Connection.* New York: New York University Press, 1997.

———. *The Palestinian Intifada.* New York: St. Martin's Press, 1998.

———. *Terror in Ireland: The Heritage of Hate.* Novato, CA: Presidio Press, 1981.

O'Brien, Brendan. *The Long War: The IRA and Sinn Fein.* 2nd ed. Syracuse, NY: Syracuse University Press, 1999.

O'Day, Alan. *Terrorism's Laboratory: The Case of Northern Ireland.* Aldershot, UK: Dartmouth, 1995.

Pardo-Maurer, R. *The Contras, 1980–1989: A Special Kind of Politics.* New York: Praeger, 1990.

Patterson, Henry. *The Politics of Illusion: A Political History of the IRA.* London: Serif, 1997.

Pelt, Robert Jan van. *The Case for Auschwitz: Evidence from the Irving Trial.* Bloomington: Indiana University Press, 2002.

Peretz, Don. *Intifada: The Palestinian Uprising.* Boulder, CO: Westview Press, 1990.

Peri, Yoram, ed. *The Assassination of Yitzhak Rabin.* Stanford, CA: Stanford University Press, 2000.

Pettigrew, Joyce. *The Sikhs of the Punjab: Unheard Voices of State and Guerilla Violence.* London: Zed Books, 1995.

Poole, Deborah, and Gerardo Renique. *Peru: Time of Fear.* London: Latin American Bureau, 1992.

Quandt, William B. *Between Ballots and Bullets: Algeria's Transition from Authoritarianism.* Washington, DC: Brookings Institution Press, 1998.

Ramsey, Robert. *The Corsican Time Bomb.* Manchester, UK: Manchester University Press, 1983.

Ranstorp, Magnus. *Hizb'Allah in Lebanon: The Politics of the Western Hostage Crisis.* London: Palgrave, 1997.

Rapoport, David C., ed. *Inside Terrorist Organizations.* London: Frank Cass, 2001.

Rashid, Ahmed. *Jihad: The Rise of Militant Islam in Central Asia.* New Haven, CT: Yale University Press, 2002.

———. *Taliban: Militant Islam, Oil and Fundamentalism in Central Asia.* New Haven, CT: Yale University Press, 2000.

Reader, Ian. *Religious Violence in Contemporary Japan: The Case of Aum Shinrikyo.* Honolulu: University of Hawaii Press, 2000.

Reich, Walter, ed. *Origins of Terrorism: Psychologies, Ideologies, Theologies, States of Mind.* Washington, D.C.: Woodrow Wilson Center Press, 1998.

Ressa, Maria A., *Seeds of Terror: An Eyewitness Account of Al-Qaeda's Newest Center of Operations in Southeast Asia.* New York: Free Press, 2003.

Reeve, Simon. *The New Jackals: Ramzi Yousef, Osama bin Laden and the Future of Terrorism.* Boston: Northeastern University Press, 1999.

Reische, Diana L. *Arafat and the Palestine Liberation Organization.* New York: Watts, 1991.

Roxburgh, Angus. *Preachers of Hate: The Rise of the Far Right.* London: Gibson Square Books, 2002.

Rubin, Barry. *Revolution until Victory?: The Politics and History of the PLO.* Cambridge, MA: Harvard University Press, 1994.

———. *The Transformation of Palestinian Politics: From Revolution to State-Building.* Cambridge, MA: Harvard University Press, 1999.

Rubin, Michael. *Into the Shadows: Radical Vigilantes in Khatami's Iran.* Washington, DC: Washington Institute for Near East Policy, 2001.

Ruiz, Bert. *The Colombian Civil War.* Jefferson, NC: McFarland, 2002.

Russell, Philip L. *The Chiapas Rebellion.* Austin, TX: Mexico Resource Center, 1995.

Ryan, Henry Butterfield. *The Fall of Che Guevara.* New York: Oxford University Press, 1998.

Saad-Ghorayeb, Amal. *Hizbu'llah: Politics and Religion.* London: Pluto Press, 2002.

Schiff, Ze'ev, and Ehud Ya'ari. *Intifada: The Palestinian Uprising—Israel's Third Front.* New York: Simon & Schuster, 1990.

Schmidt, Michael. *The New Reich: Violent Extremism in Unified Germany and Beyond.* New York: Pantheon Books, 1993.

Sela, Avraham, and Moshe Ma'oz, eds. *The PLO and Israel: From Armed Conflict to Political Solution, 1964–1994.* New York: St. Martin's Press, 1997.

Shahak, Israel, and Norton Mezvinsky. *Jewish Fundamentalism in Israel.* London: Pluto Press, 1999.

Shenfield, Stephen D. *Russian Fascism: Traditions, Tendencies, Movements.* Armonk, NY: M. E. Sharpe, 2001.

Sidahmed, Abdel Salam. *Politics and Islam in Contemporary Sudan*. Richmond, UK: Curzon Press, 1997.

Simmons, Harvey G. *The French National Front: The Extremist Challenge to Democracy*. Boulder, CO: Westview Press, 1996.

Simpson, John, and Jana Bennett. *The Disappeared*. London: Robson Books, 1985.

Singh, Sarab Jit. *Operation Black Thunder: An Eyewitness Account of Terrorism in Punjab*. New Delhi, India: Sage Publications, 2002.

Sluka, Jeffrey A., ed. *Death Squad: The Anthropology of State Terror*. Philadelphia: University of Pennsylvania Press, 2000.

Smith, Martin. *Burma: Insurgency and the Politics of Ethnicity*. Rev. ed. Dhaka, Bangladesh: University Press, 1999.

Smith, Sebastian. *Allah's Mountains: Politics and War in the Russian Caucasus*. London: I. B. Tauris, 1998.

Solovyov, Vladimir, and Elena Klepikova. *Zhirinovsky: Russian Fascism and the Making of a Dictator*. Reading, MA: Addison-Wesley, 1995.

Sperling, Susan. *Animal Liberators: Research and Morality*. Berkeley: University of California Press, 1988.

Sprinzak, Ehud. *Brother against Brother: Violence and Extremism in Israeli Politics from Altalena to the Rabin Assassination*. New York: Free Press, 1999.

Stern, Kenneth S. *Holocaust Denial*. New York: American Jewish Committee, 1993.

Stern, Steve J. *Shining and Other Paths: War and Society in Peru, 1980–1995*. Durham, NC: Duke University Press, 1998.

Strong, Simon. *Shining Path: The World's Deadliest Revolutionary Force*. London: Harper-Collins, 1992.

Sundaram, Anjali, and George Gelber, eds. *A Decade of War: El Salvador Confronts the Future*. London: Catholic Institute for International Relations, 1991.

Svoray, Yaron, and Nick Taylor. *In Hitler's Shadow: An Israeli's Amazing Journey inside Germany's Neo-Nazi Movement*. New York: Doubleday, 1994.

Taheri, Amir. *The Spirit of Allah: Khomeini and the Islamic Revolution*. London: Hutchinson, 1985.

Tambini, Damian. *Nationalism in Italian Politics: The Stories of the Northern League, 1980–2000*. London: Routledge, 2001.

Taylor, Peter. *Behind the Mask: The IRA and Sinn Fein*. Rev. ed. New York: TV Books, 1999.

———. *Loyalists: War and Peace in Northern Ireland*. New York: TV Books, 1999.

Theroux, Peter. *The Strange Disappearance of Iman Moussa Sadr*. London: Weidenfeld and Nicolson, 1987.

Thurlow, Richard. *Fascism in Britain: From Oswald Mosley's Blackshirts to the National Front*. London: Tauris, 1998.

Tibi, Bassam. *The Challenge of Fundamentalism: Political Islam and the New World Disorder*. Berkeley: University of California Press, 1998.

Toolis, Kevin. *Rebel Hearts: Journeys within the IRA's Soul*. New York: St. Martin's Griffin, 1995.

Turner, John W. *Continent Ablaze: The Insurgency Wars in Africa 1960 to the Present*. London: Arms and Armour Press, 1998.

Vague, Tom. *Anarchy in the UK: The Angry Brigade*. London: AK Press, 1997.

———. *Televisionaries: The Red Army*. London: AK Press, 1994.

Vidal-Naquet, Pierre. *Assassins of Memory: Essay on the Denial of the Holocaust*. New York: Columbia University Press, 1992.

Walker, Thomas W., ed. *Revolution and Counterrevolution in Nicaragua*. Boulder, CO: Westview Press, 1991.

Watts, Meredith W. *Xenophobia in United Germany: Generations, Modernization, and Ideology*. New York: St. Martin's Press, 1997.

Weaver, Mary Anne. *A Portrait of Egypt: A Journey through the World of Militant Islam*. New York: Farrar, Straus & Giroux, 1999.

Weinberg, Leonard B. *After Mussolini: Italian Neo-Fascism and the Nature of Fascism*. Washington, DC: University Press of America, 1979.

Weinberg, Leonard B., and William Lee Eubank. *The Rise and Fall of Italian Terrorism*. Boulder, CO: Westview Press, 1987.

Weisburd, David. *Jewish Settler Violence: Deviance as a Social Reaction*. University Park: Pennsylvania State University Press, 1989.

White, Paul. *Primitive Rebels or Revolutionary Modernizers?: The Kurdish National Movement in Turkey*. London: Zed Books, 2000.

Wickham, Carrie Rosefsky. *Mobilizing Islam: Religion, Activism, and Political Change in Egypt*. New York: Columbia University Press, 2002.

Wickham-Crowley, Timothy P. *Guerrillas and Revolution in Latin America: A Comparative*

Study of Insurgents and Regimes since 1956. Princeton, NJ: Princeton University Press, 1992.

Willan, Philip. *Puppetmasters: The Political Use of Terrorism in Italy.* London: Constable, 1991.

Williams, Paul L. *Al Qaeda: Brotherhood of Terror.* New York: Alpha, 2002.

Willis, Michael. *The Islamist Challenge in Algeria: A Political History.* New York: New York University Press, 1996.

Wilson, A. Jeyaratnam. *The Break-Up of Sri Lanka: The Sinhalese-Tamil Conflict.* Honolulu: University of Hawaii Press, 1988.

Woodworth, Paddy. *Dirty War, Clean Hands: ETA, the GAL, and Spanish Democracy.* Cork, Ireland: Cork University Press, 2001.

Wright, Joanne. *Terrorist Propaganda: The Red Army Faction and the Provisional IRA.* New York: St. Martin's Press, 1990.

Wright, Robin. *Sacred Rage: the Wrath of Militant Islam.* New York: Simon & Schuster, 1985.

Yallop, David A. *Tracking the Jackal: The Search for Carlos, the World's Most Wanted Man.* New York: Random House, 1993.

Yousefi, Naghi. *Religion and Revolution in the Modern World: Ali Shari'ati's Islam and Persian Revolution.* Lanham, MD: University Press of America, 1995.

Zadka, Saul. *Blood in Zion: How the Jewish Guerrillas Drove the British Out of Palestine.* London: Brassey's, 1995.

Zimmerman, John C., *Holocaust Denial: Demographics, Testimonies and Ideologies.* Lanham, MD: University Press of America, 2000.

ORIGINAL WORKS

Negri, Antonio. *Marx Beyond Marx: Lessons on the Grundrisse* (South Hadley, MA: Bergin & Garvey, 1984).

Index

Index

About the Author

STEPHEN E. ATKINS is Assistant University Librarian for Collection Management, Texas A&M University Libraries. He received his Ph.D. in History from the University of Iowa. He is the author of *Encyclopedia of Modern American Extremists and Extremist Groups* (Greenwood, 2002), *Dictionary of Atomic Energy* (Greenwood, 2000), which received the Booklist Editor's Choice Awards for 2000, *Terrorism: A Handbook* (1992), *Arms Control and Disarmament, Defense and Military, International Security and Peace: An Annotated Guide to Sources 1980–1987* (1989), and *The Academic Library in the American University* (1989), as well as numerous journal articles on arms control.